The Modern Gang Reader

Second Edition

Jody Miller
University of Missouri–St. Louis

Cheryl L. Maxson
University of California–Irvine

Malcolm W. Klein
University of Southern California

Roxbury Publishing Company
Los Angeles, California

Library of Congress Cataloging-in-Publication Data

The Modern Gang Reader/[edited by] Jody Miller, Cheryl L. Maxson, and Malcolm W. Klein.—2nd ed.

p. cm.

Includes bibliographical references.

ISBN 1-891487-44-2

1. Gangs—United States. 2. Juvenile delinquents—United States. I. Miller, Jody, 1966- II. Maxson, Cheryl L. III. Klein, Malcolm W.

HV6439.U5 M65 2001

364.1'06'60973–dc21

00-020277

Publisher: Claude Teweles
Managing Editor: Dawn VanDercreek
Production Editor: Carla Max-Ryan
Typography: Synergistic Data Systems
Cover Design: Marnie Kenney

Printed on acid-free paper in the United States of America. This paper meets the standards for recycling of the Environmental Protection Agency.

ISBN 1-891487-44-2

Roxbury Publishing Company
P.O. Box 491044
Los Angeles, California 90049-9044
Tel.: (310) 473-3312 • Fax: (310) 473-4490
E-mail: roxbury@roxbury.net
Web site: www.roxbury.net

Contents

* New to the Second Edition

* New to the Second Edition

Section IV: GANGS, VIOLENCE, AND DRUGS

* New to the Second Edition

Section V: PROGRAMS AND POLICIES

* New to the Second Edition

* New to the Second Edition

Foreword

Gilbert Geis
University of California, Irvine

There are many good reasons why this collection of 29 essays on gang makeup and gang behavior ought to be read widely and carefully by the general public and by students of youth behavior and juvenile delinquency. For one thing, the editors are among the most experienced and talented scholars working in the study of gangs. They are very familiar with the merits and shortcomings of what has become a vast body of published material about gangs and their selections for this book have been guided by a sure instinct for the best. They have added and subtracted from the readings that appeared in the well-received earlier edition, paying particular attention to important contributions published during the past few years. Their decisions on what to include also are based on reactions and suggestions offered by readers of the first edition.

Gang studies represent the very best work that social scientists have fashioned on the subject of crime and juvenile delinquency. This has come about in large part because the subject lends itself particularly well to the talents and orientations of academic criminologists who typically focus on "macro" issues, that is, on the larger context into which matters such as gang behavior are embedded. Unlike, say, the study of fire setting by individual juveniles, which usually involves psychological analyses of the offenders' personalities, gang research is tied to social structures and group behavior. In gangs, boys and girls and young women and young men share a common allegiance, coming together in pairs or in larger numbers in both social settings and when they commit acts of delinquency. The roles they assume within the gang hierarchy often provide telling insight into human interaction. In *Street Corner Society* (1943), a classic early study done in Boston, William Foote Whyte documented how bowling scores varied by the standing of group members. Bowlers almost always lost to members who had higher status in the group, although the winners often were not as good bowlers as those they beat. The bowling losses were not deliberate, to curry favor, but were a consequence of the subtle but powerful operations of group dynamics.

The involvement of many persons bound together, as in juvenile gang law-breaking, is not a common characteristic of criminal activity. Older offenders learn that the more people they trust the greater the risk that colleagues will turn state's evidence in order to save their own skins. Dedicated criminals tend to become loners as they accumulate years in the trade, an arrangement dictated not only by self-protection but also by their interest in not having to divide the loot. In contrast, delinquent gang members typically need to share companionship and responsibility: much of what they do in violation of the law would never take place if the perpetrators did not gain from it a sense of moral fellowship with others whom they know and value.

Another reason for the outstanding research record on this subject is that gangs usually are accessible to persons who have the patience to listen to what members say and to observe what they do in a nonjudgmental manner, or at least keep their opinions to themselves. There is an insider joke among gang researchers that the only thing more boring than being a gang member, who spends most evenings standing around on a streetcorner, is being a gang researcher whose work requires being there with the gang members. But the payoff in first-rate gang research is impressive and important.

Complicated ethical problems may arise in the course of research on gangs, such as the issue of when or if one ought to inform the authorities of a pending gang activity that may end with the death of rival gang members or of innocent people. Many gang researchers handle this matter by letting the gang kids know beforehand that they will not keep to themselves knowledge of impending potentially lethal behavior. A similar problem sometimes arises when the researcher is asked to perform a role, perhaps concealing a weapon, to help the gang. The difficulty, of course, is that access to important information may become much more difficult to obtain from gang members if the researcher is seen as uncooperative or as a possible source of trouble. For researchers, other problems regarding the confidentiality of what they have learned sometimes arise if they are faced with a court order to divulge inside information to law enforcement or judicial officials.

The study of juvenile gangs also has flourished because it is a good deal less perilous than becoming involved with most other groups, such as adult mobster syndicates, in order to learn firsthand how organized crime operates. Similarly, our knowledge about white-collar crime remains relatively primitive because access to corporate headquarters is tightly controlled.

Besides relatively easy access and its kid-glove fit with social science, especially sociological and social-psychological themes, an important reason why scholarship on gangs is so much more sophisticated than that on virtually any other aspect of illegality is that recent work has been able to build on the efforts of the giants who mined the subject during earlier times. The major pioneering studies of gangs were done at the University of Chicago, where a tradition of studying neighborhood conditions throughout the city earned the university's sociology department a reputation for being the best in the nation for several decades, from about 1915 to 1940.

The subject of Chicago gangs became the general province of Clifford R. Shaw (1895–1957) and Henry D. McKay (1899–1980). Both men hailed from small towns; Shaw from Luray, Indiana, and McKay from Orient, South Dakota. Somewhat strangely, although both had been enrolled in the sociology department's graduate program, neither earned a Ph.D., either because of an inability or an unwillingness to pass the required foreign language tests, a hurdle that now has been replaced in most universities by an examination in statistics. Shaw and McKay mapped delinquency areas, published autobiographical monographs written by local juvenile delinquents, and inaugurated the Chicago Area Project, a program that sought to mobilize community people to deal with delinquency in their midst.

Frederic M. Thrasher (1892–1962) conducted the first major study of gangs. The subtitle of Thrasher's book may seem strange: *The Gang: A Study of 1,313 Gangs in Chicago* (1927). The oddity is the number: It is unlikely that Thrasher went out and meticulously counted all the gangs in Chicago in order to arrive at the 1,313 total. Old-timers who ought to know maintain that the number was a prank by research assistants working with Thrasher. The number 1313 was part of the address of a brothel near where the gang project was housed. Thrasher himself would spend the remainder of his career teaching educational sociology at New York University, a prime setting for gang research. But he never revisited the subject. In 1959, he was injured when a bus on which he was a passenger collided with a truck. So severe was the trauma that Thrasher had to live out the remaining three years of his life in a Long Island mental hospital.

Thrasher's study was followed by three major post-World War II classics: Albert K. Cohen's *Delinquent Boys* (1955), Richard Cloward and Lloyd Ohlin's *Delinquency and Opportunity* (1960), and a seminal article by Walter Miller, "Lower-Class Culture as a Generating Milieu of Gang Delinquency" (1958).

Stripped to its barest essentials, Cohen's argument was that gangs formed as a reaction to the inability of lower-class males to achieve the goals that society stresses as worthwhile. Gang boys therefore repudiate these values and seek recognition and success within a gang structure where the kinds of skills they possess are better appreciated. For their part, Cloward and Ohlin argued that young males in the slums who show certain qualities desired by organized crime are recruited into its ranks. Others fall by the wayside, indulging in drug or other defeatist ways of life. They maintained that finding legitimate opportunities for inner-city youth would keep them from exhibiting their talents in gang affiliations.

If the caliber of the critics it attracts denotes the importance of social science research, Cloward and Ohlin's *Delinquency and Opportunity* stands high. Daniel Moynihan, recently retired after several terms in the U.S. Senate, argued that the book was inadequate as a basis for public policy and that government programs following the Cloward and Ohlin blueprint were "no more in possession of confident knowledge on how to prevent delinquency than they were in possession of a dependable formula to deal with the ill-fated Vietnamese war."

Finally, Miller, a social anthropologist, insisted that slum culture is marked by different values than those found in middle- and upper-class precincts. These include emphasis on toughness and an ability to outwit others. Of the triumvirate of early gang scholars, Miller was the only one to have spent time in direct contact with gang members, mostly in the rowdy neighborhood of Roxbury, Massachusetts. The others were primarily armchair social philosophers. Nonetheless, Miller's ideas have had the shortest shelf life. A major criticism is that he was "blaming the victim," that is, putting responsibility for gang delinquency on the values of a social class that itself is victimized in regard to such things as poor schools, inadequate medical care, and dead-end jobs. William Ryan, the originator of the term, illustrated *blaming the victim* by quoting a U.S. Senator who, Ryan alleges, inquired during a floor debate about the origins of the Second World War: "And what was Pearl Harbor doing out there?"

Social science has a tendency to hold on, perhaps overlong, to the work of those who inaugurate a line of research, particularly if the results can be shorthanded, such as for Cohen: Delinquency is a reaction to failure and an attempt to form, with others who fail, a group in which success can be achieved by changing the standards. But the truth is that the research that has been done in the half century or so since the memorable postwar contributions is many jumps ahead of earlier efforts. The work of Felix Padilla, Finn-Aage Esbensen, Scott Decker, Diego Vigil, and the three coeditors of this volume, as well as the other authors whose conclusions are set out in this reader, have inestimably advanced our understanding of gangs. What they have found, however, does not readily lend itself to simple formulas. Gangs are complicated groupings of young people and their structure and activities vary considerably. What has accumulated, as the contents of this reader demonstrate, is a core of particularly good field research and theorizing that puts the oversimplified earlier conclusions about gangs into a more full-bodied framework.

There remains a pressing need for overseas studies that look at the gang situation in different cultures. Also, the growing recognition of female gang involvement, and girls' roles and activities within gangs, is an area where important inroads have been made in scholarly research, but more work needs to be done.

Today, there is heated debate about the best way to deal with gangs. Some scholars insist that we ought to be careful not to enhance their image by the kinds of sensational news stories that the media create. The public and politicians for their part have inaugurated an almost frenzied campaign that makes gang membership virtually a crime. There is no denying that gangs can at times wreak havoc on a community, both in warfare with other gangs and in terms of intimidation and violence against innocent people. But the political reactions seem overwrought, at least to me. Perhaps the unreasonably mean attitude toward gangs has evolved because most people no longer feel free to overtly manifest ethnic and racial bias. Some of that repressed prejudice may find expression in excessively punitive responses to gangs, at least those made up of minority youth.

To find out more about gangs and to participate meaningfully in policy debates on issues such as those noted above, there is no better way to begin to master the subject than by absorbing the contents of this book. The articles in it are well crafted, thoughtful, and backed by data. They provide cutting-edge insight into a controversial and very important issue of our time. ✦

Section I

Defining and Understanding Gangs

Chapter 1
Defining and Researching Gangs

Robert J. Bursik, Jr.
and
Harold G. Grasmick

Our understanding of the nature and extent of gang behavior, and our beliefs about the actions we should take to respond to it, is highly dependent on how gang is defined and the methods used to gather information about a gang. Bursik and Grasmick draw from the extensive gang literature to illustrate both process-based and delinquency-based approaches to gang definitions. In their methodological review, they describe the inherent limitations of each major method and warn that the gang literature must be approached with an eye to these limitations. The editors of this volume share their concern and urge readers to consider the definitional stances and methodological strategies adopted by each researcher. The representativeness of the study sample, reliability of informants, and adequacy of comparison groups are critical elements of the context of gang research and the information it produces.

Peggy Sanday (1990) has provided a detailed description of the dynamics that led to a gang rape alleged to have been committed by members of a fairly well-organized, cohesive group of older adolescents in Philadelphia. Prior to this particular incident, the XYZs (a fictitious name) had already developed a widespread reputation in the neighborhood for problematic behavior. Women commonly reported that they had been verbally harassed by members of the gang who hung around drinking beer on benches along the primary street in the area. Since these benches were situated in front of their clubhouse, the group made it clear that this was their "turf" to do with as they pleased.

Although all the members of this gang were enrolled in school, the group allocated some degree of special status to those who performed poorly. One of the judges involved in the rape case noted that a statement that the XYZs had offered into evidence was "ungrammatical . . . replete with misspellings . . . garbled and incomprehensible" (Forer 1990: xvii). As Sanday has reported, new members of the community were commonly warned about the group, and women were urged to consider the potential dangers of attending the parties that were regularly thrown by the gang.

To many, this short description has all the hallmarks of classic, popular descriptions of a gang, that is, a group of inner-city adolescents, a concern with turf, harassment of local residents, an organizational structure, some degree of solidarity, and mutual participation in serious forms of illegal behavior. Sanday notes (p. 71) that during her two interviews with one of the people implicated in the gang rape, "[H]is dislike for what I was doing and his sense of superiority to people like me were expressed throughout. . . ." In general, we would guess that most readers would not consider this to be a group with which they would like to interact on a regular basis. However, we have left one very important piece of information out of our short summary of Sanday's study: these were all members of a prominent fraternity at a prestigious, upper-middle-class university; the neighborhood in question was a campus community in Philadelphia.

Perhaps some readers think that this is an inappropriate example of gang activity, for public images of such behavior usually do not include the activities of fairly affluent fraternity members at highly respected colleges. Yet consider the influential definition of a gang provided by Klein (1971:13): any

---

Reprinted from: Robert J. Bursik, Jr. and Harold G. Grasmick, *Neighborhoods and Crime: The Dimensions of Effective Community Control.*

identifiable group of youngsters who (a) are generally perceived as a distinct aggregation by others in their neighborhood, (b) recognize themselves as a denotable group (almost invariably with a group name), and (c) have been involved in a sufficient number of delinquent incidents to call forth a consistent negative response from neighborhood residents and/or law enforcement agencies. As anyone familiar with campus life is aware, all fraternities easily qualify under the first two conditions; each has a unique name, and highly visible, relatively arcane symbols (i.e., Greek letters) are used to signify membership in such groups. The third condition is the one that would disqualify many (and perhaps most) fraternities. Yet Sanday's ethnographic material clearly shows that the "XYZ" fraternity had a "dangerous" reputation on campus, and we would be surprised to find many college campuses without at least one such house. Nevertheless, despite the fact that the XYZs clearly qualified as a gang under Klein's definition and the fact that one of the judges described the similarities of this case to those involving more traditional gang members as "striking" (Forer 1990:xvi), there is no indication that Philadelphia's long-established Gang Crimes Unit had any involvement in the case.

Thus, we come to the heart of the problem: exactly how are we to define a gang? Without a generally accepted definition of the concept, it is impossible to make any kind of informed judgment concerning the nature and extent of gang behavior, much less changes that have occurred over time. Some criminologists would certainly include the XYZ case in the computation of rates of gang crimes;[1] others would object strongly to such a classification.

Likewise, what are we to make of the fact that many small, stable, rural communities have recently claimed to be the site of gang behavior? For example, a Knight-Ridder newspaper item (Wallace 1991) describes the case of Frederick, Oklahoma (population 5,200), where the local police chief believes that violent, drug-dealing gangs are staking out territory in the community. The primary basis for his conclusion is the existence of some "Bloods" graffiti in the area, a number of auto thefts, cases of shoplifting and intimidation, reports of drug dealing, and warning notes (this time from the Crips) that have been left on cars.

It is clear that one of the gravest mistakes that a community can make is to deny the existence of a gang-related problem until a series of serious incidents force the issue. Columbus, Ohio, for example, denied that it had any type of problem until members of the mayor's family were brutally attacked by people claiming gang affiliation (Huff 1989: 530–531). Therefore, the situation in Frederick might be seen as an outcome of the expansion of gang-controlled drug markets that had been widely discussed (U.S. General Accounting Office 1989). However, while the concern of the Frederick police chief certainly is understandable, a healthy degree of skepticism is warranted concerning the large number of communities who suddenly have discovered a "gang problem" in their midst. Grasmick was recently told by a high school teacher from Oklahoma City (which does have a documented gang problem), that once particular symbols (such as certain forms of dress or graffiti) became associated with gang membership in his school, they quickly became adopted by many nongang adolescents as a sign of personal rebellion.[2] Therefore, the incidents that were reported in Frederick (including the graffiti) may not be gang-related in any respect other than they represent the efforts of local youths to adopt symbols that are guaranteed to elicit a horrified reaction from the adults in their community.

There are other dynamics that also must be considered when evaluating the extent to which an area is characterized by gang activity. Many concerned communities have invited law enforcement personnel to speak to local leaders about whether they have a gang problem and, if so, what they should do about it. One of the central themes that usually emerges is that without proper action on the part of the community, it is likely to be overrun with gang-related problems in a relatively short period of time. Such messages are quickly picked up by the local media and spread to the general public. Hagedorn

(1988:30), for example, reports that the elites and the media of Milwaukee adopted an image of gang behavior that was promoted by the Chicago Gang Crimes Unit and reinforced by "scary slide shows of murders and a display of gang weapons that would make the U.S. Army run for cover." During these presentations, Milwaukee was warned that if the city failed to act "in a hard line manner," Milwaukee's gangs would be like those in Chicago within five years or less. We find this passage to be especially interesting in that one member of Oklahoma City's Gang Crimes Unit has worked especially hard to promote the image of impending gang danger across the state. Recall that the principal of the junior high that was quoted in the beginning of this chapter reported that she was told that if her community took no action, gang problems would be rampant within five years.[3]

Finally, it must be noted that since access to some federally funded law enforcement programs is more likely if a gang problem can be demonstrated in a community, some agencies may have vested interests in the "discovery" of gang activity. It is impossible to determine the extent to which the apparent diffusion of gang behavior reflects such economic considerations. However, such dynamics have been suggested as an explanation of why police estimates of the number of gangs in Phoenix increased from 5 or 6 to over 100 in a very short period of time (Zatz 1987).

It certainly has not been our intention in this section to downplay the seriousness of some gang activities or to imply that most communities are exaggerating the problems they face. Rather, we have attempted to emphasize that without a precise and parsimonious understanding of what constitutes a gang and gang behavior, it is often difficult to separate fact from mythology. Unfortunately, several factors make it very difficult to arrive at such an understanding.

Crime and Delinquency as Group Phenomena

There are very few issues concerning which criminologists usually feel confident enough to make strong declarative statements. However, the group nature of delinquency is certainly one of those issues. One of the most influential findings of the Shaw and McKay research was that almost 90 percent of the delinquent events reflected in the juvenile court records of Cook County involved two or more participants (Shaw et al. 1929:7–8). The group orientation was strongly reinforced several years later when Edwin Sutherland (1934) began to develop his influential theory of differential association, which emphasized the small-group dynamics associated with the learning of delinquent and criminal behavior. More recent work has noted some important offense-specific differences in the rates of group offending. In addition, a large proportion of offenders do not engage in illegal behavior strictly in group situations (see the review of Reiss 1988). Nevertheless, the presumed group nature of illegal behavior is a generally uncontested part of criminological lore.

There have been several important criticisms of the group hypothesis. The differential association perspective suggests that the most important sources of information concerning the techniques, motivations, and justifications for illegal behavior are intimate personal groups (see Sutherland's propositions 3 and 4). Given the apparent group nature of crime and delinquency, the intimate nature of these groups might suggest that offenses occur primarily within aggregations with temporal histories, fairly developed sets of relationships among the members, and relatively high levels of cohesiveness and solidarity. However, Klein (1969) has argued that the existence of two or more offenders in a single incident does not in itself guarantee that the event represents the outcome of such group dynamics. He criticizes in particular the influence that the Shaw and McKay findings have had on the discipline, for they were based on official records in which it is impossible to determine the actual group dynamics that may have been involved.

Klein illustrates this problem with several hypothetical examples, including one in which a relatively large number of strangers are attending a party and they happen to purchase marijuana from one of the other attendees. If the police happen to bust the party and make multiple arrests for possession, the arrest reports would most likely note that several people were involved in the incident. However, they would not constitute a group in any sociological sense of the word. Rather, these people were simply "contiguous individuals" (Klein 1969:67) who were engaged in the same behavior in the same location. Because of such conceptual ambiguities, some researchers now utilize alternative phrases (such as "co-offending"; Reiss 1988) to refer to events in which more than one person was involved but in which the existence of group dynamics is not clear.[4]

Klein certainly is not arguing that group dynamics are unrelated to criminal and delinquency behavior. Rather, he is emphasizing the need to recognize the basic distinction between the sociological notions of aggregate and group processes. In that respect, some unknown percentage of illegal behavior may be more validly viewed as a form of collective behavior in which an aggregate of relative strangers respond to a particular stimulus; this aggregate may have a very limited prior history and may disband after that particular response. There is a large body of literature that indicates that persons are more likely to engage in illegal behavior if their closest friends are involved in such behavior (see Elliott et al. 1985). However, there also is evidence that many delinquent behaviors occur in the company of individuals to whom a person has relatively weak associational bonds. Martin Gold (1970:83–94) has likened this situation to a "pickup game" of basketball in which the roster of players depends on who happens to be on the playground at the same time. That is, those present may define an opportunity as suitable for basketball (delinquency), and once the game is concluded, many of them go their separate ways. While certain interesting dynamics are involved in the definition of the situation, they have a relatively short-term relevance to the participants. These are not typically the kinds of processes that sociologists attribute to groups. As a result, some criminologists have raised important questions concerning the extent to which group solidarity is reflected in the illegal behavior of co-offenders (see Morash 1983).

Much of the confusion that has arisen in the gang literature, as well as in the public's perception of gang behavior, is due to the often interchangeable use of the words "group" and "gang" (see the criticism of Klein and Maxson 1989). For example, while Walter Miller (1980) delineates twenty different types of "law-violating youth groups," he only considers three of these to represent gangs (see Table 1.1). If the general pattern of relationships among co-offenders is much more fluid than is usually assumed, perhaps the primary distinction between group and gang crime and delinquency pertains to the internal dynamics of the aggregate that may result in a criminal event. For example, Bernard Cohen (1969:66) considers delinquent groups to represent relatively small cliques that coalesce sporadically without apparent reason and spontaneously violate the law. Cohen considers such groups to be ephemeral, with no elaborate organizational structure, name, or sense of turf. Gangs, on the other hand, are highly developed aggregates with relatively large memberships. As opposed to delinquent groups, gangs have elaborate organizations, names, senses of corporate identity, and identifications with particular territories. A similar typology has been developed by Irving Spergel (1984). The viability of such distinctions will be examined in the next section.

Defining Gang Delinquency

John Hagedorn (1988) has identified two primary ways in which the gang has been defined within the criminological literature. The first, and oldest, approach has emphasized the processes that give rise to such groups. Albert Cohen (1955), for example, defines gangs in terms of collective reactions to problems of social status, while Richard Cloward and Lloyd Ohlin (1960) focus on the interaction between legitimate and illegitimate opportunity structures. However, we feel that the most important processual defi-

Table 1.1
Types and Subtypes of Law-Violating Youth Groups

1	Turf gangs
2	Regularly associating disruptive local groups/crowds
3	Solidary disruptive local cliques
4	Casual disruptive local cliques
5	Gain-oriented gangs/extended networks
6	Looting groups/crowds
7	Established gain-oriented cliques/limited networks
7.1	Burglary rings
7.2	Robbery bands
7.3	Larceny cliques and networks
7.4	Extortion cliques
7.5	Drug-dealing cliques and networks
7.6	Fraudulent gain cliques
8	Casual gain-oriented cliques
9	Fighting gangs
10	Assaultive cliques and crowds
10.1	Assaultive affiliation cliques
10.2	Assaultive public-gathering crowds
11	Recurrently active assaultive cliques
12	Casual assaultive cliques

Reprinted from Miller (1980) by permission of the editors.

nition for understanding the relationship between neighborhood dynamics and gang behavior is that of Frederic Thrasher (1927), who defines a gang as "an interstitial group originally formed spontaneously and then integrated through conflict. . . . The result of this collective behavior is the development of tradition, unreflective internal structure, esprit de corps, solidarity, morale, group awareness, and attachment to a local territory" (p. 46).

Several aspects of Thrasher's definition are worth noting. First, "interstitial" has a dual connotation. Thrasher uses it in one sense to represent the period of life when one is neither a child nor an adult; gangs therefore are a reflection of the period of adjustment between childhood and maturity (p. 32). For this reason, Thrasher argues that such groups are relatively short-lived and that adult gangs or members are relatively rare.[5] Yet this does not mean that gangs are characterized by age homogeneity. Rather, as older members age out of the group, younger members join, leading to a set of loosely connected, age-based cliques within the gang.

Thrasher also used the term "interstitial" to refer to neighborhoods located between Chicago's central business district and "the better residential areas" (p. 6). Since these were areas characterized by neighborhood deterioration and residential turnover (p. 46), Thrasher's model is clearly a variation of the social disorganization approach. . . . The systemic implications of his approach are clearly evident in his discussion (p. 33) of the failure of "directing and controlling customs and institutions to function efficiently in the boy's experience. The spirit of this aspect of Thrasher's processual definition is evident in Spergel's (1984:201) more recent definition of integrated gangs as a reflection of the inability of primary and secondary community institutions to provide mechanisms of opportunity or control.

Second, Thrasher's emphasis on "spontaneous formation" reflects his argument that all childhood play groups represent potential forms of gangs (see pp. 23–26). Since such groups usually arise on the basis of interaction and familiarity, they tend to form around particular residential locations in a neighborhood where youths are likely to come into contact with one another. Thus, street corner groups represent the basic building block upon which Thrasher develops his thesis. The key determinant of the transition into a gang is contact with other groups (either other play groups or adults) who express disapproval or opposition to the playgroup. For example, Hagedorn (1988: 57–60) observes that fierce rivalries developed among the many breakdancing groups that arose during the early 1980s in Milwaukee; gangs sometimes emerged as a result of the fights that often broke out after competitions. Such conflict can produce an awareness of the distinction between "us" and "them" and the development of a sense of solidarity among group members. The existence of a street corner group therefore can serve as a source of protection from other groups in the neighborhood (see Spergel 1984:202).

Finally, note that delinquent or criminal activities are not mentioned in Thrasher's definition. While he certainly recognized that such activities may be facilitated by gang membership, he emphasized the variability that existed in the 1,313 groups that he identified as gangs: some are good, some are bad. Thrasher's approach emphasizes the social dynamics that may lead to cohesion among a play group and the resulting development of a gang. The relationship of gangs to delinquency is therefore a key analytical issue.

Although such process-based definitions of the gang continue to appear in the literature, Hagedorn (1988:57) notes that most current research is no longer characterized by a focus on how gangs arise within particular community contexts and how they function within those social environments. Rather, he argues that the fundamental question has become "why gang members are delinquent." The definition of Klein (1971) presented earlier in this chapter, with its criterion that the number of delinquencies committed by the group has called forth some type of negative response, represents a commonly used example of such an approach. The implications of this shift in focus are much more important than they may first appear, for illegal behavior is considered to be a definitional aspect of gang activity, whereas for Thrasher it was an empirical question.

Even more so than was the case with processual definitions, there is an enormous variety of delinquency-based definitions which have become the basis for different policies, laws, and strategies. One of the most interesting attempts to produce a definition with a broad consensual base is that of Walter Miller (1975, 1980), who asked a national sample of youth service agency staff members to respond to the questions: "What is your conception of a gang? Exactly how would you define it?" His final definition is based on the responses of 309 respondents representing 121 youth serving agencies in 26 areas of the country (Miller 1980:120), including police officers, prosecutors, defenders, educators, city council members, state legislators, ex-prisoners, and past and present members of gangs and groups (1980: 117).

Of the 1,400 definitional characteristics that were provided by his sample, Miller reports that there were six items with which at least 85 percent of the respondents agreed (1980:121): a youth gang is a self-formed association of peers, bound together by mutual interests, with identifiable leadership, well-developed lines of authority, and other organizational features, who act in concert to achieve a specific purpose or purposes, which generally include the conduct of illegal activity and control over a particular territory, facility, or type of enterprise.

Such delinquency-based definitions have been criticized for several reasons. Klein and Maxson (1989:205) call Miller's approach "discouraging" and argue that to define a concept on the basis of the results of a "vote" does not make it inherently more definitive or valid than other approaches. Yet their criticisms are not aimed solely at Miller, for they note that the definitional task is "difficult and arbitrary" and an "inherently unsatisfying task." The continued existence of a great variety of delinquency-based definitions (see Spergel 1990) suggests that consensus does not exist for any particular conceptualization (although the definition provided in Klein 1971 has been particularly influential). Ruth Horowitz (1990:43) notes that the variation in locally used definitions may be useful for understanding how the relationships among criminal justice personnel, the community, the gang, and the individual gang member are defined. Nevertheless, the lack of a standard, nationwide definition of a gang makes estimates that have been made concerning the number of youth gangs in the United States or comparisons that have been made over time or between communities relatively meaningless (Spergel 1990:180).

Some contemporary researchers have expressed a more general discomfort with all definitions that assume generalizable groups structures and processes or that equate crime with gang behavior (see Hagedorn 1988; Fagan 1989:643). Merry Morash (1983:310) argues that these approaches developed due to a growing reliance on definitions used by law enforcement and social work personnel. Since many of these agencies classify groups as gangs if violent or criminal activity is a major activity, gangs are by definition heavily involved in illegal behavior and Thrasher's question concerning the relationship between gang membership and delinquency becomes tautological (see Short 1990:160).

To illustrate the implications of such definitional assumptions, Morash created a scale of "gang likeness" based on an adaptation of Miller's definition.[6] While her analysis presents evidence that the gang-likeness variable has a significant effect on delinquency, more general peer group processes, such as the delinquent behavior of one's friends, are of much greater importance. Overall, she concludes (p. 325) that membership in a stereotyped gang is not a sufficient condition to stimulate serious delinquency. This seems to provide an important contradiction to the finding of many studies that gang members are involved in significantly higher levels of crime and drug use (see Fagan 1989). However, Klein and Maxson (1989:204) take issue with Morash's findings, noting that adolescent church or school groups could have qualified as gangs using her criteria.

Other characteristics of gangs that might be the subject of empirical investigation are also embedded into definitions such as that developed by Miller. For example, while some of the informants in Hagedorn's (1988) study reported that their gangs had fairly specialized and formalized ranks, others insisted that the structure was very informal; a few even stated that their gangs had no recognized leader (p. 92). Likewise, Joan Moore (1978:44) reports that the historical circumstances that set the context for the development of each of the age-based cliques (klikas) in Los Angeles Chicano gangs has resulted in significant differences among groupings in the same gang, each of which may have its own organizational structure (see also Keiser 1969:15).

We find the arguments of Hagedorn and Morash very persuasive, for those characteristics that are assumed by researchers such as Miller to be defining features of gangs actually exhibit a great deal of variation among groups who have been identified as gangs. Rather than taking these characteristics for granted, it would seem to be much more theoretically fruitful to examine the processes that give rise to such group variation. Perhaps one of the reasons why the Klein (1971) definition has been extremely popular is that the three criteria are extremely flexible and are relevant to a wide range of gang types.

Nevertheless, we are uncomfortable with the delinquent behavior criterion, for it makes a possible outcome of gang activity one of the defining characteristics. Klein and Maxson (1989:204) defend their position by noting that "to think of modern street gangs independent of their criminal involvement is to ignore the very factor that makes them qualitatively different from other groups of young people."[7] Despite our own misgivings concerning the presumed equivalence of gang activity and crime, there is no question that the major criterion used by many audiences in the definition of gang is the group's participation in illegal behavior (Spergel 1990:179).

Methods of Gang Research

. . . Easily the longest tradition of gang research is based on some variant of ethnographic fieldwork with gang members (or the combination of such research with supplementary forms of data collection). The work of Thrasher (1927) is exemplary in this respect. Although we know very little concerning how he actually collected his data (see Short 1963:xviii), it is clear that it represented primarily a combination of personal observation and documents that were supplemented by court records and census materials. Over the course of his seven-year study, he amassed enough material to identify 1,313 Chicago gangs.

While Bookin and Horowitz (1983) noted that fieldwork techniques had a declining popularity in sociology and predicted that they would rarely be used in future research, Horowitz (1990:37) recently has retracted that statement, for they certainly represent one of the major forms of data collection used in the study of gangs.[8] Unfortunately, ethnographers no longer have the resources at their disposal to conduct such a "census" of gangs as that of Thrasher. Therefore, the modern emphasis has been on the depth of data, rather than the breadth. Generally this is not considered a problem in fieldwork, for such research is much more concerned with the identification and analysis of process and meaning than with the ability to generalize findings to some larger population. Nevertheless, it must be emphasized that the representativeness of the gangs that have been described is not clear. Many times the gangs have been chosen on the basis of their notoriety within a community (see Keiser 1969; Muehlbauer and Dodder 1983), because of chance circumstances that bring a gang to the attention of a researcher, such as the prior participation of gang members in social service projects (Short and Strodtbeck 1965; Klein 1971; Hagedorn 1988; Harris 1988), or because of their location in particular communities upon which researchers have elected to focus (Klein 1971; Moore 1978; Horowitz 1983; Campbell 1984; Sullivan 1989; Jankowski 1991).

There are special difficulties in conducting fieldwork with gangs that do not arise in many other fields of inquiry. First, and most obviously, while most researchers are highly educated, middle-class persons, many gang members are not. It takes a skilled ethnographer to overcome the initial hostility that is often inherent to interactions with gang members (see the descriptions provided by Horowitz 1983:Chapter 1; Moore 1978:Appendix A; Hagedorn 1988:32–33). In addition to this inherent suspicion, many researchers have noted that gang members are notoriously unreliable as informants (Spergel 1990:175); Klein (1971:18) feels that "the only thing worse than the young reporter's description of a gang incident is his [sic] acceptance of the gang participant's statement about it." This problem was forcibly driven home to the first author of this book during a conversation with a friend who formerly had been a central member of one of Chicago's most notorious fighting gangs. He described with great pleasure how during times of boredom, members of his group would have an informal competition to see who could convincingly tell the most outrageous story to a social worker who had been assigned to work with the group. Therefore, the collection of valid data through fieldwork with gangs is only possible after an extended period of contact during which trust is established.

There is also a more subtle problem in the reliability of data drawn from fieldwork with gangs. An important concern in all ethnographic studies is the degree to which the presence of the researcher has a significant effect on the nature of the dynamics that are observed. For example, some of the most important studies of gang dynamics (such as that of Short and Strodtbeck 1965) have relied to a significant degree on the observations of "detached workers," that is, social service personnel who have been assigned to work with gangs in their natural settings. As Klein (1971:151) notes, those procedures that are often used to maximize contact with gangs (such as group counseling sessions or attendance at club meetings) may in fact increase group cohesiveness, which may lead to an increase in gang delinquency. In addition, the assignment of a group worker may increase the local reputation of a gang, which in turn may attract new members. Thus, the presence of a fieldworker can result in a set of group dynamics and activities that would not have occurred otherwise.

Despite these problems, ethnographic work has provided some of the most important insights that criminologists have about gangs, and much of the richest data has been obtained under situations that may have seemed doomed to failure (see Horowitz 1983). However, as we have noted, there are problems in the generalizability of such data. A second approach to gang research has attempted to overcome this limitation by incorporating surveys into the study design. While this often has been done in conjunction with ongoing fieldwork (such as Short and Strodtbeck 1965; Joe and Robinson 1980), this is not necessarily the case (Giordano 1978; Bowker et al. 1980; Morash 1983; Fagan 1989; Curry and Spergel 1991).

Many of the same problems concerning trust and hostility that characterize fieldwork studies also are present in survey-based study designs. However, two other issues make gang survey research especially problematic. The first is the sampling frame itself, that is, the population of gang members from which the respondents should be selected. Obviously, there is no "official" listing of all gang members in an area, but even if one existed, the ongoing flux in gang membership would make a list obsolete almost immediately (Short and Strodtbeck 1965: 10). The police in many communities have compiled lists of suspected gang members, but these tend to be very inaccurate. Klein (1971:19) tells the story of how he examined the files kept by the police concerning the members of a particular gang. Whereas he had the names of over 100 members, the police had less than 20 and much of their information concerning addresses and offense histories was extremely dated. One solution is to administer surveys to those people who have been identified as gang members through fieldwork (see Short and Strodtbeck). Another is to interview people known to be gang members, ask them for the names of other people who should be interviewed, and continue to build the sample of respondents through such a "snowball" approach (see Fagan 1989).

While such techniques can potentially collect a great deal of useful information concerning the characteristics and behavior of gang members, it is often desirable to compare the distributions of these variables to those found among youths not involved in gang activity.[9] However, the selection of an appropriate comparison group is very difficult. The sample survey data examined in the 1989 paper of Jeffrey Fagan (1989), for example, included only the responses of gang members, and he was only able to draw comparisons with nongang youths by comparing his findings with other published research. While Short and Strodtbeck (1965) did include nongang youths in their sample, all these respondents were affiliated in some manner with youth-serving agencies (p. 5). Therefore, the degree to which these youths are representative of nongang youths in general is not clear.

Several attempts have been made to identify gang membership and make the relevant comparisons on the basis of more broadly administered surveys (Morash 1983; Rand 1987; Spergel and Curry 1988; Curry and Spergel 1991). The validity of the information that has been collected on the basis of such study designs depends on two crucial considerations. First, how likely is it that youths involved in gangs will be represented in the sample? Some researchers have tried to maximize this possibility by drawing all or part of their sample from those youths residing in correctional facilities (Bowker et al. 1980; Morash 1983). Such approaches would tend to overrepresent those youths with extensive or especially violent offense histories. Other sampling designs are likely to underrepresent active gang members. Spergel and Curry (1988) and Curry and Spergel (1991), for example, surveyed all male students in the sixth through eighth grades at four schools in Chicago. Likewise, Fagan (1990) supplemented the gang data noted earlier with information collected from a sample of high school students residing in the same three neighborhoods and a snowball sample of dropouts. However, school-based samples are especially prone to errors in studies of delinquency since the most active delinquents may be those youths who are most likely to be truant during the time of administration. In general, it is extremely difficult to draw a representative sample of gang members.

The second consideration reflects the identification of respondents as gang members. Some surveys have simply asked the respondents if they belong to a gang (Rand 1987; Johnstone 1981). While John Johnstone presents some evidence (p. 362) to suggest that the adolescents in his sample interpreted the term "gang" consistently, he does note problems with such an assumption. Other researchers assume the existence of a continuum along which a youth group is more or less like a particular operational definition of a gang (Morash 1983; Spergel and Curry 1988; Curry and Spergel 1991). We have already noted Klein and Maxson's (1989) criticism of the scale developed by Morash for its apparent inability to differentiate among dramatically different types of youth groups. The Spergel and Curry scale is a much narrower approach to the measurement of gangs and includes such items as the flashing of gang signs, the wearing of colors, and attacking (or being attacked) in a gang-related incident. One of their most important findings is that the indicators of gang involvement scaled differently for Hispanics and African Americans, which highlights our argument that the search for a broadly relevant uniform definition of gangs may be relatively fruitless. In addition, contrary to the findings of Morash, they present evidence of a strong relationship between gang involvement and serious delinquency.

Overall, the use of surveys is no guarantee that the results of a study are any more reliable than those produced through more traditional fieldwork approaches. Rather, results are especially sensitive to the nature of the sampling design, the selection and wording of the indicators of gang membership, and the relevance of those indicators to the populations under consideration.

The final technique that has been used to collect data on gangs is based on information that has been collected by law enforcement agencies. While sometimes this information is used to supplement that derived through fieldwork or survey designs, much of the current knowledge concerning gangs is the result of studies that have been based primarily on such data (Miller 1975; Spergel 1984, 1986; Curry and Spergel 1988; Klein and Maxson 1989; Maxson et al., 1985). Bernard Cohen (1969) has argued that the Philadelphia Gang Crimes Unit uses sociologically sophisticated definitions of gang and nongang activities in its classification of criminal events. However the official classification of an offender as a gang member generally is not systematic and may not be based on reliable criteria (Klein and Maxson 1989:206).

In addition to the problem of identifying gang membership based on the information included in official records, there is an equally difficult problem in the classification of illegal events as gang-related. For example, suppose a member of a gang is arrested for the armed robbery of a convenience store. On the basis of the description of the event provided in the arrest report, it may be impossible to determine whether it was committed due to gang membership. Unfortunately, there are no national standards for the identification of a crime as gang-related. For example, the Los Angeles Police and Sheriff's Departments designate a homicide as gang-related "if either the assailant or the victim is a gang member or, failing clear identification, elements of the event, such as motive, garb, characteristic gang behavior, or attribution by witnesses, indicate the likelihood of gang involvement" (Klein and Maxson 1989:206–207). However, the Chicago Police Department uses a much more restrictive definition that is based on the evidence of "gang function or motivation" (Curry and Spergel 1988:384). Maxson and Klein (1990) note that a reclassification of the Los Angeles data on the basis of the Chicago criterion leads to a significant reduction in the estimated rate of gang homicide and question whether the massive efforts of gang control and suppression that have characterized Los Angeles would have developed if this alternative definition had been used to gauge the extent of the problem.

The existence of such definitional inconsistencies makes it very difficult to make any kind of reliable comparisons between jurisdictions concerning the level of gang activity. However, definitions may also be characterized by inconsistencies even within the same jurisdiction. For example, Curry and Spergel (1988:385) note that prior to 1986, arson, theft, burglary, and vice offenses (including those that were drug-related) were not included in the gang crime reporting system. Such changes make it nearly impossible to examine the trends in many forms of gang behavior in Chicago over time, including the changing nature of drug use and distribution that has received so much attention in other parts of the country.

Overall, the inherent limitations of the dominant forms of data collection on gangs are very serious. Therefore, in many respects, we simply cannot be as confident of our knowledge concerning gangs as we are in other areas of criminology. However, despite these problems of measurement, certain patterns have emerged in a sufficient number of studies and locations to provide at least a minimal degree of confidence in those empirical regularities. This is especially the case in gang research that has emphasized the neighborhood dynamics related to such behavior.

Notes

1. For example, our colleague John Cochran has referred to certain fraternities on the University of Oklahoma campus as "syndicates of rape" which has made him a very popular figure in the Letters to the Editor department of the school newspaper.
2. Interestingly, at least in that high school, this meant that the dominant gang continually revised its preferred style of dress to maintain a symbolic separation between it and the general school population.
3. If the Soviet Union had had five-year plans as effective as those attributed by many authorities to street gangs, it might have survived.
4. The careful reader will note that this problem is very similar to the compositional effect-group effect issue that was discussed in Chapter 2 in respect to neighborhoods. [Editors' note: See Chapter 2 of Bursik and Grasmick, *Neighborhoods and Crime: The Dimensions of Effective Community Control*. New York: Lexington Books, 1993.]
5. A very similar argument concerning the role of gangs in adolescent development has been presented by Bloch and Niederhoffer (1958).
6. Items included in the final scale reflected whether or not the group meets outside the home, if youths are typically members for four or more years, if the group usually meets in the same place, if the group comes from just one part of the neighborhood, if the group has a name, if the group contains older and younger kids, if the respondent meets with the group at least four days a week, and if the respondent takes part in several activities with the group.
7. Spergel (1990) notes that many gang researchers who once believed that gang behavior was not especially serious or lethal (such as Miller and Klein) now have come to the position that such groups are responsible for a large number of homicides and are active participants in widespread narcotics trafficking (see, for example, Miller 1975; Klein and Maxson 1985, 1989).
8. We use the term "fieldwork" in a very broad sense to refer to qualitative study designs that involve some degree of interaction between the researcher and the gang member. They can range from intensive observation conducted by the researcher over extended periods (as in Horowitz 1983; Campbell 1984; Sullivan 1989; Jankowski 1991), through the reports provided by social service workers who deal with a particular gang on a regular basis (as in Short and Strodtbeck 1965; Klein 1971; or Moore 1985), to sets of intensive, unstructured interviews with respondents identified as gang members (as in Vigil 1988 or Hagedorn 1988). Many studies have combined two or more of these techniques into a single research design.
9. In fact, the availability of such information is absolutely essential to the development of processual approaches to gangs.

References

Bloch, Herbert A., and Arthur Niederhoffer (1958). *The Gang: A Study in Adolescent Behavior.* New York: Philosophical Library.

Bookin, Hedy, and Ruth Horowitz (1983). "The End of the Youth Gang: Fad or Fact?" *Criminology* 21:585–602.

Bowker, Lee H., Helen Shimata Gross, and Malcolm W. Klein (1980). "Female Participation in Delinquent Gang Activities." *Adolescence* 59:509–519.

Campbell, Ann (1984). *The Girls in the Gang*. Oxford: Basil Blackwell.

Chambliss, William J. (1973). "The Saints and the Roughnecks." *Society* 11:24–31.

Cloward, Richard A., and Lloyd Ohlin (1960). *Delinquency and Opportunity.* New York: Free Press.

Cohen, Albert K. (1955). *Delinquent Boys.* Glencoe, IL: The Free Press.

Cohen, Bernard (1969). "The Delinquency of Gangs and Spontaneous Groups." Pp. 61–111 in *Delinquency: Selected Studies*, edited by Thorsten Sellin and Marvin E. Wolfgang. New York: Wiley.

Curry, G. David, and Irving A. Spergel (1988). "Gang Homicide, Delinquency, and Community." *Criminology* 26:381–405.

——. (1991). *Youth Gang Involvement and Delinquency: A Report to the National Youth Gang Intervention and Suppression Research and Development Project*. Office of Juvenile Justice and Delinquency Prevention, Washington, DC.

Elliott, Delbert S., David Huizinga, and Suzanne S. Ageton (1985). *Explaining Delinquency and Drug Use*. Beverly Hills, CA: Sage.

Fagan, Jeffrey (1989). "The Social Organization of Drug Use and Drug Dealing Among Urban Gangs." *Criminology* 27:633–669.

—— (1990). "Social Processes of Delinquency and Drug Use Among Urban Gangs." Pp. 183–219 in *Gangs in America*, edited by C. Ronald Huff. Newbury Park, CA: Sage.

Forer, Lois G. (1990). "Foreword." Pp. xiii–xxv in *Fraternity Gang Rape: Sex, Brotherhood, and Privilege on Campus*, by Peggy Sanday. New York: New York University Press.

Giordano, Peggy C. (1978). "Girls, Guys, and Gangs: The Changing Social Context of Female Delinquency." *Journal of Criminal Law and Criminology* 69:126–132.

Gold, Martin (1970). *Delinquent Behavior in an American City*. Belmont, CA: Brooks-Cole.

Hagedorn, John M. (1988). *People and Folks: Gangs, Crime, and the Underclass in a Rustbelt City*. Chicago: Lakeview Press.

Harris, Mary G. (1988). *Las Cholas: Latino Girls and Gangs*. New York: AMS Press.

Horowitz, Ruth (1983). *Honor and the American Dream*. New Brunswick, NJ: Rutgers University Press.

—— (1990). "Sociological Perspectives on Gangs: Conflicting Definitions and Concepts." Pp. 37–54 in *Gangs in America*, edited by C. Ronald Huff. Newbury Park, CA: Sage.

Huff, C. Ronald (1989). "Youth Gangs and Public Policy." *Crime and Delinquency* 35:524–537.

Jankowski, Martin Sanchez (1991). *Islands in the Street: Gangs and American Urban Society*. Berkeley: University of California Press.

Joe, Delbert, and Norman Robinson (1980). "Chinatown's Immigrant Gangs: The New Young Warrior Class." *Criminology* 18:337–345.

Johnstone, John W. C. (1981). "Youth Gangs and Black Suburbs." *Pacific Sociological Review* 24: 355–375.

Keiser, R. Lincoln (1969). *The Vice Lords: Warriors of the Streets*. New York: Holt, Rinehart and Winston.

Klein, Malcolm W. (1969). "On Group Context of Delinquency." *Sociology and Social Research* 54: 63–71.

—— (1971). *Street Gangs and Street Workers*. Englewood Cliffs, NJ: Prentice Hall.

Klein, Malcolm W., and Cheryl L. Maxson (1985). " 'Rock' Sales in South Los Angeles." *Sociology and Social Research* 69:561–565.

—— (1989). "Street Gang Violence." Pp. 198–234 in *Violent Crime, Violent Criminals*, edited by Neil A. Weiner and Marvin E. Wolfgang. Newbury Park, CA: Sage.

Maxson, Cheryl L., Margaret A. Gordon, and Malcolm W. Klein (1985). "Differences Between Gang and Nongang Homicides." *Criminology* 23:209–222.

Maxson, Cheryl L., and Malcolm W. Klein (1990). "Street Gang Violence: Twice As Great or Half As Great?" Pp. 71–100 in *Gangs in America*, edited by C. Ronald Huff. Newbury Park, CA: Sage.

Miller, Walter B. (1975). *Violence by Youth Gangs as a Crime Problem in Major American Cities*. National Institute for Juvenile Justice and Delinquency Prevention, U.S. Justice Department. Washington, DC: U.S. Government Printing Office.

—— (1980). "Gangs, Groups, and Serious Youth Crime." Pp. 115–138 in *Critical Issues in Juvenile Delinquency*, edited by David Schichor and Delos H. Kelly. Lexington, MA: D.C. Heath.

Moore, Joan W. (1978) *Homeboys*. Philadelphia: Temple University Press.

—— (1985). "Isolation and Stigmatization in the Development of an Underclass: The Case of Chicano Gangs in East Los Angeles." *Social Problems* 33:1–12.

—— (1988). "Introduction: Gangs and the Underclass. A Comparative Perspective." Pp. 3–17 in *People and Folks: Gangs, Crime, and the Underclass in a Rustbelt City*, by John M. Hagedorn. Chicago: Lakeview Press.

Morash, Merry (1983). "Gangs, Groups, and Delinquency." *British Journal of Criminology* 23:309–335.

Muehlbauer, Gene, and Laura Dodder (1983). *The Losers: Gang Delinquency in an American Suburb*. New York: Praeger.

Rand, Alicia (1987). "Transitional Life Events and Desistance from Delinquency and Crime." Pp. 134–162 in *From Boy to Man, from Delinquency to Crime*, by Marvin E. Wolfgang, Terence P. Thornberry, and Robert M. Figlio. Chicago: University of Chicago Press.

Reiss, Albert J., Jr. (1988). "Co-Offending and Criminal Careers." Pp. 117–170 in *Crime and Justice: A Review of Research*. Vol. 10, edited by Michael Tonry and Norval Morris. Chicago: University of Chicago Press.

Sanday, Peggy (1990). *Fraternity Gang Rape: Sex, Brotherhood, and Privilege on Campus*. New York: New York University Press.

Shaw, Clifford R., and Henry D. McKay (1931). *Social Factors in Juvenile Delinquency*. National Commission on Law Observation and Enforcement, No. 13, Report on the Causes of Crime, Volume II. Washington, DC: U.S. Government Printing Office.

Shaw, Clifford R., Frederick M. Zorbaugh, Henry D. McKay, and Leonard S. Cottrell (1929). *Delinquency Areas*. Chicago: University of Chicago Press.

Short, James F., Jr. (1963). "Introduction to the Abridged Edition." Pp. xv–liii in *The Gang*, by Frederic Thrasher. Chicago: University of Chicago Press.

—— (1990). *Delinquency and Society*. Englewood Cliffs, NJ: Prentice Hall.

Short, James F., Jr., and Fred L. Strodtbeck (1965). *Group Process and Gang Delinquency*. Chicago: University of Chicago Press.

Spergel, Irving A. (1984). "Violent Gangs in Chicago: In Search of Social Policy." *Social Service Review* 58:199–226.

—— (1986). "Violent Gangs in Chicago: A Local Community Approach." *Social Service Review* 60:94–131.

—— (1990). "Youth Gangs: Continuity and Change." Pp. 171–275 in *Crime and Justice: A Review of Research*. Volume 12, edited by Michael Tonry and Norval Morris. Chicago: University of Chicago Press.

Spergel, Irving A., and G. David Curry (1988). "Socialization to Gangs: Preliminary Baseline Report." School of Social Service Administration, University of Chicago.

—— (1990). "Strategies and Perceived Agency Effectiveness in Dealing with the Youth Gang Problem." Pp. 288–317 in *Gangs in America*, edited by C. Ronald Huff. Newbury Park, CA: Sage.

Sullivan, Mercer L. (1989). *Getting Paid: Youth Crime and Work in the Inner City*. Ithaca, NY: Cornell University Press.

Sutherland, Edwin H. (1934). *Principles of Criminology*, Second Edition. Philadelphia: J.B. Lippincott.

Thrasher, Frederic M. (1927). *The Gang*. Chicago: University of Chicago Press.

United States General Accounting Office (1989). *Nontraditional Organized Crime*. Washington, DC: U.S. Government Printing Office.

Vigil, James D. (1988). *Barrio Gangs: Street Life and Identity in Southern California*. Austin: University of Texas Press.

Wallace, Linda S. (1991). "Big-City Terror Stalks Small-Town America." *Knight-Ridder Newspaper Service*, December 26.

Whyte, William F. (1981). *Street Corner Society*. Third Edition. Chicago: University of Chicago Press.

Zatz, Marjorie S. (1987). "Chicano Youth Gangs and Crime: The Creation of a Moral Panic." *Contemporary Crises* 11:129–158. ✦

Chapter 2
The History of Gang Research

Scott H. Decker
and
Barrik Van Winkle

In this introductory section of their book Life in the Gang, *Decker and Van Winkle provide an overview of the history of research and theory concerning street gangs. Gangs were a topic of serious concern in the early part of the twentieth century, then again in the middle decades, and again beginning in the late 1980s and into the 1990s. Gang research falls in and out of favor depending upon the particular theoretical framework dominant within criminology at a given time—for instance, gang research fell out of favor in the late 1970s and 1980s when individuals—rather than groups—were of primary interest to criminologists. Although the specific theoretical premises differ among early gang researchers, there are recurrent themes outlined by Decker and Van Winkle: poverty, economic instability, population changes and migration patterns, the geographic isolation of urban youth and consequent lack of access to legitimate social institutions, and the ways in which gangs fill these voids for some youths.*

Early Gang Studies

The themes of immigration, urbanization, ethnicity, and poverty are most evident in examinations of gangs in the 1890s and at the turn of the century. The majority of such accounts were journalistic in nature. Faced with waves of immigrants from western Europe, New York found itself with a considerable level of gang activity in the late 1890s, much of it involving Irish immigrants. According to Riis (1892, 1902) young Irish (and later Italian) immigrants found integration into the economy to be difficult. Lacking activities to occupy their time, they formed gangs to provide for social and material needs. His descriptions of the gang focused on the myriad social conditions faced by the children of immigrants: poverty, poor education, poor housing, dirt and the lack of wholesome activities. Gang life was a natural outcome for such youth:

> So trained for the responsibility of citizenship, robbed of home and of childhood, with every prop knocked from under him, all the elements that make for strength and character trodden out in the making of the boy, all the high ambition of youth caricatured by the slum and become base passions,—so equipped he comes into the business of life. As a "kid" he hunted with the pack in the street. As a young man he trains with the gang, because it furnishes the means of gratifying his inordinate vanity; that is the slum's counterfeit of self-esteem. (Riis 1902, pp. 236–237)

The response to such problems was rather straightforward; occupy the time of these individuals and they will cease to be involved in gang activity. Activities such as athletics were recommended as "safety-valves" (Riis 1892, p. 131) for youthful energies.

The role of immigration in gang formation provided an important foundation for later examinations of gangs. Asbury (1928) studied gangs in New York City, especially in the Five Points area populated largely by recent Irish immigrants yet to move out of the economic underclass. He provided encyclopedic descriptions of the variety of gangs and their activities. The primary activities for these gangs were fighting, with each other as well as rival gangs. Asbury was careful to make the distinction between those who grow up in a gang and criminals who organize to perform illegal acts more effectively. He highlighted with considerable

Reprinted from: Scott H. Decker and Barrik Van Winkle, *Life in the Gang: Family, Friends, and Violence*. Copyright © 1996 by Cambridge University Press. Reprinted by permission.

detail the colorful names used by these gangs, names that included the Roach Guards, Pug Uglies, Shirt Tails, and Dead Rabbits. It is an important historical footnote that red and blue, the colors adopted by the contemporary Bloods and Crips respectively, were the colors used by the Irish gangs of New York City in the 1920s. The Roach Guards used blue as their color, and the Dead Rabbits used red as their symbol. This underscores one feature common to most American gangs throughout history, the use of symbols to identify members. Asbury also described numerous small gangs with affiliations to a larger gang, suggesting that most gang activity was concentrated around the neighborhood among a small group of friends well-known to each other.

Thrasher's Study of Gangs

Thrasher's pioneering work appeared in 1927, the first serious academic treatment of gangs. Working within the sociological paradigm of the Chicago School, Thrasher gave gangs a cultural and ecological context. Using the concepts of culture and neighborhood ecology, he sought to explain gang transmission (the intergenerational character of gangs in neighborhoods and subcultures) as part of a process of collective behavior. Gangs in Chicago were found primarily in interstitial areas. These areas were characterized by three consistent ecological features: (1) deteriorating neighborhoods, (2) shifting populations, and (3) mobility and disorganization of the slum. The "ganging process" was dynamic and produced organizations that were constantly undergoing change. In this context, Thrasher saw gangs as

> . . . the spontaneous effort of boys to create a society for themselves where none adequate to their needs exists. What boys get out of such association that they do not get otherwise under the conditions that adult society imposes is the thrill and zest of participation in common interest, more especially in corporate action, in hunting, capture, conflict, flight, and escape. Conflict with other gangs and the world about them furnishes the occasion for many of their exciting group activities. (1927, p. 37)

Thrasher found considerable variation in the definition of gangs but also noted that gangs played a variety of functions, further complicating efforts to define them in precise ways. In his view, gangs originated from the spontaneous group activity of adolescents and were strengthened by conflict. This process consists of three stages. In its earliest stage, the gang is diffuse, little leadership exists, and the gang may be short lived. Some gangs progress to the next stage, where they become solidified. Conflict with other gangs plays a notable role in this process, helping to define group boundaries and strengthen the ties between members, uniting them in the face of a common threat. The final step in the evolution of the gang occurs when it becomes conventionalized and members assume legitimate roles in society. For those groups that fail to make this transition, delinquent or criminal activity becomes the dominant focus of the group. Among Thrasher's great strengths is his description of the process by which groups form, solidify, and disintegrate. He portrayed the relationship between gangs and other forms of social organization in a figure that traces the natural history of the gang. Most notable about this figure are the poignant reminders that social associations characterize most adolescent activities, and the majority of activities are law abiding.

Activities within the gang, according to Thrasher, were diverse and motivated by typical youthful concerns, such as thrills and excitement. A number of predatory activities were observed, with stealing being the most common. Many gangs were characterized by Thrasher as conflict groups that developed out of disputes and flourished in the presence of threats from rival groups. Fighting was the preeminent activity, and clashes with members of one's own gang were as likely as those with members of rival gangs. For gang members, violence served both to unite them and to speed the adaptation of the gang to its environment. In this way, violence played an especially important function in the integration of members into the group. The threat presented by rival gangs served to intensify solidarity within the gang, especially for new members. Despite their involvement in criminal or delinquent activity, most gang members were assimilated into legitimate social activities, most often athletics.

Gangs are isolated from mainstream society both by geography and lack of access to legitimate institutional roles. This isolation contributes to the within-group solidarity so critical to Thrasher's account of gangs, but it also plays another role. It helps to explain the lack of integration into the economic, educational, and social structure of cities and serves to prevent many gang members from giving up their gang affiliations for activities of a more law abiding nature. The isolated nature of the gang also allows it to enforce its rules (such as they may be) in a manner largely unimpeded by other institutions. Order is maintained through informal mechanisms as well, particularly "collective representations" (p. 297) such as symbols, signs, and group argot. The power of the collective is seen in its role in "mutual excitation" (p. 299), promoting behavior among gang members that they would not normally engage in. Despite the attention given to the larger collective of the gang, Thrasher notes the importance of subgroups within the gang.

> The two- and three-boy relationship is often much more important to the individual boy than his relationship to the gang. In such cases a boy would doubtless forego the gang before he would give up his special pal or pair of pals. (p. 322)

It is important to note that these subgroups exist in all parts of the city, regardless of whether they are affiliated with larger gangs.

Despite the fact that Thrasher's observations of gangs are nearly seventy years old, and that the demographic characteristics of cities have changed profoundly since then, many of his conclusions have important implications for the contemporary study of gangs. The central questions he addressed—gang transmission, growth of gangs, sources of cohesion among gang members, the role of threats, the importance of collective behavior, distinguishing adolescent group behavior from gang behavior, and most importantly the role of culture in understanding gangs—remain important today. And many of his observations, especially about the role of structural variables and group process within gangs, remain critical issues for the contemporary study of gangs.

Gangs in the Sixties

The advent of the Depression and World War II induced a decline in gangs and the attention paid to them. However, the conclusion of World War II brought rapid social change to American cities, as the American economy struggled to adapt to peacetime. At the same time, northern cities experienced a massive migration of southern blacks moving to the "promised land" (Lerman 1991) of jobs and greater opportunity. In many ways, this migration mirrored earlier waves of European immigrants who had moved to the industrial cities of the northeast and Midwest seeking employment. And like many of their European counterparts who came before them, southern blacks often found their new homes to be less than hospitable places.

Theory Development

Gangs began to reemerge in cities in the 1950s and spawned a new generation of gang research, theory, and policy. Attention paid to gangs by criminologists in the 1950s and 1960s yielded important theoretical insights and policy recommendations. Building on the theoretical traditions of Emile Durkheim and Robert Merton, Albert Cohen (1955) developed the theory of status frustration to explain the process by which boys become involved in delinquent activities and gangs. Because they are judged by middle-class standards that many are ill equipped to meet, working-class and lower-class boys develop frustrations about achieving status goals. As a means of resolving these status concerns, they turn to delinquent activities and to the group affiliation of the gang. Richard Cloward and Lloyd Ohlin (1960) also built on the Mertonian tradition of emphasizing the role of shared cultural success goals and institutional means of achieving those goals. Rather than emphasizing status concerns, they focused on the blocked opportunities for achieving legitimate success faced by most working-class and lower-class boys. Because the opportunities for success were differentially distributed by neighborhood, some boys found that they lacked the access to achieving the goals society defined as important. The result was three forms of adaptations; conflict gangs, property gangs, or retreatist gangs. The adaptations resulted from the level of available opportunities and the extent to which boys were integrated in the neighborhood.

Not all commentators on gangs and youth delinquency concurred with the premise that a single set of cultural values permeated American society. For the theories of Cohen and Cloward and Ohlin, it is critical that this be the case, because the commitment to a common set of values causes status frustration (for Cohen) or blocked opportunities (for Cloward and Ohlin) and leads to delinquency. Walter Miller (1958) theorized that a far different set of values permeated lower-class culture, values that naturally lead to increased levels of delinquent and gang involvement. For Miller, six "focal concerns" defined life for lower-class boys: fate, autonomy, smartness, toughness, excitement, and trouble. Commitment to these values, as opposed to those of the dominant culture, need not be explained by lack of access to legitimate success roles. Lower-class boys learned these values as a consequence of living in their own neighborhoods where such values were dominant. Miller's approach emphasized the role of a subculture in the creation and maintenance of delinquent groups and gangs.

An important development in theory and research occurred with the appearance of Lewis Yablonsky's (1962) work on the violent gang. Drawing on Thrasher, he identified three types of gangs—delinquent gangs, violent gangs, and social gangs—indicating that the violent gang was the most persistent and problematic for society. Not unexpectedly, the role of violence looms large in every aspect of this gang. The violent gang forms in response to threats against safety, and thus represents a form of protection for its members. It has a loose structure and little formal character; for example, leaders in this gang "emerge" and membership within gang subgroups in many cases is more important than the larger gang. Violence, the defining event for members of these types of gangs, can arise over seemingly senseless matters but most often occurs in response to perceived threats against gang territory. Membership fulfills a number of needs; most importantly, it meets the psychological needs of boys incapable of finding such fulfillment in the larger society. Because of its lack of organization, Yablonsky identifies the violent gang as a "near group" (p. 272); a "collective structure" situated somewhere between totally disorganized aggregates (like mobs) and well-organized aggregates (like delinquent or social gangs).

Action Research

Much criminological work takes place in a policy vacuum; that is, the research is seldom closely coordinated with ongoing policy or programmatic initiatives. A remarkable exception to this is found in the work of four researchers: Spergel (1966), Klein (1971), and Short and Strodtbeck (1974). Each of these projects evaluated a gang intervention program that was premised on theories about gangs and gang behavior. And in each the researchers used the evaluation to revisit theories about gangs and delinquency, an occasion too rare in our field. We examine each of these because they helped to set the tone for the gang research that was to follow.

While Spergel, Klein, and Short and Strodtbeck all examined active gang and delinquency prevention programs, Spergel's work was most concerned with the practical matters of working with gangs. He analyzed the approach to gang intervention that had become popular, the detached worker. At its heart, detached street work is problem-oriented, group social work, an approach with a long history, especially in Chicago, where the Chicago Area Projects had used it for some time. In part, this approach depended on the social structure of the neighborhood or community in which it operated. Spergel argued that successful work with gang members depended on an understanding of four factors: (1) the delinquent subculture (beliefs, norms and values) within the neighborhood, (2) the delinquent group itself, (3) the individual delinquent, and (4) the agency worker. Spergel highlighted the role of delinquency theory, particularly that of Cloward and Ohlin, and argued that street work *practice* must be determined by *theoretical explanations* of delinquent groups. Spergel's work had a prescriptive orientation, offering program and intervention suggestions for street workers addressing gang and delinquent behavior.

Klein (1971) assumed both a more theoretical and analytic approach to dealing with gangs, though his analysis emerged from the "action context" of evaluating gang intervention programs. Two programs, the Group Guidance Project and the Ladino Hills Project (which operated from 1962 through 1968) formed the basis of his analysis. He notes the programmatic efforts of Mobilization for Youth in New York, the Los Angeles Youth Project, the Chicago Area Projects, and Youth for Service in San Francisco. Each of these projects held many features in common, especially the detached worker approach that took programming into the community and encouraged street workers to fully involve themselves in the gang and gang activities. Klein's theoretical antecedents include Cohen, Cloward and Ohlin, Miller, and Bloch and Niederhoffer.

Klein arrived at the unsettling conclusion that the Group Guidance Project may have increased delinquency among gang members. Specifically, he found that delinquency increased among gang members who received the most services and that solidarity among gang members seemed to increase as a result of the attention paid to the gang by street workers. This led Klein to the conclusion that gang intervention programs may have the latent consequence of contributing to the attractiveness of gangs, thereby enhancing their solidarity and promoting more violence. He paid considerable attention to issues of gang structure, particularly solidarity among gang members. He concluded that most characteristics of gang structure were difficult to differentiate from other features of adolescent street culture and that members of gangs shared most in common with other (nongang) adolescents. His conclusions that gangs and gang members contained large variation within their respective ranks reinforced his earlier observation that gangs were not monolithic.

Klein's views of leadership and the sources of cohesion within gangs were consistent with his definition of gangs and gang membership. In his view, leadership was largely age related and was not so much a specific office as it was a mixture of functions. This reinforced the notion that gangs resembled other features of youth culture (disorganized, spontaneous, short term) more than they did more formal adult structures. Further support for this contention was found in the consistent report by gang members that their primary activity was "hanging out" with other members on the street. And their delinquency was described as "cafeteria style" (p. 125) rather than a purposive, well-organized specialization. Cohesiveness, the force that keeps gangs together, was more a product of external than internal sources. That is, the bonds of gang membership do not become stronger in response to internal mechanisms (meetings, codes, signs, activities) but rather as a response to external pressures. In general, Klein found that few gang goals existed outside of those generated by external pressures, and the few internal gang norms that did exist were weak and transient. The external sources of cohesion were structural (poverty, unemployment, and weak family socialization) but also included pressures that resulted from interaction with other gangs as well as members of one's own gang. In particular, the threat of violence from another gang increased solidarity within the gang. One effect of this is that most victims of gang violence were other gang members. Of particular concern to Klein was the role membership interaction played in strengthening gang cohesiveness. The more gang members met and the more important their gang was perceived to be in the community, the stronger the bonds were between gang members. Against this backdrop, Klein saw the intervention of detached workers and gang programs enhancing gang cohesiveness, making the dissolution of the gang a greater challenge.

The Ladino Hills Project gave Klein the opportunity to build on findings from the Group Guidance Project. A specific effort was made to avoid increasing gang solidarity, an outcome that would make the gang more attractive, increase membership, and expand delinquent activities. A working premise of this approach was that programmatic "attention" paid to gangs by such institutions as the police, social workers, and the schools had the latent consequence of making the gang more attractive and should be avoided. In addition, organized gang events were discouraged. The results were encouraging in many respects, as gang cohesiveness declined during the project. Despite this, the rate of delinquency increased, particularly for more serious crimes. However, the amount of delinquency overall declined, a decline that was concentrated among "companionship" offenses. The withdrawal of adults from gang activities diminished both gang cohesion and delinquency.

Short and Strodtbeck (1974) began their analysis with a premise similar to Klein's, specifically that the War on Poverty may have increased gang solidarity. Based on research in Chicago, their conclusions are similar to those of Klein, particularly with regard to gang structure, cohesion, and activities. Short and Strodtbeck adopted an approach consistent with the poverty area research of Shaw and McKay and the group delinquency perspective found in the theories of Cohen, Cloward and Ohlin, and Thrasher. They found, however, that it was difficult to locate gangs that correspond to those described in most theories. This led them to examine in greater depth the *processes* and *values* that lead to gang delinquency. Indeed, they use the concept of values to link the social status (especially social class) of gang members to their illegitimate behavior.

Short and Strodtbeck paint a picture of gangs, gang members, and gang activities remarkably similar to that drawn earlier by Klein. Like their Los Angeles counterparts, gang members in Chicago reported that the activity that consumed the greatest amount of their time was "hanging out" on the street. Short and Strodtbeck found five specific indices of gang activity: (1) conflict, (2) institutional social activities, (3) sexual behavior, hanging out, and selling alcohol, (4) homosexuality, fathering illegitimate children, and common-law marriages, and (5) involvement in minor car-related crimes, conflict, and alcohol use. They observed that these behaviors are not greatly dissimilar from the more routine activities of adolescent males. Stated differently, these analysts were unable to find activities that consistently differentiated gang members from their nongang peers. Gangs had a shifting membership and structure, with allegiances vacillating over time. Leadership seldom had power and generally was incapable of exacting discipline from members. Concomitantly, few strong group norms laid claims on the behavior of individual gang members.

Status plays a central role in Short and Strodtbeck's explanation of gang formation and activities. Threats to the status of the gang were particularly important, and conflict emerged from disputes about the reputation of the gang. But status threats also operate at the individual level for Short and Strodtbeck. They regard threats, especially to individual status, as fundamental to understanding the origin of gangs. Three systems external to the gang provide the major sources of (and threats to) individual status: (1) adult institutions such as school and jobs, (2) community institutions in the areas that generate gangs, especially street culture, and (3) gang culture. In the course of maintaining relationships with each of these systems, gang members experience threats to their status as individuals. For Short and Strodtbeck, the gang emerges as a collective solution to status threats posed by these relationships. This solution, however, is of short duration.

As America attempted to deal with demands by racial and ethnic minorities for an increased share of economic and social justice, attention to the gangs of the 1950s and early 1960s waned. Gangs faded from public concern in the sixties, replaced by broader concerns over race, increasing crime, and urban unrest. Perhaps the decline in interest over gangs confirmed what Klein and Short and Strodtbeck had reported; gangs had little permanence and stability and, if left alone, may well fade away. Whether the attention paid to other problems caused the decline in gangs, or whether gangs simply faded from the urban scene remains an open question. Regardless of the explanation, social scientists, social workers, policymakers, and the public turned their attention to other matters. This may reflect a change in the funding priorities of the federal government, as resources for studying youth gangs were no longer available (Horowitz 1983).

References

Asbury, Herbert. 1928. *The Gangs of New York*. Garden City, NJ: Alfred Knopf.

Cloward, Richard and Lloyd Ohlin. 1960. *Delinquency and Opportunity*. Glencoe, IL: Free Press.

Cohen, Albert. 1955. *Delinquent Boys*. Glencoe, IL: Free Press.

Horowitz, Ruth. 1983. *Honor and the American Dream: Culture and Identity in a Chicano Community*. New Brunswick, NJ: Rutgers University Press.

Klein, Malcolm W. 1971. *Street Gangs and Street Workers*. Englewood Cliffs, NJ: Prentice Hall.

Lerman, Nicholas. 1991. *The Promised Land: The Great Black Migration and How It Changed America*. New York: Vintage Press.

Miller, Walter B. 1958. "Lower Class Culture as a Generating Milieu of Gang Delinquency." *Journal of Social Issues*, Volume 14: 5–19.

Riis, Jacob A. 1892 (1971). *The Children of the Poor*. New York: Arne Press.

——. 1902. *The Battle with the Slum*. Montclair, NJ: Patterson Smith.

Short, James F., Jr. and Fred L. Strodtbeck. 1974. *Group Process and Gang Delinquency*. Chicago: University of Chicago Press.

Spergel, Irving. 1966. *Street Gang Work: Theory and Practice*. Reading, MA: Addison-Wesley.

Thrasher, Frederick. 1927. *The Gang*. Chicago: University of Chicago Press.

Yablonsky, Lewis. 1962 (1973). *The Violent Gang*. Baltimore: Penguin. ✦

Chapter 3 Barrio Gangs:

Street Life and Identity in Southern California

James Diego Vigil

In this brief introduction to the book Barrio Gangs, *cultural anthropologist Vigil draws on historical, cultural, and underclass theory to frame his notions about the development and persistence of Hispanic, or Cholo, gangs. Multiple marginality results from cultural accommodation to Anglo-American lifestyles, intergenerational culture clashes, and limited opportunities for social mobility in barrio communities. The barrio street gang is a social adaptation to the economic and cultural stressors confronting young men of Mexican descent. As you read the articles presented in Sections II and III, consider the following: How can the concept of multiple marginality also be applied to the development of other ethnic gangs and female gang membership?*

A look behind the scenes of Chicano youth gang behavior is long overdue. It is important to know how the streets have become such a strong socializing force in the barrios of Southern California and why certain adolescents and youth there are particularly motivated to identify with the street gang. Many of the street gang habits and customs make better sense when considered in the context of street pressures and group identification processes. To survive in street culture, one must have a street identity. It will be revealed in this study that there are many intricacies and complexities to this street identity.

Chicano street gangs in Los Angeles and Southern California have been around for several decades (Bogardus 1926). Over the past forty years they have been viewed as a menace to society, wreaking crime and violence on the rest of the populace, or as a serious social problem with roots in the urban experience of low-income minority groups. Several explanations of Chicano gangs (McWilliams 1968; Griffith 1948; Tuck 1956; Heller 1966; Rosenquist and Megargee 1969; Klein 1971; Snyder 1977; J. Moore 1978; Horowitz 1983) advanced our understanding of the problem. However, the complexity of the street gang requires a careful separation of the cluster of factors that contribute to its formation and persistence. The lives of the street youths who comprise the barrio gang reflect multiple stresses and pressures, which result in a multiple marginality. This multiple marginality derives from various interwoven situations and conditions that tend to act and react upon one another. Although interrelated, the unfolding and interpretation of these ecological, economic, social, cultural, and psychological features of the street gang suggest a developmental sequence.

All of these considerations are integral to the relationship between multiple marginality and gang patterns. In particular, it will be clear that barrio children whose lives are most intensely affected by marginality in these dimensions are more at risk to become gang members. Moreover, use of the concept will permit an examination of gang violence and related behavior within the context of a cumulative, additive experience. My self-reflexive life history involvement with various facets of street and gang life and the life histories of different types of contemporary gang members provide insights and nuances and shifting levels of insider/outsider analysis to this perspective. This combination of ways of examining and describing the street gang will promote theory building and the integration of more narrowly focused explanations for gang phenomena that have emerged over the years.

Anyone who regularly works with street gangs can learn the answers to such questions as, Where are they located? Who are the members? What do they do and how do they do it? However, even after having gained such knowledge, few observers understand what the sources of this behavior are or when in a person's life does such behavior emerge. It is these and other such questions that should guide our discussion if we are to better comprehend the gang phenomenon. Partial, incomplete, and narrow assessments do injustice to the general public as well as to the communities where gangs are common. As an example of this narrow attitude, I once inquired of a city official, the director of community programs and affairs, what recreational and social programs were offered to the local barrio youth and whether he was familiar with some of the conditions that caused the formation of the gang. He gave a testy response: "We don't want to understand the problem, we just want to stop it." While desiring to "stop it" is understandable, such lack of analysis can only impede the official's desire.

Chicano gangs are made up largely of young males, from 13 to 25 years of age. The gang subcultural style is a response to the pressures of street life and serves to give certain barrio youth a source of familial support, goals and directives, and sanctions and guides. Although gang members typically constitute a small minority of the young in a barrio, they represent a street style that both conforms and contrasts with familiar youth patterns (Klein 1968). On the one hand, most of their time is spent in the usual cohort activities found in any neighborhood where adolescents and other youth congregate. They talk, joke, plan social events, and exchange stories of adventure and love. Their alcohol consumption and drug use shows some parallels with that of other American adolescents. Yet it is their other, violent, socially disruptive activities that distinguish gang members from most other adolescents.

Reflecting the tendency among adolescents to develop new modes of dress and speech, Chicano gang members have adopted a distinctive street style of dress, speech, gestures, tattoos, and graffiti. This style is called cholo, a centuries-old term for some Latin American Indians who are partially acculturated to Hispanic-based elite cultures (Wolck 1973). The term also reflects the cultural transitional situation of Mexican Americans in the southwestern United States; it is a process strongly affected by underclass forces and street requisites. Many of the cholo customs symbolize an attachment to and identification with the gang, although many individuals copy the style without joining the gang. As we will note, there is a wide difference among members in degree of commitment to the gang, but generally it is those members with the most problematic lives and intense street experiences who become regular members. Over the decades, the gang has developed a subculture, that is, a social structure and cultural value system with its own age-graded cohorts, initiations, norms and goals, and roles. These now function to socialize and enculturate barrio youth. Though the emergence of a gang subculture initially resulted from urban maladaption among some segments of the Mexican immigrant population, it is now a continuing factor to which new Latino immigrants must adapt. To understand developments in this area we must look to the starting point, the inception of this country's urban revolution.

Gangs in Urban Immigrant Communities

Gangs have been an urban problem in the United States since the beginning of large-scale immigration to this country before the turn of the century (Thrasher 1963 [1927]). The processes and patterns of immigrant adaption, although different in important ways, stemmed from remarkably similar sources. The early groups were European immigrants especially from southeastern Europe, who came to this country to find work and a better life. Most of them settled in urban areas and established their own communities. The process of finding work, locating a place to live, and adjusting to urban life was repeated many times over for different ethnic groups, and the Mexican immigrant population is no different in this regard.

What characterized most of these groups was their poverty, their lack of skills. As a result, they were treated as a cheap source of labor. In addition they came from different cultural and (by contemporary definition) racial backgrounds that contrasted sharply with the dominant Anglo-American one. Anglo native-born Americans tended to view the ethnically different newcomers' appearance, behavior patterns, and poverty as a single entity; the immigrants thus faced discrimination from the native born. Their cultural difference acted in two ways to affect them. One stemmed from the changes they had to make in their own cultural values, beliefs, and patterns to adjust and acculturate to Anglo-American lifestyles. The other was a result of how the dominant Anglo culture received and accommodated them. Their own attitudes and behaviors and those of the predominant society operated to affect where they would live, what they would do for a living, and how, when, and even whether they would become "Americanized" (Handlin 1951). Exploitation and discrimination, in particular, dominated the early period after their arrival and extended to the lives of their children. The pressures and anxieties of urban poverty, of the struggle toward a better life, and of overcoming feelings of ethnic and racial inferiority made immigrant cultural adaptation problematic. Such an experience often resulted in gangs.

Throughout most of this century, researchers and writers have compiled evidence on urban gangs. The focus of these accounts varies as to ethnic group, time, and place and the theoretical emphasis. Nonetheless, there is widespread agreement among writers that gangs are an urban phenomenon, particularly so in the cases of ethnic minorities (Clinard 1968), and they represent a pattern found among lower-class adolescents (Cloward and Ohlin 1960). In fact, there is a complex of other factors that makes the urban experience so remarkably uniform: a breakdown in social institutions, especially the family and schools (which often impede rather than accommodate adjustment); a first- and second-generational conflict within each ethnic group, which creates loyalty discord and identity confusions; and a noted predisposition among youth to gravitate toward street peers for sources of social associations and personal fulfillment.

Within a generation or two, most members of each early ethnic immigrant group improved their standard of living and stabilized themselves as wage earners and homemakers. Problems associated with urban adaptation, such as youth gangs, crime, poor housing, and unemployment, were initially severe. Eventually, these problems were worked through and became less serious as each group acculturated. Hence, after two generations of severe culture clash both within the ethnic community (intergenerational) and between it and the other communities, the issues that sometimes became a source of national concern, such as culture conflict, economic exploitation, and associated social disruptions, tend to dissipate.

The Nature and Persistence of Chicano Gangs

Although Mexican Americans in urban settings largely share with earlier, mostly eastern U.S. ethnics a similarity in how adaptation proceeds, there are also distinct differences between them. For one thing, Chicano youth gangs (unlike those of other immigrant groups) have shown a remarkable longevity. Moore, Vigil, and Garcia (1983) suggest reasons for this difference:

> the gangs are long-lasting, not transitory phenomena. . . . With few exceptions, the Chicano communities of Los Angeles never have been invaded by another ethnic group, nor has another ethnic group succeeded them, nor has there been total cultural disintegration. Instead, there has been more or less continuous immigration of yet more Mexicans, with a reinforcement of some of the traditional culture. (p. 183)

Mexican Americans remained more visually distinct from the majority than did the third generation descendants of European immigrants, and the continued presence of fully unacculturated Mexicans made their communities more culturally distinct.

Many families and their children experience acute poverty and limited social mobility opportunities in these barrios, and thus, over time, there developed an underclass with its own set of problems. It is from among these children that the youths most intensely involved in the gangs tend to come. As members of a persistent underclass within the Mexican American population, these youths come from households with even lower incomes than those of other barrio families and a higher incidence of stressful family situations. (This is perhaps reflective of what Auletta [1982] refers to as the 9 million, a subgroup of the 25 million below the national poverty level, who experience a grinding cycle of poverty. Recent reports seem to support the existence of this strata in urban centers [Bearak and Meyer 1985:14; NALEO 1985].) Poor school records and limited job options have combined to make them even more street oriented. As part of their survival on the streets, especially during adolescence, they adopt cultural values and customs that help shape their personal identities.

The youth gangs of Mexican Americans have arisen in the context of the broader pattern of Mexican adaptation to urban life in the United States. Mexican immigration has been the primary factor in the growth of the Mexican American population. The first large wave (1920s) brought anywhere from 1.5 million to 2 million immigrants, doubling the native Mexican American population (Samora 1971). In subsequent waves in the periods from 1940 to 1964 (4 million) and from 1969 through the 1970s (anywhere from 6 to 12 million), the population has continued to swell (Cornelius 1978). Throughout these decades of immigration, the population increasingly settled in urban areas, and today close to 90 percent of the Mexican American (native and immigrant alike) population is in urban areas (Alvírez, Bean, and Williams 1981). A recent report (Muller 1984) on foreign immigration to California since 1970 found that, of over 2 million who have legally settled there, "at least 1.3 million of them have settled in its seven southern counties" (p. 1); and this figure excludes the uncounted and undocumented (Cornelius, Chávez, and Castro 1982). Southern California, and Los Angeles particularly, is the urban area that has received most of these immigrants. Their adjustment and its social and cultural developments have taken different forms, depending on the work opportunities, places of settlement, and, generally, the standard of living attained by immigrants. Such continuous waves of immigrants ensure that there is always a large pool of second-generation Mexican Americans.

Bogardus (1926) noted that in the early years of Mexican immigration there was a "boy" gang problem and characterized it as an incipient form that could be remedied. However, in the following decades it was clear that the gang problem was becoming a serious one, with a formal structure and emerging set of norms and rules to attract and guide members (Bogardus 1943). Cultural change over the years was affected by barrio and underclass life and was particularly acute during the Depression, when even more Mexican youths experienced the intense pressures of urban poverty, especially the second generation. It is a second-generation urban American experience that, in the Chicano case, is a continually renewed phenomenon because of continued immigration. The second generation in the 1930s–1940s originated the pachuco lifestyle (a label created for those who wore zoot suits and spoke a mixed English-Spanish slang language that borrowed heavily from caló—this in turn, was a continuation of what the Gypsies had started in Spain and later was diffused, by bullfighters it seems, to Mexico [McWilliams 1968; G. C. Barker 1950]). Pachucos were a group who strove to reconcile the conflicting values and nascent pressures that urban adaptation brought; prolonged lower-class status and immobility shaped how Mexican culture was relinquished and American culture integrated into a street style. This style served as a mechanism of adaptation for many youth who needed a source of personal identification and human support, especially during the adolescent self-identification process where ego and peer groups merge to simplify age/sex identification. Pachucos were more than a "boy" gang of loosely aligned street children who participated primarily in street mischief. They had passed the incipient phase of gang formation, as pride in barrio affiliation, barrio conflicts, and some amount of drug use and abuse became a part of their lifestyle. Because most pachucos preferred to look "cool" in their zoot suits and have a good time, these damaging group activities were not as widespread or intense as those practiced in more recent decades. As the practice of negative group activities has escalated, the early generations of gang members, even most pachucos, can be viewed as a transitional form of gang.

A gang subculture eventually formed and became a pressing force in barrio life. Earlier, youths would join the boys on the street for play or mischief. Later, pachucos began to add their distinctive elements to the emerging street gang style. With the passage of time, and the perpetuation of situations, conditions, and social practices that helped to create it, the street style now works to socialize and enculturate youth to a rooted gang subculture with its own group norms and cholo role fronts. The street violence and other debilitating activities that are common features of barrio life can only be understood in terms of this subcultural socialization and its appeal to barrio youths with particular types of personal backgrounds that give rise to particular forms of self-identification processes.

In the 1980s, Chicano gangs comprise at least one-half of the four hundred gangs that exist in Los Angeles County (Decker 1983). This number, of course, is larger when the counties adjacent to Los Angeles are included. Notwithstanding the absolute number of Chicano gangs, however, only a small percentage of Chicano youth, perhaps only 4 to 10 percent of most barrios, are affiliated with gangs (Morales 1982). Of this relatively small percentage, there are subcategories (based upon degree and level of commitment) of regular, peripheral, temporary, and situational. For the most part, gang affiliation and gang-related behavior are primarily male phenomena, although many barrios also have smaller female cliques. The great majority of youths, as in other ethnic groups (cf., e.g., Whyte 1973), find other sources of identification and emulation.

The cultural style of the gang subculture arose partly as a response to street life. However, its major cultural forms are a reforging of Mexican and American patterns. This recombination, of course, borrowed heavily from the earlier pachuco syncretic formulation of creating a culture of mixed and blended elements (e.g., language). Cholos (the present term identifying the style as well as its bearers), share a cultural orientation that makes them distinct from other barrio youth. Although cholos are Americanized, either by accident or by design, they refuse or are unable to be totally assimilated (Vigil 1979; Buriel et al. 1982). In important ways they consider themselves traditionalists and retain certain Mexican customs, however attenuated, as part of their cultural repertoire. For example, they have retained the caló idiom of expression; the strong sense of group as family; the adolescent palomilla cohorting tradition (Rubel 1966), which includes many daring and bravado male patterns; and an antiauthority attitude, which is, perhaps, a reaction against gabacho (originally a term used for foreigners, such as the French in Mexico during the 1860s intervention, but now designating Anglos) racism (Vigil 1984).

The gangs that have been addressed by researchers range from those that began in the 1940s, and that have over time established more than a dozen identifiable age-graded cohorts (Moore 1978), to those of more recent vintage. An individual gang might include as many as two hundred or more, or as few as ten or twelve, members. It is mainly in the suburbs that the newer, smaller gangs are found. Older, larger gangs, on the other hand, are usually located in long-established urban and semirural barrios. Semirural barrios, and the gangs associated with them, have often been engulfed in recent years by rapidly expanding suburban growth. The deep-rooted presence of older barrio gangs has become a model and a stimulus for gang formation in other areas, as well as a major socialization factor throughout the barrio and nearby areas.

Acculturation is a major factor in a large urban region, such as the greater Los Angeles metropolitan area. Barrio and underclass life has shaped each new immigrant population in different ways, however, creating generational contrasts. As the decades pass, each generation, depending on sociocultural environment and historical conditions, becomes part of a process of cultural change and accommodation. What once began as a Mexican subculture is now transformed into different subcultures. It is in the second generation where the children of Mexican immigrants undergo acculturation shifts resembling a transitional (cholo subculture) phase. Sometimes the phase involves culture conflict, whereby both the donor culture and the host culture become problematic. This ambivalent cultural (and personal) identity makes the gang subculture attractive for a small but significant minority of barrio youth. Their lives are often regulated by the age-graded klikas (cliques, or cohorts within the gang). Older gang members also lend some sense of order to their often confused interpersonal interactions by providing vertical lines of organization (Klein 1971); and the gang's involvement in some forms of criminal behavior affords avenues for prestige and income to those who have limited chances of acquiring meaningful jobs (Moore 1978; Chicano Pinto Research Project 1979, 1981). Increasingly, in recent years, both immigrant youths from Mexico and third-generation Mexican Americans have become peripherally involved with street gangs. The Chicano Pinto Research Project (1979, 1981) has found small numbers of third-generation Chicanos, who are themselves offspring of gang members, involved in the core membership of some younger age cohorts.

Multiple Marginality and Street Adaptation

The Chicano youth gang began and grew in ecologically marginal areas of the city and surrounding countryside. It was fed by pressures generated by a marginal economic role. It is peopled by youths with marginal ethnic and personal identities. Each feature of gang life merits scrutiny by itself, but once this task is completed the next step is to search for the links between these features. For example, the interrelationships between socioeconomic condition (e.g., mother-centered households) or social event (e.g., sex identity strivings) must be assessed to understand why gangs are so important during adolescence. A multiple research strategy employing the concept of multiple marginality, which is especially useful with broad and in-depth self-reflexive and life history information, will enhance this understanding. This type of information reflects various times, places, thoughts, and events that must be unpeeled layer by layer, and thus a multiple construct facilitates such a discussion. It is a construct that views reality as a constellation of forces tending to act and react upon one another.

Multiple marginality encompasses the consequences of barrio life, low socioeconomic status, street socialization and enculturation, and problematic development of a self-identity. These gang features arise in a web of ecological, socioeconomic, cultural, and psychological factors. The use of such a concept in an analysis of Chicano youth gangs will help to avoid the difficulties stemming from single-cause examinations of previous gang studies; Cartwright et al. (1975: 25–45) have addressed such problems in the second chapter of their review of juvenile gangs. The use of the concept multiple marginality can lead to what Geertz (1973:3) has called a "thick description." Looking at various circumstances and forces in a combinative way increases our understanding of the similarities and variations found within and across groups. It also affords an opportunity to make use of an analyst's personal experiences when merited. Having watched gangs and gang members for many years as an insider has enabled me to chart the flow of events and decision-making processes of street gangs.

An eclectic multiple marginality analysis makes it possible to integrate key elements of the several theories that have been formulated to explain gang delinquency and that emerged in the middle 1950s to early 1960s. (This is no coincidence, as the post-World

War II urban explosion led to the development of problems among new minority groups, such as Puerto Ricans, blacks, and Mexican Americans, that were perhaps even more threatening than what had transpired earlier with white ethnics. These new phenomena led, in turn, to the reformation of old theories and the development of new theories.) In summary fashion, these theories are (1) male maturation process, "becoming a man" (e.g., Bloch and Niederhoffer 1958); (2) subcultural, collective solution of lower-class boys to acquire status (e.g., Cohen 1955); (3) lower-class cultural values (e.g., W. B. Miller 1958); (4) lower-class means and upper-class goals disjunctures or simplified means-goals discrepancy (e.g., Cloward and Ohlin 1960); and (5) sociopathic personalities that make "near-group" (e.g., Yablonsky 1959). There are several ways to assess these theories: they can either be reclassified as sociogenic (e.g., 3, 4) and psychogenic (e.g., 1, 2, 5) or, examined another way, as fitting within explanations that focus on strain (2, 4), cultural deviance (1–4), and (in varying degrees, all five) social control (Edgerton 1973; Dembo et al. 1984; Cartwright et al. 1975). Although the authors argue that their particular theory is most salient to the gang phenomenon, each theory accounts for only an aspect of the gang pattern. Yet, all the authors in fact rely on a number of related factors to arrive at their theoretical formulation. For example, Bloch and Niederhoffer (1958) maintain that the gang outlet for becoming a man results because society (through such phenomena as poverty, family stress, and urban disorganization) has failed them; and Cloward and Ohlin (1960), working on a variation of Merton's (1949) means/goals disjunctures, elaborate on the nature of low-income slum life to explain gang subcultural variations. This suggests that a cluster of factors needs to be examined to understand gang delinquency; Cloward and Ohlin say as much with these words: "gangs, or subcultures . . . are typically found among adolescent males in lower class areas of large urban centers" (p. 1; cf. Short and Strodtbeck 1965:19).

The multiple marginality framework better allows for descriptions and interpretations of particular (and perhaps peculiar) facts of people, time, and place. Such a larger framework simultaneously provides for a broader and more in-depth portrayal of the various realities that gang members experience. The intensity and duration of the individual or group experience in gangs as such are better gauged in this broadly integrative way. There are several marginal situations and conditions that are a part of the Mexicans' overall adaptation to urban life. In such circumstances of "long duration . . . the individual can be born into it and live his whole life in it," becoming a participant in "even the development of a 'marginal culture' " (Dickie-Clark 1966:24).

Some researchers have noted that the concept of marginality should be carefully applied because it tends to diminish the important role of lower-income workers in a capitalist economy (Peattie 1974). Perlman (1976), in providing a sweeping critical summation of marginality theory, nevertheless recognizes the need for a construct that looks "to some set of circumstances outside individual control," such as one that "explains these conditions as expressions of the social structure and the historical process" and that looks at "different dimensions of marginality and seeks rather to examine the specificity of their interaction in each instance" (p. 251).

Mexican and Mexican American labor has definitely been significant in the economic development of the southwestern United States, for example, in mining, farming, railroading, and so on. These contributions, however, have not assured them of commensurate political and economic power, as they are excluded by leaders from decision-making processes. This marginality, moreover, is maintained by structural features in the environment to which they must adapt (Kapferer 1978; Lomnitz 1977; Barrera 1979).

The background to the current gang situation is also important, for multiple marginality has cumulative, diachronic sources, especially in group history. A macro (group history), meso (family history), and micro (life history) descending order of analysis is undertaken to show through time how ecological and economic conditions create sociocultural stresses and ambiguities, which, in turn, lead to subcultural and psychological mechanisms of adjustment. Descriptions of group and family history are well documented in the archives (Bogardus 1926, 1934) and in such studies as the longitudinal investigations of Moore and her pinto (ex-convict) associates (Moore 1978; Chicano Pinto Research Project 1979, 1981; Moore and Mata 1981). Moreover, my personal life experiences with numerous families who exemplify the multiple processes that lead to gang patterns provide for a unique insider/outsider interpretive perspective to inform these life histories and to show how these personalized events of places and living actions are refracted through the prism of multiple marginality. For example, I have gone through many experiences similar to those of gang youths . . . including being set upon and beaten by gang members into whose "turf" I had strayed. Such personal experiences inform my interpretation of such events.

A macroexamination of Mexican adaptation provides the backdrop for understanding Chicano youth gangs, for there are several areas that need to be traced. Clearly, a key focus is to examine how an emergent underclass life has affected many Mexicans. The underclass phenomenon entails the longitudinal effects of poverty. The youth groups that are produced in such nascent circumstances are quite different from, for example, the earlier nonviolent "street corner" groups reported by Whyte (1973). In fact, endemic racial barriers and cultural strains have combined with status to make this so (Wolfgang et al. 1972; Bogardus 1943). The historical record of cultural and social disparagement experienced by Mexicans is indicative of such developments (Moore and Pachón 1976; Acuña 1981; Vigil 1984).

Urban adaptation for immigrant Mexican families was problematic initially and continues to be so today. Low-paying jobs led to residence in older, run-down interstices of the city, such as sections of East Los Angeles (Gustafson 1940:25–40; Ginn 1947:18–19). Such circumstances created repercussions in other social, cultural, and psychological realms. Moreover, and similar to the experience of other immigrant groups (Feldstein and Costello 1974; Shaw and McKay 1942), schools and law enforcement often operated to aggravate rather than ameliorate problems in Mexican cultural adaptations (U.S. Commission on Civil Rights 1970, 1971). This segmented integration into American society and subsequent fragmenting of traditional social practices and cultural customs resulted in a new cultural orientation. In short, economic hardships undermined social control institutions: family life became stress ridden and schooling and contacts with law enforcement were problematic. The streets and older street youths became the major socialization and enculturation agents, with the gang representing a type of street social control institution by becoming in turn a partial substitute for family (providing emotional and social support networks), school (giving instructions on how to think and act), and police (authority and sanctions to enforce adherence to gang norms). The experience created a new social identity and thus a need for a new personal identity, and for street youth, the gang, both good and bad features, became a coping mechanism to ameliorate social pressures and develop avenues for personal fulfillment.

References

Acuña, Rudy, 1981. *Occupied America: A History of Chicanos*. 2nd ed. New York: Harper and Row.

Alvírez, David, Frank D. Bean, and Dorie Williams, 1981. "The Mexican American Family." In *Ethnic Families in America: Patterns and Variations*, Charles H. Mindel and Robert W. Hobenstein (eds.), pp. 269–292. New York: Elsevier.

Auletta, Ken, 1982. *The Underclass*. New York: Random House.

Barker, G. C., 1950. *Pachuco, an American-Spanish Argot and Its Social Function in Tucson, Arizona*. Tucson: University of Arizona Press.

Barrera, Mario, 1979. *Race and Class in the Southwest: A Theory of Racial Inequality*. Notre Dame, IN: University of Notre Dame Press.

Bearak, Barry, and Richard E. Meyer, 1985. "No Tactic Yet Found to Win Poverty War." *Los Angeles Times*, August 1. [Five-part series, America and Its Poor]

Bloch, H. A., and A. Niederhoffer, 1958. *The Gang: A Study in Adolescent Behavior.* New York: Philosophical Library.

Bogardus, Emory S., 1926. *The City Boy and His Problems*. Los Angeles: House of Ralston, Rotary Club of Los Angeles.

——. 1934. *The Mexican in the United States*. USC Social Science Series, no. 8. Los Angeles: University of Southern California Press.

——. 1943. "Gangs of Mexican American Youth." *Sociology and Social Research* 28:55–56.

Buriel, Raymond, Silverio Calzada, and Richard Vasquez, 1982. "The Relationship of Traditional Mexican American Culture to Adjustment and Delinquency among Three Generations of Mexican American Male Adolescents." *Hispanic Journal of Behavioral Sciences* 4(1):41–55.

Cartwright, Desmond S., B. Tomson, and H. Schwartz, 1975. *Gang Delinquency.* Monterey, CA: Brooks/Cole.

Chicano Pinto Research Project, 1979. *A Model for Chicano Drug Use and for Effective Utilization of Employment and Training Resources by Barrio Addicts and Ex-Offenders*. Los Angeles: Final report for the Department of Labor and National Institute of Drug Abuse.

——. 1981. *Barrio Impact of High Incarceration Rates*. By Joan W. Moore and John Long. Los Angeles: Final report for National Institute of Mental Health.

Clinard, Marshal B., 1968. *Sociology of Deviant Behavior.* New York: Holt, Rinehart and Winston.

Cloward, R. A., and L. B. Ohlin, 1960. *Delinquency and Opportunity: A Theory of Delinquent Gangs*. New York: Free Press.

Cohen, Albert K., 1955. *Delinquent Boys: The Culture of the Gang*. Glencoe, IL: Free Press.

Cornelius, Wayne A., Leo R. Chávez, and Jorge G. Castro, 1982. *Mexican Immigrants and Southern California: A Summary of Current Knowledge*. University of California, San Diego, Center for U.S.-Mexican Studies, Research Report Series, no. 36.

Decker, Cathleen, 1983. "Gang-Related Murders Fall by 38 Percent in Los Angeles." *Los Angeles Times*, January 7.

Dembo, Richard, Nola Allen, and Harold J. Vetter, 1984. *A Framework for Understanding Nondelinquent and Delinquent Life Styles in the Inner City.* [N.p.]

Dickie-Clark, H. F., 1966. *The Marginal Situation*. London: Routledge, Keagan Paul.

Edgerton, Robert B., 1973. *Deviant Behavior and Cultural Theory.* Addison Wesley Module in Anthropology, no. 37. Reading, MA: Addison-Wesley Publishing Co.

Feldstein, S., and L. Costello (eds.), 1974. *The Ordeal of Assimilation: A Documentary History of the White Working Class*. New York: Anchor Press/Doubleday.

Geertz, Clifford, 1973. *The Interpretation of Culture*. New York: Basic Books.

Ginn, M. D., 1947. "Social Implications of the Living Conditions of a Selected Number of Families Participating in the Cleland House Program." M.A. thesis, University of Southern California, Department of Sociology.

Griffith, Beatrice, 1948. *American Me*. Boston: Houghton Mifflin Company.

Gustafson, C. V., 1940. "An Ecological Analysis of the Hollenbeck Area of Los Angeles." M.A. thesis, University of Southern California, Department of Sociology.

Handlin, Oscar, 1951. *The Uprooted*. New York: Grosset and Dunlap.

Heller, Celia S., 1966. *Mexican American Youth: Forgotten Youth at the Crossroads*. New York: Random House.

Horowitz, Ruth, 1983. *Honor and the American Dream: Culture and Identity in a Chicano Community.* New Brunswick, NJ: Rutgers University Press.

Kapferer, Bruce, 1978. "Structural Marginality and the Urban Social Order." *Urban Anthropology* 7(3):287–320.

Klein, Malcolm W., 1968. "Impressions of Juvenile Gang Members." *Adolescence* 3(9):53–78.

——. 1971. *Street Gangs and Street Workers*. Englewood Cliffs, NJ: Prentice Hall.

Lomnitz, Larissa A., 1977. *Networks and Marginality: Life in a Mexican Shantytown*. New York: Academic Press.

McWilliams, C., 1968. *North from Mexico—the Spanish-Speaking People of the United States*. New York: Greenwood Press.

Merton, Robert K., 1949. *Social Theory and Social Structure*. Glencoe, IL: Free Press.

Miller, Walter B., 1958. "Lower Class Culture as a Generating Milieu of Gang Delinquency." *Journal of Social Issues* 14(3):519.

Moore, Joan, 1978. *Homeboys: Gangs, Drugs, and Prison in the Barrios of Los Angeles.* Philadelphia: Temple University Press.

Moore, Joan, and Alberto Mata, 1981. *Women and Heroin in Chicano Communities*. Los Angeles: Chicano Pinto Research Project.

Moore, Joan W., and Harry Pachón, 1976. *Mexican Americans*. 2nd ed. Englewood Cliffs, NJ: Prentice Hall.

Moore, Joan W., James Diego Vigil, and Robert Garcia, 1983. "Residence and Territoriality in

Gangs." *Journal of Social Problems* 31(2):182–194.

Morales, Armando, 1982. "The Mexican American Gang Member: Evaluation and Treatment." In *Mental Health and Hispanic Americans*, Rosina M. Becerra, Marvin Karno, and Javier I. Escobar (eds.). New York: Grune and Stratton.

Muller, Thomas, 1984. *The Fourth Wave: California's Newest Immigrants*. Washington, DC: Urban Institute Press.

National Association of Latino Elected and Appointed Officials (NALEO), 1985. *Poverty's Invisible Victims: Hispanic Children; Number of Latino Poor Children Doubles in California in Past Decade*. Washington, DC: NALEO News Release.

Peattie, Lisa R., 1974. "The Concept of 'Marginality' as Applied to Squatter Settlements." In *Latin American Urban Research: Anthropological Perspectives on Latin American Urbanization*, vol. 4, ed. Wayne A. Cornelius and Felicity M. Trueblood (eds.). Beverly Hills, CA: Sage.

Perlman, Janet, 1976. *The Myth of Marginality*. Berkeley: University of California Press.

Rosenquist, C. M., and E. I. Megargee, 1969. *Delinquency in Three Cultures*. Austin: University of Texas Press.

Rubel, A. J., 1966. *Across the Tracks: Mexican Americans in a Texas City*. Austin: University of Texas Press.

Samora, J., 1971. *Los Mojados: The Wetback Story*. Notre Dame, IN: University of Notre Dame Press.

Shaw, C., and R. McKay, 1942. *Juvenile Delinquency and Urban Areas*. Chicago: University of Chicago Press.

Short, James F., Jr., and Fred L. Strodtbeck, 1965. *Group Process and Gang Delinquency*. Chicago: University of Chicago Press.

Snyder, P. Z., 1977. "An Anthropological Description of Street Gangs in the Los Angeles Area." [A working note, prepared for the Department of Justice by the Rand Corporation, Santa Monica, California.]

Thrasher, Frederic M., 1963. *The Gang*. Chicago: University of Chicago Press. [Originally published in 1927.]

Tuck, R., 1956. *Not with the Fist: Mexican-Americans in a Southwest City*. New York: Harcourt, Brace.

United States Commission on Civil Rights, 1970. *Mexican Americans and the Administration of Justice in the Southwest*. Washington, DC: U.S. Government Printing Office.

——. 1971. *Report I: Ethnic Isolation of Mexican Americans in the Public Schools of the Southwest*. Washington, DC: U.S. Government Printing Office.

Vigil, James Diego, 1979. "Adaptation Strategies and Cultural Life Styles of Mexican American Adolescents." *Hispanic Journal of Behavioral Sciences* 1(4):375–392. [UCLA Spanish-Speaking Mental Health Research Center.]

——. 1984. *From Indians to Chicanos: The Dynamics of Mexican American Culture*. Prospect Heights, IL: Waveland Press. [Originally published as *From Indians to Chicanos: A Sociocultural History*. St. Louis, MO: C.V. Mosby Co., 1980.]

Whyte, William F., 1973. *Street Corner Society*. Chicago: University of Chicago Press. [Originally published in 1943.]

Wolck, Wolfgang, 1973. "Attitudes toward Spanish and Quechua in Bilingual Peru." In *Language and Attitudes*. Roger Shuy and Ralph W. Fosold (eds.). Washington, D.C.: Georgetown University Press.

Wolfgang, Marvin, Robert M. Figlio, and Thorsten Sellin, 1972. *Delinquency in a Birth Cohort*. Chicago: University of Chicago Press.

Yablonsky, L., 1959. "The Delinquent Gang as a Near-Group." *Social Problems* 7:108–117. ✦

Chapter 4
Risk Factors for Gang Membership

Terence P. Thornberry

As Thornberry notes, two features of modern street gangs are cause for concern among researchers and policymakers. First, gang members are disproportionately involved in delinquency, particularly serious and violent offending. Second, the 1980s and 1990s witnessed a tremendous growth in the number of youth gangs and the number of cities and communities reporting gangs. Each of these trends will be addressed again in the articles that follow. Thornberry makes these points in order to highlight why it is necessary for researchers to uncover the risk factors for gang membership among youths. His work is important for both its methodological and theoretical contributions. Although many gang studies focus on gangs as the unit of analysis, the studies Thornberry discusses focus on gang members. Both the Rochester Youth Development Study and the Seattle Social Development Project adopted a developmental approach to the study of gangs and employed longitudinal survey research, tracking and reinterviewing the same group of youths from childhood through adolescence. This approach enables researchers to examine both the antecedents and consequences of gang membership, highlighting as well the transient character of gang membership for most youths. Reporting findings from both of these projects, Thornberry reviews those factors found to increase youths' risks for joining gangs.

Reprinted from: Terence P. Thornberry, "Membership in Youth Gangs and Involvement in Serious and Violent Offending." In R. Loeber and D. P. Farrington, (eds.), *Serious and Violent Juvenile Offenders*, pp. 147–166.

Since the earliest days of gang research, such as Thrasher's (1927/1963) classic study of 1,313 gangs in Chicago, scholars have noted the tremendously disproportionate contribution that gang members make to the level of crime in society. Indeed, the observation that gang members are extensively involved in delinquency—especially serious and violent delinquency—is one of the most robust and consistent observations in criminological research.

This observation has been made across time, space, and methods of data collection. Observational studies of gang behavior suggest that gang members are heavily involved in various forms of delinquent activities. This finding has been reported in the earlier research of Spergel (1964), Miller (1966), and Klein (1971), as well as many more recent observational studies such as those by J. W. Moore (1978), Hagedorn (1988), Vigil (1988), and Taylor (1990). Studies that rely on official data to compare gangs and non-gang members also have found a strong association between gang membership and delinquent activity (see Cohen, 1969; Huff, 1996a; Klein, Gordon, & Maxson, 1986; Klein & Maxson, 1989). Finally, several studies that rely on survey research techniques report higher rates of involvement in delinquency for gang members as compared to non-gang members. These include Short and Strodtbeck's (1965) classic study of Chicago gangs, Tracy (1979), Fagan, Piper, and Moore (1986), Fagan (1989, 1990), and Huff (1996a). There is general agreement that the effect of gang membership is particularly pronounced for more serious offenses and for violent offenses. Thus, gang members are not only more extensively involved in delinquency, but they also are more extensively involved in the types of delinquency that [include serious, violent offending].

Not only are gang members more involved in delinquency than nonmembers, but in recent years there has also been a tremendous increase in the number of gangs and gang members in American society. Klein (1995) reports that between 1961 and 1970 there was a 74 percent increase in the number of gang-involved cities, an 83 percent increase from 1970 to 1980, and a phenomenal 345 percent increase from 1980 to 1992 (pp. 90–91). "Gangs are no longer a big-city problem" (Klein, 1995, p. 96); they have spread to cities of all sizes.

Curry, Ball, and Decker (1996a, 1996b) report quite similar results in surveys of law enforcement agencies conducted in 1991 and 1993. Based on "conservative estimates," Curry et al. (1996a) found that 57 percent of all American cities had a gang problem in 1993 but that 87 percent of the cities with a population of between 150,000 and 200,000 reported a gang problem and 89 percent of the cities with a population of over 200,000 reported a gang problem. According to Curry et al. (1996a), "The scope of the U.S. gang problem in 1993 was conservatively estimated at 735 (705–765) jurisdictions with 8,625 gangs [and] 378,087 gang members" (p. 3). These results represent a substantial increase over those observed for 1991. Across just those 2 years, there was a 76.7 percent increase in the estimated number of gangs and a 51.9 percent increase in the estimated number of gang members.

The National Youth Gang Center (1997) surveyed over 4,000 law enforcement agencies at the end of 1995. Over half (58 percent of 2,007 respondents) of the responding agencies, covering all 50 states, reported youth gang problems during 1995. Overall, about 2,000 cities, towns, and counties reported the presence of more than 23,000 gangs with membership totaling nearly 665,000 in 1995 (National Youth Gang Center, 1997). Half of all cities and towns under 25,000 population reported gang problems.

All three of these studies are surveys of law enforcement agencies and, unfortunately, therefore, may share common sources of bias. For example, part of the increase in the number of cities with gangs may be due to a heightened awareness of gang problems in American society and an increased willingness to identify local problems as gang related. Nevertheless, the consistency of the results and the magnitude of the increase suggest there has been a substantial expansion of gang behavior in the recent past. This is alarming for several reasons. First is the sheer number of gangs and gang members in American society. Second is the percentage of cities that are currently experiencing gang problems; virtually all large cities, and well over half of all cities, report active gangs. Third is the tremendously rapid increase in the spread of gangs throughout urban America. In the space of about 10 years, gangs have spread from a relatively small number of cities to being a regular feature of the urban landscape.

Scope of This Review

Starting with the work of Thrasher in the 1920s, the research literature on gangs has expanded tremendously throughout the course of this century. Many of these studies are based on observational methods in which a researcher gains access to one or more gangs and spends a substantial period of time on the street corners with them, observing their behaviors and relationships. Other studies are comparative; researchers sample gang members and compare their behaviors and attitudes with those of nonmembers. Although our understanding of gangs and their contribution to crime and delinquency has been greatly enhanced by these studies, they have a curiously myopic quality to them. That is, both observational and comparative studies generally study gang members only during their period of active gang membership. These studies often contain little, if any, information on the lives of gang members before and after their active gang membership.[1] As a consequence, the general literature on street gangs often fails to take into account developmental and life course issues with respect to gang membership.

Several excellent reviews of the general literature on street gangs have been published recently. In particular, they include Klein's *The American Street Gang: Its Nature, Prevalence, and Control* (1995) and Spergel's *The Youth Gang Problem: A Community Approach* (1995). In addition, the second edition of Huff's book, *Gangs in America* (1996b) contains an excellent set of contemporary essays on this topic. Rather than inadequately repeating the summaries presented by Klein, Spergel, and others, this chapter places gang membership in a developmental context by focusing on both the antecedents and consequences of gang membership. Unlike much of the previous literature that studies *gangs*, in this perspective individual *gang members* are the units of analysis. This approach certainly has its disadvantages; for example, it limits our ability to study group processes and to some extent it decontextualizes the deviant behavior of gang members. Also, a developmental perspective requires longitudinal data, and virtually all longitudinal data sets that have measured gang membership have been conducted in newer or "emergent" gang cities. Thus, it is not clear whether the findings from these longitudinal studies are unique to emergent gang cities or whether longitudinal studies conducted in established gang cities (e.g., Los Angeles, Chicago) would produce similar results. It also has its advantages; it allows the study of gangs to be informed by developmental and life course perspectives and it addresses substantive issues that cannot easily be examined when the gang is the unit of analysis. This approach complements the very detailed understanding that prior research has presented about periods of active gang membership, and both types of studies are needed to fully understand the phenomenon of street gangs.

A developmental perspective is consistent with the transient character of gang membership for most gang members. Several recent longitudinal studies (described below) have shown that most gang members remain in the gang for less than 1 year and proportionately few remain members for multiple years. For example, in the Rochester Youth Development Study, 54 percent of the gang members were active for a year or less and only 21 percent were active for 3 or more years. The respective percentages in the Denver Youth Survey are 67 percent and 9 percent and in the Seattle Social Development Project, 69 percent and 14 percent. Given this distribution it is important to understand why adolescents join and leave gangs and how their period of active membership affects other life course trajectories. . . .

Risk Factors for Gang Membership

Risk factors are "individual or environmental hazards that increase an individual's vulnerability to negative developmental outcomes" (Small & Luster, 1994, p. 182; see also Werner & Smith, 1982). A risk factor approach assumes that there are multiple, and often overlapping, risk factors in an individual's background that lead to adverse outcomes. Furthermore, it posits that it is the cumulation of risk in the life course that is most strongly related to adversity (B. C. Miller, 1995).

Identifying salient risk factors, especially those that occur early in the life course, has several advantages. Theoretically, identifying factors that increase risk suggests fruitful areas for exploration in more formal causal analyses. It can also help in isolating variables that mediate or translate increased vulnerability into actually experiencing the outcome. A risk factor approach also has practical advantages. Knowledge of risk factors helps structure the design of intervention programs by identifying at-risk youths for whom prevention and treatment efforts are most warranted. Also, the identification of salient risk factors suggests substantive areas or targets for intervention efforts. Despite these advantages, there have been surprisingly few examinations of risk factors for gang membership.

This appears to be directly related to the limits of past research designs in the area of gang studies. A risk factor model examines *antecedent* conditions that increase risk for *later* outcomes and is best analyzed in longitudinal designs. Also, a risk factor model requires a general, representative sample that includes both those experiencing the outcome (i.e., gang membership) and those not experiencing it. Unfortunately, there are relatively few gang studies that combine both of these features and that follow gang members and comparison, non-gang members across time. Because of this, most prior studies are correlational studies that compare gang members and nonmembers in terms of attributes measured during periods of active gang membership. Proper temporal order is not established and it is therefore not clear whether the factors identified in these studies are actual risk factors for a later outcome. Thus, the results of prior studies suggest, rather than identify, potential risk factors for gang membership. In this section, we review the results of these studies; in the following section, we examine two current longitudinal research projects that in fact examine antecedent risk factors for later gang membership.

Prior Research

Consistent with the basic tenet of a risk factor approach that there are likely to be multiple rather than single pathways to adverse outcomes, prior research has examined risk for gang membership in a variety of domains. They include community, family, school, peer, individual characteristics, and prior problem behaviors.

Community risk factors. Living in socially disorganized areas is related to gang membership (Bowker & Klein, 1983; Curry & Spergel, 1992; J. W. Moore, 1978, 1991; Short, 1990). These findings are quite consistent with the general observation that gangs themselves tend to cluster in high-crime, socially disorganized neighborhoods (e.g., Fagan, 1996; Short & Strodtbeck, 1965; Vigil, 1988). It is not surprising, therefore, that youths who reside in those same neighborhoods are at increased risk for gang membership. These findings are also consistent with research results that suggest that the availability of drugs in the neighborhood (Curry & Spergel, 1992; Hill, Hawkins, Catalano, Maguin, & Kosterman, 1995) and the presence of gangs in the neighborhood (Curry & Spergel, 1992; Nidorf, 1988) also increase the risk that an individual will become a gang member.

Although many studies find that community characteristics increase the risk of gang membership, several studies do not. For example, Bjerregaard and Smith (1993) did not find that social disorganization or neighborhood poverty is significantly related to the risk of gang membership. Fagan (1990) also found no significant association between gang membership and social integration, neighborhood integration, and neighborhood violence. Similarly, Winfree, Backstrom, and Mays (1994) did not find that urban residence differentiates gang members from non-gang members.

Family risk factors. Several studies have examined family-based risk factors for gang membership. Some have found that low socioeconomic status or poverty is related to gang membership (Bowker & Klein, 1983; Moore, 1991; Schwartz, 1989). Structural characteristics of families have also been examined. Bowker and Klein (1983) and Vigil (1988) found that coming from single-parent families or from broken homes increases the risk of joining gangs, although Le Blanc and Lanctot (in press), in a study comparing gang and non-gang members in a Quebec sample restricted to adjudicated boys, did not. Similarly, Bowker and Klein (1983) found that larger family size is related to gang membership.

In addition to concerns about family structure, many studies have examined family management style as a risk factor for gang involvement. In general, poor family management strategies increase the risk for gang membership by adolescents (Le Blanc & Lanctot, in press; Moore, 1991; Vigil, 1988). More specifically, low family involvement (Friedman, Mann, & Friedman, 1975; Le Blanc & Lanctot, in press), inappropriate parental discipline (Winfree et al., 1994), low parental control or monitoring (Bowker & Klein, 1983; Campbell, 1990; Le Blanc & Lanctot, in press; Moore, 1991), poor affective relationships between parent and child (Campbell, 1990; Moore, 1991), and parental conflict (Le Blanc & Lanctot, in press) put youths at risk for becoming gang members. These family-based risk factors are quite consistent with those generally observed as increasing risk for involvement in delinquency (see Hawkins, Catalano, & Miller, 1992; Loeber & Stouthamer-Loeber, 1986).

There are several, more specific family factors related to the phenomenon of gang membership. One of the most consistent risk factors for involvement in a gang is having relatives in a gang (Cohen, Williams, Bekelman, & Crosse, 1994; Curry & Spergel,

1992; Moore, 1991; Nidorf, 1988). In addition, the absence of prosocial parental role models (Wang, 1994) and prodeviant norms on the part of the parents (Le Blanc & Lanctot, in press) increase risk for gang membership.

School risk factors. Educational variables have also been examined as risk factors for gang membership. Bowker and Klein (1983) reported that students who have low educational expectations are at increased risk for gang membership, a finding also observed by Bjerregaard and Smith (1993) for females but not males. Gang membership is also more likely among adolescents whose parents have low educational expectations for them (Schwartz, 1989). Poor school performance and low commitment and involvement are also correlated with gang membership (Le Blanc & Lanctot, in press). In a related vein, gang membership is associated with educational frustration (Curry & Spergel, 1992) and stress (Le Blanc & Lanctot, in press).

Teachers also play a role in predicting the likelihood of gang membership. Gang members, as compared to nonmembers, are more likely to experience negative labeling by teachers (Esbensen, Huizinga, & Weiher, 1993) and are less likely to have a teacher as a positive role model (Schwartz, 1989; Wang, 1994), although Le Blanc and Lanctot (in press) did not find low attachment to teachers to be related to gang membership.

Low school self-esteem (Curry & Spergel, 1992; Schwartz, 1989) and educational marginality (Bjerregaard & Smith, 1993) also increase the risk for gang membership. Finally, having gang members as classmates (Curry & Spergel, 1992) and getting into trouble at school (Cohen et al.,1994) are risk factors for gang membership.

Peer risk factors. Having friends who are involved in delinquency is strongly related to being a gang member (Bjerregaard & Lizotte, 1995; Bjerregaard & Smith, 1993; Bowker & Klein, 1983; Curry & Spergel, 1992; Esbensen et al., 1993; Fagan, 1990; Le Blanc & Lanctot, in press; Nidorf, 1988; Winfree et al., 1994). The relationship between deviant peers and gang membership is perhaps the strongest one observed in this literature. That is not surprising, of course, because delinquent gangs are in many ways a specific version of associations with delinquent peers.

Curry and Spergel (1992) found that having drug-using peers is a significant risk factor for gang membership for African American youths but not for Hispanic youths. Associating with peers who carry guns and weapons also increases the likelihood of gang membership (Bjerregaard & Lizotte, 1995). Several researchers report that associating with peers who were themselves gang members also increases the risk of gang membership (Curry & Spergel, 1992; Nidorf, 1988; Winfree et al., 1994). Finally, being approached to join a gang (Cohen et al., 1994) is related to gang membership.

Individual risk factors. Self-esteem is rather inconsistently related to the risk of becoming a gang member. On the one hand, Rice (1963), Schwartz (1989), Wang (1994), and Cartwright, Tomson, and Schwartz (1975) find that low self-esteem increases the likelihood of gang membership. On the other hand, Bjerregaard and Smith (1993), Bowker and Klein (1983), and Esbensen et al. (1993) have not found self-esteem to be related to gang membership.

The individual's attitudes also play a role in increasing the risk of gang membership. Winfree et al. (1994) found that progang attitudes are associated with gang membership, and Esbensen et al. (1993) found that gang members have a higher tolerance for deviance and higher levels of normlessness (see also Fagan, 1990). Le Blanc and Lanctot (in press) reported that deviant beliefs and techniques of neutralization are related to gang membership.

The most systematic investigation of individual attributes as correlates of gang membership has been undertaken by Le Blanc and Lanctot (in press). In their comparison of adjudicated gang and non-gang members, they found that gang members had significantly poorer scores on 10 of their 13 personality scales. Gang members

> share attitudes and opinions of persons in lower socioeconomic classes such as the ethic of the tough and the premature adoption of adult behaviors (value orien-

> tation). In thinking and perceiving, they tend to distort reality according to their personal needs or desires (autism). Their alienation manifests itself by the presence of distrust and estrangement in their attitudes toward others, especially toward those representing authorities. They manifest awareness of unpleasant feelings, especially of anger and frustration, and react readily with these emotions. There is also obvious discomfort concerning the presence and control of these feelings (manifest aggression). They exclude conscious awareness of feelings and emotions that an individual normally experiences, in addition it reflects one's failure to label these emotions (repression). They are reluctant to acknowledge unpleasant events or conditions met in daily living (denial). They also score high on psychoticism, which indicates that they are cold, impersonal, lacking in sympathy, unfriendly, untruthful, odd, unemotional, unhelpful, antisocial, lacking in insight and strange, with paranoid ideas that people are against them. They show emotional instability (somatic and affective), they are not happy and they have a sense of being victimized (neurotism). Finally they are sociable, adventurous, sensation seekers and impulsive (extroversion). (Le Blanc & Lanctot, in press, p. 7)

Prior problem behaviors. Finally, several studies have found that adolescents who are already involved in deviant and problem behaviors are more likely to join gangs than are adolescents who are not involved in those behaviors. For example, gang membership has been shown to be related to sexual promiscuity (Bjerregaard & Smith, 1993; Le Blanc & Lanctot, in press), loitering or hanging out (Le Blanc & Lanctot, in press), alcohol and drug use (Bjerregaard & Smith, 1993; Cohen et al., 1994; Le Blanc & Lanctot, in press; Thornberry, Krohn, Lizotte, & Chard-Wierschem, 1993), violence (Friedman et al., 1975; Le Blanc & Lanctot, in press), being a gun owner (Bjerregaard & Lizotte, 1995), and general delinquency (Curry & Spergel, 1992; Esbensen & Huizinga, 1993; Le Blanc & Lanctot, in press; Nidorf, 1988). In addition, official contact with the juvenile justice system has been shown to be related to gang membership (Cohen et al., 1994; Le Blanc & Lanctot, in press). Finally, victimization also appears to be a risk factor for gang membership (Fagan, 1990).

Recent Findings

Because most prior studies examine correlates of gang membership rather than true risk factors, this section presents more detailed findings from two longitudinal studies, the Rochester Youth Development Study and the Seattle Social Development Project (Hill, Howell, Hawkins, & Battin, 1996). The Rochester study has followed a sample of 1,000 youths from the time they were middle school students until their early 20s; the Seattle study has followed 800 youths from the time they were elementary and middle school students until their early 20s. Both studies use a self-report measure of gang membership,[2] and both measure risk factors in a number of domains. The analysis is structured so that the risk factors are antecedent to the period of gang membership. In the case of the Rochester study, risk factors are measured during the Fall semester of 1988 and are used to predict the probability of joining a gang between 1989 and 1991. In the case of the Seattle project, risk factors are measured at Grades 5 or 6 and are used to predict the probability of joining a gang during Grades 7 through 12.

Thus, the developmental period covered by the two studies is quite comparable. Because the dependent variable in these analyses is a dichotomy—gang members versus nonmembers—logistic regression models are used and the bivariate logistic R is presented in the tables.

Rochester study. Risk factors for members of the Rochester Youth Development Study are reported separately for males and females (Table 4.1). The risk factors are grouped into six domains, starting with more distal and moving to more proximal arenas. Because directional predictions can be made for these relationships, one-tailed tests are used in the Rochester analysis.

For males, in terms of community variables, growing up in neighborhoods in which there is a low level of neighborhood

Table 4.1
Risk Factors for Gang Membership, Rochester Youth Development Study

	Logistic R for Joining a Gang Between Wave 3 and Wave 9	
Risk Factor at Wave 2	*Males*	*Females*
Community		
Neighborhood disorganization	.00	.13*
Neighborhood violence	.00	.08*
Neighborhood integration	–.06*	.18*
Family		
Living with both parents	–.04*	.00
Family below poverty level	.07*	.00
Parent attachment to child	–.11*	.00
Positive parenting	.00	.00
Child attachment to parent	.00	.00
Family violence	.00	.00
Parental involvement	.00	–.14*
Supervision	–.12*	.00
School		
Parent's expectations for school	–.14*	–.14*
Subject's expectations for school	–.05*	–.30*
Commitment to school	–.16*	–.11*
Attachment to teachers	–.14*	–.18*
Peer		
Association with delinquent peers	.16*	.00
Unsupervised time spent with friends	.10*	.00
Individual		
Perceived access to drugs	.14*	.09*
Positive values about drugs	.18*	.17*
Prosocial activities	.00	.00
Depression	.11*	.00
Negative life events	.24*	.00
Self-esteem	–.08*	.00
Problem behaviors		
General delinquency	.23*	.14*
Violent delinquency	.27*	.00
Drug use	.09*	.00

*$p<.05$.

integration increases the risk of gang membership. Growing up in neighborhoods that are perceived by the parent respondents as disorganized or in which there is a high level of violence does not significantly increase the risk of gang membership, however.

Both structural and process variables in the area of the family are related to the probability of becoming a gang member. Growing up in families that are below the federally established standard for poverty or in families without both biological parents increases the risk of later gang membership. Of the family process variables, low parental attachment to the child and low parental supervision increase the probability of gang membership. The child's level of attachment to the parent, positive parenting, family violence, and involvement in family activities are not significantly related to gang membership.

School is a very potent arena for creating risk for later gang membership. Four school variables are analyzed and all are significant. Low expectations for success in school—measured both by the parent's expectations and the subject's expectations—increase the risk of gang membership. Students who have low commitment to school and who have low attachment to teachers are also at elevated risk for later involvement in gangs.

Peers have a very strong impact on later gang membership. Younger adolescent males who associate with delinquent peers and who spend more unsupervised time hanging around with friends are more apt to become gang members at some later point.

Several individual characteristics were also examined. Adolescents who perceive having easy access to drugs or who have positive values about drug use are more apt to become gang members than are their counterparts. Individuals with low self-esteem, who experience many negative life events, and who have depressive symptoms are more likely to join gangs later.

Finally, young adolescent males who use drugs and who are involved in delinquency, especially violent delinquency, are more apt to become gang members than are youths who are less involved in delinquency and drug use.

Somewhat different results are observed for the female participants. In general, there are fewer significant risk factors, which may be due to the smaller number of females in the Rochester study (75 percent of the sample are males and 25 percent are females).

Community variables have a larger impact on females than on males. Females who grow up in disorganized and violent neighborhoods are more likely to become gang members. Females who grow up in neighborhoods with high levels of social integration are also more apt to become gang members, a counterintuitive finding.

Few family factors are significant predictors of gang membership for females. In fact, only low parental involvement increases the risk of later gang membership. Family structure, family poverty, attachment, positive parenting, family violence, and supervision are not significantly related to gang membership.

School variables play a major role in accounting for the risk of gang membership for females, as they did for males. Low parental expectations and low student expectations for school success significantly increase the likelihood of gang membership. Similarly, low commitment to school and low attachment to teachers increase the likelihood of gang membership for females.

Peer effects are not significantly related to gang membership for females. Neither association with delinquent peers nor unsupervised time spent with peers is significantly related to the outcome variable.

In terms of individual characteristics, young females who perceive having easy access to drugs and who have pro-drug use values are significantly more likely to become gang members. On the other hand, prosocial activities, depressive symptoms, negative life events, and low self-esteem are not significantly related to gang membership.

Finally, of the delinquency measures only general delinquency is significantly related to the probability of later joining a gang for the females. Early involvement in violent offenses or in drug use is not statistically significant.

A brief comparison of risk factors for the males and females in the Rochester study indicates areas of both similarity and difference by gender. On the one hand, school variables, access to and values about drugs, and prior delinquency operate in generally similar ways for males and females. On the other hand, neighborhood characteristics appear to be much more important in increasing the likelihood of gang membership for the females than for the males. In contrast, family, peer, and psychological states (depression, stress, and self-esteem) are more potent predictors of gang membership for the males than the females.

Seattle study. In the Seattle study, Hill et al., (1996) conducted the risk factor analysis for male and female respondents combined (Table 4.2). One of two community risk factors is significantly related to the probability of joining a gang: Adolescents who come from neighborhoods where drugs are readily available are more apt to be gang members than are their counterparts.

Several family variables are related to the risk of gang membership. Family instability (indicated by the number of transitions in family structure) and low parental income increase the probability that adolescents will later join gangs. Low attachment to mother, family management problems, and parental proviolent attitudes all significantly increase the probability of later gang membership. Having siblings who are involved in antisocial behavior increases the risk of gang membership.

School variables are strongly related to the probability of joining gangs in Seattle. Low educational aspiration, low commitment to school, low school attachment, high levels of antisocial behavior in school, low achievement-test scores, being labeled learning disabled, and receiving low grades are each related to gang membership in the expected direction.

Peers exert a fairly substantial influence on the probability of becoming a gang member. Associating with "bad" peers increases the likelihood of gang membership, whereas associating with "good" peers and being attached to conventional peers decrease that probability.

Individual factors were also examined. Of the demographic characteristics, white and female adolescents are less likely to be gang members and African American adolescents are more likely to be gang members. In terms of individual attributes, hyperactivity and

Table 4.2
Risk Factors for Gang Membership, Seattle Social Development Project

Risk Factor at Grades 5 and 6	*Logistic R for Joining a Gang Between Grade 7 and Grade 12*
Community	
Low neighborhood attachment	.00
Availability of drugs	.24*
Family	
Family instability	.11*
Extreme economic deprivation	.14
Attachment to family	.00
Attachment to mother	–.07
Attachment to father	.00
Family bonding	.00
Family management problems	.10*
Family conflict	–.03
Parent proviolent attitudes	.13*
Family involvement	.00
Parent respondent drinking	.00
Spouse drinking	.00
Both parents drinking	.00
Sibling antisocial behavior	.10*
School	
Low educational aspiration	.10*
Low school commitment	.14*
School attachment	–.10*
School antisocial behavior	.16
Achievement test score	–.19
Labeled learning disabled	.17*
Low grades	.13*
Peer	
"Bad" peers	.15*
"Good" peers	–.13*
Attachment to conventional peers	–.15*
Individual	
Conventional beliefs	–.16*
Achenbach externalizing	.23*
Achenbach internalizing	.03
Religious service attendance	.00
Hyperactivity	.15*
Social competence	–.18*
Gender (female)	–.18*
Asian	.00
African American	.17*
Other	.00
White	–.12*
Problem behaviors	
Respondent drinking	.09*
Age at first sex	–.32*

Source: Hill, Hawkins, et al. (1996). Used with permission
*$p < .05$.

externalizing behavior problems increase the probability of gang membership and holding conventional beliefs and social competencies decrease gang membership.

Finally, involvement in prior problem behaviors increases the likelihood of becoming a gang member. Young adolescents who report drinking and who are sexually precocious have a higher probability of joining a gang than do their counterparts.

Summary

Both the earlier correlational studies and the more recent longitudinal ones in Rochester and Seattle offer a rather consistent picture of risk factors for gang membership. In line with the basic assumption of a risk factor approach, there does not appear to be any single risk factor that leads adolescents to become members of street gangs. On the contrary, risk is generated in many life domains, including community, family, school, peer, and individual characteristics. Although the specific risk factors that are significant vary somewhat across studies, it seems reasonable to conclude that youths who grow up in more disorganized neighborhoods; who come from impoverished, distressed families; who do poorly in school and who have low attachment to school and teachers; who associate with delinquent peers; and who hold prodeviant belief systems and engage in various forms of problem behaviors are at increased risk for becoming gang members.

Author's Note

This study was prepared under Grant 86-JN-CX-0007 (S-3) from the Office of Juvenile Justice and Delinquency Prevention, Office of Justice Programs, U.S. Department of Justice; Grant 5 R01 DA05512-02 from the National Institute on Drug Abuse; and Grant SES-8912274 from the National Science Foundation. I would like to thank Kim Tobin-Carambia for her assistance in developing this chapter. I would also like to thank Darnell F. Hawkins, James C. Howell, Malcolm W. Klein, Alan J. Lizotte, Walter B. Miller, and Carolyn A. Smith for helpful comments on earlier drafts.

Notes

1. There are several exceptions to this general tendency, for example, studies by Hagedorn (1988), J. W. Moore (1978, 1991), Short and Strodtbeck (1965), Tracy (1979), and Vigil (1988).
2. Other longitudinal studies of gang members referred to in subsequent sections (i.e., Huizinga, 1996; R. E. Tremblay, personal communication, November 1996) also rely on a self-report measure of gang membership.

References

Bjerregaard, B. and A. J. Lizotte. 1995. "Gun Ownership and Gang Membership." *Journal of Criminal Law and Criminology* 86:37–58.

Bjerregaard, B. and C. Smith. 1993. "Gender Differences in Gang Participation, Delinquency, and Substance Use." *Journal of Quantitative Criminology* 4:329–355.

Bowker, L. H. and M. W. Klein. 1983. "The Etiology of Female Juvenile Delinquency and Gang Membership: A Test of Psychological and Social Structural Explanations." *Adolescence* 18: 739–751.

Campbell, A. 1990. "Female Participation in Gangs." Pp. 163–182 in *Gangs in America*, edited by C. R. Huff. Newbury Park, CA: Sage Publications.

Cartwright, D. S., B. Tomson, and H. Schwartz. 1975. *Gang Delinquency*. Monterey, CA: Brooks/ Cole.

Cohen, B. 1969. "The Delinquency of Gangs and Spontaneous Groups." Pp. 61–111 in *Delinquency: Selected Studies*, edited by T. Sellin and M. E. Wolfgang. New York: John Wiley.

Cohen, M. I., K. Williams, A. M. Bekelman, and S. Crosse. 1994. "Evaluation of the National Youth Gang Drug Prevention Program." Pp. 266–275 in *The Modern Gang Reader*, edited by M. W. Klein, C. Maxson, and J. Miller. Los Angeles: Roxbury.

Curry, G. D., R. A. Ball, and S. H. Decker. 1996a. "Estimating the National Scope of Gang Crime From Law Enforcement Data." *Research in Brief*. Washington, D.C.: National Institute of Justice.

Curry, G. D., R. A. Ball, and S. H. Decker. 1996b. "Estimating the National Scope of Gang Crime From Law Enforcement Data." Pp. 266–275 in *Gangs in America*, 2nd Edition, edited by C. R. Huff. Thousand Oaks, CA: Sage Publications.

Curry, G. D. and I. A. Spergel. 1992. "Gang Involvement and Delinquency Among Hispanic and African American Adolescent Males." *Journal of Research on Crime and Delinquency* 29:273–291.

Esbensen, F. and D. Huizinga. 1993. "Gangs, Drugs, and Delinquency in a Survey of Urban Youth." *Criminology* 31:565–589.

Esbensen, F., D. Huizinga, and A. W. Weiher. 1993. "Gang and Non-Gang Youth: Differences in Explanatory Factors." *Journal of Contemporary Criminal Justice* 9:94–116.

Fagan, J. 1989. "The Social Organization of Drug Use and Drug Dealing Among Urban Gangs." *Criminology* 27:633–667.

Fagan, J. 1990. "Social Processes of Delinquency and Drug Use Among Urban Gangs." Pp. 183–219 in *Gangs in America*, edited by C. Ronald Huff. Newbury Park, CA: Sage Publications.

Fagan, J. 1996. "Gangs, Drugs, and Neighborhood Change." Pp. 39–74 in *Gangs in America*, 2nd Edition, edited by C. R. Huff. Newbury Park, CA: Sage Publications.

Fagan, J., E. Piper, and M. Moore. 1986. "Violent Delinquents and Urban Youths." *Criminology* 24:439–471.

Friedman, C. J., F. Mann, and A. S. Friedman. 1975. "A Profile of Juvenile Street Gang Members." *Adolescence* 10:563–607.

Hagedorn, John M. 1988. *People and Folks: Gangs, Crime, and the Underclass in a Rustbelt City*. Chicago: Lake View Press.

Hawkins, J. D., R. F. Catalano, and J. Y. Miller. 1992. "Risk and Protective Factors for Alcohol and Other Drug Problems in Adolescence and Early Adulthood: Implications for Substance Abuse Prevention." *Psychological Bulletin* 112: 64–105.

Hill, K. G., J. D. Hawkins, R. Catalano, E. Maguin, and R. Kosterman. 1995. *The Role of Gang Membership in Delinquency, Substance Use, and Violent Offending*. Paper presented at the annual meeting of the American Society of Criminology, Boston.

Hill, K. G., J. C. Howell, J. D.Hawkins, and S. R. Battin. 1996. "Risk Factors in Childhood for Adolescent Gang Membership: Results from the Seattle Social Development Project." Manuscript under review.

Huff, C. R. 1996a. "The Criminal Behavior of Gang Members and Nongang At-Risk Youths." Pp. 75–102 in *Gangs in America*, 2nd Edition, edited by C. Ronald Huff. Thousand Oaks, CA: Sage Publications.

Huff, C. R. 1996b. *Gangs in America*, 2nd Edition. Thousand Oaks, CA: Sage Publications.

Huizinga, D. H. 1996. *The Influence of Delinquent Peers, Gangs, and Co-offending on Violence*. Fact sheet prepared for the U.S. Department of Justice, Office of Juvenile Justice and Delinquency Prevention.

Klein, M. W. 1971. *Street Gangs and Street Workers*. Englewood Cliffs, NJ: Prentice Hall.

——. 1995. *The American Street Gang: Its Nature, Prevalence, and Control*. New York: Oxford University Press.

Klein, M. W., M. A. Gordon, and C. L. Maxson. 1986. "The Impact of Police Investigation on Police-Reported Rates of Gang and Nongang Homicides." *Criminology* 24:489–512.

Klein, M. W. and C. L. Maxson. 1989. "Street Gang Violence." Pp. 198–231 in *Violent Crime, Violent Criminals*, edited by N. Weiner and M. Wolfgang. Newbury Park, CA: Sage Publications.

Le Blanc, M. and N. Lanctot. In press. "Social and Psychological Characteristics of Gang Members According to the Gang Structure and Its Subcultural and Ethnic Makeup." *Journal of Gang Research*.

Loeber, R. and M. Stouthamer-Loeber. 1986. "Family Factors as Correlates and Predictors of Juvenile Conduct Problems and Delinquency." Pp. 219–339 in *Crime and Justice: An Annual Review of Research*, Volume 7, edited by M. Tonry and N. Morris. Chicago: University of Chicago Press.

Miller, B. C. 1995. "Risk factors for adolescent nonmarital childbearing." Pp. 201–216 in *Report to Congress on Out-of-Wedlock Childbearing*, edited by K. A. Moore. Hyattsville, MD: U.S. Department of Health and Human Services.

Miller, W. B. 1966. "Violent Crimes by City Gangs." *Annals of the American Academy of Political and Social Science* 364:96–112.

Moore, J. 1978. *Homeboys: Gangs, Drugs, and Prison in the Barrios of Los Angeles*. Philadelphia: Temple University Press.

Moore, J. 1991. *Going Down to the Barrio: Homeboys and Homegirls in Change*. Philadelphia: Temple University Press.

National Youth Gang Center. 1997. *The 1995 National Youth Gang Survey*. Washington, D.C.: U.S. Department of Justice, Office of Juvenile Justice and Delinquency Prevention.

Nidorf, B. J. 1988. *Gang Alternative and Prevention Program. Program Policy and Procedure Handbook*. Los Angeles: County of Los Angeles Probation Department.

Rice, R. 1963. "A Reporter at Large: The Persian Queens." *The New Yorker*, 39, October 19.

Schwartz, A. J. 1989. "Middle-class Educational Values Among Latino Gang Members in East Los Angeles County High Schools." *Urban Education* 24:323–342.

Short, J. F. 1990. "New Wine in Old Bottles? Change and Continuity in American Gangs." Pp. 223–239 in *Gangs in America*, edited by C. R. Huff. Newbury Park, CA: Sage Publications.

Short, J. F. and F. L. Strodtbeck. 1965. *Group Process and Gang Delinquency*. Chicago: University of Chicago Press.

Small, S. A. and T. Luster. 1994. "Adolescent Sexual Activity: An Ecological Risk-Factor Approach." *Journal of Marriage and the Family* 56: 181–192.

Spergel, I. A. 1964. *Slumtown, Racketville, Haulburg*. Chicago: University of Chicago Press.

Spergel, I. A. 1995. *The Youth Gang Problem: A Community Approach*. New York: Oxford University Press.

Taylor, C. S. 1990. "Gang Imperialism." Pp. 103–115 in *Gangs in America*, edited by C. R. Huff. Thousand Oaks, CA: Sage Publications.

Thornberry, T. P., M. D. Krohn, A. J. Lizotte, and D. Chard-Wierschem. 1993. "The Role of Juvenile Gangs in Facilitating Delinquent Behavior." *Journal of Research in Crime and Delinquency* 30:75–85.

Thrasher, F. M. 1927/1963. *The Gang*. Chicago: University of Chicago Press.

Tracy, P. E. 1979. *Subcultural Delinquency: A Comparison of the Incidence and Seriousness of Gang and Nongang Member Offensivity*. Unpublished manuscript, University of Pennsylvania, Center for Studies in Criminology and Criminal Law.

Tremblay, R. E. 1996. Personal communication, November.

Vigil, J. D. 1988. *Barrio Gangs: Street Life and Identity in Southern California*. Austin: University of Texas Press.

Wang, A. Y. 1994. "Pride and Prejudice in High School Gang Members."

Adolescence 29:279–291.

Werner, E. E. and R. S. Smith. 1982. *Vulnerable but Invincible: A Longitudinal Study of Resilient Children and Youth*. New York: McGraw-Hill.

Winfree, L. T., Jr., T. Backstrom, and G. L. Mays. 1994. "Social Learning Theory, Self-Reported Delinquency, and Youth Gangs: A New Twist on a General Theory of Crime and Delinquency." *Youth and Society* 26:147–177. ✦

Section II

Distribution and Structures of Gangs

Chapter 5
1997 National Youth Gang Survey Summary

National Youth Gang Center

While the number of cities reporting gang problems slowly increased from the 1950s to 1980, a dramatic, accelerating increase since 1980 has been suggested by several scholars using nonrepresentative samples. By using careful sampling techniques and projections, the National Youth Gang Center (NYGC) has established a large set of figures for street gangs and gang members. In reviewing these figures, keep in mind that the definition of gangs used by the NYGC is purposely broad; because of this, some reporting police departments may include youth groups that do not fit more traditional definitions found within the gang literature and discussed elsewhere in this reader. Nonetheless, their efforts are an important first attempt to establish baseline information about gangs and gang members throughout the United States.

The 1997 National Youth Gang Survey was the third annual survey administered by the National Youth Gang Center. Almost 5,000 law enforcement agencies throughout the United States were surveyed, representing the largest national gang survey to date. The majority of survey recipients were part of a statistically representative sample that allowed the data to be extrapolated for the Nation as a whole. The 1997 survey used the same sample as the 1996 survey, allowing both comparative and trend analysis. The data collected from these surveys provide valuable information about the extent of the youth gang problem in the United States.

The findings of the 1997 National Youth Gang Survey are summarized below:

- An estimated 4,712 cities and counties, more than half (51 percent) of all respondents, reported active youth gangs in 1997. This represents a small decrease from 1996, when an estimated 4,824 cities and counties, 53 percent of all respondents, reported active youth gangs. Moreover, small decreases between 1996 and 1997 in the percentage of respondents reporting gangs were found for each area type. Although all of these decreases were small, large cities showed the largest decrease. Large cities continued to have the highest percentage (72 percent) of jurisdictions with active youth gangs, followed by suburban counties (56 percent), small cities (33 percent), and rural counties (24 percent).
- The prevalence of gangs varied considerably by region. The percentage of jurisdictions reporting active youth gangs ranged from 74 percent in the West to 31 percent in the Northeast.
- Population also greatly affected the prevalence of active youth gangs in 1997. For all area types, the percentage of jurisdictions with active youth gangs increased as population increased.
- The estimated number of youth gangs and gang members also decreased between 1996 and 1997. In 1997, an estimated 30,500 youth gangs and 815,896 gang members were active in the United States, compared with an estimated 31,818 youth gangs and 846,428 gang members in 1996. Despite these decreases in the overall number of youth gangs and gang members, the estimated number of youth gangs in small cities increased substantially (20.5 percent) between 1996 and 1997. In addition, the estimated number of youth

gang members increased by 38.5 percent in rural counties and 5.7 percent in small cities.

- The average number of youth gangs and gang members per jurisdiction increased as population increased in both 1996 and 1997. For cities and counties with populations of 1–9,999, there was considerable growth (percentage-wise) between the relatively low numbers of gangs and gang members reported in 1996 and the low numbers, compared with other population ranges, reported in 1997. However, the growth of the gang problem in these less populated areas is cause for concern and deserves further attention. Most population ranges, however, showed a decrease.

- An estimated 3,341 member-based youth gang homicides were committed in the United States in 1997, of which 1,880 were motive-based. Large cities accounted for almost two-thirds of the total estimated number of member-based homicides and nearly three-quarters of the motive-based homicides.

- The crimes respondents most frequently reported as having a high degree of gang member involvement were aggravated assault and larceny/theft (28 percent), followed by motor vehicle theft (27 percent), burglary (26 percent), and robbery (13 percent). However, gang member involvement in all of the above crimes decreased between 1996 and 1997.

- Approximately 42 percent of the youth gangs in the United States were involved in the street sale of drugs for the purpose of generating profits for the gang. The average percentage of youth gangs involved in the street sale of drugs was higher in large cities and suburban counties than in small cities and rural counties. Regionally, the average percentages ranged from 50 percent in the Northeast to 30 percent in the West. The percentage of youth gangs involved in the street sale of drugs also varied directly with population.

- Approximately 33 percent of youth gangs in the country were estimated to be involved in drug distribution for the purpose of generating profits for the gang. The average percentage of youth gangs involved in drug distribution was highest in large cities (31 percent), followed by suburban counties (29 percent), rural counties (29 percent), and small cities (25 percent). Additionally, youth gangs involved in drug distribution were most prevalent in the Midwest (35 percent) and least prevalent in the West (21 percent). Population size had little effect on the percentage of youth gangs involved in drug distribution.

- Respondents estimated that, nationwide, youth gang members were responsible for 33 percent of crack cocaine sales, 32 percent of marijuana sales, 16 percent of powder cocaine sales, 12 percent of methamphetamine sales, and 9 percent of heroin sales. The average percentages of crack cocaine and heroin sales varied significantly between area types and were highest in large cities and suburban counties. Additionally, sales of crack cocaine, heroin, and methamphetamine by youth gang members varied significantly by region. Crack cocaine sales were most prevalent in the Midwest (38 percent), heroin sales were most prevalent in the Northeast (15 percent), and methamphetamine sales were most prevalent in the West (21 percent).

- Nationwide, gang migration increased between 1996 and 1997. Eighty-nine percent of respondents indicated that they experienced some gang migration into their jurisdictions during 1997, up from 84 percent in 1996. In addition, approximately 23 percent of youth gang members in the country were estimated to be migrants in 1997, up from 21 percent in 1996. In both years, the average percentage of youth gang migrants was highest in small cities and jurisdictions in the Midwest.

- The vast majority (70 percent) of respondents cited social factors as reasons why youth gang members migrated to their jurisdictions. Establishing drug markets was the second most cited reason (15 percent), followed by avoiding law enforcement crackdowns (14 percent), participating in illegal ventures other than those related to drugs (12 percent), getting away from the gang life (9 percent), and other reasons (6 percent).
- Approximately two-thirds of respondents indicated that their agencies had some type of specialized response unit to address their gang problem. Thirty-five percent reported having a youth/street gang unit or officer(s), 18 percent said they had a gang prevention unit or officer(s), and 29 percent indicated they had a unit that combined both types of response. Large cities and jurisdictions in the West were the most likely to have a specialized response unit. In addition, the prevalence of specialized response units increased as population increased.
- Despite the slight decrease in gang activity between 1996 and 1997, most respondents (45 percent) felt that the gang problem in their jurisdictions in 1997 was staying about the same, 35 percent indicated it was getting worse, and 20 percent felt it was getting better. In contrast, 49 percent of respondents to the 1995 survey believed that their problem was getting worse, 41 percent said it was staying about the same, and 10 percent reported it was getting better. Most suburban and rural county respondents (43 percent) to the 1997 survey felt their youth gang problem was getting worse. Regionally, respondents in the South believed their gang problem had worsened in 1997.

The National Youth Gang Center will continue to analyze these data, and subsequent surveys will gather additional information in areas that require further examination. Other researchers also will have access to the NYGC database for analysis. ✦

Chapter 6
Gang Members on the Move

Cheryl L. Maxson

Along with the recognition of the increased proliferation of gangs across the country came various attempts to explain this change. By far the most common of these attempts was to invoke the migration of gang members from major crack cocaine markets, such as Los Angeles, to smaller cities to establish new markets. In this article, Maxson reviews some of the definitional issues and earlier studies of gang migration. She then reports the results of a new national survey of both chronic and emergent gang cities, using police experts as informants on the principal reasons for gang migration. The crack marketing explanation, although applicable in certain situations, generally does little to explain gang proliferation.

In recent years, local government officials, law enforcement officers, and community organizations have witnessed the emergence and growth of gangs in U.S. cities once thought to be immune to the crime and violence associated with street gangs in large metropolitan areas. Police chiefs, mayors, school officials, community activists, and public health officials have gone so far as to identify this proliferation as an epidemic. Reports of big-city gang members fanning out across the nation seeking new markets for drug distribution have added fuel to concerns about gang proliferation and gang migration.

Reprinted from: Cheryl L. Maxson, "Gang Members on the Move." In *Juvenile Justice Bulletin*, October, pp. 1–11.

The increase in gang migration has generated the need for the issue to be assessed based on empirical evidence. As local communities attempt to address gang-related problems in their areas, it is critical that they have a clear understanding of patterns of gang migration and an accurate assessment of local, or indigenous, gang membership.

This Chapter explores how key terms such as *gang, gang proliferation,* and *gang migration* are defined; how and whether gang migration affects gang proliferation; and trends reported in research literature. This Chapter is based in part on work supported by the National Institute of Justice (NIJ) and an article previously published in the *National Institute of Justice Journal* (Maxson, Woods, and Klein, 1996). Findings from a recent University of Southern California (USC) study on street-gang migration are also discussed (Maxson, Woods, and Klein, 1995).

Clarifying the Concepts

Defining the Terms 'Gang,' 'Gang Proliferation,' and 'Gang Migration'

Gang. There has been much debate over the term "gang," but little progress has been made toward widespread acceptance of a uniform definition. Some researchers prefer a broad definition that includes group criminal and noncriminal activities, whereas law enforcement agencies tend to use definitions that expedite the cataloging of groups for purposes of statistical analysis or prosecution. Variations in the forms or structure of gangs make it difficult to put forth one standard definition (Klein and Maxson, 1996). For example, researchers have attempted to draw a distinction between street gangs and drug gangs (Klein, 1995). Drug gangs are perceived as smaller, more cohesive, and more hierarchical than most street gangs and are exclusively focused on conducting drug deals and defending drug territories. Street gangs, on the other hand, engage in a wide array of criminal activity. Drug gangs may be subgroups of street gangs or may develop independently of street gangs. For the purposes of this Chapter and the national surveys on gang migration conducted by

USC, gangs were defined as groups of adolescents and/or young adults who see themselves as a group (as do others) and have been involved in enough crime to be of considerable concern to law enforcement and the community (Maxson, Woods, and Klein, 1995). In the USC survey, drug gangs were included in the overall grouping of gangs, but members of motorcycle gangs, prison-based gangs, graffiti taggers, and racial supremacy groups were excluded to narrow the focus to street gangs.

Another challenge in defining the term "gang" is the fluctuating structure of these groups. Over the course of adolescence and young adulthood, individual members move in and out of gangs, continually affecting the gangs' structure (Thornberry et al., 1993). The terms "wannabe," "core," "fringe," "associate," "hardcore," and "O.G." (original gangster) reflect the changing levels of involvement and the fact that the boundaries of gang membership are penetrable. Some researchers argue that the term "member" was created and used by law enforcement, gang researchers, and individuals engaged in gang activity with only a loose consensus of generalized, shared meaning.

Gang proliferation. The term "gang proliferation" indicates the increase in communities reporting the existence of gangs and gang problems (Knox et al., 1996). While gangs have existed in various forms, degrees, and locations in the United States for many decades, the sheer volume of cities and towns documenting recent gang activity cannot be denied. Some of this increase may be attributed to a heightened awareness of gang issues, redirection of law enforcement attention, widespread training, and national education campaigns. Nevertheless, gangs exist in locations previously unaffected and attract a larger proportion of adolescents than in the past.[1]

Gang migration. The already difficult task of defining gangs is compounded when the relationship between gang migration and proliferation is addressed. Gang migration—the movement of gang members from one city to another—has been mentioned with increasing frequency in State legislative task force investigations, government-sponsored conferences, and law enforcement accounts at the Federal, State, and local levels (Bonfante, 1995; Hayeslip, 1989; California Council on Criminal Justice, 1989; Genelin and Coplen, 1989; McKinney, 1988; National Drug Intelligence Center, 1994, 1996). For the USC study, migration was broadly defined to include temporary relocations, such as visits to relatives, short trips to sell drugs or develop other criminal enterprises, and longer stays while escaping crackdowns on gangs or gang activity. More permanent changes, such as residential moves (either individually or with family members) and court placements, were also included. Individuals in the study did not have to participate in gang activity in the destination city to be considered gang migrants. This broad definition of gang migration allowed researchers to investigate the degree of gang-organized and gang-supported expansion of members to other locations, of which little evidence was found. It also allowed researchers to examine variations in gang activity in the destination city and the many reasons for relocating. If the concept of migration was limited to individuals or groups traveling solely for gang-related purposes or at the direction of gang leaders, the patterns of migration would change drastically. Further, collective gang migration is rare, but the migration of individual gang members is not.

Another complication in defining gang migration is the distinction between migrant gang members (migrants) and indigenous gang members, which often fades over time. As migrants settle into new locations, sometimes joining local gangs, their identities may evolve to the point to which their prior gang affiliation no longer exists. This process of assimilation into local gang subcultures has not been addressed in research literature, because law enforcement officers and researchers have only recently begun to discuss gang migration. In future studies, researchers should consider at what point a migrant gang member is no longer perceived as a migrant but as a local gang member in the new location.

The Influence of Gang Migration on Gang Proliferation

The primary focus of this Chapter is to assess whether gang migration has played a major role in gang proliferation. Migrant gang members may stimulate the growth of gangs and gang membership through a variety of processes, such as recruiting locals to establish a branch of the gang in previously unaffected areas. This approach, described as the importation model, involves efforts by gang members to infuse their gang into new cities, primarily to establish new drug markets and other money-making criminal enterprises (Decker and Van Winkle, 1996). This is also referred to as gang franchising (Knox et al., 1996) and gang colonization (Quinn, Tobolowsky, and Downs, 1994). Alternatively, migrants may establish a new gang without structural affiliation to an existing gang. Furthermore, if a sufficient number of individuals from a gang move to a new location, they may replicate a migrant subset of their former gang. No matter what process is used, new local gangs will most likely emerge in response to territorial challenges or perceived protection needs. The city with a single gang is a rare phenomenon (Klein, 1995). Regardless of the pattern of new gang initiation, gang member migration would create an increase in both the numbers of gangs and gang membership.

Another way migrant gangs may stimulate gang proliferation is by introducing new and exciting cultural distinctions from existing gangs. In a city in which gangs exist but are not firmly established, migrant gang members may act as cultural carriers of the folkways, mythologies, and other trappings of more sophisticated urban gangs. They may offer strong distinctions from other gangs and cause a rivalry with existing gangs, such as the rivalry between the Bloods and Crips in southern California and between the People and Folks in the Midwest. Most of the respondents in the 1993 USC phone survey reported that migrants influence local gang rivalries, gang dress codes, and recruiting methods (Maxson, Woods, and Klein, 1995). In addition, the solidification of local gang subcultures may increase the visibility or attractiveness of gangs to local youth. It may also influence the growth of rival gangs.

Conversely, there are a variety of circumstances in which migrant gang members have little or no impact on gang proliferation. If the geographic location allows, migrants may retain their affiliation with their original gangs by commuting to old territories or they may simply discontinue gang activity altogether. In cities with relatively large and established gangs, it is unlikely that migrant gang members would have a noticeable effect on the overall gang environment.

An important related issue is the impact of migrant gang members on local crime patterns.[2] Migrants are generally perceived as contributing to both increased levels of crime and the seriousness of criminal activity (Maxson, Woods, and Klein, 1995). The 1993 USC survey involved telephone interviews with law enforcement in 211 cities that experienced gang migration in 1992. Most of the cities involved in the survey (86 percent) reported that migrant gang members contributed to an increase in local crime rates or patterns primarily in theft (50-percent increase), robbery (35-percent increase), other violent crimes (59-percent increase), and, to a lesser extent, drug sales (24-percent increase). The small increase in drug sale activity can most likely be attributed to competition from established local drug markets. The survey also showed that the type of criminal gang activity was changing to include increased use of firearms and more sophisticated weapons (36-percent increase). Carjackings, firebombings, residential robberies, drive-by shootings, and advanced techniques for vehicle theft were also cited on occasion. Changes in the targets of criminal activity and the use of other technological advances were mentioned less frequently.

What Previous Studies Show

The following is a summary of the research literature on the relationship between migration and proliferation. Local law enforcement agencies have become increasingly aware of the usefulness of maintaining systematic information on gangs, yet such data bases hardly meet the scientific standards of reliability and validity. Therefore, the results of the studies described in this section should be viewed as exploratory.

Although a number of national studies dating back to the 1970s have documented an increase in the number of cities and smaller communities reporting street gang activity, the numbers reported by these studies vary (Miller, 1975, 1982; Needle and Stapleton, 1983; Spergel and Curry, 1990; Curry, Ball, and Fox, 1994; Klein, 1995; Curry, 1996). Variations in localities reporting gang activities are attributed to the use of different sampling frames in the national surveys. While the surveys are not compatible, each reports increased gang activity. Miller's 1996 compilation of data from several sources documents gang proliferation during the past three decades and shows that in the 1970s, street gangs existed in the United States in 201 cities and 70 counties (many with cities included in the former count) (Miller, 1996). These figures climbed to 468 and 247, respectively, during the 1980s and to 1,487 and 706 in the 1990s. A nationwide survey conducted by the National Youth Gang Center (NYGC) reported that in 1995 gangs existed in 1,492 cities and 515 counties (OJJDP, 1997). The figures reported by Miller and NYGC are considerably higher than the estimate of 760 jurisdictions reported by Curry and his associates (Curry, Ball, and Decker, 1996) and the projection of 1,200 gang cities derived from the 1992 USC national mail survey (reported in Maxson, Woods, and Klein, 1995). Similarly, the National Drug Intelligence Center (NDIC) reported a much smaller figure of 265 for cities and counties reporting gang activity in 1995 (NDIC, 1996). Of these 265 cities and counties, 182 jurisdictions reported gang "connections" to 234 other cities, but the nature of these relationships was not elaborated on (D. Mehall, NDIC, personal communication, August 20, 1996). With the exception of the Mehall report and that of Maxson, Woods, and Klein (1995), none of the studies addressed the issue of gang migration on a national scale.

With few exceptions, findings on gang migration reported in research literature contrast sharply with the perspectives presented by the media, government agencies, and law enforcement reports. Several researchers have studied gangs in various cities throughout the United States and examined their origin and relationships to gangs in larger cities (primarily Chicago) to examine correlations between gang migration and proliferation on a more regional scale.

Gangs in the Midwestern United States

In 1983, Rosenbaum and Grant identified three Evanston, IL, gangs as "satellites" of major Chicago gangs, but proceeded to emphasize that they "are composed largely of Evanston residents, and in a very real sense, are Evanston gangs" (p. 15). They also found that two indigenous gangs, with no outside connection, contributed disproportionately to levels of violence and were, therefore, "almost totally responsible for increasing fear of crime in the community and forcing current reactions to the problem" (Rosenbaum and Grant, 1983:21). In contrast, the Chicago-connected gangs maintained a lower profile and were more profit oriented in their illegal activities, aspiring "to be more like organized crime" (Rosenbaum and Grant, 1983:21). In other words, the gangs indigenous to Evanston seemed to be more of a threat to the community than the Chicago-based gangs. The conclusion can be drawn that in this particular study, the migration of gangs into Evanston only minimally affected the proliferation of gang activities.

In an extensive study of Milwaukee gangs in 1988, 18 groups were found to use the names and symbols of major Chicago gangs, including identification with such gang confederations as People versus Folk (Hagedorn, 1988). In questioning gang founders on the origins of the gangs, it was determined that only 4 of the 18 were formed directly by gang members who had moved from Chicago to Milwaukee. Further, these members maintained only slight ties to their original Chicago gangs. Despite law enforcement claims to the contrary, no existence of a super-gang (i.e., Chicago) coalition was found in Milwaukee. Founding gang members strongly resented the idea that their gang was in any way tied to the original Chicago gangs (Hagedorn, 1988). In this study, Hagedorn concludes that gang formation in Milwaukee was only minimally affected by the migration of Chicago gangs. If anything, the influence was more cultural than structural, because gangs in smaller cities tend to follow big-city gang traditions and borrow cultural aspects from these gang images.

Further supporting the notion that gang migration only minimally affects proliferation is a 1989 study that determined that gangs in Columbus and Cleveland, OH, originated from streetcorner groups and breakdancing/rapping groups and also from migrating street-gang leaders from Chicago or Los Angeles (Huff, 1989). The study found no evidence that Ohio gangs were directly affiliated with gangs from other cities, particularly Chicago, Detroit, or Los Angeles.

In 1992, researchers examined the role that Chicago gangs played in the emergence of youth gangs in Kenosha, WI (Zevitz and Takata, 1992). Based on interviews with gang members, police analyses, and social service and school records, the study concluded that "the regional gangs in this study were products of local development even though they had a cultural affinity with their metropolitan counterparts. . . . We found no convincing evidence that metropolitan gangs had branched out to the outlying community where our study took place" (Zevitz and Takata, 1992:102). Regular contact between some Chicago and Kenosha gang members reflected kinship or old neighborhood ties rather than the organizational expansion of Chicago gangs.

These findings are echoed in a 1996 study of 99 gang members in St. Louis (Decker and Van Winkle, 1996). A minority (16 percent) of those interviewed suggested that gangs reemerged in St. Louis, MO, through the efforts of gang members from Los Angeles. Several of these migrants had relocated for social reasons, such as visiting relatives. The study also found that St. Louis gangs were more likely to originate as a result of neighborhood conflicts influenced by popular culture rather than from big-city connections.

> The powerful images of Los Angeles gangs, conveyed through movies, clothes, and music, provided a symbolic reference point for these antagonisms. In this way, popular culture provided the symbols and rhetoric of gang affiliation and activities that galvanized neighborhood rivalries. (Decker and Van Winkle, 1996:88)

Another study on gang migration in 1996 surveyed 752 jurisdictions in Illinois (Knox et al., 1996). (Because only 38 percent of the law enforcement agencies responded, these findings should be interpreted cautiously.) The majority of respondents (88 percent) reported that gangs from outside their area had established an influence, that one-fifth or more of their local gang population was attributable to recent arrivals (49 percent), that parental relocation of gang members served to transplant the gang problem to the area (65 percent), and that some of their gang problem was due to gang migration (69 percent). The study concluded that, while the impact of migration varies, "it is still of considerable interest to the law enforcement community" (Knox et al., 1996:78).

Gangs in the Western United States

In a study of drug sales and violence among San Francisco gangs, 550 gang members from 84 different gangs were interviewed (Waldorf, 1993). Of these, only three groups reported relationships with other gangs outside San Francisco. The report concluded that

> . . . most gangs do not have the skills or knowledge to move to other communities and establish new markets for drug sales. While it is true they can and do function on their own turf they are often like fish out of water when they go elsewhere. . . . They are not like organized crime figures (Mafia and Colombian cocaine cartels) who have capital, knowledge and power . . . while it might be romantic to think that the L.A. Bloods and Crips are exceptional, I will remain skeptical that they

are more competent than other gangs. (Waldorf, 1993:8)

To the contrary, a 1988 study of inmates in California correctional institutions and law enforcement and correctional officials suggested high levels of mobility among "entrepreneurial" California gang members traveling long distances to establish drug distribution outlets and maintaining close ties to their gangs of origin (Skolnick et al., 1990; Skolnick, 1990). Among all the empirical studies conducted in this area, Skolnick's resonates most closely with the reports from law enforcement previously cited (Bonfante, 1995; Hayeslip, 1989; California Council on Criminal Justice, 1989; Genelin and Coplen, 1989; McKinney, 1988; National Drug Intelligence Center, 1994, 1996).

> Against a backdrop of escalating violence, declining drug prices, and intensified law enforcement, Los Angeles area gang-related drug dealers are seeking new venues to sell the Midas product—crack cocaine. . . . Respondents claim to have either participated in or have knowledge of Blood or Crip crack operations in 22 states and at least 27 cities. In fact, it appears difficult to overstate the penetration of Blood and Crip members into other states. (Skolnick, 1990:8)

But the sheer presence of Crips and Bloods in States other than California is a poor indicator of gang migration. The 1996 NDIC survey identified 180 jurisdictions in 42 States with gangs claiming affiliation with the Bloods and/or Crips. At the same time, the NDIC report cautions against assuming organizational links from gang names.

> It is important to note that when a gang has claimed affiliation with the Bloods or Crips, or a gang has taken the name of a nationally known gang, this does not necessarily indicate that this gang is a part of a group with a national infrastructure. While some gangs have interstate connections and a hierarchical structure, the majority of gangs do not fit this profile. (NDIC, 1996:v)

Gangs in the South Central United States

In a 1994 study of 9 States located in the south central United States, 131 municipal police departments were surveyed; 79 cities completed the mail survey (Quinn, Tobolowsky, and Downs, 1994). Respondents in 44 percent of small cities (populations between 15,000 and 50,000) and 41 percent of large cities (populations greater than 50,000) stated that their largest gang was affiliated with groups in other cities. It is unknown whether the perceived affiliation was based on structural links or on name association. Nearly three-fourths of the 792 gang cities that responded to the 1992 USC mail survey reported that at least some indigenous gangs adopted gang names generally associated with Los Angeles and Chicago (e.g., Bloods, Crips, Vicelords, Gangster Disciples, or Latin Kings). Approximately 60 of these cities had no gang migration.

The National Survey on Gang Migration

In 1992, the University of Southern California conducted a mail survey of law enforcement personnel in approximately 1,100 U.S. cities. The survey was distributed to all cities with a population of more than 100,000 and to more than 900 cities and towns that serve as likely environments for street gangs or gang migration.[3] Law enforcement officials suggested municipalities to include in the survey, and all cities with organizations that investigate gangs were included. To increase the survey pool, the survey asked respondents to list cities to which their local gang members had moved. This sample is best characterized as a purposive sample of gang cities—it is neither representative of all U.S. cities and towns, although all large cities are enumerated fully, nor all gang cities.[4] This survey captured data on the largest number of cities with gangs identified at the time (and a majority of the cities identified by the NYGC survey in 1995) and is the only systematic enumeration of U.S. cities experiencing gang migration to date. Repeated mailings and telephone follow up resulted in completion of the survey by more than 90 percent of those polled.

To develop descriptions about the nature of gang migration and local responses to it, extensive telephone interviews were conducted with law enforcement officers in 211 cities that reported the arrival of at least 10 migrant gang members in 1991. Interview participants were sampled from a larger pool of 480 cities that cited at least moderate levels of gang migration. Other facets of the study included interviews with community informants and case studies, including personal interviews with migrant gang members.[5]

A primary limitation of this research design is the necessity to rely on law enforcement for depictions of the scope and nature of gang migration. Locally based ethnographic approaches—based on the systematic recording of particular human cultures—would lend a more comprehensive view of the migration situation in individual cities. The USC case studies involved a range of informants whose depictions sometimes contrasted markedly with law enforcement's assessment of the issue. The attempt to extend beyond law enforcement to community respondents produced mixed results, because informants were generally less informed about migration matters in the city as a whole and tended to focus on particular neighborhoods of interest. It would seem that law enforcement is the best available source of information on national patterns of gang migration, but the reader should be wary of the limitations on law enforcement as a source of information on migration. These limitations include the occupational focus of law enforcement on crime (i.e., if migrants are not engaged in a lot of crime, they are less likely to come to the attention of law enforcement), the lack of local data bases with systematically gathered information about migration, and the definitional challenges described earlier in Clarifying the Concepts. Given these limitations, the results from this study should be

Figure 6.1
Cities Experiencing Gang Member Migration Through 1992

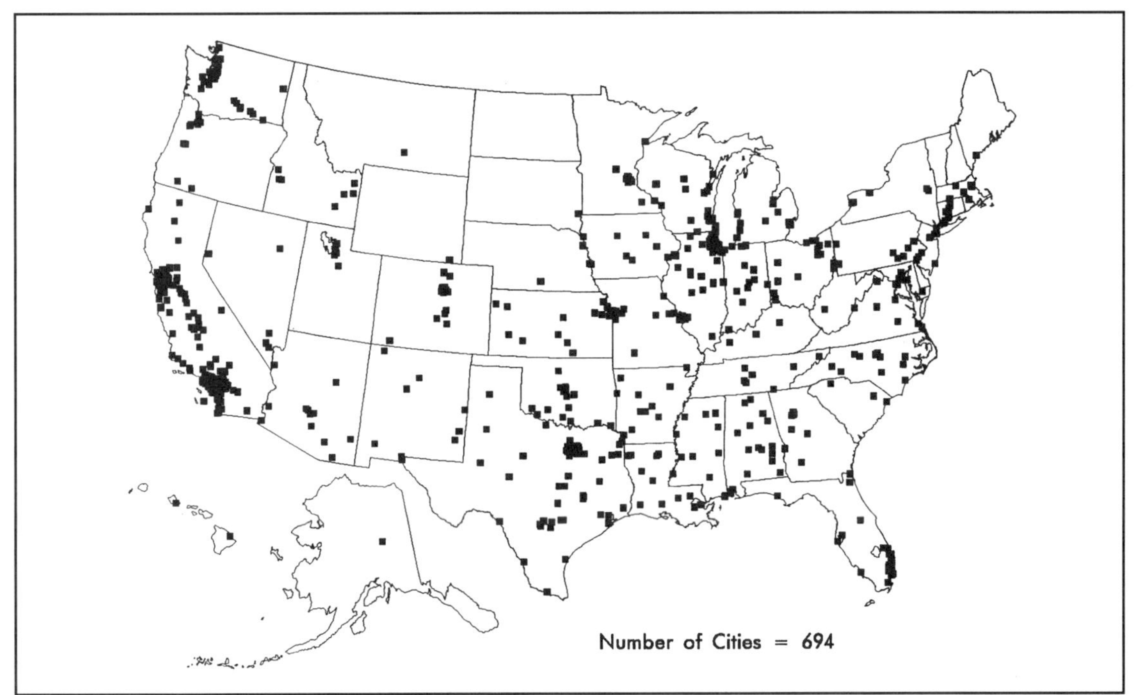

viewed as exploratory until replicated by further research.

Study Findings

The National Scope of Gang Migration

Approximately 1,000 cities responded to the 1992 mail survey, revealing 710 cities that had experienced gang migration by 1992. The widespread distrution of these cities is reflected in Figure 6.1.[6] Only three States had not experienced gang migration by 1992—New Hampshire, North Dakota, and Vermont. The concentration of migration cities in several regions—most dramatically southern California and the Bay area, the area surrounding Chicago, and southern Florida—may obscure the geographic distribution. Forty-four percent of migration cities are located in the western region of the country, with slightly less prominence in the mid-western (26 percent) and southern (25 percent) portions of the country. Only 5 percent of the migration cities are situated in the northeastern region of the country.

Approximately 80 percent of cities with a population of more than 100,000 have migrant gang members. The overall sample cannot address the proportion of all smaller cities with migration, but the distribution of migration cities by population, shown in Figure 6.1, suggests that this is an issue confronting cities of all sizes. That nearly 100 towns with populations of 10,000 people or less experienced gang migration is striking. This phenomenon is a manifestation of the motivations to relocate and the potential influences of migrant gang members on small-town life and overtaxed law enforcement resources. Moreover, because smaller cities are less likely to have longstanding gang problems, gang migration could be a catalyst for the onset of local gang problems.

The sheer number of cities with migrant gang members and the widespread geographic distribution of these cities across the country is dramatic, but the volume of gang migration presents a far less alarming picture. Survey respondents provided an estimate of the number of migrants that had arrived in their city the year prior to survey completion.[7] Just under half (47 percent) of the 597 cities providing an estimate reported the arrival of no more than 10 migrants in the prior year. Only 34 cities (6 percent) estimated the arrival of more than 100 migrants during this period. The significance of such numbers would vary by the size of the city, but the large number of cities reporting insubstantial levels of migration suggests that gang migration may not represent a serious problem in many cities.

Survey respondents were asked to provide a demographic profile of migrant gang members. The typical age reported ranged from 13 to 30, and the mean and median age was 18. Female migrants were uncommon; more than 80 percent of the cities noted five or fewer. Compared with the ethnic distribution of gang members nationally, migrant gang members were somewhat more likely to be black. Approximately half of the cities polled in the survey reported that at least 60 percent of migrant gang members were black; predominantly Hispanic distributions emerged in 28 percent of the cities. The predominance of Asian (14 cities or 7 percent) or white (2 cities) migrant gang members was unusual.

Gang Migration and Local Gang Proliferation

The potential for gang migration to have a harmful impact on local gang activity and crime rates may increase substantially if migrant gang members foster the proliferation of local gang problems in their destination cities. This is a pivotal issue, and data of several types are available for elaboration. The characteristics of cities with local gangs can be compared with those of cities with migrant gangs to establish the parameters of the relationship. Of particular interest are the dates of local gang formation and migration onset. Law enforcement perceptions about the causes of local gang problems are also relevant. Lastly, the motivations of gang members to migrate and their patterns of gang activity upon arrival must be considered.

Through the survey of 1,100 cities, it was found that most, but not all, cities that have local gangs also have migrant gang members. Conversely, nearly all cities with gang migration also have local gangs. The 1992 survey identified 792 cities with local gangs; of these cities, 127 (16 percent) reported no experience with gang migration (Table 6.1). Only 45 of the 710 identified migration cities (6 percent) had no indigenous gangs. This simple comparison yields 172 cities (22 percent) in which migration could not have caused the emergence of local gangs, at least through 1992. The large proportion of cities with both local and migrant gang members made it difficult to detect any differences between local gang and migrant gang cities. Distributions across city size categories and geographic region are negligible (data not shown).

Table 6.1
Cities With Local Gangs or Gang Migration

	No Gang Migration	Gang Migration
Cities with no local gangs	182	45
Cities with local gangs	127	665

Source: Maxson, Woods, and Klein (1995).

Another pertinent point of comparison from the survey is the date of onset of local gangs and the year in which migrant gang members first arrived in cities with local and migrant gang members. (These data are shown in Figure 6.2 with some loss of cases due to the respondents' inability to estimate at least one of the dates.) Only 31 of the cities with local gangs (5 percent) reported the onset of gang migration at least 1 year prior to the emergence of local gangs. Most cities (54 percent) had local gangs prior to gang migration. Adding these 344 cities (i.e., those with local gangs before migrants) to the prior figure of 172 cities that have just one or the other gang type yields a total of 516 cities that clearly challenge the notion of migration as the cause of local gang proliferation. While the picture for cities with coincidental onset of the two types of gang members is ambiguous, it seems reasonable to conclude that cities in which migration provides the catalyst for indigenous gang formation are the exception rather than the rule.

The telephone interviews confirm this pattern; the majority of informants (81 percent) disagreed with the statement, "Without migration, this city wouldn't have a gang problem."

Figure 6.2
710 Gang Migration Cities by Population

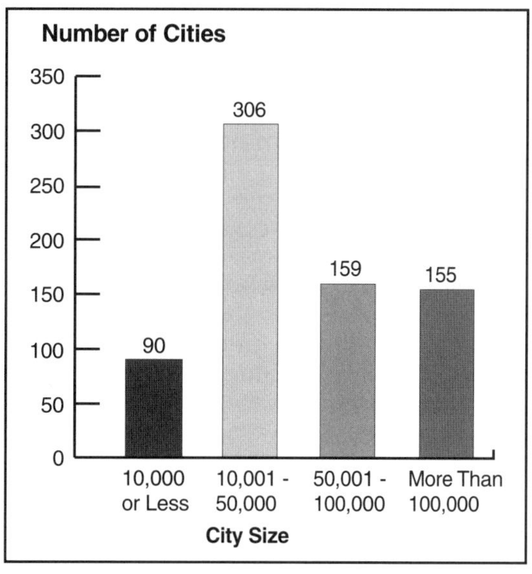

It can be argued that the concern over gang migration is most pertinent to emerging gang cities. The national gang surveys (Miller, 1996) discussed earlier have shown that the major proliferation of gang cities has occurred since the 1980s.[8] Nearly 70 percent of the 781 gang cities that could provide a date of emergence reported one after 1985. These cities can be characterized as "emergent" rather than "chronic" gang cities (Spergel and Curry, 1990). Emergent gang cities are equally as likely to report gang migration as chronic cities (84 percent of the cities in each group). However, cities with gang onset after 1985 are significantly less likely to report that local gangs preceded gang migration (40 percent versus 88 percent), as might be expected when they are compared with cities with longstanding local gang problems. Emergent cities are more likely to experience the onset of local gangs and migrants in the same year as opposed to chronic cities (53 percent versus 11 percent). The majority of respondents interviewed from emergent gang cities believed that migration was not the cause of local gang problems. This figure was significantly lower for emergent gang cities (73 percent) than for chronic gang cities (93 percent). This shows that the conclusion that migration is not generally the catalyst for gang proliferation holds up, but the exceptions to this general rule can most often be found in emergent gang cities.

Patterns of Gang Migration

Examination of the reasons gang members migrate to other cities and their patterns of gang affiliation in the new city show that migration is not a major catalyst of gang proliferation. Survey interviewers asked participating officers to choose from a list of reasons why most gang members moved into their cities. The most frequently cited reason was that gang members moved with their families (39 percent). When this was combined with the reason of staying with relatives and friends, 57 percent of the survey respondents believed that migrants relocated primarily for social reasons. Drug market expansion was the second most frequently cited motivation (20 percent of cities) for migrating. When this was combined with other criminal opportunities, it created a larger category of illegal attractions, or "pull" motivators, in 32 percent of cities reporting an influx of migrant gangs. "Push" motivators that forced gang members to leave cities, such as law enforcement crackdowns (8 percent), court-ordered relocation, or a desire to escape gangs, were cited in 11 percent of migrant-recipient cities.

Are these patterns of motivation for migrating different in cities with emergent gangs as compared with those cities with chronic local gang problems? The data shown in Table 6.2 provide evidence that they clearly are not. Emergent gang cities have nearly equal proportions of socially motivated gang migration as chronic gang cities. "Pull" motivators (primarily drug market expansion) and "push" motivators are less frequent reasons for gang member relocation than social motivations in both types of city.

Table 6.2
Most Frequent Reasons for Migration Reported by Chronic and Emergent Gang Cities

Motivation	Chronic Gang Cities (*n*=73)	Emergent Gang Cities (*n*=111)
Social	41 (56%)	63 (57%)
"Pulls"	22 (30%)	37 (33%)
"Pushes"	10 (14%)	11 (10%)

Note: "Pull" motivators (e.g., drug markets) are those that attract gang members to relocate in specific locations. "Push" motivators, such as law enforcement crackdowns, are those that force gang members to leave cities and relocate elsewhere.

There are no differences between the two types of gang cities with regard to patterns of migrant gang activity. Approximately one-third (38 percent) of survey respondents stated that gang migrants established new gangs or recruited for their old gangs; 36 percent reported that gang migrants joined existing local gangs or exclusively retained affiliation with their old gangs. The proportions of each in chronic and emergent gang cities are quite similar (data not shown). Thus, data on motivations for migrating and on migrant patterns in joining gangs provide little support for the view of migrants as primary agents of gang proliferation and no evidence for differential impact on emergent gang cities.

Conclusion

The interpretation of these results should be tempered by an awareness of the limitations of the USC study methodology. The surveys used to collect data relied heavily on law enforcement as a source of information. A logical next step would involve using an array of informants, including courts, schools, and social service providers in addition to community residents and gang members. It should also be noted that the USC data are cross-sectional in nature and cannot adequately describe second- or third-

Figure 6.3
Dates of Onset of Local Gangs Versus Migration

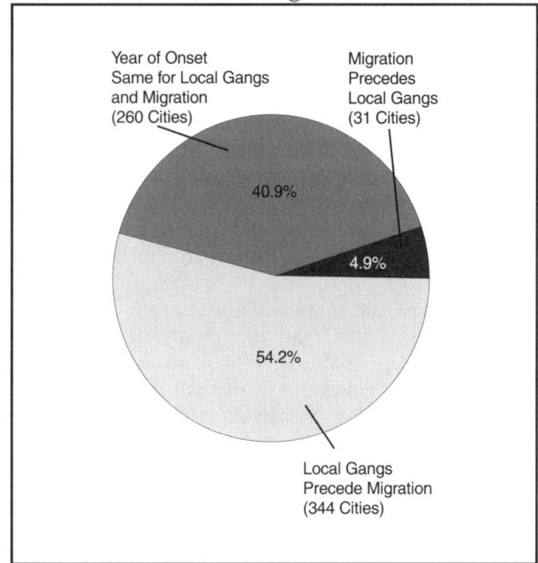

order waves of migration, wherein some individuals may travel from city to city.[9] Another untapped dimension in the USC survey was termed "indirect migration," in which one gang is influenced by another gang that was influenced by a third gang. For example, Pocatello, ID, gangs were heavily influenced by Salt Lake City gangs, which were started by gang members from Los Angeles (R. Olsen, Pocatello Police Department, personal communication, September 24, 1996). Other patterns of sequential mobility were reported on during the USC interviews, but did not occur with sufficient frequency to warrant further analysis.

The findings from the 1992 and 1993 USC surveys provide evidence that gang member migration, although widespread, should not be viewed as the major culprit in the nationwide proliferation of gangs. Local, indigenous gangs usually exist prior to gang migration, and migrants are not generally viewed by local law enforcement as the cause of gang problems. This pattern is less evident in cities in which gangs have emerged more recently, but these municipalities are no more likely to experience gang migration than chronic gang cities. Moreover, the motivations for gang member relocation (i.e., more often socially motivated than driven by crime opportunities) and patterns of gang participation (equally likely to join existing gangs as to retain original affiliation in order to initiate new gangs or branches) do not distinguish migrants in the two types of cities. Proponents of the "outside agitator" hypothesis of gang formation as described by Hagedorn (1988) will find little support in the data available from the USC national study.

On the whole, the USC findings agree with the research literature on gangs cited earlier. Many of the researchers—Rosenbaum and Grant (1983), Hagedorn (1988), Huff (1989), Zevitz and Takata (1992), Decker and Van Winkle (1996), and Waldorf (1993)—found that gang formation was only minimally affected by the diffusion of gang members from other cities. The findings reported by some researchers—Skolnick et al. (1990) and NDIC (1994, 1996)—are less consistent with those reported in the USC study. The Skolnick et al. and NDIC studies focused heavily on drug issues and may have disproportionately represented cities with drug-gang migration or with migrants that moved for drug expansion purposes.[10] Such cities reflect a distinct pattern of gang migration—older gang migrants, traveling longer distances, staying for briefer periods (see Maxson, Woods, and Klein, 1995, for full presentation of these analyses). Research that focuses on drug matters may fail to capture more prevalent trends. Although more often the subject of media coverage, migration for drug distribution purposes is less common than other types of migration. The differential patterns of gang migration, and their effects on local communities, require more research.

In addition, the USC findings are difficult to compare with those reported by Knox et al. (1996). Respondents in the Knox et al. study presented a widespread perception of outside gang influence. This may be the result of exposure to the media and products of the entertainment industry. Klein (1995) and others have suggested that the diffusion of gang culture in the media plays a key role in the proliferation of gang membership. Our nation's youth are hardly dependent on direct contact with gang members for exposure to the more dramatic manifestations of gang culture, which is readily accessible in youth-oriented television programming, popular movies, and the recent spate of "tell-all" books from reputed urban gang leaders. The nature of this influence and its impact on gang participation and expansion have not been investigated systematically but are crucial in understanding fully the dynamics of gang proliferation.

Cities with emerging gang situations should examine the dynamics of their own communities before attributing their gang problems to outside influences. Socioeconomic factors, such as persistent unemployment, residential segregation, and the lack of recreational, educational, and vocational services for youth, are more likely sources of gang formation or expansion than is gang migration.

Notes

1. Few studies attempt to assess the proportion and age of adolescent gang members within a given area. Recent information on self-identified membership from longitudinal projects for representative samples in Denver, CO, and Rochester, NY, (Thornberry and Burch, 1997) is available from the OJJDP-funded Program of Research on the Causes and Correlates of Delinquency. Approximately 5 percent of youth living in "high-risk" neighborhoods in Denver indicated that they were gang members in any given year (Esbensen, Huizinga, and Weiher, 1993). In Rochester, 30 percent of the sample reported gang membership at some point between the beginning of the seventh grade and the end of high school (Thornberry and Burch, 1997). To address the issue of gang proliferation within Denver or Rochester, new samples would need to be examined to determine whether the proportion of youth joining gangs in these cities has increased since the initial sampling period (nearly 10 years ago).

   Prevalence estimates derived from law enforcement identification of gang members have been challenged, as when Reiner (1992) reported that, according to the gang data base maintained for Los Angeles County, 9.5 percent of all men ages 21 to 24 were identified gang members. However, this proportion increased to 47 percent when the analysis was limited to black males ages 21 to 24. This figure has been generally recognized as a vast overstatement of black gang membership.
2. Whether or not migrants provide a catalyst to local gang proliferation, their impact on local crime is of considerable concern to law enforcement.
3. It should be noted that incorporated cities (of all population sizes) were the unit of analysis in this study; unincorporated areas were not included. Whenever cities contracted law enforcement responsibilities to sheriff's departments or State police, such agencies were pursued as respondents. Letters were addressed to the head agency official with a request to pass the survey on to the individual in the department most familiar with the gang situation within the city jurisdiction.
4. A random sample of 60 cities with a population of between 10,000 and 100,000 was surveyed for gang migration or local street-gang presence. Projections from this sample indicate a much larger number of U.S. cities with gang migration than have been identified to date.
5. These data are not presented in this report. Also not included are data from interviews with law enforcement in 15 cities that reported drug-gang migration only. This report refers to street-gang, rather than drug-gang, migration. See earlier discussion under Clarifying the Concepts for the distinction between the two types.
6. A few cities with gang migration were not included in this map because respondents were unable to specify the year of the first arrival of gang members from other cities.
7. A separate estimate of the total number of migrants was discarded as less reliable than the annual estimate. Even the annual estimate should be considered with caution, as few departments maintained records on gang migration. Some officers had difficulty generalizing to the city as a whole, based upon their own experience, and many migrants presumably do not come to the attention of the police.
8. Klein (1995) provides a highly illustrative series of maps displaying dates of onset of local gang problems using data gathered in the migration study.
9. The interviews with migrant gang members gathered data on multiple moves, but there were too few instances from which to generalize. The author acknowledges Scott Decker

for his observation of this limitation of the study design.

10. The Skolnick and NDIC studies employed purposive rather than representative sampling techniques.

Acknowledgements

Support was provided by the National Institute of Justice, grant #91-IJ-CX-K004. Malcolm Klein was co-principal investigator of the study and research assistance was provided by Kristi Woods, Lea Cunningham, and Karen Sternheimer. The author gratefully acknowledges the participation of personnel in hundreds of police departments and community agencies, along with several dozen gang members. Useful comments on an earlier draft were provided by Malcolm Klein, Walter Miller, James Howell, and Scott Decker.

References

Bonfante, J. 1995. Entrepreneurs of crack. *Time*, February 27.

California Council on Criminal Justice. 1989. *State Task Force on Gangs and Drugs: Final Report*. Sacramento, CA: California Council on Criminal Justice.

Curry, G. D. 1996. National youth gang surveys: A review of methods and findings. Unpublished. Tallahassee, FL: National Youth Gang Center, Institute for Intergovernmental Research.

Curry, G. D., Ball, R. A., and Decker, S. H. 1996. "Estimating the national scope of gang crime from law enforcement data." In *Gangs in America*, 2d ed., edited by C. R. Huff. Thousand Oaks, CA: Sage Publications.

Curry, G. D., Ball, R. A., and Fox, R. J. 1994. *Gang Crime and Law Enforcement Recordkeeping*. Research in Brief. Washington, DC: U.S. Department of Justice, Office of Justice Programs, National Institute of Justice.

Decker, S., and Van Winkle, B. 1996. *Life in the Gang*. New York: Cambridge University Press.

Esbensen, F. A., Huizinga, D., and Weiher, A. 1993. Gang and non-gang youth: Differences in explanatory factors. *Journal of Contemporary Criminal Justice* 9:94–116.

Genelin, M., and Coplen, B. 1989. Los Angeles street gangs: Report and recommendations of the countywide Criminal Justice Coordination Committee. Unpublished report of the Interagency Gang Task Force. Los Angeles: Interagency Gang Task Force.

Hagedorn, J. 1988. *People and Folks: Gangs, Crime, and the Underclass in a Rustbelt City*. Chicago: Lakeview Press.

Hayeslip, D. W., Jr. 1989 (March/April). Local-level drug enforcement: New strategies. *NIJ Reports* 213:2–6. Washington, DC: U.S. Department of Justice, Office of Justice Programs, National Institute of Justice.

Huff, C. R. 1989. Youth gangs and public policy. *Crime & Delinquency* 35:524–37.

Klein, M. W. 1995. *The American Street Gang*. New York: Oxford University Press.

Klein, M. W., and Maxson, C. L. 1996. Gang structures, crime patterns, and police responses. Unpublished final report. Los Angeles: Social Science Research Institute, University of Southern California.

Knox, G. W., Houston, J. G., Tromanhauser, E. D., McCurrie, T. F., and Laskey, J. 1996. Addressing and testing the gang migration issue. In *Gangs: A Criminal Justice Approach*, edited by J. M. Miller and J. P. Rush. Cincinnati, OH: Anderson Publishing Company.

Maxson, C. L., Woods, K. J., and Klein, M. W. 1995. Street gang migration in the United States. Unpublished final report. Los Angeles: Social Science Research Institute, University of Southern California.

Maxson, C. L., Woods, K. J., and Klein, M. W. 1996 (February). Street gang migration: How big a threat? *National Institute of Justice Journal* 230: 26–31. Washington, DC: U.S. Department of Justice, Office of Justice Programs, National Institute of Justice.

McKinney, K. C. 1988 (September). *Juvenile Gangs: Crime and Drug Trafficking*. Chapter. Washington, DC: U.S. Department of Justice, Office of Justice Programs, Office of Juvenile Justice and Delinquency Prevention.

Miller, W. B. 1975. Violence by youth gangs and youth groups as a crime problem in major American cities. Unpublished. Washington, DC: U.S. Department of Justice, National Institute of Juvenile Justice and Delinquency Prevention.

Miller, W. B. 1982 (Reissued in 1992). *Crime by Youth Gangs and Groups in the United States*. Washington, DC: U.S. Department of Justice, Office of Justice Programs, Office of Juvenile Justice and Delinquency Prevention.

Miller, W. B. 1996. The growth of youth gang problems in the United States: 1970–1995. Unpublished. Tallahassee, FL: National Youth Gang Center, Institute for Intergovernmental Research.

National Drug Intelligence Center. 1994. *Bloods and Crips Gang Survey Report*. Johnstown, PA: National Drug Intelligence Center.

National Drug Intelligence Center. 1996. *National Street Gang Survey Report*. Johnstown, PA: National Drug Intelligence Center.

Needle, J. A., and Stapleton, W. V. 1983. *Police Handling of Youth Gangs*. Washington, DC: U.S. Department of Justice, Office of Justice Programs, Office of Juvenile Justice and Delinquency Prevention.

Office of Juvenile Justice and Delinquency Prevention. 1997. *1995 National Youth Gang Survey.* Summary. Washington, DC: U.S. Department of Justice, Office of Justice Programs, Office of Juvenile Justice and Delinquency Prevention.

Quinn, J. F., Tobolowsky, P. M., and Downs, W. T. 1994. The gang problem in large and small cities: An analysis of police perceptions in nine states. *The Gang Journal* 2(2):13–22.

Reiner, I. 1992. *Gangs, Crime, and Violence in Los Angeles*. Los Angeles: Office of the District Attorney of Los Angeles County.

Rosenbaum, D. P., and Grant, J. A. 1983. *Gangs and Youth Problems in Evanston*. Report. Evanston, IL: Northwestern University, Center for Urban Affairs and Policy Research.

Skolnick, J. H. 1990. *Gang Organization and Migration*. Sacramento, CA: Office of the Attorney General of the State of California.

Skolnick, J. H., Correl, T., Navarro, T., and Rabb, R. 1990. The social structure of street drug dealing. *American Journal of Police* 9(1):1–41.

Spergel, I. A., and Curry, G. D. 1990. Strategies and perceived agency effectiveness in dealing with the youth gang problem. In *Gangs in America*, edited by C. R. Huff. Newbury Park, CA: Sage Publications.

Thornberry, T. B., and Burch, J. H. II. 1997 (June). *Gang Members and Delinquent Behavior Chapter.* Washington, DC: U.S. Department of Justice, Office of Justice Programs, Office of Juvenile Justice and Delinquency Prevention.

Thornberry, T. B., Krohn, M. D., Lizotte, A. J., and Chard-Wierschem, D. 1993. The role of juvenile gangs in facilitating delinquent behavior. *Journal of Research in Crime and Delinquency* 30(1): 55–87.

Waldorf, D. 1993. When the Crips invaded San Francisco: Gang migration. *The Gang Journal* 1(4).

Zevitz, R. G., and Takata, S. R. 1992. Metropolitan gang influence and the emergence of group delinquency in a regional community. *Journal of Criminal Justice* 20(2):93–106. ✦

Chapter 7
Gangs in the United States and Europe

Malcolm W. Klein[1]

Klein accomplishes several objectives in this article. He provides the first report of the recent emergence of street gangs in a number of Western European cities. He also presents a picture of five types of gang structures emerging in his research with co-editor Maxson. Finally, he applies the five structures to the initial brief descriptions of European gangs to test the applicability of this structural approach, developed in the United States, to the gangs being described in Europe. A considerable amount of overlap between the two continents is suggested.

The general aim of this report is to bring up to date portions of the material published recently (Klein, 1995) on street gangs in the United States and Europe, much of which was current only through 1992. This will be done in two ways: by reporting on new material on European street gangs gathered since 1992,[2] and by describing and applying new information on the *structure* of American street gangs. The emphasis throughout will be on *street gangs*, a term which, in this article, is used to indicate a group-accepted and acknowledged orientation toward anti-social or criminal activities. It includes some specially focused groups such as street-level drug sales groups but not organized, upper-level distribution systems and cartels. It includes some hate groups such as a number of skinheads, but not terrorist groups. It excludes prison gangs, motorcycle gangs, football hooligans, and the many youthful groups at school and elsewhere that may occasionally dabble in delinquent activities but do not orient themselves around these (see Klein, 1995, for a more complete discussion of street gang definitional issues).

Quite obviously, gangs in some form have existed in many eras and in many places, but when and where is essentially unknowable due to the absence of careful descriptions and acceptable or common definitions. The word "gang" can be found in Chaucer and Shakespeare. It is forever associated in the public's mind now with the romanticized and grossly inaccurate depictions in *West Side Story* and Marlon Brando's *The Wild Ones*. Europeans—lay, professional, and scholar alike—often deny the existence of street gangs in their countries because their groups do not resemble these stereotyped depictions of cohesive, leader-dominated, violent aggregations. Such denial is inappropriate because the image is journalistic, not scientific. American gangs are generally rather loosely organized, with ephemeral leadership and only sporadic violence in an otherwise humdrum, boring existence.

Many Americans, too—lay, professional, and scholar—accept a stereotype that seldom mirrors reality. I have had many interviews with gang observers throughout the U.S. who offer reasoned depictions of their gangs and then add, "but they're not like your typical Los Angeles-style gangs," not realizing that most of "ours" are like most of theirs.

Fortunately, for the purposes of the updating report, I can avoid disputes about the gangs in ancient Greece or Palestine or Mongol China, and in a report on the U.S. and Europe, I can avoid the complications of gang-like descriptions from more recent times in Africa and Asia. Readers seeking lists of nations with some form of gang experience can profitably refer to Clinard and Abbot (1973), Covey et al. (1992), Klein (1995) and Spergel (1995). The concern in this paper is with the

---

Reprinted from: *European Journal on Criminal Policy and Research*, 4:2, pp. 63–80. "Gangs in the United States and Europe," by Malcolm W. Klein.

most recent developments in Europe and the U.S. only.

Gangs in Europe in 1992

I summarize briefly here what I learned while travelling to and from my temporary 1992 home at the National Center for Crime Prevention in Stockholm. For those who prefer that Scandinavia and Europe not be included under the same umbrella, I beg their indulgence. The combining of the two is a convenience for my own purposes.

My purpose at that time was to determine the degree to which American-style gangs might exist in Europe. This was prior to the data collection reported later in this paper on American street gang structures, so it would be more accurate to say that I was seeking any existence of the "traditional" form of American gang structures, with large numbers of members separated into age-graded subgroups. I wanted to ascertain whether the American street gang, as I described it, was in fact a unique American phenomenon.

I should state at the onset that my 1992 exposures were not complete. All of Eastern Europe, with the exception of Russia, was omitted. Italy, France, and Portugal were omitted, as were Scotland, Ireland, and Norway. I was able to ascertain that street gangs seemed to be absent in Spain (in 1992—prior years were different), Finland, Holland, and Slovenia (which did report networks of troublesome youth, but not gangs).

The trail I followed started in Sweden. Sarnecki's (1986) work in the mid-1980s, although initially labelled as gang research, really was about loose and rapidly changing networks of small-city youth who got into some trouble with the police. Their transitional status and level of delinquency involvement did not upon further study justify their being thought of as street gangs. Yet soon thereafter a form of street gang did evolve in Stockholm which was soon found elsewhere. Located in housing projects on the outskirts of the city, these groups were composed principally of second-generation immigrant youth, the progeny of guest workers and refugees. They were more ethnically mixed than American minority gangs, typically coming from such backgrounds as Morocco, Yugoslavia, Greece, Lebanon and Turkey. Also unlike most American gangs, they were not territorial or "turf" conscious, and were not involved in intergang rivalries. But like American gangs they did have a strong sense of special group identity; they developed special symbols, dress, and argot; and they oriented themselves around a versatile pattern of criminal behavior. Living on the edge of town, they typically gathered in the evening to ride the subway into the central city areas where their crimes were committed—smash-and-grab burglaries, robberies, "rolling" of drunks or unwary tourists, drinking and loitering in selected spots. On one evening's tour with a Stockholm police officer, I found them gathered at the open market at Kungsgatan and in the underground area of Sergelstorg. When their night's predations were concluded, they returned to their homes by subway in a pattern seen later in Zurich, Frankfurt, and Stuttgart. An article on this pattern was later aptly subtitled by a journal editor, "commuting to turf" (Klein and Gatz, 1993).

Three other cities—Zurich, Stuttgart, and Frankfurt—revealed very much the same pattern, although with some variation. In Zurich, there were also some centrally located groups preparing to become gangs; the police called them "toys" for toy gangsters. In Frankfurt, the groups had learned to discard distinctive markings and names to avoid police detection, and flirted with drug distribution. In Stuttgart, football hooligans were more of a concern than the commuting gangs, since Stuttgart's reputation in the soccer world served as a magnet. Each city reported a different mix of foreign ethnicities in its gangs, although Eastern Europe, North Africa, and the Near East were generally prominent. But Chile, for instance, contributed to the mix in Zurich.[3]

With this pattern of suburban, ethnic street gangs established for several cities, I turned to England and found a very different picture. In London and Manchester, there were street gangs, and they were often composed of foreign-born members—Chinese, Pakistani, Indian, and Jamaican seemed the principal groups. However, unlike the groups across the Channel, these gangs were found in more central city areas, were ethnically more pure, and were often quite territorial. Most different of all, they were drug gangs. Their principal focus was on the sale of drugs. Their "territories" were both residential and market-oriented. In function and form, including the use of violence in the furtherance of their business affairs, they more closely resembled the newly emergent drug gangs reported in a number of American cities, most particularly Detroit, Atlanta, and Washington, D.C. But whereas these new American drug gangs were primarily involved with crack cocaine, the British groups revolved around hashish and heroin. The principal problem groups were reported to be the Jamaican gangs—"Yardies," as they are called.

There may have been other British cities involved—Liverpool and Nottingham were mentioned—but the heavy action was repeatedly attributed to London and Manchester. The latter city, with its rapidly deteriorating housing projects ("estates") in the Moss Side district, most closely resembled inner-city American areas that have traditionally spawned street gangs.

In all of the above—Sweden, Germany, England—the 1992 depiction was of a variety of street gangs which did not correspond well to the traditional American structure of age-graded cliques within a larger territorially-based agglomeration of youth. Elsewhere, however, such structures were clearly identified. These were in Berlin, Brussels, and a number of cities of the Volga region in Russia. The Berlin picture was particularly striking, and documented by police gang intelligence officers, refugee officials, and an active gang worker agency. Arising in protective reaction to right-wing extremist groups in the mid-1980s, second- and third-generation immigrant youth had formed gangs in deteriorated inner city areas such as Kreuzberg, as well as Wedding and Tiergarten. They adopted such names as Black Panthers, Fighters, Bulldogs, Bomber Boys, Club 7, and Aderpower. In Kreuzberg, the 36ers were highly visible with their graffiti in typical American-style block letters, in English.

The Berlin police gang intelligence officers provided some data on these groups, and when I sketched the structure of a traditional American turf gang for them, they exclaimed in unison, "Yes, yes, that's it" with what seemed to me to be relief that finally someone had recognized what they were dealing with. The gang worker agency confirmed this picture, adding that the violence potential of some of these groups was such that the street workers, for their own safety, were instructed only to work with the younger, less threatening cliques.

The Berlin gangs were the first I encountered that clearly fit the best documented of the American gang structures. Soon thereafter, I was given a brief but similar depiction for Brussels; inner-city second- and third-generation immigrant youth had formed age-graded cliques, bound together by territorial identification, with the typical versatile crime patterns and intergang rivalries. Five such gangs were reported, along with several other, smaller groups focused on thefts from automobiles. I did not have occasion to visit Brussels, and a brief, tourist's-eye view in 1995 failed to locate outward signs of gang activity. Nonetheless, there is new confirmation of these gangs from a Belgian research team that is about to launch a major field study of them.

Finally, there is the case of Russia. As part of a criminal justice delegation that visited Moscow, Kiev, and St. Petersburg, I failed to turn up evidence of street gangs in those cities, although other forms of organized crime were alluded to with regularity. However, further east, a set of about a dozen cities have yielded reports of street gangs remarkably similar to those I was seeking. "We borrow the worst from the West," commented an official of the National Procuracy. Russian scholars differentiate between these street gangs and a far larger collection of "Informal Youth Groups" (IYG). The street gangs, collectively referred to as the "Kazan Phenomenon" because that city seems to be the most intensely involved, are—not surprisingly—composed principally of ethnic minorities. They are described as territorial, large, with age-graded subgroups, criminally oriented and versatile in crime pattern, having clear intergang rivalries, and patterns of cohesiveness that probably exceed those typically found in the U.S. Various of the Russian writers predict a worsening of their street gang situation as economic failures increase, ethnic nationalism rises, and effective social controls weaken further.

Street Gang Structures in the United States: New Data

As part of an extended series of gang studies initiated in the 1990s (gang formation, gang resistance, gang member migration, gang proliferation), my colleagues and I undertook the first attempt to establish the national prevalence of different gang structures in the U.S. Several steps were involved.

Interviews with police gang experts in 260 cities helped to establish structural dimensions that had meaning for the police and could help to distinguish between gang types. Such dimensions as age, ethnicity, subgrouping, membership size, criminal versatility, and territoriality were promising variables. Gang cohesiveness and leadership proved far less discriminating. These interviews also revealed that these police experts showed little consensus on terminology for types of gangs or levels of gang member involvement. They all revealed that the police often classify gangs according to presumed crime patterns, but seldom according to structural characteristics. To typologize street gangs from police-derived information could not fruitfully be pursued by direct questioning on "types" of gang structures, but might be approached inductively by reference to structural dimensions from which types could be derived.

Interviews with a stratified sample of 60 police gang experts confirmed the above conclusions and established six reliable dimensions along which these experts could describe the gangs best known to them. These six were subgrouping, size, age range, duration (years in existence), territoriality, and criminal versatility. Ethnicity (black, Hispanic, Asian, white, mixed) proved to be less discriminating than we had expected. Possible crime specialization was omitted because it was not a structural dimension and because it was to be used later in our research program as a dependent variable tested empirically in relationship to the different structural types.

On the basis of the data from the sixty city police respondents, *scenarios for five gang structures* were derived and pre-tested with a small number of police gang experts whose knowledge we had come to respect over several years of contact. The five scenarios are reproduced below as taken from our final report (see Figure 7.1). Other details can be found in Maxson and Klein, 1995.

Five Gang Types

The traditional gang. "Traditional" gangs have generally been in existence for twenty or more years; they keep regenerating themselves. They contain fairly clear subgroups, usually separated by age: OGs or Veteranos, Seniors, Juniors, Midgets, and various other names are applied to these different age-based cliques. Sometimes the cliques are separated by neighborhoods rather than age. More than other gangs, traditional gangs tend to have a wide age range, sometimes as wide as from nine or ten years of age into the thirties. These are usually very large gangs, numbering one hundred or even several hundred members. Almost always, they are territorial in the sense that they identify strongly with their turf, 'hood, or barrio, and claim it as theirs alone. In sum, this is a large, enduring territorial gang with a wide range and several internal cliques based on age or area.

The neotraditional gang. The "neotraditional" gang resembles the traditional form, but has not been in existence as long—probably no more than ten years, and often less. It may be medium-size—say fifty to one hundred members—or also into the hundreds. It probably has developed subgroups or cliques based on age or area, but sometimes may not. The age range is usually smaller than in the classical traditional gangs. The neotraditional gang is also very territorial, claiming turf and defending it like the traditional gang. In sum, the

Figure 7.1
Characteristics of Five Gang Types

	Traditional	Neotraditional	Compressed	Collective	Speciality
Duration	long-lasting	10 years or less	short history	10 to 15 years	under 10 years
Size	large	medium to large	small	medium to large	small
Subgroups	distinct subgroups	distinct subgroups	no subgroups	no subgroups	no subgroups
Age range	wide		narrow	medium to wide	usually narrow
Territory	strongly territorial	strongly territorial			territorial
Other					narrow criminal focus

neotraditional gang is a newer territorial gang that looks on its way to becoming traditional in time. Thus at this point it is subgrouping, but may or may not have achieved the size and wide age range of the traditional gang. The subgrouping, territoriality, and size suggest that it is evolving into the traditional form.

The compressed gang. The "compressed" gang is small—usually in the size range of up to fifty members—and has not formed subgroups. The age range is probably narrow—ten or fewer years between the younger and older members. The small size, absence of subgroups, and narrow age range may reflect the newness of the group, in existence less than ten years and maybe for only a few years. Some of these compressed gangs have become territorial, but many have not. In sum, compressed gangs have a relatively short history, short enough that by size, duration, subgrouping and territoriality, it is unclear whether they will grow and solidify into the more traditional forms, or simply remain as less complex groups.

The collective gang. The "collective" gang looks like the compressed form, but bigger and with a wider age range—maybe ten or more years between younger and older members. Size can be under a hundred, but is probably larger. Surprisingly, given these numbers, it has not developed subgroups, and may or may not be a territorial gang. It probably has a ten- to fifteen-year existence. In sum, the collective gang resembles a kind of shapeless mass of adolescent and young adult members that has not developed the distinguishing characteristics of other gangs.

The specialty gang. Unlike these other gangs that engage in a wide variety of criminal offenses, crime in this type of group is narrowly focused on a few offences; the group comes to be characterized by the "specialty." The specialty gang tends to be small—usually fifty or fewer members—without any subgroups in most cases (there are exceptions). It probably has a history of less than ten years, but has developed well-defined territory. Its territory may be either residential or based on the opportunities for the particular form of crime in which it specializes. The age range of most specialty gangs is narrow, but in others is broad. In sum, the specialty gang is crime-focused in a narrow way. Its principal purpose is more criminal than social, and its smaller size and form of territoriality may be a reflection of this focused crime pattern.

These five scenarios were then sent to a *random sample of 200 police experts* in towns and cities known to experience street gang problems. This sample represents approximately 800 cities in the U.S. which we have documented as being gang-involved (Klein, 1995). Respondents were asked a number of questions about their jurisdiction's gangs, particularly in relation to the five scenarios. From an 80 percent return, we note several findings.

- The five structural types encompassed the vast majority of the 2,860 gangs involved in the responses, far exceeding our hopes.

- No additional structural types emerged.
- The most prevalent type was the compressed gang (39 percent), followed by the neotraditional form (24 percent). Since most research on American gangs has been carried out on the traditional form, which accounted for only 15 percent, a call for careful research on compressed gangs is obviously in order. This result also forces me to reconsider my 1992 approach to locating American-style gangs in Europe, as reported earlier.
- Some external validation of the five types was obtained in that they did differ, according to the 200 respondents, on such items as:
    - ❑ *Size*: traditional gangs averaged 182 members, specialty gangs averaged 24 members.
    - ❑ *Ethnicity*: traditional gangs, 57 percent Hispanic; collective, 47 percent black, while white and Asian predominated in no category.
    - ❑ *Arrest volume*: traditional gangs averaged 10.9 arrests per month, specialty averaged 5.7.
    - ❑ *Arrests per member*: specialty gangs averaged 0.29 per month, while traditional averaged 0.16 per month.
    - ❑ *Duration*: 52 percent of cities with traditional gangs had gang onset prior to 1986, while only 22 percent of cities with specialty gangs did so.
    - ❑ *City size*: collective gangs were located in cities over 100,000 in population in 52 percent of the cases, whereas other structures were found in these large cities in from 28 to 36 percent of the cases.
    - ❑ *Predominance*: cities showing a preponderance of any one structure are most likely to report compressed gangs, least likely to report collective gangs. Traditional gangs are the predominant form in only 10 percent of cities showing predominance of any form.

The success of this inductive approach to deriving predominant street gang structures in the U.S. clearly calls for independent validation by other researchers. It is also important to determine how these different structures relate to crime patterns, a process made difficult by the problems of police recording of gang crimes in most cities. Most other attempts at gang typologies have relied on ethnographic observations of gang activity; that is, they are really crime typologies, not structural. A structural typology, it seems to me, holds far more conceptual promise for its relationship to both group and contextual variables. Gangs are groups that are spawned by social contexts. Comparative research on street gangs needs an appreciation for the specific group and group member properties of gangs, and needs to be applicable and testable in a variety of contexts—different cities and different countries.

As a tentative first step in this direction, the next section reviews my 1992 observations in Europe by reference to the five gang types described earlier. I emphasize, however, the term *tentative*. My notes from 1992 were clearly not informed by the new structural findings.

Five Types of Street Gangs in Europe, 1992

Some of the structural applications seem obvious. The Berlin, Russian, and perhaps Belgian gangs were of the traditional form—large, subgrouped, criminally versatile, territorial, with some strong intergang rivalries. While it is true that all were composed of ethnic minorities, this is true of almost all other types as well. It is not true of skinhead groups, if one wants to think of them as specialty gangs. From what I know of such groups in the U.S., Germany, and Stockholm, the only problem with that categorization would be territoriality. Berlin also included neotraditional gangs, not surprising since the onset of Moroccan and Turkish groups was in response to attacks by supremacist groups in the mid-eighties at the earliest. That leaves little time for the self-regenerating element typical of traditional gangs.

Also fairly clear is that the English gangs in London and Manchester best fit the specialty scenario. These are drug gangs, specifically, the most common of the American specialty gangs as well (since the outbreak of crack cocaine in the mid-eighties).

Reviewing what I learned of the suburban, "commuter" gangs of Stockholm, Zurich, Frankfurt, and Stuttgart, they strike me as non-territorial compressed gangs, the most common form found in the U.S., where their territoriality is also a non-defining dimension. Whether the location of many of these gangs in the outskirts of European cities yields an important difference from inner-city compressed gangs in the U.S. is a question I cannot answer. One could hypothesize, for instance, that the inner-city location is more likely to lead to intergang rivalries due to physical proximity of gangs, and that in time the resulting increase in gang cohesiveness will lead these inner-city groups into longer duration and, therefore, into the more traditional form. Only time will tell, since the bulk of the compressed gangs in America are new formations, as they are in Europe.

In any case, even this tentative review of the 1992 situations suggests that traditional or neotraditional gangs, compressed gangs, and specialty gangs in the form of skinheads and drug gangs were in existence during my earlier observational period, and therefore the typology may indeed be reasonably applicable and useful. Certainly it applies a more differentiating palate to the European gang landscape and provides a framework for more careful comparative observations than I can supply from the other side of the ocean.

European Gangs Beyond 1992

In preparing this report, I have contacted about 20 colleagues throughout Europe. Most of these were unable to report any new gang developments since 1992. It is not clear in each case whether this is due to the absence of gangs, the absence of research on gangs, or my informants' lack of familiarity with new material. In any case, I cannot offer anything of value in response to inquiries about Slovenia, Italy, Switzerland, France or Spain. However, there is some new information from Belgium, England, Sweden, Holland, and Germany.

It must be stressed that the material on developments in these five countries between 1992 and 1996 should be viewed tentatively. For the most part, it is not based on solid empirical research, nor do I have any of my own personal observations upon which to rely. Rather, as the reader will see, the material is an amalgam of colleagues' views I have solicited, of newspaper articles, of magazine articles, and of professional publications only a very few of which directly speak to street gang issues.

Further, my occasional attempts to apply the five-structure category system to the gangs described below are admittedly speculative. The raw data required for accurate documentation have not been forthcoming. Nonetheless, speculation seems worthwhile. At the very least, it allows us to consider the parallels between European and U.S. street gangs. More hopefully, it provides the foundation for building a more adequate characterization of European gangs, both as similar to and distinct from their American counterparts. Of this much I am at least convinced, that during my period of attending to the European street gang situation, it has become more prevalent and, given the context of nonnative immigrant and refugee populations, promises to increase in intensity as well.

Belgium. Belgian researcher Lode Walgrave has provided some information obtained from the gang unit first established by the Public Prosecutor in Brussels, in 1991. The very fact of the unit's existence would seem to confirm the official concern over the gang description offered earlier. By 1996, the few large gangs are reported by the unit to have evolved into a larger number of small, more mobile gangs. Fourteen such groups are noted, with 138 "hard core" members (and therefore an equal or larger number of fringe members) concentrated primarily in only two of the nineteen municipalities of the Brussels region. Given the prosecutorial source of the data and the absence of operationally clear definitions or structural characteristics, Walgrave suggests we be alert to bias in the depictions offered so far.[4]

England. The best description here might simply be that gang activity is worsening. The famous killing of an innocent 14-year-old boy in Manchester in 1992 has now been characterized as a "hit" upon a known drug gang member, who dressed in gang style and had stashed away a substantial amount of secret funds. A following gang truce in the Moss Side area is said to have broken down in 1995 with "ruthless gangs" now involved in a new spate of assaults in "the Bronx" of Manchester. That same year, 1995, saw official acknowledgment of rival gangs in Liverpool. What was unclear was the basis of the rivalries—ethnic disputes, territorial claims, drug markets, and control of the criminal enterprises have all been suggested.

But it is in London that gang activity seems to be of greatest concern. In part, this seems to be fueled by the increasing availability of crack cocaine. In 1993, the National Criminal Intelligence Service (NCIS) catalogued at least 10 murders attributed to crack distribution, with still more likely but not confirmed due to reporting problems. In 1994, crack-selling gangs in the Mozart estate and territorial street gangs in the Four Corners estate drew substantial public and media attention. In 1995, the stabbing to death of a school headmaster drew widespread attention, and was soon attributed to that gentleman's intervention in a rivalry between street gangs modelling themselves after London's Chinese triads.

Finally, in the aftermath of a major violence outbreak in Manchester's Moss Side district, it was announced that the NCIS was giving serious consideration to a new gang crackdown. Initial reports were of a proposal to appoint a gang czar in charge of a 100 million pound, 1,000 staff antigang force at the national level. While this may represent a considerable over-reaction and quite possibly a wasteful bureaucratic response, it signals the increasing concern for England's status as a gang-involved nation. In almost all the reports from England, it should be added that whites are less often noted as gang members. Most are minority and/or immigrant groups clearly located in inner-city, deteriorating areas. The days of the Mods, Rockers, and Teddy Boys are long gone.

Sweden. Two Swedish research teams are engaged in studies that will provide some data on that country's gang situation. Jerzy Sarnecki has recently initiated a new study of "youth networks" in Stockholm, but it will be some time before the data become available and the issue of network vs. gang can be clarified (cf. Sarnecki, 1986). The Stockholm Project, directed by Per-Olof Wikstrom, has been gathering data on community characteristics and youth for several years now. Wikstrom reports that these include some gang data which have yet to be analyzed by his research team.

For the time being, then, we are limited to print media reports, but fortunately these are somewhat more informed and less sensational than is often the case in many countries. Three newspaper articles, all appearing in 1995, give evidence of a growing gang problem in Stockholm, with increased public attention to the problem compared to the 1992 situation. The first of these is a summary of a police report which maps out gang locations in the metropolitan area. Two patterns are reported; Swedish groups—usually described as skinheads—and immigrant groups.

Gang descriptions are minimal in this report. What is emphasized are the social conditions which spawn the immigrant gangs, and the recruitment of younger members to maintain their existence. The Swedish police, it seems, have now discovered the "inner city" problem, whether it is located downtown or in the suburban housing project areas. They have recognized that gangs can emerge from more innocent youth groupings, and that youth gangs can easily become seriously bothersome criminal gangs.

A second article carries the description further by reference to one group—the "Skarholmen Gang"—which fits perfectly the immigrant commuter gang description of 1992, coming downtown to the Kunsgatan area for their evening diversions. To the extent that interviews with several gang members permit the placement on the gang dimensions, they strongly suggest classification of the Skarholmen Gang as a compressed gang. A third article reveals the visibility of the gang situation. The skinhead groups have proliferated, with combined membership mounting into the several hundreds. If one considers their characteristics—small, criminally focused, each of a few year's duration, and territorial—then these fit generally with our scenario for specialty gangs.

The immigrant gangs, described as now occasionally including some Swedish members, have appeared in far more locations than before. Some of this is said to be movement due to police pressure, a fact made feasible by the non-territorial nature of compressed gangs which most of these are. The reporting team from the newspaper *Svenska Dagbladet* surveyed the situation in all 25 political units (communes) within Stockholm county, using a base of almost 60 police districts. Although the article refers to criminal youth gangs, a number of the instances seem more to resemble small informal networks that only occasionally cause problems.

But in at least 20 districts, the description seems to merit the gang designation. In some of these, only one gang is listed while in others several distinct gangs are noted. They seem to be equally divided between the compressed and specialty (some skins, some not) categories. Significantly, there are now a number of reported gang rivalries and intergang fights, something not noted a few years ago. Given the importance of intergang rivalries to gang cohesiveness and perpetuation, it seems entirely feasible that Stockholm has now become a "gang city" similar to many of the newly emergent gang cities in the U.S., and may well be on the road to developing traditional or neotraditional gangs as in Berlin, the Volga cities, and perhaps Brussels.

There are some generalizations that emerge from this comprehensive report from the Stockholm area. Most of the groups are young, with ages in the teens and early twenties. They are generally small, ranging in size from ten to forty members. Their violence level, despite the emerging rivalries, appears to be rather low with few lethal outcomes. Firearm use is rare, in a country where firearm proliferation has been held in check. It is a picture that suggests the need for immediate attention to the etiology of gangs, not merely their control. Leaving the gang problem to the police alone could, as it has in many American settings, lead to solidification of street gangs.

Holland. Next to Sweden, I have spent more time in Holland than any other European country. Through 1992, I assiduously sought information on possible street gangs, especially since I viewed Amsterdam as a most likely location for their emergence. But try as I might, I could not confirm any gang formation, nor even get responses from researchers said to be in a position to speak to the issue. Holland seemed to be gang free.

Now, the picture is far more ambiguous. A rather amazing news report from The Hague in 1994 reports street gangs in existence for some years—fifteen groups according to the police, of small but highly active juveniles and young adults. They are described as criminally versatile with all the stylistic clothing, colors, and hand signs of Los Angeles gangs, and call themselves either Crips or Bloods in direct imitation of Los Angeles gangs. They are territorial, using the American designation of "posses" or "sets" with membership categories of Peewees, Baby Gangsters, and "OGs" (Original Gangsters). If the description is at all accurate—it combines police, street worker, and news reporter sources—then this remarkable Americanized picture places street gangs, probably best categorized as compressed, clearly in the Dutch experience.

Academic research reports make the case less clear. Two articles by Van Gemert (1995a and b) use my own definition of gangs to discuss whether Moroccan groups in Amsterdam and Rotterdam can be considered to be gangs. He also refers to such groups in Utrecht. One of these groups, the Panthers in Amsterdam, is a self-defined gang with versatile crime patterns. Others are viewed sceptically, since Moroccan culture would yield groupings with cultural norms indigenous to that background but easily misperceived as gang-like from the outside. In Rotterdam, Van Gemert decides against the gang designation for similar groups, but in doing so seems to use a too stereotypical picture of American gangs to draw his conclusion. In contrast, he does apply the gang terminology to the Turkish group that was eventually broken up by police pressure.

Arie Kuijvenhoven, writing about Rotterdam in 1995 as well and employing the same Klein criteria, clearly places both Moroccan and Turk groups in the gang category. The groups are small, aged 15 to 25 years, nonterritorial, criminally active and versatile. With a number of them adopting the Los Angeles Crips and Bloods terminology and imagery, they seem remarkably similar to the groups reported in The Hague: compressed street gangs.

Thus, while street gangs may not be rampant in Holland, their presence whether over-stated or not is certainly more obvious than it was to this writer in 1992. Van Gemert's culturally-based cautions are well taken, but cannot easily be used to deny gang presence. It seems more appropriate, in the spirit of describing a potentially growing social problem, to add three or four Dutch cities to the two or three in England, one in Sweden, one in Belgium, one in Switzerland, three in Germany, and up to ten in Russia. Given the inadequacy of data from other countries, this list of twenty or more gang locations is probably an undercount, but still no match for the 800 or more American gang cities.

Germany. A colleague well-positioned to make such judgements reports that there has been no observed change in the Berlin street gang situation in the past few years. He does note, however, an increase in youth violence from small cliques of four to eight members, each with common ethnic or neighborhood ties: "So you have the necessary ingredients, but they usually disintegrate before gangs can form" (C. Ohder, personal communication).

I have received more bibliographic information from German colleagues than from any others. However, this tends to be even more confusing because the preponderant topic has become terrorism against immigrant groups. It is unclear in some instances when ethnic terrorism melts into gang-like structures such as skinheads, and whether German skinheads structurally resemble the specialty skin groups of the U.S. or Sweden. Willems (1995) for instance provides a thoughtful categorization of right-wing extremist groups which includes some gang-like activity in opposition to refugee/immigrant groups. Kersten (1995) typologizes German youth groups into cliques, hooligans, and skins, with the first of these emphasizing territorial defensive battles and rivalries. Elsewhere, Kersten (1993) uses some gang materials to illuminate issues of masculinity and the social construction of manliness.

A hint of gang structure comes from a description (Koster-Schilling, 1994) of a five-member girls' specialty gang (thefts from cars) in Duisberg. It was a mixed ethnic, inner-city clique that broke off from a larger, male-dominated structure but later disintegrated due to internal dissension. An article by Gruner (1993) describes an intervention applied to a group of young school boys, mostly immigrants in Hamburg, whose delinquent pattern was influenced by older, more sophisticated youth. Another article, equally on the periphery of gang issues, discusses violence in three different contexts: at-risk youth, affluent youth, and the "halbstarken" of prior decades in Germany (Hafeneger, 1993). One article clearly describing street gangs emerged from my search (Arnold and Stuwe, 1993). Published about Frankfurt just one year following my visit, it really doesn't count as new information, but does serve to confirm my impressions. I noted earlier the tendency for Frankfurt gangs to abandon names and distinguishing characteristics in order to evade police attention. Arnold and Stuwe see this a bit differently, as the abandonment of gang locales or turfs, but then adopting residentially-based names. I suspect these authors and I relied on some of the same police informants, and interpreted the material slightly differently. But the gangs were there, contributing increasing levels of criminal acts. Arnold and Stuwe report about 25 such groups with age ranges, size, and non-hierarchical structure that place them in the compressed gang category, with both German and immigrant composition.

Discussion

Disentangling street gangs from other youthful structures in Europe, already difficult due to the ambiguities and variations in gang patterns, is complicated by the existence of xenophobic terrorism and the place of skinhead groups. Willems (1995) provides an analysis of violence and crimes against foreigners in Germany. Ninety-five percent of perpetrators were men, 75 percent being under 20. Further, over 90 percent of the incidents involved group offenses, and 30 percent of these involved skinhead groups. In the U.S., I can classify many skinhead groups as specialty gangs. If their form is similar in Europe, as I am led to believe in many instances, then the ambiguities at one extreme of violence are well illustrated.

At the other end are those youthful groups such as mentioned in Berlin by Ohder, and many, many others based on school and residence patterns that are groups, but not gangs as described in the five scenarios or discussed in *The American Street Gang*. Fixing the boundaries between gang and nongang, if now somewhat easier than it was some years ago, is nevertheless something of an art, still. Van Gemert's discussion of the Dutch situation adds the complexity of concretizing a conception of gangs in the context of differing ethnic cultural patterns. This much seems clear: Europe is not overrun with street gangs. And this much is also clear: Europe does have a number of cities affected by street gangs. Policy makers, of both the welfare and justice persuasions, will increasingly be called upon to "deal" with gangs via prevention, intervention, or suppression programs or some mix of the three. If these policy makers follow our American example, they will formulate their programs in almost total ignorance of and appreciation for available empirical knowledge of street gangs. European nations have the opportunity to be far wiser than we Americans have been. My principal recommendation is that some European researcher, or better yet a team of researchers, plan and mount a research program on the etiology, epidemiology, and structures of gangs in Europe. A comparative analysis would be particularly useful, especially one that paid special attention to the ethnic complexities involved. Social and enforcement programmes must be sensitive to ethnic differences, as well as acknowledging that street gangs comprise a variety of structures. My book title, *The American Street Gang*, is a misnomer. There is no one generic form, only similarities among diverse forms. American gang policies are still based on a gross, generalized (and usually erroneous) conception. European research could help to prevent a repeat of our U.S. failures to deal effectively with gangs.

Notes

1. University of Southern California, Social Science Research Institute, Allan Hancock Foundation B-51A, Los Angeles, California 90089-0375, USA.
2. The 1992 description of European street gangs was based on personal visits to and descriptions of a number of sites, along with material provided generously by many colleagues. The European update is based solely on written material collected at my request by many of these same colleagues: I have not been able to repeat my personal visits. Thus I am deeply indebted for their help to Alexis Aronowitz, Bojan Dekleva, David Farrington, Uberto Gatti, Boo Johannson, Hans-Jurgen Kerner, Joachim Kersten, Claudius Ohder, Nancy Pedersen, Walter Specht, Hans van Throtha, Lode Walgrave, and Helmut Willems. In addition, I have been aided immeasurably by friendly volunteer translators of non-English material: Robbert Flick, Eli Heitz, Jovanka Nikolic, Dirk Vanderklein, Lode Walgrave, and Dallas Willard.
3. At one point, I was alerted to a gang situation in Lucerne, but this turned out to be an ill-stated reference to some temporary political skirmishing. Still, it did justify a two-day excursion to that absolutely charming Swiss town.

4. Better Brussels data will become available within two years from the aforementioned research project being launched there. Some of the information from the gang unit is reported in Janssens and Janssen, 1996.

References

Arnold, T., G. Stuwe. Jugend-Gewalt-Gangs der zweiter Migrantengeneration. *Sozialmagazin*, vol.18, no. 6,1993, pp. 40–47.

Clinard, M. B., D. J. Abbott. *Crime in Developing Countries: A Comparative Perspective*. New York, Wiley, 1973.

Covey, H. C., S. Menard, R. J. Franzese. *Juvenile Gangs*. Chicago, Thomas, 1992.

Grüner, M. Eine Bande im Stadtteil. *Pedagogik*, vol. 43, no. 3, 1993, pp. 21–23.

Hafeneger, B. "Herumtreibend, halbstark, luxus verwahriost": Jugend (Jungen) und Gewalt in den fünfziger Jahren Neue. *Praxis*, vol. 23, no.1, 1993, pp. 114–120.

Janssens, S., C. Janssen. Jong en goed gek: jeugdbendes in Brussel. *Politeia*, no. 3, 1996, pp. 9–14.

Kersten, J. Männlichkeitsdarstellungen in Jugendgangs. In: P-A. Albrecht, A. Ehlers, F. Lamott et al. (eds.), *Festschrift für Horst Schüler—Springoram*. Köln, Carl Heymanns Verlag, 1993.

Kersten, J. Feinbildkonstruktionen, Konfrontation und Konflikt als Darstellung von sozialer Geschlechtszugehörigkeit. *Widersprüche*, no. 56/57, pp. 103–117.

Kersten, J. Kriminalität und Jugendkriminalität in Deutschland. Paper presented at the Goethe Institut Chicago symposium, Youth cultures in complex societies, October 23, 1995.

Klein, M. W. *The American Street Gang New York*. New York, Oxford University Press, 1995.

Klein, M. W., M. Gatz. Europe's new gangs break American pattern: Commuting to turf. *Psychology International*, vol. 4, no. 2, 1993, pp. 1–11.

Köster-Schilling, S. Im Zuge der Gleichberechtigung: Mädchen als Diebesbande. *Kriminalistik Verlag*, vol. 48, no. 2, 1994, pp. 118–119.

Kuijvenhoven, A. Een bende in de stad: Jeugdbendes in Los Angeles, Parijs, Rotterdam en Sharpeville. *Het Tijdschrift voor de Politie*, October 1995, pp. 13–16.

Maxson, C. L., M. W. Klein. Investigating gang structures. *Journal of Gang Research*, vol. 3, no. 1, 1995, pp. 33–40.

Sarnecki, J. *Delinquent Networks*. Stockholm, National Council for Crime Prevention, 1986.

Spergel, I. *The Youth Gang Problem*. New York, Oxford University Press, 1995.

Van Gemert, F. Amerikaanse gangs en Nederlandse jeugdbendes. In: E. Rood-Pijpers, B. Rovers, F. van Gemert, C. Fijnaut (eds.), *Preventie van jeugdcriminaliteit in een grote stad* Sanders Instituut, Faculteit der Rechts geleerdheid, 1995a, pp. 69–105.

Van Gemert, F. Marokkaanse jeugdbendes in Rotterdam-Zuid? In: E. Rood-Pijpers, B. Rovers, F. van Gemert, C. Fijnaut (eds.), *Preventie van jeugdcriminaliteit in een grote stad* Sanders Instituut, Faculteit der Rechts geleerdheid, 1995b, pp. 265–300.

Willems, H. Development, patterns, and causes of violence against foreigners in Germany; social and biographical characteristics of perpetrators and the process of escalation. *Terrorism and Political Violence*, vol. 7, no.1, Spring 1995, pp. 162–181. ✦

Chapter 8
A Tale of Two Cities:
Gangs as Organized Crime Groups

Scott H. Decker, Tim Bynum, and Deborah Weisel

Abstract

This article examines the extent to which street gangs are becoming organized crime groups. Active gang members were asked about gang structure and organization, gang activities, and relationships between their gang and other groups. Gang members were interviewed in an emerging gang city, San Diego, and an established gang city, Chicago. Members of one African-American and one Hispanic gang were interviewed in each city. Roughly equal numbers of members were imprisoned and on probation. The results suggest that, with the exception of the Gangster Disciples in Chicago, there is little evidence that gangs are assuming the attributes of organized crime groups.

Here, *Decker and his colleagues review the organizational structures and behaviors of four major street gangs. By describing various characteristics to be expected in well-organized criminal groups, they are able to test the stereotype of organized street gangs offered in the media and by many criminal justice agencies. The data come from the gang members themselves, with somewhat contrasting results. In San Diego, neither of the two major gangs appears to fit the picture of organized gangs. In Chicago, one of the two infamous gangs, the Black Gangster Disciples, does approach the status of an organized criminal gang. The other, the Latin Kings, does not. In considering these data, the reader may wish to keep in mind findings reported elsewhere that most American street gangs are far more similar to those in San Diego than those in Chicago. Thus, most street gangs are less organized and less violent than the depictions one finds in news reports, movies, and television.*

Reprinted from: Scott H. Decker, Tim Bynum, and Deborah Weisel, "A Tale of Two Cities: Gangs as Organized Crime Groups." In *Justice Quarterly*, 15, pp. 395–425.

Are street gangs becoming organized crime groups? Do gangs exhibit the characteristics of continuing criminal enterprises? Considerable speculation exists about these issues (Orvis 1996), but hard evidence is more difficult to find. Although law enforcement (Fox and Amador 1993), media sources, and some government agencies (Conley 1993) provide support for this view, little empirical evidence has been gathered to address these questions.

Gang research has exploded in the past decade. Spurred in part by increased federal funding, researchers have "rediscovered" gangs (Bookin-Weiner and Horowitz 1983; Maxson and Klein 1990). Yet despite the abundance of research, a number of important questions remain unanswered. For example, little is known about the evolution of gangs into organized crime groups. Are gangs disorganized aggregations of predatory individuals that commit a number of crimes, or do they purposively engage in crimes motivated and organized by the gang according to formal-rational criteria? The answer to this question has important implications for both prevention and intervention. In addition, it bears on a central question about the nature of criminal behavior—its level of organization.

Groups, Gangs, and Crime

The structure of gangs and gang activity is an important issue in our understanding of gangs specifically, and of crime in general. Indeed, this is one of the most significant topics in criminology and criminal justice today because of its implications for our understanding of both criminal behavior and criminal justice policy. This issue has been framed largely in the context of drug sales.

In their review of the role of gangs in drug sales, Decker and Van Winkle (1995) describe two competing views. The instrumental-rational view is reflected in the work of Skolnick et al. (1988), Padilla (1992), Sanchez-Jankowski (1991), and Taylor (1990). These authors describe gangs as well-organized entrepreneurs who employ traditional economic strategies of marketing, structure, and amassing profits that are reinvested in the gang. The gangs depicted in these works have a vertical structure, enforce discipline among their members, and are quite successful in defining and achieving group values. A contrasting view is found in the work of several well-known gang researchers including Hagedorn (1988), Klein, Maxson, and Cunningham (1991), and Fagan (1989). They describe gang drug sales in sharply different terms, emphasizing the informal-individual characteristics of many youth gangs, and the consequent difficulties in organizing activities, consensus, and investments. According to this view, gangs are diffuse, self-interested, and self-motivated aggregations of individual members, most of whom sell drugs for themselves. The results of Decker and Van Winkle's (1995) St. Louis field study are compatible with the latter conclusion. Their findings support a view of drug sales as a rather haphazard, individually focused activity.

The debate over the organizational nature of drug sales by street gangs offers an important theoretical framework for the current study. That debate also provides a link to a larger issue, the organization of criminal activities. At the heart of this controversy is a question: To what extent can offenders announce and embrace common goals, motivate others to join them in a common enterprise, and maintain a monetary and emotional commitment to the group enterprise of crime? Fortunately the criminological literature is applicable to these issues, and it generally supports a view that street criminals are ineffective in achieving these goals. Einstadter (1969), Conklin (1972), and Wright and Decker (1997), who studied robbers, concluded that armed robbers generally do not plan their crimes, nor do they organize their activities effectively. Bennett and Wright (1984), Wright and Decker (1994), Cromwell, Olsen, and Avery (1991), and Tunnel (1992) interviewed active residential burglars. In each of these studies the researchers concluded that burglars act in a rather disorganized manner—most often caused by drugs, drink, or the desire to impress their friends.

Beyond burglars and robbers lurks a broader group of street criminals, particularly those who engage in petty theft and drug sales. Best and Luckenbill (1994) discuss how street criminals can be grouped into categories. Although they offer several different typologies, these authors add that a typology does not imply obedience or structure among individuals within that typology. Indeed, they suggest that independence among offenders is the norm, and that social organization is largely absent from these individuals' criminal involvement. This view is supported by Irwin (1972), a researcher and ex-inmate who argues that "disorganized criminals" are:

> . . . the largest category of active criminals, [which] includes the less skilled, less sophisticated thieves who spend most of their time while not in prison hanging around, waiting for something to come along, and engaging in unplanned, unprofitable petty crimes, often on impulse. (p. 122)

Although Irwin uses the word group to refer to these individuals, it hardly reflects the instrumental-rational views of group crime. Similarly, Adler (1985) suggests that although individual drug sellers are enmeshed in an organization, that organization is more a consequence of social life as a series of relationships than the well-orchestrated efforts of a coordinated group.

In this study we examine four gangs: one African-American and one Hispanic in each of two cities, San Diego and Chicago. We seek to determine how extensively these four gangs have taken on the characteristics of organized crime groups. This issue is framed in three specific contexts: (1) the nature of gang organization, (2) the nature of gang activities, and (3) the nature of gang relationships. On the basis of interviews with key informants, some on probation and some imprisoned, we provide both qualitative and quantitative evidence on these issues.

Methods

We interviewed gang members in two cities. Using the dichotomy developed by Spergel and others, we sought to include one city that represented established gang cities, and another that represented "emerging" gang cities, where gangs were not intergenerational. We chose Chicago because it is widely regarded as the city where gangs have operated continuously for the longest time, are most highly organized, and have begun to penetrate institutional activities such as politics and neighborhood organization. The group of "emerging" gang cities was much larger. As noted by Spergel and Curry (1990), Curry, Ball, and Fox (1994), Curry, Ball, and Decker (1996), and Klein (1995), the number of cities in which law enforcement representatives report the presence of gangs has grown dramatically in the last 15 years. We chose San Diego because it is in California, is easily accessible to Los Angeles (and Los Angeles gangs) by automobile, has a base of knowledge about local gangs (Pennell 1994; Sanders 1994), and is similar to many other emerging gang cities.

We chose these cities and these gangs for strategic reasons. Little comparative research on gangs or gang cities can be found in the literature. Both the Latin Kings and the Gangster Disciples in Chicago have been targeted by the attorney general for federal prosecution. No San Diego gangs have received similar attention, however. This fact strengthens the argument that Chicago and San Diego represent diverse cities and allow for varied tests of the hypothesis of gangs as organized crime groups. The opportunity to compare gangs within and across cities is a strong rationale for the current study because the literature lacks and needs such a comparison.

We asked key law enforcement officials and social service providers in each city to identify their city's most organized gangs. To aid in the identification process, we asked officials to consider variables such as leadership structure, involvement in crime, relationships with other gangs, and relationships with other social institutions. In late 1994 and early 1995, we conducted more than 20 such interviews in each city on two separate occasions. The respondents provided a very short list of gangs in each city. Ethnic composition was an additional criterion for selection. Both Chicago and San Diego contain many African-American and Hispanic gangs; we selected one gang composed primarily of members of each group.

We chose two well-known Chicago gangs, the Latin Kings and the Gangster Disciples. Each has existed in some form for at least two generations; this suggests that they have had substantial impact on neighborhoods. In addition, law enforcement officials and social service providers stated almost unanimously that they were the most highly organized gangs in Chicago. In San Diego we chose the Lincoln Park Piru (also known as the Syndo Mob) and the Logan Heights Calle Treinte (also known as the Red Steps).

Our next task was to design a sampling strategy. We used official agencies as our catchment locations, and within each agency we collected a convenience sample of available and willing subjects. Such samples may not be representative, but in-depth interviews with key informants create a picture of their lives and concerns. Each city has a specialized gang probation unit, and numerous members of each gang were on probation. We believe that gang members on probation are more heavily involved in crime, tend to be older, and consequently would be more knowledgeable respondents about organized gang activities than individuals recruited solely from a street sample. We also believe that many of the most seriously involved gang members, especially in well-organized gangs, are in prison. After all, organized criminal activities are attracting increased attention from law enforcement officials, resulting in more arrests, convictions, and sentences. On the basis of interviews conducted with law enforcement officials, we knew that this was the case in Chicago, and we had reason to believe that the situation was similar in San Diego. Therefore we also interviewed members of each gang who were in prison.

The sampling strategy called for interviews with 10 to 15 members of each gang in probation offices and in prison. This would result in 20 to 30 interviews with members of each gang, approximately half drawn from probation and half from prison. In each case we attempted to recruit "key informants" (McCall 1978)—individuals with long tenure in the gang, and in a position to know about its activities, relationships, and structure. We offered respondents 20 dollars for participation; they could participate only after signing a human subjects consent form. Interviews were conducted by graduate students. In California, the prison interviews were conducted at the R. J. Donovon Correctional Facility; in Illinois they were conducted at the Joliet Prison. At each prison, interviews were held in a private room by an independent researcher. Our sample of subjects is described in Table 8.1.

In all, 85 active gang members were interviewed: 41 from San Diego and 44 from Chicago. In San Diego, a disproportionate share of the total (68 percent) came from probation. The explanation for this deviation from our sampling strategy provides important insights for the primary goal of the study. Our primary goal is to determine whether gangs are becoming like organized crime groups and assuming the features of continuing criminal enterprises: engaging in organized criminal activities, establishing relationships with traditional organized crime groups, and using legitimate activities and relationships to expand influence and control for criminal, gang-related purposes.

The differences between an emerging gang city such as San Diego and a traditional gang city such as Chicago are quite evident in these explorations. In San Diego, despite cooperation from a variety of local, state, and federal criminal justice agencies, we could not easily locate members of either gang. The explanation we received from each source we interviewed (including most gang members) was that both the Logan Heights Calle Treinte and the Lincoln Park Syndo Mob had been dismantled through aging out, splintering, and vigorous law enforcement, prosecution, and incarceration. This point is remarkable because less than a year before initiating interviews with gang members, each of these gangs was identified as the most highly organized and most likely to become like an organized crime group. This situation suggests that even the most

Table 8.1
Gang Members Interviewed, by City

	Chicago		San Diego	
	GD	Kings	Logan Heights Calle Treinte	Lincoln Park Piru Syndo Mob
Source				
Prison	15	4	10	4
Probation	11	14	10	17
Total	26	18	20	21
Characteristics				
Mean age	27	24	24	22
Mean age joined gang	13	15	13	13
Percentage arrested in gang-related crime	50	76	80	57
Mean years of membership	14	9	11	8

highly organized gang, at least in an emerging gang city such as San Diego, can fade rather rapidly from the street gang scene.

In Chicago, our results followed the sampling plan more closely. Twenty-six interviews were conducted with Gangster Disciples, an African-American gang: 15 in prison and 11 on probation. Eighteen interviews were conducted with the Latin Kings, the Hispanic gang selected in Chicago. We were more successful in interviewing Latin Kings on probation than in prison, unlike the Gangster Disciples. This was not unexpected because, early in the study, we met with individuals involved in a project conducted by Irving Spergel in the Pilsen and Little Village areas. The lead interviewers for that project told us that we might find it difficult to gain cooperation from Latin Kings who were incarcerated because gang members, once in prison, became resistant to outsiders' efforts, and gang permission was required to conduct such interviews. Consequently we interviewed only four imprisoned Kings and 14 on probation.

A key feature in all gang research is the need to distinguish between the activities of the larger enterprise known as the gang and the activities of individual members or small groups of members who operate outside the gang's influence. Such a distinction has even greater implications for the present study because gang members can engage in behaviors outside their gang that resemble organized crime. We dealt with this crucial issue by prompting respondents to distinguish between their activities as part of the gang and their activities as individuals. Such efforts were aided by specific questions about activities such as racketeering, influence peddling, money laundering, counterfeiting, and prostitution rings, which typically are associated with organized crime. Each gang member was instructed to indicate the activities he engaged in, and whether he did so as an individual or as part of the gang.

Findings

We have organized the results of our interview findings around three major categories: gang structure and organization, gang activities, and relationships with other groups. In examining the extent to which gangs are becoming like organized crime groups, a key indicator is how well organized they are to carry out gang activities. Accordingly, we sought to determine whether gangs had levels of membership and leaders, held regular meetings, had written rules, and owned legitimate businesses. Taken together, such features may indicate a structure similar to those found in organized crime.

The second set of indicators concentrated on the criminal activities pursued by gangs and gang members. Many of these activities centered on drugs, such as selling drugs, organizing drug sales, supplying large quantities of drugs, or using drug money for gang purposes. In addition, we asked questions about firearms, specifically sale and possession of guns by gang members. Finally, we asked whether there were consequences for gang members who left the gang.

A third important element of gangs' increasing organization and sophistication is their relationships with other gangs and with legitimate groups such as neighborhood stores. We probed this area by asking whether gangs met together, sold drugs together, committed crime together, or partied together. We also sought to determine how extensively street gangs maintained relationships with prison gangs and with legitimate political and neighborhood groups. Overall we found a striking consensus between the prison groups and the probation groups within gangs.

To summarize, differences between Chicago and San Diego gangs on most dimensions were much greater than differences between gangs in the same city or between catchment areas for the same gang within a city. In other words, Chicago gangs are considerably more highly organized than their counterparts in San Diego. This finding is not especially surprising, given our selection criteria for cities and gangs. Because of their similarities, we have grouped together the prison and the probation gang members for analysis.

Table 8.2
Gang Organization

	Chicago		San Diego	
	GD	Kings	Calle	Syndo Mob
Levels of Membership	90% (22)	94% (16)	8% (12)	9% (21)
Leaders	100% (26)	94% (18)	30% (20)	52% (21)
Regular Meetings	85% (26)	82% (17)	30% (20)	29% (21)
Written Rules	81% (26)	81% (16)	0% (17)	0% (18)
Pay Dues	83% (25)	73% (15)	6% (17)	6% (17)
Political Activities	84% (25)	27% (15)	26% (19)	12% (21)
Legitimate Businesses	77% (22)	69% (13)	61% (13)	47% (15)
Consequences for Leaving the Gang	23% (22)	60% (15)	11% (18)	6% (18)

Note: Numbers in parentheses are cases with valid responses.

Gang Organization

The gangs from Chicago—the Gangster Disciples and the Latin Kings—are more highly organized than their San Diego counterparts on every measure (see Table 8.2). Between the Chicago gangs, the Gangster Disciples are higher on five of eight indicators; in only two measures (levels of membership and consequences for leaving the gang) is the percentage of King members higher. The cultural significance of the gang to the Latin Kings may account for this difference. San Diego gangs report no written rules, few dues, and virtually no political activities. In Chicago, however, more than three-quarters of members report these activities for their gang. Clearly, the Chicago gangs are more highly organized than their San Diego counterparts. The meaning of these percentages can be seen more fully below, in the gang members' responses.

Levels of membership. Differentiation within the organization is an important indicator of the level of gang organization. In general, the less differentiation between roles or levels of membership within the gang, the less highly developed the organization, and the less effective it can be in generating goals and producing compliance among members in the pursuit of those goals. We found well-defined roles among Chicago gangs, but considerably fewer among the gangs in San Diego. This difference reflects the "emerging" nature of the gang situation in San Diego, as well as the longer history of Chicago gangs. Even some Chicago gang members, however, expressed uncertainty about levels of membership.

One imprisoned Gangster Disciple (#003) identified the levels of membership as "King, . . . Board of Directors, the Generals, and First Captains. The rest is just the membership, the enforcers." This view was seconded by several Gangster Disciples from the probation sample. One respondent stated,

> You got the king, you got the chiefs, you got the—wait a minute, let me go down the line. You go the prince . . . next in line. Then you got the don, they call it the don. Something like a war counselor or something. Then you got chief of forces, then you got the generals, then the lieutenants. (#010)

Further insight into the Gangster Disciples' level of organization was offered by another incarcerated subject:

> Larry Hoover was king, and that's the highest you can get right there. Coming from him, they go down to BMs, board members. From there, they walk it on down to little generals and lieutenants and all that, and then you have the foot soldiers. (#004)

Despite these Gangster Disciples' claims about different levels of membership, other members were considerably less specific. One (#072, incarcerated) told us that there were "up people, down people"; another (#005) reported that there were "killers, cowards, and ones that party." These insights hardly reflect the role differentiation of a highly organized group.

Gangster Disciples from the probation sample offered a similar perspective on this issue. One member (#051) identified eight different levels of membership, including foot soldiers, first coordinator, second coordinator, literature coordinator, exercise coordinator, regents, governor, and board member.[1] These roles were identified as well by Subject #063, who also added the role of treasurer. Commenting on the overall structure, he noted, "It's pretty cool." Two members of the probation sample denied that there were different levels of membership, and indicated that everyone was equal.

Latin Kings described fewer and less precise distinctions between levels of membership. A probationer (#030) said there were "gangbangers on the street, and the older guys." Another King on probation mentioned "foot soldiers and chiefs." The most common distinction offered was between a lower level of membership (gangbangers on the street, foot soldiers, pee-wees) and leaders (crowns, older guys [OGs]).

San Diego gang members reported considerably lower levels of role differentiation, and described the different roles less precisely. In general, we found no substantial differences in role differentiation between the Lincoln Park Piru and the Logan Heights Calle Treinte. Many members of the San Diego gang seemed confused by the question, as in this exchange:

> INT: Are there different levels of membership in your gang?
>
> #022: Oh yeah.
>
> INT: What levels are there?
>
> #022: I don't know them by name but there are different levels.
>
> INT: Like what kind of levels?
>
> #022: Levels of power.
>
> INT: How many levels of power are there?
>
> #022: I don't know the process, about three or four I would say.
>
> INT: What is the lowest level of power?
>
> #022: Most of those people are youngsters, teenagers barely coming in or trying to hang with them or trying to be cool, I would say.

Other San Diego gang members could name only two or three categories of membership. Usually these were based on age, such as "youngsters" or "old gangsters," "children, teenagers, and adults," "young G, old G, all kinds of stuff," or "young homies and old homies."

Others denied that there were levels of membership. A Lincoln Park member on probation said,

> No. There is nobody called the shot caller. That's prison shit. That's only in prison. There ain't no shot caller. (#027)

His remarks were echoed by a Logan Heights member, also on probation, who said, "There ain't no shot callers. It's got nothing to do with a gang either. Most Mexicans have respect for our elders. You start growing older, you teach the young ones respect for their elders."

The comments about respect in this Hispanic gang were also evident in the response of an imprisoned member:

> INT: Are there different levels of leadership in your gang?
>
> #029: Not really. It depends on how everybody treats you. If you respect somebody you get that respect back. We don't got no leaders or nothing. Nobody tells anybody what to do.

In sum, our results support the contention that the Chicago and the San Diego gangs show important differences in the degree of organizational differentiation. In the emerging gang city, few members could cite distinctions between levels of membership or duties associated with those levels. In Chicago, however, role differentiation was greatest for the Gangster Disciples, though some of it appeared to take on a "mythic" character.

Leaders. A second characteristic of well-organized groups is the presence of leadership roles. We asked gang members to elaborate specifically on the presence of leaders within their gangs, and whether those leaders had any special roles, responsibilities, or skills. Again, the city was the most important dimension on which our results varied. Gangs in Chicago, especially the Gangster Disciples, told us that their gang had leaders, and those leaders performed functions different than those of regular members. The Latin Kings also described a leadership category, though less clearly defined. In contrast, virtually none of the San Diego gang members could tell us anything about leaders.

Gangsters Disciples identified leadership roles in quite distinct terms. Gangster Disciples in prison stated that leaders "make sure all laws and policies are being adhered to" (#009), "give orders" (#003), "are supposed to be the thinkers" (#004), and "sit back and just put out a plan or whatever to [their] generals" (#010). A member on probation (#017) offered an expanded view of the role of leaders, which included making sure members attend school, get a job, and practice good hygiene. The nature of leadership among the Gangster Disciples is not dissimilar to that in many other supergangs, where leadership often reflects a mythic quality.

Latin Kings provided less specific details in identifying the roles and responsibilities of leadership within their gang. Respondent #049, an imprisoned King, told us that leaders "make the overall decisions"; #019, currently on probation, said that the leader "is the one that got the say so." A number of Kings identified a specific leadership role, the Inca, who gives orders to the Cacina. These roles and titles reflect the Latin Kings' strong cultural orientation, a feature common to Hispanic gangs (Moore 1978; Vigil 1988). In general, leaders among the Latin Kings occupied less instrumental, though not less important roles than leaders of the Gangster Disciples.

In San Diego, a less clearly defined picture of leadership emerged. Few Lincoln Park Pirus could specify whether leaders existed. Two Pirus on probation (#022 and #039) reported that leaders could no longer be distinguished from regular members. Logan Heights members provided equally vague definitions of leadership. Leadership roles were defined clearly only in regard to drug sales where leaders supplied drugs.

We found little evidence of defined leadership roles within these gangs. The lone exception was the Gangster Disciples, where our respondents consistently identified specific leadership responsibilities. In general, highly evolved, effective organizations are characterized by clear leadership roles and responsibilities. This was not true of the other three gangs.

Regular meetings. Meetings are an important characteristic of organized groups. They accomplish a variety of functions, including enhancing group cohesion, communicating responsibilities, and disseminating information. Almost all of our respondents told us that their gang held meetings, though the character of these meetings varied considerably.

Gangster Disciple members provided the clearest, most consistent answers to our questions about gang meetings; yet even these hardly depict a "businesslike" gathering. A Gangster Disciple on probation (#012) described meetings as "an hour of nonsense talking." Similarly, #017 said, "We talk, we talk. It ain't no meeting, we all just talk." Gangster Disciples in prison described more structured, more purposive meetings. That purpose was variously described as "discussing the programs, problems that may develop" (#003) and "discuss[ing] what's going on and the problems and stuff like that, or finances" (#001).

Latin Kings offered a slightly different view of their meetings. Dues generally were collected, and a concern about the welfare of the neighborhood (reflecting the salience of Hispanic culture) was a usual topic for such gatherings. But these assemblages, too, were informal. "We discuss what has happened, what's been going on, and if a situation occurs we talk about that situation and what we are going to do about it" (#014).

Meetings among San Diego gangs were even more informal; typically they focused on social activities. Lincoln Park gang members talked about holding meetings at a nearby park, which centered around barbecues, drinking beer, and talking to women. Another member (#061) described the meetings as "like a family reunion." The majority of Pirus, however, denied that their gang held meetings.

> INT: Do you have regular meetings or anything?
>
> #037: Ain't no motherfucking meetings, they ain't organized, none of them.

Logan Heights members had a similar view of their "meetings." They named barbecues and other social gatherings as the occasions when gang members held meetings. Many Calle Treinte members couldn't distinguish between parties or informal gatherings and meetings. One member on probation described meetings (such as they were) in the following terms:

> We just talk about whatever is going on, stuff like that, how we are going to meet girls, what happened to this person or that person, these people are doing this so what are we going to do about it? (#058)

Among the gangs we interviewed, meetings were not formal, nor were they dedicated to achieving specific purposes. More often they reflected their members' informal, social concerns and were held by "happenstance" whenever a number of members ran into each other.

Written rules. Another characteristic of organized groups is their commitment to formal rules to enforce discipline and maintain order among members. Rules express important organizational values, provide a means of forging consensus, and allow organizations to announce their boundaries by punishing unacceptable conduct. The great majority of the gang members we interviewed [in Chicago] stated that their gangs did have rules. When rules existed, their character and their enforcement varied considerably within and between gangs.

Almost all Gangster Disciples reported that their gang had rules; most said that the rules were written. Those rules reflected values central to the gang, and included prohibitions against activities such as "stealing, secrecy, and silence. Secrecy and silence is . . . the one they drill mostly in the head" (#009).

Secrecy plays a large role in the Gangster Disciples, as we learned in a number of interviews:

> INT: What were the most important rules?
>
> #010: No stealing, no members . . . hurt each other, no dope, no homosexual activity. The other ones I can't . . . reveal to you. We have an oath we have to swear about certain things we can't say. If we was on the stand [in court] we couldn't say it, we would just have to go to prison.

Many Disciples made references to the "sixteen laws" that each member must study and learn by heart. Although Gangster Disciple rules are written, one member on probation made an observation that nicely captures what many individuals told us about the rules: "Basically it's common sense" (#012).

Latin Kings also identified a number of rules, though these were less formal, and generally were directed toward individual standards of conduct. Respondent #019, currently on probation, told us that the most important rules were related to prohibitions against gang members' use of cocaine and PCP. No King could identify written rules or a constitution, as had their Gangster Disciple counterparts. A King in prison (#014) said the rules were "Once a King always a King, and don't have no rapists or heroin users."

Not surprisingly, San Diego gangs had very few rules; the rules that existed were more "street norms" than written prohibitions against specific forms of conduct. A Lincoln Park member on probation (#022) said that all the rules were verbal. Another member on probation (#027) denied the existence of written rules.

> INT: Are the rules written down?
>
> #027: No. It's no bullshit like the whole gang is gonna sit down and listen to some rules. I guess you make up the rules as you go along. It's called a learning process. Everybody knows the rules. Everybody knows you don't go running your goddamn mouth snitching, everybody know you not supposed to be getting your ass whipped and not doing nothing about it.

We made a similar finding for the Logan Heights gang members we interviewed. The rules were informal, not written down, and had the stature of lore. Prohibitions against "snitching" were high on the list. Respondents denied the existence of rules and described them more as "loyalty."

Not surprisingly, the view of rules in these gangs is consistent with the indicators of gang organization discussed above. Only the Gangster Disciples stand apart from the other gangs in that they have a written constitution, acknowledged by all members.

Gang Activities

The general pattern observed for measures of gang organization held for gang activities, though to a lesser degree (see Table 8.3). Though a higher percentage of Chicago gang members reported involvement in criminal activities, the differences between Chicago and San Diego gangs were smaller than in the findings on organization. Although the Chicago gangs are more highly organized, their San Diego counterparts hardly lag behind them in criminal activities. One conclusion to be drawn from this set of findings is that levels of organization are not necessarily linked to increased involvement in crime.

We found the greatest difference between gangs in the two cities for the variable measuring whether gang leaders supply drugs for sale: Approximately one-third of each San Diego gang, but nearly two-thirds of Chicago gang members, reported that this was the case. This finding underscores the central and established role of leaders in Chicago gangs. Considerable similarities also exist between gangs in the same city; this fact emphasizes the role of city context for understanding gangs' organization and activities.

Activities are an important measure of gang organization. Here we examine five specific spheres of activity: specialization within the gang, organization of drug sales, use of money made in gang endeavors, ownership of legitimate businesses, and gang involvement in political activities. We do not merely seek to learn whether gang members are involved in these activities; we wish to determine how extensively activities are organized by the gang, involve a large proportion of gang members, and serve gang goals.

Specialization. Specialization in a particular set of activities is a characteristic of organized groups. Specialization requires expertise and technical skills in a defined area, recruitment and development of members with such skills, and establishment of a reputation for that activity. We found little evidence that any of the four gangs we examined had developed such specialization.

The Gangster Disciples we interviewed expressed no consensus about specialized activities of their gang. One (#003) responded that the gang was known as "go-getters" in their housing project (Cabrini Green); others (#010) said they were known for drugs

Table 8.3
Gang Activities

	Chicago		San Diego	
	GD	Kings	Calle	Syndo Mob
Members Sell Drugs	100% (23)	100% (17)	100% (20)	100% (21)
Gang Organizes Drug Sales	74% (23)	80% (15)	63% (19)	72% (18)
Gang Leaders Supply Drugs	62% (21)	67% (15)	29% (14)	37% (19)
Drug Profits Used for Gang Activities	79% (19)	100% (10)	65% (17)	56% (18)
Gang Sells Guns	67% (24)	77% (13)	74% (19)	71% (17)
Members Own Guns	72% (25)	53% (17)	50% (20)	50% (20)

Note: Numbers in parentheses are cases with valid responses.

and pistols (#010), "banging" (#004), and "talk" (#013). Responses from Gangster Disciple members on probation were equally diverse and unfocussed: Politics (#012), drug sales (#048), and a form of "neighborhood protection" (#051) were the primary responses. One respondent elaborated:

> Well basically, you know, they ain't really known for nothing special . . . because there is a lot of stores and stuff around there. They probably recognize us for being positive towards the women because we don't mess around like that. Even [when] we see people . . . out there prostituting, we talk to them . . . like, "How come you doing this? How old are you?" One girl actually told me she was 15 years old. I told her, "You know what? If you was my sister, I would beat the shit out of you, just like that." (#051)

The Latin Kings' responses were more focused; a number of members mentioned "drugs" as their specialization. Others mentioned "helping families" (#021), engaging in violence (#031), or sponsoring parties (#050). The Kings, however, expressed little consensus about their areas of specialization.

Responses from the San Diego gangs were equally nonspecific. A number of Lincoln Park Pirus mentioned that their gang specialized in selling drugs, gambling (#075), being "fierce" (#042), and shooting (#035). Two members (#045, #046) told us that the gang didn't specialize in anything. Members of the Logan Heights Red Steps found it equally difficult to identify areas of specialization. Most could not easily comprehend the question, and reported that their gang engaged in diverse activities.

Organization of drug sales. Drug sales are a major activity among street gang members, and the four gangs we interviewed were no exception. A majority of the members of each gang told us that the gang played an active role in organizing drug sales, either by providing large amounts of drugs, managing money, or specifying roles in the sales. If gangs are evolving into organized crime groups, they are most likely to do so in areas involving considerable amounts of money, such as street drug sales. By choosing the two most highly organized gangs in Chicago, the city widely acknowledged to contain the most highly organized gangs, we test this hypothesis directly.

The Gangster Disciples are recognized as the most highly organized gang in Chicago (Knox and Fuller 1995). Thus, if any gang should show a high degree of coordination, role differentiation, control, and resource management, it should be this gang. Drug sales by Gangster Disciples sometimes resemble the activity of a well-coordinated corporate giant, though they also display less organized features. A number of subjects told us that members were required to meet certain weekly or monthly quotas of drug sales; and others specified different jobs or roles associated with drug sales. The following comments by imprisoned Gangster Disciples illustrate the level of role differentiation associated with these jobs:

> The guy who picks up the money, the guy who distributes the drugs to the customers, the guy who supplies the guy who distributes. (#003)

> Some of them be making it up, you know, mixing the drugs, some be selling it on the streets, some be distributing it to different members. (#010)

Another imprisoned Gangster Disciple described a virtual franchise operation:

> OK. Say . . . for instance I sold narcotics for eight years for the organization, and I've put away something like $800,000. I would move, take my $800,000, and invest it. . . . Say . . . I move to Alabama and I have $800,000 worth of narcotics. Now I am a member of this organization and I take my concept with me. When I get there, and once I get familiar with the area, if you got a narcotic, you are going to draw attention from those who use it. If you know a lot about the organization you could form GDs in that particular area. (#015)

Although this account hardly resembles a corporate plan for franchising new territories, it shows considerably more organization than comments by those members who indicated that the gang played little or no role in organizing drug sales. An imprisoned Gangster Disciple told us,

> Basically I don't consider [the gang] as being about drug sales. A person sells drugs on they own. The organization don't make them sell drugs. The people sell drugs on they own. (#013)

These views were echoed by several Gangster Disciples on probation.

A large number of Latin Kings participated in drug sales that were both organized by the gang and sales conducted independently. A number of Kings identified different jobs involved in selling drugs; as with the Gangster Disciples, however, these job descriptions were rather general and interchangeable among individuals. Two Kings, both on probation, said that the gang's primary role in organizing drug sales was managing money, as in this description:

> [The gang] collects the money, keeps track of the money. Wants to know exactly where all the money is going, how much profit is coming in, how much profit we will make if we sell different drugs. (#021)

Others, however, were equally eloquent in describing their independence from the gang in selling drugs: "You don't have to tell nobody what you sold. Whatever you sell, you don't have to tell them how much money you made" (#032).

The role of gangs in organizing drug sales in San Diego differed in several ways from that of Chicago gangs. Gangster Disciples and Kings could identify separate roles in drug sales, and some of the Chicago gang members pointed to a role for the gang in overseeing drug profits; San Diego gang members reported no such roles. There were few differences between the two San Diego gangs, and no important differences between the responses we received from probationers and from inmates.

Street gang drug sales in San Diego conform to the balkanized model found in a number of emerging gang cities. The informality of these sales is evidenced in the comments of respondent #024, a Logan Heights member: "They say, do you need money? If you say yeah, they give you the drugs. If you don't need money you just say no, I don't need no cash."

Most members reported that when it came to selling drugs, they were independent of the gang. Respondent #028 reported "What I make is mine. I'm the one out there on the street." This comment resonated with many of our subjects: Respondent #061 told us, "Not organized. It's just, you buy some and you sell it and you get your money."

Lincoln Park gang members reported that there was little pressure to get involved in drug sales: Those who wanted to do so, did so, but others chose not to be involved.

Respondent #026 told us that drug sales were organized. He clarified this point by telling us that the basic principle of his gang was "You don't purchase nothing from nobody you don't know." Another gang member offered a similar view of the gang in organizing drug sales:

> INT: Does the gang organize drug sales?
>
> #034: The gang don't organize nothing. It's like everybody is on they own. You are not trying to do nothing with nobody unless it's with your friend. You don't put your money with gangs.

This sentiment was echoed by respondent #042, an imprisoned member of the Lincoln Park Piru:

> INT: Does the gang organize those [drug] sales?
>
> #042: Yeah. Let me say this. You said "Do members of the gang sell drugs?" and I said yes. You said "Does the gang organize drug sales?" . . . There is people who sell drugs who are in a gang but they are selling as individuals. A gang never do it as one. Mainly it's just always individuals.

These findings are not particularly surprising, but we must explain the disparity between the fraction of gang members who say that their gang organizes drug sales (between 63 percent and 80 percent) and the responses to specific questions. Clearly gang members are heavily involved in drug sales, and gangs play a role in these sales, largely through contacts that exist within the gang and in cliques or subgroups of friends in the gang. The level of organization, however, is primitive at best, and at worst nonexistent.

Drug profits for gang activities. In understanding any organization involved in financial ventures, one must follow the flow of cash. Thus, understanding how money is managed, its flow through the organization, and how it is spent should clarify the level of gang organization. In general our respondents told us that the money they made from selling drugs remained with them for their own purposes. Most of these purposes involved items for immediate individual consumption, such as clothes, parties, cars, and jewelry.

Only one Gangster Disciple (#003) told us that individuals invested profits from drug sales in gang activities. He said that "holding reunions, buying stores, buying properties, things like that" were the primary uses to which drug profits were put. His response, however, was unique among those of our 85 respondents. Most gang members reported that profits from drug sales went to the individual responsible for selling the drugs. To most respondents this made perfect sense, because they had put themselves at risk to make the money. In a typical comment, respondent #013 said, "I never seen the money that I made go into the organization." Respondent #006 told us that it was "a lie" if anyone said that the gang invested profits from drug sales in anything; the profits were controlled solely by the individual responsible for generating them: "Please not me. If I'm gonna stand up here and sit up here and then use mine [profit] for their benefit, I don't think so. I ain't no sucker." Recall that these responses were received from Gangster Disciples, the most highly organized gang in the most highly organized gang city.

Latin Kings responded uniformly that drug profits went into their pockets. With a single exception (#053), the Kings reported that profits from drug sales went to the individual gang member, not to the gang. They identified parties, trips, bail, or funerals as the most likely uses for such profits.

Reflecting their more disorganized character, members of the San Diego gangs stated that drug profits were used for individual purposes, especially those related to individual consumption. Respondent #029, an imprisoned member of Logan Heights, told us, "A percentage of the drug money [to the gang]? Hell, no. You keep it to yourself." In keeping with the interests of other people their age, our respondents identified items such as fast food and parties as the primary uses for their drug profits. One respondent (#024) said succinctly, "Just round up everyone and let's go eat at Burger King or MacDonald's or something." Others mentioned parties, as in "Buy a keg or something for a homeboy's birthday. Somebody else will have some money and buy another one too" (#028).

Our respondents indicated that the primary (if not the sole) use of drug profits was for individual consumption. Few could identify a common use for the money they made; most denied vehemently that they would share their profits.

Ownership of legitimate businesses. One measure of increasing organization would be efforts to find legitimate activities, such as businesses, that the gang could invest in and use to expand its criminal interests. Organized crime groups historically have followed this pattern as a means of finding legitimate roles for members. In addition, legitimate businesses may give gangs the opportunity to exploit their own business-related enterprises for criminal purposes. Indeed, for crime groups, one of the great advantages of owning a legitimate business has been the ability to use that business to pressure other legitimate businesses in ways that lead to illegal profits.

For this measure, more than any other, we observed a distinct difference between the Chicago gangs. Every Gangster Disciple whom we interviewed in prison (and most of those on probation) stated that the gang itself owned legitimate businesses, and that these businesses were not merely providing low-level neighborhood services such as car washes or yard cleanup. Instead they were often quite substantial, involving considerable amounts of capital; the model categories included clothing stores, grocery stores, record shops, cleaning companies, lounges, and apartment buildings. One respondent (#010) reported that the gang had developed a construction business employing several gang members. Another (#063) said that the primary reason for owning legitimate businesses was to "launder your money." Significantly, gang members in prison were generally more aware of these activities than were members on probation. This indicates that access to information about such matters is available to older members and that prison gangs exert some control over events on the street.

The Latin King members' responses regarding the ownership of businesses contrast sharply with those of the Gangster Disciples. Roughly as many Kings told us that the gang owned businesses as told us that they did not. Many of these businesses were associated with automobiles, such as auto detailing shops, body shops, and car washes. Others stated that beeper companies were operated for the benefit of the gang.

The situation in San Diego was quite different: Only five of 41 gang members identified a gang-owned and gang-operated business. Many of the respondents in San Diego were unsure about the nature of the question, and said that gang members indeed held jobs or had worked in the past. Among Lincoln Park Pirus, gang members mentioned making rap tapes (#022) and working in nightclubs (#037) and at car washes (#078). The few Logan Heights members who identified gang businesses pointed to auto-related operations such as car washes and auto detailing.

This is the first category in which one of the gangs exhibited behavior consistent with higher levels of organization: The majority of Gangster Disciples identified legitimate businesses owned and operated by their gang. In most cases, these businesses did more than provide small-scale neighborhood services. They generated considerable sums of cash, allowing members of the Gangster Disciples to launder drug money at these locations.

Political activities. Political involvement is evidence of increased organization on the part of gangs, and facilitates their ability to influence the political process. Because of the number of patronage jobs available to elected officials, especially in cities such as Chicago, efforts to penetrate the political process bring considerable benefits.

Nearly every Gangster Disciple named political activities organized by the gang; these included passing out leaflets backing certain candidates, voter registration drives, soliciting contributions, and raising political awareness. A number of Gangster Disciples mentioned the groups "21st Century Vote" and "Growth and Development" as vehicles for the gang's political activity. These groups have been active in Chicago for the last several years, organizing neighborhood support for candidates sympathetic to their concerns. One such concern, according to respondent #016, was supporting politicians who could help Larry Hoover, the acknowledged leader of the Gangster Disciples (Knox 1995), obtain his release from prison.

By contrast, only one of the Latin Kings told us that he was involved in political activities. The modal response to our question about political involvement was that most members were unable to vote because of felony convictions. The one King who described involvement in political activities said that he had hung posters for a neighborhood candidate.

The San Diego gang members' political involvement is similar to that of the Latin Kings: Not a single Lincoln Park Piru told us that the gang was involved in political activity. One said that voting was the political activity of some members, and only two Logan Heights gang members said that the gang was active in politics. In each case, they became involved as a consequence of Proposition 187, the ballot initiative in California designed to limit immigration.

Relationships With Other Gangs

Relationships between gangs are important in attempting to determine whether gangs have come to resemble organized crime groups. Mutually reinforcing relationships built on instrumental concerns may indicate the evolution of street gangs from relatively disorganized groups to quasi-organized crime groups. Table 8.4 presents data pertaining to this issue. The San Diego gangs share more relationships with other

Table 8.4
Relationships With Other Gangs

	Chicago		San Diego	
	GD	Kings	Calle	Syndo Mob
Meet Together	79% (24)	69% (16)	11% (9)	61% (18)
Sell Drugs Together	43% (23)	53% (15)	44% (9)	53% (17)
Commit Crime Together	61% (23)	50% (14)	44% (9)	53% (17)
Party Together	88% (24)	81% (16)	100% (11)	75% (12)
Street Gangs Maintain Relationships With Prison Gangs	87% (23)	100% (14)	100% (11)	75% (12)
Prison Gang Members Maintain Relationships With Street Gangs	80% (15)	75% (4)	100% (5)	100% (1)

Note: Numbers in parentheses are cases with valid responses.

gangs than do the Chicago gangs on almost every measure, perhaps as a reflection of their social nature. Notably, the percentage of street gang members who report that they have relationships with prison gangs, and the corresponding percentage of prison gang members who report relationships with street gangs, are as high in San Diego as in Chicago, or higher. This finding deserves further exploration; we explore these and other points below, using qualitative data.

One measure of gang organization is a network of relationships between the gang and other groups. Such groups include businesses in the neighborhood, gangs in other cities, prison gangs, and other criminal enterprises that provide roles and opportunities for gangs and gang members. We explored these four areas in an attempt to determine how far gang relationships were expanding beyond the narrow circle of gang members and neighborhoods.

Relationships with neighborhood businesses. In addition to a general question about relationships between the gang and neighborhood stores, we asked whether gang members obtained credit from stores, protected stores, received payment to protect stores, extorted money from stores, or sold stolen goods to store owners. A consistent picture emerged: only the Gangster Disciples had made significant inroads into the ownership or control of neighborhood stores. The great majority of members of other gangs (Kings, Lincoln Park Pirus, and Logan Heights Red Steps) seemed to barely understand these questions, as if they had never contemplated such matters.

Gangster Disciples, however, showed considerable evidence that the gang was a presence in the operation of neighborhood stores. This may result from the large number and concentration of Gangster Disciples in many Chicago neighborhoods, as well as from the gang's more extensive ownership of legitimate businesses. Some subjects clearly misunderstood our questions about extortion, and replied that because store owners feared gang members, they and their families enjoyed a certain latitude regarding payments for merchandise. Store owners frequently sought protection against rival gangs from competing neighborhoods. Few Gangster Disciples told us that the store owners bought stolen goods from them. Customers and employees, however, were willing to do so, which may have obviated the need for store owners to engage in such practices (#008). In sum, except for the Gangster Disciple who told us that there weren't any stores left in the neighborhood (#048), this gang appeared actively involved in protection of neighborhood stores.

We found a far different picture for the Latin Kings and the two San Diego gangs. A single King told us that gang members engaged in extortion (#049), but this extortion more closely resembled individual property crime than an effort organized by the gang. Most members of the two San Diego gangs told us that they (and their gang) maintained good relationships with stores in their neighborhood. As a hallmark of these relationships, the respondents regarded themselves as regular customers valued by the store. One member told us that a local grocery extended credit to his family, a privilege that was not offered to him because of his fiscal irresponsibility. One Logan Heights member told us that there was no need to extort money or goods from store owners because "If we were going to do that we would just rob them" (#069). This comment reflects the more primitive level of organization among San Diego gangs.

Relationships with gangs in other cities. Police departments have spoken often about the "spreading tentacles" of gang membership. They imply that gangs are being franchised, primarily out of Los Angeles or Chicago, to virgin gang territory. In this model, gangs from one city find new territory, send veteran members to that territory to start new gangs, and reproduce themselves in the new city. A corollary to this argument is that networks among gangs exist across the country, exchanging cash and goods (primarily drugs and guns) throughout a complex web of cities with interrelated gangs. On the basis of interviews with knowledgeable law enforcement representatives in 1,100 cities, however, Maxson and Klein (1996) found little support for the franchise hypothesis. Instead they concluded that most gang migration occurs as a consequence of normal migratory pressures—family relocation, job opportunities, and the like—rather than because of gangs' concerted efforts to spread criminal activities.

Our results agree with Maxson and Klein's conclusions about gang migration. Nearly every respondent could name other cities that were important to their gang, where relationships with other gangs were maintained. The origins of these relationships, however, lacked the instrumental character associated with the view that gangs actively franchised themselves across the country. Much of the relationship with gangs in different cities had an expressive basis (stemming from family or peer relationships); the ability to buy or sell drugs and guns clearly added an instrumental quality.

Gangster Disciples maintained relationships with gangs in other places; these relationships were based on instrumental benefits. Gangster Disciples named a large and diverse group of such cities, states, and areas: Los Angeles, New York, Orange County (CA), Oklahoma, Hartford, Atlanta, Detroit, Rockford, St. Louis, Arizona, Houston, Miami, Little Rock, Jacksonville, Evanston (IL), Milwaukee, Virginia, The District of Columbia, Minnesota, Indiana, Iowa, Michigan, Mississippi, and the Illinois cities of Springfield, Decatur, East St. Louis, Joliet, Urbana-Champaign, and Elgin. These relationships were built primarily on the exchange of drugs and guns: "It's all about money" (#005); "drug trade, prosperous, cocaine, heroin, marijuana, anything that will sell" (#001); "drugs, money."

One member reported that the gang had been franchised from Chicago to Rockford (IL):

> Set up shop over there with someone from Chicago actually running things over there. They would get the dues, they would get the crime profits, the drug profits, things of this nature. The majority of that would come back to Chicago. (#005)

One Gangster Disciple described why he thought Chicago gangs had an advantage in expanding to other cities:

> People look at guys coming out of Chicago as crazy anyway. They got this Al Capone mentality, that's the way they look at it. (#002)

Latin Kings who commented on this issue told us that there were "Kings all over," but articulated the link between their gang in Chicago and those in other cities in far more tenuous terms. More often than not, family or friends were the basis of such relationships. A smaller number told us that they had relationships with gangs in other cities based on "drugs and money" (#071).

Despite their proximity to Los Angeles, members of both San Diego gangs used general terms to describe their relationships with gangs in other cities. They cited weak connections that provided few instrumental benefits to either party. A number of Lincoln Park Pirus described their relationship with Los Angeles gangs as based on dealing drugs together. This was an exception, however; it was more likely that "hanging out" (#039) or ties to family (#037) formed the basis of such relationships. Logan Heights gang members were divided equally over the basis of such relationships. Respondent #059 told us that "drugs" were at the heart of his gang's relationship with the Mexican Mafia; relatives and family were as important to other members. One respondent expanded on his interest in gangs in Long Beach:

> I have cousins up in Long Beach. I'll go up there with a few friends of mine, kick it there, get fucked up. Take some girls from here up there and meet them. It's a love connection. (#029)

Relationships with prison gangs. Because of their involvement in violence and drug sales, many gang members have been sent to prison in the last decade. Because prisons create the need for individual security and protection, they are perfect places for gangs to proliferate. Although the need for protection offers a rationale for the benefits of maintaining gang affiliations, there are other reasons as well. Because large numbers of gang members are imprisoned, inmates can build on existing relationships. Gang members who go to prison have a stake in maintaining ties to fellow gang members on the street because they can depend on them for monetary, influential, or criminal favors. Thus it is no surprise to find that gang members maintain relationships with gangs on the street. The nature of those relationships tells us whether gangs are becoming more highly organized and becoming more like organized crime groups.

To learn more about this subject, we asked gang members about the relationship between the street gang and gang members in prison. We began by determining whether a relationship existed between street and prison gangs, whether prison gangs called the shots on the street, and what kinds of decisions the prison gang made about street gangs' activities.

Prison gangs have operated in Illinois prisons for at least three decades, and Chicago gangs have been at the forefront of such activities. Prison gangs have considerable influence on street gangs in Chicago: Prison gangs often call the shots for the street gang, even specifying targets of violence, locations for drug sales, and other significant aspects of gang activity, criminal and noncriminal. In some ways this finding makes sense because gang leaders are likely to be older, and older gang members face greater odds of being incarcerated because of their extended involvement in criminal activities. In fact, every King and all but two Gangster Disciples told us that incarcerated gang members played a role in directing the gang's actions on the street.

The primary means of communication were mail, telephone conversations, and visits. Several subjects reported the use of cellular ("cell") phones to which members of gangs had access. One Gangster Disciple told us that his eyes had been "opened" by the prison experience:

> When you come in prison you find out the truth. I found out the people you thought was really your friends, your gang, ain't really nothing to you. It's an economical thing now. They don't believe in brotherhood. They don't believe in it. It's all about the dollar now, the dollars. Let's say you have a guy who was a big drug dealer on the street. If he was already out there on the streets and he come here, he still call the plays. A lot of people do what he tell them to do. (#003)

Those who occupied leadership positions on the street, especially if they were high in the hierarchy, such as regents or governors, exerted considerable influence on street activities from inside the prison. Most Gangster Disciples said that decisions made in prison primarily affected economic matters, especially drug sales, and had a secondary effect on violence, as in identifying targets of gang violence:

> INT: What is the nature of the relationship that you have with the gang on the street?

> #005: Monetary, drugs, women, hits, I think that about covers it. This is the Mecca right here.... Everybody wants to come to Stateville for that reason.

The view that gang leadership and decisions originate in prison was not confined to the subjects we interviewed in prison. Gangster Disciples on probation also acknowledged imprisoned individuals' active role in decisions about drug sales. Respondent #084 told us, "They are the ones that hand out spots (street locations for drug sales) and I think everything is run from prison, everything." Others stated that going to prison enhanced the members' status, making it more likely that they would assume leadership roles upon release.

Latin Kings expressed similar opinions. Indeed, every King we interviewed, whether in prison or on probation, told us that the prison played a central role in decisions about the street gang's activities. Several told us that the rules governing the gang came from the prison (#019), as did decisions about enforcing the rules and meting out penalties. "They can tell who they want to send them money for clothes and food in there" (#056). Finally, an imprisoned King told us that gangs in prison were so influential as to influence prison management; they played a role in cell assignment for individual gang members.

A different picture emerged from our interviews with the San Diego gangs. Although the great majority told us that they stayed in touch with gang members in prison (just as prison gang members stayed in touch with those on the street), such contacts were more informal and often were based on familial relations. Further, imprisoned San Diego gang members call few "shots" for street activities. Finally, ethnicity appeared to be the primary factor in prison gang association: Imprisoned gang members tended to disregard divisive gang affiliations from the street and to associate primarily on the basis of race.

A number of San Diego gang members told us that family was the primary basis of relationships between prison and street gang members. Respondent #036 said, "We have relationships with people in prison. Most of the people that be in prison be our family, our brothers, our sisters. So yes, we do know people in prison, yeah." Another respondent (#025) told us that they visited prison to see a fellow gang member only if it was a relative—an "uncle, or cousin, or something."

A similar picture emerged when we asked members whether imprisoned gang members "call shots," or order the street gang to perform certain, usually criminal tasks. Here, too, the role of family was important: Respondent #061 informed us that he had ordered such violence from prison in retaliation for someone who had "messed with" his sister. Most respondents from San Diego, however, denied that shots were called from the prison to the street:

> INT: Do the guys in prison still call the shots about drug sales?
>
> #037: They don't call no shots. Too many leaders in every gang, all the gangs like that now, too many leaders.

Respondent #038 told us that giving orders from prison was "movie stuff."

Respondent #062, an imprisoned member of Logan Heights, said,

> No. That's the thing that always cracks me up about shot callers. There is no such thing, it's just about respect.

Finally,

> INT: Can a guy in prison, if he is a drug dealer, still call shots and stuff?
>
> #080: That's bullshit. That's the movies, a myth. Not unless you are Al Capone or Scarface or something like that.

Only one San Diego gang member told us that imprisoned members still gave orders to members of the street gang (#077), but he qualified that by saying that the orders were based on respect.

Unlike their Chicago counterparts, Logan Heights and Lincoln Park members pointed to the salience of race for prison gang affiliation. Most stated that race, not prior gang affiliation, was the major unifying factor in prison:

> #041: As far as being locked up, it's a black thing and then it's a white thing and Mexican thing. The main thing is that you are black and you stick with black.

This theme was repeated by a number of respondents, including Hispanic members of the Logan Heights gang.

In sum, street gangs in both cities maintained relationships with imprisoned gang members. For Chicago gangs, these relationships were more instrumental; they provided formal links designed to enable direct input from the prison for the day-to-day operation of the street gang. In San Diego, such communication was more informal, and generally focused on issues of family or friends. Unlike the case in Chicago, few shots were called from prison.

Crime groups to join after the gang. We asked gang members whether their gang had relationships with organized crime groups, and, more important, whether there were criminal gangs with which members eventually could affiliate. This is a key issue in the possible evolution of gangs into more highly organized, more efficient forms of criminal involvement. The results of this line of questioning can be summarized quite succinctly: Not a single respondent could identify a crime group to which he could graduate, nor could any respondent identify an organized crime group with which his gang eventually could affiliate.

Conclusion

We have examined a central question in our understanding of contemporary American street gangs: the extent to which such groups are becoming more formal and evolving into organized crime groups. We examined two gangs from an emerging gang city (San Diego), and two gangs from an established gang city (Chicago), choosing one Hispanic and one African-American gang in each city. We used three spheres of gang activity to provide evidence about the nature of gang organization: gang structure, gang activities, and gang relationships.

The results provide a number of important answers to the question that motivated this study. In San Diego, the two gangs identified by law enforcement and social service providers had ceased to be central players on the street within a year of that identification. Little evidence exists to suggest that these gangs ever were on the way to becoming organized crime groups. Their disorganized character is consistent with what Sanders (1994) found in his study of San Diego gangs, and with the results of numerous studies of gangs in emerging gang cities such as St. Louis (Decker and Van Winkle 1996), Milwaukee (Hagedorn 1988), Denver, Cleveland, and Columbus (OH) (Huff 1996), Seattle (Fleisher 1995), and San Francisco (Waldorf et al., 1996).

The story for Chicago is quite different, however. The Gangster Disciples exhibited many characteristics of emerging organized crime groups. In structure, activities, and relationships, this gang has moved well beyond the rather disorganized, informal quality marking groups that have appeared in most American cities in the past decade. Gangster Disciples also apparently have forged effective and solid relationships with gangs in prison and, to a lesser extent, with gangs in other cities. Even so, there seems to be virtually no penetration into traditional organized crime groups. Latin Kings represent a model of the cultural gang: Elements of Hispanic culture have assumed a central role in the gang. Also, although the Kings are more highly organized than their San Diego counterparts, they apparently have not embarked on the course followed by their African-American counterparts.

In addition to the substantive findings presented here, we have demonstrated the importance of comparative studies of gangs. Just as single-city studies have documented the salience of neighborhood characteristics for gang structure, activities, and relationships, important city-level differences and histories affect these features of gang life as well.

Note

1. It is difficult to imagine the role played by an exercise coordinator. The image of several hundred gang members doing pushups or jumping jacks together doesn't square with

what is generally known about gang members.

References

Adler, Patricia. 1985. *Wheeling and Dealing*. New York: Columbia University Press.

Bennett, T. and R. Wright. 1984. *Burglars on Burglary: Prevention and the Offender*. Aldershot, UK: Gower.

Best, Joel and David Luckenbill. 1994. *Organizing Deviance*. Englewood Cliffs, NJ: Prentice Hall.

Bookin-Weiner, Hedy and Ruth Horowitz. 1983. "The End of the Gang: Fad or Fact?" *Criminology* 21:585–602.

Conklin, John. 1972. *Robbery*. Philadelphia: Lippincott.

Conley, Catherine. 1993. *Street Gangs: Current Knowledge and Strategies*. Washington, D.C.: National Institute of Justice, Issues and Practices.

Cromwell, Paul, Phil Olsen, and D'Aunn Avery. 1991. *Breaking and Entering: An Ethnographic Analysis of Burglary*. Newbury Park, CA: Sage.

Curry, G. David, Richard A. Ball, and Scott H. Decker. 1996. *Estimating the National Scope of Gang Crime from Law Enforcement Data*. Washington, D.C.: National Institute of Justice.

Curry, G. David, Richard A Ball, and Robert J. Fox. 1994. *Gang Crime and Law Enforcement Recordkeeping*. Washington, D.C.: National Institute of Justice.

Decker, Scott and Barrik Van Winkle. 1995. "Slinging Dope: Drug Sales and Gangs." *Justice Quarterly* 11:1001–1022.

——. 1996. *Life in the Gang: Family, Friends, and Violence*. New York: Cambridge University Press.

Einstadter, Werner. 1969. "The Social Organization of Robbery." *Social Problems* 17:64–83.

Fagan, Jeffrey. 1989. "The Social Organization of Drug Use and Drug Dealing Among Urban Gangs." *Criminology* 27:633–669.

Fleisher, Mark. 1995. *Beggars & Thieves*. Madison, WI: U.W. Press.

Fox, Robert W. and Mark E. Amador. 1993. *Gangs on the Move*. Placerville, CA: Copperhouse.

Hagedorn, John. 1988. *People and Folks*. Chicago: Lakeview Press.

Huff, C. Ronald. 1996. *The Criminal Behavior of Gang Members*. Washington, D.C.: National Institute of Justice.

Irwin, John. 1972. "The Inmate's Perspective." Pp. 117–137 in *Research on Deviance*, edited by Jack D. Douglas. New York: Random House.

Klein, Malcolm. 1971. *Streetgangs and Streetworkers*. Englewood Cliffs, NJ: Prentice Hall.

——. 1995. *The American Street Gang*. New York: Oxford University Press.

Klein, Malcolm, Cheryl Maxson, and Lea Cunningham. 1991. "Crack, Street Gangs, and Violence." *Criminology* 29:623–650.

Knox, George and Leslie Fuller. 1995. "The Gangster Disciples." *Journal of Gang Research* 3:58–76.

Maxson, Cheryl and Malcolm Klein. 1986. *Street Gangs Selling Cocaine "Rock."* Los Angeles: University of Southern California, Social Science Research Center.

——. 1990. "Street Gang Violence: Twice As Great or Half As Great?" Pp. 71–100 in *Gangs in America*, edited by C. Ronald Huff. Newbury Park, CA: Sage.

——. 1996. "Street Gang Migration: How Big a Threat?" *National Institute of Justice Journal* 228(February):26–31.

McCall, George. 1978. *Observing the Law*. New York: Free Press.

Moore, Joan. 1978. *Homeboys: Gangs, Drugs and Prison in the Barrios of Los Angeles*. Philadelphia: Temple University Press.

Orvis, Gregory P. 1996. "Treating Youth Gangs like Organized Crime Groups: An Innovative Strategy for Prosecuting Youth Gangs." Pp. 93–103 in *Gangs: A Criminal Justice Approach*, edited by J. Mitchell Miller and Jeffrey Rush. Cincinnati,OH: Anderson.

Padilla, Felix. 1992. *The Gang as an American Enterprise*. New Brunswick, NJ: Rutgers University Press.

Pennell, Susan. 1994. *Gangs in San Diego*. San Diego: San Diego Association of Governments.

Sanchez-Jankowski, Martin. 1991. *Islands in the Street*. Berkeley: University of California Press.

Sanders, William. 1994. *Drive-Bys and Gang Bangs*. New York: Aldine.

Skolnick, Jerome, T. Correl, E. Navarro, and R. Rabb. 1988. *The Social Structure of Street Drug Dealing*. Sacramento: Office of the Attorney General of the State of California.

Spergel, Irving and G. David Curry. 1990. *Survey of Youth Gang Problems and Programs in 45 Cities and 6 Sites*. Chicago: University of Chicago, School of Social Service Administration.

Taylor, Carl. 1990. *Dangerous Society*. Lansing: Michigan State University Press.

Tunnel, Ken. 1992. *Choosing Crime: The Criminal Calculus of Property Offenders*. Chicago: Nelson-Hall.

Vigil, Diego. 1988. *Barrio Gangs: Streetlife and Identity in Southern California*. Austin: University of Texas Press.

Waldorf, Dan, Craig Reinerman, and Sheglia Murphy. 1996. *Cocaine Charges*. Philadelphia: Temple University Press.

Wright, Richard and Scott H. Decker. 1994. *Burglars on the Job*. Boston: Northeastern University Press.

——. 1997. *Armed Robbers in Action*. Boston: Northeastern University Press. ✦

Chapter 9
Inside the Fremont Hustlers

Mark Fleisher

This chapter is an excerpt from Fleisher's book Dead End Kids, *based on his long-term ethnographic study of a street gang in Kansas City, Missouri. Fleisher captures the fluidity of membership as it mirrors the loose structure of a "collective" gang (see Chapter 7). In such a loosely structured gang, membership and "tightness" (cohesiveness in other gang literature) are well illustrated in Cara's listing of the subgroups in the Fremont Hustlers. Also pay attention to how different meanings are attached to words; some of these are generic, but some also constitute the special argot of such groups. The "verbal duels" described here remind us that most gang violence is verbal, not physical. The entire selection provides a rich description of the nature of street gang members' interactions and daily life.*

"Membership" in the Fremont Hustlers is a peculiar idea.[1] Wendy, Cara, and Cheri listed 72 males and females on the Fremont Hustler membership roster; however, Fremont kids don't refer to one another as members, nor do they think of themselves as having joined a gang.[2]

"Member," "membership," "join," and "gang" are static notions which fit neither the natural flow of Fremont social life nor the perceptions of Fremont kids. Even the question, Are you a member of the Fremont Hustlers? doesn't match these kids' sense of social logic. The question, Do you hang out on Fremont? makes sense to them but this question didn't bring me closer to understanding the kids' meanings for "joining a gang" and "gang membership." Fremont kids' perceptions of these issues are more complex than I had imagined.[3]

The social boundary between the Fremont Hustlers—the youth gang—and outsiders is open.[4] Fremont has no formal set of written rules (a charter) specifying what prospective members must do to be admitted and to sustain membership. There are no rules of decorum and, thus, no sanctions for violating those rules. Younger Fremont kids are not required to learn and recite a gang pledge of allegiance or attend lectures given by older members about "proper" behavior. There is no rule preventing drug sellers from being drug users. There is no rule requiring a portion of drug sale profits to be returned to a communal gang bank account or paid as tribute to the leader. There is no leader, no boss, no hierarchy that pulls all 72 kids into coherent organization.[5]

Fremont has no initiation. No one is "beaten in" or "courted in" or ordered to commit violent acts. That behavior, kids said, attracts the cops, and cops are bad for business. Cara said violent initiation is "fucked up and stupid. Who wants ta hang out with niggahs who beat ya ass?" By hanging out and establishing ties with Fremont kids, an outsider is slowly assimilated into the social life at a chill spot.

To these kids, Fremont is defined by the interaction of social histories of families; current and former love relationships; boy-boy, girl-girl, and boy-girl hostilities; envy and bitterness over possessions; current and past crime partnerships; arrests and imprisonment in jails, detention centers, and juvenile treatment facilities; histories of prior gang affiliations; and length of interpersonal affiliation. Kids who have known each other a long time, such as Cara and Wendy, stick together, although there were times when they'd vow never to speak to each other again, but that's typical among adolescents.

Kids' vocabulary helps to describe how they perceive Fremont's social arrangements. Generally speaking, Fremont kids differentiate themselves into one category defined by "time" and another by "tightness." *Tightness* refers to the intensity of a relationship. Kids who hang out together much of the time are said to be tight, and kids who are tight "do shit" (commit crimes, use drugs) together.

Tight also implies to some degree a shared social history. Most Fremont kids were members of other Kansas City youth gangs before joining the Fremont Hustlers and were together in juvenile detention and treatment facilities; however, being tight doesn't necessarily imply a long-term relationship. Kids can be tight for two weeks or four months and then become bitter enemies. Such volatility is most common among girls.[6] In July 1994, when Wendy and Janet and I met at UMKC, they had been tight for years and said they were inseparable and swore a mutual allegiance forever. Over the next year, Janet and Wendy vied for Steele Bill's attention. Janet won Bill, lost Wendy, and they haven't spoken to each other since then.

Time refers to the hours, days, weeks, and years a kid spends on Fremont. Time spent hanging out on Fremont differentiates kids into four groups. Kids who hang on Fremont most often have established closer ties than kids who don't. Those who don't hang around much are marginal to the gang's principal economic behavior, drug selling.

Kids use expressions for different time categories; I've noted in parentheses the number of days of hang-out time in each category: "here all the time" (six or seven days a week), "here a lot" (three to five days a week), "comes around" (one or two days a week), and "will be here if we need him (or her)" (several days a month). The last group includes kids who didn't appear even once on Fremont between June 1995 and February 1997, but hung out there at some time in the past. These kids are still considered to be Fremont. Fremont Hustlers who have been killed continue as members. The children of Fremont girls are Fremont, too.

A kid who is "here all the time" also is said to be in the "everyday" group. It's common in natural speech for kids to refer to the everyday group as kids "who's in the shit everyday," said Cara. The everyday and here-a-lot groups correspond to the terms *core* and *regular* members, respectively.

There is a segmentary quality to these social groups. Few kids hang out all the time, but dozens of kids are available to the Fremont Hustlers should help be needed. Wendy captured this segmentary quality: "If somebody fucks wid us," she said sternly, "we can get all the help we need."

A subtle difference exists between what it means to "hang out on Fremont" and what it means to be "down with Fremont." To be "down with Fremont" is the expression closest to our use of the term *member*. But being down with Fremont doesn't mean a kid hangs out on Fremont every day.

A number of Fremont kids have been down with other KC gangs. Cara was down with the Southside 39th Street Crips, as well as the 31st Street Eastside Crips, before hooking up with Wendy. Steele Bill has been a 24th Street Crip.

There is a finer distinction as well. I've heard kids ask another kid, "Is he (or she) Fremont or Fremont Fremont?" This is an interesting distinction. Kids, including Cheri, Wendy, Angie, and Roger, who were reared in the Fremont neighborhood and whose family history now links them to the neighborhood are denoted with the label "Fremont Fremont." Afro, by contrast, is a down with Fremont member but is not Fremont Fremont; Wendy said she had "brought him" to Fremont from the east side. Thus, a kid can be Fremont Fremont or Fremont, and either down with or hang out with Fremont. Generally speaking, boys and girls in the everyday and here-a-lot groups are Fremont Fremont and down with Fremont.

Cara, Wendy, Cheri, and I explored how they perceive Fremont social grouping.[7] This was a productive way to learn about social relations from a single-informant, or egocentric, perspective. Simple "social role" labels for gang members as defined by gang researchers, such as "core," "peripheral," "associate," "wannabe," are outsiders' categorizations and simplistic when compared with gang members' perceptions of their own social world.[8] Rather than imposing my labels on each girl's subgrouping, I asked them to give me labels.

Wendy's and Cheri's social groupings are mostly egocentric; that is, each subgrouping is defined with them at the center. The strength of the social ties is denoted with labels such as "my babies," "my real mothafuckas," "kind of cool with, but ain't seen for awhile," "my niggahs," "I'm cool with, but don't fuck with anymore," "people I don't care about," "still all right in my life," "boys I used to talk to" (former lovers), "true bitches" (or "people I hate"). Some labels denote Fremont kids' prior gang affiliation, such as Bloods, Southside (51st Street), Latin Count Brothers, and La Familia. Other labels referred to time spent on Fremont: "hardly come over," "never come over," and "used to come over." Interestingly, Fremont kids who were killed or committed suicide, as well as boys in prison, are still considered to be Fremont members. Imprisoned kids are either labeled "in prison" or are placed in some other group, such as "my mothafuckas." Tyler, a 14-year-old boy killed by Fremont TJ, is always placed in a group with kids who are alive.

Cara's view is much less egocentric than Wendy's and Cheri's, and it has a "fly-on-the-wall" quality. She divides the Fremont Hustlers into these groups: Bloods (friends of Chucky D's from the east side and former Latin Count Brothers); used to visit a lot (girls from the Seven-Miles rap group); grew up on Fremont; in prison; La Familia (members of the gang La Familia, but hang with Fremont anyway); hang together; hang out (these kids are tighter than those in hang together); hardly come around; and Southside.[9] Cara's subgroups, with kids' names and pertinent facts, are listed below.[10]

Bloods: J-Love, JC, and Joe Green

Used to visit a lot: Kiki, Erica, Felisha, JoJo, Kizzy (all members of the Seven-Miles rap-group; Felisha and Kizzy are sisters). These girls hung out on Fremont in the early days of the Fremont Hustlers. I never met any one of them, although Wendy talked about them, and in the spring of 1997 she started to hang out with several of them, because she was interested in recording rap songs.

Grew up on Fremont: Anthony Contreras, Curly Contreras (these two are brothers; they have three more brothers—Sam, Eddie, and Sal—whom Cara puts in the "hardly come around" group).

In prison: Buck, Dwayne, Snapper, Fremont TJ, Little Man, Rick. Cara put Tyler (RIP) in this category and said it includes kids "who's never coming back." Rick was a crime partner with Anthony and Curly Contreras.

La Familia (also known as KCBs, Kansas City Barrios): Tre, Jacob, JD, John, Chill, Maria, Speedy, Duce. Chill, Maria, and Speedy are cousins. Speedy's sister used to be a member of La Familia.

Hang together (A): Chucky D, Tervis (also called Earl), Steele Bill, Cara, Cheri, Wendy, Joanne, Sequoia. Sequoia is the two-year-old daughter of Joanne and Charles B., Cheri's brother (he was in prison in March 1996 and released in the summer of 1997 but returned a month later on a parole violation). Joanne has another daughter, Charlene, whose father is Chucky D.

Hang together (B): Johnny Murillo, Steve Holly, Joe Murillo, House of Pain, Cain, Greenbean, Lucky, Wayne, Taz, Zipper. Taz and Zipper were brothers. Taz was 16 when he was killed by Afro in what the police called an accidental shooting. Zipper was 15, a member of La Familia, when a Northeast member shot him in the chest, leaving a scar that looks like a zipper. Zipper is tight with Fremont, despite his affiliation with La Familia. Cheri was once pregnant by a brother of Zipper and Taz; the baby was lost in a spontaneous abortion. One of Taz's brothers told me that Afro intentionally killed Taz, and was released by the police because he is a snitch. Johnny Murillo, Steve Holly, and Joe Murillo are cousins. House of Pain and Cain are brothers.

Hang out (tight): Angie, Chica Bitch, Netta, Donna, Roger, Christina, Melissa, Rosa, Afro. Netta and Donna are sisters (they have a third sister, Teresa). Melissa and Rosa are cousins. Melissa and Lucky are siblings; Christina is their step-sister. Melissa and Lucky's father married Christina's mother. Lucky and Christina had a child born in the spring of 1996. Rosa and Joe Murillo are cousins. Rosa and Afro were lovers and had a baby girl in the fall of 1996. When Rosa was 13 she was shot in the chest by a Northeast member wielding a .38. Afro is a cousin of Cheri and her siblings, Dante and Charles B. Roger and Angie are siblings.

Hardly come around: Dallas, Frosty, Milk, Joey, the Contreras brothers (Sam, Eddie, Sal). Joey is Frosty's little brother. Milk has the dubious distinction of being the only Fremont Hustler to be initiated with a beating.[11] Cara said, "The boys whipped his ass 'cause he's stupid." The Contreras brothers are Fremont's carjackers.

Southside: Bill Bill, Little E, Tony, Scandalous Herb. Bill Bill, Little E, and Tony are brothers; Tony and Bill Bill are twins.

These are perceptions of social groupings and aren't day-to-day operational subgroups within the Fremont Hustlers. Understanding daily social, emotional, and economic dynamics is a complex issue.[12] Recording and analyzing Fremont kids' speech can offer insights.

Two-person relationships and intra- and interclique relations are marked by emotions and behavior, including passivity, standoffishness, friendliness, dependency, anger, aggressiveness, violence, vindictiveness, fearfulness, and withdrawal. These emotions and behavior are captured in the complexity of kids' speech as it's played out in daily social life.

Fremont social life is rich in jokes and laughter, as well as anger, aggression, unresolved disputes, and inter- and intragang incidents of mild to serious violence. Hardly an hour passes without some kid claiming to be pissed off about something or at someone. When one kid gets angry he usually has a lot of companions willing to talk about violence, and some of them are willing to engage in it. Talk about violence is far more common than violent acts.

A number of vocabulary terms connote the quality or affective nature of social ties and, by extension, the likelihood of violence between kids. Three such terms are *niggah*, *dog*, and *mothafucka*. In nearly all instances *niggah* is used without regard to the color of the speaker or the addressee. Sometimes *niggah* is used as a synonym for *homey*, though the terms *home, homeboy, homegirl*, and *homey* are rarely used in natural conversations.

Rather than denoting racial affiliation, *niggah* is used symbolically for more complex issues. A black, white, or Mexican Fremont boy or girl can call a black, white, or Mexican boy or girl a niggah, as long as the speaker and addressee are "cool," said Wendy.

"Niggah, you ain't shit!" is a common aggressive statement, but it isn't a racial insult to the addressee, who may or may not be black. A common use of *niggah* comes in statements such as, "That niggah over there, he got some."

In natural conversations the term *niggah* is distinguished from *nigger*. *Nigger* is always an insult, but it's a raceless insult used in an already heated conversation. *Nigger* has triggered fights even between black Fremont kids.

The term *dog* has the synonyms *ace deuce* and *number one*. To say "Wha's up, dog?" is a friendly greeting; however, "You're a dog" can, in an already tense situation, trigger a fight.

The term *mothafucka* is used commonly in natural conversations and has a range of connotations as wide as the word *fuck* in colloquial English. In friendly expressions, it is used this way: "You my mothafucka." However, the term *mothafucker*—that is, the form with the *-er* ending, like *nigger* as opposed to *niggah*—can be an insult and can be directed toward someone during an already tense verbal interaction.

Fremont girls and boys form cliques; however, girls' cliques, more so than boys, act as social units. Wendy and other girls too use the girl's term *my mothafuckas* to denote cliques; boys don't use such terms to label cliques. The term *together* is a synonym for *my mothafuckas*. Cara, Wendy, and Cheri are together, at least most of the time. This means if someone angers Wendy, Cara and Cheri will act with Wendy to support her and oppose her enemy. This works best if the girl who seeks support also controls resources the other girls need. Wendy, for example, had absolute control over her room on Fremont, and Cheri and Cara needed it as a safe spot.

Whenever Wendy got pissed off at someone, as she did at Janet for stealing Steele Bill, Cheri and Cara supported Wendy against Janet; however . . . when Wendy's resource disappeared so did her support from Cheri and Cara, and from everyone else on Fremont.

"Sticks and stones can break your bones but words will never hurt you" doesn't apply to Fremont social life. Social life rests on words and how they are uttered and on stylized forms of verbal interaction. Friendly words, angry words, misspoken words, misinterpreted words, filthy words, clean words, all sorts of words are elements in complex social and verbal scenes called verbal duels.

Verbal duels are organized by rules that allow "players" to insult one another, within limits. Verbal duels (structured verbal forms of teasing) publicly verify informal social hierarchies and release tension without violence.

A Fremont insider (a so-called member) may verbally challenge and insult an outsider, as Wendy did a teenage girl walking across Truman by the Quick Trip, but that girl remained silent and didn't exchange insults with Wendy. To do that would have instigated a verbal duel with Wendy's partners in my car, and that might have escalated into a brawl. Fremont Hustlers' membership means that only insiders verbally duel (insult, challenge) one another with impunity. Stylized verbal dueling is a privilege of membership.

Cara and Wendy tease Cheri. Cheri teases boys, and because of her reputation as an impulsive and violent girl, boys take it and leave her alone. Girls tease Angie about her hair and aggressiveness; she accepts such teasing as a sign of companionship, rarely ever retaliating with words motivated by angry emotions. In this way, friendships are denoted with teasing.

Fremont kids don't often say things to one another that outsiders would interpret as friendly and affectionate things to say. *Mothafucka, bitch, stank pussy, niggah, dog,* and other terms are signs of companionship if they are spoken correctly between kids whose relationship has already been established and allows for such talk.

Boy-girl, girl-girl, and boy-boy relationships are built on verbal duels. Boys duel by calling each other bitch; girls call each other bitch; boys call girls stank pussy; girls call each other stank pussy; girls accuse each other of sleeping around; and both toss allegations of disloyalty at partners in previous relationships. A girl who wants a boy's attention, or one who is sleeping with a boy, smiles and tolerates his teasing, insults, and accusations.[13]

Boys don't engage in verbal duels as often or as intensely as girls. Boys tease each other momentarily, calling each other bitch or pussy, but verbal dueling, even among boys in the same clique, isn't as elaborate and stylized as it is among girls.

Verbal dueling partnerships exist in pairs, triads, and cliques (four or more) of girls. Wendy, Cara, Cheri, and Angie challenge and insult one another, and emergent among them is an informal pattern of verbal dueling partners. Wendy challenges Cara more often than she does Cheri and Angie. Wendy and Cara tease and challenge Cheri more often than they do Angie. Angie and Wendy tease Cheri more often than they do Cara. Cheri is known for bursts of anger and violent behavior, and girls, as well as boys, tend not to push her.

Verbal duels are stereotyped. When a duel is happening between boys, it's never imbued with the same ferocity as a boy-girl or a girl-girl verbal duel. Nearly always, a boy-boy duel is a brief challenge of a boy's ability or willingness to fight: "You ain't shit," asserts one boy. "Fuck you, niggah. I'll kick your mothafuckin' ass" is a common retort. The "loser" (the second speaker) defers and walks away. The duel ends. A less aggressive boy wouldn't say "You ain't shit" to a more aggressive boy, who might then punch him. No one ever verbally challenges Chucky D and Afro.

Girl-boy duels happen regularly. Some girls don't duel with boys or other girls and aren't chided or judged to be cowardly for not doing it. Most girls are thrilled to insult boys with terms for male and female genitalia, for excrement, and for challenging a boy's sexual prowess and fighting ability.

Verbal duels are street theater. Verbal duels always occur in public settings, in earshot of others. Verbal duels allow girls to display bravery against boys, adjust social network alliances among themselves, and shift their romantic pairings. During a particularly loud and boisterous performance, kids circle the performers, shouting support for stylistic insults, and laughter reigns. Verbal duels sow the seeds of "domestic" and "dating" violence when such duels run amok. The rules of the verbal duel help to control kids' tendencies to carry aggressive talk too far. When a kid bends verbal dueling rules too far and breaks the unwritten code of conduct, an expected outcome is violence. Controlling their speech helps these kids control their emotions. Once speech rules have been violated, anger pours out of these kids like water gushing from a drainage pipe after a thunderstorm.

Girls always instigate duels with boys. Girl-boy duels are more theatrical than girl-girl duels. Obscenities punctuate the discourse between dueling partners. Boys call girls by the standard list of insulting terms, including *bitch, rotten bitch, stank bitch, pussy, cunt*, and *slut*, among others. Girls retaliate with a vengeance, shouting, "bastard," "prick," "pussy," "bitch," "little dick," and "cocksucker," among others. Girls call one another by the standard list of insults.

Boys and girls toy with the pronunciation of the terms *bitch* and *bastard*. They exaggerate *bitch* until it sounds like "biy-yitch." Girls exaggerate *bastard* until it sounds like "baas-TURD" (emphasis on the second syllable). These stylized pronunciations signal the end of a duel.

Verbal duels can turn violent. *Niggah* signals a challenge by a girl who wants to play-fight with a boy. Sometimes, this playful fighting escalates. One Sunday afternoon, I was interviewing Angie at the picnic table next to Wendy's. Other kids were nearby. House of Pain walked over to listen.

"Get outta here, niggah," Angie said to House of Pain. He looked at her but said nothing. She growled at him a bit more.

He responded, "Fuck you. I'll stand where I want."

She stood up. ""I calling you out, NIGGAH. Wha's up?"

Words were tossed back and forth. House of Pain ended with "You ain't shit, you stank bitch."

That should have ended the duel. He turned and slowly walked away. She kept insulting him and walked after him. House of Pain told her to stop: "Fuck you, bitch. Shut up or I'll kick your ass." That should have been Angie's cue to end it.

She continued to berate him. Wearing a very angry face, he walked up to her, grabbed her by the arm, held her close to him, curled his right hand into a fist, and repeatedly punched her thighs and shoulders. To her cries of pain, an onlooking boy said, "Fuck you, you stank bitch, whatcha do that [push him] for?" Girls paid no attention once the punching ended. They walked away and let Angie rub her wounds by herself.

This scene was awful to watch. I wondered what motivated Angie to persist to the point where words turned to punches. After all, I thought, Angie isn't new to the street, and House of Pain's short fuse is well known. Angie knew that no one would intervene if he beat her.

"Violence doesn't scare me. I'm used to it, it's normal," said Poodle Bitch in a matter-of-fact voice. "I seen shootings and drive-bys." Poodle said she had been arrested for assault in a courtroom. She had punched her mother in the face and "knocked that bitch on her fuckin' ass." Roger, Angie's brother, said "It's true," adding, "We used to get into fistfights at home too."

Notes

1. Richard A. Ball and G. David Curry, "The Logic of Definition in Criminology: Purposes and Methods for Defining 'Gangs,'" *Criminology* 33(2) (1995): 225–245, offers an excellent discussion of gang definitions.
2. The vast gang literature is synthesized nicely in Irving Spergel, *The Youth Gang Problem* (New York: Oxford University Press, 1995); and Malcolm Klein, *The American Street Gang: Its Nature, Prevalence and Control* (New York: Oxford University Press, 1995).

3. Gang researchers have systematically sought theories to explain gang formation. Frederick Thrasher's 1927 study, *The Gang* (Chicago: University of Chicago Press), was the first serious research on gangs, and since then gang researchers have created a number of categories of theories linking gangs to poverty, socioeconomic strain, social class (low class, underclass), social disorganization (neighborhood, community), family disorganization, racism, and abnormal personality development.

   Despite the search for gang theories or integrated theories of delinquency and gangs, gang researchers haven't looked into the literature on cross-cultural adolescence or on adolescent development. Thus, the focus on gangs has largely been to explain gangs' deviant aspects, with researchers virtually overlooking the universal sociocultural aspects of adolescent social processes. The fact is, most of what we call gang behavior is not especially interesting as a research phenomenon, because it's so commonly a part of adolescent culture. Kids' wishes to hang out with kids like themselves, kids' use of symbolic means (graffiti, clothes, jargon) to sort one group from another, kids' aggressiveness, the impermanence of membership in kids' social groups, kids' rebelliousness against adults, including their families, aren't unique phenomena. Cross-cultural adolescent research has shown that male adolescent aggressiveness is related to increased peer contacts (see Alice Schlegel, "A Cross-Cultural Approach to Adolescence," *Ethos* 23: 1 [1995]:24). Is it really a surprise, then, to find that large groups of American kids (a gang) do more of something (commit crime) than smaller (delinquent) groups?

   Bonnie Miller Rubin ("Today's Teens Have Plenty of Picks to Clique," *Chicago Tribune*, National section, Sunday, September 14, 1997, pp. 1, 17) points out that adolescents in large high schools stratify themselves into ranked homogeneous subgroups (skaters, preps, hip-hop, ravers, postgrunge, goths, and stoners); that some kids pretend to be members of a group they really don't belong to (wannabes); that kids shift between groups; that there's conflict between groups; that the school as the adolescent community is fragmented by these subgroups; and the parents are concerned about their kids being in the "wrong" group.

   An overemphasis on criminological theories and on adolescent male delinquents seems to have clouded our vision about adolescent delinquent females. Meda Chesney-Lind and Randall G. Shelden's excellent study of girls' delinquency (*Girls, Delinquency and Juvenile Justice* [Pacific Grove, Calif.: Brooks/Cole, 1992]) is narrowly focused on delinquency theory (ecological, strain, differential association, control, labeling) and doesn't cite studies on girls' sociopsychological development or research on nondelinquent-female relationships among themselves and with males. If we don't understand a full range of cross-cultural adolescent female behavior, how are we to pinpoint those behaviors which are unique deviant responses to a range of family and environmental stimuli? In short, we don't understand how much of what we're measuring in female (and male) delinquent and gang behavior is within the range of predictable adolescent behavior in complex urban settings. Why is this such an important issue? Unless we know which adolescent behaviors are natural (and will terminate with adolescence) and which are effects of controllable negative stimuli (family disorganization, for instance), then we won't be able to develop truly effective intervention strategies.

   Perhaps the true uniqueness of a "youth gang" is how communities respond to it. Generally speaking, decades of research show that kids in gangs are marginal in school and have been injured by family disorder, among other things. That marginality and injury don't preclude these kids from engaging in universal adolescent sociopsychological processes (homophilous groups, stratification, ranks, aggression); however, so-called gang members act out these processes in an unconventional venue, the street, which alarms adults and engenders a law enforcement (control) response instead of a parental (supportive) response. As an anthropologist observing this scene, it's alarming to watch American adults castigate and alienate their own youth and further injure already victimized adolescents. It isn't youth gangs that should bother America's lawmakers, but rather the dominant culture's response to America's most vulnerable children. America's aggressiveness and punitive reaction to youth gangs as "community evil" marks the abusive nature of our society.

4. Fremont Hustlers fit a common operational definition of gangs as a group involved in illegal activity (Finn-Aage Esbensen and David Huizinga, "Gangs, Drugs, and Delinquency in

a Survey of Urban Youth," *Criminology* 31 [1993]:565–569). I prefer the definition in Scott H. Decker and Barrik Van Winkle, *Life in the Gang* (Cambridge: Cambridge University Press, 1996), p. 31; "an age-graded peer group that exhibits some permanence, engages in criminal activity, and has some symbolic representation of membership." The notion of age-grade is important, because we know that gang members in their late teens and early twenties commit most of the violent acts (Spergel, *The Youth Gang Problem*, pp. 33–36). Thus, older gang members in consort with young boys and girls pose a serious problem in the socialization or coercion of young members to be involved in violent acts. How age distribution influences violence in male gangs and in mixed male-female gangs, like the Fremont Hustlers, has not been carefully studied.

5. Malcolm Klein, *Street Gangs and Street Workers* (Englewood Cliffs, N.J.: Prentice Hall, 1971), includes a comprehensive discussion of gang cohesion and leadership. Fremont findings support Klein's and show that external pressures, including poverty, family dysfunction, unemployment, and schools' inadequate responses to difficult kids, have a stronger effect on group cohesion than internal forces, such as a code of conduct and ethos.

6. Few publications focus specifically on females in gangs and female gangs. See, for instance, Lee Bowker and Malcolm Klein, "The Etiology of Female Juvenile Delinquency and Gang Membership: A Test of Psychological and Social Structure Explanations," *Adolescence* 18 (1983):740–751; Joan W. Moore, *Going Down to the Barrio: Homeboys and Homegirls in Change* (Philadelphia: Temple University Press, 1991); Carl Taylor, *Girls, Gangs, Women and Drugs* (East Lansing: Michigan State University Press, 1993), Anne Campbell, *The Girls in the Gang*, 2d ed. (New York: Basil Blackwell, 1991). Also see Ruth Horowitz, *Honor and The American Dream* (New Brunswick, N.J.: Rutgers University Press, 1983).

7. Using the roster elicited on my first day in Fremont, I wrote each of the names of the 72 Fremont Hustlers on its own three-by-five card. I gave the stack of cards to each girl and asked her to sort the cards into as many piles as necessary, as long as each pile had more than one card (see H. Russell Bernard, *Research Methods in Anthropology* [Newbury Park, Calif.: Sage, 1994], pp. 249–252). After each informant had created the piles, I asked why she had grouped those people together.

   Pile sorting is useful, but there are a number of difficulties in structured interviews with gang kids in noisy apartments. First, kids want to help each other put cards into piles. I had to tell bystanders to stay quiet. Second, kids see names on cards and start to tell stories about those kids. This is wonderful, but it distracts the informant from the task. Third, kids see names that disturb them. Enemies, former lovers, dead homeys, snitches, and others distract both the informant and the bystanders. If she is upset, either the informant wants to stop the pile sorting or she gets into arguments with bystanders about the names on the cards. Fourth, sorting 72 cards takes time and effort, and then enduring my questions takes even more time and effort. In the end, an hour interview becomes 90-120 minutes, or the kids just abandon the task out of boredom. Fifth, kids have other things going on at the same time. Distractions are endless. Phone calls, buzzing pagers, people knocking at the door, and other kids getting high keep the informant away from the job. Sixth, pile sorting requires good rapport with informants and a fully open channel of communication. I did this pile sorting eight months after arriving on Fremont. Kids are suspicious and without good rapport, they're likely to conceal good data by glossing over kids who are "really in the shit."

   In the end, however, pile sorting gave me insights into the internal classification of the Fremont Hustlers through the eyes of three of its longest-standing active members. With these data, I decided who would likely be the best kids to interview next and who could be passed by.

8. Labels such as "core," "peripheral," "associate," "wannabe," or synonyms of these labels, were not used by informants.

9. I elicited these categories in March 1996 and asked Cara to sort the cards as social groups had existed during the gang's 1994–1995 heyday. Social dynamics are continuous; thus, these categories should be viewed as a temporal snapshot. I recorded notes about the kinship relationships within each group, and in some cases between groups, and also noted violent incidents (perpetrator or victim) or other unique characteristics for each kid, as Cara reported them.

10. Fremont girls are in Anne Campbell's (*The Girls in the Gang*) "bad girls" category. "They are not tortured by dreams of upward mobil-

ity and have a realistic view of their chances of success in society. They have not done well in school, and when they have money, they spend it. . . . Like the boys in the neighborhood, they enjoy excitement and trouble, which break the monotony of a life in which little attention is given to the future. They like sharp clothes, loud music, alcohol, and soft drugs. They admire toughness and verbal 'smarts.' They may not be going anywhere, but they make the most of where they are" (pp. 7–8).

To be sure, Fremont girls aren't chattle, that is, possessions of gang boys. These girls are staunchly independent, although many have customary adolescent boy-girl relationships. Gang boys are more aggressive than girls and frequently try to control them; in such a case, girls play a passive role. Boy-girl pairings often display violence, as I describe and discuss later. In some cases, a girl will perceive her victimization at the hands of a boy as his affection for her, but I don't think this is unique to gang-affiliated adolescents.

I'm unconvinced that girls, like Cara and Wendy, who have been physically hurt by boys actually believe their own words ("He hit me because he loves me"). If anyone knows about violence, it's these kids, and they know from experience at home that violence isn't love. The public talk equating physical violence and interpersonal affection is a girl's culturally defined rationalization for her inability to escape such a horrible situation. If a gang girl pulls away on her own, her boyfriend will likely beat her more severely. To escape an abusive relationship, a girl needs a new suitor who's stronger and more violent than her current abusive boyfriend. This is how Chucky D and Afro succeed in relationships. No one challenges them, and girls can, in a sense, "hide" behind them. In relationships with them, however, girls pay a price, and that price is obedience and sex.

The more realistic way to escape from these boys is to become pregnant. Once real-life responsibilities face Afro and Chucky D and other Fremont boys, they flee and find new girlfriends. Although pregnant girls don't say it directly, they believe their pregnancy will soften their abusive boyfriends.

11. Anthropologists have reported that social groups with a special purpose, such as a fraternity, commonly have a rite of passage, or initiation, for the prospective members. An initiation rite is the public transformation of social status from, in the case of a gang, a non-gang member to a gang member. Such a rite of passage serves an additional function. It is also a rite of social intensification, which draws group members together and further bonds them on a collective occasion.

It's no surprise to find that a youth gang has a rite of passage. The number of gangs requiring a rite of passage is unknown, although folklore about such rites is plentiful and often apocryphal. Folklore has it that such rituals may include, for instance, being beaten by fellow members or being forced to commit a violent act. Even if such rites of passage occur, it'd be very difficult to know if these are idiosyncratic events or a core feature of gangs as a uniform expression of marginal adolescent culture. By idiosyncratic event, I mean an event that is initiated by a violent boy like Chucky D and his violent companions, who use new members as a means of satisfying their own bloodthirst (see Decker and Van Winkle, *Life in the Gang*, p. 184). In any case, a violent rite of passage certainly isn't unique to inner city gangs. In my college years, fraternities "paddled" initiates, and many still do, although paddling is members' "secret" knowledge.

Gang initiation stories have become so exaggerated that on occasion they reach the news and engender public fear. Over the winter of 1993–94 in central Illinois, local news stations broadcast that gangs were engaged in an egregious violent initiation. It was reported that gang members would drive around at night with the headlights on high beam. When an oncoming car, usually driven by an elderly person, flashed its lights signaling the high beams, the gangsters would turn around and follow the elderly driver to his home and then rob, beat, or kill him. A colleague in the California Youth Authority in Los Angeles told me that such a tale was broadcast on the news there at about the same time it appeared in central Illinois.

While doing Fremont research, Kansas City newscasts reported a violent and bizarre "new" gang initiation. A prospective gangster, the story went, would hide underneath a car in the parking lot of a KC shopping center at night, and when the driver (usually a woman holding bags) stood next to the door to unlock it, the gangster would slash at her ankles with a knife, pull her to the ground and rob her and steal her car. Such an event never occurred in Kansas City. Cara, Wendy, Afro, and Chucky D chuckled when they heard that tale. Chucky D said, "What da fuck d'ya wanna do dat for? Ya getcha clothes dirty and dey ain't no money in it."

12. Social groupings are static representations. To be sure, daily Fremont life isn't static. Pagers helped me to track changing social ties. When a kid gave me his or her pager number, it was a sign of rapport. Old fashioned "low-tech" street ethnography isn't sufficient to keep up with kids who have cars, pagers, and cellular phones, and who shift residences every week or month. "Pager" ethnography helps. I learned to use their pagers and caller identification to my advantage. Kids who know one another's pager numbers, how often kids page one another, whether or not a kid returns a page, how quickly pages are returned, who borrows a pager from whom and then puts his or her own outgoing message on that pager are good data. Boy-girl relationships are traceable with pagers. A girl might carry her boyfriend's pager, and a boy might lend his pager to a girl he wants to sleep with.

    Pager numbers are sensitive information. I never had a problem collecting information about drug selling or kids' sex lives, but when I asked for pager numbers and numbers listed on caller identification machines, I often had problems. Even after a long and close association with Cara, she was judicious in giving me caller ID numbers. Their numbers were valuable, and they told me who was contacting whom and how often. Once I had that information, I could ask about the content of the calls and move into the most intimate aspects of kids' social ties.

13. The fundamental gender-linked difference between Fremont girls' and boy' responses to one another is this: girls think about relationships as moral contracts; boys don't. Beyond the street rhetoric of the gang, girls' implicit construction of relationships, especially with boys, includes fairness, reciprocity, and equality. A girl expects that, if she pairs up with a boy and has sex with him, then he will treat her fairly and be responsive to her and their children. In what they perceive to be long-term relationships, girls feel an inherent responsibility toward the boys with whom they are involved, but the boys feels neither reciprocity nor fairness nor equality. This conflict between girls' and boys' underlying conception of the nature of interpersonal relationships is the source of boy-girl physical and emotional abuse. A baby has an important role in the unwitting moral contract between its mother and father, from a girls' perspective. ✦

Section III

Race, Ethnicity, and Gender in Gangs

Chapter 10
Race and Gender Differences Between Gang and Nongang Youths[1]

Finn-Aage Esbensen
and
L. Thomas Winfree, Jr.

Based on survey results from the Gang Resistance Education and Training program (see Chapter 24 for an overview), Esbensen and Winfree report on rates of gang participation among a sample of eighth-grade youths from fourteen cities across the United States. As these authors note, the public, policy makers, and even researchers often hold stereotypical views of who the typical gang member is, and often associate gang membership exclusively with young men from minority racial groups, including African Americans, Latinos, and Asians. Findings from the G.R.E.A.T. survey, which sampled youths in geographically and demographically diverse communities, challenge these assumptions; this survey reveals higher than expected gang participation rates both among females and among white youths. Moreover, the disproportionate involvement of gang members in criminal activities is true for female and white gang members, not just minority males. According to the authors, their findings differ considerably from other estimates of gang participation as a result of both their methodological approach and the age of their sample. They conclude by discussing both the strengths and limitations of their approach.

Abstract

Most examinations of youth gangs have been limited to a single city or a single state. In this article we examine gang affiliation in a multi-site survey of 5,935 eighth-grade students in 42 schools located in 11 cities across the United States. We use this diverse sample to examine two related issues: the demographic composition of gangs and the level of delinquent activity of gang members compared with nongang members. Our findings call into question the validity of prevailing notions about the number of girls in gangs and their level of delinquency involvement, and the number of white youths active in gangs and the extent of their illegal activities.

In the past 100 years, volumes of research have been produced describing gangs, gang members, and gang activity. Currently there is heightened concern that although the American violent crime rate is declining, the juvenile violent crime rate is increasing (Fox 1996). Some commentators attribute this increase to the increased role of juvenile gangs in drug trafficking and other illegal activities (Spergel 1995). Combined with the stereotypical image of gang members (e.g., an African-American or Hispanic male), this belief about gang-based drug sales reinforces the myth that the American crime problem is a "minority" problem. On the basis of findings reported in this paper, we are led to question how closely gang affiliation and associated criminal activity are restricted to minority males.

Methodological Issues

Juvenile gangs have often served as the focal point for delinquency research and theoretical development (e.g., Cloward and Ohlin 1960; Cohen 1955; Miller 1958; Short and Strodbeck 1965; Thornberry, Krohn,

Reprinted from: Finn-Aage Esbensen and L. Thomas Winfree, Jr., "Race and Gender Differences Between Gang and Non-Gang Youth: Results From a Multi-Site Survey." In *Justice Quarterly*, 15, pp. 505–525.

Lizotte, and Chard-Wierschem 1993). Historically the study of gangs has been descriptive (e.g., Asbury 1927; Campbell 1991; Hagedorn 1988, 1994; Moore 1978; Puffer 1912; Spergel 1966; Thrasher 1927; Vigil 1988); it has relied chiefly on observational methods, thus providing a wealth of information about specific gangs and their members. In spite of some excellent descriptive accounts provided by recent gang researchers (e.g., Campbell 1991; Decker and Van Winkle 1996; Hagedorn 1988, 1994; Harris 1988; MacLeod 1987; Sullivan 1989; Vigil 1988), we have little information about the composition of gangs relative to the adolescent population as a whole. Bursik and Grasmick (1995:154) summarize gang research by stating that the "emphasis has been on the depth of data, rather than the breadth."

More recently, social scientists have turned to two types of quantitative data. First, some gang researchers rely on law enforcement records to describe gang offenses and gang members (e.g., Curry, Ball, and Decker 1996; Curry, Ball, and Fox 1994; Maxson and Klein 1990; Spergel 1990). This body of research parallels the general picture of gang members as disproportionately male and members of ethnic/racial minorities, an image often reinforced by the popular press. Because of enforcement strategies that tend to target individuals with these characteristics, in conjunction with a general reluctance to accept the notion that girls[2] can be gang members, this finding is not surprising.

A second quantitative approach employs survey methods to study gang behavior (e.g., Esbensen and Huizinga 1993; Esbensen, Huizinga, and Weiher 1993; Fagan 1989; Thornberry et al. 1993; Winfree, Backstrom, and Mays 1994). Regardless of study design or research methodology, there is considerable consensus about the high rate of criminal offending among gang members, including crimes against person and property, substance use, and drug distribution and sale.

In spite of this consensus on behavioral traits, the demographic characteristics of gang members remain the subject of considerable disagreement. The primary purpose of the current study is to review the literature and to provide a descriptive account of the differences and similarities between gang and nongang members based on one of the largest general surveys undertaken to assess the American gang problem. We are interested in four questions related to the gender and ethnic composition of gangs:

- What percentage of gang members are female?
- Are girls in the gang as delinquent as boys in the gang?
- What is the ethnic composition of gangs?
- Are members of ethnic minorities in gangs involved disproportionately in delinquent activity?

Gender and Gang Membership

The nature and extent of female delinquency and gang membership is poorly understood. Throughout the history of criminology, female involvement in crime has been a neglected research topic, largely because of the belief that women's level of participation and seriousness of offending are too insignificant to warrant serious attention. For instance, females are not considered in the works of Cohen (1955), Cloward and Ohlin (1960), or most criminological theory and research before 1970. Even in more recent conceptualizations of female delinquency (e.g., Chesney-Lind and Shelden 1992; Triplett and Meyers 1995), female involvement in gangs is largely ignored or presented as an insignificant issue. Chesney-Lind and colleagues (1996:194) refer to girls in the gang as "present but invisible."

Estimates of the prevalence of females in gangs vary greatly, as do descriptions of their involvement in gang activities (e.g., Bjerregaard and Smith 1993; Cohen et al. 1995; Curry et al. 1994; Esbensen and Huizinga 1993; Goldstein and Glick 1994; Huff 1997; Klein and Crawford 1995). Most estimates place the figure in the single digits and perpetuate the stereotype of girls as auxiliary members relegated to gender-specific crimes (i.e., seducing males, concealing weapons, and instigating fights between rival male gangs).

Researchers, however, have begun to question this view of female delinquency. As early as 1967, Klein and Crawford (1995) reported that their caseworkers' "daily contact reports" identified 600 male and 200 female gang members. In other words, 25 percent of the Los Angeles gang members identified by caseworkers in the 1960s were female!

This estimate is consistent with results from recent general surveys. Bjerregaard and Smith (1993) report that 22 percent of girls in their high-risk sample (i.e., from socially disorganized neighborhoods) were gang members. These 60 girls accounted for 31 percent of the self-reported gang members in that survey. Cohen and her colleagues (1995) interviewed approximately 520 youths (age 10 to 18) in their evaluation of 13 drug and gang prevention programs. When program and nonprogram youths were combined, girls accounted for approximately 21 percent of self-proclaimed gang members. Esbensen and Huizinga (1993), during their four years of interviews with high-risk youths in Denver, reported that girls made up 20 to 46 percent of the gang members. When the ages of their longitudinal sample ranged from 11 to 15, 46 percent of the gang members were female. When the sample had reached the age range 13 to 19, girls accounted for only 20 percent of the gang members. These findings tend to support the belief that girls age in and out of gangs earlier than boys.

In contrast to these figures, which are derived primarily from adolescent surveys, other researchers (e.g., Curry, Ball, and Fox 1994; Goldstein and Glick 1994; Huff 1997) report that females account for fewer than 10 percent of the gang members in their studies. For example, a study of 61 large and small police departments yielded a total of 9,092 female gang members, representing less than 4 percent of the total (Curry et al. 1994). Similarly, Goldstein and Glick (1994: 9) state that "males continue to outnumber female gang members at a ratio of approximately 20 to 1."

We can identify two main sources of the discrepancy between these two sets of estimates: the research methods utilized to produce the data, and the age of the sample members. Case studies, observational studies, and studies relying on law enforcement data tend to produce lower estimates of female involvement than do general surveys. This difference may well be an artifact of differential recording policies for males and for females. In the operating manual for the Los Angeles Sheriff Department, a youth is classified as a gang member when he or she admits to gang membership. The manual, however, questions the validity of female self-nomination: "These same females will say they are members of the local Crip gang; however, evidence has shown that this is not so" (Operation Safe Streets 1995:40).

The second methodological issue, the age of the sample, may be more significant. The Esbensen and Huizinga (1993) study reported a lower percentage of girl gang members as the sample aged. Additional evidence suggests that girls mature out of gangs at an earlier age than males (e.g., Fishman 1995; Harris 1994; Moore and Hagedorn 1996; Swart 1995). According to Harris (1994), girls are most active in gangs between the ages of 13 and 16. She suggests that "by 17 or 18, interests and activities of individual members are directed toward the larger community rather than toward the gang, and girls begin to leave the active gang milieu" (p. 300). Thus gang samples consisting of older adolescents or gang members in their twenties tend to produce a substantially different picture than studies focusing on youths of middle school and high school age.

Female Delinquency and Gang Membership

Are girls as delinquent as boys, especially in gangs? The prevailing view is that girls account for very little of the violent crime in society; and this also applies to gang crime. Law enforcement data continue to report female delinquency as considerably less prevalent and less violent than male delinquency. In 1995, for example, girls under age 18 accounted for only 14.6 percent of juvenile arrests for violent crimes and 26 percent of juvenile arrests for property crimes (U.S. Department of Justice 1996:217).

With respect to female gang activity, the Denver Youth Survey reveals that girl gang members account for only a small percentage of all active offenders but commit more violent crimes than do nongang boys (Huizinga 1997). The stereotype of the girl as sex object and limited participant in the gang's delinquent activity apparently requires reexamination. For example, in Rosenbaum's (1991) study of 70 female gang members who were wards of the California Youth Authority, none of the females mentioned sex as playing a role in her gang involvement. Several of the girls in Huff's (1997) study, however, reported that they were forced to engage in sexual activity with male gang members. In a clarification of these opposing findings, Miller (1997) states that the girl's status in the gang determines whether she will be subject to forced sex with the gang boys. Thus it may be that this stereotype of gang girls as sex objects is more an artifact of the data-collection technique and of the age of the youths sampled than of the actual distribution of the behavior in the targeted population. Furthermore, the traditional focus on girls' sexual activity may have distracted attention from their "other" delinquent pursuits.

Anecdotal observations in the mass media suggest that females have become more violent and more crime-oriented in recent years. Evidence supporting such increases, however, is largely missing (see the critique of the media construction of girl gangs by Chesney-Lind, Shelden, and Joe (1996). In an attempt to address this issue of a "new violent female offender," Huizinga and Esbensen (1991) compared self-reported data from the 1978 National Youth Survey with 1989 data from the Denver Youth Survey; they found no evidence of an increase in violent offending by females. Moreover, in his comprehensive review of the literature, Spergel (1995:58) concludes that "there is no clear evidence that female gang members are increasingly involved in serious gang violence." Chesney-Lind and her colleagues (1996:189) note similarly that the "rise in girls' arrests more or less parallels increases in arrests of male youth."

Race, Ethnicity, and Gang Membership

In spite of questions about the generalizability and reliability of ethnographic gang studies, such studies have proved to be a rich source of information about the ethnic and racial composition of gangs (e.g., Campbell 1991; Hagedorn 1987; Moore 1978, 1991; Vigil 1988). This depth of coverage, however, may have engendered one of gang research's greatest racial myths: One consequence of these studies is an assumption that gang members are youths from ethnic or racial minority backgrounds (e.g., Fagan 1989; Spergel 1990). Police-based studies often support these conclusions. In the national survey conducted by Curry and colleagues (1994), approximately 90 percent of gang members are African-American or Hispanic. Spergel (1995:59) concluded his review by stating that the "dominant proportions of blacks and Hispanics identified as gang members based on police reporting seem hardly to have changed, although the numbers have increased in the past twenty years."

As with gang research in general, much of what is known about ethnicity and gangs is derived from case studies of specific gangs or cities. Yet even the more general surveys of youths do not include diverse enough samples to adequately address the race/ethnicity composition of gangs. The Denver and Rochester longitudinal studies (e.g., Bjerregaard and Smith 1993; Esbensen and Huizinga 1993; Thornberry et al. 1993) were concentrated in high-risk neighborhoods; such neighborhoods, by definition, include disproportionate numbers of racial and ethnic minorities. In the Denver Youth Survey, for instance, African-American or Hispanic youths accounted for almost 80 percent of the entire sample and approximately 90 percent of gang members (Esbensen and Huizinga 1993). Such samples hardly permit examination of gang membership by ethnicity.

The emergence of the underclass concept (Wilson 1987) as an explanation for the apparent increase in gangs (Hagedorn 1988; Vigil 1988) has focused attention on ethnic and racial minority gang membership. This perspective can be seen as an outgrowth of social disorganization theory (Shaw and McKay 1942), historically the dominant social structural explanation for gang activity. Covey, Menard, and Franzese summarize the effect of ethnicity on gang membership:

> Racial differences in the frequency of gang formation such as the relative scarcity of non-Hispanic, white, ethnic gangs (Campbell 1984) may be explainable in terms of the smaller proportion of the non-Hispanic European American population that live in neighborhoods characterized by high rates of poverty, welfare dependency, single-parent households, and other symptoms that characterize social disorganization. (1997:240)

The early gang studies by Thrasher (1927), Puffer (1912), and Asbury (1927) were a rich source of information about white urban gangs. These gangs were described according to nationality, not race or ethnicity; not until the 1950s did commentators identify gang members by race or ethnicity (Spergel 1995:8). This apparent change in gang composition is tied closely to the social disorganization of urban areas and the research focus on urban youths. As researchers expand their efforts to include a more representative sample of the general population, the problem is likely to be redefined. The 1995 National Youth Gang Survey, a survey of law enforcement agencies, illustrates how expanding the sample can affect the apparent parameters of the problem. That survey, which included nonurban law enforcement agencies, found gangs to be present in communities with fewer than 10,000 inhabitants (National Youth Gang Center 1997). With this wider coverage, it seems inevitable that the description of the demographic (especially racial) composition of gang members will change.

Gang Membership, Ethnicity, and Rates of Offending

In addition to the ethnic composition of gangs, another important issue is the extent of involvement in delinquent activity within the gang. Are minority gang youths more delinquent than white gang members? Among the researchers who have examined differential rates of adolescents' offending by race/ethnicity (e.g., Curry and Spergel 1992; Elliott and Ageton 1980; Huizinga and Elliott 1987; Lyons, Henggeller, and Hall 1992; Sellers, Winfree, and Griffiths 1993; Winfree, Mays, and Vigil-Backstrom 1994), relatively few have explored whether differences in offending exist within the gang. Two studies that compared Hispanic with Caucasian gang members produced mixed results. Lyons, Henggeller, and Hall (1992) found slightly lower rates of self-reported offending among Hispanic youths; Winfree and his colleagues (1994b) found no difference between the two groups. In their comparison of African-American with Hispanic gang members in Chicago, Curry and Spergel (1992) found higher offending rates among African-American males.

Most investigations of gang offending have been restricted to ethnically or racially homogeneous gangs. Therefore, the issue of ethnic differences in offending has rarely been explored. Many ethnographic and case studies of gang members, as discussed above, tend to have limited generalizability. Similarly, some of the general surveys reported recently have been restricted to "high-risk" areas and thus limit the ability to examine ethnic differences in offending.

In the current multi-site study, considerable population and geographic diversity allows for closer examination of the gender and ethnic composition of gangs. We use this diverse sample from 11 cities to examine the demographic characteristics of gang members in relation to nongang members and to investigate behavioral differences and similarities between males and females and four ethnic groups (whites, African-Americans, Hispanics, and Asians).

Research Design

This investigation of demographic and behavioral differences between gang and nongang youths is part of a larger evaluation of the Gang Resistance Education and Training (G.R.E.A.T.) program, a school-based gang prevention program. Therefore, evaluation objectives dictated site selection and sampling procedures. Because the G.R.E.A.T. program is administered to seventh-grade students, we surveyed eighth-grade students to allow for a one-year follow-up while at the same time guaranteeing that none of the sample members was currently enrolled in the program. We conducted this multi-site, multi-state cross-sectional survey in spring 1995. Site selection was limited to cities in which the G.R.E.A.T. program had been delivered during the 1993–1994 school year, when the targeted students were in grade 7.[3]

Site Selection

We used records provided by the Bureau of Alcohol, Tobacco, and Firearms, the federal agency supervising the G.R.E.A.T. program, to identify prospective sites that met two criteria. First, only agencies with two or more officers trained before January 1994 to teach G.R.E.A.T. were considered eligible.[4]

Second, to increase the geographic and demographic diversity of the sample, we excluded some potential cities from consideration.[5] We made exploratory contacts with more than 30 different law enforcement agencies to determine whether adequate numbers of students were participating in the classroom-based program.

Fifteen of these sites met this preliminary requirement. Reasons for exclusion at this stage varied: Some cities had not yet implemented the program; not all of the sites had processed enough students through the program in the previous year to allow for the retrospective data collection planned; and in some situations, the police had instructed all seventh-grade students, making it impossible to construct a comparison group of students who had not received G.R.E.A.T. Subsequently we submitted formal proposals requesting participation to the public school districts at these 15 sites.

We reached agreements with 11 of the sites. Three districts declined participation; at the fourth site, it was determined on closer scrutiny that all of the seventh-grade students in the district had participated in the program during the previous year. The eleven cross-sectional sites selected were Las Cruces, NM; Omaha, NE; Phoenix, AZ; Philadelphia, PA; Kansas City, MO; Milwaukee, WI; Orlando, FL; Will County, IL; Providence, RI; Pocatello, ID; and Torrance, CA. These sites provide a diverse sample. One or more can be described by the following characteristics: large urban area, small city, racially and ethnically homogeneous, racially and ethnically heterogeneous, East Coast, West Coast, Midwest, inner-city, working-class, and middle-class.

At the selected sites, schools that had offered G.R.E.A.T. during the past two years were selected and questionnaires were administered in groups to all eighth-grade students in attendance on the specified day.[6] Attendance rates varied from a low of 75 percent at one Kansas City middle school to a high of 93 percent at several schools in Will County and Pocatello.

We obtained a final sample of 5,935 eighth-grade students representing 315 classrooms in 42 different schools. Passive consent procedures (i.e., a procedure requiring parents to respond only if they do not want their child to participate in a research project) were approved everywhere but at the Torrance site. The number of parental refusals at each school ranged from zero to 2 percent (at one school). Thus participation rates (the percentage of students in attendance on the day of administration who actually completed questionnaires) varied between 98 and 100 percent at the passive consent sites. Participation rates in Torrance, where active consent procedures were required, ranged from 53 percent to 75 percent of all eighth-grade students in each of the four schools.[7]

This public school-based sample has the standard limitations associated with school-based surveys: exclusion of private-school students, exclusion of truant, sick, and/or tardy students, and the possible under-representation of "high-risk" youths. With this warning in mind, the current sample is composed of all eighth-grade students in attendance on the days when questionnaires were administered in these 11 jurisdictions. The sample includes primarily 13- to 15-year-old students attending public schools in a cross-section of communities in the continental United States. This sample is not random, and generalizations cannot be made to the adolescent population as a whole.

Students from these 11 jurisdictions, however, represent the following types of communities: large urban areas in which most of the students belong to a racial or ethnic minority (Philadelphia, Phoenix, Milwaukee, and Kansas City); medium-sized cities (population ranging between 100,000 and 500,000) with considerable racial and/or ethnic heterogeneity (Providence and Orlando); medium-sized cities with a majority of white students but a substantial minority enrollment (Omaha and Torrance); a small city (fewer than 100,000 inhabitants) with an ethnically diverse student population (Las Cruces); a small, racially homogeneous (white) city (Pocatello); and a rural area in which more than 80 percent of the student population is white (Will County). This diversity in locations and sample characteristics permits exploration of the distribution of gang affiliation and delinquent activity in an age group generally excluded from "gang research."

Measures

The questionnaires given to students consisted of demographic, attitudinal, and behavioral measures. In this paper we examine only demographic variables (gender, age, race/ethnicity, and family composition) and behavioral traits (self-reported delinquency and gang membership). Self-reported delinquency and gang affiliation were asked of respondents toward the end of the questionnaire. This reporting technique has been used widely during the past 40 years and provides a good measure of actual behavior rather than a reactive measure of police response to behavior (e.g., Hindelang, Hirschi, and Weis 1981; Huizinga 1991; Huizinga and Elliott 1987). Respondents were asked whether they had ever engaged in any of 17 distinct delinquent acts, whether they had ever used any of five different types of drugs, and whether they had ever been in a gang. Students indicating that they had engaged in these behaviors then were asked to report how many times during the past 12 months they had committed each offense. Students indicating that they had belonged to a gang were asked to answer additional gang-related questions.

We created four different measures of self-reported delinquency for the analyses reported here: property offenses, crimes against persons, drug use, and illegal drug sales (see appendix). To correct for the skewness of self-reported data, we truncated individual items at 12. Upon creation of each composite score, we truncated the score again at 12.[8]

Gang membership was determined through self-identification. As with most social phenomena, issues of definition arise.[9] By relying on self-definition, we adhere to law enforcement officers' primary criteria for identifying "official" gang members. In the current research, two filter questions introduce the gang-specific section of the questionnaire: "Have you ever been a gang member?" and "Are you now in a gang?" Given the current sample, in which almost all the respondents are under age 15, even an affirmative response to the first question followed by a negative response to the second may indicate a recent gang affiliation.

In an attempt to limit our sample of gang members to "delinquent gangs," we employed a restrictive definition of gang status: We classified as gang members only those youths who reported ever having been in a gang and who reported that their gangs engaged in at least one type of delinquent behavior (fighting other gangs, stealing cars, stealing in general, or robbing people). This strategy resulted in identification of 623 gang members, representing 10.6 percent of the sample.

Results

In this paper we focus on gender and ethnicity. To put results in perspective, however, we first provide a demographic description of the whole sample. Approximately half of the sample is female (52 percent). Most of the respondents live in intact homes (62 percent); that is, they indicated that both a mother and a father (including stepparents) were present in the home. The sample is ethnically diverse: Whites account for 40 percent of the respondents, African-Americans 27 percent, Hispanics 19 percent, Asians 6 percent, and other groups 8 percent. As would be expected with an eighth-grade sample, most of the respondents are between 13 and 15 years old; 60 percent are 14 years old. According to data provided by the school districts included in this study, the sample characteristics are similar—indeed, virtually identical—to the districts' student profiles. In Las Cruces middle schools, for example, 36 percent of the students are Caucasian, 61 percent are Hispanic, and 4 percent are classified as "other." Our Las Cruces sample is 34 percent Caucasian, 57 percent Hispanic, and 9 percent "other." In Milwaukee, our sample contains 27 percent white and 56 percent African-American students, compared with 25 percent and 61 percent respectively in the district.

At the beginning of this paper we posed two questions about the gender and ethnic composition of gangs. Table 10.1 reveals that (1) there are more girls in gangs than is commonly assumed and (2) that whites account for a larger portion of gang members than official reports suggest. In agreement with much of the emerging gang research but contrary to prevailing stereotypes about the male-dominated nature of gangs, fully 38 percent of the gang members in this eighth-grade sample are females. This figure still indicates that females are underrepresented among gang members, but to a far lesser extent than is commonly assumed when older samples are studied.

Also, contrary to popular perception, 25 percent of the gang members are white. Although minority youths account for most gang members, white youths are not as absent as "official" estimates suggest. As discussed previously, much of the previous gang literature relied on case studies of gangs or surveys limited to predominantly minority samples. This sample reveals that white youths are less likely to be involved in gangs than are African-American and His-

Table 10.1
Demographic Characteristics of Gang and Nongang Youths

	Nongang			Gang			Total Sample	
	N	Row%	Col%	N	Row%	Col%	N	Col%
Sex*								
Male	2,412	86	46	380	14	62	2,792	48
Female	2,793	92	54	237	8	38	3,030	52
	5,202	89		617	11			
Race*								
White	2,187	94	42	150	6	25	2,337	41
African-American	1,339	88	26	188	12	31	1,527	27
Hispanic	924	86	18	153	14	25	1,077	19
Asian	317	92	6	28	8	5	345	6
Other	389	81	8	94	20	15	483	8
	5,156	89		613	11			
Family Structure*								
Single-parent	1,559	86	30	249	14	40	1,808	31
Intact	3,301	92	64	292	8	47	3,593	62
Other	336	81	7	78	19	13	414	7
	5,196	89		619	11			
Age*								
13 and under	1,585	94	31	101	6	17	1,686	29
14	3,119	90	60	367	11	61	3,486	60
15 and over	468	77	9	138	23	23	606	11
	5,172	89		606	11			

*p<.001

panic youths, but not to the extent suggested by past research. In fact, if we include some of the "other" category, which includes white youths who identified themselves as American, Italian, German, Portuguese, and the like, the ethnic difference in gang membership is reduced even further.

In keeping with earlier assessments of the demographic characteristics of gangs, this sample reveals that younger youths are underrepresented in gangs and that gang members are more likely than nongang members to live with a single parent. Even in this limited age sample, the youths age 13 and under account for only 17 percent of gang members but represent 31 percent of the nongang sample. At the other extreme, 23 percent of gang members but only 9 percent of nongang members are 15 or older. A minority of all youths live in single-parent homes, but gang members report living in single-parent homes more frequently (40 percent) than do nongang youths (30 percent). These demographic characteristics suggest possible qualitative differences between gang and nongang youths' living situations.

Table 10.2 reports the mean annual rates of offending for male and female gang and nongang members. The appendix lists the individual items constituting each subset of delinquent activity. In agreement with past research, girls report lower rates of offending than do boys, with one exception: The male-female difference in drug use among gang members is not statistically significant at the .001 level. The ratio of male to female offending within the two groups (gang and nongang) is in the general range of 1.5:1; the actual range is from 1.15:1 for drug use among gang members to 2.53:1 for drug sales among nongang youths. More interesting perhaps, is the ratio of gang girls' self-reported offending relative to nongang boys' delinquency rates: For each comparison, the gang girls are considerably more delinquent than the nongang boys. For crimes against persons, the gang girls commit 2.34 offenses to every one for the nongang boys. Evidence for a link between gang membership and drug dealing (with a ratio of 5.24:1) is found in the comparison of gang girls' involvement in drug sales with that of nongang boys.

Table 10.3 presents results from an analysis comparing annual offending rates by ethnicity while controlling for gang affiliation. Among nongang members, we found no differences for rates of property offending. For crimes against person, drug sales, and drug use, the Asian youths reported the lowest levels of activity. The African American youths reported the highest levels of crimes against person; while the white, Hispanic, and "other" youths indicated the highest levels of drug use. These figures suggest the possibility of a slight degree of offense specialization by ethnicity.

Table 10.2
Self-Reported Delinquency (SRD) by Gender, Controlling for Gang Membership[a]

	Nongang		Gang		Ratio of Female Gang to Male Nongang
	Male	Female	Male	Female	
Property[b,c]	.79	.47	3.15	1.99	2.5:1
Person[b,c]	.80	.50	2.76	1.87	2.34:1
Drug Sale[b,c]	.38	.15	3.27	1.99	5.24:1
Drug Use[b]	1.08	.93	4.03	3.49	3.23:
N =	2,412	2,793	380	239	

[a] The SRD scores reflect the average number of offenses for respondents in each of these categories. To control for extreme scores, all items were truncated at 12. All composite scores were also truncated at 12.

[b] Differences between male and female nongang members were statistically significant at $p < .001$. Separate-variance t-tests were used.

[c] Differences between male and female gang members were statistically significant at $p < .001$. Separate-variance t-tests were used.

Table 10.3
Self-Reported Delinquency (SRD) by Ethnicity, Controlling for Gang Membership[a]

	White	African-American	Hispanic	Asian	Other
Nongang					
Property	.67	.55	.61	.57	.68
Person[b,c,d,e,g,h,i]	.59	.86	.53	.35	.70
Drug sale[c,e,g,i]	.24	.29	.26	.03	.36
Drug use[b,c,d,e,f,g,i]	1.15	.74	1.10	.48	1.22
N =	2,187	1,339	924	317	389
Gang					
Property[h]	3.07	2.47	2.21	3.04	3.49
Person[i]	2.45	2.53	2.22	1.70	2.77
Drug sale[c,i]	2.99	2.62	2.57	1.10	3.79
Drug use[b,d,f]	4.51	2.65	4.32	3.64	4.47
N =	150	188	153	28	94
Ratio of Gang to Nongang Offending, by Ethnicity					
Property	4.58:1	4.49:1	3.62:1	5.33:1	5.13:1
Person	3.64:1	2.94:1	4.19:1	4.86:1	3.96:1
Drug sale	12.46:1	9.03:1	9.88:1	36.67:1	10.53:1
Drug use	3.92:1	3.58:1	3.93:1	7.58:1	3.66:1

[a] The SRD scores reflect the average number of offenses for respondents in each of these categories. To control for extreme scores, all items were truncated at 12. All composite scores were also truncated at 12.
The following comparisons were statistically significant at the .01 level using separate-variance t-tests.

[b]White/African American
[c]White/Asian
[d]African-American/Hispanic
[e]African-American/Asian
[f]African American/Other
[g]Hispanic/Asian
[h]Hispanic/Other
[i]Asian/Other

A different picture emerges among the gang youths. We found relatively few statistically significant differences between the self-reported delinquent acts across the ethnic subgroups. African American gang members reported lower levels of drug use than the other groups; the Asian gang members indicated less involvement in drug trafficking than white and "other" adolescents. Overall, however, the similarities between the different groups are quite remarkable, especially in light of the ethnic differences found among nongang youths.

Table 10.3 makes clear that the gang members are significantly more delinquent than their nongang peers. Within each ethnic group, the gang youths report three to 36 times more delinquency than the nongang youths. The smallest ratio of gang to nongang activity is crimes against persons among the African-American youths. The greatest difference (36.67:1) is found between Asian gang members and nongang members with regard to drug sales.

Summary

We posed four research questions at the beginning of this paper, and attempted to address each one. First, what percentage of gang members are female? With our finding that 38 percent of gang members in our sample are female, this study contributes to the growing body of research reporting greater rates of female participation in gangs than was previously acknowledged (e.g., Bjerregaard and Smith 1993; Cohen et al. 1995; Esbensen and Huizinga 1993; Thornberry et al. 1993). Is this involvement of females in gangs a new phenomenon, or have females been systematically excluded from gang research? Although we will probably never know the answer, we contend that much of the discrepancy in estimates of female gang participation is attributable to two related methodological issues: the data-collection method and the age of the sample.

Field research, as Campbell (1991) suggests, has tended to be conducted by male researchers on male subjects; thus it has failed to identify female participants except through the eyes of male gang members. This has posed problems not only in identifying gang girls but also in describing girls' role in gangs. Older adolescents and young adults frequently serve as objects of field studies. Hagedorn (1988), for example, studied the "top dogs" in the formation of Milwaukee gangs. Campbell (1991) reports on case studies of three gang "girls," one of whom did not join the gang until her late twenties. Vigil's (1988) gang boys were 16 to 23 years old. These older samples fail to identify gang girls captured in general surveys of younger samples because the girls "mature out" of gangs earlier than boys (e.g., Harris 1994; Moore and Hagedorn 1996). Decker and Van Winkle (1996) include a much wider age range in their St. Louis study of gang members (from 13 to 29), with a mean of 16.9. Their snowball approach, however, produced only seven female gang members, compared with 92 males. Also, these gang girls "were often recruited in groups of two or through their boyfriends" (Decker and Van Winkle 1996:57). Field studies, through a combination of relying on older respondents and reliance on snowball sampling techniques, have systematically excluded girls from field studies.

The current study introduces its own limitations. The eighth-grade sample may exclude some high-risk students—that is, truants and expelled students—whose absence biases the estimates of gang membership provided in our analyses. In addition, in view of some evidence that girls exit gangs at an earlier age than boys, this young sample may over-represent the actual distribution of girls in gangs. Our purpose here is not to claim that one method or one estimate is better than the other, but to clarify the great disparity in estimates of female participation in gangs. In this spirit, we encourage future researchers to include not only multiple methods but also diverse age groups, and to consider the possibility that gangs are not the exclusive domain of young males.

Our second research question concerned the relative delinquency levels of girls and boys in the gang. Our findings do not support the notion that gang girls are mere sex objects with no involvement in the violent acts that the gang boys commit. The gang girls commit the same variety of offenses as the boys, but at a slightly lower frequency. Further, the gang girls are two to five times more delinquent than the nongang boys. These findings are consistent with recent longitudinal analyses from the Denver Youth Survey (Huizinga 1997) and Miller's (1997) fieldwork in Columbus, Ohio. It is time for a conscientious inclusion of females in the study of gangs not only for academic reasons, but also for identifying and designing gang prevention programs that include girls in the target population.

Analyses assessing the ethnic composition of gangs confirmed the stereotype that gang members are disproportionately members of ethnic and racial minorities. Although our findings are consistent with prior research, white involvement in gangs in this sample is greater (25 percent of gang members) than has generally been reported. One problem is that much of the research conducted during the past 30 years simply has been unable to address the race/ethnicity issue. Field studies are often unsuccessful in identifying white gang members or, by design, are limited to studying specific racial or ethnic groups. Decker and Van Winkle's (1996) St. Louis study, in which they found only four white gang members, is representative of field studies that fail to "recruit" white gang members. The authors state: "The racial composition of our sample merits some comment. We are aware of white gangs in the city of St. Louis that have been in existence for several years. However, we were not able to gain access to members of these gangs through our street contacts" (Decker and Van Winkle 1996:57). They add that the same limitation applied to their identification of Asian gang youths in the city.

Exclusion of white youths from gang research is not limited to field research. Surveys also tend to over sample minority populations (e.g., Esbensen and Huizinga 1993; Fagan 1989; Thornberry et al. 1993). In their study of gang affiliation in "high-risk" Denver neighborhoods, for example, Esbensen and Huizinga (1993) had a sample containing 90 percent minority youths, a disproportionate representation. This kind of sample bias does not permit a realistic assessment of the racial composition of gangs. Our research identifies a need for more surveys of the general adolescent population to clarify the extent of gang activity among different racial and ethnic groups.

The fourth research question raised the issue of differential involvement in delinquent activity by ethnicity. Although we found ethnic differences in rates of offending among nongang members, gang membership seems to be an equal opportunity promoter of delinquent behavior. All gang members, regardless of ethnicity, reported considerably higher levels of delinquency than their nongang ethnic counterparts.

By answering these four questions, we believe we have accomplished one final, critical goal: We have identified several unintentional biases inherent in most of the current gang research strategies. These biases have the potential to overestimate the male and minority composition of gangs while concurrently underestimating or ignoring female and white involvement. Other methods, however, may lead to overestimation of females' involvement in gangs and illegal activity. We believe that to contextualize the American gang problem as completely as possible, we must incorporate results from these methodologies and diverse samples. We hope that our analyses of data from this sample of eighth-grade students attending 42 public schools in 11 very different settings has contributed to an understanding of American youth gangs at the end of the twentieth century.

Appendix: Self-Reported Delinquency Scales and Items

Property Offenses: Stole or tried to steal something worth less than $50; stole or tried to steal something worth more than $50; went into or tried to go into a building to steal something; stole or tried to steal a motor vehicle.

Person Offenses: Hit someone with the idea of hurting them; attacked someone with a weapon; used a weapon or force to get money or things from people; shot at someone because you were told to by someone else.

Drug Sales: Sold marijuana; sold other illegal drugs such as heroin, cocaine, crack, or LSD.

Drug Use: Used tobacco products; used alcohol; used marijuana; paint, glue, or other things you inhale to get high; used other illegal drugs.

Notes

1. An earlier version of this paper was presented at the 1995 annual meetings of the Academy of Criminal Justice Sciences, Las Vegas. This research is supported under Award 94-IJ-CX-0058 from the National Institute of Justice, Office of Justice Programs, U.S. Department of Justice. Points of view in this document are those of the authors and do not necessarily represent the official position of the U.S. Department of Justice. We would like to thank our colleagues Fran Bernat, Libby Deschenes, Wayne Osgood, Chris Sellers, Ron Taylor, and Ron Vogel for their contributions to this research enterprise. We also acknowledge the excellent work of our research assistants, who were responsible for much of the data collection. Larry Mays and the anonymous reviewers provided valuable comments.
2. Throughout this paper we consciously use the term girls rather than young women in support of young women's movement to reclaim their power as girls, absent the negative connotations of the past. In her recent address to the Academy of Criminal Justice Sciences, Christine Alder (1997) introduced us to this new perspective.
3. In another paper, Esbensen and Osgood (1997) examined program effects, and included preexisting differences between the G.R.E.A.T. program students and the comparison group. They found no systematic demographic differences between the two groups.
4. Officers interested in becoming certified G.R.E.A.T. instructors apply for training through the G.R.E.A.T. office at the Bureau of

Alcohol, Tobacco, and Firearms headquarters. Currently there is a waiting list, but in the early years officers were trained within a few months of their initial inquiry. Our selection of sites was influenced by the number of officers who had been trained at each site. This site selection was not dictated either by the funding agency or by others involved in the G.R.E.A.T. program.

5. Because the program originated in Phoenix, cities in Arizona and New Mexico were overrepresented in the early stages of the G.R.E.A.T. program. Thus cities such as Albuquerque, Tucson, Scottsdale, and other smaller southwestern cities were excluded from the eligible pool of potential sites. At most sites it was possible to identify schools in which the G.R.E.A.T. program had been administered to some but not all of the students as seventh-grade pupils. In Will County and Milwaukee, however, it was necessary to select entire schools as the treatment and control groups because G.R.E.A.T. instruction had been delivered to or withheld from all seventh-grade pupils in those schools.

6. We wish to acknowledge the following research assistants for their contribution to the data-collection process: Karen Arboit and Lesley Harris from California State University at Long Beach; Danette Sandoval Monnet and Dana Lynskey from New Mexico State University; Lesley Brandt, Jennifer West, and Annette Miller from the University of Nebraska at Omaha; and Leanne Jacobsen from Temple University.

7. Five weeks of intensive efforts to obtain active parental consent in Torrance produced an overall return rate of 90 percent (72 percent consents and 18 percent refusals). In spite of repeated mailings, telephone calls, and incentives, 10 percent of the parents failed to return the consent form. Ninety percent of students with parental permission completed the questionnaires. (For a discussion of active parental consent procedures and their effect on response rates, see Esbensen et al. 1996.)

8. The skewness of self-report frequency data presents analytic problems. Various approaches can be used in attempts to remedy this problem, including transforming the data with the natural log, truncating at the 90th percentile (Nagin and Smith 1990), or truncating the high-frequency responses according to some conceptual reasoning. We chose to truncate items at 12 on the premise that monthly commission of most of these acts constitutes high-frequency offending. Thus we can examine these high-frequency offenders without sacrificing the detail of open-ended self-report techniques.

9. For further discussion of this definitional issue, see Decker and Kempf-Leonard (1991), Maxson and Klein (1990), or Winfree et al. (1992). We agree with Klein (1995) that the illegal activities of gangs are a matter of research and policy interest. For this reason we restrict our definition of gangs to include only youths who reported that their gangs are involved in illegal activities.

References

Alder, C. 1997. "Passionate and Willful Young Women: Confronting Practices." Presented at the annual meetings of the Academy of Criminal Justice Sciences, Louisville.

Asbury, H. 1927. *The Gangs of New York*. New York: Capricorn.

Bjerregaard, B. and C. Smith. 1993. "Gender Differences in Gang Participation, Delinquency, and Substance Use." *Journal of Quantitative Criminology* 4:329–55.

Bursik, R. J., Jr. and H. G. Grasmick. 1995. "The Collection of Data for Gang Research." Pp. 154–57 in *The Modern Gang Reader*, edited by M. W. Klein, C. L. Maxson, and J. Miller. Los Angeles: Roxbury.

Campbell, A. 1991. *The Girls in the Gang*. 2nd ed. Cambridge, MA: Basil Blackwell.

Chesney-Lind, M. and R. G. Shelden. 1992. *Girls: Delinquency and Juvenile Justice*. Pacific Grove, CA: Brooks/Cole.

Chesney-Lind, M., R. G. Shelden, and K. A. Joe. 1996. "Girls, Delinquency, and Gang Membership." Pp. 185–204 in *Gangs in America*, 2nd ed., edited by C. R. Huff. Thousand Oaks, CA: Sage.

Cloward, R. and L. E. Ohlin. 1960. *Delinquency and Opportunity*. New York: Free Press.

Cohen, A. 1955. *Delinquent Boys: The Culture of the Gang*. Glencoe, IL: Free Press.

Cohen, M. I., K. Williams, A. M. Bekelman, and S. Crosse. 1995. "Evaluation of the National Youth Gang Drug Prevention Program." Pp. 266–75 in *The Modern Gang Reader*, edited by M. W. Klein, C. L. Maxson, and J. Miller. Los Angeles, CA: Roxbury.

Covey, H. C., S. Menard, and R. Franzese. 1997. *Juvenile Gangs*. 2nd ed. Springfield, IL: Thomas.

Curry, G. D., R. A. Ball, and S. H. Decker. 1996. *Estimating the National Scope of Gang Crime from*

Law Enforcement Data. Washington, DC: U.S. Department of Justice.

Curry, G. D., R. A. Ball, and R. J. Fox. 1994. *Gang Crime and Law Enforcement Record Keeping*. Washington, DC: U.S. Department of Justice.

Curry, G. D. and I. A. Spergel. 1992. "Gang Involvement and Delinquency among Hispanic and African-American Adolescent Males." *Journal of Research in Crime and Delinquency* 29:273–91.

Decker, S. H. and K. Kempf-Leonard. 1991. "Constructing Gangs: The Social Definition of Youth Activities." *Criminal Justice Police Review* 5: 271–91.

Decker, S. H. and B. Van Winkle. 1996. *Life in the Gang: Family, Friends, and Violence*. New York: Cambridge University Press.

Elliott, D. S. and S. S. Ageton. 1980. "Reconciling Race and Class Differences in Estimates of Delinquency." *American Sociological Review* 45: 95–110.

Esbensen, F.-A., E. P. Deschenes, R. E. Vogel, J. West, K. Arboit, and L. Harris. 1996. "Active Parental Consent in School-Based Research: An Examination of Ethical and Methodological Issues." *Evaluation Review* 20:737-753.

Esbensen, F.-A. and D. Huizinga. 1993. "Gangs, Drugs, and Delinquency in a Survey of Urban Youth." *Criminology* 31:565–589.

Esbensen, F.-A., D. Huizinga, and A. W. Weiher. 1993. "Gang and Non-gang Youth: Differences in Explanatory Variables." *Journal of Contemporary Criminal Justice* 9:94–116.

Esbensen, F.-A. and D. W. Osgood. 1997. *National Evaluation of G.R.E.A.T.* Washington, DC: U.S. Department of Justice.

Fagan, J. 1989. "The Social Organization of Drug Use and Drug Dealing among Urban Gangs." *Criminology* 27:633–69.

Fishman, L. T. 1995. "The Vice Queens: An Ethnographic Study of Black Female Gang Behavior." Pp. 83–92 in *The Modern Gang Reader*, edited by M. W. Klein, C. L. Maxson, and J. Miller. Los Angeles: Roxbury.

Fox, J. A. 1996. *Trends in Juvenile Violence: A Report to the United States Attorney General on Current and Future Rates of Juvenile Offending*. Washington, DC: U.S. Department of Justice.

Goldstein, A. P. and B. Glick. 1994. *The Prosocial Gang: Implementing Aggression Replacement Training*. Thousand Oaks, CA: Sage.

Grasmick, H. G., C. R. Tittle, R. J. Bursik, Jr., and B. J. Arneklev. 1993. "Testing the Core Empirical Implications of Gottfredson and Hirschi's General Theory of Crime." *Journal of Research in Crime and Delinquency* 30:5–29.

Hagedorn, J. M. 1988. *People and Folks: Gangs, Crime, and the Underclass in a Rustbelt City*. Chicago: Lakeview.

——. 1994. "Homeboys, Dope Fiends, Legits, and New Jacks." *Criminology* 32:197–219.

Harris, M. C. 1988. *Cholas: Latino Girls and Gangs*. New York: AMS.

——. 1994. "Cholas, Mexican-American Girls, and Gangs." *Sex Roles* 30:289–301.

Hindelang, M. J., T. Hirschi, and J. G. Weis. 1981. *Measuring Delinquency*. Beverly Hills: Sage.

Huff, C. R. 1997. "The Criminal Behavior of Gang Members in Ohio, Colorado, and Florida." Presented at the annual meetings of the Western Society of Criminology, Honolulu.

Huizinga, D. 1991. "Assessing Violent Behavior with Self-Reports." Pp. 47–66 in *Neuropsychology of Aggression*, edited by J. Milner. Boston: Kluwer.

——. 1997. "Gangs and the Volume of Crime." Presented at the annual meetings of the Western Society of Criminology, Honolulu.

Huizinga, D. and D. S. Elliott. 1987. "Juvenile Offenders: Prevalence, Offender Incidence, and Arrest Rates by Race." *Crime and Delinquency* 33:206–23.

Huizinga, D. and F.-A. Esbensen. 1991. "Are There Changes in Female Delinquency and Are There Changes in Underlying Explanatory Factors?" Presented at the annual meetings of the American Society of Criminology, San Francisco.

Klein, M. W. 1995. *The American Street Gang: Its Nature, Prevalence, and Control*. New York: Oxford University Press.

Klein, M. W. and L. Y. Crawford. 1995. "Groups, Gangs, and Cohesiveness." Pp. 160–67 in *The Modern Gang Reader*, edited by M. W. Klein, C. L. Maxson, and J. Miller. Los Angeles: Roxbury.

Lyons, J.-M., S. Henggeller, and J. A. Hall. 1992. "The Family Relations, Peer Associations, and Criminal Activities of Caucasians and Hispanic-American Gang Members." *Journal of Child Psychology* 20:439–49.

MacLeod, J. 1987. *Ain't No Makin' It: Leveled Aspirations in a Low-Income Neighborhood*. Boulder: Westview.

Maxson, C. L. and M. W. Klein. 1990. "Street Gang Violence: Twice As Great or Half As Great?" Pp. 71–100 in *Gangs in America*, edited by C. R. Huff. Newbury Park, CA: Sage.

Miller, J. 1997. "Gender and Victimization Risk among Young Women in Gangs." Presented at the National Research and Evaluation Conference, Washington, DC.

Miller, W. B. 1958. "Lower Class Culture as a Generating Milieu for Gang Delinquency." *Journal of Social Issues* 14:5–19.

Moore, J. W. 1978. *Homeboys: Gangs, Drugs, and Prison in the Barrios of Los Angeles*. Philadelphia: Temple University Press.

——. 1991. *Going Down to the Barrio: Homeboys and Homegirls in Change*. Philadelphia: Temple University Press.

Moore, J. W. and J. M. Hagedorn. 1996. "What Happens to Girls in the Gang?" Pp. 205–19 in *Gangs in America*, 2nd ed., edited by C. R. Huff. Thousand Oaks, CA: Sage.

Nagin, D. S. and D. A. Smith. 1990. "Participation in and Frequency of Delinquent Behavior: A Test for Structural Differences." *Quantitative Criminology* 6:335–365.

National Youth Gang Center. 1997. *1995 National Gang Survey*. Tallahassee: National Youth Gang Center.

Operation Safe Streets (OSS) Street Gang Detail. 1995. "L.A. Style: A Street Gang Manual of the Los Angeles County Sheriff's Department." Pp. 34–45 in *The Modern Gang Reader*, edited by M. W. Klein, C. L. Maxson, and J. Miller. Los Angeles: Roxbury.

Puffer, J. A. 1912. *The Boy and His Gang*. Boston: Houghton Mifflin.

Rosenbaum, J. L. 1991. "The Female Gang Member: A Look at the California Problem." Unpublished manuscript, California State University at Fullerton.

Sellers, C. S., L. T. Winfree Jr., and C. T. Griffiths. 1993. "Legal Attitudes, Permissive Norm Qualities, and Substance Use: A Comparison of American Indian and Non-Indian Youth." *Journal of Drug Issues* 23:493–513.

Shaw, C. R. and H. D. McKay. 1942. *Juvenile Delinquency and Urban Areas*. Chicago: University of Chicago Press.

Short, J. F. and F. L. Strodtbeck. 1965. *Group Process and Gang Delinquency*. Chicago: University of Chicago Press.

Spergel, I. A. 1966. *Street Gang Work: Theory and Practice*. Reading, MA: Addison-Wesley.

——. 1990. "Youth Gangs: Continuity and Change." Pp. 171–275 in *Crime and Justice: An Annual Review of Research*, edited by N. Morris and M. Tonry. Chicago: University of Chicago Press.

——. 1995. *The Youth Gang Problem*. New York: Oxford University Press.

Sullivan, M. L. 1989. *Getting Paid: Youth Crime and Work in the Inner City*. Ithaca: Cornell University Press.

Swart, W. J. 1995. "Female Gang Delinquency: A Search for 'Acceptably Deviant Behavior'." Pp. 78–92 in *The Modern Gang Reader*, edited by M. W. Klein, C. L. Maxson, and J. Miller. Los Angeles: Roxbury.

Thornberry, T. P., M. D. Krohn, A. J. Lizotte, and D. Chard-Wierschem. 1993. "The Role of Juvenile Gangs in Facilitating Delinquent Behavior." *Journal of Research in Crime and Delinquency* 30:55–87.

Thrasher, F. M. 1927. *The Gang: A Study of One Thousand Three Hundred Thirteen Gangs in Chicago*. Chicago: University of Chicago Press.

Triplett, R. and L. Meyers. 1995. "Evaluating Contextual Patterns of Delinquency: Gender-Based Differences." *Justice Quarterly* 12:59–84.

U.S. Department of Justice. 1996. *Crime in the United States, 1995*. Washington, DC: U.S. Department of Justice.

Vigil, J. D. 1988. *Barrio Gangs: Street Life and Identity in Southern California*. Austin: University of Texas Press.

Wilson, W. J. 1987. *The Truly Disadvantaged: The Inner City, the Underclass, and Public Policy*. Chicago: University of Chicago Press.

Winfree, L. T., T. V. Backstrom, and G. L. Mays. 1994a. "Social Learning Theory, Self-Reported Delinquency, and Youth Gangs: A New Twist on a General Theory of Crime and Delinquency." *Youth and Society* 26:147–77.

Winfree, L. T., K. Fuller, T. Vigil, and G. L. Mays. 1992. "The Definition and Measurement of 'Gang Status': Policy Implication for Juvenile Justice." *Juvenile and Family Court Journal* 43: 29–37.

Winfree, L. T., G. L. Mays, and T. Vigil-Backstrom. 1994b. "Youth Gangs and Incarcerated Delinquents: Exploring the Ties between Gang Membership, Delinquency, and Social Learning Theory." *Justice Quarterly* 11:229–56. ✦

Chapter 11 Female Gang Involvement

G. David Curry

In this chapter, Curry provides a careful review of recent studies of young women's participation in youth gangs. Although there is compelling evidence that girls have consistently been involved in gangs, it has only been in the past two decades that researchers have been attentive to girls' membership in gangs. Consequently, according to Curry, suggestions that female gang involvement is on the rise should be viewed with caution. In addition, he notes that early gang research was sorely lacking in a feminist perspective, often depicting gang girls in quite stereotypic ways and gleaning information about girls in gangs from male gang members rather than the girls themselves. More recently, scholars have begun to study female gang involvement more systematically and to gather information by talking to gang girls. Much of this recent work has also been influenced by feminist criminology. However, debates about whether gang involvement for girls is "liberating" or a form of "social injury" has often splintered research on gang girls. In Curry's estimation, neither approach provides a sufficient explanation; instead, girls' gang involvement is "dialectical and contradictory in nature."

Abstract

A review of the research literature on female gang involvement identifies three central research themes. These are the need for a feminist perspective, changes in the magnitude of the problem, and the degree to which membership can be a form of liberation. A research agenda is proposed that offers examples of how a common set of theoretical issues might guide studies of both male and female gang behavior.

Reprinted from: G. David Curry, "Female Gang Involvement." In *Journal of Research on Crime and Delinquency*, 35:1, February, pp. 100–118.

Female participation in gang-related crime (Candamil 1992; Cosmos 1993; Felkenes and Becker 1995; Howell 1994), although apparently less prevalent than that of males (Curry et al. 1994; Miller 1975, 1982; Spergel 1990), has attracted much attention from policymakers, the public, and scholars. Here I review the literature on female gang involvement and set forth a research agenda that, I hope, will bring us a better understanding of male as well as female gang behavior.

Themes in Research on Female Gang Involvement

Three questions have emerged from the literature on female gang involvement: (1) Is a feminist perspective required for understanding female gang involvement? (2) Is female gang involvement increasing? (3) Is female gang involvement "liberating"?

Is a Feminist Perspective Required for Understanding Female Gang Involvement?

Over time, the research on female gang involvement has moved closer to a feminist approach that involves understanding female gang participation from the point of view of the females themselves rather than from an externally imposed male perspective. A feminist perspective is one "in which women's experiences and ways of knowing are brought to the fore, not suppressed" (Daly and Chesney-Lind 1988:498). Those who pursue a feminist perspective in developing theories of criminal behavior do so under the assumption that heretofore criminological theory has been "unable to explain adequately the phenomenon of women and crime." There is also the assumption that "unwittingly" focusing on "the activities, interests, and values of men, while ignoring a comparable analysis of women" results in a perspective that is inevitably "sexist" (Leonard 1982:182). One of the strongest arguments for a feminist perspective is the comparatively narrow range of behaviors attributed to females under the male-centered perspective. From the male-centered perspective, participation in gangs is by nature a male behavior, and females can be either tools to serve the interests of male gang members or the instrument of other social institutions antithetical to male participation in the gang.

Thrasher ([1927] 1963) in his study of Chicago gangs has been praised for his appreciation of the diversity and dynamic vitality of gang life (Hagedorn 1988:84) and as "an activist, a person committed to putting what he learned into practice so that the lives of others might be improved" (Monti 1993:17). For Thrasher gang involvement was male behavior. The female gang involvement he reported (p. 151) was by the young female "tomboy" and more transient than that of men, soon giving way to a concern with "hair" and "long skirts." Thrasher's reasons for why females did not participate in gangs both have counterparts in contemporary feminist theories of female delinquency. That "the social patterns for behavior of girls, powerfully backed by the great weight of tradition and custom, are contrary to the gang and its activities" (p. 161) could be interpreted as an early presentation of gender-based subcultural theory (Brownfield 1996), and his observation that "girls even in urban disorganized areas, are much more closely supervised and guarded than boys" (p. 161) is in keeping with power control theory as an explanation of lower levels of female participation in delinquency in patriarchal families (Hagan, Gillis, and Simpson 1987).

Still, when it came to the relationship of females to gangs, Thrasher produced a male-centered perspective that was to dominate the literature for decades. Thrasher described females as either the instruments of male gang members or the instrument of the social forces that undermine male participation. As instruments of the gang, females were portrayed by Thrasher ([1927] 1963) in terms of sexuality, "certain girls may be taken under its protection or in other cases may become members of the gang in their sexual capacity" (p. 155). His examples ranged from female participation in "orgiastic" or "immoral" gangs, "the stag party" usually involving female nude dancers (pp. 164–165), and the "gang shag" in which multiple gang members engaged in sex with the same female (p. 166). The specific way in which girls received "protection" by these activities was not made explicit. As external to the gang, females were identified by Thrasher as "the chief disintegrating force in the gang."

> For the gang boy, marriage usually means reincorporation into family groups and other social structures of work, play, and religion which family life as a rule brings with it. The gang which once supplanted the home, now succumbs to it. (p. 170)

Thrasher's male-centered view of gang life was reflected in other classic studies of gangs. Two examples serve to make the point. In Whyte's (1943) study of the Norton Street Gang, his vivid images of the "corner boys" can be contrasted to his description of the Aphrodite Club. For a period of time during Whyte's observation, the Nortons entered into an alliance with the Aphrodite Club. As a result of their association with this nondelinquent female group, relations within the structure of the male group experienced strains and, in some cases, permanent rearrangements. In a comparable way, Spergel (1964) in his study of male gangs and delinquent groups in New York City neighborhoods described the females who associated with his gang members in terms of utility associated with their gender or sexuality or as a threat to the integrity of the gang through marriage. Females "played various roles, contributing highly to the maintenance of the gang-fighting system. She was the carrier of tales—the magnifier, the distorter, and fabricator of derogatory remarks which served to instigate conflict among the various clubs" (pp. 88–89). More direct participation in conflict as "weapon-bearer" or "spy" were described. As in Thrasher, women still retained a role as gang destroyers. For Spergel, "Marriage and employment, in particular, compel the patterns of orientation and behavior previously developed during the stage of adolescent delinquency to change" (p. 148).

The research of Whyte and Spergel had as a central focus male participation in gang activity, but comparable views were generated by other studies with female gang involvement as the primary concern. Two studies of female involvement in gangs were Rice's (1963) "A Reporter at Large" and Hanson's (1964) *Rebels in the Streets*. Each elaborated on the theme that female gangs and their members are "marginal and parasitic" (Campbell 1991:17) to the greater social world of male gangs.

The shortsightedness of androcentric perspectives of female participation in gangs was revealed as research that transcended the male-centered stereotypes became available. The work of three male researchers is generally cited as beginning to transcend the male-centered stereotypes dating from Thrasher. Miller (1973) reported the results of his study of two female gangs, Brown (1977) recorded the gang-related activity of African American female gang members in Philadelphia, and Quicker (1983) studied Chicana involvement in gangs in southern California. One of Miller's gangs, the Molls, a gang of White Catholic girls, and the Holly Ho's, a gang of African American girls studied by Brown, were described as autonomous female gangs with their own female leadership and gang-based patterns of criminal involvement. The other gang studied by Miller, an African American gang, the Queens, and the Latina girl gangs reported by Quicker were affiliates or auxiliaries of male gangs, but sexual availability to male gang members was by no means a condition of membership as recorded by these researchers.

The argument that understanding female gang involvement required a feminist perspective was first enunciated in Campbell's (1984, 1991) *The Girls in the Gang*. Her research was presented as a set of social biographies of three women involved in three separate female gangs in New York City from 1979 into the early 1980s. Two were Puerto Rican and the other African American. All were mothers at the time of the study. Two were involved in female auxiliaries to male gangs. One had been a member of an autonomous female gang, but she had subsequently joined a mixed-sex gang with rules supporting a hegemonic gender structure of men over women. From her research, Campbell (1991:32) arrived at two major conclusions about female gang involvement in the early 1980s. (1) "It is still the male gang that paves the way for the female affiliate and opens the door into many illegitimate opportunities and into areas that serve as proving grounds." With some exceptions, females become involved in gang activity through male relatives or boyfriends. (2) Once involved in gangs, however, "a more visible solidarity or 'sisterhood' within the gang appears. A girl's status depends to a larger extent on her female peers." "Worth" within the gang was not a matter of relationships with males or "simple sexual attractiveness."

Campbell's findings were themes that had not been absent from prior work, such as that of Miller, Brown, and Quicker reviewed above. The perspectives of females, however, had never been emphasized as being so strikingly different from the perspectives of male gang members nor had the method of taking a female-based perspective been characterized as explicitly feminist in orientation. It could be argued that as an issue or theme in research on female gang involvement, the question of the need for a feminist perspective has historically only been an issue insofar as earlier generations of male scholars ignored the issue, and, as a result of that earlier neglect, a more recent generation of scholars feels compelled to emphasize it. Whether a feminist perspective has any meaning for theory and future research on female gang involvement other than as a manifestation of generational differences will be examined below. First, though, the other themes that have characterized research on female gang involvement will be reviewed.

Is Female Gang Involvement Increasing?

A second theme in research on female gang involvement has been the issue of whether female gang involvement is increasing. This should not be confused with the more interesting theoretical question of what the correlates of changes in levels of female gang participation might be. Likewise, this question cannot be disentangled from the question of whether gang-involvement rates for females are changing proportionally to rate changes for males (Klein 1995: 111). The idea that female involvement in gangs is increasing has often been taken for granted by researchers in the face of media and law enforcement declarations (Chesney-Lind 1993), but the idea's popularity has led Chesney-Lind, Shelden, and Joe (1996) to critique its validity.

Three national surveys of law enforcement agencies spanning two decades have gathered information on female gang involvement. Relying on data from six cities, Miller (1975) provided an estimate of the gang crime problem by gender that is still cited and used as a rule of thumb, when he noted, "A general estimate that gang members are 90 percent or more male probably obtains for all gang cities" (p. 23). Miller's 10 percent estimate was greater than his reported statistics for any of the cities included in his study. For example, in New York City, where half of the gangs identified by police were reported to have had female auxiliaries, only 6 percent of gang membership was estimated to be females. Computations from data gathered by a 1988 survey sponsored by the Office of Juvenile Justice and Delinquency Prevention (OJJDP) (Inter-University Consortium for Political and Social Research 1993; Spergel and Curry 1993) produced an estimate of 4,803 female gang members reported for 34 jurisdictions. This was 3.98 percent of all gang members reported for these jurisdictions. The 1992 National Institute of Justice survey (Curry et al. 1994) of law enforcement agencies requested available information on female gang members from agencies in the nation's 79 largest cities and smaller cities that had been included in the 1988 OJJDP survey. For 61 law enforcement jurisdictions reporting statistics for female gang members, a total of 9,092 female gang members was reported. As a percentage of the total number of gang members reported to the study for the nation, this came to only 3.65 percent. If, in an effort to control for law enforcement policies that officially excluded female gang members, gang members are only counted from cities reporting some number of both male and female gang members, the percentage increased to only 5.7 percent, still well below Miller's 10 percent estimate.

Another statistic that is used as a measure of increased female gang involvement is greater reported numbers of autonomous female gangs. Miller (1975:23) classified female gangs into three types: (1) female auxiliary gangs affiliated with male gangs, (2) mixed-sex gangs with both male and female members, and (3) independent or autonomous female gangs. His results indicated that by far the most common of these was the female auxiliary. Without doubt, the rarest of gangs involving females were independent, autonomous female gangs. Miller found only one in 1975. As he extended his study, Miller (1982:74) reported six autonomous female gangs in the Bronx and Queens, but few more in other locations. The 1988 OJJDP compiled reports of the existence of 22 "independent" female gangs. The 1992 National Institute of Justice national survey (Curry et al.1994) received reports of 99 independent female gangs spread over 35 law enforcement jurisdictions in 1991. There are, however, several problems with treating these survey results from law enforcement agencies as indicative of increasing female gang involvement.

First, the data from national surveys were not derived by using comparable methodology. Miller used official data. The OJJDP survey used estimates. The National Institute of Justice survey returned to official records statistics only. Each study emphasized differences in definitions of what constituted a gang or a gang-related crime across jurisdictions and time. Only 23 of the 34 law enforcement agencies offering 1987 percentage estimates to the 1988 OJJDP survey provided official statistics on the number of female gang members in their jurisdictions to the 1992 NIJ survey. The increase for these 23 jurisdictions, over a four-year period, was from an estimated 4,803 female gang members in 1987 to a tabulation of 4,971 female gang members in 1991. Given the time lapse, the increase was not a particularly radical one. The apparent increases in the number of "autonomous" female gangs is also subject to skepticism. Klein (1995:66) has questioned the ability of police or researchers to distinguish with any accuracy differences between Miller's typology of female gangs by gender mixture. Given the absence of uniform definitions and limited law enforcement ability to get accurate internal information on gangs, it would be unwise to place too much emphasis on the increased numbers of autonomous female gangs reported by studies of local law enforcement data. A related point is that these observed increases in statistics on female gang involvement occur within a context of even greater increases in similar statistics on male gang members. Within the context of these perceived increases in male gang participation, it might even be possible to argue that female gang participation as a proportion of male gang membership is declining.

It has also been argued that law enforcement agencies and researchers who have relied on law enforcement data have greatly underestimated the number of females in gangs. In a longitudinal survey of Denver respondents, Esbensen and Huizinga (1993) found that about 25 percent of youths self-reporting gang membership were females. This finding led Esbensen and Huizinga to suggest that the participation of females in gangs may be greatly underestimated. From her fieldwork with gangs, Moore (1991) estimated that females accounted for one third of all gang members. The difference between these survey estimates and the analyses of official records may be a methodological one. Not all delinquency is detected and not all gang members are identified by law enforcement. Given the lower levels of offending by females in comparison to males, even among gang members (addressed below), it may be that female gang members are less likely than are males to be identified as such by law enforcement agencies. Still, Curry et al. (1994:8) noted that "in a number of cities females as a matter of policy, were never classified as gang members" (p.8). In an argument linked to the first theme about the need for a feminist perspective, Chesney-Lind et al. (1996:194) has cautioned that given the "gendered habits" of many gang researchers, gang involvement by females could easily have been undercounted in the past.

Is Female Gang Involvement 'Liberating'?

The third theme that has arisen from the research on female gang involvement concerns the impact of female gang involvement on the young women participating. Is female gang involvement becoming more independent and autonomous of males? Is it in some way liberating for the females involved? Of the three themes in female gang involvement identified here, this is the only one around which a debate in the literature has arisen. From the research literature that has explicitly focused on the role of females in gangs, two divergent hypotheses have emerged. Chesney-Lind (1993) has characterized the first position as the "liberation hypothesis." The second is here labeled the "social injury hypothesis."

Campbell's (1991) conclusion that there exists among female gang members "a more visible solidarity and 'sisterhood' " (p. 31) is reached through her emphasis on how much this female independence and solidarity are reached through the diminished importance of their relationships with males. Harris (1988), who conducted in-depth structured interviews with 21 Chicana girls aged 13 to 18 who were involved in gangs in southern California, found that female members governed their own cliques and gained status through their own behavior within their cliques (pp. 125–126, 130). It is important to note that Campbell in her account of Sun-Africa and the Five Percent Nation detailed the paternalistic and sexist structure of that particular gang, and she concluded her book by emphasizing the limits of the liberation that was to be obtained through gang involvement. Harris, likewise, observed that the independence of the Chicana gang members she studied was achieved through continued resistance to recurring male gang member efforts to control and exploit them. For other research, however, the liberation hypothesis is presented with less qualification.

The two most extreme statements of the liberation theme are found in separate accounts of female gang member involvement in drug sales. Lauderback, Hansen, and Waldorf (1992) studied the Potrero Hill Posse, "a strictly independent group of young African-American women" (p. 57). Ten members of the posse were interviewed as part of a larger study of 65 gang-involved females. The evolution of the Posse paralleled Campbell's two propositions. The five posse founders learned drug selling from their boyfriends during the proliferation of crack sales in San Francisco in the late 1980s. Reportedly, the posse founders broke off on their own because they perceived the distribution of drug profits in the operation they were involved in to be unfair. At the time of the study, the Potrero Hill Posse included 22 to 23 members. Initiation into membership required having grown up in the community and proof of criminal skill through shoplifting or crack-selling ability. The major profit-making activity of the gang was a systematic and well-organized crack cocaine dealing operation.

A similar image of female involvement in gangs and drug sales was offered by Taylor (1993) from his series of case studies of female gang members in Detroit. From his analysis of gang types and infrastructure based on "structure, function, and motivation," he concluded, "Women are participating in gangs in crime as never before in urban America. And, this is not exclusive to Detroit" (p. 10). For Taylor, "A new attitude of female criminal independence is emerging. The male-female gang relationship is also being altered" (p. 23). Crucial to this change had been the involvement of female gang members in the drug trade. According to Taylor, "The dope business has empowered young and old, female and male, in many major cities" (p.9).

The "social injury hypothesis" holds that any benefit in personal liberation that girls may gain from gang involvement is outweighed by the social costs of such affiliation. The strongest proponent of the social injury hypothesis has been Moore (1991). Moore grounded her position in her interviews with a random sample of 156 male and female gang members from a population of members from two barrio gangs in two Los Angeles Mexican American communities. To some extent, Moore's results were in line with those of Campbell and Harris, with females having some level of autonomy within their cliques, but Moore based her conclusions about the greater impact in terms of social injury on the cumulative influence of gang involvement as female members made the transition into adulthood and the perspectives of male gang members toward female members.

Moore (1991) concluded that the damage that gang involvement did to the immediate and long-term social future of gang girls far surpassed that experienced by males in the same context. The stigma associated with gang involvement was particularly injurious to the social reputations of Chicana females. Few managed to escape drug addiction or gang life, and most of those required the assistance of marriage to a "reasonably square man with a reasonably stable job" (p. 129). Long-term harm on children was also a concern. While a majority of the male and female gang members studied by Moore ultimately had children (82 percent of the men and 94 percent of the women), the women (85 percent) were significantly more likely than the men (43 percent) to rear their children (p. 113). The women (22 percent) were more likely to report that their children had joined gangs than the men (only five percent) (p. 114).

Moore chastised Campbell for suggesting "that girl gangs have outgrown their sexist image" (p. 55). Moore herself found sexist attitudes prevalent among a majority of the male gang members and many of the female gang members whom she interviewed. Male gang members displayed one or more of three attitudes toward female gang members (p.54). (1) Females were not considered worthy of gang membership. (2) Males should always be dominant over females in gangs. (3) Females were regarded as sexual objects for male "gang warriors." Moore even recorded several instances in which gang females supported or assisted in the rape of other female members. Moore's emphasis on social injury has received support from other researchers. In her study of female gang members in Ohio, Miller (1996) described sexist attitudes among female gang members and incidents of sexual exploitation in mixed-sex gangs. From their study of female gang members in Hawaii, Joe and Chesney-Lind (1995) explicitly rejected the liberation hypothesis. For them, gang involvement was not an act of rebellion but an attempt of "young women to cope with a bleak and harsh present as well as a dismal future" (p. 428).

Although the disagreement between the supporters of the liberation hypothesis and the social injury hypothesis has been spirited, there is evidence for both views, and, with some reservations, there are essential elements of each from which an understanding of female, and male, gang involvement can be enhanced. The option of gang involvement for at-risk females is indeed one that may offer an opportunity for some level of "solidarity" and even limited individual liberation, while, at the same time, increasing risk of exposure to violence, loss of legitimate opportunities, and victimization by male and female gang members. From a dialectical perspective, there is really no theoretical problem in the same social activity being simultaneously rewarding and destructive. The same thing can be said about a wife in a paternalistic family structure, the worker in a capitalist economy, or the volunteer to military service (Foucault 1979). Similarly for male gang members, it may be possible that the "defiant individualist" (Sanchez Jankowski 1991) can simultaneously be the individual alienated from the community with no employment future (Hagedorn 1988).

The dialectical and contradictory nature of female gang involvement can be found even in some research supporting the liberation hypothesis. Despite the observation of Lauderback et al. (1992) that the Potrero Hill Posse was similar in nature to a family, the gang's practice was far from being a generalized "sisterhood." The ties that bound the posse together were business oriented and instrumental. A social by-product of the crack operation as administered by the posse was the recurring exploitation of nonposse females as "toss-ups," women used for sex in crack houses, and as heads of household in residences used as temporary crack houses.

The dialectical interplay of liberation and social injury was especially clear in Fishman's ([1988] 1995) observations of a Chicago female gang called the Vice Queens from her perspective as a fieldworker for the Short and Strodtbeck project from 1960 to 1963. The Vice Queens were the African American female auxiliary to the male Vice Kings. In congruence with the more male-centered views of female gang participation, the Vice Queens were described in sexually instrumental roles to their male counterparts that included being available for sex—and even bearing children and working as prostitutes. They were pictured as instigating conflicts between the Vice Kings and other male gangs and serving as weapons bearers and lookouts when conflicts were most intense. At the same time, a number of Vice Queen activities were reported that do not fit stereotypic restrictions. They engaged in property crime activities independently of the Vice Kings and participated in fighting with members of other female gangs that were independent of male conflicts. Despite, or perhaps as a result of, their sexual exploitation by the Vice Kings, a number of the Vice Queens expressed a preference for homosexual relationships with each other. Although the debate over liberation versus social injury has probably been the most spirited in the literature on female gang involvement to date, its extension, if not resolution, is discussed below as one amenable to measurement and empirical testing.

An Agenda for Research on Female Gang Involvement

An agenda for research on female gang involvement must overcome shortcomings of past research while building on the themes that have been central to that research. It should also be linked to major themes in the larger research literature on male gangs. Space prevents more than providing the simplest outline for such an agenda here.

Building on Prior Research

When reviews of the literature on gangs (female or male) are organized chronologically, the cyclical nature of the history of gang research is quite apparent. Nothing has characterized research on gangs more than a tendency to emphasize the degree to which each piece of research is a new "discovery" that more or less invalidates earlier efforts. Thanks to a contemporary revival of research on gangs, more is known about gangs and there is more ongoing research on gangs than ever before. Where links with earlier gang research have been made, there has been a preference to reach back to Thrasher, sometimes without a very careful reading of the original. The problems of evoking Thrasher in the case of studying female gang involvement have been noted above by emphasizing the narrowness associated with his male-centered approach.

It is important that the central themes of prior research neither be dismissed out of hand nor accepted without reservation. In particular, popular media presentations have taken for granted propositions such as increased female gang involvement, the growing violence of female gang members, and that gangs play a major role in the organized distribution of drugs. Scrutiny of the available research literature reveals the intellectual riskiness of generalizing from such reports.

Linking Research to Theory

As noted above, gang research on males and females has been characterized by a tendency to "invent" rather than expand or integrate existing theories of gang involvement and delinquency. In too much gang research, the facts have just been too exciting to bend to the mundane demands of more rigorous theory. An effective research agenda on female, or male, gang involvement must make the transition from simply describing gang behavior to developing and testing theories about gang behavior. In so doing, it must also move toward integrating research on gangs into the mainstream of research on delinquency and crime in general. Three theoretical themes strike me as being particularly worth pursuing.

Gangs and the theory of the urban underclass. The growth of the urban underclass (Wilson 1987) has been linked to the emergence of gang problems in Milwaukee (Hagedorn 1988) and St. Louis (Decker and Van Winkle 1996), the entrenchment of gangs in Los Angeles (Moore 1988, 1989), and the proliferation of gangs nationwide (Klein 1995:194–95). Wilson has postulated that unlike socially disadvantaged minority populations of the past, contemporary inner-city minority residents are irrevocably segregated and isolated from existing avenues of economic opportunity. The value of Wilson's theory to understanding gangs was enhanced by Bursik and Grasmick's (1993) reconstruction of Shaw and McKay's social disorganization theory. By integrating Hunter's levels of social control into social disorganization theory, Bursik and Grasmick were able to incorporate Wilson's conceptualization of the urban underclass into a community-level theory of gang problems.

A research effort that indicated the importance of macro-level social factors such as those posited by Wilson on female gang involvement was conducted by Bowker and Klein (1983). Bowker and Klein studied gang and nongang girls inside and outside the juvenile justice system. Survey results from 78 girls identified within the juvenile justice system were supplemented with official records information. Survey data were also collected from a comparison group of girls residing in the neighborhoods in which gangs were active. This second population had no record of contact with the juvenile justice system. In all, the study compared 122 gang girls and 100 nongang girls. The survey data included the results of several batteries of psychological tests. Because they found no significant differences in keeping with psychological explanations of the etiology of female gang membership, Bowker and Klein (1983) suggested that the overwhelming impact of racism, sexism, poverty and limited opportunity structures is likely to be so important in determining the gang membership and juvenile delinquency of women and girls in urban ghettos that personality variables, relations with parents, and problems associated with heterosexual behavior play a relatively minor role (pp. 750–751).

Wilson (1987:90–91) in his construction of the urban underclass theory devoted special attention to the differential impact of the social structural changes inherent in the theory on men and women. Campbell (1991:35–36) provided a good foundation for this kind of approach in her description of the way gender provided different kinds of access to the mainstream culture and economy for Puerto Rican women and men. As research efforts emerge to test the hypothetical importance of the emergence of the urban underclass in the emergence and proliferation of gang problems, it is important that this search encompass the measures of the differential impact of these social forces on males and females.

Cultural factors and gangs. The influence of cultural context was stressed by Moore in her studies of Chicano gangs in Los Angeles, and its importance has not been overlooked in other research on female gang involvement in Mexican American communities. Female participation in gangs was not the primary focus of Horowitz's (1983) study of "coming of age" in a Chicago Chicano community, but her work illustrated how interpreting gang involvement for males or females required an appreciation of the cultural context of the community setting. Horowitz observed female gangs that were both affiliated with male gangs and autonomous, but in every case, female participation emerged as a form of (largely unsuccessful) struggle against male control (p. 133). Whereas male gang involvement was pictured by Horowitz as a central component of personal identity, the role of gang involvement for females was a peripheral concern subordinate to other dilemmas facing young women.

The Chicana female gangs studied by Quicker (1983) in East Los Angeles were all affiliates of male gangs with in most cases names that were feminized versions (in Spanish) of the male gang affiliate. For the "homegirls" studied by Quicker, their role as full participants in the social life of their barrios was as important as their gang membership. The importance of cultural factors for the gang girls studied by Harris (1988) was reflected in their self-identification as *Cholas*, the female plural form of *Cholo*, a term used by Americans and more established Mexican American residents of southern California for "the poorest of the poor, marginalized immigrants" (Vigil 1990:116).

Klein (1995) has argued that a major element in the proliferation of gang problems in the United States has been the development and diffusion of a "gang culture" (p. 205). This gang culture has become integrated into a broader popular youth culture. Future research on gangs should examine ways in which such gang culture structures the relationships between, and the roles of, men and women. The research of Horowitz, Quicker, and Harris showing how gang behavior is influenced by community cultural context makes it essential that studies that focus on gender relations within gangs also be sensitive to the influences of broader cultural settings on these relationships.

Gangs and delinquency. A recurrent finding in gang research has been higher levels of delinquency associated with gang membership. Using the Denver Youth Survey, Esbensen and Huizinga (1993) found two to three times as much delinquency for gang members as nongang members. From longitudinal survey results on a representative sample of Rochester youths, Thornberry et al. (1993) also concluded that gang-involved youths were significantly more likely to report involvement in violence and other delinquency. By following youths over time, their analysis showed gang involvement to be a transitional process with delinquent activity increasing during gang involvement and declining afterward.

Differences in levels of delinquency between gang members and nongang members has held up when gender is controlled. Relying on samples of high school students and dropouts from three cities, Fagan (1990) found that both male and female gang members had higher levels of self-reported delinquent behavior than their nongang counterparts. Although male gang members exhibited higher levels of delinquent behavior than female gang members, female gang members had higher levels of delinquent behavior than nongang males. Using the Thornberry data from Rochester, Bjerregaard and Smith (1993) systematically examined gender differences in gang involvement. Increased involvement in delinquency and substance abuse were observed for both male and female gang members in comparison to nongang members, but they found surprisingly little difference in the factors that explained male and female gang involvement. The only major difference observed was that failure in school was a stronger explanatory variable for females than males.

Although research has demonstrated differences between gang members and other youths regardless of gender it has also been shown that male gang members engage in more delinquency than female gang members and especially more violent delinquency. In a series of studies that have combined analysis of official records and interviews with gang members Joe and Chesney-Lind (1995; Chesney-Lind, Shelden, and Joe 1996) found that male gang members offended more and engaged in more violence than female gang members. From the limited available law enforcement data on gang offenses by gender Curry et al. (1994) concluded that female gang offenders were proportionally more likely to have been involved in property offenses and less likely to have been involved in violent offenses. Both Klein (1995) and Spergel (1995) have emphasized these differences in levels of violence by gang member gender by drawing attention to the extremely small portions of gang-related homicides that have been attributed to female offenders respectively in Los Angeles and Chicago in recent years. For Spergel (1995) "The youth gang problem in its violent character is essentially a male problem" (p. 58).

Two papers presented at the 1996 annual meetings of the American Society of Criminology contained empirical evidence linking gender-specific attitudes toward violence and differences in violent behavior. Chesney-Lind et al. (1996) using data from their Hawaii research argued that females regardless of gang membership status are more likely than are males to consider specific behaviors as violent in nature. Deschenes et al. (1996) analyzed survey data on 5,935 eighth-grade students from 42 schools in 11 cities. They found significant differences between females and males in the neutralization of violence. Males were more likely than were females to accept physical violence and feel that violence was justified. Gang members regardless of gender were more likely to accept violence than were nongang members. Among gang members differences between males and females although not as pronounced were still observed. In multivariate logistic regression analysis these attitudinal differences were shown to be statistically significant predictors of levels of violent offending for the total population for males and for females.

A Gender-Conscious Perspective

Of the three themes central to female gang involvement identified in the first section of this article the recognition of the need for a feminist perspective may be most important as a prelude to developing more useful theories of criminal behavior. A review by Leonard (1982) of the major theoretical approaches to crime and delinquency including those that had been developed from studies of male gang involvement found anomie theory and subcultural theory (among others) inadequate to explain female criminality. Subsequent and comparable reviews reached the same conclusion (Chesney-Lind and Shelden 1992; Daly and Chesney-Lind 1988; Mann 1984). Campbell's (1984) conclusions from her review of the gang literature was a comparable revelation. This review of the literature reaches a similar conclusion that an androcentric perspective can result only in narrow interpretations that cannot encompass the empirical results of available research. A comparable example of improving the breadth of theory by the addition of a feminist perspective was suggested by Tittle (1995:22) for the study of rape. The feminist perspective defined rape as a crime of violence, an abstraction that moved rape into the same theoretical category as other forms of violent assault. Adding a feminist perspective to the study of gang involvement has resulted in similar changes in how concepts and propositions are developed that will make it possible to incorporate a greater range of themes into the research agenda on female gang involvement.

A feminist perspective brings its demands as well as its rewards. Daly and Chesney-Lind (1988) suggest that a feminist approach must deal with two theoretical problems: the "generalizability problem" and the "gender-ratio problem" (p. 517). The generalizability problem concerns the degree to which findings about male gang members can be applied to understanding and responding to female gang involvement. The gender-ratio problem concerns the differences between males and females in participating in delinquency and crime. In addition, much of what has been described as male gang involvement (Horowitz 1983; Moore 1991) can be described as "doing gender" (West and Zimmerman 1987). The degree to which female gang involvement reflects "doing gender" from a female perspective and what this means is one that must be part of the future research agenda.

As Short (1996) noted, "Gangs probably have always been more diverse than they have been portrayed in either our limited studies or in the media" (p. xi). For Moore (1991:136–137), stereotypes that emerge from the traditional view of the gang are important tools of those who would isolate and separate gang-involved youths from the rest of society. Picturing gang members as non-White minorities is one element of creating a "social cleavage" that separates them from White middle-class America. In the same way picturing gangs as quintessentially male through an act of cognitive purification is likewise part of the process of social cleavage. As all-male violent social entities gangs can be perceived as fundamentally different from the dual-gendered society in which they exist. Attention to gender as a variable requires "the understanding in any community or location, men and women assume different social roles" (Weiss 1993:2). The gender-based analysis demanded by a feminist perspective, with its focus on the social roles of men and women as different, complementary, and intersecting, offers an especially useful tool for understanding the gang-related activities of females by studying the behavior of both men and women in gang-related roles.

References

Bjerregaard, Beth, and Carolyn C. Smith. 1993. "Gender Differences in Gang Participation, Delinquency, and Substance Use." *Journal of Quantitative Criminology* 4:329–355.

Bowker, Lee H., and Malcolm W. Klein. 1983. "The Etiology of Female Juvenile Delinquency and Gang Membership: A Test of Psychological and Social Structural Explanations." *Adolescence* 18:739–751.

Brown, Waln K. 1977. "Black Female Gang Members in Philadelphia." *International Journal of Offender Therapy and Comparative Criminology* 21:221–228.

Brownfield, David. 1996. "Subcultural Theories of Crime and Delinquency." Pp. 99–123 in *Criminological Controversies: A Methodological Primer*, edited by John Hagan, A. R. Gillis, and David Brownfield. Boulder, CO: Westview.

Bursik, Robert J., and Harold G. Grasmick. 1993. *Neighborhoods and Crime: The Dimensions of Effective Community Control*. New York: Lexington Books.

Campbell, Anne. 1984. *The Girls in the Gang*. Cambridge, MA: Basil Blackwell.

——. 1991. *The Girls in the Gang*, 2d ed. Cambridge, MA: Basil Blackwell.

Candamil, Maria T. 1992. "Female Gangs: The Forgotten Ones." Washington D.C.: U.S. Department of Health and Human Services; Administration for Children, Youth, and Families.

Chesney-Lind, Meda. 1993. "Girls, Gangs, and Violence: Reinventing the Liberated Female Crook." *Humanity and Society* 17:321–344.

Chesney-Lind, Meda, Marilyn Brown, and Dae-Gyung Kwack. 1996. "Gender, Gangs, and Violence in a Multi-Ethnic Community." Presented at the annual meeting of the American Society of Criminology, November 21, Chicago, IL.

Chesney-Lind, Meda, and Randall G. Shelden. 1992. *Girls: Delinquency and Juvenile Justice*. Pacific Grove, CA: Brooks/Cole.

Chesney-Lind, Meda, Randall G. Shelden, and Karen A. Joe. 1996. "Girls, Delinquency, and Gang Membership." Pp. 185–204 in *Gangs in America*, 2d ed., edited by C. Ronald Huff. Thousand Oaks, CA: Sage.

Cosmos Corporation. 1993. *Forum on the Prevention of Adolescent Female Gang Involvement*. Washington, D.C.: ACE-Federal Reporters.

Curry, G. David, Richard A. Ball, and Robert J. Fox. 1994. *Gang Crime and Law Enforcement Recordkeeping*. Washington, D.C.: U.S. Department of Justice, National Institute of Justice Research in Brief.

Daly, Kathleen, and Meda Chesney-Lind. 1988. "Feminism and Criminology." *Justice Quarterly* 5:497–538.

Decker, Scott H., and Barrick Van Winkle. 1996. *Life in the Gang: Family, Friends, and Violence*. New York: Cambridge University Press.

Deschenes, Elizabeth, Fran Bernat Finn Esbensen, and D. Wayne Osgood. 1996. "Gangs and School Violence: Gender Differences in Perceptions and Experiences." Presented at the annual meeting of the American Society of Criminology, November 20, Chicago, IL.

Esbensen, Finn-Aage, and David Huizinga. 1993. "Gangs, Drugs, and Delinquency in a Survey of Urban Youth." *Criminology* 31:565–587.

Fagan, Jeffrey. 1990. "Social Processes of Delinquency and Drug Use among Urban Gangs." Pp. 183–219 in *Gangs in America*, edited by C. Ronald Huff. Newbury Park, CA: Sage.

Felkenes, George T. and Harold K. Becker. 1995. "Female Gang Members: A Growing Issue for Policy Makers." *Journal of Gang Research* 2:1–10.

Fishman, Laura T. [1988] 1995. "The Vice Queens: An Ethnographic Study of Black Female Gang Behavior." Presented at the annual meeting of the American Society of Criminology, November, Chicago, IL. Reprinted in *The Modern Gang Reader*, pp. 83–92, edited by Malcolm W. Klein, Cheryl L. Maxson, and Jody Miller. Los Angeles: Roxbury.

Foucault, Michel. 1979. *Discipline and Punish: The Birth of the Prison*. New York: Vintage.

Hagan, John, A. R. Gillis, and John Simpson. 1987. "Class in the Household: A Power Control Theory of Gender and Delinquency." *American Journal of Sociology* 92:788–816.

Hagedorn, John M. 1988. *People and Folks: Gangs, Crime, and the Underclass in a Rustbelt City*. Chicago: Lake View.

Hanson, Kitty. 1964. *Rebels in the Street: The Story of New York's Girl Gangs*. Englewood Cliffs, NJ: Prentice Hall.

Harris, Mary G. 1988. *Cholas: Latino Girls and Gangs*. New York: AMS.

Horowitz, Ruth. 1983. *Honor and the American Dream: Culture and Identity in a Chicano Community*. New Brunswick, NJ: Rutgers University Press.

Howell, James C. 1994. "Recent Gang Research: Program and Policy Implications." *Crime and Delinquency* 40:495–515.

Inter-University Consortium for Political and Social Research. 1993. National Archive of Criminal Justice Data. Ann Arbor: University of Michigan and Bureau of Justice Statistics.

Joe, Karen and Meda Chesney-Lind. 1995. "'Just Every Mother's Angel': An Analysis of Gender and Ethnic Variations in Youth Gang Membership." *Gender and Society* 9:408–430.

Klein, Malcolm W. 1995. *The American Street Gang*. New York: Oxford University Press.

Lauderback, David, Joy Hansen, and Dan Waldorf. 1992. "'Sisters Are Doin' It for Themselves': A Black Female Gang in San Francisco." *The Gang Journal* 1:57–72.

Leonard, Eileen B. 1982. *Women, Crime, and Society: A Critique of Theoretical Criminology*. New York: Longman.

Mann, Coramae R. 1984. *Female Crime and Delinquency*. University, AL: University of Alabama Press.

Miller, Jody. 1996. "Gender and Victimization Risk among Young Women in Gangs." Presented at the annual meeting of the American Society of Criminology, November 21, Chicago, IL.

Miller, Walter B. 1973. "The Molls." *Society* 11:32–35.

——. 1975. *Violence by Youth Gangs and Youth Groups as a Crime Problem in Major American Cities*. Washington, D.C.: Government Printing Office.

——. 1982. *Crime by Youth Gangs and Groups in the United States*. Washington, D.C.: U.S. Department of Justice, Office of Juvenile Justice and Delinquency Prevention.

Monti, Daniel J. 1993. "Origins and Problems of Gang Research in the United States." Pp. 3–25 in *Gangs: The Origins and Impact of Contemporary Youth Gangs in the United States*, edited by Scott Cummings and Daniel J. Monti. Albany: State University of New York Press.

Moore, Joan W. 1988. "Introduction." Pp. 3–17 in *People and Folks: Gangs, Crime, and the Underclass in a Rustbelt City*, by John M. Hagedorn. Chicago: Lake View.

——. 1989. "Is There an Hispanic Underclass?" *Social Science Quarterly* 70:265–283.

——. 1991. *Going Down to the Barrio: Homeboys and Homegirls in Change*. Philadelphia: Temple University Press.

——. 1993. "Gangs, Drugs, and Violence." *Gangs: The Origins and Impact of Contemporary Youth Gangs in the United States*, edited by Scott Cummings and Daniel J. Monti. Albany: State University of New York Press.

Quicker, John C. 1983. *Homegirls: Characterizing Female Gangs*. San Pedro, CA: International University Press.

Rice, Robert. 1963. "A Reporter at Large: The Persian Queens." *The New Yorker* 39(35):153–189.

Sanchez Jankowski, Martin. 1991. *Islands in the Street: Gangs and American Urban Society*. Berkeley: University of California Press.

Short, James F., Jr. 1996. "Forward: Diversity and Change in U.S. Gangs." Pp. vii–xviii in *Gangs in America*, 2d ed., edited by C. Ronald Huff. Thousand Oaks, CA: Sage.

Spergel, Irving A. 1964. *Racketville, Slumtown, Haulburg*. Chicago: University of Chicago Press.

——. 1990. "Youth Gangs: Continuity and Change." Pp. 171–275 in *Crime and Justice: An Annual Review of Research*, edited by Norval Morris and Michael Tonry. Chicago: University of Chicago Press.

——. 1995. *The Youth Gang Problem*. New York: Oxford University Press.

Spergel, Irving A. and G. David Curry. 1993. "The National Youth Gang Survey: A Research and Development Process." Pp. 359–400 in *Gang Intervention Handbook*, edited by Arnold Goldstein and C. Ronald Huff. Champaign-Urbana, IL: Research Press.

Taylor, Carl S. 1993. *Girls, Gangs, Women and Drugs*. East Lansing: Michigan State University Press.

Thornberry, Terence, Marvin D. Krohn, Alan J. Lizotte, and Deborah Chard-Wierschem. 1993. "The Role of Juvenile Gangs in Facilitating Delinquent Behavior." *Journal of Research in Crime and Delinquency* 30:55–87.

Thrasher, Frederic M. [1927] 1963. *The Gang: A Study of 1,313 Gangs in Chicago*. Chicago: University of Chicago Press.

Tittle, Charles R. 1995. *Control Balance: Toward a General Theory of Deviance*. Boulder, CO: Westview.

Vigil, James Diego. 1990. "Cholos and Gangs: Culture Change and Street Youth in Los Angeles." Pp. 116–128 in *Gangs in America*, edited by C. Ronald Huff. Newbury Park, CA: Sage.

Weiss, Carolyn. 1993, November. "Gender Research of Economic Development Planning." Presented at the Regional Research Institute, West Virginia University, Morgantown.

West, Candace, and Don H. Zimmerman. 1987. "Doing Gender." *Gender & Society* 1:125–151.

Whyte, William E. 1943. *Street Corner Society*. Chicago: University of Chicago Press.

Wilson, William J. 1987. *The Truly Disadvantaged*. Chicago: University of Chicago Press. ✦

Chapter 12 Chinese Gangs and Extortion

Ko-Lin Chin

Ethnic variations in gang formation result from differences in social and economic opportunities, community structures, and cultural values. In this article, Chin describes the involvement of Chinese youth gangs in the extortion of community businesses. According to the author, Chinese gangs are closely tied to the social and economic organization of their communities. Because the communities in which they evolve tend to be prosperous, and because they draw on Chinese subcultural norms, these gangs are able to take advantage of both legitimate and illegitimate opportunities for money and power that are not available to gang members of other ethnic groups.

Before 1965, with the exception of group conflicts among the tongs[1] in the late nineteenth and early twentieth centuries (Dillon, 1962; Gong & Grant, 1930), crime rates within the Chinese communities in North America were very low (Beach, 1932; MacGill, 1938). Chinese immigrants were generally law-abiding, hardworking, and peaceful. Official statistics show that the most common offenses were victimless crimes such as prostitution, opium smoking, drunkenness, and disorderly conduct (Tracy, 1980). Offenders were primarily adults who indulged in these culturally sanctioned recreational activities as a respite from work. Among Chinese adolescents, delinquency was also uncommon (Sung, 1977).

Reprinted from: Ko-Lin Chin, "Chinese Gangs and Extortion." In C. Ronald Huff (ed.), *Gangs in America*, pp. 129–145.

In considering the tranquility of Chinese communities in the past, however, it is important to note that before 1965 there were few Chinese teenagers in the United States, a result of the Chinese Exclusion Act passed in 1882 and the National Origins Act of 1924 (Fessler, 1983; Sung, 1979). The Immigration and Naturalization Act of 1965 was a turning point in the history of Chinese immigration because it not only made China a "preferred" nation but also established priorities for admission based largely on family relationships; those already living in the United States could initiate the immigration process for their families overseas (Kwong, 1987; Takagi & Platt, 1978).

Since 1965, the increasing number of Chinese immigrating to the United States has affected the stability of the Chinese communities in unprecedented ways. Traditional groups such as the family and district associations were ill prepared to cope with the influx. Because there were few social service agencies to help the newcomers, they were left mostly on their own to resolve housing, employment, education, and health problems (R. Chin, 1977; Huang & Pilisuk, 1977).

This breakdown in support, coupled with the growth of the Chinese population in isolated and fragmented communities, brought a corresponding increase in criminal activities among the Chinese (Bresler, 1981; Posner, 1988; President's Commission on Organized Crime, 1984; Robertson, 1977). Chinese gangs sprang up in San Francisco (Emch, 1973; Loo, 1976), Los Angeles (Los Angeles County Sheriffs Department, 1984), Boston (Roache, 1988), Toronto (Allen & Thomas, 1987), Vancouver (Robinson & Joe, 1980), and New York City (Chang, 1972; K. Chin, 1986). Although the number of active Chinese gang members is relatively small (there are no more than 2,000 Chinese gang members in the whole country), their involvement in some of the nation's worst gang-related violence (e.g., Daly, 1983) and heroin trafficking (U.S. Senate, 1986) has drawn the attention of law enforcement authorities. Recently, local and federal authorities have predicted that Chinese criminal organizations will emerge as the number one organized crime problem in the 1990s, when they become a dominant force in heroin trafficking, alien smuggling, money laundering, and other racketeering activities (U.S. Department of Justice, 1985, 1988, 1989; U.S. Department of State, 1988).

Although Chinese gangs have been active in the United States for more than 20 years, most of our knowledge about them has come from police and journalists. Other than a few scholarly studies carried out 10 or 15 years ago (Loo, 1976; Miller, 1975; Robinson & Joe, 1980), there has been no recent research on Chinese gangs. Thus it is imperative to improve our understanding of a social problem that law enforcement authorities have suggested is of paramount importance.

This chapter describes the individual and group characteristics of New York City's Chinese gangs and compares them with street gangs of other ethnic groups. Additionally, the social processes and functions of extortion—the type of illegal activity routinely and systematically committed by the Chinese gangs—also are considered.

This study was based on four types of data: ethnographic interviews, field notes, official reports and documents, and newspapers and magazines. People who were familiar with Chinese gangs or who had been victimized by gang members were interviewed, including members of the tongs and street gangs, social service providers, officials of civic associations, reporters, police officers, prosecutors, federal law enforcement officials, and victims.

To supplement interview data, I spent some time in the field. Most of my observations were made in gambling dens or bars where gang members hang out. I also reviewed and analyzed official reports and documents, and examined indictment materials and sentencing memoranda related to Chinese gangs. Finally, hundreds of English- and Chinese-language newspaper and magazine articles on Chinese gangs were collected and categorized by type of criminal organization, geographical area, and type of crime.

Demographic Characteristics

Sex

Like other ethnic gangs, Chinese gangs are composed predominantly of males. Although young females do hang around with members or live in the gangs' apartments, they are not initiated into the gangs. Except for carrying guns for their boyfriends, the girls are not involved in either property or violent crime.

Age

According to a police report, members' ages range from 13 to 37 (New York City Police Department, 1983). The mean age for the 192 registered gang members is 22.7. Most members are in their late teens or early 20s. Because the report included active, inactive, suspected, and imprisoned members, the sample may overrepresent seasoned members. Those who are new members may not yet be known to the police.

Country of Origin

In the 1960s and 1970s, most gang members were young immigrants from Hong Kong. A few were American- or Taiwan-born. Of the 25 Ghost Shadows indicted in 1985, for example, 24 were born in Hong Kong. Since the late 1970s, some Chinese gangs have recruited many Vietnam-born Chinese (President's Commission on Organized Crime, 1984). In the 1980s, many young immigrants from China were being recruited. Recently, some Korean youths also were inducted into the newly established Chinese gangs. So far, Chinese gangs have not recruited anyone who is of non-Asian origin. Most gang members, with the exception of a Taiwanese gang, speak the Cantonese dialect.

Structural Characteristics

Size

Each gang has on average about 20 to 50 hard-core members, a few inactive members, and some peripheral members. When conflicts among gangs are intense, they may seek reinforcements from other cities. Law enforcement authorities estimate a total of

200 to 400 active Chinese gang members in New York City, belonging to about nine gangs.

Organization

The structures of the gangs vary. The Ghost Shadows, for example, have four or five leaders at the top, the so-called tai lou (big brothers). Most other gangs have either one or two leaders. Under the leaders are a few "lieutenants," or associate leaders, in command of the street soldiers. At the bottom of the hierarchy are the street soldiers, who guard the streets and commit most of the extortion, robbery, and street violence. They are known as the ma jai (little horses).

Leaders maintain direct contact with certain tong elders and receive payment from them or from the gambling houses in the community. The leaders are the only liaisons between the tongs and the gangs. Leaders rarely are involved in street violence, although they give the orders. Whenever a leader wants somebody harassed or assaulted, he instructs the street leaders or members to carry out the assignment. The leader may provide the hit man with guns and pay him as a reward after he fulfills the "contract." Usually, the leader monitors the action from a nearby restaurant or gang apartment.

Although the associate leaders do not have much power in the administration of the gang, they control the ordinary members. Therefore, it is not surprising that street soldiers are more loyal to their immediate bosses than to the top leaders. Street leaders usually recruit the ordinary members. Although street leaders sometimes are involved in carrying out assignments, their usual role is that of "steerer"—they bring the street soldiers to their target and identify it for them. Street leaders do not initiate plans to attack specific people.

Among ordinary members, a few tough ones are known as "shooters"; they carry out most of the gang's assaults. The primary function of the soldiers is to watch the streets, guard the gambling places, and collect protection fees.

Most gangs have their own apartments, which are occupied mainly by street soldiers and are used as headquarters and for ammunition storage. The leaders do not live in them, although they drop by occasionally.

Except for the Ghost Shadows and the Flying Dragons, the gangs do not have splinter groups in other cities. The Ghost Shadows have chapters in Boston, Chicago, Baltimore, Houston, and Toronto, and police in New York City believe that the groups are nationally—or even internationally—linked.

Recruitment and Membership

Some youths join the gangs voluntarily, while others are coerced. Before the mid-1970s, most youths were volunteers. Members treated one another as brothers, and it appeared that there was much camaraderie among them. From the mid-1970s through the early 1980s, however, many youths joined the gangs out of fear. Gangs have employed both subtle and crude methods to recruit new members. Gang members may treat a potential member to a good meal, show him their expensive cars, and provide him with the companionship of teenage girls. Impressionable adolescents may decide to join the gang to enjoy the putative benefits of membership. If potential recruits are unimpressed by what the gang offers, gang members send street soldiers to beat them up, a crude way of convincing them that their lives are more secure if they are gang members than if they are alone.

Usually, gang members recruit youths who are vulnerable—those who are not doing well in school or who have already dropped out. Young newcomers who have little or no command of English, poor academic records, and few job prospects are the most likely to find gang life attractive and exciting. Gang youths also approach adolescents who hang around video arcades, basketball courts, bars, and street corners, and those who talk and act arrogantly. Recruitment activities are carried out by both seasoned members and those who have been in the gang for only a short time.

Once a youth decides to join the gang, he goes through an initiation ceremony that is a simplified version of the Chinese secret societies' recruiting rituals. The youth takes his oaths, burns yellow paper, and drinks wine mixed with blood in front of the gang leaders and the altar or General Kwan, a heroic figure of the secret societies. The oaths taken by new recruits are, in essence, similar to the 36 oaths of the secret societies (see Bresler, 1981; K. Chin, 1990).

Dynamic Characteristics

Conformity to peer pressure is a strong characteristic of Chinese gang members. For instance, after six Ghost Shadows abducted and raped a White woman, two of the offenders initially opposed killing the victim. When the other four argued that she had to be killed, however, the two immediately consented. Nevertheless, group cohesion appears to be weak. Intragang conflicts erupt frequently, and members sometimes transfer from one gang to another. Within a Chinese gang there are usually two or more cliques, each consisting of a leader, one or more associate leaders, and several soldiers. These cliques usually distrust and dislike one another, and the tensions among them are exacerbated easily whenever illegal gains are not distributed properly. A review of the history of Chinese gangs in New York City indicates that leaders constantly are plotting to have one another killed (K. Chin, 1990). A Chinese gang leader is more likely to be killed by his associates than by a rival.

Some intragang conflicts are instigated by tong elders who are associated with a particular clique. These mentors prefer to have a divided rather than a united gang; therefore, they intervene to ensure that no particular clique gains enough power to challenge the supremacy of the tong.

Attachment to the gang is not absolute. To date, no gang member has been attacked by his peers simply because he decided to leave the gang. If a member joins a rival gang, however, he can provoke retaliation from his former associates. On the other hand, if the leaders of the two groups involved can reach agreement about the transfer of members, changing membership and allegiance can be arranged satisfactorily.

Comparison of Chinese Gangs With Other Ethnic Gangs

How different are Chinese gangs from other ethnic gangs? Some researchers report that Chinese gangs are similar to other ethnic gangs in several ways. For instance, Robinson and Joe (1980) found that the characteristics of the Chinese gangs in Vancouver were identical to those of American gangs. The gangs Robinson and Joe studied, however, were atypical in the sense that they were not related to community organizations as Chinese immigrant gangs in San Francisco and New York City are. They resembled American street-corner gangs or athletic clubs, and were similar to the American-born Chinese gangs that were active in the early 1960s, a period when Chinese gangs were not yet institutionalized by community associations.

Like Robinson and Joe, Takagi and Platt (1978) suggest that Chinese gangs—like other ethnic gangs—are involved only in petty crimes. In their view, the tongs and other adult associations, rather than the gangs, are responsible for the organized racketeering activities and violence within the Chinese communities. Takagi and Platt's findings are not supported by other data. Violence in Chinatown is, in most instances, instigated by Chinese gangs (K. Chin, 1990).

In contrast to scholars of gang delinquency, law enforcement authorities argue that Chinese gangs are unlike other ethnic street gangs. A former captain of the New York City Police Department suggests that Chinese gangs should not even be considered as "youth" gangs because of the way they are controlled and the age of the leaders:

> [Chinese gangs] are well-controlled and held accountable to the various associations in the Chinatown area. They are the soldiers of Oriental organized crime, with strong ties to cities throughout the United States. The associations have international ties in banking, real estate, and import/export businesses and are suspected of being involved in narcotics and alien smuggling. Members of the street gangs range in age from the mid-

> teens to early twenties. The street leaders are in their early twenties and thirties, with the highest leader being a mature middle-age or senior adult generally in charge of one of the associations. (New York City Police Department, 1983, p. 3)

The data collected for this study revealed that Chinese gangs have the following unique characteristics that set them apart from other ethnic gangs. First, they are closely associated with and are controlled by powerful community organization. Second, gang leaders invest their money in legitimate businesses and spend a large amount of time doing business. Third, Chinese gangs form national or international networks. Fourth, the gangs are influenced to a great extent by Chinese secret societies and the norms and values of the Triad[2] subculture. Fifth, gang members normally do not go through various stages in which they graduate from delinquent behavior to serious crime. New members often are assigned to carry out the most serious assaults. Sixth, Chinese gangs control large amounts of money, and making money is their main motive. Finally, Chinese gangs systematically victimize the businesses in their communities in ways no ordinary street gangs possibly could. In sum, their strong affiliation with powerful adult organizations, their high level of mobility, and their businesslike methods of wiping out rivals suggest that they more closely resemble adult criminal organizations than typical youth gangs that are concerned mainly with dress codes, turf, and involvement in nonutilitarian, negativistic activities (Cohen, 1955).

According to data collected for this study, Chinese gangs resemble Cloward and Ohlin's (1960) "criminal gangs." Chinese gangs develop in ethnic communities in which adult criminal groups exist and in which the adult criminals serve as mentors and role models for the gang members. They not only provide the youths with jobs but also offer them an opportunity structure in illegitimate activities. The youths can start working as street soldiers and then go on to become lieutenants, gang leaders, and (eventually) core members of the tong. Thus, a street youth can work his way up to become a respected, wealthy community leader through the structure of illegal activities provided by adult organizations, if he can survive his years as a gang member.

Nevertheless, gangs such as the Ghost Shadows and the Flying Dragons do not strictly follow the subculture pattern in Cloward and Ohlin's classification. Their long history of street violence shows that, besides securing income, the gangs fought constantly with rival gangs to establish their power to shake down the community. This use of violence to win status is consistent with Cloward and Ohlin's definition of "conflict gangs." It is hard to imagine, in any case, how criminal gangs could protect their illegal sources of income without violently subduing rival gangs to prevent them from encroaching on their territory. Although gang involvement in street violence is not condoned by the adult organizations and is not in the best interests of the gangs themselves, apparently the gangs believe that they must instill fear in rival groups as well as in the community as a whole.

What is the evidence for Cloward and Ohlin's third delinquent subculture, the retreatist? In a study of gangs in three cities, Fagan (1989) found drug use widespread among Black, Hispanic, and White gangs, regardless of the city. Moore's (1978) Los Angeles gangs and Hagedorn's (1988) Milwaukee gangs were involved heavily in drug use and dealing. Drug use among Chinese gang members, however, is rare. Moreover, although gang leaders are involved in drug trafficking, they themselves are not drug users. Tong members do not tolerate drug use in the gangs, and the gangs themselves are reluctant to recruit anyone who uses drugs. If a member begins using drugs, he is expelled from the gang.

Thus Chinese gangs have the characteristics of two of the subcultures described by Cloward and Ohlin: the criminal and the conflict subcultures. Because gang leaders are concerned primarily with the lucrative heroin trade and investment in legitimate businesses and are closely associated with certain tong leaders, they adhere more to norms and values of the criminal subculture as depicted by Cloward and Ohlin. Young members are concerned mostly with their macho image and therefore are more prone to commit violent acts and predatory crimes. These young members seem to be most congruent with Cloward and Ohlin's conflict gangs. Consequently, instead of labeling Chinese gangs as either criminal or conflict gangs, it is perhaps more important to consider the ages and ranks of the gang members and their criminal propensities.

Unlike Chinese gangs that are closely associated with the well-established adult groups, gangs formed by young Chinese immigrants from Vietnam and Taiwan have no adult group to emulate. As a result, these gangs are not as well organized as the Chinatown gangs. Without the stable income from protection and extortion operations that Chinatown gangs enjoy, and without a lucrative commercial district to claim as a territory, Vietnamese and Taiwanese gangs are forced to become involved primarily in extortion, robbery, and burglary. These gangs resemble Cloward and Ohlin's conflict gangs because they are prone to excessive use of violence, they lack supervision by adult criminal elements, and they are outside the illegitimate opportunity structure.

Protection and Extortion

The booming economy and the gambling industry in the Chinese community have provided Chinese gangs with ample criminal opportunities. Of the businesses in the community, gambling clubs are the most in need of the gangs' protection. In order to operate smoothly, the clubs must rely on gang members to protect them and their customers from the police, intruders, and the gangs themselves. To perform these jobs, a few members are dispersed in the street where the gambling club is located. Three or four members guard the entrance, while some stay inside. Members carry beepers to communicate with one another. Street leaders in the gang's nearby apartments oversee the entire operation. Nightclubs and massage parlors owned by Chinese and catering to Chinese patrons also require protection. These businesses need gang members to protect them from members of other gangs.

Gangs supplement their primary activity of guarding gambling dens and adjacent streets with another criminal activity: systematic extortion of Chinese businesses. Police estimate that at least 80 percent to 90 percent of Chinese businesses have to pay one or more gangs regularly or occasionally. Only those merchants who are close to the hierarchy of the tongs are said to be able to avoid paying the gangs.

Techniques of Extortion

According to police officers, prosecutors, and victims interviewed, the gangs primarily use two forms of extortion. One explicit technique is for gang members to demand money. Usually, gang members approach a new business during its opening ceremony and ask for li shi (lucky money). After the owner pays, they show up again later and identify themselves as gang members, explain how the racket works, and indicate that it is better to pay than to refuse. Occasionally, gang members tell the owners that they need money for food, or to help their "brothers" who have been arrested. There are also times when gang members will ask businessmen to "invest" in their business or give them a "loan."

In the second extortion technique, the demand for money is implicit. For example, the gang members will try to sell festival-related goods such as firecrackers or plants to business establishments for an inflated price. Sometimes, gang members may simply tell store owners that protection from the gang is provided to their businesses.

Gangs employ several common practices. First, a group of youths may enter a restaurant during the lunch or dinner hour, and each of them occupies a table. They tell the manager that they are waiting for friends. They sit for hours, and they act in rowdy fashion to intimidate customers. They may fight with each other, smash the dishes, or insist on remaining in the restaurant after closing hours. An experienced manager knows what the disruptive youths want.

Second, young men may go into a restaurant and order the finest dishes on the menu. When they leave, they write "Shadows" or "Dragons" on the back of the bill and do not pay. Third, some gang members may dine in a restaurant but refuse to pay the bill. While they argue with the manager about it, two or three fellow members walk in and pretend to be customers. They appear to be sympathetic to the manager and chastise the youths who refuse to pay. When the "show" is over, a gang member calls up the manager, demands protection money, and tells the manager that if similar incidents happen in the future, his gang will protect the restaurant. This technique is known as hei bai lian (black and white faces), meaning that while members play the role of the "bad guys," leaders will act as the "good guys" who ask money from the frightened victim.

The fourth method is called tai jiau tsi (carrying a sedan chair). Gang members will try to flatter a potential victim by calling him "Big Brother" and acting as though they are his loyal followers. If the businessman is unaware of the gang's tactic and associates himself with the gang, he may find out that it is too late for him to get rid of the label "Big Brother." As a "Big Brother," the victim has no other real benefits except to provide financial support to the gang.

The fifth approach is known as wo di (literally, undercover). A gang member infiltrates a business by seeking a job there. During his tenure he collects information about the owner, where he lives, when the business will accumulate the maximum amount of cash, and other matters. The gang member provides the information to his associates to draw up an extortion or robbery plan.

Most of the time, the owners negotiate about the amount of payment, but they do not bicker about whether they are going to pay. When the gang gets a victim paying, a schedule is arranged: several hundreds dollars monthly for large stores; less than a hundred dollars per week for modest businesses. The gang usually has designated collectors and keeps records of its income from extortion.

If a retail business refuses to pay, then the gang may vandalize, burglarize, rob, or set fire to the shop. The owner then usually relents and cooperates. In some instances gangs have beaten, shot at, or killed business and retail store owners. For those who do pay, the amount demanded by crime groups escalates rapidly, or another gang will show up soon with the same demand. When businesses are no longer able to meet the gangs' demands, they close down, move to another area, or report the crime to the police. Usually, most business owners try to satisfy the gangs by paying them the first few times. Only when they find out that they have to pay more than one gang or that their payments increase rapidly will they turn to law enforcement for help.

Types of Extortion

Extortion in Chinese communities may be classified into four types. The primary objective of the first and most prevalent type of extortion is monetary gain. The offenders and victim may not know each other prior to the incident, and the extortionate act may be perpetrated without the knowledge of the tong associated with the gang. Regardless of how the victim reacts to the offender's demand, he or she is unlikely to be assaulted physically by the offender in this type of extortion.

The second type is symbolic extortion, which is used as a display of power to indicate control over a territory. Monetary gain is not the major goal; gang members usually demand only free food or other small items such as cigarettes. They also may ask for heavy discounts from restaurant owners. This type of extortion occurs almost on a daily basis, and the victims are usually small store owners or peddlers who do businesses within a tightly controlled gang territory.

The third type is extortion for revenge. Offenders extort victims because of something the victims did to the gang previously, or the gang is hired by a victim's adversary to extort the victim as a form of revenge. Because monetary gain is not the motivating factor, victims are likely to be robbed, beaten up, or killed even if they do not resist the perpetrators. Extortion is used simply as a cover for vengeance.

The fourth type is instrumental extortion, which is used to intimidate the victim into backing down in certain business or personal conflicts. In this type of extortion, the victims are also vulnerable to assault and harassment. The extortionate act is, more than anything else, a message sent to the victim by his rival through the gang members. Gang members also may rob or extort money from the victims for their own sakes. Conflicts pertaining to business territories and business or gambling debts usually result in instrumental extortion activity.

Extortion and Territory

Through extortion, the gangs assert their firm control over certain territories in New York City's Chinese communities. When two or more gangs claim control of a specific area, or when the area is occupied by a weaker gang, store owners within that territory have to pay more than the gang. Currently, Canal Street and East Broadway, the rapidly expanding streets of Chinatown, have no single powerful gang that can claim exclusive sovereignty. Consequently, some of the store owners in those areas have to pay as many as five gangs simultaneously.

The same is true for the Chinese communities in Queens and Brooklyn. Although the White Tigers, The Green Dragons, and a Taiwanese gang are the three most active gangs in these newly established communities, more powerful gangs from Manhattan's Chinatown occasionally invade the area to commit extortion. When two or more gangs are active in a particular area and attempt to extort from the same victim simultaneously, street violence erupts as a result of the power struggle.

Before 1980, most extortionate activities were confined to Manhattan's Chinatown. Only occasionally would gang members venture outside Chinatown to extort money. Beginning in 1980, however, the gangs rapidly spread their extortionate activities to other parts of Manhattan, Queens, Brooklyn, Long Island, New Jersey, and Connecticut. Unlike extortionate activities within Manhattan's Chinatown, which are mostly spontaneous and cost the victims fairly small amounts of money, out-of-state extortion is well planned, and gang members tend to demand rather large amounts.

Since 1984, businessmen in Queens and Brooklyn have been extorted frequently. Unlike in Manhattan's Chinatown, gangs in these areas have no gambling establishments from which to collect protection money. As a result, the only likely source of funds is extortion or robbery of stores in the community. The lack of knowledge about the gangs by local precincts has also contributed to the rapid increase in extortion. In addition, business owners in Queens and Brooklyn are not protected by tongs or other traditional organizations as are business owners in Manhattan's Chinatown.

Conclusion

In order to understand Asian crime groups, the research and law enforcement communities need to broaden their perspectives. Concepts that are adequate for explaining Italian, Black, and Hispanic crime groups may not be adequate for examining criminal organizations of Asian origin. Because Asian people have diverse cultural heritages, we also need to identify the unique features of each Asian ethnic group.

We can isolate three unique characteristics that cause Chinese gangs to persist. First, unlike Black and Hispanic gangs (Hagedorn, 1988; Moore, 1978), Chinese gangs are not based on youth fads or illicit drug use. Instead, they are closely related to their communities' social and economic life. This relationship enables Chinese gangs to become deeply enmeshed in the legitimate and illegitimate enterprises in their communities. Opportunities for money, power, and prestige through various ventures are bestowed on Chinese gang members. No such distinctive opportunity exists for other minority gangs.

Second, unlike other ethnic gangs—which operate primarily in deteriorated, poor neighborhoods—Chinese gangs flourish in rapidly developing and economically robust Chinese communities that are tied closely to Chinese societies in Southeast Asia. Chinese gangs thus can become engaged in economically rewarding domestic and international ventures. Other ethnic gangs are hampered by both the lack of lucrative criminal opportunities in their own neighborhoods and the absence of contacts outside those neighborhoods.

Third, Chinese gang members are embedded in the legendary Triad subculture, a subculture established and maintained by members of the Chinese secret societies. By emulating Triad initiation rites and internalizing Triad norms and values, they can claim a certain legitimacy within their communities. This legitimacy enables them to instill a level of fear that no other ethnic gangs can match, because the community does not view them merely as street thugs.

Nevertheless, the nature, values, and norms of Chinese gangs could change in the future. Chinese gangs with no ties to the tongs or Triad subculture are emerging in newly established Chinese communities. We are now observing the rise of Vietnamese-Chinese and Fujianese gangs (Badey, 1988; Meskil, 1989). Both groups are not only unfamiliar with Triad norms and values, but their criminal patterns—such as street mugging and household robbery—are markedly different from those of the traditional Triad-inspired gangs.

Author's Note

I am grateful to Colleen Cosgrove for her comments. This chapter is excerpted from *Chinese Subculture and Criminality: Non-Traditional Crime Groups in America* (Contributions in Criminology and Penology, No. 29, Greenwood Press, an imprint of Greenwood Publishing Group, Inc., Westport, CT, 1990).

Notes

1. *Tong* means "hall" or "gathering place." Tongs were first established in the United States during the mid-nineteenth century by the first wave of Chinese gold field and railroad workers as self-help groups. Bloody conflicts among the tongs are known as "tong wars." The most powerful tongs in New York City are the Chih Kung, the On Leong, and the Hip Sing. Since the 1960s, in order to improve their image, the tongs have been renamed as associations. The heads of these associations are normally influential and well-respected community leaders.
2. *Triad* means a "triangle of heaven, earth, and man." Triad societies are secret societies formed by patriotic Chinese three centuries ago to fight against the oppressive and corrupt Ch'ing dynasty. When the Ch'ing government collapsed and the Republic of China was established in 1912, some of the societies began to be involved in criminal activities.

References

Allen, G., & Thomas, L. (1987). Orphans of war. *Toronto Globe and Mail,*. 1(12), 34–57.

Badley, J. R. (1988). *Dragons and tigers*. Loomis, CA: Palmer Enterprises.

Beach, W. G. (1932). *Oriental crime in California*. Stanford, CA: Stanford University Press.

Bresler, F. (1981). *The Chinese Mafia*. New York: Stein & Day.

Chang, H. (1972). Die today, die tomorrow: The rise and fall of Chinatown gangs. *Bridge Magazine*, 2, 10–15.

Chin, K. (1986). *Chinese triad societies, tongs, organized crime, and street gangs in Asia and the United States*. Unpublished doctoral dissertation, University of Pennsylvania.

——. (1990). *Chinese subculture and criminality: Non-traditional crime groups in America*. Westport, CT: Greenwood.

Chin, R. (1977). New York Chinatown today: Community in crisis. *Amerasia Journal*, 1(1), 1–32.

Cloward, R. A., & Ohlin, L. E. (1960). *Delinquency and opportunity: A theory of delinquent gangs*. New York: Free Press.

Cohen, A. K. (1955). *Delinquent boys: The culture of the gang*. Glencoe, IL: Free Press.

Daly, M. (1983, February). The war for Chinatown. *New York Magazine*, pp. 31–38.

Dillon, R. H. (1962). *The hatchet men*. New York: Coward-McCann.

Emch, T. (1973, September 9). The Chinatown murders. *San Francisco Sunday Examiner and Chronicle*.

Fagan, J. (1989). The social organization of drug use and drug dealing among urban gangs. *Criminology*, 27(4), 633–669.

Fessler, L. W. (Ed.). (1983). *Chinese in America: Stereotyped past, changing present*. New York: Vantage.

Gong, Y. E., & Grant, B. (1930). *Tong war!* New York: N. L. Brown.

Hagedorn, J. M. (1988). *People and folks: Gangs, crime, and the underclass in a rustbelt city*. Chicago: Lake View.

Huang, K., & Pilisuk, M. (1977). At the threshold of the Golden Gate: Special problems of a neglected minority. *American Journal of Orthopsychiatry*, 47, 701–713.

Kwong, P. (1987). *The new Chinatown*. New York: Hill & Wang.

Loo, C. K. (1976). *The emergence of San Francisco Chinese juvenile gangs from the 1950s to the present*. Unpublished master's thesis, San Jose State University.

Los Angeles County Sheriff's Department (1984). *Asian criminal activities survey*. Los Angeles: Author.

MacGill, H. G. (1938). The Oriental delinquent in the Vancouver juvenile court. *Sociology and Social Research*, 12, 428–438.

Meskill, P. (1989, February 5). In the eye of the storm. *New York Daily News Magazine*, pp. 10–16.

Miller, W. B. (1975). *Violence by youth gangs and youth groups as a crime problem in major American cities*. Report to the National Institute for Juvenile Justice and Delinquency Prevention.

Moore, J. W. (1978). *Homeboys: Gangs, drugs, and prison in the barrios of Los Angeles*. Philadelphia: Temple University Press.

New York City Police Department, Fifth Precinct (1983). *Gang intelligence information*. New York: Author.

Posner, G. (1988). *Warlords of crime*. New York: McGraw-Hill.

President's Commission on Organized Crime (1984). *Organized crime of Asian origin: Record of hearing III—October 23–25, 1984, New York, New York*. Washington, DC: U.S. Government Printing Office.

Roache, F. M. (1988, January). Organized crime in Boston's Chinatown. *Police Chief*, pp. 48–51.

Robertson, F. (1977). *Triangle of death*. London: Routledge & Kegan Paul.

Robinson, N., & Joe, D. (1980). Gangs in Chinatown. *McGill Journal of Education*, 15, 149–162.

Sung, B. L. (1977). *Gangs in New York's Chinatown* (Monograph No. 6). New York: City College of New York, Department of Asian Studies.

——. (1979). *Transplanted Chinese children*. New York: City College of New York, Department of Asian Studies.

Takagi, P., & Platt, T. (1978). Behind the gilded ghetto. *Crime and Social Justice*, 9, 2–25.

Tracy, C. A. (1980, Winter). Race, crime and social policy. *Crime and Social Justice*, pp. 11–25.

U.S. Department of Justice (1985). *Oriental organized crime: A report of a research project conducted by the Organized Crime Section* (Federal Bureau of Investigation, Criminal Investigative Division). Washington, DC: U.S. Government Printing Office.

——. (1988). *Report on Asian organized crime*. (Criminal Division). Washington, DC: U.S. Government Printing Office.

——. (1989). *The INS enforcement approach to Chinese crime groups* (Immigration and Naturalization Service, Investigative Division). Washington, DC: U.S. Government Printing Office.

U.S. Department of State. (1988). *Hong Kong 1997: Its impact on Chinese organized crime in the United States* (Foreign Service Institute). Washington, DC: U.S. Government Printing Office.

U.S. Senate (1986). *Emerging criminal groups* (Hearings before the Permanent Subcommittee on Investigations of the Committee on Governmental Affairs). Washington, DC: U.S. Government Printing Office. ✦

Chapter 13 The Working Gang

Felix Padilla

In this article, Padilla provides an example of one gang that is organized around the drug trade. The reader should keep in mind that the author is describing only one type of gang structure. Padilla traces the development of this gang into a group organized around making money. He highlights the roles of legislation and the lack of economic opportunities, as well as cultural solidarity. However, in the end the author concludes that the youths' employment in drug sales finds them trapped as highly exploited workers who receive few of the benefits of their labor.

"I'm going to work," Rafael said. "I have to go and make me some bread." The day is April 17,1989. I had just finished having lunch with Rafael in a local restaurant. Rafael is a member of a Puerto Rican youth gang in Chicago that I have been studying for over two years. He was responding to one of the questions I would ask him as we departed from the restaurant.

"Where can I drive you?" I asked. Of course I knew that he was headed to the usual street location where he had been dealing drugs for several years. After dropping him off, Rafael and a friend boarded a car, which appeared to have been waiting for his arrival. They drove away from the vicinity only to return thirty minutes later carrying a large amount of merchandise he would try selling on this day.

Once back in the neighborhood, he would position himself alongside other dealers to earn a day's pay. Rafael, as well as his co-workers, were employed by one of the distributors in his gang. Like other workers, they were expected to be at the job for a certain amount of time.

Rafael's work relations with the gang are a clear illustration of the business side of the organization. This is a topic which remains veiled despite a fairly extensive scientific and journalistic literature on youth gangs. In the main, most accounts about gangs and drugs tend to consider "all" teenage drug dealing as an innate activity of the gang. However, this approach overlooks many cases of teenage drug dealing that are not affiliated with or sponsored by the gang.

There are some young men who simply establish drug-dealing networks or crews comprised of several members, but these are not gangs. They lack a formal organization and leadership stratum. Members are not expected to invest time in attending formal meetings. Nor do they pay any form of dues. Members of the network or crew do not consider this group a gang. In other cases, young people who are not affiliated with the gang manage to develop street-level dealing operations on their own. There also are instances of street-level dealing being carried out by gang members working on their own. I will demonstrate below that these three cases are unlikely to materialize where street-level dealing is controlled by a gang, though individuals continue to make attempts to establish these forms of individual undertakings.

The scholarly and journalistic writers do not make a distinction between the times when drug dealing represents a gang activity and a large portion of the earnings go to the organization and the times when drug dealing is an endeavor carried out by nongang members working only for themselves. The discussion that follows will focus primarily on street-level dealers who work for the gang, and who receive a salary for their labor. It also will touch on the experiences of several youngsters who are independent dealers, but who are still part of the gang's occupational structure. They purchase their merchandise from the gang's distributors, utilize the gang-controlled turf for retailing, and are required to pay weekly organizational dues.

The following questions will be considered. What are the reasons for the gang becoming a business organization? What does the gang look like as an entrepreneurial establishment? That is, what are its defining characteristics as a business enterprise? Which cultural elements are used by youngsters for cementing and reinforcing business relations among themselves? What is the gang's occupational structure? How does the gang generate income for itself?

Information for this chapter comes from a two-year study that I have been conducting of a Puerto Rican youth gang in Chicago. I have given the gang the fictitious name of the Diamonds. The neighborhood that serves as the Diamonds' turf is located five miles northwest of the downtown area. For the last twenty years, the neighborhood has been racially and ethnically mixed, comprised of Latino (i.e., Puerto Ricans, Mexican Americans and Cubans) and white residents. Puerto Ricans, who comprise the largest group among Latinos, often refer to this neighborhood as *Suburbia* (pronounced "sooboorbia"). Living there is perceived as a measure of social prosperity and improvement. Census reports confirm this perception. In 1980, almost 40 percent of workers were employed in white-collar occupations. Only 18 percent had incomes below the poverty line and the unemployment rate was 9 percent.

The Diamonds Become a Business Gang

The history of the Diamonds dates back approximately twenty years, a relatively short period when compared to other Latino youth gangs in Chicago. At first, the Diamonds was a musical group. Members played their music on the street or in local night clubs. In 1970, a member of the musical group was mistaken for a gang member and was killed by a gunshot fired by a youngster from a rival gang. This incident sparked the reorganization of the group into a violent gang. For the next six years the Diamonds provoked fights with other groups. During most of this time, the membership of the Diamonds was quite small. The organization did not divide itself into different sections. Some members used drugs, but in the late 1970s a major change occurred in the thrust of the operations of the gang. It began taking on a businesslike character. No longer were retaliation and violent behavior the mainstays of the organization. Money making through drug dealing came to represent the gang's chief activity. Several factors account for this change.

Controlled Substance Act

One gang member named Carmelo described one change:

> I remember this older guy from the neighborhood who wanted me to sell for him. He asked several of us to be his dealers. He was offering good money, but I was afraid. I didn't know what he was about. We knew that he was doing something, because all these people used to come to his house all the time. But he never dealt with us before, and then all of sudden he wanted us to work for him. I said no to the guy.

The event that precipitated the development of the gang into a business was the 1971 passage of the Illinois Controlled Substance Act. It carried heavy criminal penalties for adult heroin and cocaine dealers. Well aware that juveniles could always beat the penalties of the newly instituted law, adults who for the most part had controlled drug distribution and dealing up to this point, began enlisting some members from the Diamonds and other gangs to work the streets of particular neighborhoods. Some youngsters like Carmelo refused the job offers. Others agreed. It did not take them or leaders of the gang long to realize that they could profit substantially by controlling neighborhood drug dealing. In other words, these youngsters began to ask the question, why can't we develop our own business?

Gang leaders began thinking about the gang as a wholesaler or investor. It would purchase the merchandise itself and hire its own members, especially the younger ones, to sell at the street level. Because the Diamonds viewed themselves as landlords of several *puntos* or blocks in the neighborhood, the only thing still missing for developing a business operation was the necessary capital with which to purchase large amounts of drugs.

They began pulling their money together. Sometimes two or three of the older members (or leaders) would "go into business." Sometimes the group was larger. At other times, leaders would request that all members make an investment of a certain amount and use this sum for purchasing the drugs with which to open the business.

High Demand for Drugs

The rise of the business side of the gang also was ignited by the increasing demand for drugs, particularly cocaine. The increasing popularity of drug use during the 1970s and the still blossoming international cocaine trade created a situation in which demand outstripped the supply. One distributor recalls the times when, as a street-level dealer, he would sell his merchandise so easily that some customers at times were left without goods. This was the time when the demand was greater than the supply.

> Author: How would you compare selling now to years ago?
>
> Carmelo: I was dealing in the streets back in 1974 or so. We did not have the organization that we have now. Now we deal through the gang. So, that was one difference.
>
> Author: What was another difference?
>
> Carmelo: I think it was the amount of reefer and coke, but mainly reefer that were out in the streets. Cocaine was expensive, but reefer, everybody wanted reefer and we were making all kinds of money.
>
> Author: How was that possible?
>
> Carmelo: Like I told you. There was a lot of stuff out there. There were times when I would get my supply in the morning and then go back in the afternoon and get some more. My supplier wanted me out there all the time because the stuff was selling real fast. There were times when I had to turn some of my customers on to somebody else, something I never wanted to do, but if I didn't have the stuff it was better that they cop from other guys. That way they would not want to stop using it. That's what kept us going. Yeah, but, man, that was good, today, well, you seen how that is.

The Nation Coalition

When the business side of gangs grew too large, it had to be better organized. That is when gang nations were built. "My understanding of what the nation means is that we are supposed to respect other groups from the same nation," replied Rafael when I asked him to explain the meaning of the concept. He added that

> gangbanging is nothing really hard to do. In my neighborhood, you have to hang out a lot. Our chief wants us there a lot so nobody else would try to take our neighborhood from us. And we have boundaries, and a little bit of the neighborhood we share with others from the same nation, but of a different affiliation. And we have our territory and if they were to come into our territory, we wouldn't start trouble by getting loud and stuff like that. We all respect each other pretty much, and it's alright.

At a more general level, Rafael was describing the moderate and congenial relations established by rival gangs in Chicago during the early 1980s. Peaceful relations were facilitated by the division of city areas into two gang nations or alliances, People and Folks. Suburbia's various gangs came under the auspices of the latter. No one is really certain of the lineage of the nation alliance, but rumors have it that the alignment was created from formerly rival gangs that were jailed together in 1981. It is also believed that jailed, former leaders of these two parent groups continue to play a significant role in dictating the policies and practices of street gangs in Chicago.

Theoretically, the nation approach was aimed at reducing significantly the degree of intergang violence that had been so common during the 1970s. As indicated by Rafael above, nation gangs were discouraged from invading each other's territories, and agitation and harassment were not to be brought upon coalition members. Indeed, the nation coalition contributed immensely to solidifying the business operation of the gang. "Respect for each other's territories" also came to mean the sharing of the drug consumer market. Each gang was permitted to operate its business from a relatively safe turf or marketplace, selling only to those customers who voluntarily frequented there. No longer was the gang involved in efforts to take over other turfs, hoping to expand its business boundaries beyond its immediate setting. The new nation approach called for the development of a particular gang's business enterprise in its own turf, improving the image and reputation of the business, and making it more attractive to consumers.

Since drug use was so widespread, the most rational business decision was to share the market. It was no longer necessary to fight over turfs. This also freed the neighborhood of gangbanging and provided a fairly safe "shopping area" for prospective customers. A neighborhood that was known for its ongoing gangbanging activities tended to scare off customers.

Members of the Diamonds are committed to mutual understanding and harmony with other gangs but have not abstained entirely from conflict and fighting. In fact, members of the Diamonds believe that the nation alliance has broken down as gangbanging among nation gangs is becoming routine. But the significant point is that when first started, the nation alliance reduced intergang violence substantially and enabled some gangs to establish their organizations as sound business enterprises.

Perceptions of Conventional Work

Youngsters' image of "traditional" jobs was perhaps the leading force that helped to transform the gang into a business venture. These young men began turning to the gang in search of employment opportunities, believing that available conventional work would not be sufficient for delivering the kinds of material goods they wished to secure. One youngster indicated,

> There are some jobs that people can still find, but who wants them? They don't pay. I want a job that can support me. I want a job that I could use my talents—speaking, communicating, selling and a definite goal that I'd be working towards as far as money is concerned.

These young people have a pessimistic appraisal of and outlook toward jobs in the regular economy. They have become increasingly convinced that those "jobs available to them" are essentially meaningless and far from representing the vehicles necessary for overcoming societal barriers to upward mobility. Although these youngsters have been socialized with the conventional cultural belief in achieving material success, they refuse to accept the conventional means to become successful. That is, they do not accept the "American achievement ideology," reflected in middle-class norms, and shown by Horowitz, Kornblum and Williams, and others to be widely supported by ethnic and racial minority parents and teenagers.[1] The ideology stresses that success in school leads to the attainment of managerial and professional jobs, which in turn pave the way for social and economic advancement. The youngsters' own school experiences and contact with the job market, as well as the futile and frustrating efforts of adults around them to achieve social advancement through menial, dead-end jobs, contradict the American achievement ideology. These young men do not believe in the power of education to serve as the "great equalizer." Nor do they perceive conventional jobs as leading to a successful, meaningful life.

These views reflect the tension between culturally defined goals and the ineffectiveness of socially legitimate means for achieving them that Robert Merton first described and subsequent gang studies confirmed.[2] They point to the absence of avenues and resources necessary for securing rewards which society purports to offer its members.

The decision by members of the Diamonds to sell drugs was informed by their assessment of available opportunities in the regular economy as well as their high level of aspirations. Drug dealing did not arise in deliberate violation of middle-class normative aspirations. The gang represents a "counter organization" geared to achieving things valued by the larger society and countering forces weighing heavily upon their lives. In effect, these youngsters transformed the gang into an income-generating business operation in an unconventional economy in order to "make it" in conventional American society.

Social and Cultural Components of the Ethnic Enterprise

Two questions need to be addressed at this point. First, what are the distinguishing characteristics of the gang that enable it to function as a business organization? Second, what social and cultural devices did the youngsters use for organizing the gang into a reliable money-making enterprise?

The gang has developed its own culture. The gang does this in the same way that the family unit teaches its young the norms, skills, values, beliefs, and traditions of the larger society—and the ways to communicate and reinforce that culture. At the heart of the gang culture is a collective ideology that serves to protect all the members. Collectivism also serves as the major determinant of the gang's efficient development as a business operation. The members' response to their shared conditions and circumstances is collective in the sense that they form a partnership.

For the young people I studied, collectivism translates into an ideology of strength. These young men share a belief that their capacity to earn a living or improve their life can only be realized through a "collective front." In the views of a youngster by the name of Coco, "we are a group, a community, a family—we have to learn to live together. If we separate, we will never have a chance. We need each other even to make sure that we have a spot for selling."

The collectivist nature of the gang can be said to be an extension of the traditional Puerto Rican family. In Puerto Rican immigrant society, as well as in other societies from which many other ethnic and racial groups originated, the family served as the cornerstone of the culture, defining and determining individual and social behavior. Ties between families were cemented by the establishment of *compadrazco* (godparent-godchild) relationships. Relatives by blood and ceremonial ties, as well as friends of the family, were linked together in an intricate network of reciprocal obligations. Individuals who suffered misfortunes were aided by relatives and friends. When they had re-established themselves, they shared their good fortunes with those who had helped them.

That the gang is rooted in the norms of family life and tradition can be observed from the various descriptions of the gang offered by the youngsters I studied.

> Tony: My grandmother took care of me for a long time. I guess this was part of the Puerto Rican tradition at one time. Your grandmother took care of you while your mother and father were away working. Sometimes grandmothers did not believe that their son or daughter were fit to be parents so they took the responsibility of raising their grandchildren. My grandmother is my life. Anybody who messes with my grandmother has to mess with me. The same thing with my aunt.
>
> Author: Which aunt are you referring to?
>
> Tony: This is my mother's sister, which is really weird because they are the same blood but treat me so differently. My aunt is the mother I never had. We are really close. She is the person that I go to when I need someone to tell something to. She always listens to me.
>
> Author: And why does she always listen to you?
>
> Tony: My aunt is this wonderful woman, she's about 35 years old, who is really together. When I'm with her I feel like I can tell her anything that is in my mind. That's what family is all about. This is all in the blood. She cares because she is family. When you have a family, even if it's your aunt or uncle, you know you belong.

> You will always have someone looking out for you.
>
> Author: In the last interview, you talked a little about the family as it related to the gang. How similar is the gang family to what you're describing now?
>
> Tony: They are very similar. You see a family is like a fist [he pointed to his fist, clenching it and opening it to show that when it's opened it represents five fingers separated from one another]. I know that the five fingers of your hand are supposed to be related; however, what would you prefer having, a hand with five fingers or a closed fist? When the fist is closed the fingers are inseparable; when the fist is opened they stand at a distance from one another. I prefer the closed fist. That's exactly how our gang is—we are very close. To be in our gang you need to have heart. To have heart means that you are truly committed to each other; that you'll do anything for another member because he is part of your family.

In addition to stemming directly from a Puerto Rican family tradition, ethnic solidarity served as another cultural element, used by the youngsters for cementing their business relations. As Puerto Ricans, they expressed feelings of a primordial tie, of blood kinship, said to unify them. This, in turn, provided the basis for trust. As one youngster put it: "The fact that I knew that what I liked was at another person's house—they would talk to me about things like, 'we're going to listen to Salsa music, we're going to have *arroz con gandures* [rice and pot pies]' and some other stuff, I would get more attractive to that than to other things."

Part of the collectivist, communitarian foundation of the gang was also shaped by a base of local consumers or people who are referred by friends. Their willingness to become faithful customers, to continuously purchase available goods, i.e., drugs and stolen merchandise, is viewed by gang members as an indication of membership. These customers become, in the opinion of one youngster, "one of us." The same young man also said: "People from the neighborhood know that they can get smoke, cane, and other things from us. It's risky going to other places. So they protect us. We are safe with them. So we think of them as part of the business."

The significance of collectivism for gang members can be also extracted from their views about the idea of individualism. These youngsters are not in agreement with the view that the successful exercise of individual effort in pursuit of economic and social mobility is applicable to them. To them, individualism means placing oneself at a precarious position. How can they exist or survive without one another? They are fully aware that they do not possess the traditional resources, such as money and high levels of formal education, that are used by members of the middle class to negotiate and advance their individual life chances. They believe that individual effort represents a step toward obliteration. As directly put by one youngster, "By ourselves, we are nobody. We can be had without no problem." Another's remarks were just as straightforward: "This is not a game that you can win by yourself. If you want to win, you do it as a team. If you want to lose, play alone."

Individual success honors those who have achieved it. Failure, and economic failure in particular, stigmatizes those who suffer it. Such failure can only make those who have "failed" the objects of criticism or scorn. It can also be taken to mean that they are inadequate or deficient. The individualization of "success" and "failure" in American society is unacceptable as far as these young men are concerned. For this reason, collectivism is perceived as capable of giving gang members a special sense of purpose and ability—the driving force with which to pursue economic and social success.

Rules of Collectivism

The gang adopted explicit rules aimed at enforcing communitarian behavior and discipline among its members, which was translated into economic activity. Individuals who decided to work on their own were fully aware of the severe penalties associated with such behavior if it led to problems with the "law." For example, members who are apprehended by the police for selling drugs or stealing on their own may not be entitled to receive the amenities accorded to others who engage in collective action. One youngster, who spent six months in jail, describes the consequences of working alone. "I was left to rot. My people didn't come for me. We were all warned about doing shit by ourselves. I was one who paid for not listening."

Additionally, sullen individual action can lead to severe physical harm, in particular the brutal punishment embellished in one of the most traditional rituals of the gang: the Vs. As explained by one youngster, Vs stand for "violations," which are beatings dispensed to individual members for violating certain rules of the gangs. They are often used in special ceremonies, like initiations or withdrawals of members. During these occasions an individual must walk through a line comprised of other members. The number in the line could range from ten to fifty. The line walk usually lasts three to five minutes and the individual must try to defend himself from the onslaughts of those making up the ranks of the line. If an assault causes the individual to fall, he must return to the beginning of the line and start again. If he gives up, he cannot be excused from the penalty, or accepted as member, or allowed to leave the gang. The most devastating of the Vs are those involving members wishing to quit the gang and those who violate gang rules. One young man described the violations performed during cases when a member leaves the gang:

> There are no rules when they give you a V out. They can use whatever they want on you, they can kick you wherever they want, they pull you on the floor, they can punch you wherever they want, you can't fight back. You just stand there and cover up what you can cover up, and hope that they don't hit one of your weak spots.

I was informed of many instances when individuals who violated certain rules were given severe beatings. The case of Frankie is one example.

> I came out all bruised up and had a broken rib, and that was about it. I just had lumps and bruises all over my face and on my back. It was a lot on my back. But it wasn't as hard really as I thought it would be, so it went pretty fast and I just hope for the best. I wanted to come out alright [*sic*], alive, at least.

It is to the advantage of individuals to function from the collective perspective of the gang rather than on their own. As gang members, drug dealers are offered a fairly safe marketplace from which to sell their products. The gang's turf, the location in the neighborhood where drug transactions tend to occur, is to be used by members only. In cases when a particular turf has developed a reputation for carrying stocks of reliable and good merchandise, as is true for the turfs of the section of the Diamonds I studied, youngsters can be assured of having an ongoing clientele and a profitable business.

Another advantage of a collectivist approach to doing business is found in the symbolic messages this action tends to communicate, particularly to "outsiders." For example, the presence of a group of dealers on a street block or corner, usually taking turns to insure that everyone has an opportunity to make a sale, serves to discourage possible robbery attempts. Customers, users, and others not associated with the gang recognize the danger in trying to burglarize or stick up a group of dealers who are members of a particular gang. In addition, the gang provides individuals with a "reputation," serving as a defense against possible customer snitching. Customers and other individuals would be afraid and hesitant to reveal information about a particular dealer who is viewed as belonging to a particular gang. There is a widespread understanding that to snitch against one is tantamount to revealing information about the entire gang. This is an act youngsters in the streets recognize will provoke retribution and physical violence.

The gang, as representative of a collective unit, carries another advantage. It provides customers with a reputable source from which to purchase drugs and other items. In doing so, it contributes significantly to cementing seller-customer relations. Knowledge about the gang, its territory, its affiliated dealers and overall reputation present customers with the background information necessary for trusting that the merchandise they buy is authentic and good. Customers feel confident that they are not being sold a fraudulent product, or what street-level dealers call "junk."

Finally, the collective approach to selling drugs provides youngsters with protection against police invasion and apprehension. The youngsters I studied worked in groups or crews of at least three members. This work arrangement served as a reliable shield to keep each worker alert and informed of the different predators and threats around them. Otherwise, having to conduct an illicit business from an open and highly visible location, like a street corner, makes arrests a distinct possibility.

Occupational Character

The gang, as a business, is built around a fairly elementary occupational structure. Several leading jobs are found within this structure: drug suppliers/distributors, cocaine and marijuana dealers, and those involving several forms of stealing. This occupational structure, like in other business establishments, is developed in a hierarchical basis, representing a pyramid of power, prestige, authority, and information. One's position on the pyramid is correlated with one's access and possession of these attributes.

At the top level of the gang's occupational hierarchy stands the cocaine and marijuana suppliers or distributors. The number of suppliers/distributors is limited, for the smaller the number the larger the profit. Members of the Diamonds referred to their distributors/suppliers in terms of "leaders," "older guys," or simply "main heads." They thought of the distributors as individuals who had paid their dues by remaining with the gang for a very long period of time. In the process they would have gained knowledge about the drug distribution network and accumulated the necessary money for purchasing bulk quantities of drugs. Distributors hold a virtual monopoly over the purchase and supply of drugs sold by members of the Diamonds.

Author: Who did you purchase your stuff from?

Carlos: I usually bought it from my gang leaders.

Author: So there was a distributor within your gang?

Carlos: Yes, every gang has at least one distributor. There are times when a section may not have one, well these guys then buy from another distributor from the larger gang. My guess is that the older guys took trips to Florida, or meet people half-way. I heard some guys going downtown for the stash. Some of these people were into real estate, restaurants. But it's through some business and the owner of the business was handling the stuff. But this was all done by the older guys, the younger ones never got into this, they couldn't.

Author: I heard you refer to the distributor as the "older guys."

Carlos: Yes, it is the older ones who know what life is all about, who are making money and living a nice life. They are into communicating with one another and making money. But not the youth.

Distributors exercise great influence over street-level dealers through their control over drug sources. A single distributor may have as many as fifteen to twenty youngsters working for him on a regular or periodic basis. The money paid to each youngster, as well as the amount of drugs that he gives on consignment, depends on the type of relationship that is established. If he believes that an individual is not making him money, he will sever the relationship by refusing to supply him. Along with their monopoly over the supplies of cocaine and marijuana, the ability to hire and fire employees gives these distributors a considerable amount of influence over youngsters working at street-level dealing.

The distributor epitomizes success within the gang. He seduces newer members. He is not an illusion or fantasy. Rather, he embodies the dream which the larger society has denied Puerto Rican youngsters. And, in the mind of the youngsters, the distributor represents the one position within the business infrastructure of the gang that they want.

> I would see my prez and other heads, you know, two or three cars, and this and that, and they still got jobs, money, you see a bankroll in their pocket, and they be asking you what you want to eat. And this and that, and you be like, "I want to make this money and that money, I want to be like you." And he'll be like, "Ok, well I'll go buy an ounce of reefer, right, cause you ain't got the money to do it." And you know you can't do it.

Since successful drug distribution requires a great deal of secrecy, information about top-level distributors is limited. Contact between the distributor and street-level dealers is restricted to sporadic episodes, most likely involving occasions of drug dispersion and money collection. Distributors are rarely seen on the corners where drugs are presently sold.

Distributors belong to a fairly closed and exclusive club. The few individuals who remain with the gang long enough to achieve this level of job mobility are usually expected to create a new section of the gang in a different area of the neighborhood. They also might be appointed to oversee an existing section that was viewed by the leadership as nonproductive. One young man provides a precise account of the nature of the distributor's job:

> In my section, the big guys would never change. They were the distributors, the people everybody wanted to be like but couldn't. They had the control and were not going to give it to anyone. If you got big like them, you had work with another section. They didn't let you compete with them. Why should they? They were going to lose money. But I guess it's not a bad idea to create your section—it's only yours.

In effect, most workers within the Diamonds' job hierarchy occupied the position of street-level cocaine and marijuana dealers—the job directly beneath the distributor/supplier. In most cases dealers sell both drugs, though the preference is toward the cocaine business for its larger profits. Dealing cocaine and marijuana requires possessing available cash in order to purchase the drug from the supplier. Otherwise, youngsters work as sellers for the supplier who "fronts" them a certain amount of drugs—dealers receive a small percentage of the profits. There are other times when the supplier uses gang members to sell cocaine and marijuana by hiring them to make "drops" or "deposits" of specific amounts to individuals outside of the neighborhood. The profits from this job are usually small.

Because of the relatively small profits made by those working for distributors or dealers, the ultimate goal of street-level dealers is to become independent businessmen. That is, they want to amass the necessary amount of dollars to acquire and sell the product without having to share the profits with the distributor. As "independents," the youngsters know very well that the return for their investment and labor will always be higher.

> Author: How long did you stay in drug dealing?
>
> Gustavo: I'm still doing it to this day.
>
> Author: What was your biggest profit when you were working for the man?
>
> Gustavo: My biggest profit a week was about $100.00 to $150.00 a week. The profit I was making for the guy was sometimes $1,000 to $2,000.
>
> Author: So you were making very little.
>
> Gustavo: That's right. He was making all the money. There were Saturdays when I would be counting the money that I was going to take him and there were times when on a Saturday he would make $2,000.
>
> Author: Now that you're on your own, how much money do you make?
>
> Gustavo: It varies. If I go and buy $800 worth of cocaine I can make $1,600—a one hundred percent profit. If I package the stuff myself into quarter bags I can make more. Any profit to me is good, as long as it's over $100. But you see, I don't make that kind of money because I don't have the money to buy that quantity.
>
> Author: What has been the most you've ever made?

> Gustavo: I bought $400 and took out that plus another $400. And I sold that on a Wednesday, Thursday, and Friday.

Similarly, as independents, dealers determine which drugs to sell, favoring cocaine over others even though the penalties for selling it are more severe. "The money is in cocaine," indicated a youngster as he described the difference between selling cocaine and marijuana. He also stated, "I have spent a lot [of] time working the streets, selling reefers and pills, but I know that I can double whatever I make in these jobs by selling cane."

Dealers from the Diamonds tend to sell both cocaine and marijuana to local consumers, though other buyers come from the "outside." In the majority of the cases, the outside buyers are young, middle-class whites, who have learned through different ways and sources about a particular corner or street block where cocaine can be readily purchased. The thing drug dealers like most about outside buyers is that they tend to become habitual customers, making purchases throughout the course of the week.

> Author: You were telling me about some of your customers, and you mentioned how people from the neighborhood are not steady. What do you mean by that?
>
> Carmelo: Friday is the big day. It's payday. That's when most of people come out to make their kill. Actually, the whole weekend is when we sell a lot to people from around here.
>
> Author: And you would not consider that to be steady!
>
> Carmelo: Well, I guess. But, you see my white customers come around all the time. These people have money all the time and don't care about spending it. They come around on a Monday or a Thursday, whenever.
>
> Author: So are you saying that people from the neighborhood make larger purchases that last for the entire week?
>
> Carmelo: Are you kidding? No, they buy a few hits, that's all.
>
> Author: What happens to them during the week?
>
> Carmelo: We work out different things. Sometimes I just give them the stuff and they pay me on Friday. Or, they bring something that they use to trade. For example, I had a guy give me this expensive watch one time. Another left his VCR. So there are different ways that we use.

Marijuana is the most readily sold drug among the youngsters I studied. Not surprisingly, the job of marijuana dealer is the one found most often within the occupational structure of the gang. Marijuana is usually sold to local clients for a very low price. Members of the Diamonds working in marijuana dealing indicated that the common use and popularity of the drug is correlated with customers' perception of it as being relatively mild, pleasurable, and easily manageable. One dealer provided what he believes to be the reasons why users or customers prefer marijuana over other drugs like cocaine.

> Because people have the opinion that cocaine is dangerous. And marijuana you just smoke it, it's like smoking a cigarette, you just smoke and get high and that's it. There's not a real big effect on you, you don't get addicted to it. You know, some people do, but they, it's controllable, it's not as bad as cocaine—you get hooked.... You know, you get rid of marijuana fast. Marijuana goes better than cocaine.

Youngsters also believe that the legal penalties for dealing marijuana are less severe than those for dealing cocaine. This suggests another explanation for their widespread involvement in marijuana sales. From the dealers' perspective, there is no sign of any significant enforcement apparatus and no cases of severe punishment for possessors of marijuana.

Finally, at the bottom of the gang's occupational hierarchy are those youngsters who make money through stealing. The large number of youngsters involved in acts of stealing are the newer members, called the "Pee Wees" or "Littles." In many cases, stealing represents a "special mission" that Pee Wees are instructed to carry out to demonstrate their loyalty and commitment to the gang. Although these efforts are geared to "proving themselves," they still manage to generate a profit. For other youngsters, stealing becomes a way of life. They work in crews of three or four, and the major item they target is cars. These youngsters become extremely proficient in stealing cars and make a substantial amount of money, though not as much as that generated from drug dealing.

Money-Raising Capacity

Similar to other business organizations, the gang's survival depends on its capacity to develop and maintain a sound financial base. Funds are needed to meet a wide range of organizational needs, such as purchasing weapons, making rent payments, bailing members out of jail, and paying for attorney's fees. The gang's finances are managed primarily through two major sources: one is the organization's own centralized fund, referred to by youngsters as the "box," and the other represents the private funds of the drug supplier/distributor(s) within the gang.

The centralized fund or "box" is established through membership contributions or dues, paid periodically (i.e., weekly, biweekly) to the gang's treasurer. As one youngsters put it: "Without the kitty [box] we would had [*sic*] disappeared a long time ago. We needed all kinds of money to get people out of jail because for a while we were doing some heavy gang-banging. We were paying about $10–15 a week." The significance of membership dues in terms of maintaining the gang is also described in detail by another young man:

> Author: How often did you pay dues in your gang?
>
> Hector: We pretty much paid twice a month. We were paying ten dollars per crack. To me that was a lot of money.
>
> Author: What would have happened if you didn't pay?
>
> Hector: But we had to pay—if we didn't the organization would stop. There were times when the president would give us time to raise the money, but we always had to pay. And I guess when you're part of the gang, you care for it. So if you care about the gang, you always find the way to get your hands on some money. It's like if you care for your girlfriend, you always find a way to make her happy. With the gang, you had to find the money to make it happy.

Money for the centralized fund was also secured through other means, for membership dues could only raise a very limited amount. Included in these activities were the stealing and selling of weapons, car parts, and the like. While recalling his early days in the gang as a newcomer, one youngster described his working relationship with senior gang members to whom he was assigned:

> The older guys would always bring me and tell me to go steal or sell this or that. And that this would bring money for me, but most of the money had to be taken to the box for dues. They would tell me that the money would be used for getting me out of jail or any trouble that I might get into later.

A similar account was given by another youngster: "In our gang, we collected dues. Everybody had to pay. Several times I worked together with other guys pulling some jobs, we stole a car and stripped it. The guy in charge took most of the money for the box because we were empty. I guess we didn't mind that much."

The other mode for generating funds for the box is through contributions made periodically by the distributor/supplier. Because the supplier has a vested interest in the maintenance or survival of the gang, there are times when he uses his own funds for resolving certain gang-related matters. The supplier understands quite well that without his monetary donation, the gang might well fall apart. Similarly, he understands that without the gang, he could lose his business. Contributions made by the distributor are geared to protecting his workers, his street-level dealers. If they are apprehended by the police, he puts up the money for getting them out of jail. In the following exchange, Carlos provides a graphic picture of the role of the distributor as a provider toward the well-being of the organization and its members.

Author: How often did the distributor use his money to get members out of jail?

Carlos: Many. We had some times when they pull the money out of their own pockets and one of us would get bailed out. Or sometimes to pay a hospital bill or for someone who got really busted out.

Author: And why did the distributor do this?

Carlos: They would do it really out of their good-will, for the devotion they got for their own gang. And they want everybody in the hood; they figure the more of us who are out there, the better for them.

Author: What were the other reasons the distributor used his money to get people out of jail?

Carlos: One thing you have to understand that is they got their money back. The guy paid him double. It's like an investment because the guy would have to pay him two times what it cost to get him out of jail in the first place.

Author: Did you ever see this happen within your gang?

Carlos: Yes, I saw this happened several times. I even saw it where the big guy borrowed the money and charged double for getting this guy out. He needed money to pay his rent and went and got this money from some other guy and bailed this other one out.

Author: You said earlier that one reason the big guys get others out of trouble situations is to demonstrate to everybody else that they are devoted to the gang and they care for the gang. Elaborate on this.

Carlos: They want to show everybody in the gang that they are devoting everything they have into the gang to make it better. And to take, how can I say it, "look what I did for you," kind of thing. And they tell everybody, "that's why I'm leader and that's one reason I want all of you to look up to me."

Discussion

In this chapter I have provided a basic sketch of the leading components of the business youth gang. It is clear from the presentation that this kind of enterprise is quite complex. There were many factors contributing to the formation of the gang as a business operation. The examples provided indicate how external forces and conditions combined with internal cultural group dynamics to give rise to systematic and highly organized business relations among gang members.

In addition, although the description presented in the chapter suggests that the gang does indeed provide youngsters with an alternative to unemployment, it is also the case that this form of labor is highly exploitative. The street youth gang of Suburbia is far from representing a progressive cultural response to youth labor exploitation. On the contrary, it serves to reproduce that exploitation and oppression.

There are several reasons for this. Contrary to public belief, street level dealers make little money selling drugs or through stealing. In most cases, these youngsters represent another type of minimum-wage labor. The saturation of the market with mass amounts of drugs as well as the fast rise of so many gangs involved in drug selling have increased availability of drugs and decreased the cost. Youngsters' profit margins are quite small. One youngster explained this turn of events in a very interesting way. "I was planning to make enough to go legit. I wanted to do something with the money I was going to make. I know an older gang member who owns a car wash. I wanted something like that. But as I told you, I worked hard and yet I'm still standing on the corner." Another youngster put it this way:

> I guess when we joined the gang, we would see the prez and chief with so much gold and [we'd] think we're going to be the same. But then we have to face the hard facts. There is not much for most of us. But by then, you're too involved, you're a member, people see you and know you now. So you stay—you continue dealing, what else can you do?

In effect, street-level drug dealers are a cheap and permanent labor force used by a few suppliers or distributors within the gang to maintain and enhance their business interests and profits. Although the wages received from selling drugs may be higher than those earned "turning hamburgers at McDonald's," in the case of the street-level dealer upward mobility is highly unlikely. It is to the advantage of the supplier to maintain the subordination and dependency of their street-level dealers. Distributors/suppliers establish the wages of street-level dealers. Suppliers also maintain a large number of youngsters employed, establishing a very real competitive setting and compelling dealers to operate according to the rules established by suppliers.

Additionally, street-level dealing can be regarded as exploitative labor in that the occupation itself is "sporadic, having high peaks and droughts, and is full of uneven demands on [their] time"[3] (Manning and Redlinger, 1983:283). The large majority of the youngsters I studied indicated "working the block" or "standing on the corner" for a good part of their day, for there was not any established time for "making a deal." A transaction could occur at 6:00 A.M. or 12:00 midnight. In addition, competition from other dealers contributed directly to the amount of time youngsters invested working the streets or corners. As one former dealer put it:

> We used to work very long hours. There were other times that we would have to work long past 12 midnight because we got some of these people coming in on Fridays or Saturdays at 2 or 3 in the morning telling us that they just came out of after-hours and they needed it now and they would pay more for it. These were some desperate folks. But you had to deliver otherwise you would lose your clients.

Moreover, the extreme danger of drug dealing adds to the persisting strenuous nature of the occupation. These young people are the ones who do the dirty work of the business, which is often accompanied by physical harm or even death. For youngsters caught doing the gang's dirty work the common consequence is stigmatization by the larger society. Re-entering school is difficult. Obtaining employment in the conventional economy is almost out of the question.

Notes

1. Ruth Horowitz, *Honor and the American Dream* (N.J.: Rutgers University Press, 1983); William Kornblum and Terry Williams, *Growing Up Poor* (Lexington, Mass.: Lexington Books, 1985).
2. Robert K. Merton, *Social Theory and Social Structure* (Glencoe, Ill.: The Free Press, 1957); Richard A. Cloward and Lloyd Ohlin, *Delinquency and Opportunity* (New York: Free Press, 1960); Joan Moore et al., *Homeboys: Gangs, Drugs and Prison in the Barrios of Los Angeles* (Philadelphia: Temple University Press, 1978); Horowitz, *Honor and the American Dream*; Diego Vigil, *Barrio Gangs: Street Life and Identity in Southern California* (Austin: University of Texas Press, 1988).
3. Peter K. Manning and Lawrence J. Redlinger, "Drugs at Work," in *Research in the Sociology of Work*, eds., Ida H. Simpson and Richard L. Simpson (Greenwich, Conn: JAI Press, 1983), p. 283. ✦

Chapter 14
The Differences Between Street Gangs and Neo-Nazi Skinheads

Mark S. Hamm

As a result of the ways in which social researchers typically define what constitutes street gangs, white supremacist youth groups are often not classified as "gangs." Hamm argues that this distinction is a valid and important one: while street gangs tend to organize as a result of shared culture and shared experiences of oppressive social and economic conditions, skinhead groups are organized explicitly around the ideology of racism. The overt political nature of skinhead groups and of their violence makes them more aptly defined as terrorist youth subcultures, according to Hamm.

The skinheads constitute a unique criminal subculture for several important reasons. To begin with, scholars have found that gangs are a largely immigrant, adolescent, underclass phenomenon, but they have not found racism to be an organizing principle for gang membership. In those instances where racism has been discovered by gang researchers, it has usually been cited as an excuse for juvenile delinquency. That is, gang delinquency is a function of youthful rebellion against oppressive conditions caused by racism in the larger society (Cloward and Ohlin, 1960; Erlanger, 1979; Hagedorn, 1988; Spergel, 1961; Vigil, 1990).

This is not the case, though, for the neo-Nazi skinheads of North America. For them, we consistently discover that skinhead membership is an explicit function of their own strident racism.

Many scholars have also pointed out that violence, like racism, plays only a small role in gang behavior (Hagedorn, 1988; Klein, 1971; Merry, 1981; Miller, 1958; Morash, 1983; Moore, 1978; Suttles, 1968). In fact, some researchers have shown that gangs often have a positive relationship with their local communities and even serve as auxiliary police forces (Horowitz, 1987; Sanchez-Jankowski, 1991). Others have found that when gang violence does occur, it is often related to the use and/or distribution of highly addictive drugs such as heroin and crack cocaine (Fagan, 1989; Huff, 1989; Taylor, 1990), disputes over turf (Erlanger, 1979; Horowitz and Schwartz, 1974; Thrasher, 1927), ethnic and cultural differences between neighborhoods (Moore, 1978; Suttles, 1968), poverty and social disorganization (Curry and Spergel, 1988), or general economic interests (Spergel, 1984).

Once again, the evidence on the neo-Nazi skinheads stands in instructive contrast to this body of criminology. For the skinheads, violence is their signature trademark because *violence is part of their subcultural style*. Instead of turf disputes, socioeconomic disadvantage, social disorganization, drugs, or economic interests, the skinheads seem to use violence for the explicit purpose of promoting political change by instilling fear in innocent people.

This was evident in Clark Martell's Romantic Violence, Robert Heick's American Front, David Mazzella's WAR Skins, and John Metzger's Aryan Youth Movement. It was ultimately the case in the killing of Mulugeta Seraw. There are virtually hundreds of other cases where American neo-Nazi skinheads have used violence for the specific purpose of instilling fear in innocent people.

Among these cases are the following:

- On December 4, 1987, a skinhead in Tampa, Florida (Dean McKee), used an eight-inch hunting knife to kill a homeless black man sleeping in his bedroll outside a local art museum (ADL, 1988).
- On September 15, 1987, a skinhead in Van Nuys, California, used a switchblade knife to slit the throat of a Hispanic woman because she refused to turn off a cassette recording by the Miami Sound Machine (Klanwatch, 1989; field notes).
- On February 9, 1988, a skinhead in Las Vegas, Nevada, used a .38-caliber snubnosed revolver to kill a young black female clerk at a 7-Eleven store. He then turned on an elderly black female customer in the 7-Eleven, and fired two shots into her spine. No money was taken from the cash register nor were the victims sexually molested (Klanwatch, 1989; field notes).
- On April 2, 1988, four members of the Detroit Area Skinheads (DASH) used knives to murder a twenty-year-old black woman. About the murder, the leader of DASH told police, "All I could do was feel confused and happy" (Dees, 1990).
- On March 4, 1988, four skinheads from La Verne, California, assaulted an Iranian couple, their two-week-old son, and a black man who tried to intervene. On arrest, the skinheads confessed that they thought the couple was Jewish (Dees, 1990).
- On December 10, 1988, a skinhead in Reno, Nevada, used a .45-caliber Smith & Wesson revolver to kill an unidentified black male (Klanwatch, 1989; field notes).
- On February 7, 1988, eight skinheads attacked a group of homeless advocates in Santa Barbara, California, stomping them with Doc Martens and beating them with baseball bats (Klanwatch, 1989).
- On January 7, 1988, seven members of San Diego's WAR Skins assaulted a group of Vietnamese immigrants outside a restaurant near Ocean Beach (ADL, 1988c).
- On January 1, 1988, seven skinheads in Washington, D.C.'s Dupont Circle attacked a party of homosexuals and beat them with baseball bats and steel batons. One of the victims, Rodney Johnson, received a fractured skull, broken ribs, and a broken shoulder as his skinhead attackers shouted, "Die, faggot, die!" On arrest, one of the skinheads told a *Washington Post* reporter that if Johnson had died, "I don't think I would have felt any remorse about it" (ADL, 1988; Shapiro, 1990:6).
- On March 15, 1988, two skinheads approached two lesbian women outside a Philadelphia bar and beat them with beer bottles (ADL, 1988).
- On April 21, 1988, three skinheads from Halifax, North Carolina, abducted an eighteen-year-old black male and tortured him with a boa constrictor. Then the skinheads slit the young man's throat with a hunting knife, killing him (Klanwatch, 1989; field notes).
- On December 3, 1988, five skinheads in Minneapolis, Minnesota, attacked a group of black kids playing basketball. One fourteen-year-old victim was seriously beaten with a wooden club wrapped in barbed wire (Dees, 1990).
- In July 1989, eight affluent teenagers belonging to a group known as BRASH (Buffalo Rochester Aryan Skinheads) were arrested and charged with beating a thirty-year-old man. Later, members of BRASH became suspects in more than two dozen attacks against gays in the Rochester, New York, area. One skinhead suspect told police during his interrogation: "Gay bashing is when we lure a gay guy into our path and jump him. Sometimes his wallet gets stolen, but mostly we just beat him up bad" (John Brown Anti-Klan Committee, 1990a:2).
- On March 15, 1988, two members of the Los Angeles Reich Skins pled guilty to

assault with a deadly weapon for pointing a gun at a Hispanic teenager after breaking into his home (ADL, 1988).

- On June 6, 1988, a fourteen-year-old skinhead stabbed a black junior high school student three times in the back on a playground in Ventura, California (ADL, 1988).
- On February 4, 1989, a thirteen-year-old skinhead pulled a loaded .357 Smith & Wesson revolver and threatened to shoot a Glendale, California, teacher who refused to let the skinhead wear a white power T-shirt for his school yearbook picture (ADL, 1989; field notes).
- On May 4, 1989, four skinhead members of Tampa's American Front were stopped in Taveras, Florida, after two of the skinheads had pulled automatic assault rifles on an elderly black couple (ADL, 1989).
- On March 18, 1989, David Timoner was shot to death with a 9-mm automatic weapon wielded by a skinhead in Denver. The skinheads then set Timoner's car afire. During a police chase the following day, one of the skinheads took a hostage while brandishing a .22-caliber handgun, proclaiming to a police negotiator that he wanted "to go out in a blaze of glory" (ADL, 1989).
- On February 3, 1990, five members of the Confederate Hammer Skins were found guilty of putting poison gas into a Dallas synagogue's air-conditioning system, and of other racially motivated hate crimes against Hispanics at a Dallas park during the summer of 1989 (Clarke, 1991; the *New York Times*, February 4, 1990). Since then, the Confederate Hammer Skins have been linked to more than forty hate crimes in the Dallas area, including attacks on blacks and gays, and anti-Semitic and anti-Moslem vandalism (John Brown Anti-Klan Committee, 1990b; Thornburgh, 1990).

Neo-Nazi skinheads have clubbed and knifed the punk music scene into submission in Detroit, San Diego, and Los Angeles (Coplon, 1989). And following the murder of Mulugeta Seraw, Portland skinheads were implicated in forty-six hate crimes including assaults with deadly weapons (ADL, 1988; Shapiro, 1990). During 1989 alone, the Southern Poverty Law Center discovered more than 200 skinhead arrests and prosecutions throughout the United States for murder and assaults on blacks and minorities (Dees, 1990).

Finally, academic gang theorists have traditionally based their sociological models on the following proposition:

> The violent gang is a natural, lower-class interstitial institution, resulting mainly from the weaknesses of secondary institutions, such as schools, local communities and ethnic organizations, and to some extent from the weakness of primary institutions such as the family, to provide adequate mechanisms of opportunity and social control, particularly in the transition of males from youth to adulthood. (Spergel, 1984:201–2)

This means that violent gangs are a natural outgrowth of urban, underclass cultures where schools are lousy, parents don't control their children, and there is no community or ethnic organization to join when life becomes just too much for young men to endure. This is the classic sociological definition of alienation. When this happens, contemporary criminology predicts that certain young men will meet each other in the neighborhood and start a violent street gang because it is a natural product of their environment.

Yet this pre-paradigmatic construct is based on research that focuses exclusively on poor, urban, African-American, Hispanic, or Asian youth. Rarely has a study focused exclusively on a white street gang (although Short and Strodtbeck [1965] and Yablonsky [1962] offer partial exceptions). And never has a study examined a white gang that is international, rather than interstitial, in nature.

There is good reason for this. White international criminal youth subcultures are a very recent phenomenon in America. Indeed, it was not until 1986 that the word *skinhead* was even introduced into the mainstream vernacular in the United States (Coplon, 1989). As a result, social science has yet to catch up with this unique development. For example, a recent analysis entitled *Gangs in America* (Huff, 1990) includes fourteen original criminological studies of U.S. street gangs written by foremost scholars in the field of gang research. Within this 345-page volume, the word *skinhead* is not mentioned once. Nevertheless, today thousands and thousands of violent neo-Nazi skinheads are scattered throughout the United States, Great Britain, Germany, France, Spain, Holland, Belgium, Portugal, Denmark, Canada, Australia, Brazil, and Egypt (ADL, 1989; Jackson, 1991; Mücke, 1991; Seidelpielen, 1991; Ward, 1991; field notes).

These skinhead groups have emerged under various social, economic, and political conditions. Hence, they do not share a common street corner or neighborhood culture. But they do share a common ideology. According to every published account filed to date, this ideology is *neo-Nazism* supported and sustained by a specific *style* (shaved heads, Nazi regalia, Doc Martens, and racial/ethnic violence) and *music* (white power rock).

For these important reasons, then, the skinheads do not conform to the classic criminological definition of a street gang. In fact, the skinheads seem to violate this definition in a classical way. The skinheads represent something else; something with a wider agenda that is potentially more dangerous to society, and certainly more elusive to academic gang scholars. Hence, instead of viewing the skinheads as a street gang, we must define them for what they truly are. Because of their overt racism, political violence, and links to a homologous international subculture of neo-Nazism, the skinheads constitute what can best be described as a *terrorist youth subculture*.

References

ADL (Anti-Defamation League). 1989. *Skinheads Target the Schools*. New York: ADL.

——. 1988. *Young and Violent: The Growing Menace of America's Neo-Nazi Skinheads*. New York: ADL.

Clarke, Floyd I. 1991. "Hate, Violence in the United States." *FBI Law Enforcement Bulletin*, January:14–17.

Cloward, Richard A., and Lloyd E. Ohlin. 1960. *Delinquency and Opportunity*. Glencoe, IL: Free Press.

Coplon, Jeff. 1989. "The Skinhead Reich." *Utne Reader*, May/June:80–89.

Curry, G. David, and Irving A. Spergel. 1988. "Gang Homicide, Delinquency and Community." *Criminology*, 26:381–405.

Dees, Morris. 1990. Personal communication, letter.

Erlanger, Howard S. 1979. "Estrangement, Machismo and Gang Violence." *Social Science Quarterly*, 60:235–248.

Fagan, Jeffrey. 1989. "The Social Organization of Drug Use and Drug Dealing Among Urban Gangs." Criminology, 27:633–669.

Hagedorn, John. 1988. *People and Folks: Gangs, Crime and the Underclass in a Rustbelt City*. Chicago: Lakeview Press.

Horowitz, Ruth. 1987. "Community Tolerance of Gang Violence." *Social Problems*, 34:437–450.

Horowitz, Ruth, and Gary Schwartz. 1974. "Honor, Normative Ambiguity and Gang Violence." *American Sociological Review*, 39:238–251.

Huff, C. Ronald. 1989. "Youth Gangs and Public Policy." *Crime and Delinquency*, 35:524–537.

Jackson, James O. 1991. "Unity's Shadows." *Time*, July 1:6–14.

John Brown Anti-Klan Committee. 1990a. "Rich Kid Skinheads Bash Gays," *No KKK-No Fascist USA*, Winter/Spring:2.

——. 1990b. "$3 Million in Stolen Loot Linked to Nazi Skinheads," *No KKK-No Fascist USA*, Winter/Spring:2.

Klanwatch. 1989. *Intelligence Report*. Montgomery, AL: Southern Poverty Law Center.

Klein, Malcolm W. 1971. *Street Gangs and Street Workers*. Englewood Cliffs, NJ: Prentice Hall.

Merry, Sally. 1981. *Urban Danger*. Philadelphia: Temple University Press.

Miller, Walter B. 1958. "Lower-Class Culture as a Generating Milieu of Gang Delinquency." *Journal of Social Issues*, 15:5–19.

Moore, Joan W. 1978. *Homeboys*. Philadelphia: Temple University Press.

Morash, Mary. 1983. "Gangs, Groups and Delinquency." *British Journal of Criminology*, 23:309–331.

Mücke, Thomas. 1991. "Bericht über das projeckt-Miteinander statt gegeneiandeer." *Jervantal*:38–47.

Sanchez-Jankowski, Martin. 1991. *Islands in the Street: Gangs in American Urban Society*. Berkeley: University of California Press.

Seidelpielen, Eberhardt. 1991. *Krieg im den Stadten*. Berlin: Rotbuch, 34.

Shapiro, Lena. 1990. "Tom Metzger and White Aryan Resistance Sued for Murder." *No KKK-No Fascist USA*, Winter/Spring:1–6.

Short, James, F., and Fred L. Strodtbeck. 1965. *Group Process and Gang Delinquency*. Chicago: University of Chicago Press.

Spergel, Irving A. 1984. "Violent Gangs in Chicago: In Search of Social Policy." *Social Service Review*, 58:199–225.

——. 1964. *Racketville, Slumtown, Haulberg*. Chicago: University of Chicago Press.

Suttles, Gerald D. 1968. *The Social Order of the Slum*. Chicago: University of Chicago Press.

Taylor, Carl S. 1990. *Dangerous Society*. East Lansing: Michigan State University Press.

Thornburgh, Dick. 1990. Address before the Simon Wiesenthal Center, Chicago, on March 6.

Thrasher, Frederic. 1927, 1963. *The Gang*. Chicago: University of Chicago Press.

Vigil, James Diego. 1990. "Cholos and Gangs: Culture Change and Street Youth in Los Angeles." In C. Ronald Huff, ed., *Gangs in America*. Newbury Park, CA: Sage.

Ward, Dick. 1991. "Hate Groups Increase in Wake of Change." *CJ Europe*, 1:1–4.

Yablonsky, Lewis. 1962. *The Violent Gang*. New York: Macmillan. ✦

Section IV

Gangs, Violence, and Drugs

Chapter 15 Membership in Youth Gangs and Involvement in Serious and Violent Offending

Terence P. Thornberry

Drawing from his own and several additional longitudinal studies, Thornberry reviews the current state of knowledge concerning the significant relationship between youth gang membership and participation in serious and violent crime. He highlights three important findings: First, gang members are not only disproportionately involved in offending, but they are also responsible for the majority of those serious and violent acts committed by adolescents. Second, gang membership has a facilitation effect on delinquency. That is, youths have higher rates of serious and violent offending while they are active gang members than they do prior to or after they are gang-involved. Finally, gang youths' associations with delinquent peers cannot fully account for this relationship between gang membership and offending. Instead, there is something unique about gang membership itself that increases youths' participation in serious and violent crime. As Thornberry concludes, these findings indicate the importance of focusing on gang youths as targets for prevention and intervention in order to reduce crime.

Reprinted from: Terence P. Thornberry, "Membership in Youth Gangs and Involvement in Serious and Violent Offending." In R. Loeber and D. P. Farrington (eds.), *Serious and Violent Juvenile Offenders*, pp. 147–166.

The Contribution of Gang Members to the Volume of Delinquency

Prior studies have demonstrated that gang members are significantly more involved in delinquency, especially serious delinquency, than are nonmembers. Despite the uniformity of this finding, we have surprisingly few estimates of the proportion of all delinquent or criminal acts for which gang members are responsible. That is, although we know that gang members have higher rates of offending than do nonmembers, we do not know how much of the total amount of crime is attributable to them. This is an important issue: If gang members are responsible for a very large proportion of all offenses, effective gang intervention may be a necessary ingredient in efforts to reduce the overall amount of crime in society.

The most straightforward way of addressing this analytic issue is to compare the proportion of gang members in the population with their proportionate share of the number of crimes reported. For example, if gang members represent 10 percent of the population we would expect them to be responsible for approximately 10 percent of the crimes committed, if there were *no relationship* between gang membership and criminal involvement. To the extent that their proportionate share of crimes exceeds 10 percent, one can conclude that they are disproportionately contributing to the volume of crime in society. Results from four studies are presented in Table 15.1.

Fagan (1990) analyzed a general adolescent sample by combining a cluster sample of high school students and a "snowball" sample of dropouts in San Diego, Los Angeles, and Chicago. He found the prevalence of gang membership to be 23 percent during the year prior to the interview. Although only 23 percent of the population, gang members account for 67 percent of felony assaults, 66 percent of minor assaults, and 66 percent of robberies during that same time period. Fagan reported similar percentages for various forms of theft, ranging from 56 percent of minor thefts to 72 percent of felony thefts. Gang members are also disproportionately

Table 15.1
Percentage of Delinquent Acts Committed by Gang Members, Results From Four Projects

Three City Gang Study, Fagan (1990)	*%*	*Denver Youth Survey, Huizinga (1997)*	*%*
Prevalence of gang membership (1 year)	**23**	**Cumulative prevalence of gang membership (Waves 1–5)**	**14**
Percentage of offenses		**Cumulative percentage of delinquent acts**	
Felony assault	67	Serious violence	79
Minor assault	66	Serious property	71
Robbery	66	Public disorder	44
Felony theft	72	Alcohol use	42
Minor theft	56	Marijuana use	53
Extortion	60	Drug sales	87
Property damage	61		
Weapons	53		
Illegal services	70		
Alcohol use	59		
Drug use	55		
Drug sales	71		
Rochester Youth Development Study, Thornberry (1996)	*%*	*Seattle Social Development Project, Battin, Hill, Hawkins, Catalano, and Abbott (1996)*	*%*
Cumulative prevalence of gang membership (Waves 1–9)	**30**	**Cumulative prevalence of gang membership (Grades 7–12)**	**15**
Cumulative percentage of delinquent acts		**Cumulative percentage of delinquent acts**	
General delinquency	65	Minor assault	51
Serious	86	Robbery	85
Moderate	67	Felony theft	54
Minor	59	Minor theft	53
Violent	68	Damaged property	59
Property	68	Drug selling	62
Street	64	General delinquency	58
Public disorder	60		
Alcohol use	63		
Drug use	61		
Drug sales	70		

involved in weapons offenses, illegal services, drug use, and drug sales.

Thornberry (1996) examined cumulative measures of gang membership and self-reported delinquency in the Rochester Youth Development Study. Thirty percent of the Rochester sample reported being a member of a street gang prior to the end of high school. Although slightly less than one third of the population, gang members accounted for two thirds of the acts of general delinquency that were self-reported over a 4-year period, covering the junior high school and high school years. These gang members were also responsible for 86 percent of the serious acts of delinquency, 68 percent of the violent acts of delinquency, and 70 percent of the drug sales that were reported. Gang members, as compared to their share in the population, also had much higher rates of moderate and minor delinquency, property offenses, public disorder offenses, and alcohol and drug use.

Battin, Hill, Hawkins, Catalano, and Abbott (1996) report very similar patterns of results for gang members in the Seattle Social Development Project. Although gang members comprised only 15 percent of the total sample, they accounted for 85 percent of the robberies that were committed between Grades 7 and 12. They also accounted for at least 50 percent of all the other forms of delinquency measured in that project. These percentages ranged from 51 percent for minor assault to 62 percent for drug selling.

Using data from the Denver Youth Survey, Huizinga (1997) reported very similar results. Between 1988 and 1992, 14 percent of the Denver sample were gang members. They are responsible for 79 percent of the acts of serious violence, 71 percent of serious property offenses, and 87 percent of drug sales, however. They are also disproportionately involved in public disorder offenses, alcohol use, and marijuana use.[1]

The results of these studies confirm the finding of the many earlier studies that gang members have higher rates of involvement in delinquency than do non-gang members. They go beyond those results, however, to indicate that gang members, although representing a minority of the overall population, are responsible for the majority of the delinquent acts. These two findings are not duplicative. The first observation, that gang members are significantly more likely to be involved in delinquency than are non-gang members, can hold even if the second observation does not. That is, gang members could be responsible for only slightly more delinquent acts than their proportionate share in the population and still be significantly different from non-gang members. The results in these studies suggest, however, that this is not the case. Not only are gang members significantly different from non-gang members, they also account for the lion's share of all delinquent acts that are reported. Also, the proportionate contribution of gang members to delinquency is most pronounced for the more serious forms of delinquency. That is, gang members account for a very large proportion of felony offenses, serious offenses, violent offenses, and drug sales. Their contribution to more minor forms of delinquency, although still large, is somewhat muted.

The Facilitation Effect of Gang Membership on Delinquency

The previous section has shown that gang members have higher rates of delinquency than non-gang members and also that gang members account for a disproportionate share of the crime problem relative to their share of the population. Those analyses, however, do not identify the processes by which this relationship is brought about.

Thornberry et al. (1993) have identified three models that could account for this relationship. The first is a social selection model. It suggests that gangs recruit or attract individuals who are already involved in delinquency and violence. If this is the case, then prior to periods of active gang membership, gang members should be more heavily involved in delinquency and violence than are non-gang members. The second model is a facilitation model. In this model, the norms and group processes of the gang are thought to facilitate involvement in delinquency and violence. If this model is accurate, then gang members would not be particularly different from nonmembers prior to or after their periods of active gang membership; during that period, however, they would be much more extensively involved in delinquency and violence. The third model is a mixed model. It suggests that both selection and facilitation effects are at work.

In their empirical analysis, limited to the male respondents in the Rochester Youth Development Study, Thornberry et al. (1993) report strong support for the facilitation model and virtually no support for the selection model:

> Perhaps the strongest support for the social facilitation model is found in the analysis of the type of behavior most often associated with gangs—crimes against the person. . . . Gang members have higher rates of person offenses only when they are active gang members. Of particular interest is the drop-off in the rate of person crimes once boys leave the gang. The means for crimes against the person for boys when they are active members of the gang are, by and large, at least twice as high as when they are not. Clearly, being in the gang is generative of

violent behavior among these boys. (pp. 80–81)

A gang facilitation effect was also observed for general delinquency, drug sales, and to a somewhat lesser extent drug use. It was not, however, observed for property offenses.

Since the publication of these findings, several studies have replicated the facilitation effect that gang membership has on delinquency. Esbensen and Huizinga (1993) report that "prevalence rates for each type of [delinquent] behavior are highest during the gang member's year of actual gang membership" (p. 577). They also report some elevation in the prevalence of delinquency in the year prior to joining a gang. Thus, the results from the Denver Youth Survey offer support for a mixed model, combining both selection and facilitation models.

Hill, Hawkins, et al. (1996) examined this issue in the Seattle Social Development Project. For violent delinquency their results are quite similar to those reported by Thornberry et al. (1993). Mean levels of violence are particularly elevated during the year of active gang membership. Violent delinquency is only slightly elevated in the year prior to joining a gang and reduces quite substantially in the years following active gang membership. With the exception of drug sales, similar findings are observed for other types of delinquency. During periods of active gang membership, involvement in drug sales is quite high (Hill, Hawkins, et al., 1996). Unlike other forms of delinquency, however, involvement in drug sales remains high after the individual leaves the gang. This finding has also been observed in more recent analyses of the Rochester Youth Development Study data (Bjerregaard & Lizotte, 1995; Lizotte, Howard, Krohn, & Thornberry, 1997).

The most recent investigation of this issue has been conducted in the Montreal longitudinal study by Tremblay (personal communication, November 1996). The Montreal study is based on 1,034 boys who attended kindergarten in 1984 in one of 53 low socioeconomic status schools in Montreal. The screening criteria "created a homogeneous low socioeconomic status, white, French-speaking sample" (Tremblay, Pihl, Vitaro, & Dobkin, 1994, p. 733). In replicating the study by Thornberry et al. (1993), Tremblay used self-reported data on gang membership and on delinquency and drug use for the 3-year period when the respondents were 14, 15, and 16 years of age.

The results for violent offenses are consistent with the facilitation model. Violent offending is higher during the year(s) of gang membership than either prior to or following active membership. Prior to joining the gang, gang members have somewhat higher rates of violent offending than do nonmembers, but the predominant change in behavior patterns occurs during periods of active gang membership. A similar pattern is observed for general delinquency and property crimes. As reported by Hill, Hawkins, et al. (1996) and Bjerregaard and Lizotte (1995), drug selling exhibits a somewhat different pattern. Involvement in drug sales increases during periods of gang membership, and it remains high after the youth leaves the gang.

The findings by Tremblay are important for several reasons. Prior studies of the facilitation effect were conducted in American cities and based on samples of gang members that were predominantly African American or Hispanic. Tremblay shows very similar effects in a large Canadian city with an exclusively white, French-speaking sample. The similarity of results suggests that gang processes may be quite similar in diverse settings.

Controlling for Risk Factors

Gang members have higher rates of delinquency, especially violent delinquency, when they are active gang members, and it appears that gang membership facilitates this increase. It is possible, however, that gang members have elevated rates of violence, not because of a gang facilitation effect but because of the accumulation of risk in their backgrounds. As we saw in Chapter 4, gang members have substantial deficits in many social and psychological domains. As a result, it may not be gang membership that brings about the observed increase in violence; the increase may instead be caused by risk factors that are related both to gang membership and to violent behavior. Indeed, Le Blanc and Lanctot (in press) claim that Thornberry et al.'s (1993) conclusion that there is a gang facilitation effect is premature: "We tend to favor the enhancement causal model. The delinquent with lower self and social control joins a gang, and the group activates its offending. . . . To thoroughly verify the nature of the causal role of the gang longitudinal data sets should be reanalyzed controlling for self and social control characteristics of individuals" (p. 13).

To begin examining this possibility, we further examine data from the Rochester Youth Development Study.[2] Involvement in violent delinquency is grouped into the same three annual periods analyzed in Thornberry et al. (1993) and then regressed on a dummy variable indicating whether the subject was a gang member during that year and a variety of prior risk factors (Table 15.2). The inclusion of the dummy variable allows us to assess the facilitative effect of active gang membership on violent behavior net of the impact of antecedent variables. The antecedent variables are drawn from different domains and are among the strongest risk factors for gang membership and for violence (see Chapter 4 in this volume). The specific risk factors that are included are family poverty level, parental supervision, commitment to school, experiencing negative life events, prior involvement in violence, and associating with delinquent peers. The risk factors are measured at the wave prior to the year of gang membership.[3] The analysis is limited to males because of the relatively small number of female gang members at later waves.

The results in Table 15.2 suggest that the relationship between gang membership and concurrent involvement in violent delinquency is not spurious. Even when family poverty level, parental supervision, commitment to school, experiencing negative life events, prior involvement in violence, and associating with delinquent peers are held constant, gang membership exerts a strong impact on the incidence of violent behavior at all 3 years.[4] In the equation for Year 1, for example, the standardized coefficient for gang membership is .26, approximately the same magnitude of coefficients observed for prior violence (.18) and for association with delinquent peers (.32), generally two of the strongest predictors of delinquent behavior (see Thornberry & Krohn, 1997). Indeed, across the years, gang membership has the largest impact on violent behavior.

Table 15.2

Predicting the Incidence of Self-Reported Violence, Rochester Youth Development Study, Males Only (standardized OLS regression coefficients)

	Self-Reported Violence (logged)		
Risk Factor	*Year 1*[a]	*Year 2*[b]	*Year 3*[c]
Gang membership	.26***	.34***	.32***
Family poverty level	.04	–.06	.00
Parental supervision	–.10**	–.06	.01
Commitment to school	–.01	–.04	.02
Negative life events	.13***	.15***	.20***
Prior violence	.18***	.08*	.13**
Delinquent peers	.32***	.13**	.16***
R^2	.46	.31	.28
N	512	487	430

[a]Year 1 violence combines data from Waves 2 and 3; risk factors are from Wave 2.

[b]Year 2 violence combines data from Waves 4 and 5; risk factors are from Wave 3.

[c]Year 3 violence combines data from Waves 6 and 7; risk factors are from Wave 5.

*p<.05. **p<.01. ***p<.001.

Summary

Several recent longitudinal studies provide rather consistent support for the facilitation effect described by Thornberry et al. (1993). Rates of delinquency, especially violent delinquency and drug sales, are particularly high during periods of active gang membership. There is evidence of some selection effect in that gang members have somewhat higher rates of involvement in delinquency prior to joining the gang, but this effect is less consistent and less powerful than the facilitation effect. Also, there tends to be a general drop-off in delinquency following the period of gang membership, with the notable exception of drug sales. In that case, the gangs appear both to facilitate entry into drug-selling markets and to facilitate continuation of involvement in those markets even after the individual leaves the gang. Finally, the impact of gang membership on concurrent involvement in violent delinquency was examined when major risk factors are held constant. Based on results from the Rochester Youth Development Study, the gang exerts a strong facilitative effect on violent behavior even when prior involvement in violence and several important risk factors are controlled. The pattern of results reported here, using a complementary methodology, is concordant with the portrait of gang behavior that is typically presented in the ethnographic literature (e.g., Hagedorn, 1988; Klein, 1995).

Gangs and Delinquent Peer Groups

One of the most consistent correlates of delinquency is association with delinquent peers (Thornberry & Krohn, 1997). Because youth gangs obviously constitute one form of a delinquent peer group, it is not clear whether the effects of gang membership described in this chapter are a function of gang membership or simply a function of association with delinquent peers.

Several gang researchers suggest that delinquent peer groups and gangs are qualitatively different. For example, Joan Moore (1991) has concluded that "gangs are no longer just at the rowdy end of the continuum of local adolescent groups—they are now really outside the continuum" (p. 132). Klein (1995) makes a similar point: "Street gangs are something special, something qualitatively different from other groups and from other categories of law breakers" (p. 197). Although these and other gang researchers view gangs as qualitatively different, there is virtually no quantitative research investigating this hypothesis. Because of that, several recent longitudinal studies have begun to investigate this issue.

In the Rochester Youth Development Study, we classified the male respondents into five groups at each interview wave.[5] One group consists of active gang members at that wave. Respondents who were not gang members were divided into quartiles based on their score on a scale measuring their association with delinquent peers, also at that wave. The most important comparison concerns the non-gang members in the highest quartile (those with the greatest number of delinquent peers) and the gang members. If Moore and Klein are correct, gang members will have substantially higher rates of delinquency than will the non-gang members who associate with highly delinquent peer groups. If, on the other hand, gangs are simply another variant of highly delinquent peer

Table 15.3

Mean Logged Incidence of Self-Reported Violent Delinquency by Gang Membership and by Level of Delinquent Peer Groups, Rochester Youth Development Study, Males Only

	Non-Gang Members				
Interview Wave	Low Delinquent Peers	Moderately Low Delinquent Peers	Moderately High Delinquent Peers	High Delinquent Peers	Gang Members
2	.11	.17	.38	.87	1.44*
3	.05	.13	.24	.58	1.73*
4	.05	.08	.25	.64	1.44*
5	.04	.09	.22	.50	1.29*
6	.04	.05	.15	.51	1.26*
7	.03	.09	.17	.38	1.11*
8	.01	.11	.22	.32	1.57*
9	.02	.03	.15	.27	1.05*

*p<.05 (one-tailed test) between the last two groups; non-gang members with high delinquent peers versus gang members.

groups, these two groups should not differ in terms of their delinquency.

Table 15.3 presents results for the logged incidence of violent delinquency. At all eight waves, gang members report committing violent offenses at significantly higher rates than do the nonmembers who associate with highly delinquent peer groups. For example, at Wave 2 the mean number of violent offenses for the gang members is 1.44 as compared to a mean of .87 for the nonmembers who associate with highly delinquent peers. There are even larger differences at the later waves: At Wave 9 the mean for the nonmembers who associate with highly delinquent peer groups is .27, whereas the mean for the gang members is 1.05. All of the differences between the nonmembers in the highly delinquent peer group and the gang members are statistically significant.[6]

Battin, Hill, Hawkins, et al. (1996) examined this issue with Seattle data. They created three groups: (a) those youth who were ever gang members from the 7th through the 12th grades, (b) those youth who were members of non-gang law-violating youth groups, and (c) those who were neither. To establish the second group, they selected those youth who were never in a gang but for whom the majority of their three best friends had been arrested or who had done things to get them into trouble with the police. They then calculated the mean incidence of delinquency that each group reported committing between the 7th and 12th grades.

The results are quite similar to those in the Rochester study. Gang members reported substantially higher levels of involvement in all the offense types that were examined: minor assault, robbery, felony theft, minor theft, property damage, drug selling, and general delinquency. For minor assault, for example, the mean number of offenses reported by the gang members is 45.9 as compared to 14.1 for members of the law-violating youth groups. The mean number of robberies reported by gang members is 2.0, but it is only 0.2 for members of the nongang law-violating youth groups.

Finally, Huizinga (1996) examined this topic using data from the Denver Youth Survey, in which "youth aged 14–19 in 1991 were classified into four groups—those who had low, medium, and high involvement with delinquent friends, and those who were gang members" (p. 1). For both males and females, he observed higher levels of serious assaults and total assaults for the gang members as compared to the nonmembers who had highly delinquent peers. For example, among the males, 72 percent of the gang members reported involvement in serious assault, whereas only 20 percent of the nonmembers with highly delinquent peers did so. For the females, 72 percent of the gang members reported involvement in serious assault, and only 13 percent of the nonmembers with highly delinquent peers did so.

Battin, Hill, Hawkins, et al. (1996) tested this hypothesis from a causal modeling perspective. They used measures of association with delinquent peers and of gang membership to predict various forms of delinquent activity. Even when association with delinquent peers is included in the equation, the effect of gang membership is sizable and significant. This model was tested for a variety of outcomes—violence, theft, drug use, and drug selling, and for both self-reported and court-reported data—with similar results.

In line with the predictions by Klein and Moore, these three recent longitudinal studies find that gang membership appears to be qualitatively different from associating with delinquent peers in terms of its impact on delinquent behavior. Even when compared to nonmembers who associate with highly delinquent peer groups, gang members have substantially higher rates of delinquency. . . .

Discussion

The findings reported here, especially in the context of recent trend data, provide cause for great concern. Gang members are clearly major contributors to the level of serious and violent crime in American society—especially while they are active gang members. Moreover, Klein (1995), Curry et al. (1996a, 1996b), and the National Youth Gang Center (1997) report a massive expansion of gangs in recent years. As recently as the mid-1980s, gangs were found in relatively few, and generally very large, cities. By the mid-1990s, however, gangs have spread to virtually all large and middle-sized cities and to many smaller cities and towns. Given the facilitation effect that gangs appear to have on violent and serious delinquency, it is little wonder that the overall rate of these crimes for youth has increased so sharply during the past 10 years.

These findings highlight the importance of focusing on youth gangs as important targets for prevention and treatment programs. If gang members are indeed responsible for the majority of serious and violent delinquent acts, as suggested by all studies that have examined this topic, then it is unlikely that we will be successful in reducing the overall rate of serious delinquency unless we can bring gangs under control. That will not be an easy task, however.

Recent surveys to identify prevention programs that effectively reduce delinquency uniformly report that we have few, if any, truly effective gang prevention and suppression programs. In his masterful review of the scene, Klein (1995) has concluded that "the simple fact is that much of our local response and most of our state and federal responses to gang problems are way off base—conceptually misguided, poorly implemented, halfheartedly pursued" (p. 19). The conclusions reached by Spergel (1995), Howell (1995, 1998), and others are hardly more encouraging. Effectively intervening in street gangs has proven remarkably difficult.

It seems, therefore, that one of the highest priorities that we can have in our effort to reduce the level of serious and violent delinquency in American society is to develop effective intervention programs for street gangs. This is, and will be, a most difficult challenge (see Howell, 1998). It will not be done overnight and will require a carefully thought-out, long-term commitment to a "strategy of search" (see Thornberry, 1976). That is, potentially effective programs will have to be faithfully implemented and very carefully evaluated in a slow, iterative process that might eventually lead to the identification of effective programs. It is unlikely that any other approach will succeed. Yet the data reviewed in this chapter suggest the centrality of gangs to the production of serious and violent delinquency, and therefore the centrality of gang prevention to the reduction of serious and violent delinquency.

Author's Note

This study was prepared under Grant 86-JN-CX-0007 (S-3) from the Office of Juvenile Justice and Delinquency Prevention, Office of Justice Programs, U.S. Department of Justice; Grant 5 R01 DA05512-02 from the National Institute on Drug Abuse; and Grant SES-8912274 from the National Science Foundation. I would like to thank Kim Tobin-Carambia for her assistance in developing this chapter. I would also like to thank Darnell F. Hawkins, James C. Howell, Malcolm W. Klein, Alan J. Lizotte, Walter B. Miller, and Carolyn A. Smith for helpful comments on earlier drafts. ✦

Notes

1. Because cumulative measures were used in the Rochester, Seattle, and Denver analyses, some of the offenses for which the gang members are responsible were committed either prior to or subsequent to periods of active gang membership. Because of the temporal patterning of membership and offending, however (see following section), it is likely that many of these offenses were committed while the gang members were actively involved in the gang.
2. I would like to thank David Farrington also for suggesting this line of analysis.
3. There is some overlap between risk factors and gang membership in the analysis for Year 1 because, with the exception of prior violence, the risk factors are measured at Wave 2 and gang membership combines data from Waves 2 and 3. This was unavoidable as not all risk factors were measured at Wave 1.
4. Equations also were estimated excluding association with delinquent peers because of the conceptual and empirical overlap between delinquent peers and gang membership. There were no substantive changes in the results when this was done.
5. These data are based only on males because of the relatively low base rate of female gang membership at later waves.
6. We also restricted the nonmembers to those in the top decile on the delinquent peer measure and to the top *n* respondents, where *n* is equal to the number of gang members at the

particular wave. Differences between gang members and nonmembers are still large and statistically significant.

References

Battin, S., K. G. Hill, J. D. Hawkins, R. F. Catalano and R. Abbott. 1996. "Testing Gang Membership and Association With Antisocial Peers as Independent Predictors of Antisocial Behavior: Gang Members Compared to Non-gang Members of Law-violating Youth Groups." Paper presented at the annual meeting of the American Society of Criminology, Chicago.

Bjerregaard, B., and A. J. Lizotte. 1995. "Gun Ownership and Gang Membership." *Journal of Criminal Law and Criminology* 86:37–58.

Curry, G. D., R. A. Ball and S. H. Decker. 1996a. "Estimating the National Scope of Gang Crime From Law Enforcement Data." *Research in Brief*. Washington, D.C.: National Institute of Justice.

Curry, G. D., R. A. Ball and S. H. Decker. 1996b. "Estimating the National Scope of Gang Crime From Law Enforcement Data." Pp. 266–275 in *Gangs in America*, 2nd Edition, edited by C. R. Huff. Thousand Oaks, CA: Sage Publications.

Esbensen, F. and D. Huizinga. 1993. "Gangs, Drugs, and Delinquency in a Survey of Urban Youth." *Criminology* 31:565–589.

Fagan, J. 1990. "Social Processes of Delinquency and Drug Use Among Urban Gangs." Pp. 183–219 in *Gangs in America*, edited by C. Ronald Huff. Newbury Park, CA: Sage Publications.

Hagedorn, John M. 1988. *People and Folks: Gangs, Crime and The Underclass in a Rustbelt City*. Chicago: Lake View Press.

Hill, K. G., J. C. Howell, J. D. Hawkins and S. R. Battin. 1996. "Risk Factors in Childhood for Adolescent Gang Membership: Results from the Seattle Social Development Project." Manuscript under review.

Howell, J. C., ed. 1995. *Guide for Implementing the Comprehensive Strategy for Serious, Violent and Chronic Juvenile Offenders*. Washington, D.C.: U.S. Department of Justice, Office of Juvenile Justice and Delinquency Prevention.

Howell, J. C. 1998. "Promising Programs for Youth Gang Violence Prevention and Intervention." Pp. 284–312 in *Serious and Violent Juvenile Offenders: Risk Factors and Successful Interventions*, edited by R. Loeber and D. Farrington. Thousand Oaks, CA: Sage Publications.

Huizinga, D. H. 1996. *The Influence of Delinquent Peers, Gangs and Co-offending on Violence*. Fact sheet prepared for the U.S. Department of Justice, Office of Juvenile Justice and Delinquency Prevention.

Huizinga, D. H. 1997. "Gangs and the Volume of Crime." Paper presented at the annual meeting of the Western Society of Criminology, Honolulu, HI.

Klein, M. W. 1995. *The American Street Gang: Its Nature, Prevalence and Control*. New York: Oxford University Press.

Le Blanc, M. and N. Lanctot. In press. "Social and Psychological Characteristics of Gang Members According to the Gang Structure and Its Subcultural and Ethnic Makeup." *Journal of Gang Research*.

Lizotte, A. J., G. J. Howard, M. D. Krohn and T. P. Thornberry. 1997. "Patterns of Carrying Firearms Among Juveniles." *Valparaiso University Law Review* 31:375–393.

Moore, J. 1991. *Going Down to the Barrio: Homeboys and Homegirls in Change*. Philadelphia: Temple University Press.

National Youth Gang Center. 1997. *The 1995 National Youth Gang Survey*. Washington, D.C.: U.S. Department of Justice, Office of Juvenile Justice and Delinquency Prevention.

Spergel, I. A. 1995. *The Youth Gang Problem: A Community Approach*. New York: Oxford University Press.

Thornberry, T. P. 1996. *The Contribution of Gang Members to the Volume of Delinquency*. Fact sheet prepared for the U.S. Department of Justice, Office of Juvenile Justice and Delinquency Prevention.

Thornberry, T. P. 1976. "The Once and Future Promise of the Rehabilitative Idea." *Journal of Criminal Law and Criminology* 67:117–122.

Thornberry, T. P. and M. D. Krohn. 1997. "Peers, Drug Use and Delinquency." Pp. 218–233 in *Handbook of Antisocial Behavior*, edited by D. Stoff, J. Breiling and J. D. Maser. New York: John Wiley.

Thornberry, T. P., M. D. Krohn, A. J. Lizotte and D. Chard-Wierschem. 1993. "The Role of Juvenile Gangs in Facilitating Delinquent Behavior." *Journal of Research in Crime and Delinquency* 30:75–85.

Tremblay, R. E. 1996. Personal communication, November.

Tremblay, R. E., R. O. Pihl, F. Vitaro and P. L. Dobkin. 1994. "Predicting Early Onset of Male Antisocial Behavior From Preschool Behavior." *Archives of General Psychiatry* 51:732–739. ✦

Chapter 16
Defining Gang Homicide:
An Updated Look at Member and Motive Approaches[1]

Cheryl L. Maxson
and
Malcolm W. Klein

Law enforcement agencies adopt different definitional policies for tabulating and reporting "gang related" crime. A major distinction is whether gang features are fundamental to the motive of the incident or whether gang members participate regardless of the motive. Maxson and Klein apply the two definitional approaches to Los Angeles homicide data and find that the difference between the resulting case groups is less than what one might expect. Although departments using the motive definition will report far fewer numbers of gang-related crimes, the overall character of the two types of gang cases is quite similar. However, depictions of drug aspects of gang homicide appear to be influenced by definitional approach.

Attempts to develop generalizations across cities about the prevalence of gang violence need to take these definitional stances into account. However, characterizations about the nature of gang violence are less vulnerable to definitional variations. The implications of different definitional styles may be more or less important depending upon the purposes for which these data are utilized.

Reprinted from: Cheryl L. Maxson and Malcolm W. Klein, "Defining Gang Homicide: An Updated Look at Member and Motive Approaches.". In C. Ronald Huff (ed.), *Gangs in America*, 2nd ed., pp. 3–20. Copyright © 1990 by Sage Publications, Inc. Reprinted by permission.

In our chapter for the first edition of *Gangs in America* (Maxson and Klein, 1990), we presented Los Angeles homicide data from the years 1978 through 1982 to investigate the implications of two approaches to defining gang crime—the member versus motive definitions. In the current edition, we utilize homicide incidents from 1988 and 1989 to update our previous findings and to examine whether or not drug aspects introduce differences in the definitional analyses.

The recent proliferation of U.S. cities with street gang activity increases the importance of investigating the relationships between gangs, violence and drug distribution. A recent study by the authors estimates about 1,100 gang-involved cities and towns (Klein, 1995)—cities of all shapes and sizes. Curry, Ball, and Decker (1995) report a national estimate of 735 jurisdictions with a population of at least 25,000 with gang crime problems. Our law enforcement respondents share a deep concern about the violence and drug activity reportedly associated with gangs in cities both large and small.[2] Furthermore, the implications of different law enforcement approaches to definitions of street gangs, gang membership and gang-related crime extend to the vast array of cities; police officials are grappling with developing methods of counting, reporting and understanding their gang problems.

But it is to Los Angeles, one of the "traditional" gang areas, often referred to as the gang "capital" of the United States, that we turned to address our research questions. The grim figure of 779 gang homicides occurring in the county of Los Angeles in 1994 provides corroboration for this appellation (McBride, Los Angeles Sheriff's Department, personal communication, August 21, 1995). We will, as before, refer to two definitional approaches, gang member versus gang motive homicides. The first are defined as having a gang member on either the assailant or victim side; the second are defined in terms of group-loyalty vs. individual interest as the principal reason for the act. The primary research questions can be stated quite simply: Updating the implications of using member versus motive definitions of gang homicides,

- How many homicides appear to result from gang motives? Has the proportion of gang-motivated cases changed from 1978–82 levels?
- What incident and participant characteristics distinguish member-defined gang cases from motive-defined gang cases? Are there different distinguishing characteristics when each group of cases is compared with nongang cases? Are there different patterns in each of these comparisons involving 1988–89 homicides from those found in 1978–82 homicides?
- How successful are these characteristics in classifying member-defined gang versus nongang cases and motive-defined gang versus nongang homicides? Are the classification rates similar to those found in earlier years?

Combining the drug and definition issues,

- What aspects of drug involvement distinguish member-defined gang cases from motive-defined gang cases, and each from their nongang counterparts?
- Is the classification of gang (member and motive) versus nongang cases improved by the consideration of aspects of drug involvement?

Following a brief discussion of the definitional issue and an overview of the study methods, we present the current Los Angeles data to address each of the research questions. We conclude with the implications of these findings for knowledge about gang violence in Los Angeles and elsewhere.

Definitional Approaches to 'Gang-Related' Crime

Law enforcement procedures for defining gang-related crime take on increased significance in the current context of the proliferation of cities with street gang problems. Despite the resurgence of ethnographic gang studies, these are limited in both the number of gangs and the cities investigated. Law enforcement is currently the best source available for comparisons of gang prevalence and violence. The definitional approaches adopted by these newer gang cities will have a distinct impact on perceptions of the scope and nature of gang violence in this country. There is a lack of consensus among law enforcement (Curry, Ball, and Fox, 1994; Curry et al., 1995; Spergel, 1988) and, for that matter, among researchers (Curry, 1991; Ehrensaft and Spergel, 1991), regarding the optimal definitional approach. There is even disagreement as to the presumed value of adopting common definitions (Decker and Kempf-Leonard, 1991; Horowitz, 1990). Ball and Curry (1995) recently lodged the following criticism against their academic coworkers: "Unfortunately . . . few if any gang researchers and theorists have been sufficiently conscious of their own definitional stances, with the result that their definitions have carried too many latent connotations, treated correlates or consequences as properties or causes, or contributed to similar errors of logic" (p. 239). Yet, a recent symposium of street gang experts from state and local law enforcement agencies across the country issued a call for standardized definitions and provided a model based upon the consensus reached at this meeting (National Drug Intelligence Center [NDIC], 1995).

Among law enforcement agencies, there are two basic approaches to defining gang-related violence. Officials in Los Angeles and many other cities have adopted a rather broad definitional policy, designating an incident as gang-related if either the suspect or victim is a gang member. This is the approach recommended by the NDIC gathering described above. Officials in Chicago and other cities apply the more stringent criterion of a direct link to gang function. In Chicago, there must be positive evidence that gang activity or gang membership was the motive for the encounter (Block, 1991). Examples of such motives are retaliation, territoriality, recruitment, and "representing" (graffiti, wearing gang colors, shouting gang slogans, etc.) (Bobrowski, 1988). We refer to these two approaches as "gang-member" and "gang-motive" definitions. (See Maxson and Klein, 1990, for a detailed description of these definitional approaches.) A recent national survey of prosecutors in 192 jurisdictions that have addressed gangs found that equal numbers in large jurisdictions adopted each approach (Institute for Law and Justice, 1994). More small jurisdictions (59 percent) use the narrower definition, that is, a crime committed by a gang member for the benefit of a gang.

For the current study, we posed questions regarding the implications of the two definitional approaches. The first is a prevalence question: What proportion of the homicides designated as gang-involved by the member definition would also satisfy the motive requirement? This analysis has both operational and statistical significance. Gang homicides are often assigned to investigators with special gang expertise, which may produce more positive investigative outcomes (Maxson, Klein, and Gordon, 1990). The number of gang homicides reported would certainly differ. In 1994, law enforcement gang experts in the city of Los Angeles tallied 370 gang homicides, or a whopping 44 percent of all homicides occurring in the city in that year (Los Angeles Police Department, personal communication, August 23, 1995). On the other hand, the Chicago Police Department reported a 1994 figure of 293 gang homicides, a more moderate 32 percent of all homicides for that year (D. Hilbring, Chicago Police Department, personal communication, August 23, 1995).[3]

The second research question addresses the impact of the two definitional approaches on descriptions of the *nature* of gang homicide, particularly in comparison with nongang incidents. If the characteristics of the two types of gang cases are similar and the differences between gang and nongang incidents remain stable, then elements of gang violence can be compared from city to city, despite different operational approaches to defining gang-related crime. Legitimate, cross-city comparisons provide a foundation for building generalized knowledge about gangs.

That, in essence, was the conclusion we drew from the earlier analyses of two data sets made up of gang and nongang homicides that occurred in the city of Los Angeles and in county areas patrolled by the Los Angeles Sheriff's Department (LASD) (Maxson and Klein, 1990). The Los Angeles Police Department (LAPD) homicides were drawn from three station areas over the years 1979–1981; the LASD data spanned the years 1978–1982 and included all 19 station areas. The two data sets were analyzed separately, but the conclusions held for both jurisdictions: Applying the criterion of the presence of a gang motive reduced the number of gang homicides by about half, but for the most part, the qualitative differences between gang and nongang cases were constant, regardless of the definitional criteria used.

We noted some variation between the two jurisdictions, but these differences were minor in contrast with the overall stability of gang versus nongang distinctions. We confirmed the conclusions emerging from the bivariate analyses with discriminant analysis techniques, noting once again some differences, but an overall pattern of consistency between the two definitional approaches.

We wondered whether these conclusions would hold up in more recent homicides and furthermore whether drug aspects of homicides might introduce some differences in the definitional analyses that we were not able to examine in the earlier project. Thus, we were able to combine our interests in both the drug and definitional aspects of gang violence with analyses of current gang and nongang homicides while updating our prior findings.

Method

Our current study includes homicides from five station areas in South Central Los Angeles, selected due to high levels of gang and drug activity. Three of the five stations were within the jurisdiction of the LAPD and two were county areas handled by the LASD. The data from the two departments are combined for all analyses reported in this chapter.

Gang and nongang homicides occurring in the five station areas during 1988 and 1989 were sampled using a random stratified approach to yield equal numbers of each type for collection. Officer-involved shootings and the few cases handled by specialized units other than the homicide division were deleted from the population. Lists of "gang-involved" cases were supplied by each jurisdiction's specialized gang unit. Both departments employ broad definitions of gang involvement including membership of participants on either side, behavioral indications during the incident, and other gang indicators that may emerge during the course of the investigation. In a previous study, we found the application of these criteria to homicide cases to be relatively stable over time in both jurisdictions (Klein, Gordon, and Maxson, 1986; Maxson, Gordon, and Klein, 1985). The sampling procedures resulted in 201 gang and 201 nongang homicides, reflecting about two-thirds of the gang homicides and slightly less of the nongang homicides. Despite the inclusion of two station areas from the LASD jurisdiction, it should be noted that about three-fourths of these cases are from LAPD.

A team of data collectors extracted information from extensive homicide investigation files. On occasion, files could not be located, and in a few instances, access was denied by the detective in possession of the case material; these cases were replaced by randomly selected cases from the remaining population. Coded items included descriptors of the incident (e.g., setting, automobile involvement, weapons, related case charges, additional injuries, and gang motives), participants (e.g., numbers on each side, relationship, demographics of designated victims and suspects, and stated gang affiliations), and an extensive list of drug indicators (use and sales paraphernalia, drugs found in investigation, autopsy results, drug use or sales by participants, aspects of the location, and drug motives). Intercoder reliability was assessed by duplicate coding of 10 percent of the sample. Overall, reliabilities were quite high (over .90), but it should be noted that the data collection was closely supervised, with lots of involvement by senior staff in coding decisions.

Findings

Assessing the Implications of Different Definitional Approaches

We begin with the basic question of how many of the homicides labeled as gang-involved by Los Angeles gang units, utilizing the broad member definition, would retain their gang status under the more stringent motive criterion. Then moving beyond the issue of case numbers, we use the incident and participant characteristics to explore the differences between the two types of gang cases and the respective gang-nongang comparisons. Finally, discriminant analytic techniques permit an assessment of the overall impact of these variables on distinguishing gang from nongang homicides. We examine whether the motive approach produces a "purified" set of gang cases, more clearly distinct from nongang cases, with a wholly different character from homicides categorized using the member criterion.

Of the 201 homicides labeled by the gang units as gang-member involved, 120 (60 percent) also had statements of gang motives present in the case file investigation materials. Similar motive statements also appeared in 8 (4 percent) of the 201 nongang homicides.[4] Both figures are slightly higher than those found in the 1978–82 homicides. In the earlier study, 52 percent of the member-defined gang homicides and 2 percent of the nongang homicides included statements of gang motives. This difference over time may reflect changes in the nature of gang activity, increased sensitivity of law enforcement investigators to gang issues, differences in the sampling strategies employed in the two studies, or some combination of these factors.

Clearly, a narrow definition such as Chicago's would reduce the reported Los Angeles rate significantly. The revised 1994 figure for the city of Los Angeles would be in the neighborhood of 222 gang-related homicides, as compared with the 370 incidents reported using the member definition.[5] Both figures are high and represent substantial human and social costs, but one could reasonably question whether 222 homicides would have provoked the intense law enforcement and press reactions to gang activity that we have observed over the last several years in Los Angeles. Moreover, the new figure for Los Angeles is considerably lower than Chicago's total of 293. When the issue is *prevalence*, that is, the volume of gang activity, clearly comparisons between cities with different definitional styles would be quite inappropriate.

Putting aside the issue of comparative incident counts, we now turn to the question of, "So what?" If reducing the pool of gang incidents to the presumably more "pure," motivated cases does not substantially alter the descriptions of gang violence, then comparisons regarding the *nature* of gang activity between cities with different definitional policies may be quite legitimate.

We approached this issue by utilizing a series of variables describing the incidents and participants and comparing gang with nongang cases. This required construction of a new data set made up of the 128 identified gang-motive cases and a comparable group of 128 nongang cases, sampled randomly from a reconstituted population of the remaining homicides. This reconstitution was a complex procedure, but allowed those member-defined gang cases *not* meeting the motive criteria to fall within the nongang motive group. For the comparison member-defined data set, we sampled 128 gang and 128 nongang cases from the original 402 cases.[6] Table 16.1 shows the bivariate comparisons of gang-nongang differences in case characteristics, employing first the member definition and then the motive definition.

The construction of Table 16.1 permits several types of comparisons. Characteris-

Table 16.1

Characteristics of Gang and Nongang Homicides Using Member and Motive Definitions

	Member-Defined			Motive-Defined		
	Gang (n = 128)[b]	Nongang (n = 128)[b]	p[a]	Gang (n = 128)[b]	Nongang (n = 128)[b]	p[a]
Late afternoon-to-evening occurrence	49%	32%	**	52%	34%	**
Automobile present	80%	44%	***	83%	54%	***
Street location	58%	35%	***	65%	32%	***
Fear/threat of retaliation	37%	20%	**	40%	19%	***
Associated charge: violent	41%	16%	***	38%	30%	NS
Associated charge: robbery	6%	6%	NS	2%	13%	***
Gun(s) present	95%	74%	***	98%	76%	***
Other victim injuries present	38%	12%	***	38%	20%	**
Clear prior relationship	24%	48%	***	18%	47%	***
Mean number victim participants	4.13	1.79	**	4.47	1.95	**
Mean number suspect participants	2.70	1.71	***	2.83	1.95	***
Proportion male victims	.88	.73	***	.92	.78	***
Proportion male suspects	.96	.85	**	.98	.89	***
Proportion black suspects	.86	.88	NS	.84	.82	NS
Mean age victims	24.2	33.1	***	22.7	31.8	***
Mean age suspects	20.5	29.6	***	19.7	26.5	***

Notes: NS = not significant.
[a]Significance levels were determined by chi-squares or t-tests (*p<.05; **p<.01; ***p<.001).
[b]Numbers of cases included in each analysis vary according to missing values.

tics of the two types of gang cases are displayed in the first and fourth columns.[7] There is a striking similarity between the two sets of percentages and means. Motive-defined gang cases are slightly more likely to occur on the street and are slightly less likely to involve participants with a clear prior relationship than member-defined incidents. These differences are minimal and not substantially significant. In fact, comparing the incident and participant characteristics of the two types of gang cases suggests that we are not dealing with two distinct types at all. Descriptions of the nature of gang homicide categorized by either definitional approach are for all intents and purposes identical.

Does the similarity between the two types of gang cases extend to comparisons between the two groups of nongang homicides? Employing the motive definition results in the transfer of some member-defined gang cases[8] into the nongang population and may alter the aggregated character of the nongang comparison pool.

A cursory review of the second and fifth columns of Table 16.1 suggests that the two groups of nongang cases show more differences than the two sets of gang cases. Presence of automobiles, associated charges, and other (than the homicide) victim injuries are higher in nongang cases using the gang motive approach than in nongang incidents under the member approach. This pattern suggests increased gang aspects of nongang cases when the gang motive standard is applied. The direction of the slight differences in the participant characteristics (more participants, proportionally more males, more blacks, of younger ages) is consistent with this interpretation. Does this slight change in the nature of nongang homicides affect descriptions of the differences between gang and nongang incidents? The relevant comparisons are displayed by the two vertical halves of Table 16.1, with particular reference to the significance tests reported in the third and sixth columns.

The overall consistency between the two vertical halves of Table 16.1 is quite remarkable. With only a few exceptions, the same variables significantly differentiate gang from nongang homicides, and there are no reversals of direction. Consistent with the 1978–1982 incidents, the presence of associated charges seems to differentiate gang cases under one definitional approach but not the other, as exemplified by the lower proportion of nongang member-defined cases with additional violent offenses.

It appears that the motive approach is associated with a lower likelihood of gang designation when robbery is a feature of the case. This is hardly surprising and very consistent with conceptual distinctions between the member and motive definitions. Personal gain, rather than gang benefit, is more often viewed as the offender's primary motive. Perhaps more surprising is the marked similarity between the two definitional approaches in most of the incident and participant descriptors.

A more mixed picture emerges when we turn to more sophisticated, multivariate techniques in order to examine these distinctions further. Discriminant analysis organizes all the variables in such a way as to maximize their capacity to discriminate gang from nongang cases. The standardized coefficients reported in Table 16.2 show the relative contribution of each variable toward distinguishing gang from nongang incidents. The drug variables were not included in this analysis, and associated violent charges were dropped due to high correlations with other variables. The rank ordering of the size of the coefficients is provided in parentheses to facilitate the comparison between the two data sets. Eta squared (eta^2) is a measure of the ability of the discriminant function to explain the variance between gang and nongang cases.

In both data sets, mean age of suspects emerges as by far the strongest discriminator between gang and nongang incidents. The value of eta squared and the classification results are similar, although slightly higher in the motive-defined analysis. The overall pattern is one of shared variables, but in a departure from the bivariate results, three variables did not achieve sufficient discriminatory power to enter the motive-defined function. Two of these variables, mean age of victims and automobile presence, ranked quite high in the member-defined function. Consistent with the bivariate analysis, robbery as an associated case offense figured prominently in the motive function, but was the lowest-ranked variable in the member function. The rank-order correlation (rho) between the two columns of figures is a quite low .19. Further examination of the variable rankings in the discriminant analyses performed previously on the older LAPD and LASD homicide data sets shows equally low correlations.

Overall, data presented in Tables 16.1 and 16.2 do not suggest that drastic changes in the depiction of gang homicides, or in the characterization of the differences between gang and nongang incidents occur when different operational approaches to gang crime definitions are applied by law enforcement. Descriptions of the *nongang* comparison group may be more vulnerable to definitional variations, but on the whole, we find a large measure of stability in the gang/nongang comparisons, at least at the bivariate level.

Multivariate analyses are less supportive of a stance that definitional policies make little difference in depictions of the character of gang violence. Despite similarities between the results of discriminant analyses of the two data sets, there are marked differences in the contributions that a few variables make to the discriminant functions. The import of robbery as an associated charge for the motive-derived function makes sense. It is possible that victim age and automobile presence failed to enter the motive function as a consequence of special features of robbery incidents, but there were too few such cases to examine this speculation. Expanding the analysis to include drug aspects of the incident may prove useful.

Table 16.2
Gang Versus Nongang Discriminant Analysis Results: Member and Motive-Defined Comparisons

	Member Defined [a]	*Motive Defined* [a]
Mean age, suspects	–.555 (1)	–.603 (1)
Number suspect participants	.243 (2)	.239 (6)
Mean age, victims	–.224 (3)	N.S.
Automobile present	.219 (4)	N.S.
Clear prior relationship	–.207 (5)	.266 (3)
Other victim injuries present	.190 (6)	.192 (9)
Proportion male suspects	.184 (7)	.253 (4)
Proportion black suspects	.170 (8)	.239 (7)
Late afternoon-to-evening occurrence	.166 (9)	.154 (11)
Fear/threat of retaliation present	.162 (10)	.243 (5)
Number victim participants	.150 (11)	.217 (8)
Gun(s) present	.139 (12)	.179 (10)
Proportion male victims	.139 (13)	N.S.
Associated charge: robbery	–.117 (14)	–.444 (2)
Street location	N.S.	.129 (12)
Variance explained (eta^2)	.429	.461
Classification success (%)		
Gang	85.5	91.3
Nongang	71.4	75.0
Overall	80.6	83.4

Notes: NS = not significant.
[a]Weights are standardized canonical discriminant function coefficients. Negative valence indicates inverse relationship with gang. Relative rankings are noted in parentheses. Member-defined analysis includes 113 gang cases and 98 nongang cases (45 cases dropped for missing values on at least one variable). Motive-defined analysis includes 115 gang cases and 108 nongang cases (33 cases dropped for missing values).

Combining the Drug and Definition Issues

The presence of robbery as an associated case offense affects whether or not a homicide would be handled as a gang crime in departments, depending upon their different definitional policies. Drug involvement may well have a similar impact. Drug information was collected on quite specific items, most of which did not produce sufficiently high frequencies to support analyses of gang-nongang differences. This fact in itself throws some doubt on the purportedly close relationship between gangs, drugs, and violence. Alternatively, we computed variables that represent more general aspects of drug involvement and reflect the gang-drug issues in South Central Los Angeles. Most drug (excluding alcohol) mentions were coded to indicate the type of drug involved. From these, we computed a variable for any *mention of cocaine* in the case. The *presence of any type of sales* or *distributional aspect* of the case could derive from the nature of the incident location, sales involvement by participants on either side, or motives related to drug distribution. Finally *mentions of any drug-related motive* for the homicide includes conflicts over drug use, although these are far less frequent than motives stemming from drug distribution (for example, conflicts over drug territory and dealer rip-offs). In Table 16.3, we present the data on the three drug dimensions in gang and nongang incidents reflecting the two definitional approaches.

If drug sales are *not* intrinsically related to gang affairs, then one would expect the three drug dimensions to be less apparent in gang-motivated cases than in member-defined gang cases.[9] In comparing the first and fourth columns in Table 16.3, it appears that employing the gang motive definition reduces the proportion of gang cases with cocaine involvement, drug sales aspects, or drug motives (see Note 8). Two of these, cocaine involvement and the presence of drug motives, appear with similar frequency in nongang cases, regardless of whether they are "nongang" by virtue of no gang members or no gang motive (see columns two and five in Table 16.3). But the third, the proportion of nongang cases with an aspect of drug sales, is higher when the gang motive criterion is employed.

Drug aspects of the incidents do distinguish gang from nongang cases, but these vary by definitional approach. For this analysis, we tested for gang versus nongang differences by comparing columns 1 and 2 (member approach) and then, columns 4 and 5 (motive approach) in Table 16.3. The statistical tests for the significance of these respective differences are reported in the third and sixth column. Drug sales involvement separates gang member cases from nongang incidents, but not from gang-motivated cases. Neither cocaine presence nor drug motives distinguishes gang member cases from their nongang counterparts. On the other hand, both of these features differentiate motive-defined gang cases from nongang cases. These findings would be sur-

Table 16.3
Drug Characteristics of Gang and Nongang Homicides Using Member and Motive Definitions

	Member Defined			*Motive Defined*		
	Gang (n = 128)[b]	Nongang (n = 128)[b]	p[a]	Gang (n = 128)[b]	Nongang (n = 128)[b]	p[a]
Cocaine involved	37%	47%	NS	29%	48%	**
Drug sales aspect	41%	28%	*	34%	37%	NS
Drug motive mentioned	20%	27%	NS	12%	28%	***

Notes: NS = not significant.
[a]Significance levels were determined by chi-squares or t-tests (*p <.05; **p <.01; ***p <.001).
[b]Numbers of cases included in each analysis varies according to missing values.

prising to those who argue a close gang-drug-violence connection. Drug motives and cocaine involvement are *less* common in gang-motivated than in nongang homicides.

These bivariate results of the drug variables revealed interesting gang-nongang distinctions that varied between the two definitional styles. The "purification" of gang features resulting from the application of the motive approach reveals that drug aspects are important in distinguishing gang from nongang cases—cocaine and drug motives are more often featured in nongang cases.

Once again, we turned to discriminant analysis strategies to examine the relative impact of the drug variables. Unfortunately, the three drug dimensions have high intercorrelations that permitted the inclusion of only one drug variable in the multivariate analysis. A separate set of discriminant analyses was performed with the same set of incident and participant variables, plus mention of a drug motive.

As shown in Table 16.4, the drug motive variable entered both member and motive functions and ranked quite high (second) in the motive-defined data set. From the bivariate results, low ranking of drug motive in the member-defined function was not surprising. But the summary statistics (eta squared and classification) were affected only minimally by the inclusion of drug motive, nor did it appear to influence the relative contributions of the other variables. The rank-order correlations between the two member-defined functions (i.e., with and without the drug motive variable) and between the two motive-defined functions both exceeded .95. Clearly, our quest to ex-

Table 16.4

Gang Versus Nongang Discriminant Analysis Results: Member and Motive-Defined Comparisons (Drug Motive Included)

	Member Defined[a]	*Motive Defined*[a]
Mean age, suspects	−.532 (1)	−.582 (1)
Mean age, victims	−.241 (2)	N.S.
Number suspect participants	.235 (3)	.259 (8)
Automobile present	.212 (4)	N.S.
Clear prior relationship	−.200 (5)	−.309 (5)
Proportion male suspects	.198 (6)	.310 (4)
Other victim injuries present	.188 (7)	.176 (10)
Proportion black suspects	.184 (8)	.277 (7)
Fear/threat of retaliation present	.169 (9)	.278 (6)
Late afternoon-to-evening occurrence	.162 (10)	.141 (12)
Gun(s) present	.158 (11)	.195 (9)
Drug motive mentioned	***−.158 (12)***	***−.397 (2)***
Number victim participants	.146 (13)	.175 (11)
Proportion male victims	.129 (14)	N.S.
Associated charge: robbery	N.S.	−.372 (3)
Street location	N.S.	N.S.
Variance explained (eta^2)	.432	.495
Classification success (%)		
Gang	86.8	91.3
Nongang	74.5	75.9
Overall	81.3	83.9

Notes: NS = not significant.

[a]Weights are standardized canonical discriminant function coefficients. Negative valence indicates inverse relationship with gang. Relative rankings are noted in parentheses. Member-defined analysis includes 113 gang cases and 98 nongang cases (45 cases dropped for missing values on at least one variable). Motive-defined analysis includes 115 gang cases and 108 nongang cases (33 cases dropped for missing values).

plain the differential contribution of variables to gang-nongang distinctions has not been aided by the inclusion of drug motive.

Conclusion

Overall, these analyses of 1988 and 1989 incidents confirm our prior conclusions about the implications of different law enforcement policies regarding the designation of gang homicides. Adopting the narrower, motive criterion substantially reduces the number of gang homicides reported by jurisdictions confronting violent gang activity. Comparisons of rates between jurisdictions embracing different definitional approaches are clearly *not* valid unless motive information is available to restructure a member-defined population of incidents (or conversely, if member information is available on non-motive but gang member involved cases).

Cross-city comparisons of bivariate descriptions of gang, as compared with nongang, homicide characteristics *are* appropriate, but within certain limitations. On the one hand, the use of firearms, participant demographics, and the number of and relationship between participants are among the many examples of case characteristics that appear to be unaffected by definitional styles. On the other hand, comparisons of drug involvement and additional violent offenses should be approached with extreme caution.

Other general statements can be derived from the data on drug aspects of homicide. The finding that drug motives and cocaine mentions appear more commonly in nongang cases but sales involvement is more frequent in gang incidents is interesting because most of the specific drug motives mentioned concerned sales rather than use. This suggests that although participants in gang homicides are more likely to have roles in the sales or distribution of drugs, this sales involvement may be less likely to figure as a "cause" of the homicide than in nongang cases. These findings do not support a strong connection between gang drug sales and violence. If anything, the sales-violence connection seems stronger in nongang cases. In any case, the term "drug-related" is just as ambiguous as is the term "gang-related." The "involved" versus "motivated" distinctions could be applied to an analysis of drug homicides just as we have used the member versus motive categories to investigate gang homicides.

Applying motive versus more general gang involvement criteria certainly results in different prevalence rates. Drug aspects emerge less frequently in cases designated as "gang" under the motive criterion. Given the ubiquitous association between gangs, drugs, and violence in the popular media, one wonders whether the connection would be made less readily if motive became the primary consideration for police (or media) reports of violence. Different definitional approaches to labeling gang and drug aspects of homicides could result in varying social constructions about the nature of gang and drug violence connections.

Since the use of discriminant analytic techniques is relatively limited in law enforcement circles, it remains for researchers to be somewhat troubled by the multivariate results. Frankly, we are stymied as to how to interpret the intricacies of the performance of certain variables and must fall back on the customary positions of caution and the call for more research of this type. In particular, it would be helpful if data from other cities could be investigated with similar analytic techniques.

Finally, there is the issue of which approach is better, more valid, or more useful. For local law enforcement, it is probably *most* important to apply definitional policies consistently, regardless of the type of definition used. Both approaches are vulnerable to the availability of information. Motives can be quite difficult to determine, even with the resources usually devoted to homicide investigation; motive information often is not available for other types of offenses. Reliable gang rosters are quite costly to develop and maintain, require a strong commitment to intelligence gathering, and place emphasis on systematic application of criteria for gang membership.

For research purposes, the broader member approach provides the data to examine incident-based characteristics of all homicides involving gang members. Data are also available on the subset of incidents closely tied to gang function or operations. Thus, there is more information accessible to researchers with the member definition. Finally, both definitional approaches present opportunities for valid comparisons between cities, a prerequisite for developing a comprehensive understanding of the nature of gang violence.

Notes

1. This research was supported by the Harry Frank Guggenheim Foundation and the Southern California Injury Prevention center (under the auspices of the Public Health Service Centers for Disease Control grant # R49/CCR903622). We are grateful to officials in the Los Angeles Police Department and the Los Angeles Sheriff's Department for their cooperation. Many thanks also to the team of USC students who helped collect these data, under the supervision of the ever-vigilant Lea C. Cunningham. Points of view expressed herein are solely those of the authors.
2. Space limitations do not permit an extended discussion here of street gang involvement in drug distribution. Perceptions of a tight or highly organized connection between gangs and drugs have been supported by some research (Mieczkowski, 1986; Padilla, 1992; Sanchez-Jankowski, 1991; Skolnick, 1990; Taylor, 1990), but also severely challenged by many recent studies (Block and Block, 1994; Decker and Van Winkle, 1994; Esbensen and Huizinga, 1993; Fagan, 1989; Hagedorn, 1994; Klein and Maxson, 1994; Maxson, 1995; Moore, 1990; Waldorf and Lauderback, 1993). Interested readers should refer to the recent reviews of this literature by Klein (1995) and Decker (1995).
3. The 1994 figure of 293 gang homicides in Chicago represents a marked increase over the 1993 figure of 129. Follow-up inquiries with the Chicago Police Department's Crime Analysis Unit confirmed the 1994 count. This unit has the official responsibility for designating gang homicides. Officials report that the command structure implemented a new definition in 1994 and encouraged the practice of inferring gang motive in ambiguous cases. The current Chicago definition of gang-related homicides is, "The offender must be a gang member and any of the following apply: 1) the offender is engaged in any activity which furthers the gang enterprise; or 2) the by-product of the offender's gang activity results in a death."

   Crime Analysis Unit personnel report their perception that there has been a genuine increase in both turf and drug-motivated incidents, but also acknowledge that the application of the new definition would produce higher gang homicide numbers than in prior years. This exemplifies the importance of examining shifts and definitional stances; Chicago perhaps should be removed from the group of cities that are thought to employ the "Chicago definition."
4. A brief review of the summary descriptions of these cases suggested two patterns. In most cases, there was speculation about various motives without confirmatory reports by witnesses or participants. In a few cases, the drug issues dominated the gang issues. Both patterns are also present in the gang incidents with gang motives, however, so it is not clear why these eight cases were not designated as "gang" by the units.
5. It should be noted that Los Angeles city figures, rather than county, are more appropriate for comparison with Chicago.
6. Data collectors recorded all statements of gang affiliation in the investigation files. It is interesting to note that 11 percent of the member-defined gang cases had no affiliation statements while 22 percent of the member-defined nongang cases had gang members possibly involved in the incident. Apparently, even the more inclusive definitional approach based upon gang status of the participants does not result in designating all cases with gang aspects as "gang crimes." The motive-defined nongang cases had only a slightly higher percentage (29 percent) of incidents with gang members involved.
7. Because the same cases can appear in both the member and motive categories, statistical tests would be inappropriate.
8. That is, those with gang members involved but without gang motives expressed as the cause of the incident.
9. Using a database maintained by the LAPD homicide unit, Meehan and O'Carroll (1992) found a much lower rate of narcotics involvement in gang-motivated homicides. "Gang motive" was entered by detectives in 345 of the 2,162 homicides occurring between January 1, 1986, and August 31, 1988. Only 18 of

the 345 homicides also were coded positively by detectives as "narcotics involved." Meehan and O'Carroll examined investigation files on a subset (adolescent victims who died in South Central Los Angeles in a 20-month period) of the homicides in the LAPD database and report similar results. Although the number of gang-motive homicides we identified would be reduced by limitation to only those cases with clear *confirmation* of the gang motive (available in about 60 percent of the 128 homicides with gang motives mentioned in our data set), this would still not account for the much lower figure reported by Meehan and O'Carroll.

References

Ball, R. A., & Curry, G. D. (1995). The logic of definition in criminology: Purposes and methods for defining "gangs." *Criminology*, 33(2), 225–245.

Block, C. R. (1991). Early warning system for street gang violence crisis areas. Chicago: Illinois Criminal Justice Information Authority.

Block, C. R., & Block, R. (1994). Street gang crime in Chicago. *Research in Brief*. Washington, D.C.: National Institute of Justice, Office of Justice Programs, U.S. Department of Justice.

Bobrowski, L. J. (1988). Collecting, organizing and reporting street gang crime. Chicago: Chicago Police Department, Special Functions Group.

Curry, G. D. (1991, November). Measuring street gang-related homicide. Paper presentation, American Society of Criminology annual meetings.

Curry, G. D., Ball, R. A., & Decker, S. H. (1995). An update on gang crime and law enforcement recordkeeping. St. Louis: University of Missouri, Department of Criminology and Criminal Justice.

Curry, G. D., Ball, R. A., & Fox, Robert J. (1994). Gang crime and law enforcement recordkeeping. *Research in Brief*. Washington, D.C.: National Institute of Justice, Office of Justice Programs, U.S. Department of Justice.

Decker, S. (1995). Gangs, gang members and drug sales. St. Louis: University of Missouri, Department of Criminology and Criminal Justice.

Decker, S., & Kempf-Leonard, K. (1991). Constructing gangs: The social construction of youth activities. *Criminal Justice Policy Review*, 4, 271–291.

Decker, S., & Van Winkle, B. (1994). Slinging dope: The role of gangs and gang members in drug sales. *Justice Quarterly*, 583–604.

Ehrensaft, K., & Spergel, I. (1991). Police technical assistance manual. Youth Gang Suppression and Intervention Program. Chicago: University of Chicago, School of Social Service Administration.

Esbensen, F. A., & Huizinga, D. (1993). Gangs, drugs, and delinquency in a survey of urban youth. *Criminology*, 31, 565–586.

Fagan, J. (1989). The social organization of drug use and drug dealing among urban gangs. *Criminology*, 27, 633–667.

Hagedorn, J. M. (1994). Homeboys, dope fiends, legits and new jacks. *Criminology*, 32, 197–219.

Hilbring, D. (1995). Commander, Gang Crime Section, Chicago Police Department. Personal communication, August 23, 1995.

Horowitz, R. (1990). Sociological perspectives on gangs. In C. R. Huff (Ed.), *Gangs in America*. Newbury Park, CA: Sage Publications.

Institute for Law and Justice (1994). Gang prosecution in the United States. Final report prepared for the National Institute of Justice. Alexandria, VA: Institute for Law and Justice.

Klein, M. W. (1995). *The American street gang*. New York: Oxford University Press.

Klein, M. W., Gordon, M. A., & Maxson, C. L. (1986). The impact of police investigations on police-reported rates of gang and nongang homicides. *Criminology*, 24, 489–512.

Klein, M. W., & Maxson, C. L. (1994). Gangs and cocaine trafficking. In D. MacKenzie & C. Uchida (Eds.), *Drugs and the criminal justice system: Evaluating public policy initiatives*. Newbury Park, CA: Sage Publications.

Los Angeles Police Department (1995). Gang Information Section and Press Relations. Personal communication, August 23, 1995.

Maxson, C. L. (1995). Street gangs and drug sales in two suburban cities. *Research in Brief*. Washington, D.C.: National Institute of Justice, Office of Justice Programs, U.S. Department of Justice.

Maxson, C. L., Gordon, M. A., & Klein, M. W. (1985). Differences between gang and nongang homicides. *Criminology*, 23(2), 209–222.

Maxson, C. L., & Klein, M. W. (1990). Street gang violence: Twice as great, or half as great? In C. R. Huff (Ed.), *Gangs in America*. Newbury Park, CA: Sage Publications.

Maxson, C. L., Klein, M. W., & Gordon, M. A. (1990). Street gang violence as a generalizable pattern. Los Angeles: University of Southern California, Social Science Research Institute.

McBride, W. (1995). Sergeant, Operation Safe Streets, Los Angeles Sheriff's Department. Personal communication, August 21, 1995.

Meehan, P. J., & O'Carroll, P. (1992). Gangs, drugs, and homicide in Los Angeles. *American Journal of Diseases of Children*, 146, 683–687.

Mieczkowski, T. (1986). Geeking up and throwing down: Heroin street life in Detroit. *Criminology*, 24, 645–666.

Moore, J. (1990). Gangs, drugs, and violence. In M. De La Rosa, E. Y. Lambert, & B. Gropper (Eds.), *Drugs and violence: Causes, correlates and consequences*. Washington, D.C.: NIDA Research Monograph Series.

National Drug Intelligence Center (NDIC) (1995). NDIC Street Gang Symposium: Selected findings. Jonestown, PA: NDIC.

Padilla, F. (1992). *The gang as an American enterprise*. New Brunswick, NJ: Rutgers University Press.

Sanchez-Jankowski, M. (1991). *Islands in the street*. Berkeley, CA: University of California Press.

Skolnick, J. H. (1990). The social structure of street drug dealing. *American Journal of Police*, 9, 1–41.

Spergel, I. A. (1988). *Report of the Law Enforcement Youth Gang Symposium*. Chicago: University of Chicago, School of Social Service Administration.

Taylor, C. S. (1990). *Dangerous society*. East Lansing, MI: Michigan State University Press.

Waldorf, D., & Lauderback, D. (1993). Gang drug sales in San Francisco: Organized or freelance? Alameda, CA: Institute for Scientific Analysis. ✦

Chapter 17
Street Gang Crime in Chicago

Carolyn Rebecca Block
and
Richard Block

In this report prepared for the U.S. Department of Justice, the Blocks draw from extensive data on gang crime in Chicago. The definition of gang crime is limited to actions specifically linked to gang function. The complexity of the relationship between crime and gang involvement is revealed in the ebb and flow of gang homicide over a 25-year period, in the differential patterns of lethal and nonlethal violence, and in the variations in level and type of crime among the 40 major street gangs active in this city. The Blocks have pioneered the use of computer mapping to enhance intervention efforts. By identifying concentrations of gang crime in certain neighborhoods, "hotspots" can be pinpointed to focus law enforcement and prevention resources.

Street gang activity—legal and illegal, violent and nonviolent, lethal and nonlethal—occurs disproportionately among neighborhoods and population groups. Types of incidents tend to cluster and increase in bursts in specific neighborhoods and among specific gangs.

Neighborhoods often differ sharply in the predominant type of street gang-motivated

Revised and Reprinted from: Carolyn Rebecca Block and Richard Block, "Street Gang Crime in Chicago." In *Research in Brief*, December. Copyright © 1993 by the National Department of Justice, Office of Justice Programs, U. S. Department of Justice. Reprinted by permission.

Issues and Findings

Discussed in the Brief

A study supported by the National Institute of Justice of street gang-motivated violence in one major U.S. city—Chicago. Analysis of police homicide records over 26 years and gang-motivated incident records over 3 years revealed the street gang affiliation of every offender and the location of each offense, which gives a detailed picture of gang activity and the relationships of individual, gang, and neighborhood characteristics.

Key Issues

Gangs—and gang-related violence and drug trafficking—are growing problems across the country. Street gangs and the crimes in which they engage cannot be viewed as monolithic: One neighborhood may be unaffected, while nearby, another is the marketplace for a gang's drug operation or the center of lethal turf battles. Bursts of gang-related violence appear among specific gangs and suddenly stop.

Key Findings

For a 3-year period, 1987–1990, the study results included the following:

- Gang-related, high-crime neighborhoods can be classified into three types: turf hot spots, where gangs fight over territory control; drug hot spots, where gang-motivated drug offenses concentrate; and turf and drug hot spots, where gang-motivated crimes relate to both.
- Gang involvement in violence and homicide is more often turf-related than drug-related. Only 8 of 288 gang-motivated homicides were related to drugs.
- The city's four largest street gangs were identified with most of the street gang crime. Representing 51 percent of all street gang members, they accounted for 69 percent of recorded criminal incidents.
- The rate of street gang-motivated crime in the 2 most dangerous areas was 76 times that of the 2 safest.
- A gun was the lethal weapon used in almost all gang-motivated homicides. Use of high-caliber, automatic, or semiautomatic weapons dramatically increased.

These and other findings of the research have policy implications for formulating intervention strategies:

- Programs to reduce nonlethal street gang violence must be targeted to the specific street gang problems in each neighborhood.
- Effective intervention strategies must be built on continuously updated information.

Target Audience

Law enforcement officials, community leaders, policymakers, and researchers.

incidents they experience. For example, one city neighborhood may be unaffected by street gang activity, while another close by may be a marketplace for a street gang's drug operation, and yet a third may be plagued by frequent and lethal turf battles.

In addition, the chief criminal activities of one street gang often differ from those of another. For example, one outbreak of lethal street gang violence may be characterized by escalating retribution and revenge, while another may be associated with expansion of a drug business into new territory. Consequently, street gangs and the crimes in which they engage cannot be viewed as monolithic in nature.

This Research in Brief describes these and other patterns of street gang-related violence in a major U.S. city—Chicago. All available information, including Chicago police records of illegal street gang-motivated activity—from vandalism to drug offenses to violent offenses (both lethal and nonlethal)—was examined across time, neighborhood, and street gang affiliation. Individual, gang-level, and neighborhood-level characteristics were also analyzed to determine the relationships among these three factors. The results of the analysis give one of the most complete pictures of street gang crime available today.

Study Methodology

Researchers examined Chicago gang homicide data over a 26-year period, from 1965 through 1990, and detailed information on other gang-related crime from 1987 to 1990. Two methods of analysis were used to determine the extent to which neighborhoods differed in the type and concentration of street gang activity and to examine the neighborhood characteristics that were associated with high levels of lethal and nonlethal street gang activity.[1] The information analyzed was primarily from Chicago Police Department (CPD) records, which were organized into three sets of data on Chicago homicides, street gang-motivated offenses, and street gang territories. Neighborhood characteristics and population data for rate calculation were obtained from the U.S. Bureau of the Census. This information was gathered by tract and aggregated into the 77 Chicago community areas (Exhibit 1).[2]

Researchers geocoded the address of each homicide and street gang-motivated incident. Boundaries of the community areas were mapped, geocoded offenses were aggregated by community area, and offenses were analyzed in relation to population and other community characteristics. Finally, the densest concentrations (hot spot areas) of individual addresses of street gang-related incidents were identified regardless of arbitrary boundaries and related to gang turfs, gang activity, and community characteristics.

Data on Homicides

One of the largest and most detailed data sets on violence ever collected in the United States, the Chicago homicide data set contains information on every homicide in police records from 1965 to 1990.[3] More than 200 variables were collected for the 19,323 homicides in this data set. The crime analysis unit of the Chicago Police Department has maintained a summary—Murder Analysis Report (MAR)—of each homicide over the 26-year period. On the basis of these reports, 1,311 homicides were classified as street gang-motivated.

Data on Street-Gang-Motivated Offenses

This data set included information on 17,085 criminal offenses that occurred from 1987 to 1990 that were classified by the police as street gang-related. These offenses were categorized as follows:

- 288 homicides.
- 8,828 nonlethal violent offenses (aggravated and simple assault and battery).
- 5,888 drug offenses (violations related to possession or sale of hard or soft drugs).
- 2,081 other offenses (includes more than 100 specific crimes ranging from liquor law violations to intimidation, mob action, vandalism, robbery, and weapons law violations).[4]

Exhibit 1

Non-Lethal and Lethal Street Gang Motivated Crimes: 1987-1990

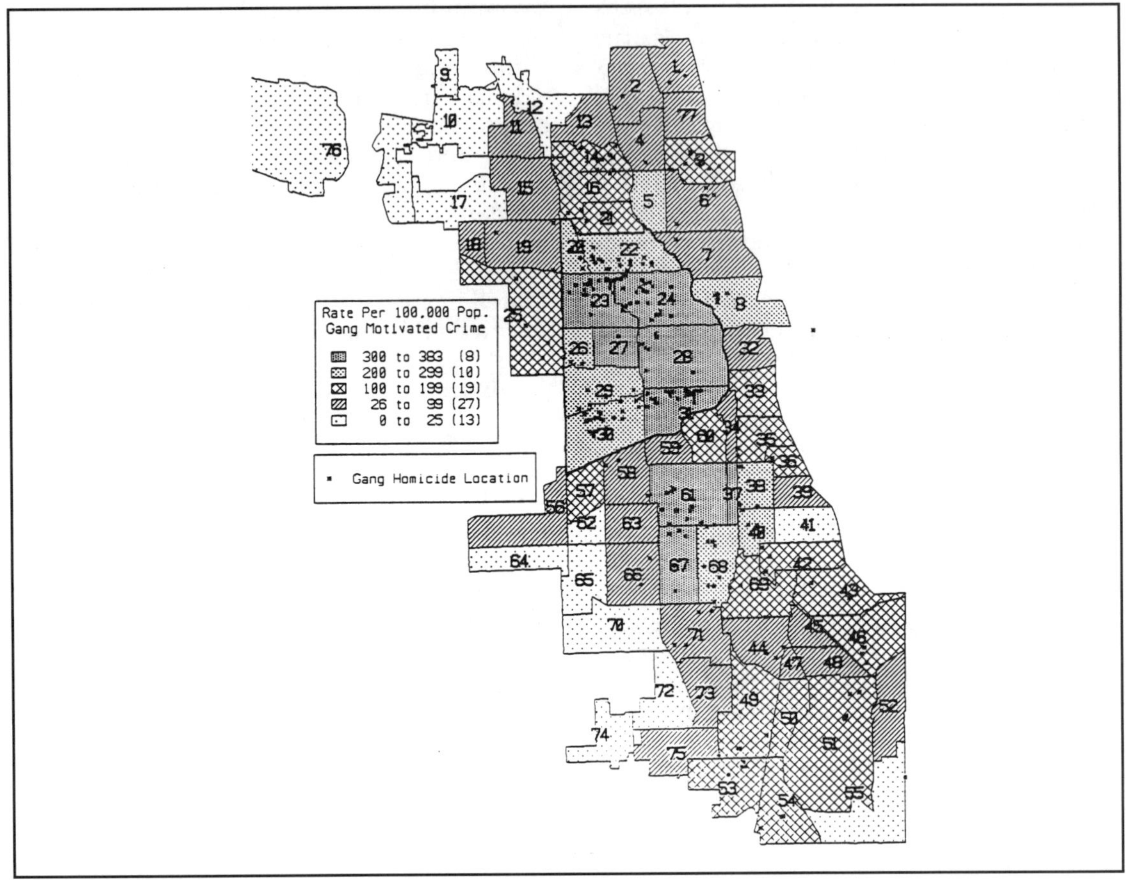

Source; Chicago Police Department.

Data on Street-Gang Territory Boundaries

This data set included the location of street gang territory boundaries in early 1991. These boundaries were based on maps drawn by street gang officers in Chicago's 26 districts, who identified the territories of 45 street gangs—both major and minor—and noted areas that were in dispute between one or more street gangs.[5]

Defining Gang Affiliation

These three data sets included several possible aspects of street gang affiliation for each incident—for example, the street gang affiliation of the offender or offenders, the affiliation of the victim or victims (if any), and the location of the incident within the boundaries of a gang's turf. In this study researchers classified street gang-motivated criminal incidents according to the affiliation of the offender(s).

Street Gangs in the City

More than 40 major street gangs are active in the city of Chicago.[6] Researchers in this study concentrated on the four largest and most criminally active street gangs, each of which was responsible for at least 1,000 police-recorded criminal incidents from 1987 to 1990:

- Black Gangster Disciples Nation (BGDN). Descended from the Woodlawn Disciples, BGDN is strongest on

Chicago's South Side. The gang is known for its turf wars with the Blackstone Rangers in the late 1960s and early 1970s and the Black Disciples in 1991.[7]

- Latin Disciples. A racially and ethnically mixed street gang allied with BGDN, the Latin Disciples operate mainly in the integrated Northwest Side neighborhoods of Humboldt Park and Logan Square.[8]
- Latin Kings. The oldest (over 25 years) and largest Latino street gang in Chicago, the Latin Kings operate throughout the city in Latino and racially and ethnically mixed neighborhoods. The gang is particularly active in the growing Mexican neighborhoods on the Southwest Side.
- Vice Lords. One of the oldest street gangs in Chicago, the Vice Lords date from the 1950s. The gang operates throughout the city, but is strongest in the very poor West Side neighborhoods that have never recovered from the destruction that followed the death of Dr. Martin Luther King in 1968.[9]

Members of BGDN and the Vice Lords are almost all black men, while the Latin Disciples and Latin Kings are predominantly Latino men. Rough police department estimates indicate that the 19,000 members of these four gangs constitute about half of all Chicago street gang members.

In the mid-1980s BGDN and the Latin Disciples formed the Folk Alliance. Soon after the Latin Kings and Vice Lords formed the People alliance. Both "super alliances" of street gangs appeared following an increase of street gang-related homicide.

The contrasting size and longevity of Chicago black and Latino street gangs is in part a reflection of the city's population dynamics. In general, the black population of Chicago has declined[10] and some black neighborhoods have been abandoned, while the Latino population has grown and the population of Latino neighborhoods has climbed. For example, over the past 25 years, the population of East Garfield Park (area 27) has fallen by 60 percent and many commercial and residential buildings have been lost, while the population of South Lawndale (area 30) has expanded by 31 percent and changed from a Czech to a Mexican neighborhood (now called Little Village).

With the growth of the Latino population and the expansion of Latino neighborhoods, many small street gangs have emerged. Given their limited territories, these small neighborhood street gangs battle each other frequently and often have to defend their turf against the more established Latino street gangs.

Definition of a Street Gang

The Chicago Police Department defines "street gang" as an association of individuals who exhibit the following characteristics in varying degrees:

- A gang name and recognizable symbols.
- A geographic territory.
- A regular meeting pattern.
- An organized, continuous course of criminality.

An incident is defined as street gang-related if the evidence indicates that the action grew out of a street gang function. Gang membership is not enough to determine gang-relatedness. To determine if an incident is street gang-related, police investigators analyze each case for application of the following criteria:

- Representing—Offenses growing out of a signification of gang identity or alliance (such as hand signs, language, and clothing).
- Recruitment—Offenses relating to recruiting members for a street gang, which include intimidating a victim or witness.
- Extortion—Efforts to compel membership or to exact tribute for the gang.
- Turf violation—Offenses committed to disrespect another gang's territory.
- Prestige—Offenses committed either to glorify the street gang or to gain rank within the gang.
- Personal conflict—Conflicts involving leadership or punitive action within the rank and file of a gang.
- Vice—Activities generally involving the street-level distribution of narcotics by street gang members.
- Retaliation—Acts of revenge for offenses against the gang by rival gang members.[11]

Exhibit 2

Street Gang Incidents: 1987–1990 Four Largest and Other Gangs

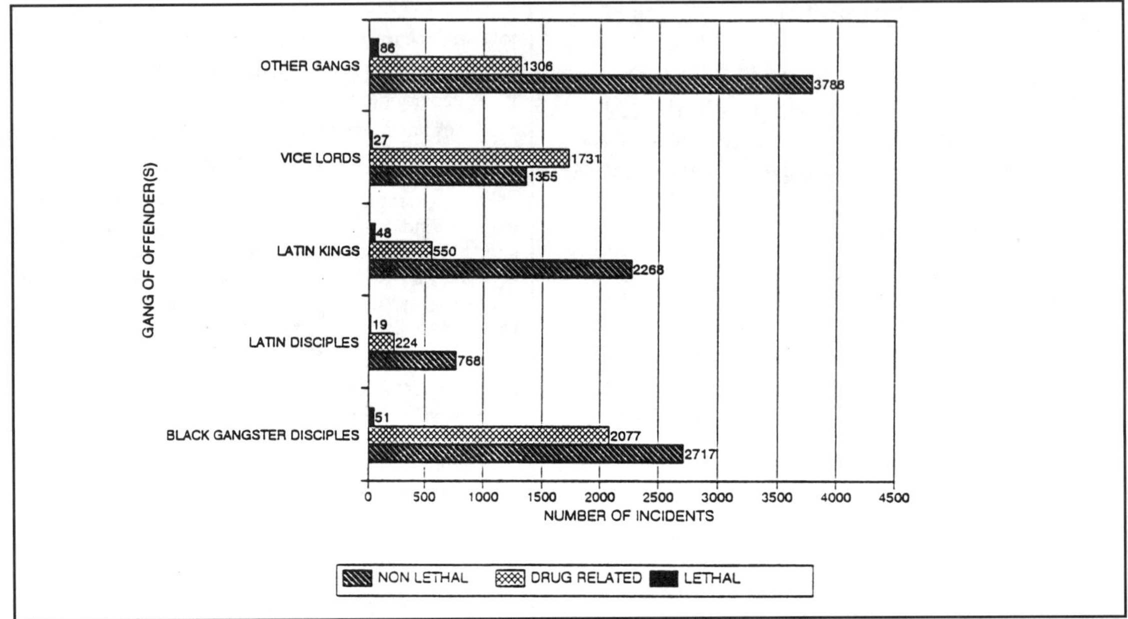

Criminal Activities of Street Gangs

From 1987 to 1990, the four largest street gangs were also the most criminally active. They accounted for 69 percent of all street gang-motivated crimes and 56 percent of all street gang-motivated homicides in which the street gang affiliation of the offender was known. Of the 17,085 street gang-motivated offenses recorded during this period, BGDN was responsible for 4,843 offenses; the Vice Lords for 3,116; the Latin Kings for 2,868; and the Latin Disciples for 1,011.

However, taken as a whole, street gangs other than the top four were responsible for more police-recorded offenses (5,207 from 1987 to 1990) than any one of the top four. Many of these smaller street gangs were relatively new, predominantly Latino, and fighting among themselves over limited turfs.

Drug Offenses

The four major street gangs varied sharply in the degree to which drug crimes dominated their illegal activity (Exhibit 2). For example, of the 2,868 incidents committed by the Latin Kings from 1987 through 1990, only 19 percent were drug offenses, compared to 56 percent of the 3,116 incidents attributed to the Vice Lords. More incidents of cocaine possession (the most common drug offense) were attributed to the Vice Lords or to the Black Gangster Disciples Nation than to all other street gangs combined. The Vice Lords were also active in heroin possession offenses, with twice as many incidents attributed to them than to all other street gangs combined.

The reintroduction of heroin to Chicago by the Vice Lords and Black Gangster Disciples Nation was particularly disturbing to police and community workers. From 1987 to 1990, the number of incidents of possession of white heroin rapidly escalated from 11 to 165, while possession of brown heroin declined from 77 to 64, probably reflecting the reentry of Asian heroin into the Chicago market. Meanwhile, the number of incidents of hard drug possession involving the Latin Kings, Latin Disciples, and other street gangs remained low.

Only 8 of the 288 street gang-motivated homicides between 1987 and 1990 were drug related.[12] Five of these, all of which oc-

Exhibit 3

Non-Lethal Street Gang Crimes: Four Largest and Other Gangs

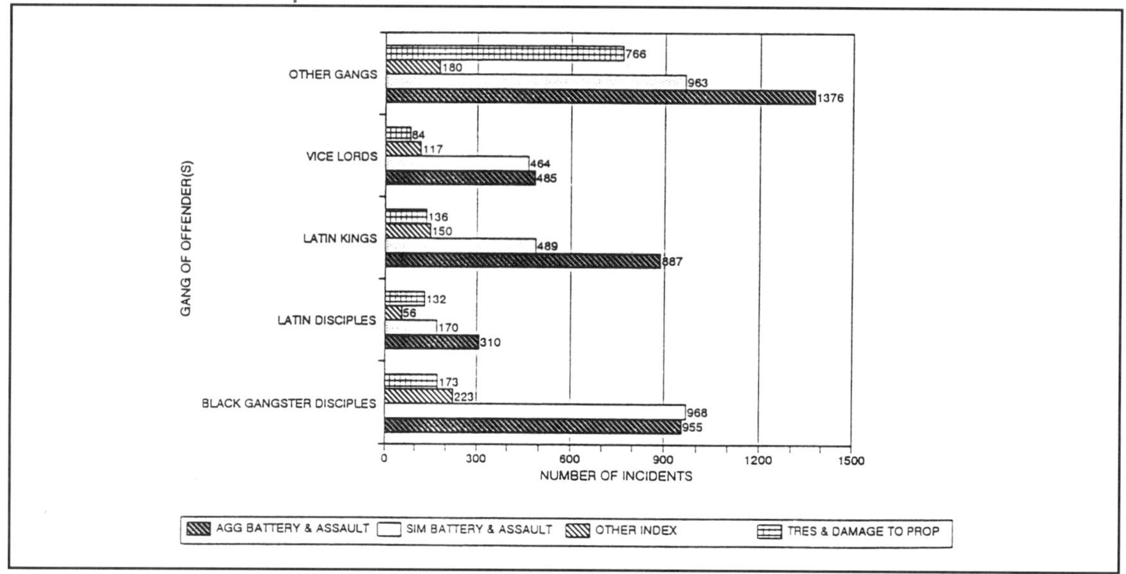

curred in 1989 or 1990, were related to the business of drugs. As researchers in Los Angeles also found, the connection between street gangs, drugs, and homicide was weak and could not explain the rapid increase in homicide in the late 1980s.[13]

Competition, Violence, and Other Confrontations Over Turf

Most of the nonlethal, nondrug offenses attributed to street gangs were violent confrontations (assault and battery) or damage to property (graffiti); see Exhibit 3. Other Index crimes such as robbery and burglary were relatively rare, and only six sexual assaults were determined to be street gang-motivated from 1987 to 1990.[14]

Violent incidents involving the Vice Lords or BGDN were evenly divided between simple battery and assault (no weapon) and aggravated battery and assault. Offenses attributed to the Latin Disciples, Latin Kings, or smaller street gangs (which were also mostly Latino) were more likely to be aggravated than simple assault or battery.

The Vice Lords' West Side turf (see Exhibit 4) was remarkably free of graffiti. The gang was so much in command that they did not need many physical markers to identify their turf. In contrast, the constricted turfs of the smaller street gangs were well marked with graffiti and other identifiers. Driving south on Pulaski Road from Vice Lords' turf in North Lawndale (area 29) toward Two Sixers', Deuces', and Latin Vikings' territories in South Lawndale (area 30), researchers observed a remarkable transformation in neighborhoods. In North Lawndale stood many abandoned factories and apartments and empty lots, but not much graffiti. In thriving South Lawndale (Little Village), buildings were covered with multiple layers of insignia. Competing for scarce territory, the street gangs in Little Village had to identify and violently defend their domains.

Both the amount of graffiti and number of violent turf defense incidents appear related to competition. West Side gangs knew which neighborhoods were under the Vice Lords' control and infrequently challenged that control. In contrast, battles between rival street gangs were a regular occurrence in the expanding Mexican neighborhoods on the Southwest Side. Thus, symbolic "face maintenance," graffiti contests, and violent territorial defense actions were relatively

Exhibit 4
Street Gang Motivated Homicide, Other Violence, and Drug Crimes: 1987–1990

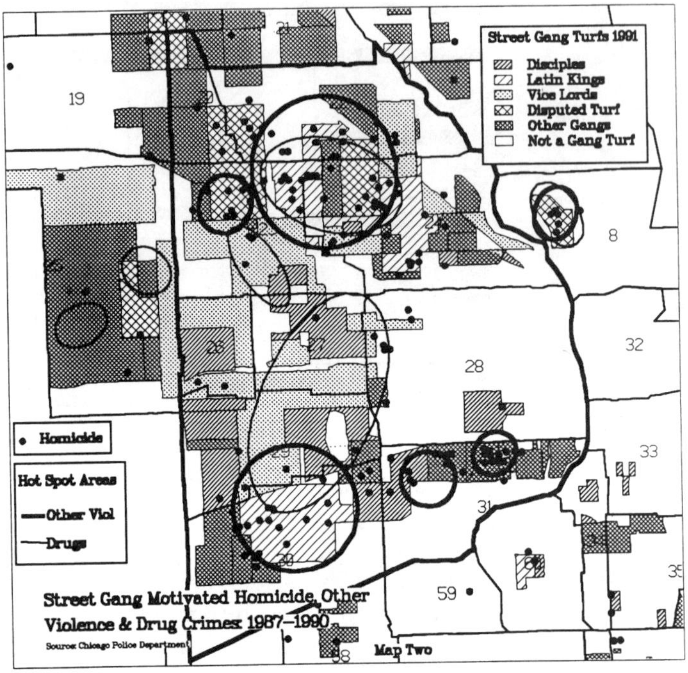

Exhibit 5
Street Gang Motivated Homicides: 1965–1990 (Number and Rate per 100,000)

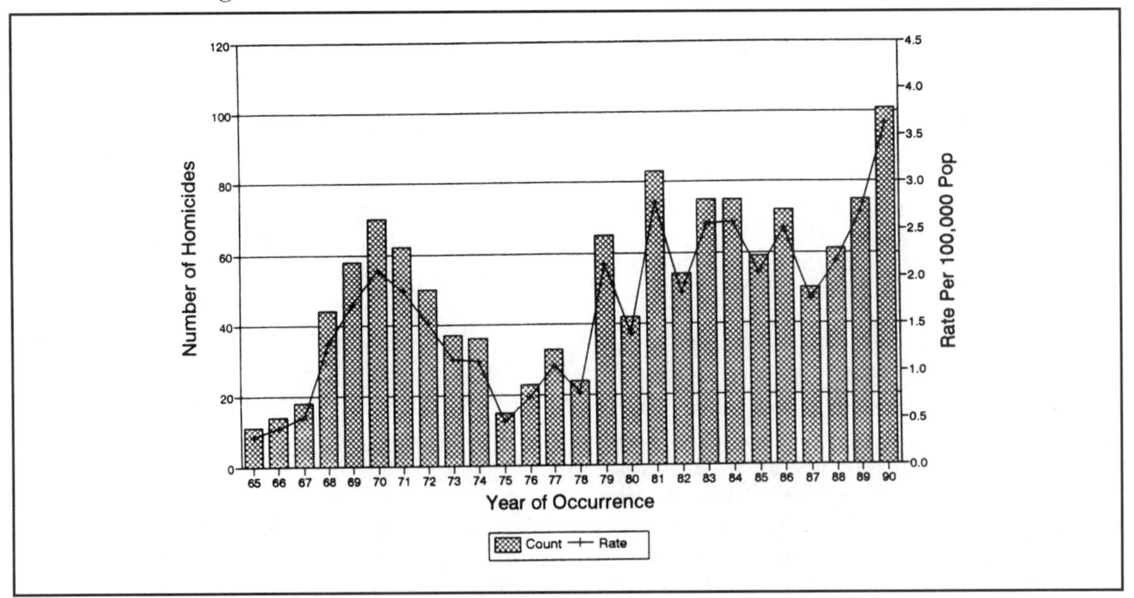

frequent in street gangs more threatened by competition.

Trends in Homicides

In contrast to domestic or acquaintance killings, street gang homicides occurred in bursts (Exhibit 5).[15] Years with only a few homicides were punctuated by years with many. In 1965 only 11 street gang-motivated homicides occurred (2.8 percent of all homicides); but in 1970, 70 occurred (8.7 percent of the total). The risk of being murdered in a street gang confrontation was more than five times higher in 1970 than in 1965. This early surge in homicide reflected BGDN wars on Chicago's South Side.

By 1975 the number of street gang-motivated homicides was again as low as the mid-1960s, even though 1974 and 1975 were record years for other types of homicide. This brief respite was followed by eruptions of lethal street gang violence in 1979 and again in 1981, when there were 65 and 83 deaths, respectively. However, the formation in the mid-1980s of the two gang super alliances, People and Folk, may have brought relative stability in street gang-motivated violence for a few years. Only 50 street gang-motivated homicides were recorded in 1987, and the total number of Chicago homicides reached the lowest point in 20 years.

Unfortunately, the rivalries that developed both between and within alliances in the mid-1980s generated even more violence later in the decade when street gang-motivated homicide increased sharply to 101 in 1990 (then an all-time high) and surpassed that to 121 in 1991 and 133 in 1992. Although the overall level of homicide also increased rapidly in those years, street gang-motivated homicide increased faster. It accounted for 12 percent of all homicides in 1990 and was responsible for 33 percent of the total increase from 1987 through 1990.

If street gang-motivated homicide is directly related to other street gang-motivated incidents and if the proportion of incidents with a lethal outcome does not change, then the pattern over time of lethal incidents should parallel the pattern of nonlethal incidents. Although the data show some similarity in the short-term pattern of street gang-motivated lethal versus nonlethal incidents, the overall trend is very different (see Exhibit 6).[16]

- In 1987, 1 street gang-motivated homicide occurred for every 44 street gang-motivated personal violence offenses known to the police.
- In 1990 there was 1 death for every 20 police-recorded crimes of personal violence.

Indeed, the number of street gang-motivated deaths in a typical month increased sharply over the 3-year period, even though the number of nonlethal violent incidents declined slightly. These divergent trends in lethal and nonlethal violence indicate that the proportion of incidents with a lethal outcome has increased.

The Role of Guns

One explanation for the increasing lethality of street gang-motivated violent incidents could be an increase in gang use of guns. From 1987 to 1990, the proportion of nonlethal streetgang-motivated violent offenses that were committed with a gun increased slightly from 27.3 percent to 31.5 percent. In contrast, a gun was the lethal weapon in almost all streetgang-motivated homicides—96 percent in 1987 and 94 percent in 1990.

Furthermore, the proportion of murder weapons that were automatics or semiautomatics increased from 22 percent to 31 percent over the 3 years (from 11 to 31 deaths from 1987 to 1990). In addition, deaths by large-caliber guns (38 or greater) increased from 13 in 1987 to 39 in 1990.

Overall the number of street gang-motivated homicides increased from 51 in 1987 to 101 in 1990. The number killed with an automatic or semiautomatic (any caliber) or with a nonautomatic gun of 38 caliber or greater increased from 24 to 70 from 1987 to 1990. Virtually the entire increase in the number of street gang-motivated homicides seems attributable to an increase in the use of high-caliber, automatic, or semiautomatic weapons.

Exhibit 6

Trends in Street Gang-Motivated Violence: Lethal and Nonlethal (3 Month Moving Averages)

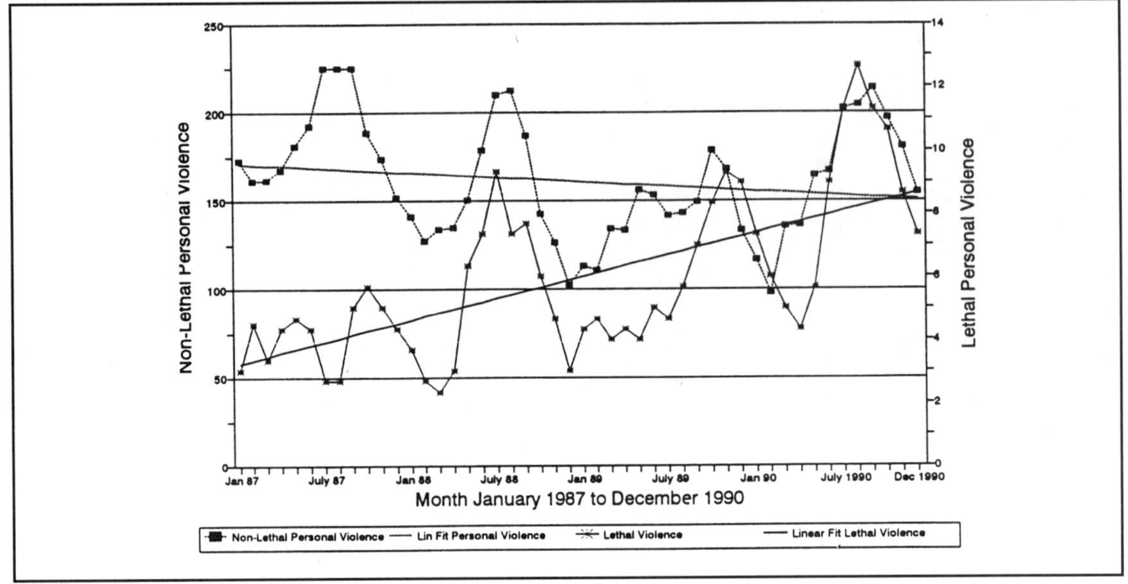

Street Gang Activity by Community Area

Every community area in Chicago had at least one street gang-motivated offense between 1987 and 1990. However, the two most dangerous communities, East Garfield Park (area 27) and Humboldt Park (area 23), had a mean annual rate of street gang-motivated crimes (381.5) that was 76 times the mean annual rate (5.0) in the two least dangerous neighborhoods, Mt. Greenwood (area 74) and Edison Park (area 9); see Exhibit 1. The community areas with the highest levels of street gang-motivated crime were on the West Side (areas 23, 24, 27, 28, and 31); in the south central neighborhoods of New City (area 61) and Fuller Park (area 37); and in West Englewood (area 67), the scene of a burst of street gang violence in 1990 and 1991.

Homicides

Street gang-motivated homicides were also concentrated in two corridors on the Northwest and Southwest Sides. Of Chicago's 77 community areas, 17 had no street gang-motivated homicide from 1965 to 1990. Many had only one. None of the 13 community areas with the lowest rates of street gang-motivated crime had a street gang-motivated homicide between 1987 and 1990. At the other extreme, the Lower West Side (area 31) averaged more than 6 street gang-motivated homicides per 100,000 people per year over that same time period.

The risk of becoming a homicide victim or offender was far higher for young Latino men than for other Latinos or for non-Latino whites, and equal to that for young black men. The risk of homicide for other Latinos was not exceptionally high,[17] but the risk of homicide for non-Latino blacks was higher than for non-Latino whites, regardless of age or gender, and higher than for all Latinos except young men.

These individual differences were reflected in community differences as well.

Community Differences

Black neighborhoods with high rates of street gang homicide also had high rates of other forms of homicide. But this was not necessarily true in other communities. For example, the mostly mixed and Latino neighborhoods on the Northwest and Southwest Sides had many street gang-motivated killings, but relatively few killings for other reasons.[18] As a result, the rate of street gang-motivated homicide and the rate of other forms of homicide from 1987 though 1990 were only weakly correlated (.287) across community areas.

Compared to the relationship over time (Exhibit 6), the relationship between lethal and nonlethal violence across geographic areas appeared to be higher, but the strength of the relationship depended on the type of violence. Five of the six community areas with the highest rates of street gang-motivated nonlethal personal violence (assault and battery) also ranked among the six with the highest rates of street gang-motivated homicide. In contrast, only one of the six community areas that had the highest rate of street gang-motivated drug crime in the years 1987 to 1990 also ranked among the top six in street gang-motivated homicide rates. Only one community area, Humboldt Park (area 23), ranked among the top six in all three rates—street gang-motivated lethal violence, nonlethal personal violence, and drug offenses. Overall the correlation across the 77 community areas between rates of street gang-motivated drug crime and homicide was moderate (.401), while the correlation was much stronger (.728) between street gang-motivated homicide and rates of street gang-motivated assault and battery.

Hot Spot Areas of Street Gang Activity

Fifty-one percent of the city's street gang-motivated homicides and 35 percent of nonlethal street gang-motivated offenses occurred in 10 community areas on the West Side. Three kinds of neighborhood situations can be seen in this West Side map (Exhibit 4).[19]

- Neighborhoods with a turf hot spot area (heavy concentration of nonlethal personal violent activity to defend turf).
- Neighborhoods with a drug hot spot area (heavy concentration of street gang-motivated drug offenses).
- Neighborhoods plagued by both a turf and drug hot spot area.

Residents in these neighborhoods tend to view street gang activity very differently. For example, a resident living in a drug hot spot area is likely to consider the neighborhood street gang problem to be primarily a drug problem. A resident living in a turf hot spot area may consider the neighborhood street gang problem to revolve around violent defense of turf. And a resident of a community in which a drug and a turf hot spot area intersect experiences the worst of both.

In specific neighborhood areas, the link between incidents of street gang-motivated nonlethal and lethal personal violence was far stronger than that between drug crimes and lethal violence. For example, street gang-motivated homicides tended to occur within or close to the boundaries of turf hot spot areas, and only rarely in drug hot spot areas except when a drug hot spot area intersected a turf hot spot area.[20] Of the 169 street gang-motivated homicides in the 10 community areas shown in Exhibit 4, 94 occurred in hot spot areas, as follows: 37 in neighborhoods where a drug hot spot area and a turf hot spot area intersected (28 in Humboldt Park, 4 in Little Village, and 5 in Cabrini Green), 48 in turf hot spot areas only, and 9 in drug hot spot areas only. The turf hot spot area in Little Village (in the southwest corner) experienced more than 7 homicides per square mile, while the Pilsen hot spot area (southeast corner) experienced 48, and the turf hot spot area around Humboldt Park, which intersected with a drug hot spot area, was the site of 16 homicides per square mile over the 3-year period.

Highlights of Major Findings

This study painted a more complete picture of the reality of street gang crime than is usually the case in studies of gangs. By analyzing police records of lethal and nonlethal streetgang-motivated crimes, examining temporal and spatial patterns of those crimes, and describing the criminal activities of Chicago's four largest street gangs, researchers sought to uncover typical patterns of street gang life.

The patterns of street gang activity can be summarized as follows:

- Chicago's largest street gangs can be identified with most of the city's street gang crime. These four street gangs (representing about 10 percent of all street gangs and 51 percent of the estimated number of all street gang members) accounted for 69 percent of police-recorded street gang-motivated criminal incidents and 55 percent of all streetgang-motivated homicides from 1987 to 1990.

- Street gangs varied in the types of activities in which they were engaged. Some specialized in incidents of expressive violence while others focused on instrumental violence (see "Expressive Versus Instrumental Violence"). For example, the Vice Lords and BGDN were much more involved in acts of instrumental violence (such as possession or sale of drugs), while the Latin Disciples, Latin Kings, and smaller gangs specialized in acts of expressive violence (such as turf defense). Most of the criminal activity in smaller street gangs centered on representation turf defense. The most lethal street gang hot spot areas are along disputed boundaries between small street gangs.
- Types of street gang crime clustered in specific neighborhoods. Street gangs specializing in instrumental violence were strongest in disrupted and declining neighborhoods. Street gangs specializing in expressive violence were strongest and most violent in relatively prosperous neighborhoods with expanding populations.
- The rate of street gang-motivated crime in the 2 most dangerous Chicago communities was 76 times that of the 2 safest. However, every community area in Chicago had at least one street gang-motivated criminal incident between 1987 and 1990.
- Most of the lethal gang-related crimes occurred in neighborhoods where street gang activity centered on turf battles, not in neighborhoods where street gang activity focused on drug offenses. Of 288 street gang-motivated homicides from 1987 to 1990, only 8 also involved drug use or a drug-related motive.
- A gun was the lethal weapon in almost all Chicago street gang-motivated homicides from 1987 to 1990. Incidents involving a high-caliber, automatic, or semiautomatic weapon accounted for most of the increase in homicides over this period.
- Many community areas with high levels of lethal and nonlethal street gang-motivated personal violence and homicide had relatively low levels of other forms of homicide. Although hot spot areas of street gang-motivated drug offenses were usually low in street gang homi-

Expressive Versus Instrumental Violence

A growing body of literature indicates that violence is not one type of event but many.[21] Almost all acts of lethal violence begin as another type of confrontation—for example, as an argument between spouses, a fight or brawl between acquaintances, a robbery, an act of sexual violence, or a street gang confrontation—that escalates to death. To understand lethal violence, the reasons why some—and only some—of these violent events become lethal must first be understood. The answer differs for those fatal and nonfatal "sibling" offenses such as assault homicide and assault compared to robbery homicide and robbery, which occupy different points on the expressive-versus-instrumental continuum.

In general, the dynamics of a violent situation are governed by the degree to which *expressive* versus *instrumental* motives predominate as the assailant's primary and immediate goal. In an expressive violent confrontation, the primary goal is violence or injury itself, and other motives are secondary. In contrast, the primary purpose of an act of instrumental violence is not to hurt, injure, or kill, but to acquire money or property. In addition, situational factors—such as possession of a weapon—that might affect the likelihood of a fatal outcome operate differently in expressive and instrumental confrontations.

Street gang-motivated violence often contains many expressive aspects—such as impulsive and emotional defense of one's identity as a gang member, defense and glorification of the reputation of the gang and gang members, and expansion of the membership and territory of the gang. Though some of these turf activities may involve acquisition, the primary motive is expressive. On the other hand, other types of street gang violence, such as formation and maintenance of a lucrative drug business and other entrepreneurial activities, are fundamentally instrumental. In this study researchers found that some gangs specialized in expressive violence, while others specialized in instrumental violence.

cide, some were high in other kinds of homicide.

Policy Implications

As this report shows, street gang violence has been a continuing problem in Chicago since the late 1960s. The years 1990, 1991, and 1992 broke records for street gang violence, and the number of incidents continued to grow in 1993.

Intervention programs whose aim is to reduce nonlethal street gang violence will probably also reduce lethal violence. To be effective, however, these intervention programs must be built on a foundation of current information about the types of street gangs and street gang activity in each specific neighborhood.

As shown by this research, street gang-motivated crime is not random. In Chicago it occurred in specific neighborhoods and was concentrated in limited time periods. Some street gangs spent much of their time defending or expanding their turf while others were actively involved in the business of illegal drugs. Programs to reduce street gang-motivated violence must recognize these differences. For example, a program to reduce gang involvement in drugs in a community in which gang members are most concerned with defense of turf has little chance of success.

Furthermore, because the predominant type of street gang activity in a neighborhood may change from year to year or month to month, and because the level of street gang-motivated violence tends to occur in spurts, effective intervention strategies must be built on continuously updated information.

Another focus of control over gang violence should be on weapons. The death weapon in almost all gang-motivated homicides in Chicago was a gun, and much of the increase in gang-motivated homicides from 1987 to 1990 was an increase in killings with large-caliber, automatic, or semiautomatic weapons. Therefore, reducing the availability of these most dangerous weapons may also reduce the risk of death in street gang-plagued communities.

Street gang membership, street gang-related violence, and other illegal street gang activity must be understood in light of both long-term or chronic social patterns, and current or acute conditions. Street gang patterns and trends reflect not only chronic problems, such as racial and class discrimination and adjustment of immigrants, but also acute, often rapidly changing problems stemming from the existing economic situation, weapon availability, drug markets, and the spatial arrangement of street gang territories across a city.

Obviously, the chronic problem of street gang violence cannot be solved with a quick fix; the ultimate solution rests on a coordinated criminal justice response, changes in educational opportunities, racial and ethnic attitudes, and job structure. On the other hand, while waiting for these long-term strategies to take effect, lives can be saved and serious injury prevented by targeting the causes of short-term or acute escalations in violence levels.[22]

Notes

1. Two types of spatial analysis were used: correlational community area analysis and identification of hot spot areas of dense street gang activity concentrations. Hot spot areas were identified using the hot spot ellipse capability of the STAC (Spatial and Temporal Analysis of Crime) package, which was developed by the Illinois Criminal Justice Information Authority. STAC used an iterative search that identified the densest clusters of events on the map, calculated a standard deviational ellipse fitting each cluster, and mapped the events and the ellipses. STAC delineated, regardless of artificial boundaries, the areas of the map that contained the densest clusters of events. It was thus a data base-driven, objective tool for identifying nonarbitrary summary areas from the actual scatter of events on the map. For further information about STAC, see C. R. Block, "Hot Spots and Isocrimes in Law Enforcement Decision-making," paper presented at the Conference on Police and Community Responses to Drugs: Frontline Strategies in the Drug War, University of Illinois at Chicago, December 1990.
2. Community areas are aggregations of census tracts, usually including several neighbor-

hoods but sometimes only one, identified by an official name and number. Since the Chicago School sociologists first identified them in the 1930s, a plethora of data has been collected and analyzed by community area. For more detail, see Exhibit 1 and Chicago Factbook Consortium, *Local Community Fact Book: Chicago Metropolitan Area* (Chicago: University of Illinois Department of Sociology, 1980).

3. Data from 1965 through 1981 are currently available in the National Archive of Criminal Justice Data of the Inter-University Consortium for Political and Social Research, and a completely updated data set from 1965 through 1990 is being prepared for the archive. The ultimate source of all information for all years was the Murder Analysis Report (MAR), a two-page summary of each homicide maintained since 1965 by the Crime Analysis Unit of the Chicago Police Department. Since its inception in 1965, MAR has consistently flagged cases in which there was positive evidence that the homicide was motivated by street gang activity.

4. Although a single incident may have involved multiple offenders or multiple victims, data were analyzed at the incident level. If more than one offense occurred in an incident, the incident was classified according to the most serious violation. All data are from 1987 to 1990, except for homicides; the homicide data include murders that occurred from 1965 to 1990.

5. It is quite possible that the territories defined by police officers differ from the territories that would be defined by street gang members, agency workers, community members, or even by police officers assigned to another division such as narcotics. Also, because street gangs disappear, merge, or change names over time, it would have been preferable to have a turf map that was contemporaneous with the street gang incident data. However, the turfs are probably a fairly accurate representation of the later part of the study period.

6. Chicago Police Department, Gang Crime Section, "Street Gangs" (internal report), 1992.

7. In the 1960s and 1970s, the Woodlawn Disciples battled the Blackstone Rangers (later called the Black P Stone Nation and then changed to El Rukins), which resulted in an upsurge in homicides. In 1991, renamed BGDN, the gang fought the normally allied Black Disciples gang for control of Englewood.

8. Much of the discussion on gang structure, history, and current activities depends upon two police department sources: L. J. Bobrowski, "Collecting, Organizing, and Reporting Street Gang Crime," paper presented at the annual meeting of the American Society of Criminology, Chicago, 1988; and Chicago Police Department, "Street Gangs," 1992.

9. R. J. Sampson and W. J. Wilson, "Toward a Theory of Race, Crime, and Urban Inequality," paper presented at the annual meeting of the American Society of Criminology, San Francisco, 1991.

10. C. R. Block, "Lethal Violence in the Chicago Latino Community," in *Homicide: The Victim-Offender Connection*, ed. A. V. Wilson (Cincinnati, OH: Anderson Pub. Co., 1993), 267–342.

11. For further information, see Bobrowski, "Collecting, Organizing and Reporting Street Gang Crime," and Chicago Police Department, "Street Gangs," 1992.

12. A homicide was defined as drug-related if drugs were a motivation for the crime or if the victim or offender was under the influence of drugs during the incident. Drug-motivated homicides included those involving the business or sale of drugs, those that resulted from a crime committed to get drugs or money for drugs, those that resulted from an argument or confrontation about drugs, and "other" (such as an infant starving to death because both parents were high). This definition follows that of P. J. Goldstein, "The Drugs/Violence Nexus: A Tripartite Conceptual Framework," *Journal of Drug Issues* 14 (1985): 493–506. Note that drug-related information was not available for nonlethal incidents.

13. M. W. Klein, C. L. Maxson, and L. C. Cunningham, " 'Crack,' Street Gangs, and Violence," *Criminology* 29(4) (1991): 701–717.

14. Non-Index offenses, such as intimidation, mob action, and weapons and liquor law violations, are not shown in Exhibit 3.

15. Yearly totals in Exhibit 5, which refer to the year of occurrence of the homicide (year of the incident) may differ from police totals, which refer to the year in which the police "booked" the offense.

16. The data here are 3-month moving averages.

17. C. R. Block, "Lethal Violence in the Chicago Latino Community," 1993.
18. R. Block and C. R. Block, "Homicide Syndromes and Vulnerability: Violence in Chicago's Community Areas Over 25 Years," in *Studies on Crime and Crime Prevention*, v. 1. (Oslo/Stockholm: Scandinavian University Press, 1992), 61–87.
19. Because of space considerations, the actual locations of the drug or nonlethal violent incidents that formed the basis for these hot spot areas are not depicted in Exhibit 4. The location of street gang-motivated homicides, which were not included in the calculation of the hot spot area ellipses shown on the map, are depicted by black dots.
20. Note that only nonlethal offenses, not homicides, were included in the calculation of hot spot areas depicted in Exhibit 4.
21. For more information on this issue, see R. Block and C. R. Block, "Homicide Syndromes and Vulnerability," 1992.
22. The authors acknowledge also the assistance of the Chicago Police Department in preparing this study, especially Commander Robert Dart of the Gang Crime Section, Commander James Maurer of Area Four Violent Crimes, Gang Crimes Specialist Lawrence J. Bobrowski of the Bureau of Operational Services, and Detective Al Kettman (retired) of the Crime Analysis Unit. Findings and conclusions of the research reported here are those of the authors and do not necessarily reflect the official position or policies of the U.S. Department of Justice.

References

Block, Carolyn Rebecca. "Hot Spots and Isocrimes in Law Enforcement Decisionmaking." Paper presented at the Conference on Police and Community Responses to Drugs: Frontline Strategies in the Drug War. University of Illinois at Chicago, December 1990.

——. "Lethal Violence in the Chicago Latino Community." In *Homicide: The Victim-Offender Connection*, ed. Anna V. Wilson. Cincinnati, OH: Anderson Pub. Co., 1993, pp. 267–342.

Block, Carolyn Rebecca, and Richard Block. "Beyond Wolfgang: An Agenda for Homicide Research in the 1990s." *Journal of Criminal Justice* 14 (1992): 31–70.

Block, Richard, and Carolyn Rebecca Block. "Homicide Syndromes and Vulnerability: Violence in Chicago's Community Areas Over 25 Years." *Studies on Crime and Crime Prevention*, v. 1. Oslo/ Stockholm: Scandinavian University Press, 1992, pp. 61–87.

Bobrowski, Lawrence J. "Collecting, Organizing, and Reporting Street Gang Crime." Paper presented at the annual meeting of the American Society of Criminology, Chicago, 1988.

Chicago Factbook Consortium. *Local Community Fact Book: Chicago Metropolitan Area, 1980*. Chicago: University of Illinois Department of Sociology, 1980.

Chicago Police Department, Gang Crime Section. "Street Gangs." Internal report, 1992.

Curry, G. David, and Irving Spergel. "Gang Homicide, Delinquency, and Community." *Criminology* 26(3) (1988): 381–405.

Goldstein, Paul J. "The Drugs/Violence Nexus: A Tripartite Conceptual Framework." *Journal of Drug Issues* 14 (1985): 493–506.

Klein, Malcolm W., Cheryl L. Maxson, and Lea C. Cunningham. "'Crack,' Street Gangs, and Violence." *Criminology* 29(4) (1991): 701–717.

Sampson, Robert J., and William Julius Wilson. "Toward a Theory of Race, Crime, and Urban Inequality." Paper presented at the annual meeting of the American Society of Criminology, San Francisco, 1991.

Spergel, Irving A. "Youth Gangs: Continuity and Change." In *Crime and Justice: A Review of Research*, vol. 12, eds. Michael Tonry and Norval Morris. Chicago: University of Chicago Press, 1990, pp. 171–275.

Wacquant, Loic, and William Julius Wilson. "Poverty, Joblessness, and the Social Transformation of the Inner City." In *Welfare Policies for the 1990s*, eds. Phoebe H. Cottingham and David T. Ellwood. Cambridge, Mass.: Harvard University Press, 1989, pp. 70–102. ✦

Chapter 18
Drive-bys

William B. Sanders

In this chapter from Gangbangs and Drive-bys, *Sanders describes several features of what has become the quintessential form of gang violence, the drive-by shooting. The author approaches these events as strategic interactions, reinforced by the grounded values and norms of gang culture and yielding considerable benefits to identity and status. Although Sanders relies on law enforcement sources, supplemented with interviews with San Diego gang informants, his framework of analysis contrasts markedly with other researchers' use of police data. His focus on situational interactions reinforces the importance of group dynamics in understanding gang behavior.*

Introduction

This chapter closely examines one of the key violent situations associated with gang life: drive-by shootings. I have attempted to explore this phenomenon from several different angles in order to provide a fully developed understanding of it. First, it is examined in terms of a historical background to see how drive-bys replaced other types of gang violence as a favored tactic. Then, using Erving Goffman's concept of strategic interaction, we evaluate drive-bys as a strategy. Further using Goffman's notions of character and identity developed in situations, we see how a gang identity can be found in the context of a drive-by. Finally, we look at the different types of situations where drive-bys develop and how they develop.

The Drive-by Shooting in the Context of Gang Warfare

A drive-by shooting occurs when members of one gang drive a vehicle into a rival gang's area and shoot at someone. As used here, the drive-by is a hit and run tactic and does not include situations where members of one gang, who happen to have guns, arrive at a location in a car, and then later on encounter rival gang members and use their guns. However, drive-bys do include situations where gang members drive to a location, find a target, jump out of the car, chase the victim down, and then flee in the car after the shooting. The idea of a drive-by is that it is a hit-and-run maneuver, and whether or not someone temporarily leaves their car is not considered analytically important. The following examples provide a sense of the range of types of drive-by shootings:

> The victims, some members of Da Boys, were at home. Some Be Down Boys drove up, got out of the car and shot at the victims, their car, and dog. After firing several shots, they got back in their car and drove away.

> Members of Eastside Piru were hanging out in front of a liquor store when a car drove by. Some Crips in the car said, "What's up, Blood?" The Pirus ignored them and walked away. After a Piru member refused to come over to their car, the Crips began firing, hitting the victim three times. Then the Crips drove away.

> A member of the Neighborhood Crips was sitting on a wall when he heard a car drive up. He turned to look at the car and then turned back. At this point he was shot in the head. The victim ran into a friend's house, noting only that the shooter was wearing red. [Red is the color of the Crips' rivals, the Bloods/Pirus.]

> Some VELs were standing in front of their house when two 70s on a motorcycle drove by and shot a pistol at the house and car, hitting the car.

Reprinted from: William B. Sanders, *Gang-bangs and Drive-bys: Grounded Culture and Juvenile Gang Violence.* (New York: Aldine de Gruyter)

Some Varrio Market Street boys were standing outside when four VELs drove up and yelled, "Encanto, Encanto!" and asked, "Where are you from?" When the victims replied "Varrio Market!" the VELs started shooting.

Sometime after World War II, gangs introduced the term japping to refer to hit and run attacks (Klein, 1971:24). The term came from certain unorthodox strategies used in the war by Japanese soldiers, especially shooting from hidden positions behind Allied lines. It was an unconventional mobile warfare discovered by the gangs. Walter Miller (1975:36–38) used the term foray to characterize these mobile tactics. This type of gang warfare is in contrast to the melee or rumble, where gangs would meet at appointed places and times to do battle in large groups.

In the traditional East Coast cities with high density populations, narrow streets, and congested traffic, a foray was often conducted on foot or bicycle. The neighborhoods are relatively close, and gang members were able to make a quick attack, and get back to the safety of their own area before the other gang could mobilize for a counterstrike. It would even be possible to make a hit-and-run attack using public transportation, such as the subway.

On the West Coast, particularly in Southern California, the neighborhoods are further apart, more spread out, more likely to be on the ground level, and have lower density. There is an excellent road system and relatively little public transportation. The automobile is the primary mode of transportation, and using the freeway system, an attacker can quickly return to his home base miles away from the site of the shooting. It was in this type of situation that the drive-by shooting developed.

Table 18.1

Percentage of All Gang Assaults That Are Drive-by Shootings

Year	Drive-bys
1981	23.7
1988	40.8

In San Diego, there was an increasing use of the drive-by shooting from the early 1980s to the end of the decade. Table 18.1 shows the jump in drive-by shootings as a percentage of gang attacks from the early 1980s to the later part of the decade. As can be seen, the drive-by almost doubled in proportion to non-drive-by assaults from the beginning to the end of the decade.

Strategic Interaction and Drive-by Shootings

Analytically, we can understand drive-by shootings as a rational reaction to the conditions of gang warfare. Erving Goffman (1969:100–101) describes strategic interaction as those situations where people come together under conditions of mutual fatefulness. The players in these situations attempt to dope out what the other is going to do, and make the best possible move to maximize their chances of surviving the encounter. Since the level of violence used has escalated in the situations of gang warfare, they are literally life-and-death ones.

As situations come to be more and more those of life and death, the notion of chivalry takes on a different tone. In encounters with knives and clubs, one could well spare the life of (or limit the wounds upon) an opponent. It was not only a chivalrous move, it was one that may be repaid later, and as such, was a strategic move. A victor who did not finish off an opponent with a fatal blow or shot could receive as much honor for chivalry as he could for ending the opponent's life. The value was in the honor, not just the victory.

In gang warfare, as it became clear that face-to-face encounters with manufactured guns should be short in duration, the automobile was seen as a resource to make such meetings as brief as possible. Only in situations of pure recklessness would an assembled group stand before opponents who were displaying firearms.

When manufactured firearms began to be used by gangs on a large scale in the 1970s, the old style rumble was replaced without ceremony by the foray (Miller, 1975). In the wide open spaces of Southern California, the drive-by became the adopted style of the foray.

In the context of gang warfare the drive-by shooting is the military equivalent of getting hit by an unseen shell. Since there is an almost constant enemy but there are not constant staged battles, a drive-by is something that can happen anywhere, any time. What's more, a drive-by is hidden in the normal appearances of its surroundings (Goffman, 1971:238–282). A car driving down San Diego streets is a normal occurrence, and like all such mundane events is seen but unnoticed. When bullets or shotgun pellets suddenly begin spewing from a car, it is too late. Since about 80 percent of all drive-by shootings were in the evening or at night (between 6 p.m. and 6 a.m.), noting a vehicle belonging to a rival gang is even more problematic. The following case provides an instance where the most mundane of situations can be transformed into a deadly one:

> The victim, a Syndo Mob member, was working inside his car on the back window. He saw a white van back down the alley. When the van's passenger side door came in front of his car, a Piru pointed an Uzi machine gun at him and fired eighteen rounds, hitting his car several times but missing him.

Given the swift and deadly nature of drive-by shootings, gang members live in a very real situation of sudden death. Considering the stances to unpredictable danger, Goffman suggests postures that can be "deer-like, ever ready to be startled, . . . cow-like, slow to be mobilized, or lion-like, unconcerned about predators and wary chiefly when stalking prey" (1971:242–243). One might expect the general stance to be either deerlike, especially when separated from fellow gang members, or lionlike, demonstrating heart to the gang. However, a good deal of the postures of the targets appeared to be cowlike. This could be due to the frequent use of alcohol and drugs by gang members. Since partying was a major pastime for gang members, and parties consisted of drinking, illicit drug use, dancing, and sex, it would be trying indeed to maintain full alert on such occasions. Intoxicated gang members make easy targets. The following illustrates a relaxed interlude being transformed into a situation of high alarm:

> A member of the Neighborhood Crips and his girlfriend were sitting on what was described as an "electrical box" [possibly a phone company switching box]. He heard several shots fired and pulled his girlfriend towards him when he realized she had been shot.

. . . The term kicking back was used by gang members to convey a desired stance of relaxing or having fun. Not only was this a general term favored by youth in the area, gang members used it to describe everything from parties to hanging out at their favorite haunts. Jankowski (1991:81) found the identical term and sentiment used among Chicano gangs.

Returning to the relaxed stance that seemed to be a dominant posture of the targets of the drive-by shootings, we can understand their lack of alertness in terms of kicked-back situations. Goffman (1961:37) explains fun in terms of spontaneous involvement. To be spontaneously involved is to disattend to all but the unfolding moment. If one must concern oneself with external matters that take attention away from being engrossed in kicking back, then one cannot enjoy the fun of the gathering. At parties, a sure bore is one who brings up unpleasant chores at the office, unfinished homework, a dying relative, or anything else that takes away from being caught up in the moment of the gathering. Constant reminders of the possibility of a drive-by and the need for alertness are also undesirable in kicked-back situations, because they put a damper on the spirit of the occasion. Furthermore, one who shows too much alertness may be accused of lacking the heart for gang life. So, for those with a nervous alertness, there is a need to manage the impression that they are indifferent to the dangers of drive-bys, and they may in fact let down their guard in the performance of doing so.

To the extent people can disattend to external matters in a situation, we can say they are at ease (Goffman, 1961:41–45). Tension is defined as a "sensed discrepancy between the world that spontaneously becomes real to the individual, or the one he is able to accept as the current reality, and the one in which he is obliged to dwell" (Goffman, 1961:43). For the gang members, kicking back and enjoying any ease contrasts dramatically with the state of alertness necessary to survive a drive-by shooting. Since the weather in Southern California is conducive to year-round outdoor activity, gang members spend a good deal of time outside. In about 90 percent of the cases, the victims were outside when attacked in a drive-by shooting. In several cases, those who were shot outside were spillovers from an indoor party. The following is typical of a kicked-back occasion that was disrupted by a drive-by:

> Some VELs were leaving a party when a car drove by with some boys who yelled "Logan, Logan" and shot them. Later, several other people who were at the party showed up at the hospital with stab and gunshot wounds.

The irony of gangs is that the very kicked-back lifestyle that is an important part of their life is disrupted by the tension of drive-by shootings, another part of gang life.

In the aftermath of drive-by shootings where someone is actually killed or severely wounded, the reaction of the gang members and others in the neighborhood is disbelief that it really happened. Even though violence is a major part of gang life in terms of topics of conversation, tattoos proclaiming violence, and carrying weapons, that actual situation of violence always produces trauma.

So the unprepared posture often taken in the face of danger appears to be more a matter of denial than it is of either bravery or ignorance. There may be a temporary alertness after a drive-by against a gang, but it seems to be short-lived. In one instance, a boy from the Shelltown gang had been murdered two weeks prior to a drive-by shooting where a second Shelltown member was gunned down. The denial cannot be maintained indefinitely, and some gangs do post sentries and/or have their gatherings in cul-de-sacs or other locations where drive-by shootings are difficult. However, the overall attitude is one that recognizes the drive-by shooting as a possibility, but gangs filter it out as an external matter. To give it too much attention takes away from the vida loca (the crazy life), but to be wholly unaware of it can have fatal consequences. So drive-bys are viewed as something to avoid (as a target), hoping oneself is not the victim.

Grounded Values and the Drive-by Shooting

Up to this point we have discussed drive-by shootings primarily from the point of view of the target: a contingency in the life of a gang member. Now, I would like to examine drive-by shootings from the point of view of the shooters. How can we understand what it takes to get in a car with one's homeboys and deliberately go hunting for someone to shoot? It is true that some drive-bys seem to be unplanned in that someone just happens to have a gun in a car and starts shooting, but interviews with former gang members show that drive-bys can be fairly deliberate hunting expeditions for human quarry.

One argument explaining deliberate initiated violence is to classify individuals who do such things as sociopaths, psychopaths, or some similar label implying that they are violent and without scruples or conscience. Likewise, we could argue that the core gang members suffer from sociopathic maladies, as did Yablonsky (1962) and that those with these dysfunctions are attracted to the most violent element of gangs. Thus, we would conclude, boys who engage in drive-by shootings are really suffering from individual problems and would be violent no matter what.

There are several problems with such individualistic arguments. First of all, they tend to be tautological. To wit: if a person engages in drive-by shootings he must be sociopathic, and sociopaths are defined as those who are involved in drive-by shootings. The same problem existed in pre-classical criminological thought. The offensive act and offensive person are wrapped together into a single entity: evil (Sylvester, 1972:3). Distinctions between the evil act and evil actor become blurred. Second of all, gangs are a group phenomenon. If sociopaths are persons without regard for others, they would not be subject to or care about others in their gang. Since observers of gang life report that there is very much a concern for the options of fellow gang members, it would be difficult to argue for a sociopathic personality generating gang behavior. On their own, sociopaths or psychopaths may generate all kinds of bizarre behavior, but involvement in a drive-by shooting in cooperation with fellow gang members in a car hardly seems to fit in with the wholly antisocial nature of this personality type. Finally, those who seem to fit the sociopathic and psychopathic labels tend to be loners, and the nature of their offenses is different from patterned crime.

Gang members involved in drive-by shootings talk about their feats in the same displaced way that bomber pilots talk of hitting targets. The gang boys are proud of the fact that they had the heart to point the gun and pull the trigger at an enemy, not necessarily that they may have killed someone. Short and Strodtbeck (1964:25–29), in their examination behind why gangs fight, point out that gang boys need to maintain status. They get the status by performing well in gang-gang encounters. In quoting gang boys' elation after one such encounter, Short and Strodtbeck illustrate the combined pride and tension relief: "Baby, did you see the way I swung on that kid?" "Man, did we tell them off?" "Did you see them take off when I leveled my gun?" "You were great, baby. . . ." The tension was relieved. They had performed well and could be proud (1964:26).

Those who could not or would not perform by going along on a drive-by were judged as lacking heart. They could still be part of the gang, but like the rear echelon troops in a battle zone, they are given no hero status or meaningful medals.

The gang, as a group or organization, provides the situation of the drive-by shooting. We might say that in the same way that situations have realized resources as described by Goffman (1961:28), gangs too have realized resources. One of the resources that can be realized by gang membership is participation in a drive-by shooting. The guns, the cars, the rival, and even the accounts (Scott and Lyman, 1968:46–62) are gang-provided resources.

Of the gang-provided resources, the least important are the guns and automobiles. Virtually anyone can get cars and guns in San Diego without much trouble. However, coming up with murderous rivals and the accounts necessary for shooting at them is another matter. The rivals are generated as part of gang lore, accidental encounters, and contingency of ethnic group and location. As part of gang lore, images of rivals as cowardly, venal, dangerous, and worthy of disdain are passed on from one generation to the next. The rivalry between the Crips and Bloods/Pirus in San Diego is traced to a rivalry in Los Angeles, one that had nothing to do with anyone in San Diego. When the gangs in San Diego started using Crips and Bloods/Pirus in their names, they based their rivalry on the Los Angeles gangs' lore. Within the lore are the accounts for any enmity between the two groups. Likewise, an accidental encounter between non-rival gangs may result in a fight or a killing. Once that occurs, a vendetta may be established that will work into a full-time rivalry. Finally, a rivalry may simply crop up because of the proximity of two gangs. The 70s and VELs are the Mexican-American gangs nearest to one another, and that seems to be the basis for their rivalry. Likewise, since ethnic lines are generally uncrossed boundaries in San Diego gang life, two gangs such as the West Coast Crips (African-American) and the Calle 30 (Mexican-American) are not rivals although they are adjacent and even part of the same area.

Knowing the accounts, justifications, and meanings generated in gang life to participate in drive-by shootings is core to understanding gang violence. One of the most difficult matters to resolve in this research was how to make sense of a kid sticking a gun out the window of a car and intentionally shooting another human being. Gang members learn accounts or vocabularies of motives (Mills, 1940:904–913) in gang situations. For example, a gang boy who is attacked and beaten, shot at, or stabbed has two experiences. First, he has empirical evidence of a physically painful and/or frightening experience. Second, he has a rational experience in that he seeks a reason—a motive or account—for the experience. The rational account is not an automatic calculation of costs and benefits in the classical or neoclassical sense. The rational account is weighing the empirical experience against ways of talking about what has happened.

A middle-class youth who was subject to a near-miss in a drive-by shooting would be given the account that he was in the wrong place. He would be given advice to avoid those situations by avoiding the neighborhoods where gangs exist. Low-income nongang youths in the community who cannot avoid such neighborhoods will be given advice to avoid certain individuals or places in the neighborhood. However, gang youths who experience being a target of a drive-by are provided with very different accounts. They hear about revenge, heart, courage, balls, honor, and perhaps even how weak the attacker is if no one is harmed. So the rational experience of the gang boy is one of dealing with the problem by means other than avoidance. Even the meekest members of the gang are glad there are other members who have the heart to drive by and "mess up" their rivals. Instead of hearing about the futility of endless vendettas, gang boys come to understand that only a powerful counterstrike can thwart future drive-bys. The gang's honor is at stake, but the honor is more than saving face. If a gang is seen to have honor, it is seen as a gang that should not be trifled with. As such, it is a safer, more rational, gang. So instead of being merely an act of vengeance, a drive-by shooting is seen as a rational action to protect the gang. Those in the role of drive-by shooters are seen as protecting not only the gang's honor but also its life and limb.

The accounts and understanding of what a drive-by shooting means as a protective measure are grounded in the gang-generated situations. The values and norms surrounding and justifying drive-bys, either as a rational battle plan in view of the available weapons or as a defensive act to stave off drive-bys in one's own patch, find their specific meaning in the way the gangs talk about the situations of their occurrence. In turn, the talk is justified by the empirical reference of what happens in their neighborhoods and to them as gangs.

Action and the Drive-by Shooting

Goffman (1967:185) defines action as taking on fatefulness for its own sake. A drive-by shooting clearly has the makings of a fateful situation. It is risky in that those who drive by and shoot at a rival may become the target themselves, or they may be caught by the police. It is consequential since what occurs in the occasion of the drive-by will almost certainly have significant effects on the shooters' future.

Horowitz and Schwartz (1974) argue that honor in gangs is a key to understanding their violence. One can gain honor by acting bravely in a gang encounter, establishing character for oneself and possibly robbing it from an opponent. Since character contests make up a part of gang warfare, both individually and collectively, we must examine the drive-by in this light. As noted above, not all members of a gang have the mettle to sit in a car with a gun and go hunt rival members. Those who do can demonstrate they have character or heart. This is understood in Goffman's (1967:214) use of the term character. To wit, a gang boy has the opportunity to demonstrate he has the ability to act coolly and deliberately even though alarms may be going off inside that tell him to get out of the car and away from the danger.

At the same time there is a concrete, grounded situation in which to establish character, there is the excitement in taking chances. The adrenaline that pumps through one in the face of danger creates a heightened awareness, but its effects must be kept in check to demonstrate coolness. Once the firing begins, the pent up feelings can be released in firing the gun or listening to it go off, and there is a spontaneous involvement in the moment. Also, there is the excitement of the recognition of the fellow gang members. Their praise for heart and bravery provide another high in the aftermath of the shooting. All of the excitement is grounded in the drive-by shooting. In the telling of the drive-by, future drive-bys are preordained, for the telling provides the grounds for others to establish themselves and feel the thrill of danger.

Normative and Strategic Interaction in Drive-by Shootings

Goffman (1969:130) notes that while it is possible to conceive of strategic interaction as free of norms, it is usually very difficult in reality. We can examine drive-by shootings as purely tactical moves based on the most efficient way to do in a rival, but upon closer examination, there is a good deal else that goes on and does not go on to make the move a purely strategic one.

Above we noted that norms appear not to keep gangbangers from blasting away at dwellings with non-gang members inside, but because norms against shooting at dwellings where a rival's family members may be present are not included in the moral code of the gang does not mean that norms do not exist at all. There do seem to be norms against singling out an innocent relative of a gang member and shooting at him or her. The lack of remorse shown by gang members when asked about killing babies, small children, and women is not an attitude of condoning such killings. It is a reflection of their view of reality. They will readily defend themselves by pointing out they were not trying to harm innocents, but that is one of the unfortunate side effects of gang warfare—just like any other warfare. In the same way that the rules of war "protect" noncombatants from being shot at intentionally, women and children have never been protected from the consequences of area shelling or bombing. As long as they can demonstrate that they did not knowingly and intentionally kill non-gang members, they can maintain a normatively correct posture.

Emergent Norms in a Drive-by

While it was possible to gather data on the events of a drive-by shooting during the immediate time of the shooting, it was not possible to gather much data on what led up to the shooting. In other words, there were few data that show how a drive-by emerges. From the data that were collected, widely different circumstances seem to be involved.

In one case, a police informant was at a party with some Logan gang members. As the party developed, gang members became more intoxicated with alcohol, drugs, or both and decided to "hit" the Sherman gang. It is not clear whether they decided to do the drive-by first and then became intoxicated to bolster their resolve, or after becoming intoxicated the idea of a drive-by seemed like a good one. In interviews with a former gang member, it seemed that he and his fellow gang members were "loaded" a good deal of the time, regardless of the situation. Thus, while drugs and/or alcohol may have been present in drive-by situations, they do not seem to explain how the kernel of the idea of a drive-by developed since the same state of intoxication was present when drive-by shootings were the furthest thing from gang members' minds.

In another shooting where data were available concerning the events that led up to the drive-by, two of the people in the shooting car were literally innocent bystanders. It involved a girl whose boyfriend's brother was a gang member. The following transcript excerpts show how the drive-by evolved:

> [F]irst, it started from my house and it was about 4 o'clock in the afternoon. Me and my boyfriend were talking inside this car and we decided to go for a ride around the block cause he wanted to drive. And around two blocks away from my house, we saw his brother. And uh, he asked us to stop the car so he can get in the car with us. So when uh, we stopped the car, he asked us to go to another block to pick up two of his friends. When we went out there, we saw two of his friends with something in their hands. We . . . picked them up. They asked me to open the trunk of the car. First, I didn't want to but then my boyfriend told me to do it. Cause, uh, well he probably thought it was something else but he didn't know if they had a gun with them. Whatever they had in their hands that was in the back of my car.

> So they get in the car and we left. So they asked us to go where I live at.
>
> We went down there, and they went across the street to pick up a friend. We stopped the car and [name] got out of the car and went to pick up [name]. So when [he] come out of the house, he had a gun with him. A small gun with him. And then, uh, he got into the car and he told us to drive. I didn't want to. My boyfriend didn't want to either. But then [the boy with the gun] pulled my hair, and he told me to do it. He told me "Come on girl, do it." So my boyfriend, he got out of the car and he said, "Don't be pulling her hair" and [the boy with gun] said, "Man, don' start nothing with me right now. I'm drunk, I'm loaded right now." So my boyfriend told me, "[girl's name] get in the car and then let's go." But then uh, first, uh, my boyfriend was talking so when we, he found out what they put into the trunk was two guns, a gun, he didn't want to talk no more. He wanted to stay [at the girl's house]. And then, he told me to stay too, I didn't want to. I said "Whatever my car was . . ." [the car belonged to the girl.]
>
> And he pointed the gun to him [girl's boyfriend]. I don't know if he mean it to point it to him or not but I know he pointed to him, he said, "Man, let's get out of here." So my boyfriend said, "We better go before we get shot." So we go into the car, and we started driving around by the park, I don't know the name of the park. And when we saw two guys come. They were coming around by the park, [the boy with the gun] said, "Man, stop. Stop the car." [At this point, the girl narrating the drive-by was in the back seat of her own car with her boyfriend. Two of the boys in the front seat jumped out of the car and began shooting at the boys in the park, hitting one.]

If the girl was telling the truth and was not involved with the gang members from the outset, it appears that the situation for a drive-by was an opportunistic one. That is, it was known that someone had guns and wanted to shoot at a rival gang. When the opportunity of an available automobile came about, the gang members took over the car and went looking for targets. When they found the targets, they simply shot at them.

The transformation of the situation of one from "driving around" to a drive-by started when the guns were brought into the car and the driver and her boyfriend were forced to accompany the shooters. Since the girl and her boyfriend were unwilling participants, they were under the coercive rule of the gun and not the rules of situated norms. The two others in the car who did not participate in the shooting were "along for the ride" and made no attempt to gain the release of the girl and her boyfriend. Their lack of action and failure to indicate they did not want to be along suggests they were non-shooting drive-by participants. It was an exciting outing for them. (Indeed, it may have been an exciting outing for all of them, and after deciding who was going to take the fall for the offense, the others may have openly cooperated with the police.)

More data on the nature of the emergent norms in drive-by shootings is needed. The accounts provided by researchers like Jankowski are reflections of commonsense reasoning by the gang members in the context of their social reality. However, such accounts tell us little of how actual situations of gang violence evolve or about the situations themselves. Like we do with other data that have emerged in the study of crime, we tend to want to know more about the actors than the situations they create and in turn become caught up. However, since the actors are behaving in the way they are because of the nature of the situation, we need to know more about those situations.

Situations of Drive-by Shootings

In looking at some situations where drive-by shootings occur, we can get an inkling of the strategies and norms behind these attacks. The kinds of situations that occur prior to a drive-by shooting are often vague, but we will attempt to classify those that are the most common and provide some examples to see the characteristics of the situations and shootings.

Emergent Arguments

The type of drive-by that occurs more or less accidentally or spontaneously emerges out of arguments. Typically, some gang members in a car with a gun will say something to a person in a rival's neighborhood. Often the statement will be a gang challenge. For example, the following driving-shooting occurred when three Little Africa Pirus encountered four Eastside Pirus. Since usually Pirus fight Crips, this incident stands as an exception to the unstated alliance, but the example clearly illustrates the type of situation where cars and guns are used in emergent arguments:

> Three Little Africa Pirus were at a stoplight at an intersection when a car with four Eastside Pirus pulled up next to them. One of the Little Africa Pirus said, "What's up blood?" to the boys in the other car. After some further verbal exchanges, one of the Eastside Piru members pulled out a handgun and shot several bullets into the Little Africa Pirus' car. Two of the occupants were wounded, and jumped out of the car and ran to a nearby gas station. The Eastside Pirus drove off.

It is possible that the shooter thought the boys in the Little Africa Pirus' car were Crips, since the statement, "What's up blood?" often prefaces a shooting by the Crips. (The Pirus preface their attacks of Crips with "What's up, cuz?")

Sometimes, the targets may actually initiate the violence. These are cases where the target says or does something to intentionally antagonize the shooters in the car. For example, the following cases illustrate interchanges that resulted in a shooting from a passing car:

> Three East Side Pirus were in front of their house lifting weights when a car with West Coast Crips drove by and one of the occupants shouted, "Fuck the Pirus!" The Pirus left the yard and walked down the street, where the car passed them again. The second time it passed, a shotgun was pointed at them from the rear window. One of the Pirus, who apparently did not see the shotgun, threw a rock at the car. The car continued down the street, made a U-turn, and came back toward the Pirus. As it passed the third time, two shots were fired from the car, hitting one of the Pirus in the back.

A third type of emergent argument occurs when there is an immediate attack on the drivers and counter-attack by the shooters in the car. This type of emergent argument typically occurs when a car with known rival gang members appears in another gang's home territory and is recognized. The target gang mobilizes and attacks the drivers. The following incident, described by non-gang and gang witnesses, involved the West Coast Crips and Lincoln Park Pirus:

> Two West Coast Crips drove into a parking lot in front of a fried chicken franchise and record store that was the home territory of the Lincoln Park Pirus. When they drove into the lot, they were recognized by the Lincoln Park Pirus, who began attacking them. A non-gang witness said, "I pulled into the lot and everybody was throwing rocks and bottles at each other. These dudes got out of this green Chevy that was parked in front of Dr. J's lot and started shooting. There were two people in the car. The driver got out of the car and fired six shots. There was one other guy in the car. Then they both jumped in the car and tried to run over some of the people that were throwing rocks at them."

A Lincoln Park Piru, who was shot and wounded in the drive-by, provided the following account of the same incident.

> I was just standing on Lowe's lot with a couple of my homeboys, and these two dudes in a six-nine Chevy pulled onto the lot. I don't know either one of them by name but I know they were from the Coast [West Coast Crips]. I had seen them around a couple of times before. There was an "18 and over" party at the record shop. A couple of my homeboys and them got into an argument and my homeboys said something like, "fuck the Coast." Then the dude that was driving pulled out a gun. It looked like he really meant to shoot me 'cause he pointed the gun right at me. I hear a couple of shots, and then I knew I was hit, but I kept on running. I got dizzy and fell down. The next thing I remember the paramedics were there.

Such encounters provide members of both gangs with enough evidence that they showed heart, demonstrated character, and were generally tried-and-true gangbangers. The shooters in the car could claim they took on a numerically superior group and wounded one. The target gang could claim they faced a gun with mere rocks and bottles. Furthermore, the situation grounded the beliefs of both gangs in empirical experience, giving them substance. It showed the necessity of fighting back, the nefarious nature of each other's opponents, and the reality of establishing character. All of these could further be attributed, positively, from the gang boys' perspective, to gang affiliation.

Hanging Out

The situation of the last two examples of emergent argument were also examples of drive-bys occurring in situations where the target gang is hanging out. A distinction is made here between emergent arguments and hanging out as situations of drive-by shootings on the basis of one generating a situated reason for the shooting. In emergent arguments, the shooter can always point to something that the target did or said on the shooting occasion that resulted in the shooting. In the preceding example, something was said or some action was taken by the target gang before the shooting gang began firing.

The difference between a hanging-out situation and one of emergent argument is that in a hanging-out situation, the target has little time to say or do anything before the shooting starts. We can review emergent argument situations and say that were it not for the fact that the target gang *did* say or do something to antagonize the shooter, the shooting may not have occurred. In other words, we can argue that emergent argument situations are in part *situationally victim precipitated*. That means that something the target group did *in the situation* of the drive-by shooting helped justify the shooting.

By contrast, hanging-out situations, while they may be victim precipitated, are not situationally victim precipitated. For example, suppose a gang crosses out another gang's *placaso* (gang signature). The gang whose *placaso* has been defaced justifies a drive-by shooting against the offending gang. They execute the drive-by later that day, that week, or even that month. We can say that the gang who crossed out the *placaso* contributed to its being targeted for a drive-by. In that sense, the drive-by is victim precipitated. However, it is not *situationally* precipitated because the offending action occurred in an occasion separate from the drive-by. The following is an example of this type of hanging-out situation that was precipitated by a member of the target gang. The shooter had been beaten up by some Neighborhood Crips. The drive-by was in retaliation for the "jumping" (beating). The following was related by the shooting victim:

> I was talking to a couple of fellows at Gompers Park . . . when we saw this car turn the corner at Hilltop and Carolina. It started moving toward us. They were yelling "Piru" several times, and we all started running. I could hear them yelling "Piru," and I also hear one of them yell, "What are you running for, blood?" While I was running away, I saw the passenger behind the driver point what appeared to be a double barrel shotgun and fire two shots. . . . [T]he first shot hit me in the back, and I continued running toward 47th Street, through the park. We kept on running until we were somewhere near C Street and Myron helped carry me to a house where he called the police.

As can be seen from the example, there was nothing that the targets did in the situation to precipitate the shooting during the occasion of the shooting. However, it became clear in the investigation that the shooter was involved in the drive-by because of an earlier offense by Neighborhood Crips. Thus, the case is victim-precipitated but not situationally so.

Parties

In most ways there is not a lot of difference between a drive-by targeting a group hanging out and one that targets a party. Parties were selected as targets because they provided an opportunity for a gang to show it would fearlessly attack a massed rival, and party gatherings provided large targets. The shooters may also have considered parties a good target since the party-goers were likely to be intoxicated and not be able to quickly respond:

> Some Shelltown homeboys were at a birthday party for one of the boys' grandmother when some VELs drove by. One Shelltown boy was standing on the street when two VELs got out of the car and said, "Where are you from?" He replied, "Shelltown," and they responded, "Encanto, Encanto!" [VEL is an acronym for Varrio Encanto Locos—roughly translated it means, "The crazy guys from the Encanto neighborhood."] The Shelltown boy ducked down when the VELs began shooting at him before they drove off.

The details of the shooting itself are little differentiated from one where shots are fired in a hanging-out situation. In some of the drive-by shootings observed at parties, it was noted that there tended to be a larger grouping, and girls were more likely to be present. In some of the drive-bys at parties, girls in fact were wounded. Since females are not usually targeted in drive-bys, they are considered innocent bystanders, but there does not seem to be remorse or embarrassment when girls or other innocent bystanders are shot. The view is, "They shouldn't party with those guys if they don't want get shot at."

Another reason that gangs target parties is to enhance their reputation. This can occur when there is little or no past conflict between the gangs. By hitting a party, there is an immediate and wide recognition of the event since the party is likely not only to attract most of the gang members, but also others who attend the occasion as dates or guests of gang members. In one such event, the Spring Valley Locos attacked a Shelltown party. The Shelltown boy who was gunned down in the drive-by was considered a fringe member and had no record of violence himself. In interviews after the incident the partygoers all said that there was no rivalry between the two gangs. Since the gangs were separated by about twelve miles, they did not attend the same schools, and they had no common territorial boundary, it was unclear why the attack occurred. Eventually, some Shelltown boys pointed out that Spring Valley Locos wanted to enhance their reputation. The attack and killing would get around and the Spring Valley Locos would be seen as a gang of heart.

Since two weeks prior to the drive-by, a Shelltown boy had been killed in the Spring Valley Locos territory, it would seem that the Spring Valley Locos had already made their reputation as a dangerous gang. An alternative accounting would be that the Spring Valley Locos attack was to thwart a *payback* (revenge attack) by Shelltown. Jankowski (1991:164) cited fear of being attacked by a rival as a reason to strike first. The first strike is supposed to generate fear that attempts at revenge will call on more retaliation. From this research, it appears that fear is not so much a *factor* as Jankowski used the term, but rather it is a gang *account*. That is, in the vocabulary of motives for engaging in a drive-by shooting, *fear* is an acceptable account if presented correctly. None of the gang members want to appear cowardly in front of their fellow gang members, and so fear must be presented as a rationally grounded reason instead of a gut reaction. In citing Jankowski's own example, we can see the rational account more so than the fear:

> That's it man, we attack the [rival gang's name] and leveled some impressive destruction. . . . No, I don't know if they were planning to attack us or not. If they weren't thinking of it now, they would have had to think of it in the future, so it was best we got them now. (Jankowski, 1991:164)

The account may have implied fear, but it also implied an empirically grounded account for making an attack based on what other gangs honor. Whether it is running from fear or leaping into a situation bringing on honor and the identity associated with it is not so important as was the fact that the reasoning is considered a valid accounting of the events by gang members. Thus, it is not context-free rationality, but rather a rationality grounded in the gang culture, which itself is reflexively grounded in the gang situations.

Business Competition

In the early 1980s, business competition did not appear to be a reason for gang violence at all in San Diego. However, by 1988, many of the gang-related drive-by shootings, especially among African-American gang members, did appear to be connected to the sale and distribution of crack cocaine.

The profits from the sale of crack cocaine were so great that the African-American gangs were all engaging in it to some extent. With wider distribution, sales and profits would increase. In an attempt to expand their business, Los Angeles gangs attempted to take over some of the San Diego areas serviced by local African-American gangs. When this occurred, the rivalry between the local Crips and Pirus was suspended while both gangs fought off the challenge from Los Angeles. However, the Los Angeles gangs were not going to be run off easily. The following attack was made by a Los Angeles gang on West Coast Crips:

> Two West Coast Crips and a non-gang member were walking along the sidewalk when a car drove by and shot at them with an automatic rifle (machine gun). The non-gang member was suspected in a shooting a few days previously.

The non-gang member with the two Crips may have been involved in drug deals, and the gang violence thus may have been a reflection of violence among drug dealers for customers. The increase in drive-by shootings in 1988 makes it clear that something occurred that year to make the number increase so dramatically. Since crack cocaine was introduced to the neighborhoods primarily through African-American gangs at that time, sales competition is hypothesized to be a primary cause.

Non-Person Targets

In addition to shooting at people who could be seen, targets in drive-by shootings also were physical objects that belonged to targets. Most common were automobiles and houses. In the cases of targeting automobiles, it was fairly clear whether or not someone was in the car. However, houses were sometimes occupied and sometimes not.

Shooting at a gang member's house or car can cause damage to the physical target, breaking windows, and putting holes in the stucco walls and metal car panels. In addition, such attacks threaten the victim, and the shooters can claim they have caused a loss of face for the rival gang.

The most problematic issue that arises in examining drive-by shootings at houses is the nature of norms in the context of strategic interaction. While gang members are definitely the desired target if anyone happens to be at home, there is a good chance that others in the house may be wounded or killed. Do norms exist that protect innocent family members? They do not seem to, for drive-by shootings include shooting at houses when parents and siblings of gang members are at home. A former gang member recalled when his family at dinner had to dive for the floor as a rival gang sprayed the house with bullets. He was the only gang member in the family even though he had several brothers and sisters.

Conclusion

Drive-by shootings have become synonymous with gang violence. As a strategy in the context of rival gangs armed with manufactured firearms, it is far superior to other forms of gang warfare. A gang can hit a target miles away from its home territory, and then speed away unscathed. In these situations, gang members can build an identity as having "heart" and live to tell about it. While risky in terms of counterstrikes by the rival gang and police apprehension, a drive-by can be conducted by virtually anyone who can ride in a car and shoot a gun. As such, this type of violence is the most deadly and is likely to be a continuing source of gang power.

References

Goffman, Erving. 1961. *Encounters: Two Studies in the Sociology of Interaction.* Indianapolis, IN: Bobbs-Merrill.

——. 1967. *Interaction Ritual.* Garden City, NY: Doubleday.

——. 1969. *Strategic Interaction*. Philadelphia: University of Pennsylvania Press.

——. 1971. *Relations in Public*. New York: Harper and Row.

Horowitz, Ruth and Gary Schwartz. 1974. "Honor, Normative Ambiguity, and Gang Violence." *American Sociological Review* 39 (April): 238–251.

Jankowski, Martin Sanchez. 1991. *Islands in the Street: Gangs and American Urban Society*. Berkeley: University of California Press.

Klein, Malcolm W. 1971. *Street Gangs and Street Workers*. Englewood Cliffs, NJ: Prentice Hall.

Miller, Walter B. 1975. *Violence by Youth Gangs and Youth Groups as a Crime Problem in Major American Cities*. Washington, D.C.: U.S. Department of Justice.

Mills, C. Wright. 1940. "Situated Actions and Vocabularies of Motive." *American Sociological Review* 5: 904–913.

Scott, Marvin B. and Sanford Lyman. 1968. "Accounts." *American Sociological Review* (February): 46–62.

Short, James F. and Fred L. Strodtbeck. 1964. "Why Gangs Fight." *Transaction* I (6, Sept.–Oct.): 25–29.

Sylvester, Sawyer F., Jr. 1972. *The Heritage of Modern Criminology*. Cambridge, MA: Schenkman.

Yablonsky, Lewis. 1962. *The Violent Gang*. New York: Macmillan.✦

Chapter 19 Gun Ownership and Gang Membership

Beth Bjerregaard
and
Alan J. Lizotte

The prior articles in this section document the elevated risk for serious violence and homicide among gang members. Accessibility to firearms and the willingness to use guns to settle disputes and increase status are important issues in the gang/violence nexus. In this article, Bjerregaard and Lizotte examine the relationship between owning a gun and joining a gang. In particular, they are interested in whether gun ownership precedes or follows gang membership. Do gangs foster gun activity or are gun owners specifically recruited into gangs? Longitudinal interviews from the Rochester Youth Development Study provide data to address this issue. These authors find that gangs are likely to recruit gun owners into their ranks. As will be seen in the articles in Section V, juvenile gun ownership has emerged as a critical vector for gang violence prevention.

Introduction

The problem of gang-related violence is not a new phenomenon, yet public concern over the rising violence perpetrated by juveniles has led to a renewed interest in the study of juvenile gangs. Whereas gangs used to be predominantly confined to large urban centers such as Los Angeles, Chicago, or New York City, today's gangs appear to be increasingly present in medium and small-sized cities previously believed to be immune to gang activity.[1] The increased visibility of gangs, coupled with the growing fear of juvenile crime, has led researchers and others to conclude that there is an association between gangs and crime. While researchers have been studying gangs since the turn of the century, criminologists are once again placing a greater emphasis on understanding the prevalence and dynamics of gang-related crime. This recent research overwhelmingly concludes that gang members tend to be more violent than those who are not gang members.

Recently, researchers discovered some alarming trends in the gangs they have studied: the gangs of today appear to be more violent in nature than the gangs of the first half of the century.[2] The activities that gangs participate in appear to be changing; gang members now engage more frequently in serious crimes, drug-related behavior, and firearms use.[3] While all these changes are of great concern to policymakers and criminal justice professionals, it is the latter of these changes, the increased use of firearms by gang members, that creates perhaps the most disturbing scenario. Cities across the United States have noticed an alarming trend in gang use of firearms and there is some evidence that gang related homicides have increased over the decades.[4] Likewise, conflicts between gangs and gang members are becoming increasingly more deadly due to the use of firearms.[5]

Several researchers attribute the increasingly violent nature of gangs to the increased availability of firearms.[6] Gang members today have access to an extremely sophisticated arsenal of weaponry. However, it is unclear whether the observed increase in the violent activities of juveniles and the apparent increase in gang activity is related to the observed increase in the availability and sophistication of firearms in the juvenile population.

Reprinted from: Beth Bjerregaard and Alan J. Lizotte, "Gun Ownership and Gang Membership." In *The Journal of Criminal Law & Criminology*, volume 86, pp. 37–58.

The purpose of this Chapter is to examine the relationship between gun ownership, gun use, and gang membership. In particular, this research is concerned with the causal order of the relationship between illegal gun ownership and gang membership. If gang membership is related to the ownership of firearms and the causal order between the two can be discerned, criminal justice policymakers across the country will be presented with a unique opportunity for change. The research could help determine whether gangs foster gun activity or whether gun possession leads to gang membership. If the result is that gangs do in fact foster gun activity, such information will be particularly useful in that it will allow us to improve our strategies to reduce the violent and delinquent activities of gangs. Therefore, gang membership and gun ownership also need to be examined in the context of their contributions to violent and serious crime. Understanding the role of firearms in gangs will enhance our understanding of gang behavior, which may in turn be useful in combating violent criminal activity by gangs.

Gangs and Delinquent Behavior

Scholars have placed considerable attention on examining the extent to which gang members engage in delinquent behavior. As early as 1927, Thrasher, in his observational study of 1,313 gangs in Chicago, concluded that gang members were more involved in delinquency than youths who were not involved in gangs.[7] Subsequent research has confirmed these findings. There has been a high degree of consensus among researchers examining this relationship. Utilizing an array of methodological techniques, researchers have almost unanimously concluded that gang members are far more likely to be delinquent than their non-gang counterparts. This relationship has been confirmed by both observational and self-report studies[8] and by those examining official data.[9]

While these researchers all agree that gang members are more delinquent than non-gang members, there is some controversy as to the nature of delinquent behavior by gang members. Many of the early studies on gang behavior concluded that gang members were frequently involved in minor forms of delinquency or, as Klein stated, a "garden variety" of delinquent activities.[10] However, this picture of gang related delinquency appears to be changing. More recently, scholars agree that gang violence is becoming both more frequent and more deadly.[11] Specifically, research indicates that gang members are involved in the most serious and violent types of offenses.[12] Given this recent shift in gang behavior, it becomes increasingly important to discover the factors that might be contributing to this shift in delinquency patterns among gang members.

Gangs and Weapons

Several researchers have attributed these observed increases in both the frequency and seriousness of gang-related crime to the increased availability of weapons among the juvenile population.[13] For example, in 1975 Miller found that in a typical gang about half of the members are likely to own a gun.[14] In fact, some of the gang members we interviewed made statements such as "everybody's got them; they have them either on their persons or in their homes" and "in this city (L.A.) a gang is judged by the number and quality of weapons they have; the most heavily armed gang is the most feared; for our gangs, firepower is the name of the game." While it is likely that these statements are somewhat exaggerated, there is little question that most gang members today either own a gun or have access to a large number of weapons. More recently, Hagedorn also discovered that nearly 50 percent of the gang members interviewed said they possessed more than one firearm and a large majority claimed to have at least one handgun.[15] Similarly, Lizotte, Tesoriero, Thornberry and Krohn found that over half of the juveniles who reported being in a gang also reported owning guns for "protection."[16] Taylor found that 70 percent of the gang members interviewed reported having a gun in their home, thereby having access to a firearm.[17]

While these statistics are extremely troublesome, the picture becomes even more alarming when one considers the weapons themselves. Not only have researchers revealed an increase in the availability of firearms in gangs, but they also point out that weapons today are far more sophisticated and lethal than the weapons of the past. Whereas weapons like brass knuckles and homemade zip guns dominated gangs in the 1930s through the 1950s, today gangs possess a far more deadly variety of weaponry, including sawed-off or unadulterated rifles and shotguns, along with handguns of all sizes and types (e.g., 22 cal., 38 cal., .357, 45 cal., and 9 mm. among others) and semiautomatic weapons (e.g., AK-47, Uzi, MAC-10, MAC-11).[18] For example, Andrew Hague of the Dade County Attorney's Office states that "Dade County gangs are very heavily armed," adding that it is "not uncommon for police to retrieve very sophisticated weapons, including AK-47's, MAC-10's, derringers, and 9mm's."[19]

This changing nature of weaponry has influenced the very nature of gang behavior, particularly in terms of gang conflicts. In 1975, Miller stated that "probably the single most significant development affecting gang-member violence during the present period is the extraordinary increase in the availability and use of firearms to effect violent crimes. This development is in all likelihood the major reason behind the increasingly lethal nature of gang violence."[20]

Researchers have found that gang members are being arrested in increasingly large numbers for violent offenses such as assault with a deadly weapon, shooting incidences, batteries, and homicides.[21] Los Angeles police and sheriff's data indicate that guns were present in 80 to 82 percent of all gang-related homicides, which is about 15 to 20 percent higher than homicides committed by individuals who are not associated with a gang.[22] Block and Block found that a gun was the lethal weapon in 94 to 96 percent of all street gang-motivated homicides in Chicago.[23] These changes in gun ownership among gang members not only result in an increase in gang violence, but also help spread violence to nearby communities. Further, today gang shootings tend to be unplanned and spontaneous events.[24] The rumbles of yesteryear have been replaced by activities such as drive-by shootings. Thus, it appears that gang-related violence is taking on a new quality and becoming increasingly lethal in nature. This change appears to be directly attributable to the role of firearms in a gang.

Gun Ownership and Gang Membership

Prior research has postulated a relationship between gun ownership and gang membership, but the causal order of this relationship is unclear. While it appears that there is certainly an association between gang membership, gun ownership, and delinquent behavior, researchers at this point have little empirical knowledge of the dynamics of this relationship. For example, it is entirely possible that gangs perform a self-selection process by recruiting their members from juvenile populations where firearms are readily available and perhaps utilized prior to gang membership. However, it is equally plausible that juveniles are socialized into the gun culture by virtue of their gang membership and activity. In other words, the nature or the organization of a gang may facilitate the gun ownership of its members. Finally, it is feasible that both of these factors operate simultaneously to enhance the gun ownership of gang members.

The purpose of this Chapter is to explore the nature of the temporal relationship between gun ownership and gang membership. This Chapter also considers the impact of a gang on delinquency. Longitudinal data from the Rochester Youth Development Study (RYDS) are utilized to examine the causal nature of these relationships. RYDS is an ongoing longitudinal study of delinquency and drug use among a sample of 987 youths and their primary caretakers in Rochester, New York. Specifically, this Chapter addresses the following research questions:

1. Are gang members more likely than non-gang members to own firearms for sport and/or for "protection"?

2. If gang members are more likely to own specific types of firearms, does gun ownership precede gang involvement, does gang membership precede gun involvement, or do both of these operate at the same time?
3. If gang members own guns, does it influence their delinquent behavior, especially in terms of serious offenses and gun-related offenses?
4. Do relationships between gang membership and gun ownership remain stable when the demographic and social characteristics of the juveniles are held constant?

Data and Methods

The data for this study were obtained from the RYDS, a longitudinal panel study examining the causes and correlates of juvenile delinquency in a high-risk urban sample. Adolescents and their primary caretakers were interviewed at six month intervals, commencing when subjects were in the seventh or eighth grades. The total panel consisted of 987 students who attended the seventh and eighth grades of the Rochester public schools during the 1987–88 school year. An important aim of the sampling strategy was to ensure that students at high risk for delinquent behavior were included in the sample. To facilitate this goal, the sample was stratified to over-represent high-risk youths. Males were over sampled (75 percent versus 25 percent) because they are more likely to be involved in serious delinquent behavior. In addition, students who resided in high crime areas were over sampled on the assumption that these youths were at higher risk for delinquent involvement. In order to identify high crime areas, each census tract in Rochester was assigned a resident arrest rate, which reflects the proportion of the tract's adult population arrested in 1986. Subjects were then sampled with probabilities proportionate to the arrest rate in their area of residence. Since the true probability of a juvenile living in a particular tract is known, the sample can be weighted to reflect a true random sample of the population. The multivariate analysis reported below is weighted.[25]

Since information on both gang membership and gun ownership was not collected until later waves of data collection, the current analysis is based on data collected at Waves 7 through 9. Waves are conducted at six month intervals. The subjects were sixteen and seventeen years of age at Wave 8. Because girls rarely own guns, whether for sport or protection, the present analysis is based on 656 male adolescents who remained in the panel during Waves 7 through 9. Table 19.1 shows the characteristics of subjects. The retention rate for the entire sample is 89 percent at Wave 7, 87 percent at Wave 8 and 88 percent at Wave 9. With respect to age, sex, race/ethnicity, and census tract, subjects at Wave 7 through 9 are remarkably similar to the subjects at Wave 1 of the panel. Thus, attrition does not appear to have had an effect on the characteristics of our respondents.

Table 19.1
Sample Characteristics (N=656)

Race	
White	19.1%
African-American	62.8%
Hispanic	18.1%
Age	
16	.3%
17	15.5%
18	39.9%
19	36.9%
20	7.3%
$\bar{X}$ = 18.35	
Gang	
Never been a gang member	88.7%
Gang member during at least 1 wave	11.3%
Gun ownership	
Never owned	79.4%
Owned during at least 1 wave	20.6%

Table 19.1 shows that the majority of the subjects in our sample are minorities. The average age of the juveniles in this sample is eighteen. Slightly over 10 percent of the sample reported being a gang member at some time over the eighteen month period studied in this analysis and one-fifth of the sample

Table 19.2
Coding of Variables

		X̄	S.D.
1. Gun for Protection Purposes	Subject owns gun (handgun, pistol, revolver, shotgun, or rifle) for protection.	.09	.28
2. Gun for Sport	Subject owns gun for sport-hunting, target practice.	.06	.23
3. White	0=Other 1=White	.19	.39
4. Hispanic	0=Other 1=Hispanic	.18	.39
5. Delinquent Values	Variable measuring student's commitment to delinquent values. Higher score indicates more commitment. Ranges from 1–4.	1.56	.51
6. Parent Gun Ownership	Indicates that parent owns a gun for sport.	.05	.22
7. Peer Gun Ownership	Indicates subject has friends who own a gun for protection.	.36	.48
8. Future Gang Member	A subject who is not currently in a gang, but joins in the subsequent wave.	.02	.15
9. Current Gang Member	A subject who is currently in a gang.	.05	.23
10. Past Gang Member	A subject who is not currently in a gang, but who was a member in the preceding wave.	.05	.22

DELINQUENCY SCALES

General Delinquency
* Carried weapon
* Used weapon with idea of seriously hurting someone
* Hit someone with idea of hurting them
* Threw objects at people
* Used weapon to get money or things
* Physically hurt someone to get them to have sex
* Damaged property
* Set fire
* Avoided paying
* Stole less than $5
* Stole $5-$50
* Stole $50-$100
* Stole more than $100
* Shoplifted
* Snatched purse
* Stole something from car
* Bought/sold stolen goods
* Went for a joyride
* Stole a car
* Forged a check
* Used a credit card without permission
* Cheated someone by selling them something worthless
* Sold marijuana
* Sold other drugs

Serious Delinquency
* Broke into building
* Stole $50-$100
* Stole more than $100
* Stole a car
* Used weapon with idea of hurting someone
* Involved in gang fight
* Used weapon to get money or things
* Physically hurt someone to get them to have sex

Street Delinquency
* Stole $50-$100
* Stole more than $100
* Stole a car
* Broke into building
* Used weapon with idea of hurting someone
* Used weapon to get money or things
* Physically hurt someone to get them to have sex
* Involved in gang fight
* Snatched purse
* Stolen something from a car
* Sold marijuana
* Sold hard drugs
* Knowingly bought, sold, or held stolen goods or tried to do any of these things

Drug Sales
* Sold marijuana
* Sold other drugs

Gun Related Crime
* Used a gun to make someone give you money or things
* Attacked someone with a gun
* Used a gun while in a gang fight

reported owning a gun during this same time period.

Measurement

The variables used in the analysis are presented in Table 19.2. Specifically, there are four types of variables utilized in this study: gang membership, gun ownership, delinquent behavior, and several control variables used in the multivariate analysis.

The present study utilizes a self-report measure of the respondents' participation in a street gang or "posse." Respondents who identified themselves as gang members were considered to be members for purposes of this analysis. Yet defining a gang is one of the most challenging tasks facing gang researchers today. Horowitz argues that we lack sufficient knowledge concerning gangs to allow us to form precise definitions, and she also suggests that confining the definition of a gang to specific criteria may foreclose important debate and theory.[26] Winfree et al. found that more restrictive measures of defining gang involvement, requiring both initiation rites and some external symbols of membership, were associated with less delinquency than the less restrictive measures of definition, such as self-identification as a gang member.[27] Many researchers agree that self-definition is a central aspect of gang membership.[28] Furthermore, allowing for self-definition avoids the issue of confounding the definition of gang membership with gang behavior. Therefore, a self-report measure is most appropriate for the purposes of this analysis.

Gun ownership is measured by the adolescent's self-reported ownership of a handgun, pistol, revolver, shotgun, or rifle—not a BB or pellet gun. Two measures of gun ownership were created, gun ownership for protection purposes and gun ownership for sporting purposes. Respondents were considered to own a gun for protection purposes if they reported owning any of the above firearms for protection, whether or not they owned the gun for other purposes such as hunting or sport. Respondents were considered to own a gun for sporting purposes if they reported that they owned their guns solely for the purposes of hunting or target practicing and the like. An average of 9 percent of the subjects own guns for protection while an average of 6 percent own guns for sport. Boys who own guns for sport are much more likely to own rifles and shotguns. Those who own for protection tend to own handguns, sawed-off rifles, and shotguns.[29] Protection owners are much more likely to be involved in gangs and criminal activity.[30]

Since past research has found that peers introduce boys to protective gun use,[31] subjects were asked if they have friends who own guns for "protection" (Peer Gun Ownership). Thirty-six percent (252) reported having friends who do. Similarly, prior research suggests that parents often introduce boys to sport gun use.[32] Therefore, parents' sport gun ownership is also included in our analysis. Five percent (35) of the parents own guns for sport. Because we are interested in examining socialization effects, a ten item scale measuring the boy's commitment to delinquency values is also included (Cronbach's Alpha = .91).

Race and ethnicity are related to both gang and gun activity. Because of this relationship, dummy variables indicating whether the subject is white or Hispanic are included in the analysis.

The delinquency measures are derived from the RYDS' self-report index. They were adapted from the National Youth Survey[33] and modified by the Denver Youth Survey.[34] Respondents were asked if they had, during the past six months, engaged in a series of forty-four delinquent behaviors. If a respondent answered in the affirmative, he was asked how often he did so and also asked to describe the most serious incident. Coders screened the delinquency items in order to ensure that only "actionable" offenses were analyzed. This was done to ensure that trivial offenses (e.g., sibling rivalries) were excluded. Five sub-scales are used in the following analysis: general delinquency, serious delinquency, street crimes, drug sales, and gun-related crime.

The general scale of delinquency consists of twenty-four delinquency items selected to represent a variety of delinquent activities. The range of offenses includes thefts, drug sales, weapons offenses, and vandalism. The serious delinquency scale consists of eight delinquency items, covering such offenses as using a weapon to hurt someone, robbery, forced sex, theft over $50, and breaking and entering. Thirteen items make up the street crime measure. These offenses concentrate on serious offenses that are likely to occur in public settings. The drug sales measure consists of two items measuring sales of both marijuana and hard drugs. Three offenses are used to measure gun-related crime: robbery, attacking someone with a gun, and using a gun during a gang fight.

Results

1. The Relationship Between Gang Membership and Gun Ownership

The research first examines the relationship between gang membership and gun ownership. Specifically, are gang members more likely to own guns than non-gang members? Table 19.3 examines the relationship between gang membership and gun ownership, as well as other characteristics and behaviors of gun owners.

The results clearly illustrate that gang members are significantly more likely to own guns for protection purposes than non-gang members. For example, at Wave 7, 24 percent of gang members own guns for protection, while only about 7 percent of non-gang members do so. Guns owned for sporting purposes are no more likely to be owned by gang members than by non-gang members. These results are consistent across the

Table 19.3
Relationship Between Gang Membership and Gun/Weapon Behavior for Males

	Wave 7	Wave 8	Wave 9
Own Protection Gun			
Gang Member	24.4%[a]	30.6%[a]	36.7%[a]
Non-Gang Member	7.4%	7.7%	7.7%
Own Sport Gun			
Gang Member	0%[b,c]	11.1%	13.3%
Non-Gang Member	5.4%	5.7%	5.3%
Peer Gun			
Gang Member	64.4%[a,c]	77.8%[a]	86.7%[a]
Non-Gang Member	34.3%	34.2%	35.7%
Other Weapon for Protection			
Gang Member	40.0%[a,c]	47.2%[a]	60.0%[a]
Non-Gang Member	24.4%[c,d]	23.7%	18.4%
Other Peer Weapon			
Gang Member	75.6%[a]	80.6%[a]	83.3%[a]
Non-Gang Member	37.6%	36.8%	37.2%
Carry Gun			
Gang Member	15.6%[a]	22.2%[a]	26.7%[a]
Non-Gang Member	4.1%	3.8%	4.3%

Significance tests: P<.10
a=Gang vs. Non-gang
b=Wave 7 with Wave 8
c=Wave 7 with Wave 9
d=Wave 8 with Wave 9

Wave 7 -	Gang Members	N=45
	Non-Gang	N=607
Wave 8 -	Gang Members	N=36
	Non-Gang	N=600
Wave 9 -	Gang Members	N=30
	Non-Gang	N=608

three waves examined. Furthermore, while not always statistically significant, for gang members both protection and sport ownership seem to increase over time, possibly indicating an increase of gang members' gun ownership with age. There is no visible trend in the rates of gun ownership for non-gang members over time.

Additionally, gang members are also more likely than non-gang members to have peers who own guns for protection; the percentage of gang members having such peers increases over time. By Wave 9, nearly 87 percent of gang members have friends who own guns for protection. Although lower in magnitude, this trend is similar to the observed increase in protection gun ownership for gang members over the three waves. Both of these findings suggest that the age of the respondent may have an influence on both the respondent's chance of owning a gun for protection and the chance that their peers will own guns. As the juvenile matures, he may be more likely to become involved with firearms. Further, non-gang members are far less likely to have peers who own guns. The percentage of those who have such peers remains steady at its low level over time.

Table 19.3 also shows that gang members and their friends are more likely to own other types of weapons such as knives or clubs. Furthermore, this weapons ownership increases over time for gang members and their peers. By Wave 9, 60 percent of the subjects who are gang members have weapons other than firearms for protection and 83 percent have peers who own other types of weapons. However, weapon ownership is much lower and decreases for non-gang members and remains stable for their friends.

Finally, gang members are significantly more likely than nongang members to carry guns. In Wave 7 more than 15 percent of gang members carry a gun, and this increases, although not significantly so, to more than 26 percent at Wave 9. This is contrasted by non-gang members, who rarely carry a gun (approximately 4 percent).

Overall, the results clearly demonstrate that gang membership is significantly related to both protection gun ownership and weapons ownership. Furthermore, there is an association between gang membership and peers with guns for protection; gang members have peers who own guns for protection and are more inclined to carry their weapons outside of the home.

2. Temporal Ordering of the Relationship Between Gang Membership and Gun Ownership

Having established that the relationship between gang membership and gun ownership exists, the second task of this research was to discern its temporal ordering. Do gangs influence the protective gun ownership of members, or do gangs recruit youths already involved in the gun subculture?

The unique advantage of utilizing a longitudinal data set is that it allows one to assess the temporal ordering of these variables; longitudinal data allows a determination as to whether juveniles' sport and protective gun ownership occurs prior to, during, or after their gang participation.

In order to discern the nature of this relationship, three measures of gang membership were utilized and compared to non-gang members. First, future gang members represent subjects who were not in a gang in a preceding wave (7 or 8), but who joined a gang in a subsequent wave (8 or 9). Current gang members were those youths who reported being in a gang during the current wave. Juveniles who were in a gang in a preceding wave but who were not currently in a gang were considered to be past gang members.[35] Non-gang members were those youths who never reported being a member of a gang.

Table 19.4 shows prevalence rates for the same variables reported in Table 19.3, in addition to the five delinquency items measured in each of these four categories of gang membership.

The findings clearly indicate that gang membership enhances gun ownership for protection purposes. While future gang members have somewhat inflated rates of gun ownership for protection purposes over non-gang members (23.1 percent versus 14.2 percent), current gang members are clearly more likely to own guns for protection than nongang members (30.9 percent versus 14.2

percent). The rate of protection gun ownership for current gang members is only slightly and not significantly higher than that of future gang members. This may suggest that gangs are likely to recruit members who already own guns for protection. Furthermore, the juveniles' rate of gun ownership for protection purposes drops to a level similar to that of non-gang members after the juvenile has left a gang (13.2 percent versus 14.2 percent). This finding suggests that those who are recruited into a gang are not interested in protection gun activity and are likely to drop out of a gang.[36] Again, these relationships are observed only for guns owned for protection purposes rather than for sporting purposes. A similar pattern is also observed for weapons other than firearms, which is not statistically significant, and for carrying guns outside the household, which is statistically significant.

Findings concerning peer ownership of guns for protection purposes and weapons other than guns further support the enhancement perspective. The prevalence of peer gun ownership and weapons ownership for both non-gang members and future gang members is similar, 55.1 percent versus 53.8 percent. However, once in a gang, the percentage of peers owning both guns for protection and weapons increases significantly to nearly 78 percent. Furthermore, once the youths drop out of a gang, their peers' ownership rates decline to rates comparable to that of non-gang members, 52.8 percent.

Similar patterns are observed when examining the delinquent behavior of these juveniles. Future gang members are more likely than non-gang members to have been involved in serious delinquency and street delinquency. For all types of delinquency, once the juvenile joins a gang his involvement in these activities is significantly higher than either non-gang members or future gang members. Yet, when these juveniles leave a gang, the percentage of youths involved in these behaviors drops again to rates that are comparable to those of the non-gang members. The exceptions to this are found in the serious and street delinquency scales, where the percentage of youths involved in these types of delinquency decreases after a juvenile leaves a gang but still remains slightly inflated from those who never joined a gang. More importantly, this type of relationship is also observed for gun-related crimes. Again, current gang members are more likely than

Table 19.4

Relationship Between Gang Membership and Gun/Weapon Behavior and Delinquent Behavior for Males

	Non-Gang Members (N=548)	Future Gang Members (N=39)	Current Gang Members (N=81)	Past Gang Members (N=32)
Protection Gun[a,e]	14.2%	23.1%	30.9%	13.2%
Sport Gun	8.4	12.8	9.9	7.5
Weapon Protect	39.4	46.2	46.9	39.6
Peer Gun[a,b,e]	55.1	53.8	77.8	52.8
Peer Weapon[a,b,d,e]	58.8	51.3	79.0	52.8
Serious Delinq.[a,b,d,e,f]	30.5	51.3	74.1	45.3
General Delinq.[a,b,e]	56.8	64.1	90.1	66.0
Street Delinq.[a,b,d,e,f]	35.4	53.8	80.2	52.8
Drug Sales[a,b,e]	10.2	7.7	34.6	17.0
Gun Delinquency[a,b,e]	3.1	2.6	13.6	0.0
Carry Gun[a,e]	8.6	12.8	21.0	5.7

Significance Tests: P <.10
a=Current with Past
b=Current with Future
c=Past with Future
d=Non-gang with Future
e=Non-gang with Current
f=Non-gang with Past

past, future, or non-gang members to be involved in this type of criminal activity.

The results of this analysis clearly indicate that gang membership increases the prevalence of guns for protection and weapons ownership, and affects peer behaviors and delinquent offending. However, these results also provide some support for the possibility of a selection process. Future gang members are the closest in terms of their prevalence rates to current gang members, frequently having prevalence rates slightly above those of both non-gang members and prior gang members. Once a youth leaves a gang, it appears that he also leaves behind the gun subculture and the delinquent activity. Prevalence rates of past gang members are very much comparable to those of non-gang members. It may be that these youths never really fit into a gang and that they were not interested in the deviant aspects of a gang. In other words, once they discovered that other gang members were involved in gun ownership and other forms of serious delinquency, they made the decision to leave the gang.

3. Multivariate Analysis Determining Causal Order

Having established a relationship between gang membership and protection gun ownership, the final question to be addressed is whether past, present, and future gang membership are significant predictors of gun ownership when other factors are held constant. Including separate independent variables measuring past, present, and future gang membership in equations predicting the type of gun owned helps determine the causal order of the gang-gun relationship. In the equations, the coefficient for past gang membership indicates the impact of gang membership in Wave 7 on gun ownership in Wave 8. One might think of this as the residual effect of gang membership on future gun ownership. The coefficient for future gang membership measures the opposite causal effect; it assesses the impact of gun ownership at Wave 8 on gang membership at Wave 9. In other words, it measures the forces that propel gun owners into gangs. The coefficient for current gang member on gun ownership measures the contemporaneous effect of gang membership on gun ownership. In addition, controlling for other relevant variables allows us to ascertain if the observed relationships between past, present, and future gang membership and gun ownership might in fact be due to other extraneous factors. For example, prior research has found a strong relationship between the race of a juvenile and both gang membership and gun ownership.[37] It is possible that the high percentage of minorities in gangs may also account for the high percentage of guns in gangs. Additionally, gangs may either attract youths who possess delinquent values or foster the development of those delinquent values once a youth joins a gang; again, youths with delinquent values may be more likely to own guns in the gang setting. The multivariate analysis allows us to examine the relationship between gun ownership and gang membership while controlling for these other factors. Specifically, the race of the juvenile, the delinquent values held by the juvenile, the rate of peer gun ownership for protection, and parental sport gun ownership are examined in relation to the juveniles' probability of owning a gun.[38] These variables are thought to reflect both the extent of the juvenile's commitment to a delinquent lifestyle (delinquent values, gang membership) and parental socialization of gun ownership (parent sport ownership).

Since the dependent variable of gun ownership is trichotomous, multinomial logistic regression is used to estimate this equation.[39] In this analysis sport gun ownership and protection gun ownership are simultaneously contrasted with no gun ownership. Table 19.5 reports the logistic regression coefficients, standard errors, and the percentage change in probability of joining a gang, given a one unit increase in each of the independent variables.[40]

The results show that African-Americans, those who have peers who own protection guns, and future and current gang members are the most likely to own a gun for protection purposes. Whites are 7 percent less likely to own guns for protection than are African-Americans. Additionally, juveniles who have peers who own guns are 31 percent more likely to own a gun for protection pur-

Table 19.5
Multinomial Logistic Regression Predicting Gun Ownership for Males (N=631)[a]

	Parameter Estimates Protection Gun	Parameter Estimates Sport Gun	t value[b]
White	−1.76*	2.09**	−5.25
	.93	.46	
	(−.07)	(.28)	
Hispanic	−.44	−1.20	
	.49	1.29	
	(−.03)	(−.04)	
Delinquent Values	.25	.24	
	.36	.44	
	(.02)	(.01)	
Parent Sport Gun Ownership	−.22	1.68**	−2.10
	1.19	.47	
	(−.02)	(.20)	
Peer Gun Ownership	1.89**	.98**	2.07
	.45	.43	
	(.31)	(.09)	
Future Gang Member	1.75**	XX[c]	
	.77		
	(.27)		
Current Gang Member	.99**	1.25**	
	.52	.64	
	(.12)	(.12)	
Past Gang Member	.16	XX[c]	
	.72		
	(.01)		

*P<.10
**P<.05
[a]Parameter estimates are provided with standard errors underneath. Probabilities are in parentheses.
[b]Tests for significance of difference between subsample coefficients.
[c]Parameters could not be estimated due to a lack of cases.

poses than those without peers who own guns. Moreover, both future and current gang membership positively influence a juvenile's probability of owning a gun for protection by 27 percent and 12 percent respectively. Finally, past gang members are not significantly different from non-gang members.

The variables predicting gun ownership for protection purposes differ somewhat from those predicting gun ownership for sporting purposes. Whites are 28 percent more likely to own a gun for sport than are African-Americans.[41] Further, while peer gun ownership has an effect on sport gun ownership, the magnitude of its influence is significantly reduced when compared to those who own guns for protection purposes. Juveniles with peers who own guns for protection are 31 percent more inclined to own a gun for protection than those with peers who do not own guns for protection, while juveniles with peers who own a gun for sport are only 9 percent more likely to own a gun for protection purposes. Tests for differences between these coefficients show them to be statistically significant. Furthermore, while current gang membership is predictive of sport gun ownership, there are too few cases of future or past gang members owning sport guns to estimate the effects of these variables on sport gun ownership. The only unique predictor of sport gun ownership is parental sport gun ownership, indicating that parents who own guns for sport are probably socializing their children into a culture of sport gun ownership, but not protective gun ownership.

The multivariate analysis presents us with a slightly different picture of the relationship between gang membership and gun ownership. Future gang membership emerges as a strong predictor of protection gun ownership; being a prospective gang member increases a juvenile's chance of protection gun ownership by 27 percent. That is, protection gun ownership causes future gang membership, suggesting that gangs successfully recruit those who already own guns for protection. Interestingly, these findings suggest that once a juvenile is in a gang, he is equally likely to own both sport and protective guns.[42] Again, these results suggest an environment that fosters the possession of weapons both for protection and for use in crime.

Discussion and Conclusions

Overall, the results of this study clearly indicate that gang members are significantly more likely to own guns than non-gang members. These findings are also consistent for weapons other than guns. Furthermore, gang members are more likely to have peers who own guns for protection and to carry their weapons outside the home.

More importantly, the longitudinal analysis allows us to examine the nature of this relationship. While gangs do appear to influence gun ownership, the nature of that influence is slightly more complex than previous researchers have acknowledged. Those youths who eventually join a gang display slightly inflated rates of both gun ownership and delinquency before they become gang members. There are two possible explanations for this observation. First, it may be that gangs recruit juveniles who already show a propensity for involvement in these delinquent activities. Second, it may be that the youths who are involved in the illegal firearms subculture and delinquent behavior are also the same youths who are likely to be attracted to a gang. In either case, these results provide some support for the notion that a selection process is occurring. The strongest support for the occurrence of a selection process is found in the socialization perspective as discussed by Thornberry et al.: those youths who are currently involved in gangs clearly exhibit the highest prevalence rates of both gun ownership and delinquency.[43] These findings indicate that a gang milieu fosters illegal activities, including both delinquent behavior and firearms ownership.

Youths who drop out of a gang experience a decrease in their levels of participation in both the gun subculture and in delinquent behaviors. Those youths who dropped out and who did not own firearms were also unlikely to own firearms during their gang membership. Quite possibly, these youths were neither interested in the gun subculture nor in participating in illegal activities; once they realized that these activities were a part of a gang subculture, they left the gang.

These conclusions have several implications. The findings concerning current gang members lend support for the learning perspective. Previous theorists such as Akers, Sutherland and Cressey, and Cloward and Ohlin stress the importance of learning criminal behavior.[44] Gangs provide youths with both an environment which is conducive to learning criminal values and behaviors and to techniques for engaging in those activities. It is important to note that this is true mainly for delinquency; once a juvenile enters a gang, he learns that delinquent activities and gun ownership are an acceptable part of gang membership. These results also offer some support for the idea that gangs may establish their own criteria for attaining status within the group setting, and frequently that status is established by engaging in delinquent activities.[45]

With regards to gun ownership, only minimal support exists for the learning perspective. Gangs appear much more likely to recruit from juveniles who already own guns. This implies that juveniles who already own guns for protection may be joining a gang because they are attracted to the role of weapons in a gang. This view is further supported by the fact that the juveniles who drop out of a gang were not likely to own guns while in a gang.

From a policy perspective, this research suggests that society may be able to target juveniles who are susceptible to gang recruitment and aim our intervention strategies at this narrower population. Since joining a gang is also associated with a marked increase in both gun ownership and participation in illegal activities, and since leaving a gang is related to a decrease in delinquent activities, it becomes increasingly important that society institute policies to remove these juveniles from a gang once they become involved.

Finally, these findings have implications for future research. Further examination of the factors that predict future gang involvement is needed. The findings from this study suggest that gangs may be more likely to recruit certain types of juveniles; for example, those who already own guns for protection purposes. Additionally, there is a need to further develop our understanding of the dynamics and consequences of gang membership. How and why does gang membership encourage the ownership of firearms? These results imply that while gun ownership is closely related to delinquency within a gang, the gun culture may operate in a slightly different way. Protective gun ownership influences the probability that a youth will join a gang, but it also influences his behavior once he is in a gang. Since juveniles appear to leave these behaviors behind once they leave a gang, it becomes increasingly more important to identify strategies that would be successful at drawing youths out of a gang.

Notes

1. *See, e.g.*, Dan Bryant, *Communitywide Responses Crucial for Dealing with Youth Gangs*, JUVENILE JUSTICE BULLETIN 2 (1989); JOHN M. HAGEDORN, PEOPLE AND FOLKS: GANGS, CRIME AND THE UNDERCLASS IN A RUSTBELT CITY 20–21 (1988); New York State Division For Youth, Reaffirming Prevention, REPORT OF THE TASK FORCE ON JUVENILE GANGS (1990); Irving A. Spergel, *Youth Gangs: Continuity and Change*, in 12 CRIME AND JUSTICE: A REVIEW OF RESEARCH 171, 182 (Michael Tonry & Norval Morris eds., 1990).
2. Bryant, *supra* note 1, at 2–3; H. C. COVEY ET AL., JUVENILE GANGS 32 (1992); WALTER B. MILLER, CRIME BY YOUTH GANGS AND GROUPS IN THE UNITED STATES 76 (1982).
3. MILLER, *supra* note 2, at ch. 5–6; Malcolm W. Klein & Cheryl L. Maxson, *Street Gang Violence*, in VIOLENT CRIME AND VIOLENT CRIMINALS 198–226 (Neil Alan Weiner & Marvin E. Wolfgang eds., 1989).
4. MILLER, *supra* note 2, at 76; Klein and Maxson, *supra* note 3, at 218.
5. MILLER, *supra* note 2, at 76; Klein and Maxson, *supra* note 3, at 218.
6. ARNOLD P. GOLDSTEIN, DELINQUENT GANGS: A PSYCHOLOGICAL PERSPECTIVE 39 (1991); HAGEDORN, *supra* note 1, at 143–144; Klein & Maxson, *supra* note 3, at 219; MILLER, *supra* note 2, at 41; JOAN W. MOORE, GOING DOWN TO THE BARRIO: HOMEBOYS AND HOMEGIRLS IN CHANGE (1991); JAMES F. SHORT & FRED L. STRODTBECK, GROUP PROCESS AND GANG DELINQUENCY 77 (1965); Carolyn R. Block & Richard Block, *Street Gang Crime in Chicago*, NATIONAL INSTITUTE OF JUSTICE RESEARCH IN BRIEF 7 (1993); Lisa Porche-Burke & Christopher Fulton, *The Impact of Gang Violence: Strategies for Prevention and Intervention*, in SUBSTANCE ABUSE AND GANG VIOLENCE 85, 89 (Richard C. Cervantes ed., 1992); Joseph F. Sheley & James D. Wright, *Gun Acquisition and Possession in Selected Juvenile Samples*, in NATIONAL INSTITUTE OF JUSTICE RESEARCH IN BRIEF 9 (1993); James F. Short, *New Wine in Old Bottles? Change and Continuity in American Gangs*, in GANGS IN AMERICA 223, 227 (C. Ronald Huff, ed., 1990); Spergel, *supra* note 1, at 190–191; Jerome S. Stumphauzer et al., *Violence by Street Gangs: East Side Story?* in VIOLENT BEHAVIOR: SOCIAL LEARNING APPROACHES TO PREDICTION, MANAGEMENT, AND TREATMENT 68, 69 (R. B. Stuart ed., 1981).
7. FREDERIC M. THRASHER, THE GANG 374–90, 413 (1927).
8. CLIFFORD R. SHAW & HENRY D. MCKAY, JUVENILE DELINQUENCY AND URBAN AREAS 173 (1969); SHORT & STRODTBECK, *supra* note 6, at 2; Finn-Aage Esben-

sen & David Huizinga, *Gangs, Drugs and Delinquency in a Survey of Urban Youth*, 31 CRIMINOLOGY 565, 573 (1993); Jeffrey Fagan, *The Social Organization of Drug Use and Drug Dealing Among Urban Youth*, 27 CRIMINOLOGY 633, 648 (1989) [hereinafter *Social Organization of Drug Use*]; Jeffrey Fagan, *Social Processes of Delinquency and Drug Use Among Urban Gangs*, in GANGS IN AMERICA, *supra* note 6, at 83; Jeffrey Fagan et al., *Violent Delinquents and Urban Youths*, 24 CRIMINOLOGY 439, 443 (1986); Terrence P. Thornberry et al., *The Role of Juvenile Gangs in Facilitating Delinquent Behavior*, 30 J. RES. CRIME & DELINQ. 55 (1993).

9. Block & Block, *supra* note 6; Albert K. Cohen, *The Delinquency of Gangs and Spontaneous Groups*, in DELINQUENCY: SELECTED STUDIES (J. Thorsten Sellin and Marvin E. Wolfgang eds., 1969); Malcolm W. Klein et al., *The Impact of Police Investigation on Police-Reported Rates of Gang and Non-gang Homicides*, 24 CRIMINOLOGY 489, 492–500 (1986); Klein & Maxson, *supra* note 3, at 71.
10. Malcolm W. Klein, *Offense Specialization and Versatility Among Juveniles*, 24 BRIT. J. OF CRIMINOLOGY 185–86 (1984); see also, MALCOLM W. KLEIN, STREET GANGS AND STREET WORKERS (1971); Walter B. Miller, *The Impact of a "Total-Community" Delinquency Control Project*, 10 SOC. PROBS. 168, 181 (1962).
11. COVEY ET AL., *supra* note 2, at 32; HAGEDORN, *supra* note 1, at 143; MILLER, *supra* note 2, at 516; Bryant, *supra* note 1, at 2; Cohen, *supra* note 9; Klein & Maxson, *supra* note 3, at 218–219; Stumphauzer et al., *supra* note 6.
12. MILLER, *supra* note 2, at 72; Cohen, *supra* note 9, at 80; Fagan, *Social Organization of Drug Use*, *supra* note 8, at 647; C. Jack Friedman et al., *A Profile of Juvenile Street Gang Members*, 10 ADOLESCENCE 563 (1975); Klein & Maxson, *supra* note 3, at 221–22; Walter B. Miller, *Gangs, Groups, and Serious Youth Crime*, in CRITICAL ISSUES IN JUVENILE DELINQUENCY 115 (David Shichor & Dellos H. Kelly eds., 1980).
13. GOLDSTEIN, *supra* note 6, at 35; HAGEDORN, *supra* note 1, at 144; MILLER, *supra* note 2, at 41–42; MOORE, *supra* note 6; SHORT & STRODTBECK, *supra* note 6, at 77; Block & Block, *supra* note 6, at 7; Klein & Maxson, *supra* note 3, at 218–19; Porche-Burke & Fulton, *supra* note 6; Sheley & Wright, *supra* note 6, at 4–5; Short, *supra* note 6; Spergel, *supra* note 1, at 191; Stumphauzer et al., *supra* note 6.
14. MILLER, *supra* note 2, at 41.
15. HAGEDORN, *supra* note 1, at 144.
16. Alan J. Lizotte et al., *Patterns of Adolescent Firearms Ownership and Use*, 11 JUST. Q. 51, 65 (1994).
17. CARL S. TAYLOR, DANGEROUS SOCIETY 130 (1990).
18. COVEY ET AL., *supra* note 2, at 29; MILLER, *supra* note 2, at 42; Block & Block, *supra* note 6, at 7; Spergel, *supra* note 1, at 190; Del Stover, *A New Breed of Youth Gangs is on the Prowl and a Bigger Threat Than Ever*, 173 AM. SCH. BOARD J. 19, 20–21 (1986).
19. Bryant, *supra* note 1, at 4.
20. MILLER, *supra* note 2, at 76.
21. *Id.* at 41; Irving A. Spergel, *The Violent Gang in Chicago: A Local Community Approach*, 60 SOC. SERVICE REV. 94, 94–95 (1986).
22. Klein & Maxson, *supra* note 3, at 219.
23. Block & Block, *supra* note 6, at 7.
24. RUTH HOROWITZ, HONOR AND THE AMERICAN DREAM: CULTURE AND IDENTITY IN A CHICANO COMMUNITY 80–81 (1983).
25. For a more detailed description of the sampling procedures utilized by the RYDS see, Margaret Farnworth et al., *Technical Report No. 1: Sampling Design and Implementation*, Rochester Youth Development Study (1990); Terence P. Thornberry et al., *The Consequences of Respondent Attrition in Panel Studies: A Simulation Based on the Rochester Youth Development Study*, 9 J. QUANTITATIVE CRIMINOLOGY 127, 133–34 (1993).
26. Ruth Horowitz, *Sociological Perspectives on Gangs: Conflicting Definitions and Concepts*, in GANGS IN AMERICA, *supra* note 6, at 37.
27. L. Thomas Winfree et al., *The Definition and Measurement of "Gang Status": Policy Implications for Juvenile Justice*, 43 JUV. & FAM. CT. J. 29, 34–36 (1992).
28. M. G. HARRIS, CHOLAS: LATINO GIRLS AND GANGS (1988); Fagan, *Social Organization of Drug Use, supra* note 8, at 658; Winfree *supra* note 27, at 34–36; Richard G. Zevitz & Susan R. Takata, *Metropolitan Gang Influences and the Emergence of Group Delinquency in a Regional Community*, 20 J. CRIM. JUST. 93, 104 (1992).
29. Lizotte et al., *supra* note 16, at 67.
30. *See id*. For more detail on this coding scheme.
31. *Id.*

32. *Id.*
33. DELBERT S. ELLIOT ET AL., EXPLAINING DELINQUENCY AND DRUG USE 9–10 (1985).
34. David A. Huizinga et al., *Are There Multiple Paths to Delinquency?* 82 J. CRIM. L. & CRIMINOLOGY 83, 108–09 (1991).
35. For those youths who were gang members in more than one wave, prevalence rates were calculated using their most recent wave of gang activity. Youths had two chances to be counted as both past and future gang members. For example, if a youth was in the gang in Wave 7 but had dropped out in Wave 8, he was counted as a past member and prevalence rates were calculated for his Wave 8 gun ownership. Similarly, a youth who was in the gang in Wave 8, but dropped out in Wave 9 was also counted as a past gang member, and his prevalence rates were calculated for his Wave 9 gun ownership.
36. Additional analysis supports this assumption. The majority of youths who eventually drop out of the gang did not own guns while they were in the gang.
37. Lizotte et al., *supra* note 16, at 52, 65. For a discussion of the relationship between race and gang membership, see generally Spergel, *supra* note 1.
38. For a description of these variables, see Table 19.2. For purposes of this analysis, future, past, and current gang membership was calculated using Wave 8 as a reference point. For example, a past gang member is a youth who was a member in Wave 7 but had dropped out by Wave 8. The independent variables for this analysis are also from Wave 8, with the exception of the measured parental gun ownership, which was only included in Wave 7 of the data collection.
39. *See* DAVID W. HOSMER & STANLEY LEMESHOW, APPLIED LOGISTIC REGRESSION (1989) for a discussion on multinomial logistic regression.
40. *See* Trond Petersen, *A Comment on Presenting Results From Logit and Probit Models*, 50 AM. SOC. REV. 130 (1985) for a discussion of translating logistic regression coefficients into probabilities.
41. This may be the reason for the recent large increase in the homicide rate for African American teenagers. See Lois A. Fingerhut et al., Firearm and Non-firearm Homicides Among Persons 15 Through 19 Years of Age: Differences by Level of Urbanization, United States, 1979 Through 1989, 267 JAMA 3048, 3051 (1992).
42. Supplementary analysis reveals that while gang members who own guns for both protection and sporting purposes are equally likely to be involved in general types of delinquent behavior, the protection gun owners are slightly more likely to be involved in the more serious forms of delinquency.
43. Thornberry et al., *supra* note 8, at 58.
44. RONALD L. AKERS, DEVIANT BEHAVIOR: A SOCIAL LEARNING APPROACH 39–60 (1985); EDWIN H. SUTHERLAND & DONALD R. CRESSEY, CRIMINOLOGY 220 (1978); RICHARD A. CLOWARD & LLOYD E. OHLIN, DELINQUENCY AND OPPORTUNITY: A THEORY OF DELINQUENT GANGS 148–49 (1960).
45. ALBERT K. COHEN, DELINQUENT BOYS: THE CULTURE OF THE GANG 65–67 (1955); SHORT & STRODTBECK, *supra* note 6; Walter B. Miller, *Lower-Class Culture as a Generating Milieu of Gang Delinquency*, 14 J. SOC. ISSUES 5 (1958). ✦

Chapter 20
Gender and Victimization Risk Among Young Women in Gangs

Jody Miller

In this chapter, Miller suggests that research should focus not only on gang members' disproportionate involvement in offending, but also on the ways in which gang membership increases youths' risks for violent victimization. Research has shown a strong relationship between participation in delinquency and victimization risk. Miller examines how this relationship is shaped by gender, by exploring the experiences of gang girls. She suggests that female gang members are less likely than male gang members to be the targets of serious physical violence by rival gang members. This is largely because they are less involved in serious delinquency than gang boys. However, they do face considerable risks within their gangs of physical and sexual mistreatment, especially when male gang members view them as lesser members of their groups. Consequently, not only is victimization risk in gangs related to delinquent activities, it is also a gender-based phenomenon.

Abstract

Research has documented the enhancement effects of gang involvement for criminal offending, but little attention has been given to victimization. This article examines how gang involvement shapes young women's risks of victimization. Based on interviews with active gang members, the author suggests that (1) gang participation exposes youths to victimization risk and (2) it does so in gendered ways. Young women can use gender to decrease their risk of being harmed by rival gangs or other street participants by not participating in "masculine" activities, such as fighting and committing crime. However, the consequence is that they are viewed as lesser members of their gangs and may be exposed to greater risk of victimization within their gangs. The author suggests that more research is needed to examine whether and how gang involvement enhances youths' exposure to victimization risk and that researchers should maintain a recognition of the role of gender in shaping these processes.

An underdeveloped area in the gang literature is the relationship between gang participation and victimization risk. There are notable reasons to consider the issue significant. We now have strong evidence that delinquent lifestyles are associated with increased risk of victimization (Lauritsen, Sampson, and Laub 1991). Gangs are social groups that are organized around delinquency (see Klein 1995), and participation in gangs has been shown to escalate youths' involvement in crime, including violent crime (Esbensen and Huizinga 1993; Esbensen, Huizinga, and Weiher 1993; Fagan 1989, 1990; Thornberry et al., 1993). Moreover, research on gang violence indicates that the primary targets of this violence are other gang members (Block and Block 1993; Decker 1996; Klein and Maxson 1989; Sanders 1993). As such, gang participation can be recognized as a delinquent lifestyle that is likely to involve high risks of victimization (see Huff 1996:97). Although research on female gang involvement has expanded in recent years and includes the examination of issues such as violence and victimization, the oversight regarding the relationship between gang participation and

Reprinted from: Jody Miller, "Gender and Victimization Risk Among Young Women in Gangs." In *Journal of Research in Crime and Delinquency*, volume 35, pp. 429–453.

violent victimization extends to this work as well.

The coalescence of attention to the proliferation of gangs and gang violence (Block and Block 1993; Curry, Ball, and Decker 1996; Decker 1996; Klein 1995; Klein and Maxson 1989; Sanders 1993), and a possible disproportionate rise in female participation in violent crimes more generally (Baskin, Sommers, and Fagan 1993; but see Chesney-Lind, Shelden, and Joe 1996), has led to a specific concern with examining female gang members' violent activities. As a result, some recent research on girls in gangs has examined these young women's participation in violence and other crimes as offenders (Bjerregaard and Smith 1993; Brotherton 1996; Fagan 1990; Lauderback, Hansen, and Waldorf 1992; Taylor, 1993). However, an additional question worth investigation is what relationships exist between young women's gang involvement and their experiences and risk of victimization. Based on in-depth interviews with female gang members, this article examines the ways in which gender shapes victimization risk within street gangs.

Gender, Violence, and Victimization

Feminist scholars have played a significant role in bringing attention to the overlapping nature of women's criminal offending and patterns of victimization, emphasizing the relationships of gender inequality and sexual exploitation to women's participation in crime (Arnold 1990; Campbell 1984; Chesney-Lind and Rodriguez 1983; Daly 1992; Gilfus 1992). In regard to female gang involvement, recent research suggests that young women in gangs have disproportionate histories of victimization before gang involvement as compared with nongang females (Miller 1996) and gang males (Joe and Chesney-Lind 1995; Moore 1991). Moreover, there is evidence that young women turn to gangs, in part, as a means of protecting themselves from violence and other problems in their families and from mistreatment at the hands of men in their lives (Joe and Chesney-Lind 1995; Lauderback et al., 1992).

This is not surprising, given the social contexts these young women face. Many young women in gangs are living in impoverished urban "underclass" communities where violence is both extensive and a "sanctioned response to [the] oppressive material conditions" associated with inequality, segregation, and isolation (Simpson 1991:129; see also Sampson and Wilson 1995; Wilson 1996). Moreover, violence against women is heightened by the nature of the urban street world, where gendered power relations are played out (Connell 1987), crack markets have intensified the degradation of women (Bourgois and Dunlap 1993; Maher and Curtis 1992), and structural changes may have increased cultural support for violence against women (Wilson 1996).

The social world of adolescence is highly gendered as well (Eder 1995; Lees 1993; Thorne 1993). It is a period in which peer relationships increase in significance for youths, and this is magnified, especially for girls, with increased self-consciousness and sensitivity to others' perceptions of them (Pesce and Harding 1986). In addition, it is characterized by a "shift from the relatively asexual gender system of childhood to the overtly sexualized gender systems of adolescence and adulthood" (Thorne 1993:135). Young women find themselves in a contradictory position. Increasingly, they receive status from their peers via their association with, and attractiveness to, young men, but they are denigrated for their sexual activity and threatened with the labels slut and ho (Eder 1995; Lees 1993). The contexts of adolescence and the urban street world, then, have unique features likely to make young women particularly vulnerable to victimization. Thus, for some young women, gang involvement may appear to be a useful means of negotiating within these environments.

However, as Bourgois (1995) notes, actions taken to resist oppression can ultimately result in increased harm. Among young women in gangs, an important question to examine is how participation in gangs itself shapes young women's risk of victimization, including the question of whether gang involvement places girls at higher risks of victimization because of a potential increased involvement in crime. Lauritsen et al., (1991) found that "adolescent involvement in delinquent lifestyles strongly increases the risk of both personal and property victimization" (p. 265). Moreover, gender as a predictor of victimization risk among adolescents decreases when participation in delinquent lifestyles is controlled for (Lauritsen et al. 1991). That is, much of young men's greater victimization risk can be accounted for by their greater participation in offending behaviors. Among gang members, then, involvement in crime is likely associated with increased risk for victimization. Gang girls' participation in crime is thus an important consideration if we hope to understand the relationship between their gang membership and victimization risk.

Girls, Gangs, and Crime

Research comparing gang and nongang youths has consistently found that serious criminal involvement is a feature that distinguishes gangs from other groups of youths (Bjerregaard and Smith 1993; Esbensen and Huizinga 1993; Esbensen et al.,1993; Fagan 1989,1990; Klein 1995; Thornberry et al.,1993; Winfree et al., 1992). Until recently, however, little attention was paid to young women's participation in serious and violent gang-related crime. Most traditional gang research emphasized the auxiliary and peripheral nature of girls' gang involvement and often resulted in an almost exclusive emphasis on girls' sexuality and sexual activities with male gang members, downplaying their participation in delinquency (for critiques of gender bias in gang research, see Campbell 1984, 1990; Taylor 1993).

However, recent estimates of female gang involvement have caused researchers to pay greater attention to gang girls' activities. This evidence suggests that young women approximate anywhere from 10 to 38 percent of gang members (Campbell 1984; Chesney-Lind 1993; Esbensen 1996; Fagan 1990; Moore 1991), that female gang participation may be increasing (Fagan 1990; Spergel and Curry 1993; Taylor 1993), and that in some urban areas, upward of one-fifth of girls report gang affiliations (Bjerregaard and Smith 1993; Winfree et al., 1992). As female gang members have become recognized as a group worthy of criminologists' attention, we have garnered new information regarding their involvement in delinquency in general, and violence in particular.

Recent research on female gang involvement indicates that the pattern of higher rates of criminal involvement for gang members holds for girls as well as their male counterparts (Bjerregaard and Smith 1993; Esbensen and Winfree 1998; Thornberry et al., 1993). The enhancement effect of gang membership is most noticeable for serious delinquency and marijuana use (Thornberry et al., 1993). Bjerregaard and Smith (1993) summarize:

> The traditional gang literature has generally suggested that gang membership enhances delinquent activity, and particularly serious delinquent activity for males, but not for females. In contrast, our study suggests that for females also, gangs are consistently associated with a greater prevalence and with higher rates of delinquency and substance use. Furthermore, the results suggest that for both sexes, gang membership has an approximately equal impact on a variety of measures of delinquent behavior. (p. 346)

An interesting counterpart is provided by Bowker, Gross, and Klein (1980), who suggest there is evidence of "the structural exclusion of young women from male delinquent activities" within gangs (p. 516). Their (male) respondents suggested that not only were girls excluded from the planning of delinquent acts, but when girls inadvertently showed up at the location of a planned incident, it was frequently postponed or terminated. Likewise, Fagan (1990) reports greater gender differences in delinquency between gang members than between nongang youths (pp. 196–97). Male gang members were significantly more involved in the most serious forms of delinquency, whereas for alcohol use, drug sales, extortion, and property damage, gender differences were not significant.

However, Fagan also reports that "prevalence rates for female gang members exceeded the rates for non-gang males" for all the categories of delinquency he measured (see also Esbensen and Winfree 1998). Fagan (1990) summarizes his findings in relation to girls as follows:

> More than 40 percent of the female gang members were classified in the least serious category, a substantial difference from their male counterparts [15.5 percent]. Among female gang members, there was a bimodal distribution, with nearly as many multiple index offenders as petty delinquents. Evidently, female gang members avoid more serious delinquent involvement than their male counter parts. *Yet their extensive involvement in serious delinquent behaviors well exceeds that of non-gang males or females.* (p. 201, my emphasis)

Few would dispute that when it comes to serious delinquency, male gang members are involved more frequently than their female counterparts. However, this evidence does suggest that young women in gangs are more involved in serious criminal activities than was previously believed and also tend to be more involved than nongang youths—male or female. As such, they likely are exposed to greater victimization risk than nongang youths as well.

In addition, given the social contexts described above, it is reasonable to assume that young women's victimization risk within gangs is also shaped by gender. Gang activities (such as fighting for status and retaliation) create a particular set of factors that increase gang members' victimization risk and repeat victimization risk. Constructions of gender identity may shape these risks in particular ways for girls. For instance, young women's adoption of masculine attributes may provide a means of participating and gaining status within gangs but may also lead to increased risk of victimization as a result of deeper immersion in delinquent activities. On the other hand, experiences of victimization may contribute to girls' denigration and thus increase their risk for repeat victimization through gendered responses and labeling—for example, when sexual victimization leads to perceptions of sexual availability or when victimization leads an individual to be viewed as weak. In addition, femaleness is an individual attribute that has the capacity to mark young women as "safe" crime victims (e.g., easy targets) or, conversely, to deem them "off limits." My goal here is to examine the gendered nature of violence within gangs, with a specific focus on how gender shapes young women's victimization risk.

Methodology

Data presented in this article come from survey and semistructured in-depth interviews with 20 female members of mixed-gender gangs in Columbus, Ohio. The interviewees ranged in age from 12 to 17; just over three-quarters were African American or multiracial (16 of 20), and the rest (4 of 20) were white. The sample was drawn primarily from several local agencies in Columbus working with at-risk youths, including the county juvenile detention center, a shelter care facility for adolescent girls, a day school within the same institution, and a local community agency.[1] The project was structured as a gang/nongang comparison, and I interviewed a total of 46 girls. Gang membership was determined during the survey interview by self-definition: About one-quarter of the way through the 50+ page interview, young women were asked a series of questions about the friends they spent time with. They then were asked whether these friends were gang involved and whether they themselves were gang members. Of the 46 girls interviewed, 21 reported that they were gang members,[2] and an additional 3 reported being gang involved (hanging out primarily with gangs or gang members) but not gang members. The rest reported no gang involvement.

A great deal of recent research suggests that self-report data provide comparatively reliable and valid measures of youths' gang membership (see Bjerregaard and Smith 1993; Fagan 1990; Thornberry et al., 1993; Winfree et al.,1992). This research suggests that using more restrictive measures (such as initiation rituals, a gang name, symbolic systems such as colors or signs) does not change substantive conclusions concerning gang members' behaviors when comparing self-defined gang members to those members who meet these more restrictive definitions.

Although most researchers agree that the group should be involved in illegal activities in order for the youth to be classified as a gang member (see Esbensen et al., 1993; Esbensen and Huizinga 1993; Fagan 1989), other research that has used self-nomination without specifying crime as a defining feature has nonetheless consistently found serious criminal involvement as a feature that distinguishes gangs from other groups of youths (Fagan 1990; Thornberry et al., 1993; Winfree et al., 1992). All the gang members in my sample were members of groups they described as delinquent.

Cooperation from agency personnel generally proves successful for accessing gang members (see Bowker et al., 1980; Fagan 1989; Short and Strodtbeck 1965). However, these referrals pose the problem of targeting only officially labeled gang youth. I took several steps to temper this problem. First, I did not choose agencies that dealt specifically with gang members, and I did not rely on agency rosters of "known" gang members for my sample. As a result of the gang/nongang comparative research design, I was able to avoid oversampling girls who were labeled as gang members by asking agency personnel to refer me not just to girls believed to be gang involved but also any other girls living in areas in Columbus where they might have contact with gangs. Second, although I was only moderately successful, throughout the project I attempted to expand my sample on the basis of snowball techniques (see Fagan 1989; Hagedorn 1988). I only generated one successful referral outside of the agency contexts. However, I was successful at snowballing within agencies. Several girls I interviewed were gang involved but without staff knowledge, and they were referred to me by other girls I interviewed within the facilities. Thus, in a limited capacity, I was able to interview gang members who had not been detected by officials. Nonetheless, my sample is still limited to youths who have experienced intervention in some capacity, whether formal or informal, and thus it may not be representative of gang-involved girls in the community at large.

The survey interview was a variation of several instruments currently being used in research in a number of cities across the United States and included a broad range of questions and scales measuring factors that may be related to gang membership.[3] On issues related to violence, it included questions about peer activities and delinquency, individual delinquent involvement, family violence and abuse, and victimization. When young women responded affirmatively to being gang members, I followed with a series of questions about the nature of their gang, including its size, leadership, activities, symbols, and so on. Girls who admitted gang involvement during the survey participated in a follow-up interview to talk in more depth about their gangs and gang activities. The goal of the in-depth interview was to gain a greater understanding of the nature and meanings of gang life from the point of view of its female members. A strength of qualitative interviewing is its ability to shed light on this aspect of the social world, highlighting the meanings individuals attribute to their experiences (Adler and Adler 1987; Glassner and Loughlin 1987; Miller and Glassner 1997). In addition, using multiple methods, including follow-up interviews, provided me with a means of detecting inconsistencies in young women's accounts of their experiences. Fortunately, no serious contradictions arose. However, a limitation of the data is that only young women were interviewed. Thus, I make inferences about gender dynamics, and young men's behavior, based only on young women's perspectives.

The in-depth interviews were open-ended and all but one were audiotaped. They were structured around several groupings of questions. We began by discussing girls' entry into their gangs—when and how they became involved, and what other things were going on in their lives at the time. Then we discussed the structure of the gang—its history, size, leadership, and organization, and their place in the group. The next series of questions concerned gender within the gang; for example, how girls get involved, what activities they engage in and whether these are the same as the young men's activities, and what kind of males and females have the most influence in the gang and why. The next series of questions explored gang involvement more generally—what being in the gang means, what kinds of things they do together, and so on. Then, I asked how safe or dangerous they feel gang membership is and how they deal with risk. I concluded by asking them to speculate about why people their age join gangs, what things they like, what they dislike and have learned by being in the gang, and what they like best about themselves. This basic guideline was followed for each interview subject, although when additional topics arose in the context of the interview we often deviated from the interview guide to pursue them. Throughout the interviews, issues related to violence emerged; these issues form the core of the discussion that follows.

Setting

Columbus is a particular type of gang city. Gangs are a relatively new phenomenon there, with their emergence dated around 1985 (Maxson, Woods, and Klein 1995). In addition, it is thriving economically, experiencing both population and economic growth over the last decade (Rusk 1995). As such, it is representative of a recent pattern of gang proliferation into numerous cities, suburbs, and towns that do not have many of the long-standing problems associated with traditional gang cities, such as deindustrialization, population loss, and the deterioration of social support networks (see Curry et al., 1996; Hagedorn 1988; Klein 1995; Maxson et al., 1995; Spergel and Curry 1993). Even as Columbus has prospered, however, its racial disparities have grown (Columbus Metropolitan Human Services Commission 1995:17). In fact, in relative terms (comparing the gap between African Americans and whites), racial disparities in measures such as income and percentage poverty in Columbus are equal to or even greater than in many cities experiencing economic and population declines.[4]

According to recent police estimates, Columbus has about 30 active gangs, with 400 to 1,000 members (LaLonde 1995). Most of these groups are small in size (20 or fewer members) and are either African American or racially mixed with a majority of African American members (Mayhood and LaLonde 1995). Gangs in Columbus have adopted "big-city" gang names such as Crips, Bloods, and Folks, along with the dress styles, signs, and graffiti of these groups, although gangs are and have been primarily a "homegrown" problem in Columbus rather than a result of organized gang migration (Huff 1989). Local police view these groups as criminally oriented, but not especially sophisticated. On the whole, gangs in Columbus seem to match those described in other cities with emergent gang problems—best characterized as "relatively autonomous, smaller, independent groups, poorly organized and less territorial" than in older gang cities (Klein 1995:36).

The young women I interviewed described their gangs in ways that are very much in keeping with these findings. All 20 are members of Folks, Crips, or Bloods sets.[5] All but 3 described gangs with fewer than 30 members, and most reported relatively narrow age ranges between members. Half were in gangs with members who were 21 or over, but almost without exception, their gangs were made up primarily of teenagers, with either one adult who was considered the OG ("Original Gangster," leader) or just a handful of young adults. The majority (14 of 20) reported that their gangs did not include members under the age of 13.

Although the gangs these young women were members of were composed of both female and male members, they varied in their gender composition, with the vast majority being predominantly male. Six girls reported that girls were one-fifth or fewer of the members of their gang; 8 were in gangs in which girls were between a quarter and a third of the overall membership; 4 said girls were between 44 and 50 percent of the members; and 1 girl reported that her gang was two-thirds female and one-third male. Overall, girls were typically a minority within these groups numerically, with 11 girls reporting that there were 5 or fewer girls in their set.

This structure—male-dominated, integrated mixed-gender gangs—likely shapes gender dynamics in particular ways. Much past gang research has assumed that female members of gangs are in auxiliary subgroups of male gangs, but there is increasing evidence—including from the young women I spoke with—that many gangs can be characterized as integrated, mixed-gender groups. For example, from interviews with 110 female gang members in three sites (Boston, Seattle, and Pueblo, Colorado), Curry (1997) found integrated mixed-gender gangs to be the predominant gang structure of female gang members, with 57.3 percent of girls describing their gangs as mixed-gender.[6] It is likely that gang structure shapes both status orientations and criminal involvement among gang members (Brotherton 1996), and that these differences may also be mediated by ethnicity (Brotherton 1996; Joe and Chesney-Lind 1995; Moore and Hagedorn, 1996). Generalizability beyond mixed-gender, predominantly African American gangs in emergent gang cities, then is questionable.

Gender, Gangs, and Violence

Gangs as Protection and Risk

An irony of gang involvement is that although many members suggest one thing they get out of the gang is a sense of protection (see also Decker 1996; Joe and Chesney-Lind 1995; Lauderback et al.,1992), gang membership itself means exposure to victimization risk and even a willingness to be victimized. These contradictions are apparent when girls talk about what they get out of the gang, and what being in the gang means in terms of other members' expectations of their behavior. In general, a number of girls suggested that being a gang member is a source of protection around the neighborhood. Erica,[7] a 17-year-old African American, explained, "It's like people look at us and that's exactly what they think, there's a gang, and they respect us for that. They won't bother us. . . . It's like you put that intimidation in somebody." Likewise, Lisa, a 14-year-old white girl, described being in the gang as empowering: "You just feel like, oh my God, you know, they got my back. I don't need to worry about it." Given the violence endemic in many inner-city communities, these beliefs are understandable, and to a certain extent, accurate.

In addition, some young women articulated a specifically gendered sense of protection that they felt as a result of being a member of a group that was predominantly male. Gangs operate within larger social milieus that are characterized by gender inequality and sexual exploitation. Being in a gang with young men means at least the semblance of protection from, and retaliation against, predatory men in the social environment. Heather, a 15-year-old white girl, noted, "You feel more secure when, you know, a guy's around protectin' you, you know, than you would a girl." She explained that as a gang member, because "you get protected by guys . . . not as many people mess with you." Other young women concurred and also described that male gang members could retaliate against specific acts of violence against girls in the gang. Nikkie, a 13-year-old African American girl, had a friend who was raped by a rival gang member, and she said, "It was a Crab [Crip] that raped my girl in Miller Ales, and um, they was ready to kill him." Keisha, an African American 14-year-old, explained, "if I got beat up by a guy, all I gotta do is go tell one of the niggers, you know what I'm sayin'? Or one of the guys, they'd take care of it."

At the same time, members recognized that they may be targets of rival gang members and were expected to "be down" for their gang at those times even when it meant being physically hurt. In addition, initiation rites and internal rules were structured in ways that required individuals to submit to, and be exposed to, violence. For example, young women's descriptions of the qualities they valued in members revealed the extent to which exposure to violence was an expected element of gang involvement. Potential members, they explained, should be tough, able to fight and to engage in criminal activities, and also should be loyal to the group and willing to put themselves at risk for it. Erica explained that they didn't want "punks" in her gang: "When you join something like that, you might as well expect that there's gonna be fights. . . . And, if you're a punk, or if you're scared of stuff like that, then don't join." Likewise, the following dialogue with Cathy, a white 16-year-old, reveals similar themes. I asked her what her gang expected out of members and she responded, "to be true to our gang and to have our backs." When I asked her to elaborate, she explained,

> Cathy: Like, uh, if you say you're a Blood, you be a Blood. You wear your rag even when you're by yourself. You know, don't let anybody intimidate you and be like, 'Take that rag off.' You know, 'you better get with our set.' Or something like that.
>
> JM: Ok. Anything else that being true to the set means?
>
> Cathy: Um. Yeah, I mean, just, just, you know, I mean it's, you got a whole bunch of people comin', up in your face and if you're by yourself they ask you what's your claimin', you tell 'em. Don't say 'nothin.'
>
> JM: Even if it means getting beat up or something?
>
> Cathy: Mmhmm.

One measure of these qualities came through the initiation process, which involved the individual submitting to victimization at the hands of the gang's members. Typically this entailed either taking a fixed number of "blows" to the head and/or chest or being "beaten in" by members for a given duration (e.g., 60 seconds). Heather described the initiation as an important event for determining whether someone would make a good member:

> When you get beat in if you don't fight back and if you just like stop and you start cryin' or somethin' or beggin' 'em to stop and stuff like that, then, they ain't gonna, they'll just stop and they'll say that you're not gang material because you gotta be hard, gotta be able to fight, take punches.

In addition to the initiation, and threats from rival gangs, members were expected to adhere to the gang's internal rules (which included such things as not fighting with one another, being "true" to the gang, respecting the leader, not spreading gang business outside the gang, and not dating members of rival gangs). Breaking the rules was grounds for physical punishment, either in the form of a spontaneous assault or a formal "violation," which involved taking a specified number of blows to the head. For example, Keisha reported that she talked back to the leader of her set and "got slapped pretty hard" for doing so. Likewise, Veronica, an African American 15-year-old described her leader as "crazy, but we gotta listen to 'im. He's just the type that if you don't listen to 'im, he gonna blow your head off. He's just crazy."

It is clear that regardless of members' perceptions of the gang as a form of "protection," being a gang member also involves a willingness to open oneself up to the possibility of victimization. Gang victimization is governed by rules and expectations, however, and thus does not involve the random vulnerability that being out on the streets without a gang might entail in high-crime neighborhoods. Because of its structured nature, this victimization risk may be perceived as more palatable by gang members. For young women in particular, the gendered nature of the streets may make the empowerment available through gang involvement an appealing alternative to the individualized vulnerability they otherwise would face. However, as the next sections highlight, girls' victimization risks continue to be shaped by gender, even within their gangs, because these groups are structured around gender hierarchies as well.

Gender and Status, Crime and Victimization

Status hierarchies within Columbus gangs, like elsewhere, were male dominated (Bowker et al., 1980; Campbell 1990). Again, it is important to highlight that the structure of the gangs these young women belonged to—that is, male-dominated, integrated mixed-gender gangs—likely shaped the particular ways in which gender dynamics played themselves out. Autonomous female gangs, as well as gangs in which girls are in auxiliary subgroups, may be shaped by different gender relations, as well as differences in orientations toward status, and criminal involvement.

All the young women reported having established leaders in their gang, and this leadership was almost exclusively male. While LaShawna, a 17-year-old African American, reported being the leader of her set (which had a membership that is two-thirds girls, many of whom resided in the same residential facility as her), all the other girls in mixed-gender gangs reported that their OG was male. In fact, a number of young women stated explicitly that only male gang members could be leaders. Leadership qualities, and qualities attributed to high-status members of the gangs—being tough, able to fight, and willing to "do dirt" (e.g., commit crime, engage in violence) for the gang—were perceived as characteristically masculine. Keisha noted, "The guys, they just harder." She explained, "Guys is more rougher. We have our G's back but, it ain't gonna be like the guys, they just don't give a fuck. They gonna shoot you in a minute."

For the most part, status in the gang was related to traits such as the willingness to use serious violence and commit dangerous crimes and, though not exclusively, these traits were viewed primarily as qualities more likely and more intensely located among male gang members.

Because these respected traits were characterized specifically as masculine, young women actually may have had greater flexibility in their gang involvement than young men. Young women had fewer expectations placed on them—by both their male and female peers—in regard to involvement in criminal activities such as fighting, using weapons, and committing other crimes. This tended to decrease girls' exposure to victimization risk comparable to male members, because they were able to avoid activities likely to place them in danger. Girls could gain status in the gang by being particularly hard and true to the set. Heather, for example, described the most influential girl in her set as "the hardest girl, the one that don't take no crap, will stand up to anybody." Likewise, Diane, a white 15-year-old, described a highly respected female member in her set as follows:

> People look up to Janeen just 'cause she's so crazy. People just look up to her 'cause she don't care about nothin'. She don't even care about makin' money. Her, her thing is, 'Oh, you're a Slob [Blood]? You're a Slob? You talkin' to me? You talkie' shit to me?' Pow, pow! And that's it. That's it.

However, young women also had a second route to status that was less available to young men. This came via their connections—as sisters, girlfriends, cousins—to influential, high-status young men.[8] In Veronica's set, for example, the girl with the most power was the OG's "sister or his cousin, one of 'em." His girlfriend also had status, although Veronica noted that "most of us just look up to our OG." Monica, a 16-year-old African American, and Tamika, a 15-year-old African American, both had older brothers in their gangs, and both reported getting respect, recognition, and protection because of this connection. This route to status and the masculinization of high-status traits functioned to maintain gender inequality within gangs, but they also could put young women at less risk of victimization than young men. This was both because young women were perceived as less threatening and thus were less likely to be targeted by rivals, and because they were not expected to prove themselves in the ways that young men were, thus decreasing their participation in those delinquent activities likely to increase exposure to violence. Thus, gender inequality could have a protective edge for young women.

Young men's perceptions of girls as lesser members typically functioned to keep girls from being targets of serious violence at the hands of rival young men, who instead left routine confrontations with rival female gang members to the girls in their own gang. Diane said that young men in her gang "don't wanna waste their time hittin' on some little girls. They're gonna go get their little cats [females] to go get 'em." Lisa remarked, "girls don't face as much violence as [guys]. They see a girl, they say, 'we'll just smack her and send her on.' They see a guy—'cause guys are like a lot more into it than girls are, I've noticed that—and they like, 'well, we'll shoot him.' " In addition, the girls I interviewed suggested that, in comparison with young men, young women were less likely to resort to serious violence, such as that involving a weapon, when confronting rivals. Thus, when girls' routine confrontations were more likely to be female on female than male on female, girls' risk of serious victimization was lessened further.

Also, because participation in serious and violent crime was defined primarily as a masculine endeavor, young women could use gender as a means of avoiding participation in those aspects of gang life they found risky, threatening, or morally troubling. Of the young women I interviewed, about one-fifth were involved in serious gang violence: A few had been involved [in] aggravated assaults on rival gang members, and one admitted to having killed a rival gang member, but they were by far the exception. Most girls tended not to be involved in serious gang crime, and some reported that they chose to exclude themselves because they felt ambivalent about this aspect of gang life. Angie, an African American 15-year-old explained,

> I don't get involved like that, be out there goin' and just beat up people like that or go stealin', things like that. That's not me. The boys, mostly the boys do all that, the girls we just sit back and chill, you know.

Likewise, Diane noted,

> For maybe a drive-by they might wanna have a bunch of dudes. They might not put the females in that. Maybe the females might be weak inside, not strong enough to do something like that, just on the insides. . . . If a female wants to go forward and doin' that, and she wants to risk her whole life for doin' that, then she can. But the majority of the time, that job is given to a man.

Diane was not just alluding to the idea that young men were stronger than young women. She also inferred that young women were able to get out of committing serious crime, more so than young men, because a girl shouldn't have to "risk her whole life" for the gang. In accepting that young men were more central members of the gang, young women could more easily participate in gangs without putting themselves in jeopardy—they could engage in the more routine, everyday activities of the gang, like hanging out, listening to music, and smoking bud (marijuana). These male-dominated mixed-gender gangs thus appeared to provide young women with flexibility in their involvement in gang activities. As a result, it is likely that their risk of victimization at the hands of rivals was less than that of young men in gangs who were engaged in greater amounts of crime.

Girls' Devaluation and Victimization

In addition to girls choosing not to participate in serious gang crimes, they also faced exclusion at the hands of young men or the gang as a whole (see also Bowker et al., 1980). In particular, the two types of crime mentioned most frequently as "off-limits" for girls were drug sales and drive-by shootings. LaShawna explained, "We don't really let our females [sell drugs] unless they really wanna and they know how to do it and not to get caught and everything." Veronica described a drive-by that her gang participated in and said, "They wouldn't let us [females] go. But we wanted to go, but they wouldn't let us." Often, the exclusion was couched in terms of protection. When I asked Veronica why the girls couldn't go, she said, "so we won't go to jail if they was to get caught. Or if one of 'em was to get shot, they wouldn't want it to happen to us." Likewise, Sonita, a 13-year-old African American, noted, "If they gonna do somethin' bad and they think one of the females gonna get hurt they don't let 'em do it with them. . . . Like if they involved with shooting or whatever, [girls] can't go."

Although girls' exclusion from some gang crime may be framed as protective (and may reduce their victimization risk vis-à-vis rival gangs), it also served to perpetuate the devaluation of female members as less significant to the gang—not as tough, true, or "down" for the gang as male members. When LaShawna said her gang blocked girls' involvement in serious crime, I pointed out that she was actively involved herself. She explained, "Yeah, I do a lot of stuff 'cause I'm tough. I likes, I likes messin' with boys. I fight boys. Girls ain't nothin' to me." Similarly, Tamika said, "girls, they little peons."

Some young women found the perception of them as weak a frustrating one. Brandi, an African American 13-year-old, explained, "Sometimes I dislike that the boys, sometimes, always gotta take charge and they think sometimes, that the girls don't know how to take charge 'cause we're like girls, we're females, and like that." And Chantell, an African American 14-year-old, noted that rival gang members "think that you're more of a punk." Beliefs that girls were weaker than boys meant that young women had a harder time proving that they were serious about their commitment to the gang. Diane explained,

> A female has to show that she's tough. A guy can just, you can just look at him. But a female, she's gotta show. She's gotta go out and do some dirt. She's gotta go whip some girl's ass, shoot somebody, rob somebody or something. To show that she is tough.

In terms of gender-specific victimization risk, the devaluation of young women suggests several things. It could lead to the mistreatment and victimization of girls by members of their own gang when they didn't have specific male protection (i.e., a brother, boyfriend) in the gang or when they weren't able to stand up for themselves to male members. This was exacerbated by activities that led young women to be viewed as sexually available. In addition, because young women typically were not seen as a threat by young men, when they did pose one, they could be punished even more harshly than young men, not only for having challenged a rival gang or gang member but also for having overstepped "appropriate" gender boundaries.

Monica had status and respect in her gang, both because she had proven herself through fights and criminal activities, and because her older brothers were members of her set. She contrasted her own treatment with that of other young women in the gang:

> They just be puttin' the other girls off. Like Andrea, man. Oh my God, they dog Andrea so bad. They like, 'Bitch, go to the store.' She like, 'All right, I be right back.' She will go to the store and go and get them whatever they want and come back with it. If she don't get it right, they be like, 'Why you do that bitch?' I mean, and one dude even smacked ha. And, I mean, and, I don't, I told my brother once. I was like, 'Man, it ain't even like that. If you ever see someone tryin' to disrespect me like that or hit me, if you do not hit them or at least say somethin' to them. . . .' So my brothers, they kinda watch out for me.

However, Monica put the responsibility for Andrea's treatment squarely on the young woman: "I put that on her. They ain't gotta do her like that, but she don't gotta let them do her like that either." Andrea was seen as "weak" because she did not stand up to the male members in the gang; thus, her mistreatment was framed as partially deserved because she did not exhibit the valued traits of toughness and willingness to fight that would allow her to defend herself.

An additional but related problem was when the devaluation of young women within gangs was sexual in nature. Girls, but not boys, could be initiated into the gang by being "sexed in"—having sexual relations with multiple male members of the gang. Other members viewed the young women initiated in this way as sexually available and promiscuous, thus increasing their subsequent mistreatment. In addition, the stigma could extend to female members in general, creating a sexual devaluation that all girls had to contend with.

The dynamics of "sexing in" as a form of gang initiation placed young women in a position that increased their risk of ongoing mistreatment at the hands of their gang peers. According to Keisha, "If you get sexed in, you have no respect. That means you gotta go ho'in' for 'em; when they say you give 'em the pussy, you gotta give it to 'em. If you don't, you gonna get your ass beat. I ain't down for that." One girl in her set was sexed in and Keisha said the girl "just do everything they tell her to do, like a dummy." Nikkie reported that two girls who were sexed into her set eventually quit hanging around with the gang because they were harassed so much. In fact, Veronica said the young men in her set purposely tricked girls into believing they were being sexed into the gang and targeted girls they did not like:

> If some girls wanted to get in, if they don't like the girl they have sex with 'em. They run trains on 'em or either have the girl suck their thang. And then they used to, the girls used to think they was in. So, then the girls used to just just come try to hang around us and all this little bull, just 'cause, 'cause they thinkin' they in.

Young women who were sexed into the gang were viewed as sexually promiscuous, weak, and not "true" members. They were subject to revictimization and mistreatment, and were viewed as deserving of abuse by other members, both male and female. Veronica continued,"They [girls who are sexed in] gotta do whatever, whatever the boys tell 'em to do when they want 'em to do it, right then and there, in front of whoever. And, I think, that's just sick. That's nasty, that's dumb." Keisha concurred, "She brought that on herself, by bein' the fact, bein' sexed in." There was evidence, however, that girls could overcome the stigma of having been sexed in through their subsequent behavior, by challenging members that disrespect them and being willing to fight. Tamika described a girl in her set who was sexed in, and stigmatized as a result, but successfully fought to rebuild her reputation:

> Some people, at first, they call her 'little ho' and all that. But then, now she startin' to get bold. . . . Like, like, they be like, 'Ooh, look at the little ho. She fucked me and my boy.' She be like, 'Man, forget y'all. Man, what? What?' She be ready to squat [fight] with 'em. I be like, 'Ah, look at her!' Uh huh. . . . At first we looked at her like, 'Ooh, man, she a ho, man.' But now we look at her like she just our kickin' it partner. You know, however she got in that's her business.

The fact that there was such an option as "sexing in" served to keep girls disempowered, because they always faced the question of how they got in and of whether they were "true" members. In addition, it contributed to a milieu in which young women's sexuality was seen as exploitable. This may help explain why young women were so harshly judgmental of those girls who were sexed in. Young women who were privy to male gang members' conversations reported that male members routinely disrespect girls in the gang by disparaging them sexually. Monica explained,

> I mean the guys, they have their little comments about 'em [girls in the gang] because, I hear more because my brothers are all up there with the guys and everything and I hear more just sittin' around, just listenin'. And they'll have their little jokes about 'Well, ha I had her,' and then and everybody else will jump in and say, 'Well, I had her, too.' And then they'll laugh about it.

In general, because gender constructions defined young women as weaker than young men, young women were often seen as lesser members of the gang. In addition to the mistreatment these perceptions entailed, young women also faced particularly harsh sanctions for crossing gender boundaries—causing harm to rival male members when they had been viewed as nonthreatening. One young woman[9] participated in the assault of a rival female gang member, who had set up a member of the girl's gang. She explained, "The female was supposingly goin' out with one of ours, went back and told a bunch of [rivals] what was goin' on and got the [rivals] to jump my boy. And he ended up in the hospital." The story she told was unique but nonetheless significant for what it indicates about the gendered nature of gang violence and victimization. Several young men in her set saw the girl walking down the street, kidnapped her, then brought her to a member's house. The young woman I interviewed, along with several other girls in her set, viciously beat the girl, then to their surprise the young men took over the beating, ripped off the girl's clothes, brutally gang-raped her, then dumped her in a park. The interviewee noted, "I don't know what happened to her. Maybe she died. Maybe, maybe someone came and helped her. I mean, I don't know." The experience scared the young woman who told me about it. She explained,

> I don't never want anythin' like that to happen to me. And I pray to God that it doesn't. 'Cause God said that whatever you sow you're gonna reap. And like, you know, beatin' a girl up and then sittin' there watchin' somethin' like that happen, well, Jesus that could come back on me. I mean, I felt, I really did feel sorry for her even though my boy was in the hospital and was really hurt. I mean, we coulda just shot her. You know, and it coulda been just over. We coulda just taken her life. But they went farther than that.

This young woman described the gang rape she witnessed as "the most brutal thing I've ever seen in my life." While the gang rape itself was an unusual event, it remained a specifically gendered act that could take place precisely because young women were not perceived as equals. Had the victim been an "equal," the attack would have remained a physical one. As the interviewee herself noted, "we coulda just shot her." Instead, the young men who gang-raped the girl were not just enacting revenge on a rival but on a young woman who had dared to treat a young man in this way. The issue is not the question of which is worse—to be shot and killed, or gang-raped and left for dead. Rather, this particular act sheds light on how gender may function to structure victimization risk within gangs.

Discussion

Gender dynamics in mixed-gender gangs are complex and thus may have multiple and contradictory effects on young women's risk of victimization and repeat victimization. My findings suggest that participation in the delinquent lifestyles associated with gangs clearly places young women at risk for victimization. The act of joining a gang involves the initiate's submission to victimization at the hands of her gang peers. In addition, the rules governing gang members' activities place them in situations in which they are vulnerable to assaults that are specifically gang related. Many acts of violence that girls described would not have occurred had they not been in gangs.

It seems, though, that young women in gangs believed they have traded unknown risks for known ones—that victimization at the hands of friends, or at least under specified conditions, was an alternative preferable to the potential of random, unknown victimization by strangers. Moreover, the gang offered both a semblance of protection from others on the streets, especially young men, and a means of achieving retaliation when victimization did occur.

Lauritsen and Quinet (1995) suggest that both individual-specific heterogeneity (unchanging attributes of individuals that contribute to a propensity for victimization, such as physical size or temperament) and state-dependent factors (factors that can alter individuals' victimization risks over time, such as labeling or behavior changes that are a consequence of victimization) are related to youths' victimization and repeat victimization risk. My findings here suggest that, within gangs, gender can function in both capacities to shape girls' risks of victimization.

Girls' gender, as an individual attribute, can function to lessen their exposure to victimization risk by defining them as inappropriate targets of rival male gang members' assaults. The young women I interviewed repeatedly commented that young men were typically not as violent in their routine confrontations with rival young women as with rival young men. On the other hand, when young women are targets of serious assault, they may face brutality that is particularly harsh and sexual in nature because they are female—thus, particular types of assault, such as rape, are deemed more appropriate when young women are the victims.

Gender can also function as a state-dependent factor, because constructions of gender and the enactment of gender identities are fluid. On the one hand, young women can call upon gender as a means of avoiding exposure to activities they find risky, threatening, or morally troubling. Doing so does not expose them to the sanctions likely faced by male gang members who attempt to avoid participation in violence. Although these choices may insulate young women from the risk of assault at the hands of rival gang members, perceptions of female gang members—and of women in general—as weak may contribute to more routinized victimization at the hands of the male members of their gangs. Moreover, sexual exploitation in the form of "sexing in" as an initiation ritual may define young women as sexually available, contributing to a likelihood of repeat victimization unless the young woman can stand up for herself and fight to gain other members' respect.

Finally, given constructions of gender that define young women as nonthreatening, when young women do pose a threat to male gang members, the sanctions they face may be particularly harsh because they not only have caused harm to rival gang members but also have crossed appropriate gender boundaries in doing so. In sum, my findings suggest that gender may function to insulate young women from some types of physical assault and lessen their exposure to risks from rival gang members, but also to make them vulnerable to particular types of violence, including routine victimization by their male peers, sexual exploitation, and sexual assault.

This article has offered preliminary evidence of how gender may shape victimization risk for female gang members. A great deal more work needs to be done in this area. Specifically, gang scholars need to address more systematically the relationships between gang involvement and victimization risk rather than focusing exclusively on gang members' participation in violence as offenders. My research suggests two questions to be examined further, for both female and male gang members. First, are gang members more likely to be victimized than nongang members living in the same areas? Second, how does victimization risk fluctuate for gang members before, during, and after their gang involvement? Information about these questions will allow us to address whether and how gang involvement has an enhancement effect on youths' victimization, as well as their delinquency.

With the growing interest in masculinities and crime (see Messerschmidt 1993; Newburn and Stanko 1994), an important corollary question to be examined is how masculinities shape victimization risk among male gang members. The young women I interviewed clearly associated serious gang violence with the enactment of masculinity and used gender constructions to avoid involvement in those activities they perceived as threatening. Young men thus may be at greater risk of serious physical assaults, because of their greater involvement in serious gang crime and violence, and because gender constructions within the gang make these activities more imperative for young men than for young women.

Notes

1. I contacted numerous additional agency personnel in an effort to draw the sample from a larger population base, but many efforts remained unsuccessful despite repeated attempts and promises of assistance. These included persons at the probation department, a shelter and outreach agency for runaways, police personnel, a private residential facility for juveniles, and three additional community agencies. None of the agencies I contacted openly denied me permission to interview young women; they simply chose not to follow up. I do not believe that much bias resulted from the nonparticipation of these organizations. Each has a client base of "at-risk" youths, and the young women I interviewed report overlap with some of these same agencies. For example, a number had been or were on probation, and several reported staying at the shelter for runaways.
2. One young woman was a member of an all-female gang. Because the focus of this article is gender dynamics in mixed-gender gangs, her interview is not included in the analysis.
3. These include the Gang Membership Resistance Surveys in Long Beach and San Diego, the Denver Youth Survey, and the Rochester Youth Development Study.
4. For example, Cleveland, Ohio, provides a striking contrast with Columbus on social and economic indicators, including a poverty rate double that found in Columbus. But the poverty rate for African Americans in Cleveland is just over twice that for whites, and it is more than three times higher in Columbus.

5. The term set was used by the gang members I interviewed to refer to their gangs. Because they adopted nationally recognized gang names (e.g., Crips, Bloods, Folks), they saw themselves as loosely aligned with other groups of the same name. This term was used to distinguish their particular gang (which has its own distinct name, e.g., Rolling 60s Crips) from other gangs that adopted the broader gang name. I will use the terms set and gang interchangeably.
6. This was compared to 36.4 percent who described their gangs as female auxiliaries of male gangs, and only 6.4 percent who described being in independent female gangs (Curry 1997; see also Decker and Van Winkle 1996).
7. All names are fictitious.
8. This is not to suggest that male members cannot gain status via their connections to high-status men, but that to maintain status, they will have to successfully exhibit masculine traits such as toughness. Young women appear to be held to more flexible standards.
9. Because this excerpt provides a detailed description of a specific serious crime, and because demographic information on respondents is available, I have chosen to conceal both the pseudonym and gang affiliation of the young woman who told me the story.

References

Adler, Patricia A. and Peter Adler. 1987. *Membership Roles in Field Research*. Newbury Park, CA: Sage.

Arnold, Regina. 1990. "Processes of Victimization and Criminalization of Black Women." *Social Justice* 17 (3):153–166.

Baskin, Deborah, Ira Sommers, and Jeffrey Fagan. 1993. "The Political Economy of Violent Female Street Crime." *Fordham Urban Law Journal* 20:401–417.

Bjerregaard, Beth and Carolyn Smith. 1993. "Gender Differences in Gang Participation, Delinquency, and Substance Use." *Journal of Quantitative Criminology* 4:329–355.

Block, Carolyn Rebecca and Richard Block. 1993. "Street Gang Crime in Chicago." *Research in Brief*. Washington, D.C.: National Institute of Justice.

Bourgois, Philippe. 1995. *In Search of Respect: Selling Crack in El Barrio*. Cambridge, UK: Cambridge University Press.

Bourgois, Philippe and Eloise Dunlap. 1993. "Exorcising Sex-for-Crack: An Ethnographic Perspective from Harlem." Pp. 97–132 in *Crack Pipe as Pimp: An Ethnographic Investigation of Sex-for-Crack Exchanges*, edited by Mitchell S. Ratner. New York: Lexington Books.

Bowker, Lee H., Helen Shimota Gross, and Malcolm W. Klein. 1980. "Female Participation in Delinquent Gang Activities." *Adolescence* 15 (59):509–519.

Brotherton, David C. 1996. "'Smartness,' 'Toughness,' and 'Autonomy': Drug Use in the Context of Gang Female Delinquency." *Journal of Drug Issues* 26 (1):261–277.

Campbell, Anne. 1984. *The Girls in the Gang*. New York: Basil Blackwell.

——. 1990. "Female Participation in Gangs." Pp. 163–182 in *Gangs in America*, edited by C. Ronald Huff. Beverly Hills, CA: Sage.

Chesney-Lind, Meda. 1993. "Girls, Gangs and Violence: Anatomy of a Backlash." *Humanity & Society* 17 (3):321–344.

Chesney-Lind, Meda and Noelie Rodriguez. 1983. "Women under Lock and Key: A View from the Inside." *The Prison Journal* 63 (2):47–65.

Chesney-Lind, Meda, Randall G. Shelden, and Karen A. Joe. 1996. "Girls, Delinquency, and Gang Membership." Pp. 185–204 in *Gangs in America*, 2nd ed., edited by C. Ronald Huff. Thousand Oaks, CA: Sage.

Columbus Metropolitan Human Services Commission. 1995. *State of Human Services Report—1995*. Columbus, OH: Columbus Metropolitan Human Services Commission.

Connell, R. W. 1987. *Gender and Power.* Stanford, CA: Stanford University Press.

Curry, G. David. 1997. "Selected Statistics on Female Gang Involvement." Paper presented at the Fifth Joint National Conference on Gangs, Schools, and Community, March, Orlando, FL.

Curry, G. David, Richard A. Ball, and Scott H. Decker. 1996. "Estimating the National Scope of Gang Crime from Law Enforcement Data." *Research in Brief*. Washington, D.C.: National Institute of Justice.

Daly, Kathleen. 1992. "Women's Pathways to Felony Court: Feminist Theories of Lawbreaking and Problems of Representation." *Review of Law and Women's Studies* 2 (1):11–52.

Decker, Scott H. 1996. "Collective and Normative Features of Gang Violence." *Justice Quarterly* 13 (2):243–264.

Decker, Scott H. and Barrik Van Winkle. 1996. *Life in the Gang*. Cambridge, UK: Cambridge University Press.

Eder, Donna. 1995. *School Talk: Gender and Adolescent Culture*. New Brunswick, NJ: Rutgers University Press.

Esbensen, Finn-Aage. 1996. Comments presented at the National Institute of Justice/Office of Juvenile Justice and Delinquency Prevention Cluster Meetings, June, Dallas, TX.

Esbensen, Finn-Aage, and David Huizinga. 1993. "Gangs, Drugs, and Delinquency in a Survey of Urban Youth." *Criminology* 31 (4):565–589.

Esbensen, Finn-Aage, David Huizinga, and Anne W. Weiher. 1993. "Gang and Non-Gang Youth: Differences in Explanatory Factors." *Journal of Contemporary Criminal Justice* 9(2):94–116.

Esbensen, Finn-Aage and L. Thomas Winfree. 1998. "Race and Gender Differences between Gang and Non-Gang Youth: Results from a Multi-Site Survey." *Justice Quarterly* 15(3):505–525.

Fagan, Jeffrey. 1989. "The Social Organization of Drug Use and Drug Dealing Among Urban Gangs." *Criminology* 27(4):633–667.

——. 1990. "Social Processes of Delinquency and Drug Use among Urban Gangs." Pp. 183–219 in *Gangs in America*, edited by C. Ronald Huff. Newbury Park, CA: Sage.

Gilfus, Mary. 1992. "From Victims to Survivors to Offenders: Women's Routes of Entry and Immersion into Street Crime." *Women and Criminal Justice* 4(1):63–89.

Glassner, Barry and Julia Loughlin. 1987. *Drugs in Adolescent Worlds: Burnouts to Straights*. New York: St. Martin's.

Hagedorn, John M. 1988. *People and Folks: Gangs, Crime and the Underclass in a Rustbelt City*. Chicago: Lake View Press.

Huff, C. Ronald. 1989. "Youth Gangs and Public Policy." *Crime and Delinquency* 35(4):524–537.

——. 1996. "The Criminal Behavior of Gang Members and Nongang At-Risk Youth." Pp. 75–102 in *Gangs in America*, 2nd ed., edited by C. Ronald Huff. Thousand Oaks, CA: Sage.

Joe, Karen A. and Meda Chesney-Lind. 1995. "Just Every Mother's Angel: An Analysis of Gender and Ethnic Variations in Youth Gang Membership." *Gender & Society* 9(4):408–430.

Klein, Malcolm W. 1995. *The American Street Gang: Its Nature, Prevalence and Control*. New York: Oxford University Press.

Klein, Malcolm W. and Cheryl L. Maxson. 1989. "Street Gang Violence." Pp. 198–213 in *Violent Crime, Violent Criminals*, edited by Neil Weiner and Marvin Wolfgang. Newbury Park, CA: Sage.

LaLonde, Brent. 1995. "Police Trying to Contain Gang Problem." *The Columbus Dispatch*, September 3, p. 2A.

Lauderback David, Joy Hansen, and Dan Waldorf. 1992. " 'Sisters Are Doin' It for Themselves': A Black Female Gang in San Francisco." *The Gang Journal* 1(1):57–70.

Lauritsen, Janet L. and Kenna F. Davis Quinet. 1995. "Repeat Victimization Among Adolescents and Young Adults." *Journal of Quantitative Criminology* 1(2):143–166.

Lauritsen, Janet L., Robert J. Sampson, and John H. Laub. 1991. "The Link Between Offending and Victimization Among Adolescents." *Criminology* 29(2):265–292.

Lees, Sue. 1993. *Sugar and Spice: Sexuality and Adolescent Girls*. New York: Penguin.

Maher, Lisa and Richard Curtis. 1992. "Women on the Edge of Crime: Crack Cocaine and the Changing Contexts of Street-Level Sex Work in New York City." *Crime, Law and Social Change* 18:221–258.

Maxson, Cheryl L., Kristi Woods, and Malcolm W. Klein. 1995. *Street Gang Migration in the United States*. Final Report to the National Institute of Justice.

Mayhood, Kevin and Brent LaLonde. 1995. "A Show of Colors: A Local Look." *The Columbus Dispatch*, September 3, pp. 1–2A.

Messerschmidt, James W. 1993. *Masculinities and Crime: Critique and Reconceptualization of Theory*. Lanham, MD: Rowman and Littlefield.

Miller, Jody. 1996. "The Dynamics of Female Gang Involvement in Columbus, Ohio." Paper presented at the National Youth Gang Symposium, June, Dallas, TX.

Miller, Jody and Barry Glassner. 1997. "The 'Inside' and the 'Outside': Finding Realities in Interviews." Pp. 99–112 in *Qualitative Research*, edited by David Silverman. London: Sage.

Moore, Joan. 1991. *Going Down to the Barrio: Homeboys and Homegirls in Change*. Philadelphia: Temple University Press.

Moore, Joan and John M. Hagedorn. 1996. "What Happens to Girls in the Gang?" Pp. 205–218 in *Gangs in America*, 2nd ed., edited by C. Ronald Huff. Thousand Oaks, CA: Sage.

Newburn, Tim and Elizabeth Stanko. 1994. *Just Boys Doing Business?: Men, Masculinities and Crime*. New York: Routledge.

Pesce, Rosario C. and Carol Gibb Harding. 1986. "Imaginary Audience Behavior and Its Relationship to Operational Thought and Social Experience." *Journal of Early Adolescence* 6 (1):83–94.

Rusk, David. 1995. *Cities without Suburbs*. 2nd ed. Washington, D.C.: The Woodrow Wilson Center Press.

Sampson, Robert J. and William Julius Wilson. 1995. "Toward a Theory of Race, Crime, and Urban Inequality." Pp. 37–54 in *Crime and Inequality*, edited by John Hagan and Ruth D. Peterson. Stanford, CA: Stanford University Press.

Sanders, William. 1993. *Drive-Bys and Gang Bangs: Gangs and Grounded Culture*. Chicago: Aldine.

Short, James E. and Fred L. Strodtbeck. 1965. *Group Process and Gang Delinquency*. Chicago: University of Chicago Press.

Simpson, Sally. 1991. "Caste, Class and Violent Crime: Explaining Differences in Female Offending." *Criminology* 29(1):115–135.

Spergel, Irving A. and G. David Curry. 1993. "The National Youth Gang Survey: A Research and Development Process." Pp. 359–400 in *The Gang Intervention Handbook*, edited by Arnold P. Goldstein and C. Ronald Huff. Champaign, IL: Research Press.

Taylor, Carl. 1993. *Girls, Gangs, Women and Drugs*. East Lansing: Michigan State University Press.

Thornberry, Terence R., Marvin D. Krohn, Alan J. Lizotte, and Deborah Chard-Weirschem. 1993. "The Role of Juvenile Gangs in Facilitating Delinquent Behavior." *Journal of Research in Crime and Delinquency* 30(1):75–85.

Thorne, Barrie. 1993. *Gender Play: Girls and Boys in School*. New Brunswick, NJ: Rutgers University Press.

Wilson, William Julius. 1996. *When Work Disappears: The World of the New Urban Poor.* New York: Knopf.

Winfree, L. Thomas, Jr., Kathy Fuller, Teresa Vigil, and G. Larry Mays. 1992. "The Definition and Measurement of 'Gang Status': Policy Implications for Juvenile Justice." *Juvenile and Family Court Journal* 43:29–37 ✦

Chapter 21
Youth Gang Drug Trafficking

James C. Howell
and
Debra K. Gleason

For the past two decades, the role of gangs in drug distribution and associated impacts on violence levels has garnered intense attention from law enforcement, public officials, and the media. Gang researchers have responded with a variety of studies and have examined the relationship between gangs, drugs, and violence with the full range of methods described in Chapter 1. Here, Howell and Gleason utilize data gathered from law enforcement respondents to the National Youth Gang Survey. They describe widespread involvement by gang members in drug sales and find a strong correlation between drug sales and involvement in other forms of criminal activity. However, gang control of drug distribution appears to be concentrated in a small number of areas and among adult, rather than juvenile, gang members. The finding that relatively few jurisdictions have serious youth drug trafficking problems is an important consideration as we turn to the programs and policies presented in Section V.

Nationally representative data on the extent and nature of youth gang involvement in drug trafficking, as perceived by law enforcement agencies, are available for the first time. Based on results from the 1996 Youth Gang Survey, this Chapter provides baseline data and analysis on the epidemiology of youth gang drug trafficking, including age, sex, and race/ethnicity of involved gang members; the relative extent of the problem in urban, suburban, and rural areas; and the involvement of youth gangs in other crimes.

This Chapter specifically examines several issues related to youth gang drug trafficking (see Howell and Decker, 1999; Klein, 1995; Klein, Maxson, and Cunningham, 1991; Moore, 1990). Some researchers contend that many youth gangs were transformed into drug trafficking operations during the crack cocaine epidemic in the latter part of the 1980s. Others contend that the extent of youth gang involvement in drug trafficking is unclear (for a review of this literature, see Howell and Decker, 1999). The present analysis will address the involvement of youth gangs and gang members in drug trafficking. However, the connection between youth gang drug trafficking and other crimes remains unclear. According to popular perception, youth gangs are directly involved with drug sales, and drug sales inevitably lead to other crimes. While several gang studies have found a weak causal relationship between youth gang involvement in drug sales and violent crime, other studies have shown the transformation of youth gang wars into drug wars. From existing studies, it has been difficult to distinguish traditional youth gangs from drug gangs. National data relevant to these and other issues are now available for the first time.

Responses to the 1996 National Youth Gang Survey (Moore and Terrett, 1998; National Youth Gang Center, 1999a), conducted by the National Youth Gang Center (NYGC), were analyzed for this Chapter. The survey gathered data from law enforcement agencies on two measures of youth gang drug trafficking: gang member involvement in drug sales and gang control of drug distribution. "Distribution" implies organizational management and control, as opposed to individual involvement in selling drugs directly to individual buyers. Unfortunately, the wording of the survey question on gang control of drug distribution may not have elicited responses that distinguished between street-level control of drug sales to individual buyers and organizational control of drug distribution by gangs. The 1997 National Youth Gang Survey asked respondents to report on the distribution of drugs for the purpose of generating profits for the gang. Analysis of these data is under way. Nevertheless, the 1996 survey provides information on the age, gender, and race/ethnicity of youth gang members and on the demographic characteristics of responding jurisdictions. The survey data also permit an examination of the interrelationship of youth gangs, drug trafficking, and other crime involvement.

Law enforcement agencies continue to be the best and most widely used source of national information available on gangs. However, this source has some important limitations (Curry, Ball, and Decker, 1996; Maxson, 1992; Maxson, 1998). First, many agencies do not collect gang data in a standardized manner. Automated gang databases are becoming more common, but they are typically used for gathering criminal intelligence rather than recording gang crime. Local law enforcement databases are designed to track and support apprehension of individual gang members—not to compile gang crime statistics. Second, law enforcement agencies are sometimes affected and constrained by political considerations (e.g., when they are pressured politically to pursue certain types of crimes), and a gang problem may tend to be either denied or exaggerated (Huff, 1989). Third, agencies and individuals within agencies often have different definitions of what constitutes a gang or a gang incident, and perceptions of the problem vary with the expertise and experience of the observer. Varying definitions of youth gangs continue to complicate analysis of comparative gang data. Fourth, police normally investigate crimes, not gangs. Compiling national gang data through surveys of law enforcement agencies involves asking the agencies "to provide . . . a service they may not routinely provide for local assessment and policy making" (Curry, Ball, and Decker, 1996, p. 33).

Survey Methods

The Sample

The 1996 National Youth Gang Survey was sent to a sample of 3,024 police and sheriff's departments in October 1997. It consisted of a 14-item questionnaire that elicited information on gang-related drug activity and other aspects of youth gangs (National Youth Gang Center, 1999a). This sample included four subsamples:

- All police departments serving cities with populations greater than 25,000.
- A randomly selected sample of police departments serving cities with populations between 2,500 and 25,000.
- All "suburban county" police and sheriff's departments.
- A randomly selected sample of "rural county" police and sheriff's departments.[1]

Nonrespondents (n=1,512) received followup calls beginning 2 months after the survey was mailed. After the followup calls, the response rate increased from 50 percent to 87 percent of the 3,024 jurisdictions that received the survey. Response rates for the above subsamples varied, but not significantly. Large cities and suburban counties had the highest response rate (88 percent), followed by small cities and rural counties (86 percent). In a few cases, respondents elected not to respond to one or more survey questions. In such cases, the agency was excluded from the analysis for the affected question(s). A total of 1,385 respondents (53 percent of the respondents who returned survey forms) reported gang problems. Among these, 1,005 agencies responded to the question regarding gang member involvement in drug sales, and 1,139 responded to the question regarding gang control of drug distribution. These responses were analyzed for this Chapter.

Measures

The 1996 National Youth Gang Survey placed limited restrictions on local jurisdictions' definitions of a "youth gang." For the purposes of the survey, a "youth gang" was defined as "a group of youths or young adults in your jurisdiction that you or other responsible persons in your agency or community are willing to identify or classify as a 'gang.' "[2] Respondents were asked to exclude motorcycle gangs, hate or ideology groups, prison gangs, and other exclusively adult gangs.

Respondents were asked two questions regarding gang involvement with drugs. The first open-ended question[3] asked, "In your jurisdiction, what percent of drug sales do you estimate involve gang members?" The second question was "What proportion of drug distribution do you estimate gangs control or manage in your jurisdiction?" Respondents were asked to choose the answer "that fits best" among the following options: "all of it," "more than half," "less than half," "less than one-fourth," "none," or "do not know."

Information on the age of gang members was obtained by a single question: "Considering all the members of the gangs you are reporting on, what is your estimate of the percentage who are: under age 15, 15–17, 18–24, over 24, do not know?" Only responses that totaled 100 percent were used in this and the gender and race/ethnicity questions described below.

Information on the sex of gang members was obtained by a single question: "What is the percentage of all of the members of the gangs you are reporting on who are: male, female, do not know?"

Information on the racial/ethnic identity of gang members was obtained by a single question: "For your jurisdiction, what percentage of all gang members do you estimate are: African American/black, Hispanic/Latino, Asian, Caucasian/white, or other (please identify)?"

Responses to these questions regarding age, sex, and race/ethnicity of gang members were used in the analyses for this Chapter. Moore and Terrett (1998) and the National Youth Gang Center (1999a) have used responses to one question in the survey (asking for the number of gang members in respondents' respective jurisdictions) as a base for calculating the absolute percentage of gang members falling into age, gender, and race/ethnicity categories.[4]

Information on gang member involvement in criminal activity (other than drug sales and control of drug distribution) was obtained using the following question: "Please indicate the degree to which gang members are estimated to have engaged in the following offenses in your jurisdiction in 1996." The listed offenses were aggravated assault, robbery, larceny/theft, burglary/breaking and entering, and motor vehicle theft. Survey recipients were provided four response categories: high, medium, low, and not involved. No attempt was made to elicit the number of offenses for which gang members were arrested in 1996 because such data generally are not available (see Curry, 1996).

Two questions were used to determine the year of onset of gang problems in particular jurisdictions. First, respondents were asked, "Have you had gang problems in your jurisdiction prior to 1996?" Those respondents who answered "yes" to this question were asked, "In approximately what year did gangs begin to pose a problem in your jurisdiction?"

Findings

This section summarizes analyses that were conducted for this Chapter. Readers are reminded that "drug trafficking" refers to gang member involvement in drug sales and gang control of drug distribution. A report, *Youth Gangs, Drugs, and Crime: Results From the 1996 National Youth Gang Survey*, which includes all tables and statistical tests (Howell and Gleason, 1998), is available from the National Youth Gang Center. Readers are referred to the full report for statistical significance tests. In this Chapter, the term "significant" is used to describe relationships between variables at or above the 0.05 level of statistical significance. Virtually every correlation and proportional difference examined in the reported analyses is statistically significant at or above the 0.001 level. Observations involving small numbers of respondents are so noted by footnotes.

Drug Sales

On average, respondents estimated that 43 percent of the drug sales in their jurisdiction involved gang members. Rather than using the average response, it was determined that more meaningful observations could be made by aggregating responses into groups and referring to the percentage of all responses within each group for analyses in this Chapter. Gang member involvement in drug sales was divided into three response ranges: low (0–33 percent), medium (34–66 percent), and high (67–100 percent).[5] This classification of responses revealed that 47 percent of all drug sales involved gang members at a low level, 26 percent at a medium level, and 27 percent at a high level. While the average for the entire response range (0–100 percent) was 43 percent, this division shows that the preponderance of responses fell into the low range (33 percent or less).[6]

In another part of the survey, respondents were asked if they included "drug gangs" in their responses to a question regarding whether they had active gangs (National Youth Gang Center, 1999a).[7] More than half (57 percent) of the respondents who said they had active gangs included drug gangs in the scope of their youth gang definition.[8] Because youth gangs are difficult to define, consensus is difficult to reach. Whether or not respondents included drug gangs in their youth gang definition greatly affected the distribution of responses on gang member involvement in drug sales.[9] Respondents who included drug gangs in their youth gang definition reported a much larger proportion of drug sales involving gang members than did respondents who did not include drug gangs in their definition. In jurisdictions that did not include drug gangs in their definition, two-thirds of the respondents said that as much as 33 percent of their drug sales involved gang members. In contrast, in jurisdictions that included drug gangs, two-thirds of the respondents said that as much as 70 percent of their drug sales involved gang members.

Drug Distribution

Respondents indicated that gangs did not control or manage most of the drug distribution in their jurisdictions. More than two-thirds of the respondents reported gang control of drug distribution at none to less than half; nearly half (47 percent) of the respondents said that gangs "control or manage" less than one-fourth of all drug distribution in their localities.[10] In contrast, less than one-third of respondents said gangs controlled more than half of the drug distribution in their jurisdictions.

Again, the inclusion of drug gangs in respondents' definitions of youth gangs greatly affected the distribution of responses on gang control of drug distribution. Only 12 percent of the respondents in jurisdictions that did not include drug gangs said gangs controlled or managed more than half of the drug distribution. In contrast, in jurisdictions that included drug gangs, 41 percent of the respondents said gangs controlled or managed more than half (or all) of the drug distribution. Thus, the effect of including drug gangs in respondents' youth gang definition skewed responses toward a higher level of gang control of drug distribution.

Demographic Factors

Gender. Females represented a smaller proportion of gang members in jurisdictions that reported gang member involvement in drug sales and gang control of drug distribution. Although they were only slightly less prevalent in jurisdictions that reported high levels of gang member involvement in drug sales, they were significantly less likely to be members of gangs that controlled drug distribution. In the 12 jurisdictions[11] that reported gang control of all of the drug distribution and also reported the gender of gang members, females represented only 6 percent of gang members, compared with a national average of 11 percent (National Youth Gang Center, 1999a).[12] Conversely, in jurisdictions that reported no gang control of drug distribution, females represented almost 15 percent of gang members.

Age. Regardless of the extent of gang member involvement in drug sales, respondents estimated that the largest proportion of their gang members were juveniles (ages 15 to 17) (see Table 21.1).[13] However, the prevalence of gang members age 18 and older increased in jurisdictions in which the level of gang member involvement in drug sales was "moderate" or "high." There tended to be fewer gang members ages 15 to 17 in these jurisdictions.

A more distinct age-related pattern was observed with respect to gang-controlled drug distribution (see Table 21.2). Respondents who said gangs controlled none of the drug distribution estimated that 79 percent of their gang members were juveniles (age 17 or younger). In contrast, in the 12 jurisdictions that reported gang control of all drug distribution and also reported the age of gang members,[14] respondents estimated that 42 percent of their gang members were juveniles and that 58 percent were young adults (age 18 and older). Thus, on average, the prevalence of young adult gang members increased significantly as gang control of drug distribution increased.

The average age of gang members also was affected by population characteristics in jurisdictions that responded to the two questions about drug trafficking. In the largest jurisdictions (those with populations of 250,000 or more), gangs consisted of approximately equal proportions of juveniles and young adults. Two age-related trends were observed in smaller jurisdictions. The percentage of juvenile gang members increased significantly, while the percentage of young adult gang members decreased significantly as population size decreased.

Table 21.1
Level of Gang Member Involvement in Drug Sales, by Age of Gang Members (Unweighted*)

	Age			
Level of Involvement	**Under 15**	**15–17**	**18–24**	**Over 24**
67–100% (*n*=232)	20%	43%	30%	7%
34–66% (*n*=217)	20	44	30	6
0–33% (*n*=407)	23	47	26	4
0–100% (*n*=856)	21	45	28	5

Notes: The percentages within each level of involvement may not equal 100 percent due to rounding; *n* = the number of observations.

* The averages reported in this table do not account for the number of gang members reported in each jurisdiction.

Table 21.2
Level of Gang Control of Drug Distribution, by Age of Gang Members (Unweighted*)

	Age			
Level of Control	**Under 15**	**15–17**	**18–24**	**Over 24**
All (*n*=12†)	10%	32%	47%	11%
More than half (*n*=279)	19	42	31	8
Less than half (*n*=220)	23	43	29	5
Less than one-fourth (*n*=401)	21	49	26	4
None (*n*=58)	31	48	19	1
Overall average‡ (*n*=970)	21	46	28	5

Notes: The percentages within each level of involvement may not equal 100 percent due to rounding; *n* = the number of observations.

* The averages reported in this table do not account for the number of gang members reported in each jurisdiction.

† Caution should be exercised in interpreting these data because fewer than 20 observations were available for estimation. Twelve jurisdictions that said gangs control all of the drug distribution also provided information on the age of gang members.

‡ These averages were derived from the estimates of respondents who responded to the questions regarding drug distribution.

In sum, age varied more significantly with gang control of drug distribution than with gang member involvement in drug sales. Older gang members appear to be much more involved in drug distribution than with drug sales. A significant age shift was also observed with respect to population size. Gang members age 18 and older were significantly more involved in both the sale and distribution of drugs in larger jurisdictions.

Race/Ethnicity. Table 21.3 shows that Caucasian and Hispanic gang members were significantly more prevalent in jurisdictions with low levels of gang member involvement in drug sales (0–33 percent) and that African American gang members were significantly more prevalent in jurisdictions with high levels of gang member involvement in drug sales (67–100 percent).[15] At the low level of drug sales, 23 percent of gang members were African American, 34 percent were Hispanic, and 34 percent were Caucasian. In contrast, at the high level of drug sales, 50 percent of gang members were African American, 24 percent were Hispanic, and 22 percent were Caucasian.

African American gang members were most prevalent in jurisdictions reporting high levels of gang control of drug distribution (see Table 21.4). Their proportion increased from 18 percent in jurisdictions reporting no gang control of drug distribution to 59 percent in the 14 jurisdictions reporting gang control of all drug distribution and also reporting the race/ethnicity of gang members.[16] Other racial/ethnic groups were significantly more prevalent in jurisdictions reporting a low degree of gang control of drug distribution. For example, in jurisdictions reporting gang control of less than one-fourth of drug distribution, 36 percent of gang members were Caucasian, and in jurisdictions reporting gang control of all drug distribution, only 18 percent were Caucasian. The same pattern was evident for Hispanics and Asians.

In sum, the greater the prevalence of African American gang members in the jurisdiction, the larger the proportion of drug sales accounted for by gang members and the greater the extent of gang control of drug distribution. The opposite pattern was observed for all other racial/ethnic groups, except for "others,"[17] whose prevalence did not change significantly.

The Drug Trafficking Context

Population size. Gang involvement in drug trafficking (member sales and gang control of drug distribution) was spread throughout various population categories, but gangs were estimated to control slightly more of the drug distribution in large cities than in suburban areas, small cities, towns, and rural counties. The prevalence of gang member involvement in drug sales was approximately equal in suburban areas, small cities, towns, rural counties, and the largest cities, and none of the differences among population categories were statistically significant for either type of drug trafficking.

Table 21.3
Level of Gang Member Involvement in Drug Sales, by Race/Ethnicity of Gang Members (Unweighted)*

Level of Involvement	Race/Ethnicity				
	African American	Hispanic	Caucasian	Asian	Other
67–100% (*n*=250)	50%	24%	22%	3%	1%
34–66% (*n*=235)	38	26	28	6	2
0–33% (*n*=427)	23	34	34	7	2
0–100% (*n*=912)	34	29	29	6	2

Notes: The percentages within each level of involvement may not equal 100 percent due to rounding; *n* = the number of observations.

*The averages reported in this table do not account for the number of gang members reported in each jurisdiction.

Table 21.4
Level of Gang Control of Drug Distribution, by Race/Ethnicity of Gang Members (Unweighted)*

Level of Control	Race/Ethnicity				
	African American	Hispanic	Caucasian	Asian	Other
All (*n*=14†)	59%	19%	18%	4%	1%
More than half (*n*=287)	50	24	21	4	1
Less than half (*n*=235)	35	29	28	5	3
Less than one-fourth (*n*=423)	22	32	36	7	2
None (*n*=61)	18	30	43	8	0
Total/Average‡ (*n*=1,020)	33	29	30	6	2

Notes: The percentages within each level of involvement may not equal 100 percent due to rounding; *n* = the number of observations.

*The averages reported in this table do not account for the number of gang members reported in each jurisdiction.

†Caution should be exercised in interpreting these data because fewer than 20 observations were available for estimation. Fourteen jurisdictions that said gangs control all of the drug distribution also provided information on the race/ethnicity of gang members.

‡These averages were derived from the estimates of respondents who responded to the question regarding drug distribution.

Gang member involvement in drug sales and gang control of drug distribution were substantial in small cities, towns, and rural counties with populations under 25,000. Nearly one-third of respondents in these jurisdictions said gang members accounted for two-thirds or more of all drug sales. Nearly one-fourth of respondents in these areas said gangs controlled more than one-half of the drug distribution. Overall, population is not a factor in the presence or absence of drug trafficking; gang drug trafficking occurs in populations of all sizes.

Geographical region. Both gang member involvement in drug sales and gang control of drug distribution varied significantly across the four major geographic regions.[18] The average proportions of drug sales estimated to involve gang members were as follows: Northeast, 41 percent; Midwest, 47 percent; South, 45 percent; and West, 38 percent. Gang control of drug distribution was significantly lower in the Northeast (10 percent) than in the other three regions: Midwest, 29 percent; South, 35 percent; and West, 25 percent.

The prevalence of particular racial/ethnic groups also varied significantly among the four geographic regions on both drug trafficking measures. With respect to drug sales, the greatest magnitude of variation was reported for Hispanics. While they represented 58 percent of the gang members in the West, they represented only 17 percent of gang members in the Midwest. Thus, Hispanics were greatly overrepresented in the West. In contrast with their national average within gangs (34 percent), African Americans were overrepresented in the Midwest (36 percent) and South (49 percent) regions and greatly underrepresented in the West (12 percent). Compared with their national average (29 percent), Caucasians were somewhat overrepresented in the Northeast (31 percent) and Midwest (38 percent) and underrepresented in the West (19 percent). Almost identical patterns were observed for gang control of drug distribution.

Year of gang problem onset. The onset year of gang problems in jurisdictions significantly affected both drug sales and control of drug distribution by gangs (see Table

Table 21.5
Period of Gang Problem Onset, by Average Percentage of Drug Sales Involving Gang Members (Unweighted)*

Period of Onset	Average Percentage of Drug Sales
Before 1980 (*n*=69)	45%
1981-85 (*n*=60)	48
1986-90 (*n*=278)	47
1991-92 (*n*=162)	43
1993-94 (*n*=220)	41
1995-96 (*n*=52)	35
Average Percentage (*n*=841)	44

Note: *n* = the number of observations.
*The averages reported in this table do not account for the number of gang members reported in each jurisdiction.

Table 21.6
Period of Gang Problem Onset, by Average Percentage of Drug Distribution Controlled/ Managed by Gangs (Unweighted)*

Period of Onset	Degree of Drug Distribution
Before 1980 (*n*=76)	44%
1981-85 (*n*=63)	47
1986-90 (*n*=314)	42
1991-92 (*n*=185)	34
1993-94 (*n*=235)	32
1995-96 (*n*=73)	24
Average Percentage (*n*=946)	37

Note: *n* = the number of observations.
*The averages reported in this table do not account for the number of gang members reported in each jurisdiction.

21.5). In general, larger proportions of drug sales were attributed to gang members in "older" gang localities than in "newer" ones. However, gang members were not as extensively involved in drug sales in the oldest gang jurisdictions (in which gang problems began before 1980) as in jurisdictions in which onset occurred between 1981 and 1990. Jurisdictions reporting onset between 1981 and 1985 show the highest level of gang member involvement in drug sales. Jurisdictions in which gang problems emerged after 1985 show lower levels of gang member involvement in drug sales, and these levels decrease in each subsequent time period of onset through 1995–96. Thus, gang members in "newer" gang problem jurisdictions were much less likely than those in "older" gang problem jurisdictions to be involved in drug sales.

Onset year had an even stronger effect on gang control of drug distribution (see Table 21.6).[19] The peak gang problem onset period for gang control of drug distribution was 1981 to 1985, after which gang control of distribution declined in each subsequent time period for gang problem onset through 1995–96. The average percentages shown in Table 21.6 indicate that gangs control significantly less of the drug distribution in "newer" gang problem jurisdictions than in "older" ones.

The Drug Sales-Distribution Connection

The overlap between gang member involvement in drug sales and gang control of drug distribution was significant, as expected. In the 15 jurisdictions that reported gang control of all drug distribution, every respondent reported that gang members were responsible for two-thirds or more of all drug sales. Conversely, when the reported percentage of drug sales involving gang members dropped to one-third or less, 80 percent of respondents said gangs controlled less than one-fourth of the drug distribution. In other words, if gang members are involved in either drug sales or drug distribution, then they (or gangs in their jurisdiction) are likely to be involved in both activities. Similarly, in jurisdictions in which gang members are not actively involved in drug sales, gangs tend not to be actively involved in control of drug distribution.

The Gang, Drugs, and Crime Connection

Drug trafficking and criminal involvement. In another analysis (National Youth Gang Center, 1999a, pp. 34–35), gang members tended to be involved in larceny/theft, followed by aggravated assault, motor vehi-

Figure 21.1
Level of Gang Member Involvement in Drug Sales, by Level of Gang Member Involment in Related Offenses (Unweighted)*

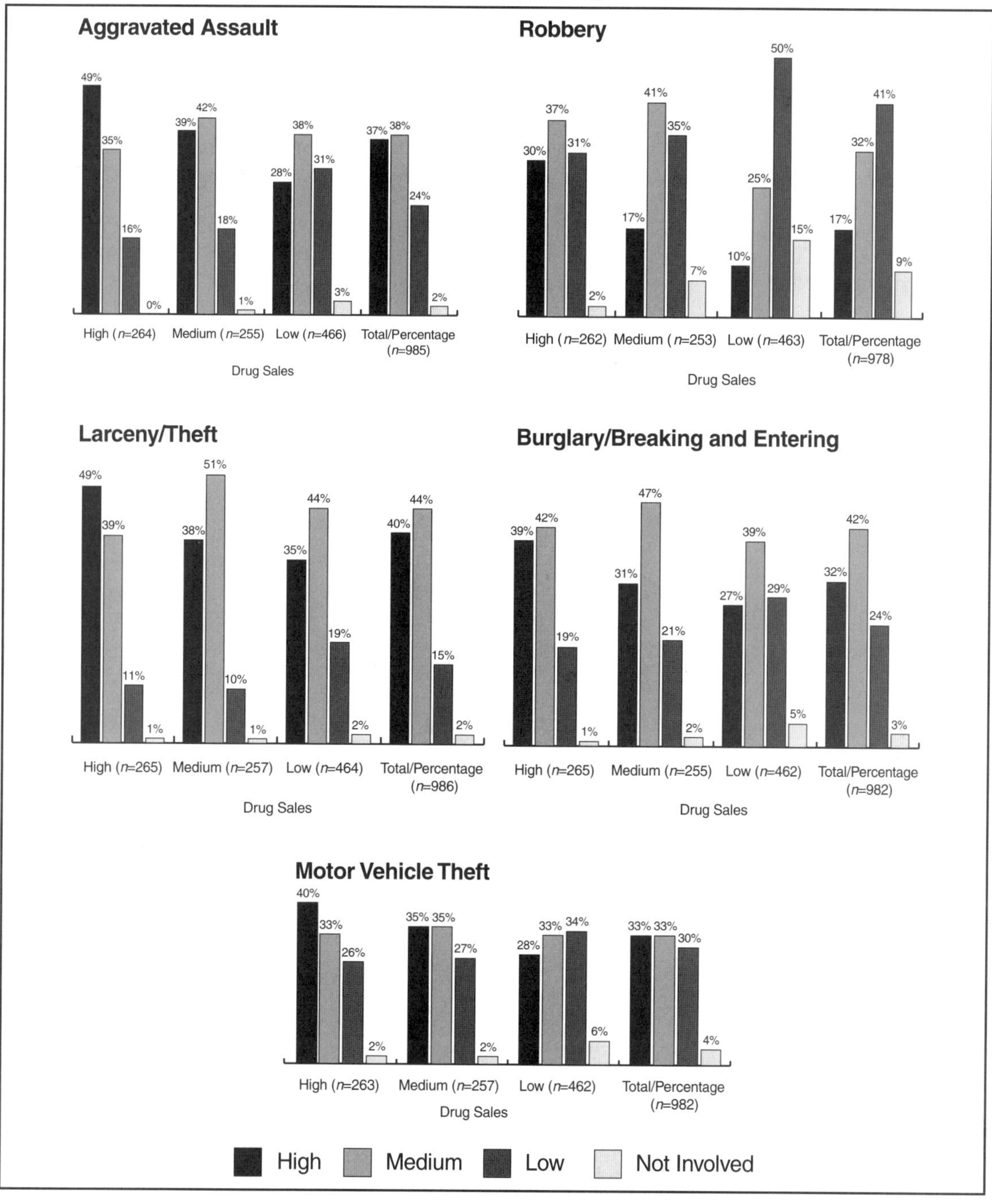

Notes: These bar graphs show the percentages of gang members involved in criminal offenses at high, medium, and low levels when involvement in drug sales is at high, medium, and low levels.
n = the number of observations. "High" = 67–100 percent; "Medium" = 34–66 percent; "Low" = 0–33 percent.
* The averages reported in this table do not account for the number of gang members reported in each jurisdiction.

cle theft, and burglary, in that order. Gang members were not reported to be extensively involved in robbery; almost half of the respondents reported "low" degrees of gang member involvement in this offense.

Figure 21.1 shows the degree to which gang members were reported to be involved in specific criminal offenses given their level of involvement in drug sales. The five measured offenses were aggravated assault, robbery, larceny/theft, burglary/breaking and entering, and motor vehicle theft. The bar graphs show the degree to which gang members were reported to be involved in the five offenses at four levels (high, medium, low, and not involved) for each of three categories representing the proportion of drug sales involving gang members (high, medium, and low). For example, Figure 21.1 shows that in jurisdictions in which gang member involvement in drug sales was estimated to be "high," 49 percent of gang members were involved in aggravated assault to a "high" degree, 35 percent to a "medium" degree, and 16 percent to a "low" degree.

A similar pattern was evident for the remaining four offenses. As gang member involvement in drug sales increased, the degree of gang member involvement in robbery, larceny/theft, burglary/breaking and entering, and motor vehicle theft increased significantly at the high level of criminal involvement. In jurisdictions reporting a high level of gang member involvement in drug sales, an average of 49 percent of all gang members were estimated to be involved to a high degree in aggravated assault and larceny/theft. In the same jurisdictions, 40 percent of gang members were estimated to be involved to a high degree in motor vehicle theft, 39 percent in burglary/breaking and entering, and 30 percent in robbery. Similar crime patterns were observed for jurisdictions reporting a high degree of gang control of drug distribution.

The overlapping percentages in Figure 21.1 do not clearly reveal how changes in each measure—drug trafficking and involvement in other crimes—are affected by changes in the other. Separate analyses for gang member drug sales and gang control of drug distribution (reported in Howell and Gleason, 1998) showed significant correlations between the two measures of drug trafficking and other crimes. The correlation was strongest for robbery, followed by aggravated assault, then other offenses. Howell and Gleason's analysis also showed very high correlations between various crimes other than drug trafficking. In fact, the strongest correlations were between robbery and aggravated assault, followed by robbery and motor vehicle theft, then robbery and either drug sales or drug distribution (in all jurisdictions that responded to the drug trafficking questions).[20]

When gang members are involved in one form of criminal activity, they are likely to be involved in other types of crimes. As Klein (1995) observed, involvement in "cafeteria-style" (widely varied) crime is typical in youth gangs. Studies of gang members within large adolescent samples show that gang members engage in a wide variety of offenses besides drug trafficking,[21] including drug and alcohol use, public disorder, property damage, theft, extortion, robbery, carrying illegal guns, and many other general acts of delinquency. Fighting with other gangs is also common. Gang members in an 11-city survey of middle school students said that the most characteristic feature of their gang was fighting with other gangs (Esbensen, Deschenes, and Winfree, 1999). Multivariate analyses[22] of the relationships between gang member involvement in drug trafficking and criminal offenses will be required, because other variables, such as intergang conflicts, may be influencing gang involvement in criminal offenses.

Program Implications

Although gang member involvement in drug sales is spread across all population categories, it accounts for a substantial proportion of the drug sales in less than one-fourth of all jurisdictions reporting youth gang problems in the 1996 National Youth Gang Survey. Youth gang control of drug distribution affects about one-third of gang problem jurisdictions. Drug gangs may be more prevalent in these localities, which would increase the proportion of involved gangs. Active control of drug distribution by youth gangs appears to be more prevalent in heavily populated jurisdictions in which young adults (age 18 and older) are more prevalent among youth gang members (see Tables 21.1 and 21.2).

It appears that a relatively small number of jurisdictions have serious youth gang drug trafficking problems. Klein's (1995) national survey of law enforcement agencies produced a similar finding. In Klein's interviews with gang experts in police departments in 261 "notable gang cities," only 14 percent reported a major role of youth gangs in drug distribution, and distinct drug gangs were reported in 16 percent of the cities (1995, p. 36). In most of these cities, the drug gangs did not represent the majority of the gangs. Overall, 72 percent of the cities "reported the gang-crack connection to be moderate, weak, or nonexistent."

There is some evidence that the most affected jurisdictions are cities in which gang problems first emerged in the early 1980s. Cities with newer youth gang problems are much less likely to have youth gangs that control drug trafficking enterprises. Each jurisdiction needs to assess the youth gang problem carefully to determine whether or not drug trafficking is a major cause for concern. A thorough assessment should consider at least the specific characteristics of the gangs, the sex and ages of gang members, the crimes gangs commit and the victims of their crimes, and the localities or areas they affect. No assumptions should be made about youth gang problems in a particular community before an assessment is performed.

As a first step, jurisdictions experiencing youth gang problems should attempt to distinguish between bona fide youth gangs and drug gangs. In some localities, the latter appear to account for much of the drug trafficking that law enforcement agencies attribute to youth gangs. This distinction has important implications for interventions, particularly law enforcement investigation and interdiction tactics. Drug gangs, also called "crack" gangs, grew out of the narcotics trade—not out of youth gangs (Klein, 1995; Moore, 1990). Klein and Maxson's (1996) law enforcement survey in 201 cities found that "specialty drug gangs" constituted only 9 percent of all gangs. Nevertheless, these drug gangs may be responsible for a significant proportion of drug sales and violence in some cities. Although the 1996 National Youth Gang Survey did not ask respondents to report the existence or number of drug gangs, their inclusion in gang definitions makes a significant difference in law enforcement estimates of gang involvement in drug trafficking. Unfortunately, researchers "do not know enough . . . to attempt to differentiate between drug gangs and the broad array of groups that comprise street gangs" (Klein, 1995, p. 130). However, Klein (Table 21.7) suggests several common differences between (youth) street gangs and drug gangs that—as a starting point—can help jurisdictions differentiate between the

Table 21.7
Common Differences Between Street Gangs and Drug Gangs

Street Gangs	Drug Gangs
Various ("cafeteria-style") crimes.	Crime focused on drug business.
Larger groups.	Smaller groups.
Less cohesive organization.	More cohesive organization.
Ill-defined roles for members.	Market-defined roles for members.
Code of loyalty.	Requirement of loyalty.
Residential territories.	Sales market territories.
Members may sell drugs.	Members do sell drugs.
Controlled by intergang rivalries.	Controlled by competition.
Younger, on average, but wider age range.	Older, on average, but narrower age range.

Source: Adapted from Klein (1995), p. 132.

two and develop appropriate responses for both (see Klein, 1995, p. 132).

Successfully breaking up youth gang drug operations may require different approaches, depending on the type of gang (Howell and Decker, 1999). Because youth gangs generally are involved only in street-level drug distribution, the proceeds of which typically are used for personal consumption, providing legitimate ways of earning money may be an effective intervention strategy. Suppression approaches (formal and informal social control procedures) may be more effective with drug gangs (see the Bureau of Justice Assistance's 1997 prototype for police suppression of drug gangs).

Several youth gang programs hold promise for reducing drug trafficking. OJJDP's Comprehensive Community-Wide Approach to Gang Prevention, Intervention, and Suppression Program model (also known as the Spergel model), currently being tested in five demonstration sites (Bloomington, IN; Mesa and Tucson, AZ; Riverside, CA; and San Antonio, TX), appears to be a promising broad approach to combating a wide range of gang crimes, including drug trafficking (for descriptions of these programs, see Burch and Kane, 1999). Preliminary data from this initiative suggest a reduction of drug use and selling among targeted gang youth. An early pilot of the comprehensive model, Chicago's Gang Violence Reduction Program, which targeted two of the city's most violent gangs, showed overall effectiveness, including reduction of drug selling among program clients when a combination of sanctions and coordinated services were delivered to them (Spergel and Grossman, 1997). The Tri-Agency Resource Gang Enforcement Team (TARGET) integrates and coordinates the work of the Westminster Police Department, the Orange County, CA, District Attorney, and the Orange County Probation Department in removing gang leadership and the most chronic recidivists from the community (Capizzi, Cook, and Schumacher, 1995; Kent et al., in press). The JUDGE (Jurisdictions United for Drug Gang Enforcement) program in San Diego, CA, is an example of multiagency coordination of investigations, prosecutions, and sanctions of violent members of drug-trafficking gangs (Bureau of Justice Assistance, 1997). Another multiagency strategy, Boston's enforcement, intervention, and prevention initiative (Kennedy, 1997; Kennedy et al., 1996), targets the city's most dangerous gang and drug offenders using a variety of enforcement-oriented strategies.

Programs that provide alternatives to gang life for active gang members also hold promise for reducing involvement in drug sales. Many gang members would give up drug selling for reasonable wages (Huff, 1998). Two inner-city gang programs that provide such job opportunities for gang members appear particularly promising in this regard: the National Center for Neighborhood Enterprises (1999) Violence-Free Zone initiatives, and the Los Angeles Homeboy Industries and Jobs for a Future (Gaouette, 1997). Many other programs that provide alternatives to gang involvement can also help reduce gang member drug trafficking, such as the Boys and Girls Clubs' Targeted Outreach program (see Howell, in press, for detailed information on this and other promising approaches). School-based antigang curriculums, such as Gang Resistance Education and Training (G.R.E.A.T.), appear promising for preventing gang involvement (Esbensen and Osgood, 1999), but other interventions may be needed to prevent adolescent involvement in drug selling. Preventing early initiation into drug use is a promising avenue, because early onset of drug use is a major risk factor for gang membership (Hill et al., 1999), and drug use is a precursor to drug trafficking (Van Kammen, Maguin, and Loeber, 1994).

Selected interventions should be community specific and based on thorough assessments of gang crimes. As Block and Block (1993, p. 9) caution, "A program to reduce gang involvement in drugs in a community in which gang members are most concerned with defense of turf has little chance of success." The most promising comprehensive models for dealing with bona fide youth gangs are built on collaboration among all sectors of the community and the juvenile justice system (Burch and Chemers, 1997; Howell, in press).

The criminal activities of youth gangs have important program and policy implications. Data from the 1996 National Youth Gang Survey support earlier studies that show the criminal versatility of youth gangs (Klein, 1995, p. 68; Miller, 1992; Thornberry, 1998). Drug trafficking is only one of many types of crimes committed by youth gangs. Thus, it is not surprising that drug crimes are highly correlated with robbery, aggravated assault, burglary, larceny-theft, and motor vehicle theft. Although gang member involvement in drug sales and gang control of drug distribution were strongly correlated with gang member involvement in all of the other five measured criminal offenses, the survey results did not suggest a particular pattern of criminal activity. The data suggest that gang drug trafficking may take place concurrently with other criminal activities, rather than cause other crimes. Further research on this relationship is needed.

In their review of the gangs, drugs, and violence connection, Howell and Decker (1999) concluded that most youth gang violence is not related to drug trafficking. Decker and Van Winkle (1994) concluded that most violent crimes committed by youth gangs are related to intergang and interpersonal conflicts. The analyses reported in this Chapter support Howell and Decker's conclusion. Youth gang interventions should be designed to prevent and reduce all types of criminality—not just drug crimes.

Conclusion

Youth gang involvement in drug sales and distribution is widespread, cutting across all demographic sectors, particularly age, race/ethnicity, geographic region, and population categories. However, according to law enforcement agency responses to the 1998 National Youth Gang Survey, extensive gang involvement in drug trafficking appears to be concentrated in a relatively small number of jurisdictions.

Every jurisdiction experiencing a gang problem needs to assess its specific problem before deciding on a response.[23] A different community response likely will be needed for different types of gangs involved in drug trafficking. Adult criminal organizations that control drug distribution systems and drug gangs are susceptible to suppression strategies (Bureau of Justice Assistance, 1997). Youth gangs may be less tractable because they are embedded in the social and cultural fabric of communities and integrally related to the adolescent developmental period. They require a more comprehensive response that combines prevention, intervention, and suppression strategies (Burch and Chemers, 1997).

Acknowledgments

This Chapter was prepared under Cooperative Agreement 95-JD-MU-K001 to the Institute for Intergovernmental Research from the Office of Juvenile Justice and Delinquency Prevention, U.S. Department of Justice.

Points of view or opinions expressed in this document are those of the authors and do not necessarily represent the official position or policies of OJJDP or the U.S. Department of Justice.

James C. Howell, Ph.D., is an Adjunct Researcher at the National Youth Gang Center (NYGC), Institute for Intergovernmental Research, Tallahassee, FL. Debra K. Gleason is a Microsystems Analyst at NYGC.

The authors are grateful to John Moore at NYGC and David Curry at the University of Missouri–St. Louis, who reviewed earlier drafts and made very helpful suggestions for improvements to this Chapter.

Notes

1. See National Youth Gang Center (1999a) for detailed information on sample selection, survey methodology, and results of analyses to date (see also Moore and Terrett, 1998, for a summary of results).
2. In the remainder of this Chapter, unless otherwise noted, the term "gang" refers to youth gangs.
3. Unless response categories are noted, questions that follow were open ended.
4. Thus, weighted counts could be used in the analyses for this Chapter pertaining to age, gender, and race/ethnicity. This procedure was not deemed appropriate for this Chapter because this analysis focuses on significant

differences in gang characteristics in different jurisdictions given various levels of involvement in drug activity, rather than on generating prevalence data. Moreover, use of weighted estimates would be misleading for analysis of covariation between variables.

5. Respondents who said "do not know" or whose estimates totaled more than or less than 100 percent were excluded from all analyses.
6. In an analysis not included in this Chapter, the spectrum of responses (0–100 percent) was divided into those that were above and those that were below the midpoint (that is, 50 percent of all drug sales). As a result, 54 percent of all responses fell below the midpoint, 34 percent fell above it, and the remaining 12 percent of responses were exactly 50 percent. An examination of the polar (lowest and highest) quadrants showed that in the lowest quadrant, 40 percent of the respondents estimated that gang members were involved in one-fourth or less of all drug sales. In the highest quadrant, 23 percent of all respondents estimated that gang members were involved in three-fourths or more of all drug sales. Thus, nearly two-thirds (63 percent) of all respondents fell into the extreme quadrants.
7. See page 265 of this Chapter for characteristics that distinguish bona fide gangs from drug gangs according to Klein (1995, p. 132).
8. Jurisdictions that included drug gangs in their responses were included in all analyses for this Chapter.
9. The authors are grateful to David Curry, University of Missouri—St. Louis, for suggesting this line of analysis.
10. This estimate might have been lower if respondents had been asked to make a distinction between street-level and organizational control of drug distribution.
11. Readers are cautioned that this observation involves a small number of respondents.
12. Readers should recall that the average percentage—not a percentage of the total number of gang members—is used in this analysis. Females represented 10 percent of the total number of gang members reported by all respondents (National Youth Gang Center, 1999a).
13. The average percentage, rather than a percentage of the total number of gang members, is used in this analysis. Of the total number of gang members reported by all respondents, 16 percent were estimated to be under age 15, 34 percent ages 15 to 17 years old, 37 percent ages 18 to 24, and 13 percent over age 24 (National Youth Gang Center, 1999a).
14. Readers are cautioned that this observation involves a small number of respondents.
15. The average percentage—not a percentage of the total number of gang members—is used in this analysis. Hispanics represented 44 percent of the total number of gang members reported by all respondents; African Americans, 35 percent; Caucasians, 14 percent; Asians, 5 percent; and others, 2 percent (National Youth Gang Center, 1999a).
16. Readers are cautioned that this observation involves a small number of respondents.
17. Nationally, only 2 percent of gang members were identified as belonging to "other" racial/ethnic groups. This category primarily consisted of American Indian (45 percent), Polynesian (27 percent), Middle Eastern (8 percent), and Haitian (5 percent) gang members (National Youth Gang Center, 1999a).
18. Uniform Crime Reports regions, as defined by the Federal Bureau of Investigation.
19. Table 21.6 was constructed using a formula that converted responses to the drug distribution question into interval responses from 0 to 100 percent (1, all, 100 percent; 2, more than half, 75 percent; 3, less than half, 37.5 percent; 4, less than one-fourth, 12.5 percent; and 5, none, 0).
20. Analysis of the data using Goodman and Kruskal's gamma to measure associations between each of the two drug trafficking measures and other crimes (Howell and Gleason, 1998) found that all were statistically significant. The pairs with the strongest association were gang control of drug distribution and robbery, followed by gang member drug sales and robbery. The association between aggravated assault and either drug trafficking measure was next in strength.
21. See Thornberry (1998) for a summary of four major studies.
22. Multivariate techniques of analysis examine which variables account for most of the variance when other factors are taken into account.
23. For an assessment process that can be adapted for any size jurisdiction, see National Youth Gang Center, 1999b.

References

Block, R., and Block, C. R. 1993. *Street Gang Crime in Chicago*. Research in Brief. Washington, DC: U.S. Department of Justice, Office of Justice Programs, National Institute of Justice.

Burch, J. H., and Chemers, B. M. 1997. *A Comprehensive Response to America's Youth Gang Problem*. Fact Sheet. Washington, DC: U.S. Department of Justice, Office of Justice Programs, Office of Juvenile Justice and Delinquency Prevention.

Burch, J., and Kane, C. 1999. *Implementing the OJJDP Comprehensive Gang Model*. Fact Sheet. Washington, DC: U.S. Department of Justice, Office of Justice Programs, Office of Juvenile Justice and Delinquency Prevention.

Bureau of Justice Assistance. 1997. *Urban Street Gang Enforcement*. Washington, DC: U.S. Department of Justice, Office of Justice Programs, Bureau of Justice Assistance.

Capizzi, M., Cook, J. I., and Schumacher, M. 1995. The TARGET model: A new approach to the prosecution of gang cases. *The Prosecutor* March/April:18–21.

Curry, G. D. 1996. National youth gang surveys: A review of methods and findings. Unpublished report prepared for the National Youth Gang Center, Tallahassee, FL.

Curry, G. D., Ball, R. A., and Decker, S. H. 1996. Estimating the national scope of gang crime from law enforcement data. In *Gangs in America*, 2d ed., edited by C. R. Huff. Thousand Oaks, CA: Sage, pp. 21–36.

Decker, S. H., and Van Winkle, B. 1994. Slinging dope: The role of gangs and gang members in drug sales. *Justice Quarterly* 11(4):583–604.

Esbensen, F., Deschenes, E. P., and Winfree, L. T. 1999. Differences between gang girls and gang boys: Results from a multi-site survey. *Youth and Society* 31(1):27–53.

Esbensen, F., and Osgood, D. W. 1999. Gang Resistance Education and Training (GREAT): Results from the National Evaluation. *Journal of Research in Crime and Delinquency* 36(2):194–225.

Gaouette, N. 1997. Hope rises at Homeboy Bakeries in L.A. *Christian Science Monitor* (Sept. 15):1.

Hill, K. G., Howell, J. C., Hawkins, J. D., and Battin, S. R. 1999. Childhood risk factors for adolescent gang membership: Results from the Seattle Social Development Project. *Journal of Research in Crime and Delinquency* 36(3):300–322.

Howell, J. C. In press. *Youth Gang Programs and Strategies*. Chapter. Washington, DC: U.S. Department of Justice, Office of Justice Programs, Office of Juvenile Justice and Delinquency Prevention.

Howell, J. C., and Decker, S. H. 1999. *The Youth Gangs, Drugs, and Violence Connection*. Chapter. Washington, DC: U.S. Department of Justice, Office of Justice Programs, Office of Juvenile Justice and Delinquency Prevention.

Howell, J. C., and Gleason, D. K. 1998. Youth gangs, drugs, and crime: Results from the 1996 National Youth Gang Survey. Unpublished report. Tallahassee, FL: National Youth Gang Center.

Huff, C. R. 1989. Gangs and public policy. *Crime and Delinquency* 35(4):524–537.

Huff, C. R. 1998. *Comparing the Criminal Behavior of Youth Gangs and At-Risk Youth*. Research in Brief. Washington, DC: U.S. Department of Justice, Office of Justice Programs, National Institute of Justice.

Kennedy, D. M. 1997. Pulling levers: Chronic offenders, high-crime settings, and a theory of prevention. *Valparaiso University Law Review* 3(2):449–484.

Kennedy, D. M., Piehl, A. M. and Braga, A. A. 1996. Youth violence in Boston: Gun markets, serious youth offenders, and a use-reduction strategy. *Law and Contemporary Problems* 59(1):147–196.

Kent, D. R., Donaldson, S. I., Wyrick, P. A., and Smith, P. J. In press. Evaluating criminal justice programs designed to reduce crime by targeting repeat gang offenders. *Evaluation and Program Planning* 24.

Klein, M. W. 1995. *The American Street Gang*. New York: Oxford University Press.

Klein, M. W., and Maxson, C. L. 1996. Gang structures, crime patterns and police responses. Unpublished report. Los Angeles: University of Southern California, Social Science Research Institute.

Klein, M. W., Maxson, C. L., and Cunningham, L. C. 1991. Crack, street gangs, and violence. *Criminology* 29(4):623–650.

Maxson, C. L. 1992. Collecting data from investigation files: Descriptions of three Los Angeles gang homicide projects. In *Questions and Answers About Lethal and Non-Lethal Violence*, edited by C. R. Block and R. Block. Washington, DC: U.S. Department of Justice, Office of Justice Programs, National Institute of Justice.

Maxson, C. L. 1998. Gang homicide. In *Studying and Preventing Homicide*, edited by D. Smith and M. Zahn. Thousand Oaks, CA: Sage, pp. 197–219.

Miller, W. B. 1992. (Revised from 1982). *Crime by Youth Gangs and Groups in the United States*. Washington, DC: U.S. Department of Justice,

Office of Justice Programs, Office of Juvenile Justice and Delinquency Prevention.

Moore, J. W. 1990. Gangs, drugs, and violence. In *Drugs and Violence: Causes, Correlates, and Consequences*, edited by M. De La Rosa, E. Y. Lambert, and B. Gropper. NIDA Research Monograph 103. Rockville, MD: U.S. Department of Health and Human Services, National Institutes of Health, National Institute on Drug Abuse, pp. 160–176.

Moore, J. P., and Terrett, C. 1998. *Highlights of the 1996 National Youth Gang Survey*. Fact Sheet. Washington, DC: U.S. Department of Justice, Office of Justice Programs, Office of Juvenile Justice and Delinquency Prevention.

National Center for Neighborhood Enterprise. 1999. *Violence-Free Zone Initiatives*. Washington, DC: National Center for Neighborhood Enterprise.

National Youth Gang Center. 1999a. 1996 National Youth Gang Survey. Washington, DC: U.S. Department of Justice, Office of Justice Programs, Office of Juvenile Justice and Delinquency Prevention.

National Youth Gang Center. 1999b. Rural gang initiative: A guide to assessing a community's youth gang problem. Unpublished report. Tallahassee, FL: National Youth Gang Center.

Thornberry, T. P. 1998. Membership in gangs and involvement in serious and violent offending. In *Serious and Violent Juvenile Offenders: Risk Factors and Successful Interventions*, edited by R. Loeber and D. P. Farrington. Thousand Oaks, CA: Sage, pp. 147–166.

Van Kammen, W., Maguin, E., and Loeber, R. 1994. Initiation of drug selling and its relationship with illicit drug use and serious delinquency in adolescent boys. In *Cross-National Longitudinal Research on Human Development and Criminal Behavior*, edited by E. G. M. Weitekamp and H. J. Kerner. Netherlands: Kluwer, pp. 229–241. ✦

Section V

Programs and Policies

Chapter 22 Gangs, Neighborhoods, and Public Policy

John M. Hagedorn

Urban underclass conditions have spread across the United States in ways that parallel the growth of gangs. Recognizing this pattern and the connection between the lack of effective social institutions, poverty, and gangs, Hagedorn presents a public policy strategy that emphasizes investing in the communities from which gangs emerge. His work is in contrast to much of the popular policy of the contemporary era, which merely emphasizes suppression and overlooks the need to combat the conditions that lead to gangs.

Abstract

This article uses research from three recent Milwaukee studies to show that deindustrialization has altered some characteristics of youth gangs. Gang members tend to stay involved with the gang as adults, and many have turned to the illegal drug economy for survival. Poor African-Americans in neighborhoods where gangs persist have both similarities and differences to Wilson's underclass concept. What characterizes these neighborhoods is not the absence of working people but the absence of effective social institutions. Public policy ought to stress jobs and investment in underclass neighborhoods, evaluation of programs, family preservation, and community control of social institutions.

Reprinted from: John Hagedorn, "Gangs, Neighborhoods, and Public Policy." In *Social Problems*, 38:4, November, 1991, pp. 529–542.

Are today's youth part of an "underclass"? What policies should communities adopt to control their gang problem? Based on recent gang research and experience in reforming Milwaukee's human service bureaucracy, we can address these questions and suggest practical local policies that go beyond the usual nostrums of "more cops" and "more jobs."

In the last few years a number of researchers have suggested that today's gangs have changed in some fundamental ways and may be part of an urban minority "underclass" (Moore 1985, Short 1990b, Taylor 1990, Vigil 1988). The nature of the "underclass," however, has been the subject of controversy (Aponte 1988, Gans 1990, Jencks 1989, Ricketts, Mincy, and Sawhill 1988, Wilson 1991). This paper uses data gathered from three different Milwaukee studies over the past five years to examine the changing nature of Milwaukee's gangs, the characteristics of Milwaukee's poorest African-American neighborhoods, and the relationship between gangs and neighborhoods.

For the first study, completed in 1986, 47 of the founding members of Milwaukee's 19 major gangs, including 11 of the 19 recognized leaders, were interviewed (Hagedorn 1988). That study described the origins of Milwaukee gangs, their structure and activities, and documented how gangs came to be seen as a social problem. It also tracked the education, employment, drug use, incarceration experience, and the level of gang participation of the 260 young people who founded the 19 gangs, including the 175 founders of 12 African-American male gangs.

A brief follow-up study in spring of 1990 looked at the patterns of drug abuse and the structure of gang drug dealing in three African-American gangs. This pilot study tracked the employment, incarceration, and drug use status of the 37 founding members of the three gangs since the original study. It began a process of exploring the relationship between Milwaukee gangs and drug dealing businesses or "drug posses."

Finally, as part of a human services reform plan, Milwaukee County commissioned a needs assessment in two neighborhoods where several of Milwaukee's gangs persist (Moore and Edari 1990b). Residents were hired to survey heads of households drawn from a probability sample of 300 households in ten census tracts in two neighborhoods. These neighborhoods had a high percentage of residents living in poverty and a clustering of social problems associated with the "underclass."

This article first looks at how Milwaukee gangs have changed due to deindustrialization. Second, the paper explores some volatile social dynamics occurring within poor but still heterogeneous African-American neighborhoods. Finally, based on the analysis of gangs and their neighborhoods, other underclass research, and on the author's own experience in reforming the delivery of social services, the article suggests several local policies to strengthen and assist community institutions with gang troubles.

Macro-Economic Trends and Gangs in Milwaukee

The underclass has been conceptualized as a product of economic restructuring that has mismatched African-Americans and other minority workers with radically changed employment climates (Bluestone and Harrison 1982, Kasarda 1985, Sullivan 1989). Milwaukee epitomizes this mismatch: between 1979 and 1986 over 50,000 jobs were lost or 23 percent of Milwaukee's manufacturing employment (White et al. 1988:2–6). African-American workers were hit especially hard. In 1980 prior to the downturn, 40 percent of all African-American workers were concentrated in manufacturing (compared to 31 percent of all city workers). By 1989 research in five all-black Milwaukee census tracts found that only about one quarter of all black workers were still employed in manufacturing (Moore and Edari 1990b). African-American unemployment rates in Milwaukee have reached as high as 27 percent over the past few years.

Another way to view economic changes in the African-American community is to look at social welfare over the last thirty years. Like European immigrants before them, African-Americans came to Milwaukee with the hopes of landing good factory jobs (Trotter 1985) and large numbers succeeded. But as industrial employment declined and good jobs were less available, reliance on welfare increased (Piven and Cloward 1987:83). In 1963, when black migration to Milwaukee was still rising, fewer than one in six of Milwaukee's African-Americans were supported by AFDC. However by 1987, nearly half of all Milwaukee African-Americans and two thirds of their children received AFDC benefits. Seven out of every ten Milwaukee African-Americans in 1987 were supported by transfer payments of some kind accounting for half of all 1987 black income in Milwaukee County (Hagedorn 1989a).

Coinciding with reduced economic prospects for African-Americans, Hispanics, and other working people, gangs reemerged in Milwaukee and other small and medium-sized cities across the Midwest. While the popular notion at the time was that these gangs had diffused from Chicago, gangs in Milwaukee and the Midwest developed from corner groups and break-dancing groups in processes nearly identical to those described by Thrasher fifty years before (Hagedorn 1988, Huff 1989). The economy may have been changing, but the way gangs formed had not.

In 1986 we interviewed 47 of the 260 Milwaukee gang founders or members of the initial groups of young people who started the 19 major gangs in the early 1980s. At the time of our interviews, the founders were all in their early twenties and at an age when young people typically "mature out" of gang life. We asked the 47 founders to report on the current status of all the members who were part of the gang when it started. To our surprise, more than 80 percent of all male gang founders were reported as still involved with the gang as twenty to twenty-five year old adults.

We concluded at the time that the economic basis for "maturing out" of a gang—those good paying factory jobs that take little education, few skills, and only hard work—was just not there any more. As Short wrote in a recent review of gang literature, "There is no reason to believe that boys hang together in friendship groups for reasons that are very different now than in the past. . . . What has changed are the structural economic conditions . . ." (Short 1990a).

Moore (1991) has also documented economic effects of deindustrialization on the "maturing out" process of Chicano gangs. She finds that members of recent gang cliques in East Los Angeles are less likely to have found good jobs than members of older gang cliques. She concludes, "It is not that the men from recent cliques were more likely to have dropped out of the labor market, nor were they more likely to be imprisoned. It may be that they could not get full-time stable jobs."

Table 22.1
Employment and Adult Gang Involvement

	% Black Male	% Hisp. Male	% Wht. Male	% Female
Full Time	9.7	10	10	8.6
Part Time	14.0	0	40	11.4
Unemployed	70.3	82.5	40	63.0
Involved with the Gang as an Adult	81.1	70	100	8.6
Totals	N=175	N=40	N=10	N=35

The difficulty in finding a good job today is offset by the abundance of part-time jobs in the illegal drug economy. In preparation for a proposal to the National Institute on Drug Abuse to examine the impact of drug abuse and drug dealing on Milwaukee's gangs, we updated our rosters on the current status of the 37 founding members of three African-American gangs. By 1990, less than one in five (19 percent) of the founders, now in their mid to late twenties, were engaged in full-time work. However, three times as many of the founders (59 percent) graduated from the gang into drug "posses" or high-risk small businesses selling drugs. "High risk" is perhaps an understatement. Almost all of the 37 (86 percent) had spent significant time in prison since 1986, most for drug offenses. Three quarters (76 percent) had used cocaine regularly within the last three years and three had been murdered. While five of the 37 were said to be working as entrepreneurs (called "hittin' 'em hard"), the others involved with drug distribution worked part time ("makin' it") or sporadically ("day one")

Table 22.2
1990 Status of 37 Founding Members of Three African-American Gangs

Involved in Regular Sales of Cocaine	Used Cocaine Routinely Since 1987	Spent Time in Prison	Presently Working Full Time	Murdered
59%	76%	86%	19%	8%
N=22	N=28	N=32	N=7	N=3

and continued to live on the margins.

As Don, a leader of the 1-9 Deacons told us in 1985: "I can make it for two or three more years. But then what's gonna happen?" The answer to Don's question is now clear. The lack of access to good jobs has had a direct effect of making illegal drug sales, no matter how risky, more attractive to Milwaukee's gang founders as an occupation for their young adult years.

Frederick Thrasher pointed out sixty years ago: "As gang boys grow up, a selective process takes place; many of them become reincorporated into family and community life, but there remains a certain criminal residue upon whom gang training has for one reason or another taken hold" (Thrasher 1963:287). The loss of entry level manufacturing jobs appears to have turned Thrasher's "selective process" on its head. Today most of the young adult gang founders rely on the illegal economy for guarantees of survival. It is only the "residue" who, at this time in Milwaukee, are being "reincorporated into family and community life."

There are also some indirect effects of economic changes. In Milwaukee most of the founders still identify somewhat with their old gang and often hang out in the same neighborhoods where they grew up, coexisting with a new generation of gang youth. This mixing of older members of drug "posses" with younger siblings and other young gang members has produced disturbing intergenerational effects. Older gang members with a street reputation employed in the fast life of drug dealing are modeling dangerous career paths for neighborhood youth. These intergenerational effects also appear in Anderson's latest work (1990). He finds that "old heads," older residents who upheld and disseminated traditional values, are being replaced by new "old heads" who "may be the product of a street gang" and who promote values of "hustling," drugs, and sexual promiscuity (103). This "street socialization" may contribute to reproducing an underclass rather than socializing young people into conventional lifestyles (Short 1990b, Vigil 1988).[1]

In summary, contemporary gangs have changed from the "delinquent boys" of fifties literature: There is a growing relationship between the youth gang, illegal drug-based distribution, and survival of young adult gang members in a post-industrial segmented economy. Clearly, powerful economic forces are affecting contemporary gangs as Wilson and other underclass theorists would predict. But when we take a closer look at the impact of economic, demographic, and institutional changes on processes within Milwaukee's poorest African-American neighborhoods, the situation becomes more complicated.

Gangs and Neighborhood Segmentation

Gangs have always been associated with neighborhoods and African-American gangs have been no exception. Thrasher found "Negroes" had "more than their share" of gangs (Thrasher 1963:132) as far back as the 1920s. In the neighborhood that Suttles studied, gangs were functional "markers" or signs by which neighborhood youth could know who may be harmful and who is not and thus were an important part of a neighborhood's search for order. Suttles' black gangs were not in any significant way distinct from white ethnic gangs (Suttles 1968: 157). Similarly, the black Chicago gang members that Short and Strodtbeck (1965: 108) studied were quite similar to nongang black youth though they were more lower class than white gang members. Until the 1960s, the sociological literature largely viewed black gangs as functional parts of black neighborhoods.

But things have been changing. Perkins, summarizing the history of black Chicago gangs, wrote that gangs first became disruptive to their communities in the late 1960s due to the influence of drugs, corrupting prison experiences, and the failure of community-based programs (Perkins 1987:40–42). Cloward and Ohlin theorized that housing projects and other big city "slums" tended to be disorganized and "produce powerful pressures for violent behavior among the young in these areas" (Cloward and Ohlin 1960:172). They correctly predicted that "delinquency will become increasingly violent in the future as a result of the disintegration of slum organization" (203).

Increasing violence in central cities has prompted angry responses from residents. Cooperation by broad elements of the black community with police sweeps of gang members in Los Angeles and elsewhere and the founding of "mothers against gangs" and similar organizations throughout the country are examples of community hostility to gangs. Gangs today are seen by both law enforcement and many community residents as basically dysfunctional. Today's gangs are a far cry from the "Negro" street gangs of Suttles' Addams area which contained the "best-known and most popular boys in the neighborhood" (Suttles 1968:172).

Based on our Milwaukee interviews, we concluded that gang members reciprocated the hostility of "respectables." While the gang founders were hostile toward police and schools as expected, they also severely criticized African-American community agencies which they felt were mainly "phoney." The black founders agreed their gangs were dysfunctional for their neighborhoods: two thirds of those we interviewed insisted that their gang was "not at all" about trying to help the black community. Some were shocked at even the suggestion that their gang would be concerned about anything but "green power" (i.e., money). The role model of choice for many of the founders we interviewed was not Dr. Martin Luther King,

Jesse Jackson, or any African-American leader, but Al Capone.

One explanation for this intracommunity alienation in Milwaukee is the peculiar way black gangs formed. Gang formation in Milwaukee coincided with desegregation of the schools: a one-way desegregation plan that mandatorally bused only black children. While gangs originally formed from neighborhood groups of youth in conflict with youth from other neighborhoods, busing complicated the situation. School buses picking up African-American students often stopped in many different neighborhoods, mixing youth from rival gangs and transforming the buses into battlegrounds. Gang recruitment took place on the buses and in the schools as well as from the neighborhood. The black founders told us in 1985–86 that a majority of the members of their gangs no longer came from the original neighborhood where the gang formed.

Consequently, when the gang hung out on neighborhood corners, they were not seen by residents as just the "neighbors' kids" messing up. "I'll tell your Mama" did not work when no one knew who "mama" was or where she lived. Informal social controls were ineffective, so calling the police became the basic method to handle rowdiness and misbehavior as well as more serious delinquency. Hostility between the gangs and the neighborhood increased with each squad car arriving on the block.

A second explanation for intra-community hostility is provided by 1989 research in five of Milwaukee's poorest and all-black census tracts (Moore and Edari 1990b) where several of the gangs I had studied were founded. These neighborhoods exhibit many of the criteria of an "underclass" area, but they also differ in many respects from very poor ghetto neighborhoods described by Wilson and others.

Household income of the tracts was very low—1980 census data (before the eighties downturn) show more than 30 percent of the families in the five tracts living below poverty. The five tracts experienced a 42 percent population loss between 1960 and 1985. In 1989, when the interviews were completed, most (53.8 percent) respondents received AFDC and nearly twenty percent (19 percent) did not have a phone. A majority of residents in the five tracts presently live below the poverty line. The tracts certainly qualify as "underclass" areas by standard definitions (Ricketts and Mincy 1988).

But these neighborhoods are not uniformly poor. One quarter of the residents (28.6 percent) owned their own home—fifteen percent less than the city-wide average but still a stable base within a very poor neighborhood. Half of the household heads lived at their current residence for five or more years. While stable employment had drastically declined in these tracts since 1980, still nearly one third of working respondents had held their current job for 10 or more years. Unlike the "densely settled ghetto areas" Sampson describes (1987:357) where residents have "difficulty recognizing their neighbors," 80 percent of the Milwaukee respondents said the best thing about their neighborhood was their "neighbors." Nearly three in five (59.2 percent) visited with neighbors at least once a week.

More striking were strong kinship ties, supporting earlier work by Stack (1974) and others. Nearly half of all respondents visited their parents every day and over ninety percent visited their parents monthly. An even higher percentage visited siblings at least once a month. Finally, more than three quarters belonged to families that held family reunions—and 77 percent of those respondents regularly attended those reunions. Even child protective clients, who are among the most transient residents, had extensive kinship networks (Moore and Edari 1990a).[2]

But the neighborhoods are not regarded positively by most residents. Less than one fifth (19.7 percent) said the neighborhood was a "good place to live," and 52 percent said they would move if they could. While the respondents liked their neighbors as the best thing about their community, the top three worst things were said to be drugs (64 percent), violence (52 percent), and gangs (20 percent). About half said things had gotten worse the past two years, and a majority (54.5 percent) believed things will continue to get worse. And the problems were not "around the corner" or in an adjacent neighborhood, but right on the blocks where the interviews took place. The interviewers were often told by respondents to not go to a certain house or to avoid a certain side of the street because of dangerous drug or gang problems.

The area also has few basic social institutions. Zip code 53206 is a 20 by 20 square block area with 40,000 residents in the heart of Milwaukee, containing the census tracts where the interviews took place. This area has no large chain grocery stores. There are no banks or check-cashing stores in the entire zip code area. Bars and drug houses are in plentiful supply and the area has the highest number of Milwaukee drug arrests. Still, in 1989, this zip code area did not have a single alcohol/drug treatment facility. Even community agencies are located overwhelmingly on the periphery of 53206, circling the neighborhoods they serve, but not a part of them.[3] Community programs, churches, and social workers were seldom mentioned by survey respondents as a resource to call in times of neighborhood trouble.[4]

In summary, while these poor African-American neighborhoods have characteristics of Wilson's notion of the underclass, they also exhibit important differences. On the one hand, central city Milwaukee neighborhoods have been getting poorer due to deindustrialization and have experienced substantial population loss. They are home to the poorest and most troubled of all Milwaukee's residents. The area's lack of basic institutions is reminiscent of descriptions by Thrasher (1927) and Shaw and McKay (1969) and supports aspects of Wilson's underclass thesis.

On the other hand, large numbers of working class African-American families still reside in these neighborhoods. Some want to leave but cannot because of residential segregation (Massey and Eggers 1990) or lack of affordable housing. But many stay because they want to. Rather than neighborhoods populated overwhelmingly by a residue left behind by a fleeing middle and working class, as Wilson described, Milwaukee's "underclass" neighborhoods are a checkerboard of struggling working class and poor families, coexisting, even on the same block, with drug houses, gangs, and routine violence.

This ecological coexistence explains much of the intra-community tension between poor and working families and underclass gangs. Clearly when drug deals gone bad turn into midnight shoot-outs, residents of a neighborhood will be scared and angry. Contrary to Wilson's claim, events in one part of the block or neighborhood are often of vital concern to those residing in other parts (Wilson 1987:38). With a lack of effective community institutions, residents can either ignore the gunshots in the night, arm themselves for self-protection, call "911"—or give in to the fear and despair by moving out.[5]

While Milwaukee neighborhoods are not the socially disorganized underclass area reported by Wilson, neither are they the highly organized neighborhoods described by Whyte (1943) or Suttles (1968). Milwaukee's poor neighborhoods have segmented and an uneasy peace reigns between nervous factions. Suttles (1968) saw the 1960s Addams area as representing "ordered segmentation," where firm boundaries between ethnic neighborhoods helped make "a decent world within which people can live" (234). Instead, Milwaukee's neighborhood segments have become a prime source of instability.

This picture of neighborhood segmentation is consistent with Anderson's portrait of "Northton," a poor African-American community in a large eastern city (Anderson 1990). "Old heads" in Northton are not so much missing, as they have become demoralized and their advice shunned (78–80). Respectable residents are confronted by a growing street culture that increases community distrust of young people, victimizes neighborhood residents, and lures children into dangerous activities (92). Police simplistically divide the neighborhood between the "good people" and those linked to drug trafficking (202–203). Conflict between neighborhood segments inevitably increases, and "solidarity" is sacrificed to the imposed order of police patrols, vigilante justice, and prisons.

These heterogeneous but segmented neighborhoods in "Northton" and Milwaukee may be characteristic of many "underclass" communities across the United States (Jencks 1990). How to stabilize such neighborhoods is one of the major policy debates of the nineties.

Gangs, Neighborhoods, and Public Policy

In light of these findings, what do we make of this contradictory picture of gangs and their neighborhoods? What policies ought to be followed? The data suggest the drug economy nourishes in large part because of the absence of good jobs. It is hard to argue with the response from a 1986 interview:

> Q: OK. We're at the end here. The Governor comes in. He says, Darryl, I'm gonna give you a million dollars to work with gangs. Do what you want with it.
>
> A: Give 'em all jobs.

But while jobs are certainly needed, there is no reason to believe hundreds of thousands of good paying entry-level jobs will appear anytime soon from either the private or public sector. In the absence of sufficient jobs, pressure will continue to mount for more police and more prisons as the policy option of choice to curtail violence. This militarization of our neighborhoods is inevitable unless community residents and public officials can be persuaded that alternative policies are plausible and can be effective. But what alternative policies should be advocated?

One popular option is to work with city hall and call for more federal resources to come to cities. While we clearly need more resources, a more critical issue is how money is spent. As Spergel says in summarizing his recommendations in the *National Youth Gang Survey* "the implication of our findings is that more resources alone for police or even human service programs would not contribute much to dealing effectively with the youth gang problem" (Spergel and Curry 1990:309). In the absence of institutional reform and guarantees that resources will get to those that need it, more resources alone will not necessarily contribute to solving gang problems.[6]

The development of effective policy will require a struggle within cities over where new and existing programs are physically located, who will be served, and how the massive public bureaucracies (which gobble most resources intended for the poor) should be structured. Rather than proposing specific new model gang programs or narrowly calling for a federal office of gang control (Miller 1990), our data suggests a focus on strengthening neighborhood social institutions. Our experience in reforming Milwaukee's human service system suggests that we should adopt four policies to strengthen neighborhood-level social control.

1. Public spending and private investment must be concentrated in the most impoverished areas. This does not mean spend more human service dollars "for" the underclass by funding well-intentioned programs run by middle-class white providers located on the periphery of the poorest neighborhoods. Rather, I suggest we should insist that money be spent mainly on programs physically located in underclass neighborhoods, run by people with ties to the neighborhoods they intend to serve. This policy has the effect of targeting programs for the underclass while also strengthening minority agencies or creating new agencies within very poor neighborhoods. These agencies provide not only services but also can provide jobs for neighborhood residents. As employment opportunities increase and better funded local agencies become centers for social action, pressures for working- and middle-class residents to flee should decrease.

For example, in Milwaukee, close examination of where human service dollars were spent by zip code exposed that less than 1 percent of $100 million of Department of Health and Human Service contract dollars in 1988 was spent on programs located in two of Milwaukee's poorest zip code areas (53206 and 53204). These two areas contain only eight percent of Milwaukee County's population but are home to 25 percent of Milwaukee's human service clients. These figures were used by our reform administration to direct several million dollars in purchase contracts to agencies physically located in the two zip code areas, helping build an institutional infrastructure. Boarded up buildings are being rehabilitated to house the new agencies, employing neighborhood youth in the rehabbing effort.

Redirecting existing money is not an easy task. When we sent more than "crumbs" to neighborhood organizations, the mainly white traditional agencies—which are located downtown or in integrated, more stable neighborhoods—howled "reverse discrimination" and lobbied against us. Funding new programs is a zero sum game: if agencies located in poor neighborhoods are to get funded, agencies located elsewhere stand to lose. Those providers will almost certainly have more political power and connections than poor neighborhood organizations.

But as our research shows, while very poor neighborhoods have been devastated by economic and demographic changes, they also have important strengths to build on. The residents who live in poor neighborhoods need stable, well-funded agencies and institutions in which to participate. This recommendation is a call for sustained local political struggle over where money is spent to better stabilize impoverished neighborhoods.

2. Programs should be fully evaluated to see if they are having a positive impact on gangs or those most in need. It is not only important where the money is spent, but it is also critical whether anyone besides the agency or bureaucracy benefits. The inability of traditional agencies to serve the "hard to reach" has a long history: the Chicago Area Project (Schlossman, Zellman, and Schavelson 1984) was initiated to fill just such a gap. Geis cites the 1960s New York City Youth Board as an example of the need for innovative programming to replace the traditional agencies which were unable "to respond readily to new ideas and approaches" (Geis 1965:43). And some programs do "work." Lizbeth Schorr lists numerous contemporary programs that have been effective and could be replicated (Schorr 1988).

Large public bureaucracies are seldom concerned with formal results of programs. Once programs are funded, their continuation is often all that is offered as proof of effectiveness. In Milwaukee, research on agencies which received more than $20 million dollars worth of contracts to work with delinquents discovered the Department of Social Services kept no records at all of client outcomes of these programs. Funding decisions were based almost solely on routine approval of the re-funding of those agencies funded the year before (Hagedorn 1989b).

Programs thus continue with no regard for their effectiveness for clients. Lindblom points out the apparent absurdity that "In an important sense, therefore, it is not irrational for an administrator to defend a policy as good without being able to specify what it is good for" (Lindblom 1959:84). James Q. Wilson, in a forum on "Can Government Agencies be Managed?" recommended the novel idea that managers be judged on program results, a prospect he doubted would happen because "It is in no one's interest in Washington, D.C.," to do it (Wilson 1990:33). Many organizational theorists have pointed out that program evaluation serves only ceremonial functions for public bureaucracies (Meyer and Rowan 1981, Weick 1976). If sociologists are not among those insisting that social programs be evaluated and show results for the clients they are intended to serve, who will?

3. Fund family preservation programs. One of the most encouraging developments in the past decade in social work has been family preservation programs (Nelson, Landsman, and Deutelman 1990). These short-term intensive empowerment model programs which focus not on an individual client but rather the needs of the entire family have been remarkably successful.[7] In dozens of states and cities these programs, many of them modeled after the successful "homebuilders" projects funded by the Edna McConnell Clark Foundation, have reduced out of home placements and helped families learn how to stay together during a crisis.

Families where an older sibling is involved with gangs may be ideal candidates for these types of intensive, coordinated efforts. Our data show that many child protective clients have extensive family networks whose strengths could be utilized by intensive interventions. Milwaukee received a $1 million dollar grant from the Philip Morris Companies to fund a "homebuilders" model program. An agency located in one of the poorest areas of the city was awarded the contract to implement the program and collaborate with the public school system. As noted above, there was considerable resistance to the program from elements within the social welfare bureaucracy where family-based, results-oriented programming was viewed as a threat to business as usual (Nelson 1988). Yet, strategies were developed to confront the opposition, and the program was implemented.

4. *Finally, large public bureaucracies should become more neighborhood based and more open to input from clients and the neighborhoods they serve.* Reminiscent of the 1960s community control movement (Altschuler 1970), current research suggests that social control is least effective when imposed by outside forces. Community controls are strengthened most when informal community level networks are voluntarily tied to external bureaucracies and other resources (Figueira-McDonough 1991).[8] Public dollars for social programs today are largely used to support "street level bureaucrats" whose structure of work often makes it difficult to deliver services that improve the quality of life of their clients (Lipsky 1980). Diverse reform trends in policing, education, and social services all stress more community involvement in public bureaucracies (Chubb and Moe 1990, Comer 1972, Goldstein 1977, Kamerman and Kahn 1989). These reforms, insofar as they increase client and neighborhood control and break down existing bureaucratic barriers, merit support.

While Lipsky and others comment that it will be difficult to reform public bureaucracies in the absence of social movement (Lipsky 1980:210, Wineman 1984:240), unfavorable conditions should not be an excuse for inaction. The Milwaukee experience of creating multi-disciplinary teams of human service workers, moving them into the neighborhoods, and creating neighborhood councils to increase accountability is one example of such a reform.

Conclusion

Deindustrialization has altered the nature of gangs, creating a new association between the youth gang, illegal drug-based distribution, and survival of young adult gang members in a post-industrial segmented economy. While it would be a mistake to see all gangs as drug-dealing organizations, the lack of opportunity for unskilled delinquents creates powerful strains on gang members to become involved in the illegal economy. Without a major jobs program, illegal traffic in drugs and related violence seem likely to continue at unacceptable levels (Goldstein 1985, Johnson et al. 1989).

Although neighborhood changes are clearly relevant to gang activities, Wilson's characterization of the underclass as living in neighborhoods from which middle and working class African-Americans have fled and abandoned social institutions (Wilson 1987:56) does not fully apply in cities like Milwaukee. Instead, there are deteriorating neighborhoods with declining resources and fractured internal cohesion. In cities like Milwaukee, it is not the absence of working people that define underclass neighborhoods but more the absence of effective social institutions. Without community controlled institutions, conventional values will have diminished appeal, neighborhoods will segment, solidarity will weaken, and working residents will continue to flee. The research on Milwaukee is consistent with the basic tenet of social theory, that the lack of effective institutions is related to crime and delinquency. The data support Spergel and others who call for "community mobilization and more resources for and reform of the educational system and job market" (Spergel and Curry 1990:309) as the most effective approach to gang control.

This article does support Wilson and others who call for massive new federal job programs. While lobbying for new state and federal job programs, social scientists should also focus on ways to encourage private and public investment in poor neighborhoods and advocate for more community control of social institutions. This means a stepped up involvement by academics in the workings of the large public bureaucracies which control resources needed to rebuild these communities.[9]

In the words of C. Wright Mills, bureaucracies "often carry out series of apparently rational actions without any ideas of the ends they serve" (Mills 1959:168). All too often the ends public bureaucracies serve are not helpful for poor communities. This article can be read as a call for social scientists to step up the struggle to make public bureaucracies more rational for the truly disadvantaged.[10]

Notes

1. Moore (1991) also finds a mixing of gang cliques in Los Angeles gangs. Short's (1990a) 1960 Nobles were mainly employed in the early 1970s when they were restudied, in contrast to Vicelords, virtually all of whom had more prison experience, many of whom still identified with the Vicelords and were involved in illegal operations more than a decade after they were first studied.
2. Child protective clients, however, more than other residents, turned to police for help with problems than asking help from their relatives or neighbors.
3. In contrast, zip code 53204, a predominantly Hispanic area home to several Hispanic gangs, is dotted with community agencies, banks, merchants, and grocery stores. While this area is a neighborhood of first settlement for Mexican immigrants, it does not have the characteristics of social disorganization of the predominantly African-American 53206 neighborhoods. Those who use "percent Hispanic" as a proxy for social disorganization should take note of these findings (cf. Curry and Spergel 1988:387).
4. There are other institutions in the area with a high profile, particularly law enforcement. But the strong police presence plays to a mixed review. While most residents (38.3 percent) called the police for any serious problems in the neighborhood before they called relatives or friends, one in eight (12.1 percent) listed police as one of the three top "bad things" about the neighborhood. Police are still viewed with suspicion and fear in African-American communities.
5. It must be remembered, however, that the illegal drug economy, while disruptive, is also sustained by a local demand. Workers in drug houses assert that most Milwaukee cocaine sales are to people within the neighborhood, not to outsiders (in contrast to Kornblum and Williams [1985:11]). But when illegal activities bring trouble to the neighborhood, particularly violence, police are often welcomed in ousting drug dealers and combatting gang problems (Sullivan 1989:128).
6. City hall may be as capable today of using academics against Washington for its own purposes as Washington in the sixties was adept at using academics to attack city hall (Gouldner 1968, Piven and Cloward 1971).
7. Recent control group evaluations have questioned these programs' effectiveness in reducing out of home placements. The main conclusion from the evaluations is the incapacity of social service bureaucracies to refer the appropriate clients to the programs. The evaluations found family preservation programs are so effective that social workers try to place families in the programs even though they do not fit project guidelines (cf. Feldman 1990, Schuerman et al. 1990, Yuan 1990). These evaluations also point out the important role social scientists can play in insisting programs be properly implemented.
8. This was also Suttles' conclusion: as community ties to external forces increased, so did its internal social control—it became more "provincial" (1968:223–224). Social disorganization and social control, Sullivan also points out, is not linear, but varies widely between poor neighborhoods (Sullivan 1989: 237).
9. This recommendation is not a call for revisiting the Chicago Area Project which relied on private financing and performed a "mediating role" with local institutions (Schlossman and Sedlak 1983, Sorrentino 1959), nor is it a call for a new war on poverty with built in antagonism between city hall and short lived federally funded agencies (Marris and Rein 1967, Moynihan 1969). Rather, it is a call for academics to directly engage in local struggles over how and where large public bureaucracies distribute existing resources.
10. This article is based on several previous papers. The first was presented on April 24, 1990, to the U.S. Conference of Mayors in Washington, D.C. Two others were presented

at the 85th Annual ASA Meetings, also in Washington D.C., August, 1990. Joan Moore, Carl Taylor, Howard Fuller, and Clinton Holloway made helpful comments on various earlier drafts. *Social Problems'* anonymous reviewers also added valuable insights. Correspondence to Hagedorn, University of Wisconsin–Milwaukee, Urban Research Center, P.O. Box 413, Milwaukee, WI 53201.

References

Altshuler, Alan A. 1970. *Community Control, The Black Demand for Participation in Large American Cities*. New York: Pegasus.

Anderson, Elijah. 1990. *Streetwise: Race, Class, and Change in an Urban Community.* Chicago: University of Chicago Press.

Aponte, Robert. 1988 "Conceptualizing the underclass: An alternative perspective." Paper presented at Annual Meetings of the American Sociological Association. August. Atlanta, Georgia.

Bluestone, Barry, and Bennett Harrison. 1982. *The Deindustrialization of America: Plant Closings, Community Abandonment, and the Dismantling of Basic Industry.* New York: Basic Books.

Chubb, John E., and Terry M. Moe. 1990. *Politics, Markets, and America's Schools*. Washington, D.C.: The Brookings Institute.

Cloward, Richard, and Lloyd Ohlin. 1960. *Delinquency and Opportunity*. Glencoe, IL: Free Press.

Comer, James P. 1972. *Beyond Black and White*. New York: Quadrangle Books.

Curry, G. David, and Irving A. Spergel. 1988. "Gang homicide, delinquency, and community." *Criminology* 26:381–405.

Feldman, Leonard. 1990. "Evaluating the impact of family preservation services in New Jersey." Trenton, NJ: New Jersey Division of Youth and Family Services.

Figueira-McDonough, Josefina. 1991. "Community structure and delinquency: A typology." *Social Service Review* 65:68–91.

Gans, Herbert J. 1990. "The dangers of the underclass: Its harmfulness as a planning concept." New York: Russell Sage Foundation, Working Paper #4.

Geis, Gilbert. 1965. "Juvenile gangs." Washington, D.C.: President's Committee on Juvenile Delinquency and Youth Crime.

Goldstein, Herman. 1977. *Policing a Free Society.* Cambridge, MA: Ballinger Publishing.

Goldstein, Paul J. 1985. "The drugs-violence nexus: A tripartite conceptual framework." *Journal of Drug Issues* 15:493–506.

Gouldner, Alvin. 1968. "The sociologist as partisan: Sociology and the welfare state." *The American Sociologist* May:103–116.

Hagedorn, John M. 1988. *People and Folks: Gangs, Crime, and the Underclass in a Rustbelt City.* Chicago: Lakeview.

——. 1989a. "Roots of Milwaukee's underclass." Milwaukee, WI: Milwaukee County Department of Health and Human Services.

——. 1989b. "Study of youth released from residential treatment, day treatment, and group homes in 1989." Milwaukee, WI: Milwaukee County Department of Health and Human Services.

Huff, C. Ronald. 1989. "Youth gangs and public policy." *Crime and Delinquency* 35:524–537.

Jencks, Christopher. 1989. "Who is the underclass—and is it growing?" *Focus* 12:14–31.

Johnson, Bruce, Terry Williams, Kojo Dei, and Harry Sanabria. 1989. "Drug abuse in the inner city." In *Drugs and the Criminal Justice System*, ed. Michael Tonry and James Q. Wilson. Chicago: University of Chicago.

Kamerman, Sheila B., and Alfred J. Kahn. 1989. "Social services for children, youth, and families in the United States." Greenwich, CT: The Annie E. Casey Foundation.

Kasarda, John D. 1985. "Urban change and minority opportunities." In *The New Urban Reality*, ed. Paul E. Peterson, 33–65. Washington, D.C.: The Brookings Institute.

Kornblum, William, and Terry Williams. 1985. *Growing Up Poor.* Lexington, MA: Lexington Books.

Lindblom, Charles E. 1959. "The Science of 'Muddling Through.'" *Public Administrative Review* 19:79–88.

Lipsky, Michael. 1980. *Street-Level Bureaucracies: Dilemmas of the Individual in Public Services*. New York: Russell Sage.

Marris, Peter, and Martin Rein. 1967. *Dilemmas of Social Reform, Poverty, and Community Action in the United States*. Chicago: University of Chicago.

Massey, Douglas S., and Mitchell L. Eggers. 1990. "The ecology of inequality: Minorities and the concentration of poverty, 1970–1980." *American Journal of Sociology* 95:1153–1188.

Meyer, John M., and Brian Rowan. 1981. "Institutionalized organizations: Formalized structure as myth and ceremony." In *Complex Organizations: Critical Perspectives*, ed. Mary Zey-Ferrell and Michael Aiken, 303–321. Glenview, IL: Scott, Foresman, and Company.

Miller, Walter. 1990. "Why the United States has failed to solve its youth gang problem." In

Gangs in America, ed. C. Ronald Huff, 263–287. Beverly Hills, CA: Sage.

Mills, C. Wright. 1959. *The Sociological Imagination*. London: Oxford University Press.

Moore, Joan W. 1985. "Isolation and stigmatization in the development of an underclass: The case of Chicano gangs in East Los Angeles." *Social Problems* 33:1–10.

——. 1991. *Going Down to the Barrio*. Philadelphia: Temple University Press.

Moore, Joan W., and Ronald Edari. 1990a. "Survey of Chips clients: Final report." Milwaukee: University of Wisconsin–Milwaukee Urban Research Center.

——. 1990b. "Youth initiative needs assessment survey: Final report." Milwaukee: University of Wisconsin–Milwaukee.

Moynihan, Daniel P. 1969. *Maximum Feasible Misunderstanding: Community Action in the War on Poverty*. New York: The Free Press.

Nelson, Douglas. 1988. "Recognizing and realizing the potential of 'family preservation.'" Washington, D.C.: Center for the Study of Social Policy.

Nelson, Kristine, Miriam J. Landsman, and Wendy Deutelman. 1990. "Three Models of Family-Centered Placement Protection Services." *Child Welfare* 69:3–21.

Perkins, Useni Eugene. 1987. *Explosion of Chicago's Street Gangs*. Chicago: Third World Press.

Piven, Frances Fox, and Richard A. Cloward. 1971. *Regulating the Poor: The Functions of Public Welfare*. New York: Pantheon.

——. 1987. "The contemporary relief debate." In *The Mean Season: The Attack On the Welfare State*, ed. Fred Block, Richard A. Cloward, Barbara Ehrenreich, and Frances Fox Piven, 45–108. New York: Pantheon.

Ricketts, Erol, and Ronald Mincy. 1988. "Growth of the underclass: 1970–1980." Washington, D.C.: Changing Domestic Priorities Project, The Urban Institute.

Ricketts, Erol, Ronald Mincy, and Isabel V. Sawhill. 1988. "Defining and measuring the underclass." *Journal of Policy Analysis and Management* 7:316–325.

Sampson, Robert J. 1987. "Urban black violence: The effect of male joblessness and family disruption." *American Journal of Sociology* 93:348–382.

Schlossman, Steven, and Michael Sedlak. 1983. "The Chicago Area Project revisited." Santa Monica, CA: Rand Corporation.

Schlossman, Steven L., Gail Zellman, and Richard Schavelson. 1984. *Delinquency Prevention in South Chicago*. Santa Monica, CA: Rand Corporation.

Schorr, Lisbeth. 1988. *Within Our Reach*. New York: Doubleday.

Schuerman, John R., Tina L. Pzepnicki, Julia H. Littell, and Stephen Budde. 1990. "Some intruding realities." Chicago: University of Chicago, Chapin Hall Center for Children.

Shaw, Clifford R., and Henry D. McKay. 1969. *Juvenile Delinquency and Urban Areas*. Chicago: University of Chicago.

Short, James F. 1990a. "Gangs, neighborhoods, and youth crime." Houston, TX: Sam Houston State University Criminal Justice Center.

——. 1990b. "New wine in old bottles? Change and continuity in American gangs." In *Gangs in America*, ed. C. Ronald Huff, 223–239. Beverly Hills, CA: Sage.

Short, James F., and Fred L. Strodtbeck. 1965. *Group Process and Gang Delinquency*. Chicago: University of Chicago.

Sorrentino, Anthony. 1959. "The Chicago Area Project after 25 years." *Federal Probation* 23:40–45.

Spergel, Irving A., and G. David Curry. 1990. "Strategies and perceived agency effectiveness in dealing with the youth gang problem." In *Gangs in America*, ed. C. Ronald Huff, 288–309, Beverly Hills, CA: Sage.

Stack, Carol B. 1974. *All Our Kin*. New York: Harper Torchback.

Sullivan, Mercer L. 1989. *Getting Paid: Youth Crime and Work in the Inner City*. Ithaca, NY: Cornell University Press.

Suttles, Gerald D. 1968. *The Social Order of the Slum*. Chicago: University of Chicago.

Taylor, Carl. 1990. *Dangerous Society*. East Lansing: Michigan State University Press.

Thrasher, Frederick. [1927] 1963. *The Gang*. Chicago: University of Chicago.

Trotter, Joe William. 1985. *Black Milwaukee: The Making of an Industrial Proletariat 1915–1945*. Chicago: University of Illinois.

Vigil, Diego. 1988. *Barrio Gangs*. Austin: University of Texas Press.

Weick, Karl E. 1976. "Educational organizations as loosely coupled systems." *Administrative Science Quarterly* 21:1–19.

White, Sammis, John F. Zipp, Peter Reynolds, and James R. Paetsch. 1988. "The Changing Milwaukee Industrial Structure." Milwaukee: University of Wisconsin–Milwaukee, Urban Research Center.

Whyte, William Foote. 1943. *Street Corner Society*. Chicago: University of Chicago.

Wilson, James Q. 1990. "Can government agencies be managed?" *The Bureaucrat* 9:29–33.

Wilson, William Julius. 1985. "Cycles of deprivation and the underclass debate." *Social Service Review* 59:541–559.

——. 1987. *The Truly Disadvantaged*. Chicago: University of Chicago.

——. 1991. "Studying inner-city social dislocations: The challenge of public agenda research." *American Sociological Review* 56:1–14.

Wineman, Steven. 1984. *The Politics of Human Services*. Boston: South End Press.

Yuan, Ying-Ying T. 1990. "Evaluation of AB 1562 in-home care demonstration projects." Sacramento, CA: Walter R. McDonald and Associates. ✦

Chapter 23
G-Dog and the Homeboys

Celeste Fremon

Given the vast array of gang intervention approaches and the sometimes hopeless sense that nothing works, we include this inspirational story of one individual's efforts to make a difference. In the following article, Fremon describes the one-man gang reform program found in Father Gregory Boyle of East Los Angeles. He offers schooling, job programs and counseling to the gang members in his community, as well as a caring, supportive relationship with these youths. While he touches the lives of so many of the gang members around him, it remains inevitable that the efforts of one person can do little to diminish the escalation of gang activity and violence.

At exactly 7 p.m. on an uncommonly warm night in early March, 1990, some 300 mourners, most of them members of the Latino gang the East L.A. Dukes, descend upon Dolores Mission Church at the corner of 3rd and Gless streets in Boyle Heights. They arrive by the carload and cram themselves into the scarred wooden pews that fill the sanctuary. As they file into the small stucco building, they cast edgy glances toward the street, as if expecting trouble. They are here for the funeral of Hector Vasquez, a.k.a. Flaco, 17, killed by a single shot to the head two nights before in a drive-by incident that took place at the nearby Aliso Village housing project.

The attire worn this night conforms to the unwritten gang code of dress. Girl gang members wear their hair long at the bottom and teased high at the crown, their lipstick blood-red. The boys sport perfectly pressed white Penney's T-shirts, dark Pendleton shirts and cotton work pants called Dickies, worn four sizes too big and belted, a contemporary interpretation of the old pachuco style. About 20 boys and girls wear sweat shirts emblazoned with iron-on Old English lettering that reads: "IN LOVING MEMORY OF OUR HOMIE FLACO R.I.P."

Outside the church, the police are very much in evidence. A couple of black-and-whites sit, just around the corner, motors running. Two beige unmarked cars, the kind favored by the LAPD's special gang unit, and one plain white Housing Police sedan continuously circle the block.

At first, the mood in the church is tense, expectant. But when taped synthesizer music throbs from loudspeakers, the sound seems to open an emotional spigot. The shoulders of the mourners start to shake with grief.

Behind the altar, a bearded man in glasses and priest's vestments sits quietly, watching the crying gangsters. When the music ends, Father Gregory Boyle rises and, taking a microphone, steps down to a point smack in front of the first row of mourners. From a distance, with his receding hair line and beard going to gray, he looks well past middle age. Up close, he is clearly much younger, not yet even 40.

Boyle takes a breath. "I knew Flaco for a long time," he says, his gaze traveling from face to face in the pews. "He used to work here at the church. I knew him as a very loving, great-hearted and kind man." Boyle pauses. "And now we shouldn't ask who killed Flaco, but rather *what* killed him. Flaco died of a disease that is killing La Raza, a disease called gang-banging." The crowd shifts nervously.

"So how do we honor Flaco's memory?" Boyle asks. "We will honor him best by doing what he would want us to do." Another pause. "He would want us to stop killing each other."

All at once, there is a commotion in the sixth row. A hard-eyed kid of 18 with the street name Magoo stands bolt upright and makes his way to the center aisle. Slowly, deliberately, he walks down the aisle, until he stands in front of Boyle, staring the priest straight in the eye. Then he turns and walks out a side door.

The air in the church is as brittle as glass when Boyle begins speaking again: "If we *knew* Flaco and *loved* Flaco, then we would stop killing each other."

Four more gangsters stand and walk out. Boyle's face reddens and then turns pale, as the mourners wait to see what he will do. Finally his jaw sets. "I loved Flaco," he says, his eyes starting to tear. "And I swear on Flaco's dead body that he would want us to stop killing each other."

The words explode in crisp, stunning bursts like so many rounds of live ammunition. Two more gang members get up and leave—but these boys walk with their heads down, their gaits rapid and scuttling. The rest of the mourners sit stock still, transfixed by the ferocity of Boyle's gaze. "We honor his memory," he says quietly, "if we can do this."

Father Gregory Boyle is the pastor of Dolores Mission Church, which serves a parish that is unique in several ways. First, it is the poorest in the Catholic Archdiocese of Los Angeles—it is dominated by a pair of housing projects: Pico Gardens and Aliso Village. Second, within the parish boundaries, which enclose about two square miles of Boyle Heights east of the Los Angeles River, seven Latino gangs and one African-American gang claim neighborhoods. This means that in an area smaller than the UCLA campus there are eight separate armies of adolescents, each equipped with small- and large-caliber weapons, each of which may be at war with one or more of the others at any given moment.

The Clarence Street Locos is the largest of the gangs, with close to 100 members; Rascals is the smallest, with 30 or so. The rest—Al Capone, the East L.A. Dukes, Cuatro Flats, The Mob Crew (TMC, for short), Primera Flats and the East Coast Crips (the single black gang in this predominantly Latino area)—hover in size from 50 to 80 teen-age boys and young men. However large the membership, the "'hood," or territory, that each gang claims is minuscule—no more than a block or two square. A member of one gang cannot safely walk the half-block from his mother's apartment to the corner store if that store is in enemy territory—much less walk the five or 10 blocks (across as many 'hoods) to reach his assigned junior high or high school.

According to statistics compiled by the Hollenbeck Division of the LAPD, gang-related crimes in East Los Angeles were up a sobering 20 percent from 1989 to 1990 and are rising again, up 11 percent over the same period last year. It is hardly surprising, therefore, that in his five years as parish priest Greg Boyle has buried 17 kids who were shot to death by rival gang members, and two who were shot to death by sheriff's deputies.[1] He himself has been in the line of fire seven times.

This is the tragic heart of the barrio, a bleak and scary part of Los Angeles that much of the rest of the city would like to block from its consciousness. Here junkies and baseheads pump gas for handouts at self-service filling stations, and bullet craters in the stucco walls of houses and stores serve as mnemonic devices, reminders of where this kid was killed, that one wounded. Yet surface impressions are not the whole of the matter in this parish: Beyond the most insistent images of gang violence, poverty and despair, a more redemptive vision comes into focus, a vision that comes clearest around Father Boyle.

Boyle lives simply. He wears the same burgundy zip-front sweat shirt every cold day, and the same rotating selection of five shirts when the days are sunny. His sleeping quarters are half a mile from the church, in a 1913-vintage two-story clapboard dwelling that he shares with six other Jesuits.

His days are long. They start at 7 a.m., often with a trip to Juvenile Court to testify in a gang member's behalf. They end close to midnight when Boyle takes one last bicycle ride around the projects to make sure that no trouble is brewing. In between, along with two assistants at Dolores Mission, he performs the conventional range of pastoral duties: saying Mass, hearing confessions, officiating at weddings and funerals or simply working in his monastic-cell of an office, dealing with parish business.

Whenever the door to Boyle's office opens, gang members swoop in like baby chicks for a feeding. They come to him to have their hair cut, to ask for a job through his Jobs for a Future program, to sign up to feed the homeless (to comply with court-ordered community service), to ask for admission to Dolores Mission Alternative, the school that he started as a sort of Last Chance U. for gang members. But mostly they come to hang out, to talk, to tease and be teased, to laugh. Around Boyle, the gangsters' defensive "screw you" expressions drop away. Twelve-year-old wanna-bes and 20-year-old tough-eyed *veteranos* jockey to be the favored child and sit next to Boyle in his car on his daily errands. They aren't afraid to cry in his presence. They find any excuse to touch him. The gangsters have even christened Boyle with his own placa, his street name: G-Dog. But most simply call him G.

"G. is always there when you need him," says one precariously reformed gangster. "I don't have a dad. So I think of him like my father. Even when I was in jail, he always had time to talk to me. Even when nobody else was there for me. And, you know, when I wanted to stop gang-banging, sometimes I would have so much anger that I wanted to do something, kill somebody. But I would talk to Father Greg and he would help me so I didn't explode inside. He's the one we can all look up to."

The term "dysfunctional family," one of the fashionable buzz phrases of the 90s, acquires a special meaning in the Dolores Mission parish. Not long ago, on a whim, Boyle sat down at his computer and made a list of all the gang kids who immediately came to mind. Next to each name he wrote a coded description of the youth's family situation: "AB" for father absent; "A" for alcoholic father; "AA" for alcoholic and abusive; "ABU" for just plain abusive, "S" for stepfather, "I" for intact original family.

"I didn't stack the deck or anything," he explains. "I just wrote down 67 names sort of stream-of-consciousness. I found that most fathers were absent. The second biggest categories were alcoholic and alcoholic/abusive." Out of 67 kids, only three had intact families with fathers who were not alcoholic or abusive.

Pick three, any three, of the gang members that hover around Boyle's door and delve into their family dynamics and the stories will disturb your sleep. There is Bandito[2], whose father died two years ago of a heroin overdose. There is Smiley[2], whose father is continually drunk and abusive. There is Gato[2], whose basehead mother sold his only warm jacket to buy another hit. Or Gustavo Martinez, Javier Villa and Guadelupe Lopez—Grumpy, Termite and Scoobie, respectively.

Grumpy's father was gone long before he was born. His mother beat him with the plug-end of the television cord, with the garden hose, a spiked belt—anything she could find. The beatings were so severe that she was jailed several times for child abuse. Some abusive parents are by turns affectionate and rejecting. Not this mother. In all the years of Grumpy's upbringing, he never received a birthday gift or a Christmas gift or even a card.

"Imagine," says Boyle, "not one piece of concrete evidence of caring from a parent throughout a whole childhood."

In Termite's case, the blows were not to the body. His mother always professed great love for him. His father never hit him. What his father did was tell him he was worthless, despicable and generally a bad seed. Even now, when Boyle drops Termite at home, a call will sometimes come minutes later. It will be Termite pleading to sleep in Boyle's office for the night. "My dad locked me out," he will say.

"I know he cares about me," says Termite, as if the words are a spell capable of making it so. But when pushed on the subject he averts his eyes. "I guess mostly he just acts like I'm not there."

Sometimes it is not the parents but life in the barrio that provides the abuse. Scoobie's last memory of his alcoholic father was when he was 3; his dad knocked his mother off her feet, cuffed Scoobie to the floor and snarled: "What're you lookin' at?" Scoobie's mother gathered her kids and fled. However, the hotel in which she found shelter was so crime-ridden that, before he was 5, Scoobie witnessed three lurid murders, virtually on his doorstep. Add to that the problems of a young single mother with no resources and no child care and the picture becomes still bleaker.

Scoobie's mother padlocked her pre-school-age children in a darkened hotel room while she went to work for the day. "She was trying to keep us safe," says Scoobie. When he is asked if his childhood had any happy times, he thinks for a moment: "I remember this one day when my mom took us all to the park and let us run around. It was so great, you know. For once we weren't stuffed up in that little room. And we felt, I don't know, just—free!"

So what does a barrio kid do when family and society have failed him? When he turns 14 or 15, he joins a gang, a surrogate family, where he finds loyalty, self-definition, discipline, even love of a sort. "We all want to be attached to something," says Diego Vigil, an anthropology professor at USC who has studied gangs. "We want to connect and commit. If we can't find anywhere else to connect and commit, we'll connect and commit to the streets. The gang takes over the parenting, the schooling and the policing."

On a Sunday afternoon in January, 1991, Father Boyle takes Scoobie and Grumpy shopping for clothes. Both of them are large kids, bulky and muscular, each with a proclivity for fast, funny patter delivered half in English, half in Spanish. They are members of the Mob Crew and the Clarence Street Locos, respectively—traditionally friendly gangs whose neighborhoods are close to the church. Scoobie is 19 and Grumpy is 20, both *veteranos*, both too old to attend Dolores Mission Alternative. They are desperate to find employment. Their shopping destination is Sears. The idea is to get them non-gangster attire to wear to job interviews.

In the men's department, Boyle pulls out pants and shirts for them to try on. He is careful to choose light colors. Grumpy and Scoobie keep edging back in the direction of the gangster look: dark colors and a baggy fit.

"Hey G., these pants are too tight," wails Scoobie. In reality, the pants fit perfectly.

"They're fine," Boyle counters, and Scoobie relents.

"Look," Boyle says to Scoobie and Grumpy as he hands the cashier a Sears credit card, "I'm spending a lot of bank on this today, and the deal is you have to be dressed and in my office every morning at 9 a.m., ready to look for work." The two nod obediently and assure Boyle that they will indeed comply.

Both Scoobie and Grumpy are staying in Casa Miguel Pro, the temporary residence that Dolores Mission maintains for homeless women and children. "I'm trying an experiment in letting them stay there," Boyle explains. "A lot of folks aren't exactly thrilled that I'm doing this. But right now neither of them has anywhere else they can go."

After the shopping trip, Scoobie irons his new tan pants and shirt striped in shades of blue. Next he takes a bath. Finally he puts on the freshly pressed clothes and looks in a communal mirror.

"That ain't me . . ." he says softly to the mirror. He stands back a little and looks again. "I look like a regular person," he says, his expression so happy it borders on giddiness. "Not like the police say, not like another *gang member*."

When Greg Boyle first came to Dolores Mission in early July, 1986, at age 32 the youngest pastor in the L.A. Archdiocese, he hardly seemed likely to become "the gang priest." Raised in comfortable Windsor Square on the outskirts of Hancock Park, one of eight children of a third-generation dairyman, he attended Loyola High School, the Jesuit-run boys' school on Venice Boulevard, from 1968 to 1972. It was a wildly inspiring four years for an idealistic Catholic kid. His teachers led peace marches protesting the Vietnam War, and activist Jesuits were making news all over the country as liberation theology—which marries social justice to spiritual renewal—came to full flower.

Boyle spent the next 13 years in religious training, culminating in his 1984 ordination in Los Angeles. He was posted to Bolivia, the poorest country in the Western Hemisphere, where he became the parish priest in a small village. The experience radicalized the young, middle-class priest from Southern California. "Bolivia turned me absolutely inside out," says Boyle. "After Bolivia my life was forever changed." He realized he wanted to work with the poor. And few places were poorer than Dolores Mission.

Boyle's first year in the parish was tense and difficult. The priest before him had been a venerable *Mexicano*, and the community was slow to warm up to an Anglo, especially one so young. Since so few parishioners came to him, he decided to go to them. Every afternoon without fail, Boyle walked for hours through the neighborhood, particularly through the housing projects where most of his parishioners lived. He talked to people, listened to their complaints, played with their children. Over time he noticed that the majority of the complaints centered upon one issue: gangs.

Boyle made an effort to get to know the gangsters. He began by learning their names. At first, they brutally rejected the *gavacho* who spoke only passable Spanish. But he kept going back to them. "And you know," he says, "at some point it becomes sort of flattering that the priest knows who you are." Then he started going to Juvenile Hall to visit when kids got locked up, bringing messages from their homeboys. Or he'd rush to the hospital if they got shot.

He noticed that the kids who got into the most trouble were the kids who were not in school, and the reasons they were not in school were invariably gang-related. Either they had gotten kicked out of school because they had been fighting with enemy gang members, or the school itself was in enemy territory and deemed unsafe by the kids.

So in September, 1988, Father Boyle and one of his associates at Dolores Mission, Father Tom Smolich, opened a junior high and high school for gang members only. Dolores Mission Alternative was started on the third floor of Dolores Mission Elementary, the church's grammar school. Through home study and specially designed classes, the school aimed to get the kids back on an educational track, or at the least to help them pass the high-school equivalency exam.

Boyle also started hiring gang members to work around the church at $5 an hour. "And before I knew it there was no turning back," he laughs. "I felt like I sort of related to the gang members. They were fun and warm and eternally interesting. So gradually," he says, "it became a ministry within a ministry."

The rest of the parish, however, didn't find the gangsters quite so "warm" and "interesting." They saw only hair-netted homeboys doing heaven-knows-what in the same building with uniformed parochial-school children. Worse yet, these same "criminal types" were hanging out at the church as if it was their personal clubhouse. In the fall of 1989, Boyle's most virulent critics circulated a petition asking then-Archbishop Roger M. Mahony to remove him from the parish altogether.

Things came to a head one October night. Boyle had called a meeting to clear the air. The school basement was packed with Boyle supporters and *contras* when a swarm of gang members unexpectedly walked in, underlining the tension in the room. One by one, the homies got up and talked: "We're human beings, and we need help. And Father Greg is helping us."

Slowly the tension began to lift. Parish parents rose to speak: "Father Greg is right," they said. "These gang members are not the enemy. They are our children. And if we don't help them no one will."

That was the turning point. The parish stopped fighting Boyle's programs and began adopting them as their own. In short order, the Comité Pro Paz en el Barrio, the Committee for Peace in the Barrio, was formed to address the gang situation. Parish mothers who had never before attended so much as a PTA meeting suddenly became activists in the gangsters' behalf, organizing a peace march, holding a gang conference.

"What is going on at Pico-Aliso is very different than anything else I've seen elsewhere in the city," says Yolanda Chavez, for the last two years Mayor Tom Bradley's official liaison to the L.A. Latino community. "A lot of people are well-meaning, but they don't help people organize themselves. They do things for them. Father Greg's goal is always to help the people help themselves. He has become a focal point for their strength, empowering the community to provide the gang members with alternatives."

Scoobie has been job-hunting for three weeks straight, but now he is sitting in Boyle's office and he looks terrible. His lips and jaw are bruised and swollen. His hands are cut up, and an incisor on the lower left side of his jaw is broken. He has just returned from the dentist. Boyle will pay the dental bills, which may be close to a thousand dollars.

It happened two nights ago, says Scoobie, when he was stopped by two uniformed police officers. He was doing nothing in particular—just hanging out with the homies when the officers ordered him up against a car with his hands over his head. "Then they pushed me down on my knees," he says. Scoobie responded with a four-letter suggestion. At that point, according to Scoobie, one of the cops hit him in the mouth with a billy club. Then, he says, the cops made him lie down spread-eagled and stepped on his hands. Finally the police let him go without an arrest.

One of the activist parish mothers, Pam McDuffie, took Scoobie to the Hollenbeck Police Station to report the incident. The case is currently under investigation by Internal Affairs, but Boyle believes Scoobie's story implicitly. "This is one of many, many cases of the police beating the kids down," he says.

A few days after Scoobie's trip to the dentist, there is new trouble. Boyle arrives at his office in the morning to find a message on his answering machine. "Hey G.," says a young voice, "tell Grumpy I don't have the money for the gun but I'll have the money soon." Boyle stares at the machine boggle-eyed. It is nearly inconceivable that someone would leave such a message with him.

Boyle goes upstairs to Grumpy's room, and in a kind of false wall in the closet he finds a gun-cleaning kit and a metal strongbox. The box is heavy and the lid is stuck. Boyle carts it down to his office and shuts the door before prying the lid open. Inside, he finds $178 in cash, a neat list of investors and a box of 9-millimeter Beretta shells.

Boyle shuts the box, puts it in a desk drawer and waits for Grumpy's inevitable appearance. The confrontation goes as follows:

"Do you have a gun?"

"No, G."

"Are you collecting money for a gun?"

"No, G."

Boyle opens the drawer to reveal the strong box. "You've really let me down," he says quietly.

Grumpy's face turns to stone. "When do you want me to leave?" he asks. Then eyes averted and brimming, he turns and walks out.

Two hours later Grumpy is back. "G., I know I let you down! I let you down, *gacho*! I let you down big time!"

Boyle cannot bring himself to make Grumpy leave. "I know tough love is sometimes required," he philosophizes later. "I just don't know how tough the love should be."

A solution to the gang problem has been eluding Los Angeles Police Department for decades, and from law enforcement's point of view, the "love" should be very tough indeed. The ongoing police anti-gang program is dubbed Operation Hammer. "Hammer is a strategy in which we keep the pressure on," says Captain Nick Salicos, recently of the Hollenbeck Division. "On a Friday or a Saturday night, we go out with 30 or 40 officers to known gang locations and arrest gang members for anything we can. Drinking beer in public. Anything." If the crime can be shown to be gang related, and the arrestee is a known gang member, the sentence can be "enhanced"—made longer.

"The police try to make life as miserable as possible for gang members," Boyle says, "which is really redundant since gang members' lives are already miserable enough, thank you very much. And they hate me, I guess, because, No. 1, I refuse to snitch on gang members. No. 2, they can't understand how I could care about these kids. And I can't understand why they insist on criminalizing every kid in this community."

A visit to Hollenbeck Police Station reveals that Boyle is correct; the police don't like him much. Mention the priest's name to most Hollenbeck officers and there is invariably much rolling of eyes, followed by remarks that range from the suggestion that Boyle is "well-meaning but dangerously naive" to veiled charges that he is an accessory to gang crimes to intimations that he is under the influence of Communists.

A ride-along in a black-and-white provides an instructive perspective. The streets seem meaner from inside a patrol car. The stares the police gather are hostile, threatening. "Although our job is to try to prevent gang crime," explains Detective Jack Forsman of the LAPD's special gang unit, CRASH (Community Resources Against Street Hoodlums), "more often than not we can do little more than pick up the pieces once a crime has been committed."

"What I don't get," adds another officer who requested anonymity, "is why Father Boyle refuses to preach against using guns and being in gangs."

The remark infuriates Boyle. "Aside from the fact that it just isn't true," he bristles, "it has no respect for the complexity of the issue. It's Nancy Reagan writ large: 'Just Say No' to gangs. I would say getting kids out of gangs is the whole point of my work here. But what is ultimately persuasive is a job and self-esteem and education and having the kid feel that he or she can put together in his or her imagination a future that is viable. Now I can sit there and say, 'Get out of the gang!' but I don't know what value that would have. If any of this is going to be successful, you have to accept folks where they are. What they always get is: 'Where you are is a horrible place and you'd better change.' Well, look how successful that's been."

Boyle sighs wearily. "Part of the problem," he says, "is that when you're poor in the city of Los Angeles, you're hard-pressed to imagine a future for yourself. And if you can't imagine a future, then you're not going to care a lot about the present. And then anything can happen."

Although his approach is controversial, Boyle is by no means the only person working with gangs who decries the Just Say No approach as simplistic. "We have tried that," says Chavez from Mayor Bradley's office, "and it hasn't worked. Force hasn't worked. Police harassment hasn't worked. Jail and Juvenile Hall hasn't worked. Without options, gangs will thrive."

Mary Ridgeway and John Tuchek are the two officers in the L.A. County Probation Department's East L.A. Gang Unit who deal with arrested juveniles from Pico Gardens or Aliso Village. "There is the illusion," says Tuchek, "that we are rehabilitating these kids. And I'm here to tell you that the truth is we aren't even trying to rehabilitate them. We used to. But that doesn't happen down here any more. That's why what Father Greg is doing is so important. He's their only resource."

Ridgeway puts it another way. "At best, we can only deal with a fraction of the kids for a very short period of time, while he's there for all of them, all of the time. Father Greg and I are, in many ways, coming from a different point of view philosophically," she continues. "There are kids that I think should be locked up who he is reluctant to give up on—like a kid we both know who, fortunately, now is in Soledad. He was trouble every minute he was out on the streets."

"But, see," she smiles, "Father Greg loves everybody. In all my years in probation I've met maybe two people who have his courage. He's the kind of person we all wish we could be."

In the month after Boyle finds Grumpy's gun fund, the Pico-Aliso gangs begin to turn up the heat. By early March, Boyle is depressed. "Things have been awful around here," he says one Monday morning. It seems that Looney, an East Coast Crip, was killed on Thursday as a payback for Clown, a Primera Flats kid who was shot by a Crip in September, 1990.

"That's how the game works," says Boyle grimly. The night after Looney was killed, two Latinos, one a transient and the other a basehead, were killed. No one is sure if these killings were gang-related or not. Moreover, the Crips and Al Capone, gangs that have traditionally gotten along, have had two fights in less than 48 hours.

The bad news didn't stop there. At about 8 p.m. on Saturday night, a kid from the Clarence Street Locos was headed down Gless Street to buy a beer when a Cuatro Flats kid approached him. Words were exchanged. Immediately each boy marched off to find his homies. In seconds, members of both gangs appeared from around corners, like magic rabbits, and began mad-dogging and dissing each other—glaring and shouting insults. A kid named Diablo from Cuatro hit Solo from Clarence, and someone yelled, "It's on!" War had been declared.

Suddenly, 80 gang members were blocking the intersection of 4th and Gless. Fists were flying, heads were bashed, ghetto blasters were swinging. All the while voices screamed, "It's on. It's on!"

It was then that Boyle showed up, almost by chance. He had just dropped a kid off at home when he saw traffic backed up, he pulled over and raced to investigate. Then the situation became surreal. Into a tangle of brawling gangsters ran Boyle, grabbing arms and shrieking every four-letter word he could think of. At his screamed orders, the Clarence group backed up. Cuatro stopped swinging and halted its advance. On the edge of the action, kids on bikes still circled, shotguns bulging underneath their Pendletons.

Finally, Boyle was able to herd the Clarence kids across 4th and down Gless; the Cuatro force moved off, dispersing into the neighborhood.

Afterward, Boyle was walking alongside Mando, who, with his identical twin, has a lot of juice with the Clarence Street Locos. "You *yelled* at us, G.," said Mando, shaking his head in genuine shock. "You used the *F word*!"

"In the moment," says Boyle later, "I'll do any damn thing that works."

It's raining. Four homies—Termite, Grumpy, Green and Critter—are hanging out in Boyle's office as he opens mail and does paper work.

Critter, a slim, handsome kid with long, fringed eyelashes and a heartbreaker's smile, rubs Boyle's ever-expanding forehead with the palm of his hand as Boyle unsuccessfully bats him away. "I'm rubbing your bumper for luck, G.!" says Critter, moving in for another rub.

"Hey, G.," interrupts Grumpy, "How come you're in such a good mood?" Turning to Green: "Have you ever noticed that whenever G. is in a good mood it rains?" Grumpy pauses, possessed of a new thought. "Hey, you think maybe G. is actually Mother Nature in disguise? That means the drought is his fault, right? You think the drought is your fault, G.?"

Boyle looks up at Grumpy. "Here's a letter here from a couple who want to adopt a child," he says, deadpan. "What do you think, Grumps? You think it's right for you?"

"Only if the *madre* is proper," sniffs Grumpy. Meanwhile, the imagined scene of an unsuspecting young couple being introduced to their new "child"—a 6-foot, 200-pound tattooed homie named Grumpy—throws the rest of the room into spasms of hilarity.

Grumpy is discouraged about his job prospects. He has been answering want ads for weeks to no avail, he says. "You go in there and you fill out an application. Then they say they'll call you but you can tell they're looking at your tattoos and they're not gonna, you know? It's like, when you leave, you see your application flying out the window made into a paper airplane."

Nonetheless, Grumpy has heard that applications are being taken at the post office on 1st Street. "C'mon, let's go," he says to Green.

"Nah," says Green, "they won't hire us."

"C'mon homes," Grumpy persists. "Let's just try it. Let's go." He attempts to drag Green.

"C'mon homes." But Green remains immovable. Finally, Grumpy sits back down with a sigh. No one goes to the post office this day.

After the homies vacate his office, Boyle stares dolefully at his checkbook. "Right now, I have a hundred dollars in the bank. And I have to pay the kids working for me on Friday." He looks up. "But, you know, it's weird. Somehow the money always shows up. It usually happens on Thursday, my day off. There'll be no money in the bank on Wednesday and then I'll come in on Friday and there'll be a couple of checks on my desk. Checks coming from nowhere when they had to come—that's happened at least 50 times since I first came here." Boyle pauses. "It's not like I think it comes from God. My spirituality doesn't really take that form. But I do feel that if the work is meant to be done, somehow there'll be a way."

"Now all I have to do is find $150,000 to give kids jobs this summer," he continues. "Invariably, the violence in the neighborhood decreases in direct proportion to how many kids are working at any given time."

With the Jobs for a Future program, Boyle usually has three or four construction and maintenance crews working on church projects. In addition, he is on the phone daily to local businesses asking them to hire homies. "We will pay their salaries," he tells the potential employers. "All you have to do is give them a place to work." Boyle adds: "Of course, it would be great if the employers would pay the salaries. But unfortunately, that rarely happens."

"The myth about gang members and jobs," says Boyle, "is how're you gonna keep 'em down on the farm when they're making money hand over fist selling drugs—the implication being that they will never want to accept an honest job. Well, I have kids stop me on the street every single day of the week asking for jobs. And a lot of times these are kids I know are slanging, which is the street term for selling crack cocaine. I always say, 'If I get you a job, it means no more slanging.' And I've never once said that to a kid who didn't jump at the chance to do an honest day's work instead of selling drugs."

Four days later it is Saint Patrick's Day, a generally uneventful Sunday until Grumpy approaches Boyle, his clothes and hands covered in paint. "Oh, I've been doing some painting at Rascal's house," he says, in answer to Boyle's questioning look. Then he screws his face into a grimace. "You know, G.," he says. "I'm not going to look for a job anymore."

Boyle's expression darkens. "Why?" he asks.

"I'm just not going to," replies Grumpy. "No more job hunting."

Boyle looks truly distressed by this news. "What are you talking about . . . ?" Boyle begins.

"Nope. I'm not looking for a job any more," is all Grumpy will say.

Boyle throws up his hands. "What the hell am I supposed to do? Support you for the rest of your life?"

Finally, Grumpy's face breaks into a gigantic grin. "I'm not going to look for a job any more BECAUSE I FOUND A JOB, G.," he shouts. "I'm a painter! I'm painting stereo speakers!"

The rest of the day, Boyle cannot restrain himself. He tells Grumpy how proud he is, over and over. Grumpy tries to stay cool but his happiness is obvious and irrepressible.

Termite is one of the regulars in and around Boyle's office. He is 16, has the huge, dark eyes of a yearling deer and a smile that unfolds fast, wide and bright. His hair is cut Marine short, shaved by Boyle with the No. 4 attachment of the church's clippers. On his upper lip there sprouts a pale hint of brown velvet. When he is happy, Termite's face is transformed into that of a deliciously mischievous child. In repose, his expression suggests someone waiting patiently for a punishment. At all times, his shoulders slump more than is natural.

Termite is a Clarence Street Loco, jumped into the gang less than a year ago. So far, his gang-banging has been confined to compulsive tagging: Walk in any direction from Dolores Mission and you soon see the spray-painted message "CSL *soy* Termite." Termite is not a kid drawn to violence. "I don't mind if you want to go head up," he says. "But it would be better if nobody had guns."

Since last summer, Termite has been pestering Boyle for a job. Finally, the priest has talked a local self-storage company into hiring two homies, courtesy of Dolores Mission. Termite and Stranger, a kid from The Mob Crew, get the call.

The timing is fortuitous. Termite's father has just gone to visit family in Mexico, and with the weight of his dad's anger briefly lifted, Termite is a new person. Instead of partying with the homies till all hours, he asks Boyle to drive him home before dark every night. He has all but stopped tagging and has started showing up at the alternative school every day.

The day before Termite and Stranger are to start work, Boyle drives them to meet their new boss, the manager of the storage company, a matter-of-fact woman named Yolanda. The boys listen quietly while she explains their duties—gofering and general cleanup. Afterward Boyle takes the two kids to McDonald's to celebrate.

"We won't let you down, G." says Termite.

One week later, events have derailed Termite's promise. On the first Sunday in April, at about 5 p.m., Boyle is driving across 1st Street, from East L.A. Dukes territory in Aliso Village toward the church. He sees a group of five Clarence kids, Grumpy and Termite among them, running in Pecan Park near the baseball diamond. It is not a playful run. Termite has a long stick under his jacket, as if he's packing a shotgun. On instinct, Boyle turns to look behind him and sees a group of East L.A. Dukes near home plate, also running. The Dukes are sworn enemies of the Clarence Street Locos.

Boyle swerves his car to a halt on the wrong side of the street, rolls down his window and yells to the Clarence kids to get the blankety-blank out of there. Amazingly they do. As he raises his hand to open his door, there is a terrifying BOOM-BOOM-BOOM-BOOM-BOOM. Just behind Boyle's head, the car's rear window on the driver's side shatters. When the shooting stops, Boyle gets out to confront the Dukes. They disappear fast as lightning.

Later, he drives back into Dukes territory. This time he finds them. "Did you want to f-kin' kill me?" he yells, hoping to shock them into a new state of consciousness. "I prayed you would hit me so then maybe it would end. I'd be willing to die to end this." The Dukes stare at him, then at the missing car window and the bullet holes in his car, one in the door frame no more than an inch from where Boyle's head had been. They murmur frantic, ineffectual apologies.

Then one boy looks up just in time to see two gangsters on the hill above them—East Coast Crips. An instant later the noise comes again: BOOM-BOOM-BOOM-BOOM-BOOM-BOOM. Everyone dives behind Boyle's car as the sky rains bullets. Miraculously, no one is hit. Instead a bullet has punctured the car's right rear tire, just missing the gas tank, and come to rest inside the trunk.

The next day, Boyle wakes up with no obvious ill effects from the near misses except for a piercing headache. The pain is localized just behind his ear, where neck meets skull. In other words, about where the doorframe bullet would have hit if it had taken only a slightly different course.

As usual, violence spawns more violence. On Monday morning, when Boyle arrives at the church, he gets a call from Yolanda, the manager of the storage facility where Termite and Stranger are working. She is going to have to fire Termite, she says. It seems that on Friday he not only crashed the facility's motorized cart, but, when he was supposed to remove graffiti from a wall, he replaced it with new inscriptions: "CSL *soy* Termite."

It does not strike Boyle as entirely coincidental that Termite's father returned from Mexico a few hours before Termite began this orgy of acting out. Nor does it help matters that the mood of the Clarence homies in general is restless. Two Clarence Street homeboys have been killed by Dukes since January, 1990, and Clarence has not yet retaliated. After yesterday's shooting, they will probably begin to feel intolerably pressed. And most of the pressure will fall on the little heads, the younger gang members like Termite who have yet to prove themselves.

Boyle takes Termite to lunch to break the bad news about the job. First he gives him a stern lecture about responsibility and consequences. Then he turns Good Cop and assures Termite that losing the job is not the end of the world. "You know I'll never give up on you," Boyle says. *"Te quiero mucho,"* he says finally. *"Como si fueras mi hijo"* ("I love you as if you were my son"). At this, Termite starts to cry. Once started he cries for a long while.

At the end of the day, Termite's actions are swinging farther out of control; he gets into a fight with one of his own homies. When Boyle sees him again, he is covered in blood.

"It's nothin'," he mumbles.

Then at about 2 the next afternoon, Father Smolich sees Termite deep in Dukes territory with a can of spray paint; he is crossing out Dukes graffiti and replacing it with his own. It is a dangerously provocative act, considering the events of the last two days. Smolich demands that Termite hand over the spray can. Termite dances rebelliously away.

Two hours later, Termite is back in Clarence territory, on the pay phone at the corner of Third and Pecan streets talking with his girlfriend, Joanna. He sees Li'l Diablo[2], another "new bootie" from Clarence, walking north toward 1st Street and Pecan Park, and sensing that something is up, he follows. All at once, Termite sees what is up: Li'l Diablo has a gun, and there is a group of Dukes gathered in the park. Termite watches as Li'l Diablo raises the gun, a .22, and fires one shot into the air. The Dukes scatter, running for the projects across 1st Street. Li'l Diablo drops his weapon and runs in the other direction.

At first Termite follows him. But then, on an impulse he cannot later adequately explain, Termite turns back and picks up the gun. Then he points it in the direction of the by-now faraway Dukes and empties it. Most of the bullets fall harmlessly to the pavement. However, one bullet strays into an apartment on Via Las Vegas, where a 6-year-old girl named Jackie is watching television with her mother. Jackie kicks up her small foot just in time for it to meet the bullet. Blood spurts, and her mother begins to scream.

Holding the empty gun, Termite stands on the sidewalk still as a statue for a long moment. Finally he runs.

In short order, the neighborhood is alive with rumor, and word of what has happened quickly reaches Boyle. It is hours before he finds Termite, milling nervously with some other homies a block from the church. Wordlessly, Termite climbs into Boyle's car.

"I know what happened," Boyle tells him. "Did you do it?"

There is a silence. "Yeah," Termite says without meeting Boyle's gaze.

Boyle informs him that he has hit a little girl. Termite is horrified. "A lot of people say," Boyle tells him, "that in order to be a man you have to shoot a gun. But I'm telling you that isn't true. The truth is, in order to be a man you need to take responsibility for your actions. That means you need to turn yourself in."

Termite starts to protest. Then he is quiet for a long while. "Let's go, G." he says finally.

Inside Hollenbeck Police Station, two CRASH officers order Termite to spread his legs. As the officers briskly frisk him, he stands with his lips pursed, trying not to cry.

Everyone who meets Greg Boyle seems to go through the same two-step process. Step one is as follows: "Hey, this guy is really some kind of a saint!" And then step two: "There's got to be a dark side."

Yet when you get to know Boyle well, you find no ominous recesses of the psyche or murky hidden agendas. There are small things: a healthy-size ego, or the way he at times seems more quarrelsome with the police than might be necessary. But nothing you'd call dark. What you do find, however, is a man in the grip of a paradox.

The other priests at Dolores Mission, however fond they are of the gang members, admit that they keep an emotional distance between themselves and a situation that can be overwhelming and tragic on a daily basis. For Boyle, there seems to be no distance. He cares for the gang members as if they were literally his own children. Certainly it is Boyle's offer of unconditional love that is the source of his magic. Pure love heals. But what happens if you give your heart to 10 dozen kids, many of whom will die violently and young, the rest of whom are dying slow deaths of the spirit?

"Burn-out is the cost, I think," Boyle says. "Because I'm so invested in each kid, tragedies and potential tragedies kind of get into my gut in a way they probably don't get into other folks'." He laughs nervously. "A lot of it is the classic ministerial occupational hazard of co-dependency, where you get too invested. Only it's kind of writ larger here, I think. And it's also parental. It's like, 'Oh my God, my kid hasn't come home yet and it's midnight' times a hundred."

The analogy of Boyle as parent can lead to still riskier territory. If you ask most parents what they would die for, they reply, "My children." Boyle grows uncharacteristically quiet when the question is posed to him. "I would die for these kids," he says finally. "I don't know how that would play itself out. But I don't think there would be any question. It's not a choice, you know," he says. "It just is."

This is not the first time Boyle has considered the possibility. The day the Dukes' gunfire hit his car and came within an inch of killing him, he realized that a line had been crossed. It was not that they had tried to kill him; it was that they had known he was in the line of fire and they had shot anyway.

Two weeks later he had another close call. Late at night, Boyle was walking one of the younger kids home when the boy whispered, "Look out." Boyle turned to see gangsters, guns at the ready, creeping along the bushes that fringe the Santa Ana Freeway on the east edge of Aliso Village. They were headed toward a group of TMC homies. But this time, seeing Boyle, no one shot.

"It was very similar to the day that the Dukes shot," Boyle says. "But that time I arrived a split second too late and the action had already been put in motion. This time I think I arrived just early enough to stop it."

"As I walked home that night I felt so weird. I kept saying to myself, 'I really think this is where my life will end. I'm going to die in this barrio.' "

He pauses, his eyes searching some interior distance. "But you know, what should I do differently? Would I not have intervened that day between Clarence and East L.A.? Just kept driving instead? I don't think that would be possible."

"So what should I do differently?"

The question hangs in the air like smoke after a fire.

Even Dukes were impressed by the fact that Termite had turned himself in. "That's *firme*! That's *firme*!" they said. But Termite's father assessed his actions differently. We could have gotten you to Mexico, he told Termite, his voice scathing. "Can't you do anything right?"

At Termite's court hearing, his fortunes take an unexpected turn. His public defender—a fast-talking, upwardly mobile fellow named Brady Sullivan—not only undermines a witness's testimony but also gets Termite's confession thrown out on a Miranda violation. Termite is set free.

As far as Boyle is concerned, this is good news and bad news. The good news is that a sensitive kid with no prior record will not get two to five in a California Youth Authority lockup. "Termite is a wonderful, wonderful kid," Boyle says. "And he shot a little girl. A lot of people can't hold those two thoughts together. But, the task of a true human being is do precisely that."

The bad news is that Termite will not go on a badly needed, if enforced, vacation. Instead, he will be back in the neighborhood and back in the gang life.

At first, Termite is euphoric at being free. But soon, reality sets in; the Dolores Mission neighborhood is no longer a safe place for him. His mother talks about sending him to live with an aunt in San Bernardino or his grandmother in Mexico, but Termite doesn't want to go. He says he wants to be near his girlfriend Joanna, a sunny-natured girl of 14. His mother relents on the condition that Termite stay away from the church and the projects.

For two weeks straight, Termite spends his days cooped up in a darkened house with his dad, who works at night. Predictably, it isn't long before the situation blows itself to smithereens. Termite is back hanging out, staying at friends' houses, tagging everything he can find, particularly in East L.A. Dukes territory.

Word is soon on the street that Termite is a marked man. His mother has answered the phone at home and heard the death threats. "It's hard to know what to do," Boyle worries out loud. "I don't want him to feel boxed in. When that happens a kid is likely to feel that the only thing to do is to go out in a blaze of glory, or take somebody else out in a blaze of glory."

When it is mentioned to Termite that he is all but asking to be killed, he cocks his head quizzically. "Sometimes I just don't care. Sometimes I feel like I want to die," he says, then looks away, "and I don't know why."

A week later, the inevitable has happened: Termite has been shot. He was hanging out with homies from both Clarence and TMC near the corner store at Gless and 4th. A truck whizzed by and dozens of bullets were fired. Only one connected. It grazed the left side of Termite's head above his ear and blew a crater an inch-and-a-half deep and six inches in diameter in the stucco wall behind him. There was lots of blood, but no serious damage.

No one knows for sure who the shooters were—or who the intended target was. But Termite believes he knows. "I didn't tell anybody," he says, "but I was thinking while I was lying there on the ground, 'This bullet was meant for me.' "

Like the volume of a boom box turned up notch by notch, the violence around Dolores Mission grows in frequency and intensity as the days move from spring to summer and on toward fall. Grumpy gets a bullet in the stomach. Two Jobs for a Future construction workers are shot on two different nights. Thumper, from Cuatro Flats, who was out walking with his girlfriend, has his hair parted down the middle by a bullet that skimmed neatly across the top of his skull. Sniper, from TMC, is shot twice in the shoulder and once below the heart. All his wounds are through-and-throughs—the .38-caliber bullets passed straight through his body and out again. An hour and a half after he is rushed to White Memorial Hospital emergency room, Sniper is back on the street, a jacket over his bandages. "He has no insurance so they wouldn't give him any pain killers," says Boyle, "not even some Tylenol."

And yet there are bright spots. Grumpy recovers and is still employed. Green finds a job making conga drums. Scoobie makes it onto one of Boyle's construction crews, and his foreman gives him rave reviews. The morning after Critter receives his diploma from Roosevelt High School (with some help from Mission Alternative) on the stage of the Shrine Auditorium, he starts a new job at a downtown law firm. "I think maybe after a while they're going to let me do some computer work," says Critter happily. "I told 'em I got an A-plus in my last computer class."

And then there is Termite. After he was shot, he asked if he could move into Casa Miguel Pro with Grumpy. "Casa Pro is supposed to be for mothers and children," explains Boyle. "If I let Termite in it would just open the flood gates. Grumpy genuinely has nowhere else he can go, but if I gave a room to every kid who has an intolerable family situation I could fill up Casa Pro plus the Hilton."

In the end Boyle found a compromise. He told Termite he could sleep on the floor of his office. For a time, things seemed to settle down.

Then, a few weeks later, the shooting starts again. Boyle is at Aliso Village talking to a group of TMC homies when unidentified gangsters open fire with automatics and "gauges"—shotguns. The shooting goes on for nearly two minutes. But, as is often the case, the gangsters are bad shots and no one is seriously hurt.

The next day, Termite is picked up by the police. He had been wandering in Dukes territory, carrying a loaded .38. He pleads guilty to a carrying a concealed weapon and is given a minimum sentence—approximately six months—in a county probation department youth camp.

It is 9:55 p.m. and Boyle has finished his bicycle rounds through the projects; things are quiet and he grows contemplative. "You know," he says, "people are always asking me what I consider to be my victories. But I can never think of things that way. With these kids, all you can do is take one a day at a time. A lot of days it's two steps forward and four steps back. On other days it's like the line in Tennessee Williams' play, 'A Streetcar Named Desire': 'Sometimes there's God so quickly.' Then it's joy upon joy, grace upon grace."

Grace or none, it is clear that Boyle loves this place and the job. "You go where the life is," he says. "And the life for me is here in this parish—especially with these kids. The happiness they bring me is beyond anything I can express in words. In the truest and most absolute sense, this work is a vocation." He laughs softly. "And for good or ill I can do no other."

There is an irony here. In July, 1992, Greg Boyle will in fact "do other." A Jesuit is normally assigned to a particular post for six years, no more. The goal is detachment—it should be the work, not the person, on which redemption depends.

Next summer marks the end of Boyle's assignment as pastor of Dolores Mission. He is then expected to spend the next 12 months in prayer, study and renewal before he takes his final vows. (Jesuits wait until a man hits his middle years before final vows are offered.)

"After that," says Boyle, "I'll probably be able to come back here in some capacity, maybe as director of the school." But not even this is a sure thing.

When asked what effect his departure will have on the homeboys, Boyle is quick to be reassuring. "It'll be fine. The structures are in place now—the school, the Comité Pro Paz, the Jobs for a Future program. I am by no means irreplaceable at Dolores Mission."

Maybe, and maybe not. A look into the faces of the gang members who love Boyle as they love no one else in the world makes you wonder. One thing is sure: For good or ill, by this time next year, Father Gregory Boyle will be gone.[3]

Notes

1. Editors' note: The article was written in 1991. By the end of 1994, Father Boyle had buried his 39th gang member in this parish.
2. The name of this gang member—and others so marked—has been changed.
3. Editors' note: And in 1994, Father Boyle returned to continue his work with his "homies," finding jobs and burial sites. ✦

Chapter 24 The National Evaluation of the Gang Resistance Education and Training (G.R.E.A.T.) Program[1]

Finn-Aage Esbensen

Public health practitioners embrace primary prevention strategies to reduce the frequency of unhealthy behaviors. Primary prevention efforts are directed toward a whole population rather than those at highest risk (secondary prevention) or those already involved in the behavior (tertiary prevention). Unlike Father Boyle's work with established gang members described in Chapter 23, the G.R.E.A.T. program is a primary prevention program that exposes all eighth graders to a gang prevention curriculum. In this article, Esbensen describes the results of two approaches to evaluating the program's impact. The findings of the cross-sectional study suggested the program was moderately successful in preventing youths from joining gangs. However, the more thorough, longitudinal research found the same percentage of gang members among youths who received G.R.E.A.T. and those who did not. The author offers several possible explanations for these divergent results and discusses the challenges that evaluators confront in assessing the effectiveness of gang prevention programs.

Finn-Aage Esbensen, "The National Evaluation of the Gang Resistance Education and Training (G.R.E.A.T.) Program."

Overview

Youth delinquent gangs received considerable academic and media attention during the 1990s. Much of this attention focused on the violence and drug dealing in which gang members are involved. Despite this widespread concern with gangs, there has been a paucity of research and evaluation of prevention and intervention programs. In this chapter, I report on a multiyear, multifaceted evaluation of one school-based gang prevention program in which uniformed law enforcement officers teach a nine-week curriculum to middle school students.

The Gang Resistance Education and Training (G.R.E.A.T.) program was developed in 1991 by law enforcement agencies in the greater Phoenix area. The primary purpose of the G.R.E.A.T. program was to reduce gang activity and to educate a population of young people as to the consequences of gang involvement.

From October 1994 through September 2000, the National Institute of Justice (NIJ) funded a National Evaluation of the G.R.E.A.T. program. Two separate objectives guided the evaluation design. The first objective was to conduct a process evaluation, that is, to describe the program and its components, and to assess the program's fidelity. The second objective was to assess the effectiveness of G.R.E.A.T. in terms of attitudinal and behavioral consequences.

The process evaluation consisted of two different components: (1) assessment of the G.R.E.A.T. officer training, and (2) observation of officers actually delivering the program in school classrooms. For the outcome analysis, three different strategies were developed. First, a cross-sectional study was conducted in which 5,935 eighth-grade students in 11 different cities were surveyed to assess the effectiveness of the G.R.E.A.T.

program. Second, a five-year longitudinal, quasi-experimental study was conducted in six different cities. Third, parents, teachers, and law enforcement officers were surveyed to determine their level of satisfaction with the program and its perceived effectiveness.

Problem Statement

In spite of years of research and years of suppression and intervention efforts, the American gang scene is poorly understood and far from being eliminated. There is a lack of consensus about the magnitude of the gang problem, the extent and level of organization of gangs, and most importantly, what should be done to address the gang issue. Some of the epidemiological and etiological confusion can be traced to different methodologies and different theoretical perspectives. Disagreement about policy can be attributed largely to political agendas and to a shortage of evaluations of strategies enacted to address the gang phenomenon. To address the latter issue, a number of gang-specific programs with evaluative components were implemented at both the local and national level during the 1990s.

With respect to knowledge about gangs, information has been derived from a variety of research methodologies and countless studies. Sections I–IV of this reader provide an overview of the multitude of issues involved in gang research. Of particular interest in this chapter is discussion of the extent to which a gang prevention program can be implemented in middle schools and with what degree of success.

The G.R.E.A.T. Program

The Gang Resistance Education and Training (G.R.E.A.T.) program is a school-based gang prevention program taught by uniformed police officers. G.R.E.A.T. was developed in 1991 by Phoenix Police Department officers in cooperation with officers representing other Phoenix area police departments. The Bureau of Alcohol, Tobacco, and Firearms, the Federal Law Enforcement Training Center, and representatives from five local law enforcement agencies (Phoenix, AZ; Portland, OR; Philadelphia, PA; La Crosse, WI; and Orange County, FL) share responsibility for and oversight of the current program. Since its inception, G.R.E.A.T. has experienced rapid acceptance by both law enforcement and school personnel. Evidence for this is its adoption by numerous law enforcement agencies across the country; as of January 2000, more than 3,500 officers from all fifty states and the District of Columbia had completed G.R.E.A.T. training.

The stated objectives of the G.R.E.A.T. program are (1) "to reduce gang activity" and (2) "to educate a population of young people as to the consequences of gang involvement." The curriculum consists of nine lessons offered once a week to middle school students, primarily seventh graders. Officers are provided with detailed lesson plans containing clearly stated purposes and objectives. In order to achieve the program's objectives, the nine lessons cover such topics as conflict resolution, goal setting, and resisting peer pressure. Discussion about gangs and how they affect the quality of people's lives are also included. The nine lessons are listed below:

1. Introduction—Acquaint students with the G.R.E.A.T. program and presenting officer.
2. Crimes, Victims and Your Rights—Students learn about crimes, victims, and the impact on school and neighborhood.
3. Cultural Sensitivity/Prejudice—Students learn how cultural differences impact their school and neighborhood.

4/5. Conflict Resolution (2 lessons)—Students learn how to create an atmosphere of understanding that would enable all parties to better address problems and work on solutions together.

6. Meeting Basic Needs—Students learn how to meet their basic needs without joining a gang.
7. Drugs/Neighborhoods—Students learn how drugs affect their school and neighborhood.

8. Responsibility—Students learn about the diverse responsibilities of people in their school and neighborhood.
9. Goal Setting—Students learn the need for goal setting and how to establish short- and long-term goals.

Process Evaluation

Of primary importance in the process evaluation was determining if the program described in written documents was, in fact, the program delivered. In this section, I will briefly describe the procedures used to assess program fidelity. During the first year of the evaluation, members of the research staff observed five officer training sessions. In addition to enhancing the researchers' understanding of the program, these observations allowed for assessment of the training program and the appropriateness of instructional techniques. The consensus of the evaluators was that these training sessions were well organized and staffed by a dedicated group of officers (Esbensen and Osgood 1997).

Our next concern was to assess the extent to which the officers brought the materials learned at training to the classroom. A total of 87 lessons were observed by one or two trained observers in six different cities and 14 different schools. Each observer noted the extent to which the officers adhered to the lesson outline and conformed to the lesson content. As with the training sessions, the consensus was that the officers did a commendable job of presenting the materials as they were taught in the G.R.E.A.T. officer training. On the basis of these two observational components, we concluded that the program was delivered with a high degree of conformity to the written description (Sellers, Taylor, and Esbensen 1998).

Outcome Evaluation

Although the development of the G.R.E.A.T. curriculum was not theory driven, the design of the National Evaluation was. The theories judged to be most relevant to the program were social learning theory (Akers 1985) and self-control theory (Gottfredson and Hirschi 1990). The identification of relevant theoretical constructs is critical to the short-term evaluation of prevention programs because prevention necessarily takes place well before the outcome of major concern (gang membership) is likely to occur. Thus, the evaluation placed considerable emphasis on theoretical constructs that were logically related to the program's curriculum and that were both theoretically and empirically linked to gang membership and delinquency (Grasmick et al. 1993; Hawkins and Catalano 1993; Huizinga, Loeber, and Thornberry 1994; Winfree, Vigil-Backstrom, and Mays 1994). It was maintained that if the program had positive effects on those variables in the short term, then it held promise for long-term benefits of reducing serious gang delinquency. Decisions about the potential value of G.R.E.A.T. could not wait for research that would track program participants through their entire adolescence to determine whether they ever joined gangs or participated in serious delinquency. Nor would the expense of such research be justified without evidence of short-term effects.

Winfree, Esbensen, and Osgood (1996) elaborated on the relationship between the G.R.E.A.T. curriculum and the theoretical constructs included in this evaluation. For example, lesson four of G.R.E.A.T. (Conflict Resolution) deals with concepts closely linked to self-control theory's anger and coping strategies. Lesson 5 (Meeting Basic Needs) has conceptual ties to the risk-taking element of self-control theory. Lessons 6, 7, and 8 include elements addressing delayed gratification and impulsive behavior by attempting to teach responsibility and goal setting, including personal and career goals.

Elements of social learning theory appear in lessons 1, 3, and 4. These lessons introduce definitions of laws, values, norms, and rules supportive of law-abiding behavior. Tolerance and acceptance (lesson 3), for instance, are presented as values that reduce conflict and, subsequently, violence. Further, lesson 4 addresses conflict resolution and steps students can take to ward off negative peer influences.

Measures

The questionnaires administered to students participating in both the cross-sectional and longitudinal studies were identical. Measures included in the student questionnaires can be divided into three main categories: attitudinal, cognitive, and behavioral. Although the attitudinal measures included in these instruments can be classified as measures of five different theoretical perspectives (social learning, social control, social strain, labeling, and self-concept) and have been used for testing theoretical propositions in other publications (Deschenes and Esbensen 1999; Esbensen and Deschenes 1998; Winfree and Bernat 1998), they will be referred to as attitudinal variables in the subsequent discussion. The following questionnaire items are representative of the diversity of questions answered by the student respondents:

- There are gang fights at my school.
- My parents know who I am with if I am not at home.
- Sometimes I will take a risk just for the fun of it.
- Police officers are honest.
- If your group of friends were getting you into trouble at home, how likely is it that you would still hang out with them?
- I'll never have enough money to go to college.
- It's okay to tell a small lie if it doesn't hurt anyone.
- I try hard in school.
- Being in my gang makes me feel important.

In addition to attitudinal items, the students were requested to complete a self-report delinquency inventory. This technique has been used widely during the past 40 years and provides a good measure of actual behavior rather than a reactive measure of police response to behavior (e.g., Hindelang, Hirschi, and Weis 1981; Huizinga and Elliott 1986; Huizinga 1991). The types of behaviors comprising this 17-item inventory included status offenses (e.g., skipping classes without an excuse), crimes against property (e.g., purposely damaging or destroying property; stealing or trying to steal something worth more than $50), and crimes against persons (e.g., hitting people with the idea of hurting them; attacking someone with a weapon). Additionally, students were asked about drug use, including tobacco, alcohol, and marijuana. Given that the focus of the G.R.E.A.T. program was on gang prevention, a series of questions asked the students about their involvement in gangs and the types of gang activities in which they and their gang were involved.

Analysis Issues

Prior to a discussion of program effectiveness, several methodological issues need to be addressed. G.R.E.A.T. is a school-based program, delivered simultaneously to entire classrooms rather than separately to individual students. For analysis of program effectiveness, this poses a problem concerning the appropriate unit of analysis: individuals, classrooms, or schools. If students from the same classroom tend to be more similar to one another than to students from other classrooms, then treating individuals as the primary unit of analysis is likely to violate the standard statistical assumption of independence among observations (Judd and McClelland 1989:403–416). When this assumption does not hold, we risk the possibility of concluding that there is a reliable treatment effect when it is, in fact, idiosyncratic to only a few classes, or we may fail to establish the statistical significance of a small but very consistent effect.

For the independence assumption to hold, *all* similarity within classes must be explained by the treatment effect and control variables. In most cases there are many other sources of similarity as well, such as which trainer delivered the program, the teacher's classroom management style, and all extraneous factors that determine which students end up in which classrooms. Though it is possible that an analysis would succeed in accounting for all such differences between classes, it is more prudent to assume that this may not be the case. Although it would be ideal to use an analysis strategy that allows for the possible nonindependence within classrooms by including classrooms as a unit of analysis, we could not do this with the cross-sectional data. It was not possible to reconstruct the seventh-grade class configuration with the available data. It was possible, however, to use *school* as a level of analysis and thus be able to control for school differences and, indirectly and in a more limited way, officer and teacher characteristics. In the longitudinal survey, we randomly assigned classrooms to G.R.E.A.T. or non-G.R.E.A.T. and were thus able to conduct those analyses using *classroom* as a unit of analysis.

Cross-Sectional Design–1995

The first outcome analysis was based on the cross-sectional survey completed in the spring of 1995. In this cross-sectional design, two *ex-post facto* comparison groups were created to allow for assessment of the effectiveness of the G.R.E.A.T. program. Because the program was taught in seventh grade, eighth-grade students were surveyed to allow for a one-year follow-up while at the same time guaranteeing that none of the sample was currently enrolled in the program. Eleven cities met all the required conditions for participation in the National Evaluation: Las Cruces, NM; Omaha, NE; Phoenix, AZ; Philadelphia, PA; Kansas City, MO; Milwaukee, WI; Orlando, FL; Will County, IL; Providence, RI; Pocatello, ID; and Torrance, CA. These sites provide a diverse sample. One or more of the selected sites can be described by the following characteristics: large urban area, small city, racially and ethnically homogeneous, racially and ethnically heterogeneous, East Coast, West Coast, Midwest, inner-city, working class, or middle class (Esbensen and Winfree 1998).

Within the selected sites, schools that offered G.R.E.A.T. during the past two years were selected and questionnaires were administered to all eighth graders in attendance on the specified day. This resulted in a final sample of 5,935 eighth-grade students from 315 classrooms in 42 different schools. Passive parental consent procedures were approved in all but the Torrance site[2]. That is, parents had to sign a form indicating that they did not want their child to participate in the survey. The absence of such a form indicated "passive parental consent." The number of parental refusals at each school ranged from 0 to 2 percent. Thus, participation rates (the percentage of students in attendance on the day of administration actually completing questionnaires) varied between 98 and 100 percent at the passive consent sites.

Demographic Characteristics

Approximately half of the sample was female (52 percent) and most lived in intact homes (62 percent)—respondents indicated that both a mother and father were present in the home, including stepparents. The sample was ethnically diverse, with whites accounting for 40 percent of respondents, African-Americans 27 percent, Hispanics 19 percent, Asians 6 percent, and others 8 percent. As expected with an eighth-grade sample, most of the respondents were between 13 and 15 years of age, with 60 percent being 14 years old. The vast majority reported having parents with a minimum educational level of a high school diploma, with a sizable number having mothers and/or fathers with some college-level education. It is worth noting that approximately 25 percent of the respondents did not know their father's highest level of education and 20 percent did not know their mother's.

With respect to gang affiliation, some interesting insight to self-reported gang membership is revealed. As with most social phenomena, definitional issues arise. In the current research, two filter questions introduce the gang-specific section of the questionnaire: "Have you ever been a gang member?" and "Are you now in a gang?" Given the current sample, with almost all the respondents under the age of 16, even affirmative responses to the first question followed by a negative response to the second may still have indicated a recent gang affiliation. Relying upon responses to the first question as an accurate reflection of the magnitude of the gang problem, fully 17 percent (994 youths) of the sample indicated that they had belonged to a gang at some point in their lives. This contrasts with nine percent (522) indicating that they were currently gang members.

Comparison Group

A primary concern for assessing program impact was determination of whether the students who participated in the G.R.E.A.T. program were comparable to those who did not. The treatment group (G.R.E.A.T. participants) and the comparison group (nonparticipants) were defined through answers to the question "Did you complete the G.R.E.A.T. program?" Of the 5,836 respondents who answered the question (99 students did not respond), 2,629 (45 percent) reported they had completed the program. The 3,207 (55 percent) who did not became the comparison group.

However, the schools varied substantially in the number of students who reported they had or had not completed the G.R.E.A.T. program. Because the precision with which program impact can be established at each school depends on the number of students in *both* participant and nonparticipant groups, schools with few students in one of the groups could contribute relatively little to the evaluation. Therefore, analysis of the treatment and comparison groups was replicated using a restricted sample of 28 schools in which there were at least 15 students in each group, participants and nonparticipants.

Because data were gathered on only a single occasion, a year after completion of the program, it was necessary to compare the participants and nonparticipants using statistical controls to rule out the possibility that differences between them were attributable to various background characteristics. Questions were asked in the survey to determine background characteristics that could be associated with the outcome measures. The analysis controlled for five characteristics:

1. Sex.
2. Race (white, African American, Hispanic, Asian American, and other).
3. Age (because only eighth-grade students participated in the evaluation, there was little variation in age).
4. Family status (as reflected in the adults with whom the youths resided).
5. Parental education (defined as the highest level attained by either parent).

Background Characteristics

Not surprisingly, there were differences among the 42 schools in terms of racial composition and socioeconomic status (as reflected by family status and parental education). The analysis, which controlled for differences between schools, found a few small but statistically significant differences in background characteristics between the treatment and comparison groups.

Ideally, the treatment and comparison groups should have been matched, but this could not be expected in a *post hoc* evaluation, such as this study. The pattern of group differences in background characteristics was ambiguous, but it did not appear especially problematic to determining the impact of the G.R.E.A.T. program. Comparisons of the treatment and comparison groups revealed no systematic bias. Demographic characteristics indicating high or low risk for delinquency and/or gang membership were found in both groups. In the comparison group, 15-year-old students were overrepresented while in the treatment group African-American youths were overrepresented. Similarly, there were fewer females in the comparison group but more youths from single-parent homes. Given this inconsistent pattern and the small size of group differences, it was concluded that the outcome measures were not a product of preexisting differences between the G.R.E.A.T. and comparison students.

Outcome Results

Findings from the cross-sectional study indicated that G.R.E.A.T. appeared to be meeting its objectives of reducing gang affiliation and delinquent activity. The students who reported completing the G.R.E.A.T. program reported *lower* levels of gang affiliation (9.8 percent of G.R.E.A.T. students reported gang membership compared to 11.4

percent of the comparison group) and self-reported delinquency. These differences were small but statistically significant. Not only was the aggregate measure of delinquency lower for the G.R.E.A.T. group, but so were most of the subscales, for example, drug use, minor offending, property crimes, and crimes against persons. No differences between the groups were found for rates of victimization or selling drugs.

A number of differences also were found for attitudinal measures. As discussed above, G.R.E.A.T. lessons are aimed at reducing impulsive behavior, improving communication with parents and other adults, enhancing self-esteem, and encouraging students to make "better" choices. The cross-sectional survey results revealed that one year after completing G.R.E.A.T., the G.R.E.A.T. students reported better outcomes, that is, more positive attitudes and behaviors than students who did not complete the program (see Box 24.1).

Box 24.1: Cross-Sectional Design Outcomes

Students completing the G.R.E.A.T. program reported more positive attitudes and behaviors than did the comparison group of students. They reported:

- Lower rates of self-reported delinquency.
- Lower rates of gang affiliation.
- More positive attitudes toward the police.
- More negative attitudes about gangs.
- Having more friends involved in prosocial activities.
- Greater commitment to peers promoting prosocial behavior.
- Higher levels of perceived guilt at committing deviant acts.
- More commitment to school.
- Higher levels of attachment to both mothers and fathers.
- More communication with parents about their activities.
- Fewer friends involved in delinquent activity.
- Lower likelihood of acting impulsively.
- Lower likelihood of engaging in risky behavior.
- Lower levels of perceived blocks to academic success.

(*See* Esbensen and Osgood 1999 for further discussion of these results.)

Longitudinal Research Design

The cross-sectional evaluation of the G.R.E.A.T. program reported above contains several methodological limitations. That design lacked a pre-test measure and required the *ex-post facto* creation of a comparison group. While statistical procedures were used to strengthen the validity of that design, it is generally considered a weak design (e.g., Sherman et al. 1997). The longitudinal research strategy implemented in the second phase of the National Evaluation, with a quasi-experimental research design and random assignment of classrooms to treatment, serves two very important functions. First, this assignment process should create groups of G.R.E.A.T. and non-G.R.E.A.T. students at equal risk for future delinquency and gang involvement. Second, the longitudinal research design greatly increased statistical power for detecting program effects by controlling for previous individual differences and examining change over time.

Site Selection

Six cities were selected for inclusion in the longitudinal phase of the National Evaluation. The first criterion was the existence of a viable G.R.E.A.T. program. A second criterion was geographical location. It was desired to include an East Coast city (Philadelphia, PA), a West Coast location (Portland, OR), the site of the program's inception (Phoenix, AZ), a Midwest city (Omaha, NE), a nongang city (Lincoln, NE), and a small "border town" with a chronic gang problem (Las Cruces, NM). Clearly, some consideration was given to proximity to the location of the research office (Lincoln). A third criterion was the cooperation of the school districts and the police departments in each site.

Quasi-Experimental Research Design

The longitudinal study includes relatively equal-sized groups of treatment (G.R.E.A.T.) and control (non-G.R.E.A.T.) students in the seventh grade at five of the sites and sixth-grade students in the sixth (Portland). Table

24.1 reports the number of schools, classrooms, and students at each of the sites. Because G.R.E.A.T. is a classroom-based program, assignment was implemented for classrooms rather than for individual students. When data were pooled across sites, there was a large enough sample of classrooms for confidence in our results, even when classrooms were used as the unit of analysis. The longitudinal sample consists of 22 schools, 153 classrooms, and more than 3,000 students (all students whose names appeared on class lists at the beginning of the school year).

The "random" assignment process was a critical feature of this research design. During late summer and early fall of 1995, procedures for assignment of classrooms to experimental and control conditions were developed at each of the 22 middle schools participating in the longitudinal study. Because the G.R.E.A.T. program was implemented differently at each site, unique solutions were required to implement random assignment at each site and, in some situations, at each school. The exact nature of the process was dependent on what was possible at each site, but in all cases the goal was to minimize the potential for differences between the sets of treatment and control classes. Working in conjunction with principals, teachers, and G.R.E.A.T. officers, "random" samples were derived at each site. These various procedures resulted in 76 G.R.E.A.T. classrooms representing 1,871 students and 77 control classrooms with 1,697 students.

Active Consent Procedures

The University of Nebraska Institutional Review Board approved a research design that allowed passive parental consent (students were included unless specifically prohibited by parents) during the pre- and post-test data collection. These surveys were conducted two weeks prior to and two weeks following completion of the G.R.E.A.T. program. Active parental consent (students were excluded unless written approval for participation was obtained from parents) was required for the subsequent annual surveys. These procedures were also approved by each of the participating school districts.

A modified Dillman (1978) total design method was utilized to obtain the active consent forms, although the specific procedures varied slightly in terms of timing and sequencing across the six sites. The following serves as an "ideal type" of the procedures that were followed. Three direct mailings were made to parents of survey participants. Included in the mailings were a cover letter (both English and Spanish versions were included in Phoenix and Las Cruces), two copies of the parent consent form for student participation, and a business reply envelope. All parents not responding after the second mailing were contacted by telephone. School personnel also cooperated by distributing consent forms and cover letters at school.

The results of the active consent process (see Table 24.1) led to an overall retention of 57 percent of the initial sample. (For a more detailed discussion of the active consent process and examination of the effects of active consent procedures on the representativeness of the sample, consult Esbensen et al. 1999). All together these efforts cost in excess of $60,000 in terms of supplies, personnel time, telephone, and mailing costs.

Questionnaire Completion Rates

The completion rates for the student survey were excellent. Of the 2,045 active consents obtained at the six sites, 1,758 (86 percent) surveys were completed during the one-year follow-up and 1,550 (76 percent) were competed in the two-year follow-up (see Table 24.1). Given the multisite, multischool sample, combined with the fact that respondents at five of the six sites made the transition from middle school to high school between the year-one and year-two surveys, this completion rate is commendable. Hansen and colleagues (1985) examined attrition in a meta-analysis of 85 longitudinal studies and reported an average completion rate of 72 percent for the 19 studies with a 24-month follow-up period. Few of these 19 studies included multisite samples. Tebes, Snow, and Arthur (1992) report on the attrition rates from middle school to high

Table 24.1
National Evalutation of G.R.E.A.T. Completion Rates

SITE	TOTAL SAMPLE SIZE	G.R.E.A.T.	NON-G.R.E.A.T.	ACTIVE CONSENT SAMPLE SIZE	CONSENT			PRE-TEST	POST-TEST	1 YR	2 YR
					YES	NO	NO RETURN				
		Classroom / Student N			N (%)			N (%)			
Las Cruces	626	11 / 280	17 / 346	301	301 (48)	71 (11)	254 (41)	518 (83)	519 (83)	275 (91)	242 (80)
Lincoln	653	13 / 324	13 / 329	425	425 (65)	79 (12)	149 (23)	595 (91)	351 (83)	388 (91)	366 (86)
Omaha	672	20 / 363	20 / 309	470	470 (70)	48 (7)	154 (23)	440 (94)	414 (88)	390 (83)	354 (75)
Philadelphia	465	9 / 286	6 / 179	228	228 (49)	28 (6)	209 (45)	388 (83)	317 (68)	174 (76)	147 (64)
Phoenix	569	11 / 316	10 / 253	300	300 (53)	54 (9)	215 (38)	493 (87)	434 (76)	250 (83)	195 (65)
Portland	583	12 / 302	11/ 281	321	321 (55)	58 (10)	204 (35)	502 (86)	468 (80)	281 (88)	246 (77)
TOTAL	3568	76 / 1871	77 / 1697	2045	2045 (57)	338 (9)	1185 (33)	2936 (82)	2503 (80)	1758 (86)	1550 (76)

* Completion percentages based on Total Sample for Pre-Test and Post-Test, all sites except Omaha
Completion percentages based on Active Consent Sample for 1 Year and 2 Year Follow-Ups
Completion percentages for Omaha based on Active Consent Sample for Pre-Test, Post-Test, 1 Year and 2 Year Follow-Ups

school. In their study examining differential attrition for different age groups, they report losing 41.3 percent of their sample between eighth and ninth grade!

For the year-two follow-up, considerable difficulty was introduced into the retention of the student sample. As the cohort moved from middle school to high school, combined with normal mobility patterns, we found students enrolled in more than 10 different high schools each in Omaha, Phoenix, and Philadelphia. It thus became necessary to contact school officials at these schools, whether fewer than 10 respondents or more than 100 were enrolled at the school. In some instances, these new schools were in different districts, which required approval from the necessary authorities to survey their students. In spite of these logistical concerns, we successfully obtained completed questionnaires from 76 percent during the 24-month follow-up survey.

Outcome Results

Of particular interest in the longitudinal design is assessment of within-individual change over time (for a detailed discussion of the longitudinal results, consult Esbensen et al., 2000). The results reported here are based on examination of immediate (post-test) and intermediate (one- and two-year follow-up surveys) program effects.

The longitudinal sample differs from the cross-sectional sample on some of the demographic characteristics. Those completing the pre-test are younger, representing sixth- and seventh-grade students with a modal age of 12 (60 percent); a higher percentage of students are white (46 percent), fewer are African American (17 percent), but there is approximately the same representation of Hispanics (19 percent) and others (16 percent). With respect to sex and family structure, the longitudinal sample is virtually identical to the cross-sectional, with 51 percent females and 61 percent living in two-parent households.

The assignment of classrooms to G.R.E.A.T. and non-G.R.E.A.T. was relatively successful in establishing comparable groups. Some differences were noted but the only statistically significant difference was for race; more white youths were in the comparison group while the treatment group consisted of proportionately more African-American and Hispanic youths. A review of attitudinal and behavioral measures collected in the pre-test indicated that the comparison group was slightly more pro-social than the G.R.E.A.T. group (e.g., more positive attitudes to police, more negative attitudes about gangs, more peers involved in pro-social activities, and lower rates of self-reported delinquency). The analysis strategy, however, controls for school, classroom, and preexisting differences between groups.

The longitudinal analysis failed to replicate the cross-sectional results. There were no consistent behavioral or attitudinal differences between those students who were assigned to G.R.E.A.T. and those who were assigned to the control classrooms. For instance, in both the year-one and year-two follow-up surveys, the same percentage (3 percent in both years—see Box 24.2 for a discussion of defining and measuring gang membership) of students in the G.R.E.A.T. and control groups reported being gang members.

The current analyses were restricted to the year-one and year-two follow-up surveys. Analyses incorporating the year-three and year-four follow-up surveys are in progress. Thus, unlike the cross-sectional study that found consistent differences between the G.R.E.A.T. and non-G.R.E.A.T. groups, the longitudinal study found no short-term or intermediate effects of the G.R.E.A.T. program on either attitudes or behavior. Of importance is assessing why these different research strategies (the cross-sectional versus the longitudinal) produced different results. Possible explanations for the different results are discussed in Conclusions and Policy Implications.

Two additional analysis strategies were conducted to more fully explore the possibility of finding programmatic effects. The first alternative strategy restricted the analysis to those cities in which both the G.R.E.A.T. program and the evaluation design were best implemented. The second approach examined program impact based on the classifica-

Box 24.2: Gang Definition and Gang Measurement

As discussed in Section I of this book, there is a lack of agreement about the definition of *gang* or *gang member*. To highlight this point, consider some of the issues involved. In the cross-sectional study, we classified respondents as gang members if they answered "yes" to the question "Have you ever been a gang member?" and also indicated that the gang was involved in at least one of four delinquent activities (gang fights, thefts, assaults, or robberies). In that study we used the "ever" question because the average respondent was 14 years of age and any gang affiliation would have been relatively recent. This produced a prevalence rate of 10.6 percent. However, had we chosen a different definition, we could have concluded that from 2.3 percent to 16.9 percent of the students were gang members! For example, if we had only used the single question "Have you ever been a gang member?" 16.9 percent of the responses were "yes". On the other hand, if we had limited our definition to students who were currently core members of an organized delinquent gang, then our gang members would be reduced to only 2.3 percent. Further, in the longitudinal study, we find that only 9 percent of the year-one respondents reported ever being a gang member, slightly more than half the findings in the cross-sectional study. And only 3 percent indicated that they were currently members of a delinquent gang. Why this difference? Is it because of sampling differences? The cross-sectional study included a more diverse sample of cities than did the longitudinal study. What about the fact that the cross-sectional surveys were anonymous (students did not provide their names) and the longitudinal surveys were confidential? Did the active consent process reduce the number of gang members in the sample? Remember that 33 percent of the parents failed to respond to the request for their children to participate in the evaluation. Does the fact that this was the third data collection point affect the responses? Was there a "testing effect"? From a policy standpoint, it is clear that which definition you choose can have serious implications not only for research but also for policy consideration. Does it make sense, for instance, to have a general prevention program when only 2 percent of the students are involved in the behavior you are trying to prevent?

tion of respondents into high- and low-risk categories.

In terms of the quality of program implementation, three of the six cities were categorized as having greater program fidelity to the G.R.E.A.T. program model than the other three sites (i.e., officer experience, strength of local organization of G.R.E.A.T.). With respect to the research design, we were more successful in some cities than in others in eliciting student participation in the evaluation. Thus, program effects were assessed in optimal circumstances by limiting the sample to the cities with the highest quality program implementation and the classrooms with most adequate participation rates. Results from the cross-sectional analysis of program impact suggested that G.R.E.A.T. is more effective for students who are at higher risk of future problems of delinquency and gang membership. Thus, in the longitudinal analysis, separate analyses contrasted program effectiveness for students displaying both high and low risk for involvement in delinquency and gang activity. Neither of these alternative strategies produced results that differed from the initial longitudinal results; we found no systematic differences between the G.R.E.A.T. students and the control group.

Conclusions and Policy Implications

The Gang Resistance Education and Training program is one of a myriad of gang prevention efforts being employed to reduce adolescent involvement in crime and gangs. As other programs await evaluation results, the preliminary findings of this study supported continuation of G.R.E.A.T. The process evaluation assessing the officer-training program as well as the observation of officers delivering the program indicated a high degree of program fidelity. Additionally, the results from the cross-sectional survey of 5,935 eighth-grade students conducted during spring 1995 suggested that students who participated in G.R.E.A.T. reported significantly more pro-social behaviors and attitudes, including less gang membership and less delinquency, than students who did not take part in the program. This one-year follow-up survey supported the idea that trained law enforcement personnel can serve as prevention agents as well as enforcers of the law.

These cross-sectional results, however, needed to be viewed with caution. Some differences existed between the two groups prior to the introduction of the program. Although most of these differences were controlled through available statistical techniques, an experimental design with random assignment would provide a stronger test of program effect.

The quasi-experimental longitudinal design was implemented in six cities and the current results rely on data obtained from the pre- and post-tests administered during the fall and winter of the 1995–96 academic year. One- and two-year follow-up surveys were obtained during the fall of 1996 and 1997. Additional surveys not yet ready for analysis were collected during 1998 and 1999, eventually allowing for assessment of long-term (four-year) effects. Contrary to the cross-sectional study, no programmatic effect was found. The two groups (G.R.E.A.T. and non-G.R.E.A.T.) were comparable on all measures, both before and after treatment.

This discrepancy in findings between the cross-sectional and longitudinal studies raises several methodological and conceptual issues:

- Were the cross-sectional results an artifact of the research design?
- Was the cross-sectional sample more diverse, especially with respect to the inclusion of more high-risk students?
- Is there an effect of analyzing cases grouped by official assignment to the program that produces different results than reliance upon subjects' self-reports of program completion?
- Is it possible that the mandated active-parental consent process contributed to a more homogeneous sample in the longitudinal study?
- Is it possible that the schools experienced a saturation or contamination effect? That is, G.R.E.A.T. officers had been assigned to the schools for a number of years and had contributed to a school-wide change in attitudes and behaviors.
- Is it reasonable to expect a nine-lesson "canned" curriculum can have an effect on students' attitudes and behaviors?

Clearly, these methodological issues defy a firm response. I pose them merely to acknowledge that different samples and different research designs, even though utilizing the same method and survey instruments, may introduce unique effects that affect outcomes. We can address some of these issues. First, analyses examining the differential attrition possibility indicate that the active consent sample did not differ significantly from the initial sample (Esbensen et al. 1999).

Second, the analyses restricted to the three sites in which both the program and evaluation were best implemented included two sites in which the G.R.E.A.T. program was in the first year of implementation in the selected schools. Results from those sites did not differ from those for the entire sample. On the basis of comparison of the cross-sectional and longitudinal samples, it is evident that the cross-sectional sample included a more racially and ethnically diverse sample, as well as including a broader geographic representation. We attempted to address this concern by examining site-specific analyses for cities included in both studies. In three cities, there was considerable overlap between schools participating in the cross-sectional and longitudinal studies. In these cases, the same pattern of results persisted—significant program effects in the cross-sectional study but not in the longitudinal. To date, we have not analyzed the longitudinal data based on self-reported program completion, as this would defy the logic of random assignment. Methodological issues aside, is it reasonable to expect that a nine-hour program can measurably change student attitudes and behaviors? The majority of school-based prevention programs, even those with more intense and prolonged treatment dosages, do not produce measurable program effects (see, for example, Sherman et al. 1997). This is especially true for curriculum-based programs, such as G.R.E.A.T.

Where does this leave us with regard to policy? Can officers be effective providers of treatment? Given the lack of consistent findings for G.R.E.A.T., this is an important question. However, from a school safety perspective, and from a community policing perspective, it may be reasonable to continue this strategy. School administrators commented during both formal and informal interviews that the officers were welcome in the schools because their presence promoted a feeling of safety. Additionally, there has been a resurgence of interest in school resource officers and in proactive policing strategies. G.R.E.A.T. and other school-based prevention programs such as DARE and law-related education can possibly be integrated into the role of school resource officers. Teachers and parents appear to be quite satisfied with the G.R.E.A.T. program. According to surveys administered to these groups, the majority of teachers and parents were in favor of school-based prevention programs, in favor of officers instructing students, and generally supportive of the G.R.E.A.T. program.

A lingering question, however, remains. With the absence of a measurable program effect, is it reasonable to continue the program because people feel good about it? Unlike many other programs with no evaluation data or with evaluations that report no effect, G.R.E.A.T. administrators responded to the results of this evaluation. When the results (the lack of program effect) were conveyed to the G.R.E.A.T. administration, the reaction was "Well, what can we do to make it a successful program?" At their request, a group of G.R.E.A.T. representatives, members of the National Evaluation research team, and experts in school-based prevention programs undertook a critical review of the G.R.E.A.T. curriculum and the overall structure of the program. This group reviewed the curriculum within the context of the evaluation results and within the context of successful school-based prevention programs. The group provided the G.R.E.A.T. administration with a report detailing a number of recommended changes and modifications to the existing program. These suggestions are currently being reviewed by G.R.E.A.T.'s governing body members for possible implementation.

It remains to be seen whether these changes to the G.R.E.A.T. program will produce positive outcomes for future recipients of the program. While the G.R.E.A.T. program is in the process of developing a family component to supplement its school curricula, to what extent can such individual-based prevention programs effect gang involvement? A significant reduction in gang activity may be too much to expect from any program if the more fundamental causes and attractions of gangs (i.e., social, structural, community, and family conditions) are not simultaneously addressed.

Note

1. This chapter is a compilation of evaluation results published or presented in various venues. My sincere thanks and indebtedness are due to my colleagues, without whom this research would not have been possible: T. J. Taylor, Dana Lynskey, Adrienne Freng, Lesley Brandt, Wayne Osgood, Chris Sellers, Tom Winfree, Libby Deschenes, and Fran Bernat. Additionally, I would like to thank the numerous respondents (students, parents, teachers, and law enforcement officers) who provided their time and assistance in the completion of this evaluation. This research was supported under award #94-IJ-CX-0058 from the National Institute of Justice, Office of Justice Programs, U.S. Department of Justice. Points of view in this document are those of the author and do not necessarily represent the official position of the U.S. Department of Justice.
2. Active parental consent was required in the Torrance site. See Chapter 10, this volume, for a discussion.

References

Akers, Ronald L. 1985. *Deviant Behavior: A Social Learning Approach*. 3d ed. Belmont, CA: Wadsworth.

Deschenes, Elizabeth Piper, and Finn-Aage Esbensen. 1999. "Violence and Gangs: Gender Differences in Perceptions and Behavior." *Journal of Quantitative Criminology* 15: 53–96.

Dillman, Don A. 1978. *Mail and Telephone Surveys: The Total Design Method*. New York: Wiley.

Esbensen, Finn-Aage, and Elizabeth Piper Deschenes. 1998. "Boys and Girls in Gangs: Are There Gender Differences in Attitudes and Behavior?" *Criminology* 36: 799–828.

Esbensen, Finn-Aage, Michelle H. Miller, Terrance J. Taylor, Ni He, and Adrienne Freng. 1999. "Differential Attrition Rates and Active Parental Consent." *Evaluation Review* 23: 316–335.

Esbensen, Finn-Aage, and D. Wayne Osgood. 1997. *Research in Brief*. National Evaluation of

G.R.E.A.T. Washington, D.C.: U.S. Department of Justice.

——. 1999. "Gang Resistance Education and Training (G.R.E.A.T.): Results from the National Evaluation." *Journal of Research in Crime and Delinquency* 36: 194–225.

Esbensen, Finn-Aage, D. Wayne Osgood, Terrance J. Taylor, Dana Peterson Lynskey, and Adrienne Freng. 2000. "Longitudinal Results from the National Evaluation of the Gang Resistance Education and Training (G.R.E.A.T.) Program." Washington, D.C.: National Institute of Justice.

Esbensen, Finn-Aage, and L. Thomas Winfree, Jr. 1998. "Race and Gender Differences Between Gang and Non-Gang Youth: Results from a Multi-Site Survey." *Justice Quarterly* 15: 505–526.

Gottfredson, Michael R., and Travis Hirschi. 1990. *A General Theory of Crime*. Stanford, CA: Stanford University Press.

Grasmick, Harold G., Charles R. Tittle, Robert J. Bursik, Jr., and Bruce J. Arneklev. 1993. "Testing the Core Empirical Implications of Gottfredson and Hirschi's General Theory of Crime." *Journal of Research in Crime Delinquency* 30: 5–29.

Hansen, William B., Linda M. Collins, C. Kevin Malotte, C. Anderson Johnson, and Jonathan E. Fielding. 1985. "Attrition in Prevention Research." *Journal of Behavioral Medicine* 8: 261–275.

Hawkins, J. David, and Richard F. Catalano. 1993. *Communities That Care: Risk-Focused Prevention Using the Social Developmental Model*. Seattle, WA: Developmental Research and Programs, Inc.

Hindelang, Michael J., Travis Hirschi, and Joseph G. Weis. 1981. *Measuring Delinquency.* Beverly Hills, CA: Sage Publications.

Huizinga, David. 1991. "Assessing Violent Behavior with Self-Reports." In Joel Milner (ed.) *Neuropsychology of Aggression*. Boston, MA: Kluwer.

Huizinga, David, and Delbert S. Elliott. 1986. "Reassessing the Reliability and Validity of Self-Report Delinquency Measures." *Journal of Quantitative Criminology* 2: 293–327.

Huizinga, David, Rolf Loeber, and Terence P. Thornberry. 1994. *Urban Delinquency and Substance Abuse*. Washington, D.C.: U.S. Department of Justice.

Judd, Charles M., and Gary H. McClelland. 1989. *Data Analysis: A Model-Comparison Approach*. New York: Harcourt Brace Jovanovich.

Sellers, Christine S., Terrance J. Taylor, and Finn-Aage Esbensen. 1998. "Reality Check: Evaluating a School-Based Gang Prevention Model." *Evaluation Review* 22: 590–608.

Sherman, Lawrence W., Denise Gottfredson, Doris MacKenzie, John Eck, Peter Reuter, and Shawn Bushway. 1997. *Preventing Crime: What Works, What Doesn't, What's Promising*. Washington, D.C.: National Institute of Justice.

Tebes, Jacob K., Davis L. Snow, and Michael W. Arthur. 1992. "Panel Attrition and External Validity in the Short-Term Follow-Up Study of Adolescent Substance Use." *Evaluation Review* 16: 151–170.

Winfree, L. Thomas, Jr., and Frances Bernat. 1998. "Social Learning, Self-Control, and the Illicit Drug Use Patterns of Eighth-Grade Students: A Tale of Two Cities." *Journal of Drug Issues* 28: 539–558.

Winfree, L. Thomas, Jr., Finn-Aage Esbensen, and D. Wayne Osgood. 1996. "Evaluating a School-Based Gang Prevention Program: A Theoretical Perspective." *Evaluation Review* 20: 181–203.

Winfree, L. Thomas, Jr., Teresa Vigil-Backstrom, and G. Larry Mays. 1994. "Social Learning Theory, Self-Reported Delinquency, and Youth Gangs: A New Twist on a General Theory of Crime and Delinquency." *Youth and Society* 26: 147–177. ✦

Chapter 25
The Tri-Agency Resource Gang Enforcement Team:
A Selective Approach to Reduce Gang Crime

Douglas R. Kent
and
Peggy Smith

Kent and Smith describe one Southern California city's approach to gang control—an all-out suppression program that emphasizes selective targeting of gang leaders and hardcore recidivists by focusing and coordinating police, probation, and prosecution resources. An evaluation after the second year of implementation found programmatic success in the arrest and conviction of a high proportion of the targeted gang members, and a reduction in serious gang-related crime. The possible displacement of gang activity into neighboring jurisdictions or changes in the type of criminal activity engaged in by gang members was not addressed by the evaluation, but the preliminary results suggest that focused efforts of this type can produce positive effects in smaller gang cities.

Introduction

The City of Westminster's gang crime intervention program is an innovative multi-agency approach to fighting gang-related crime. It places the staff of the City Police Department, County Probation Department and the District Attorney's office together in the same location at the police facility, to focus on a very select group of gang leaders and recidivist criminals. This model is intended to maximize communication and coordination among the different agencies and to amplify their ability to suppress gang activity.

The program's design is particularly innovative because of its systemic approach to gang violence and the justice system's response to it. Rather than simply focusing on the policing issues involved, the City of Westminster is addressing enforcement, case preparation, witness support, prosecution, and sentencing disposition. This intervention consists of intensive investigation, vertical prosecution, or probation supervision efforts by experts in the field of gang crime using new legal tools available to them.

The program was implemented in January, 1992 after the Westminster Police Department, the Orange County Probation Department and the Orange County District Attorney's office entered into a Memorandum of Understanding establishing an interagency program. The goal of the Tri-Agency Resource Gang Enforcement Team (TARGET) program is to increase the flow of intelligence information between cooperating agencies, and to ensure a well-coordinated effort aimed at decreasing violent gang crimes.

The cooperative agreement between these discrete criminal justice agencies established a research committee for purposes of evaluating program effectiveness and providing feedback on program operations. All cooperating agencies are represented on the research committee which has met regularly to develop the research plan, review data collection strategies and assist in evaluating research information.

This chapter contains portions of a department report describing the organization and activities of the program and which documents evidence of its success. This chapter will: (1) describe the mission and goals of the program; (2) provide an overall description of how the program works; (3) describe the activities of its operational components; and (4) describe the impact observed on gang-related crime in the community.

TARGET Mission and Key Concepts

Mission and Goals

The TARGET program mission statement is to reduce gang-related criminal activity by: (1) Removing selected hardcore target subjects that impact the City of Westminster; (2) Gathering intelligence information on gangs as well as individual gang members for use in criminal investigations and trial preparation; (3) Developing innovative techniques toward controlling gangs; (4) Developing personnel expertise in detecting and analyzing gang crime; and (5) Documenting the effectiveness of program efforts.

The prevention of future criminal activity of selected hardcore target subjects is to be accomplished by keeping them in custody. The purpose of the TARGET team is to develop target subject selection criteria, share relevant information with other agencies and follow-up with intensified investigation, probation supervision, and prosecutorial efforts. Intelligence information is shared with other agencies, for investigative as well as training purposes. Networking and interfacing with other departmental bureaus, as well as refining information storage and retrieval systems improves the use of gang intelligence information. Innovative techniques toward gang control are explored, including utilization of Street Terrorism Enforcement and Prevention (STEP) Act laws, use of civil law in addition to criminal law to fight gang crime, as well as the increased awareness of criminal gang activity on the part of patrol officers. Finally, interest in identifying the effect of the program on crime in the City is of central importance to the program.

The research committee identified the following operational program goals: (1) Vigorous arrests of identified target subjects; (2) Effective prosecution and conviction of target subjects; (3) Vigilant supervision of target subject probationers; (4) Expanded intelligence and information-sharing between cooperating agencies; (5) Development and implementation of innovative crime-reduction tools; and (6) A reduction in gang-related crime from the baseline year, 1991 to first year of full operation, 1993. Each of these outcomes is addressed in later sections of this report.

Two Key Concepts

The TARGET model is based upon two key concepts: (1) Selective intervention: efficient deployment of resources directed at incarcerating gang leadership and the most chronic recidivists; and (2) Multiple-agency cooperation: the use of a focused, coordinated team representing three levels of the criminal justice system, whose members are able to maximize the efforts of all other members.

Selective intervention. Given limited resources, law enforcement agencies are increasingly faced with the task of searching for ways to maximize impact on public safety. There is evidence that suggests that a small proportion of recidivist criminals account for a disproportionately large share of crime. Sociological studies of two birth cohorts have reported that a small percent of repeat offenders were responsible for a disproportionate share of crime (Wolfgang, Figlio, & Sellin, 1972; Wolfgang, 1983). For example, Wolfgang et al. (1972) found that 18 percent of juveniles who had committed at least one crime were responsible for 52 percent of crime committed by that cohort.

Some studies have suggested that a selective intervention approach, focusing law enforcement efforts on individuals predicted to commit serious crimes frequently in the future, may be promising for reducing crime. The Repeat Offender Project, a specialized police unit in Washington, D.C. was organized to investigate and prosecute crimes committed by individuals believed to have been committing five or more felony offenses per week. An evaluation study yielded evidence of success, and concluded that selective apprehension units provide a promising strategy for major urban police departments (Martin & Sherman, 1986). However, the utilization of selective intervention approaches have been shown to be difficult. Such difficulties have been articulated well by Struckhoff (1987). Further, concerns that disadvantaged groups might be more likely to be designated as high rate offenders have been expressed (Decker & Salert, 1987).

The concept of selective intervention was employed in the design of the TARGET program. Criminal histories and law enforcement intelligence information were used to select hardcore recidivists and gang leaders. The program then directed its multi-agency coordinated efforts toward this relatively small percentage of chronic offenders. These chronic offenders were individuals who were expected to account for a disproportionate share of gang crime in the community. Thus, placing these offenders in custody was expected to result in a reduction of gang crime in the community.

Multiple-agency cooperation. Program personnel, when operating as a team, fall under the general direction of the Detective Bureau Lieutenant and include: (1) a Police Department component (one sergeant and two police investigators); (2) a Probation Department component (one full time and one part time Deputy Probation Officer); (3) a prosecution component (one senior Deputy District Attorney and a District Attorney's Investigator); and (4) support staff (one Police Service Officer, one Special Service Clerk, and a part-time intern).

The prosecutor and probation officer are relocated from county facilities several miles away to the police department where they share an office with police investigators and support staff. Each team member interacts face-to-face with the others on a regular and ongoing basis. Because each is aware of the daily activities of other team members, coordinated action is greatly facilitated.

This approach essentially combines each of the justice system components into a single unit located at the front end of the criminal justice system. Team members select habitual offenders or gang leaders for vigorous surveillance and prosecution. When a crime is committed, however small, the defendant and the case undergo intensive investigation and prosecution for the most serious charges possible. The prosecutor and probation officer are able to direct their full attention to offenders affecting the City of Westminster. The prosecutor is able to give his maximum effort to each new offense, no matter how minor. The probation officer is able to give each new charge a heightened level of attention as well. When convicted, target subjects are either incarcerated or placed on probation under rigorous, gang-terms conditions. These conditions are then vigorously enforced by TARGET team probation officers.

Information-sharing with other agencies has proven to be tremendously useful in many criminal investigations. Internal information-sharing efforts include information bulletins and training for patrol officers. Team members have also become resource persons on the criminal activities of gangs, not only within the department, but also across agency and jurisdictional lines. Team members have presented gang suppression information at two conferences, the California Gang Investigators Conference and the Association of Criminal Justice Research. Furthermore, gang intelligence information furnished by the team has assisted other agencies in clearing gang-related crimes in many communities in the region.

The TARGET Model

The TARGET model uses intelligence-gathering and information-sharing to assist in the identification and appropriate selection of individuals and gangs for multi-agency intervention. Selection of specific hardcore gang members and intervention in their criminal activities should have an impact on future crime rates.

The first task of program implementation was to identify all gang members having contact with police officers in the City of Westminster. Prior to program implementation, there was no centralized database on known gang members. Because the program relies on selective identification of gang members, according to specified legal criteria, an early task of the implementation year was to establish central record-keeping on known gang members. All three agencies participated cooperatively in this process, and by December, 1993, had identified 2,158 known gang members having contact with Westminster Police Department over the past five years.

Of these gang members, information on individuals who are verifiable gang members is entered into the county-wide information database called the General Reporting Evaluation And Tracking (GREAT) System. Since 1990, 647 individuals have been verified by Westminster law enforcement officers as meeting GREAT gang membership verification criteria. A description of these 647 verified gang members and selection criteria are provided in the following section. From this group of 647 individuals, either individuals or the entire membership of a gang is targeted for program intervention. Figure 25.1 describes how the program intervention on selected gang members is expected to impact gang-related crime in the community.

Targeting Individual Gang Members

From this population of 647 verified gang members, individual target subjects are selected (77 by the end of 1993), then monitored for new criminal activity. . . . When a violation occurs, the incident is subject to intensified investigation by program detectives. When arrests are made, target subjects, as well as co-defendants, face vertical prosecution, enhanced penalties under a criminal law statutory scheme directed toward street gang activity and aggressive probation supervision. Thus, the prosecutor and probation officer join police on the front end of the criminal justice system—they are often integrally involved in developing case strategies before an arrest occurs.

Police detectives provide surveillance of identified gang members, investigate most gang-related crimes, maintain gang intelligence files, identify subjects to be targeted, and conduct probation searches with the deputy probation officer (DPO). The DPO provides intensive supervision of a caseload of hardcore gang members who have special "gang terms" (non-association with other gang members) of probation, authorizes probation searches, provides surveillance of known gang hangouts and provides needed information regarding probationer gang members.

Both police detectives and the DPO work with the Deputy District Attorney (DDA) and DA Investigator in gathering evidence for prosecution of probation violations and/or additional crimes committed. The intelligence information obtained on the gang membership serves an additional function as

Figure 25.1
Components Model of the Tri-Agency Resource Gang Enforcement Program

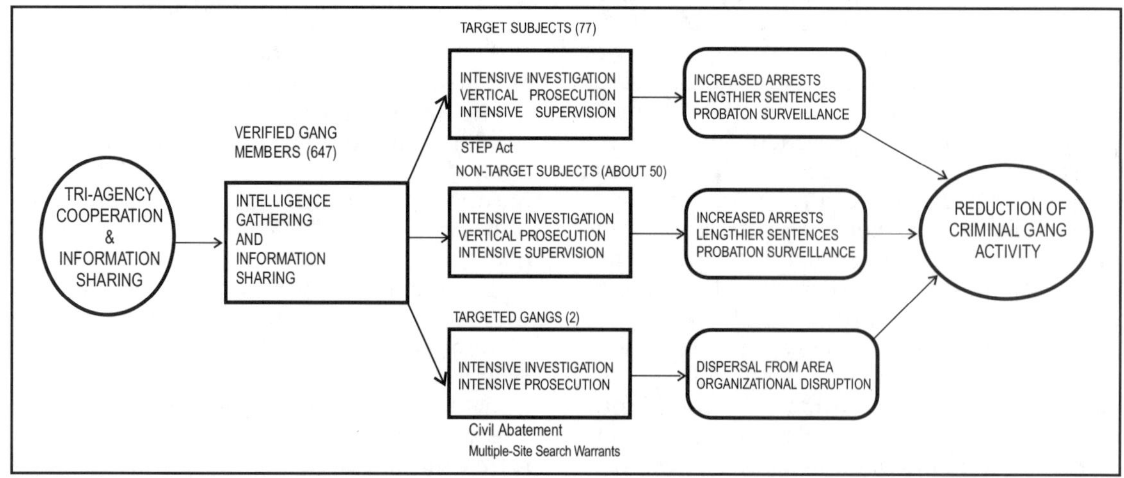

evidence in seeking enhanced sentencing under the STEP Act. The district attorney focuses efforts solely on the City of Westminster's target subject and other gang-related cases. He provides vertical prosecution (handling the case from filing to sentencing), enhances search warrant capabilities, and provides aggressive prosecution of probation violators. The DA investigator assists in trial preparation and witness management and protection.

Further, gang members may be legally served with a notice (although not required) informing individual gang members of the criminal nature of the member's gang and of the penal consequences for continued participation in the gang. The STEP Act involves a comprehensive series of laws and procedures dealing with criminal street gangs. It makes active participation in a criminal street gang a crime and adds additional sentence time to certain gang-related felonies. Meeting the various STEP Act gang membership verification criteria requires substantial documentation on gang membership and activity in a specific geographic area.

Non-Target Subjects

Individuals who associate with target subjects and participate in crimes committed by target subjects often become part of the case prosecuted by the TARGET DDA. When non-target subjects (about 50 by the end of 1993) are co-defendants or are believed to be involved in the criminal activities of a target subject, they too receive heightened attention by the TARGET team. On occasion, when the seriousness of a case warrants intensive service, other gang-related cases are investigated and prosecuted by the TARGET team.

Targeting the Entire Membership of a Gang

In addition to targeting specific individuals committing gang-related crimes, attention has also been focused on the entire membership of certain gangs. Target team detectives identify the group to be targeted and gather legal evidence of its impact on the community. This requires very specific and detailed information on each member in the gang and proof of gang affiliation. An innovative legal tool is now being used to suppress the activity of an entire gang. Under a process known as civil abatement, the entire membership of a gang is sued in civil court to abate an area of the city in which they engage in criminal activity.

The TARGET team DDA, in association with the City Attorney, sue the entire gang to abate a specified geographic area. Gang members are then served with a court order that prohibits members from associating with each other in a specified area of the community. This prohibition of association with other gang members disrupts the basic enabling mechanism of gang activity-group behavior. Violation of the court abatement order is punishable as criminal contempt of court. A major advantage of the civil abatement process is that any patrol officer (not just TARGET team detectives) can arrest an individual gang member for violating the court order.

An additional strategy used in intensive prosecution of criminal gang activity is the use of multiple-site search warrants. These warrants are becoming an important part of gang crime investigation because of the group context in which the crimes occur. Court orders are sought for multiple-sites because weapons, ammunition, and evidence are often shared among the group's membership. Multiple-site search warrants require much greater expertise in preparation than single-site warrants. When a serious gang-related crime is being investigated, multiple residential searches send a strong message to suspects that the crime committed is being vigorously pursued.

Program Outcomes

In the case of targeted individuals, arrests, lengthy sentences, and probation violations are expected. Each of these outcomes is expected to result in physical restrictions, either through incarceration and/or parole or probation restrictions. When the entire membership of a gang is targeted, dispersal from the area and organizational disruption is expected. By focusing enforcement efforts on a small number of selected target subjects and selected gangs, the program is expected to reduce a disproportionately large share of gang-related crime in the community.

Two years of program implementation and operation have produced significant progress in identifying and addressing the gang-related crime problem in the city of Westminster. To date, the program has accomplished the following:

- Identified and documented 2,158 gang members having contact with Police Officers in Westminster over the past five years.
- Identified and verified 647 individual gang members since 1990.
- Identified 95 gangs having two or more contacts with police in Westminster since 1992. Of these, members of 59 gangs were interviewed two or more times by police.
- Targeted 77 verified gang members for intensive investigation, probation supervision and prosecution. Of the 77 (12 percent of 647 verified gang members) subjects targeted for the high probability of their future involvement in crime, 53 (69 percent) are now in custody.
- Documented a 62 percent decrease in serious gang-related crime occurring in the same period that 53 (8 percent of 647 verified gang members) had been placed in custody.
- Found that 71 percent of victims of violent crimes committed by Westminster's hardcore gang members are innocent civilians.
- Initiated civil abatement procedures against two highly active gangs.
- Provided expertise in investigations, search warrants and prosecutions to criminal justice professionals in other agencies and jurisdictions.
- Supervised an average caseload of 52 probationers regarded as hardcore gang members.
- Prosecuted 145 cases involving 168 gang member defendants and achieved a 99 percent conviction rate since the program was implemented.
- Improved abilities to quantify unit operations and conducted statistical analyses of data on verified gang members.

The TARGET program has established procedures for documenting the criminal activities of gang members contacted by police, and developed computerized databases for storing essential subject characteristics and crime data. The ability to systematically identify and track gang-related criminal activity is a major advance over previous record-keeping procedures. The multi-agency team has demonstrated a significant impact on target subjects' ability to commit crime and the amount of gang-related crime in Westminster. Future indications of program effectiveness will focus on maintaining current low levels of gang-related crime. With only one year of full operation the TARGET program has demonstrated its ability to impact the criminal activity of street gangs in the City of Westminster.

References

Decker, S. H. & Salert, B. (1987). Selective incapacitation: A note on its impact on minorities. *Journal of Criminal Justice*, 15, pp. 287–299.

Martin, S. E. & Sherman, L. W. (1986). Selective apprehension: A police strategy for repeat offenders. *Criminology*, 24, pp. 155–173.

Struckhoff, D. R. (1987). Selective incapacitation: Good theory, bad practice. *Corrections Today*, 49, p. 30.

Wolfgang, M. E. (1983). Delinquency in two birth cohorts. *American Behavioral Scientist*, 27, pp. 75–86.

Wolfgang, M. E., Figlio, R. M., & Sellin, T. (1972). *Delinquency in a birth cohort*. Chicago: University of Chicago Press. ✦

Chapter 26
Pulling Levers:
Getting Deterrence Right

David Kennedy

The Boston Gun Project achieved a national reputation as a promising strategy to reduce gun violence and is in the process of being tested in several other cities in the United States. Like the TARGET program described in Chapter 25, this intervention rests on the application of deterrence principles by criminal justice agencies to targeted gang members. However, in his description of the Boston Gun Project model, Kennedy asserts that this strategy incorporates community policing and problem-solving policing approaches to shape the application of deterrence. Compare the activities described here with the approach taken in Reno (Chapter 27) and Los Angeles (Chapter 28). Which of these interventions is consistent with strengthening neighborhood-level social control, as outlined in Chapter 22?

May 1997, Lowell, Massachusetts

One by one, 20 of Lowell's worst young troublemakers are brought into a meeting with 14 representatives of 7 city and State agencies. In 2 additional meetings, the authorities meet with a group of 35 less chronic offenders and 16 members of a city street gang. The message basically is the same as Boston's. "We just wanted to tell you that we know who you are," says assistant district attorney Michael Ortiz. "If you continue to get into trouble, you're going to end up in jail, or hurt, or even dead. But if you want to get out of a gang or back into school, or you want a job or counseling, we're here to help."[1]

Reprinted from: David Kennedy, "Pulling Levers: Getting Deterrence Right." In *National Institute of Justice Journal,* July, 1998.

August 29, 1996, Boston, Massachusetts

More than 20 members of the Intervale Posse, a street gang in Boston's Roxbury neighborhood, are arrested in an early-morning sweep after a nearly 9-month investigation. Fifteen of the arrestees face Federal drug charges and 10-year minimum mandatory sentences; many face even stiffer sanctions. In the weeks after the arrests, Boston's Ceasefire Working Group—composed of frontline members of the Boston Police Department's gang unit, the departments of probation and parole, the U.S. Attorney's and county prosecutor's offices, the Office of the State Attorney General, school police, youth corrections, social services, and others—meets with gangs around the city, goes to youth detention facilities to talk with inmates, and speaks to assemblies in Roxbury public schools. The message Ceasefire members deliver is simple and direct:

> The city is not going to put up with violence any longer. We know who's behind the gang violence. We're warning gangs to stop; if they don't, there are going to be consequences. There are people here who want to help you—we can offer services, job training, protection from your enemies, whatever you need—but the violence is going to stop. The Intervale Posse was warned, they didn't listen, and they're gone. This doesn't have to happen to you. Just put your guns down.

June 1997, Minneapolis, Minnesota

A dozen members of the Bogus Boyz, a street gang composed of members ejected from other gangs and notorious for street violence, are arrested on Federal weapons charges after a short, intensive investigation spearheaded by the Minneapolis Police Department's gang unit, in cooperation with Federal authorities. At the same time, teams of police and probation officers hit the streets to visit some 250 individuals identified by the gang unit as the city's most chronic gang offenders. The teams tell the gang members:

> The Bogus Boyz' arrests were no accident. The Bogus Boyz were violent, and their violence won them this treatment. This is how the city is doing things from now on. We've got a dozen agencies, from probation to the Feds, meeting regularly and focusing on gang violence. Where we find it, we're going to act.

Gang officers visit injured gang members—victims of assaults by other gangs—in the hospital and say to them:

> This is a terrible thing that's happened to you. But understand, we're going to deal with it. Retaliation will not be tolerated. Remember the Bogus Boyz.

Can we make deterrence work? Criminal justice agencies have always tried, but the results—whether of preventive patrol or the death penalty—have always been dubious. The three vignettes on Boston, Lowell, and Minneapolis highlight a new approach to crafting deterrence strategies, and in the larger tales that lie behind them there is reason to be optimistic. In Boston, youth homicide fell by two-thirds after the Ceasefire strategy was put in place in 1996. In Lowell, youth assaults declined; according to Lowell High School headmaster William Samaras, who had been dealing with gang conflicts among students, there was "an immediate quieting effect on the school."[2] In Minneapolis—one of several Midwestern cities that had experienced an increasing homicide rate—homicide fell by 45 percent citywide in the months after the city kicked off its homicide prevention strategy with the Bogus Boyz' arrests. None of these operations were controlled experiments, and a detailed evaluation of the Boston intervention is still under way. But the experiences to date are interesting enough to support an exploration of the basic crime-control logic that was applied to the work in Boston, Lowell, and Minneapolis and that is currently being explored in a number of other jurisdictions.

The basic approach was developed in Boston as part of the National Institute of Justice-supported Boston Gun Project, an attempt to bring problem-solving policing to bear on the city's youth homicide problem. A two-part intervention—the Ceasefire Strategy—emerged from the Gun Project's research and planning phase. One part mounted a direct law enforcement attack on the illicit market that was supplying youths with firearms. The other part was what the Gun Project's interagency working group eventually came to call a "pulling levers" strategy: deterring violent behavior by chronic gang offenders by reaching out directly to gangs, setting clear standards for their behavior, and backing up that message by "pulling every lever" legally available when those standards were violated. The deceptively simple operation that resulted made use of a wide variety of traditional criminal justice tools but assembled them in fundamentally new and different ways. (See Box "What It Isn't, and What It Is.") It may be that the basic "pulling levers" logic can be applied in a variety of settings and against a range of different crime and public safety problems. And it may be that "pulling levers" can, where applicable, substantially alter the balance of power between the authorities and offenders.

The Traditional Approach: Deterrence Through Case Processing

Criminal justice has sought to generate deterrence in a variety of ways: police agencies through patrol and rapid response, probation and parole agencies through supervision, prosecutors and judges by focusing attention and sanctions on repeat and violent offenders, and the like. The main engine for creating deterrence, however, has been the basic case-processing mechanisms of the criminal justice process: the apprehension, prosecution, and sanctioning of offenders. In this model, deterrence is generated by the threat that an offender will face a formal penalty for the crime he has committed. We calculate—and presume that offenders calculate—this threat on the basis of the expected costs, imposed by the criminal justice process, on offenders for the crimes that they commit.

Unfortunately, both scholarship and everyday experience suggest that the deterrent power of this strategy has not been great. It is not hard to see why. Most crimes are neither reported to nor observed by the police; in many types of crimes, such as drug dealing and prostitution, both parties to the transaction actively strive for concealment. And the majority of crimes that are reported do not result in an arrest. In 1994, 12,586,227 offenses were known to the police; only 21.4 percent were cleared by arrest.[3] When police make an arrest, it generally takes some time for the case to make its way through to a disposition. In 1992, the average number of days between arrest and conviction for felony cases disposed by State courts was 173.[4] Finally, most of the resulting sentences are not terribly severe; it is estimated that 52 percent of all felony convictions result in probation.[5] Traditional probation is the most extensively used sanction in the correctional system. About 60 percent of offenders under correctional supervision are on probation.[6] And while research has repeatedly suggested that the certainty and swiftness of sanctions matters more than their severity, most of the political and policy debate has centered on increasing sanctions. Debates center on the death penalty and three-strikes laws, not on clearance rates for violent crimes or the workloads of prosecutors and judges.

The resulting weakness of deterrence is perhaps particularly vexing where chronic offenders are concerned. It has long been known that a relatively small number of criminals offend at very high rates, are repeatedly arrested and sanctioned, and—if only by virtue of their continued offending—demonstrate a particular resistance to both deterrence and rehabilitation. This is a particular problem where violent offending is concerned. Not all chronic offenders are violent offenders, but a large proportion of violent crimes are committed by chronic offenders, who commit not only crimes of violence but also property crimes, drug crimes, disorder offenses, and the like. Such offenders are themselves victimized at very high rates. Boston Gun Project research, for example, showed that youth homicide was concentrated among a small number of serially offending gang-involved youths. Only about 1,300 gang members—less than 1 percent of their age group citywide—in some 61 gangs were responsible for at least 60 percent, and probably more, of all the youth homicide in the city. These gang members were well known to authorities and tended to have extensive criminal records.

Pulling Levers in Boston

Deterring violence by this group of chronic offenders became a central Gun Project goal. The "pulling levers" strategy the Gun Project Working Group designed was built on a simple but crucially important realization: Chronic offending made these youths, and the gangs they formed, extremely vulnerable. Authorities had a large and varied menu of ways—"levers to pull," as the Working Group came to call them—they could impose costs on these gangs. They could disrupt street drug activity, focus police attention on low-level street crimes such as trespassing and public drinking, serve outstanding warrants, cultivate confidential informants for medium- and long-term investigations of gang activities, deliver strict probation and parole enforcement, seize drug proceeds and other assets, ensure stiffer plea bargains and sterner prosecutorial attention, request stronger bail terms (and enforce them), and even focus potentially severe Federal investigative and prosecutorial attention on, for example, gang-related drug activity.

This was, of course, not news to the authorities. There were two problems: It was impossible to give all the gangs this kind of heightened attention all the time, and occasional crackdowns, while useful in the short term, had little long-term impact. The ability to deliver overwhelming crackdowns, however, was not in doubt. The Working Group's innovation—again, simple but important—was to make it clear to gangs that violence would draw such crackdowns and then continue to communicate with gangs as the resulting strategy unfolded.

This changed the game rather dramatically. From a world in which the cost to a gang of committing a homicide was, perhaps, that a gang member would be caught and prosecuted (while "street" benefits such as a reputation for toughness accrued to the gang as a whole), the cost soared. Added to the original risk would be everything else the authorities could bring to bear: cash-flow problems caused by street drug market disruption, arrests for outstanding warrants, the humiliation of strict probation enforcement, even the possibility of severe sanctions brought by Federal involvement. Those costs were borne by the whole gang, not just the shooter. As long as the authorities were confident that they knew what gangs were involved in a particular act of violence, as they usually were, these penalties were certain; the Working Group could always figure out ways to reach out and touch particular gangs. They were also swift: Drug market

What It Isn't, and What It Is

It is worth noting that while a "pulling levers" strategy like Ceasefire may seem to be like certain existing criminal justice approaches, they are different in important ways. Ceasefire was not, for instance, a targeted prosecution strategy: No attempt was made to systematically take chronic offenders off the street. It was not a strategy for use against gang crime as such. It was not an antigang strategy to disrupt or dismantle Boston's gangs. Rather, it was an attempt to deter and control the particular problem of gang-related violence. If gangs refrained from violence but continued to commit other crimes, the normal workings of police, prosecutors, and the rest of the criminal justice community attended to them. But if they hurt people, Ceasefire members came calling.

It is possible to sketch the essence of what "pulling levers" encompasses. What follows is the basic structure, along with the key differences from more traditional deterrence approaches.

(1) Select a "target category" of behavior to be addressed, such as gang violence. (Traditional deterrence approaches have much broader targets, such as "offending" or "gang offending.")

(2) Assemble an array of agency capacities that can be deployed in the service of the strategy. In Boston, for example, the Ceasefire Working Group included police; probation; parole; Federal and local prosecutors; the Bureau of Alcohol, Tobacco and Firearms; school police; youth corrections; and gang outreach workers. Other agencies and groups that became deeply involved included clergy, the Drug Enforcement Administration (DEA), the Immigration and Naturalization Service, and neighborhood groups. (Traditional deterrence approaches tend to rely primarily on the routine workings of the police, prosecutors, and corrections.)

(3) Deliver a direct and explicit "retail deterrence" message to a relatively small target audience regarding what kind of behavior will provoke a special response and what that response will be. (Traditional deterrence approaches vaguely "send signals" to a large and indeterminate population, generally promise only arrest and prosecution as a response, and do not focus services and other opportunities on the same population in a complementary fashion.)

(4) Follow through. In Boston, the Ceasefire Working Group met roughly every 2 weeks, in addition to constant informal communication, to assess the violence problem in the city and craft necessary responses. (Traditional deterrence approaches are generally unable to deliver a sustained and focused response.)

(5) Continue to communicate with the target audience as the strategy unfolds. (Traditional deterrence approaches rely on the routine workings of criminal justice agencies to send signals to offenders and do not draw explicit cause-and-effect connections between the behavior of the target population and the behavior of the authorities.)

(6) Select, if desired, a new category of target behavior. If the original target behavior is controlled, a new one—overt drug trafficking, domestic violence—may be selected. (Traditional deterrence approaches do not take a strategic approach to winning selected battles in a manner of the public's choosing.)

disruption, increased disorder enforcement, warrant service, probation attention, and the like could be deployed within days of a violent event. Rather than an uncertain, slow, and often nonsevere response to violence, the response with the Ceasefire strategy became certain, rapid, and of whatever range of severity the Working Group felt appropriate.

Talking regularly to the gangs served a number of purposes. Originally, the Working Group wanted to make sure that gangs knew about this new policy—so they could comply if they wished—and to tell other gangs when a gang was being punished for violence. The Working Group also wanted to make clear to gangs that while violence would bring strong attention, refraining from violence would not win them a "pass" to deal drugs or do other crimes: This was, in language the Working Group used explicitly in the gang meetings, "a promise, not a deal." Other purposes emerged as the strategy was actually implemented. One objective was to make cause and effect clear: to explain to the city's gangs that a particular drug raid, for example, was but a means to an end and was not about drugs as such but a penalty being imposed for violence. Another purpose was to bolster the Working Group's own credibility: to be able to say to gangs, in effect, "We said it, we meant it, and here's proof of that: Here's what they did, here's what we did, here's how you steer clear." Another goal was to give gangs that appeared to be on the verge of trouble a dose of what the Working

Group came to think of as "retail deterrence": to reach out to them directly, one on one and face to face, and make it clear that violence would bring a strong response.

Perhaps most important, however, was that the Working Group came to realize that communication allowed the creation of a fundamentally different balance of power between the authorities and the streets. The Working Group could deploy, at best, only a few severe crackdowns at a time. But like an old-West sheriff facing down a band of desperadoes with one bullet in his gun, direct communication with gangs allowed the Working Group to say, "We're ready, we're watching, we're waiting: Who wants to be next?" And, as with the sheriff, when that message was clear and credible, not only did nobody want to be next, it was not necessary to fire the shot. So it appears to have transpired in Boston. There was one serious crackdown in May 1996, followed by another—the one described above—in August 1996. Enforcement actions of the severity of the Intervale crackdown have not been necessary since.

Strategies Against Other Problems

It is interesting to consider applying the "pulling levers" strategy to other important crime problems. Imagine a city with 20 active street drug markets and associated problems of violence, disorder, and the involvement of juveniles as corner dealers, lookouts, and drug couriers. Such drug markets are notoriously resistant to ordinary enforcement attention. A "pulling levers" strategy could begin by creating channels of communication with each drug market: through beat officers, probation officers, community representatives, even posters and fliers. On, for example, May 15, the authorities send the following message to all 20 markets:

> We have three serious crackdowns ready to deploy. They will involve heavy police and probation presence, warrant service, and the like. Those arrested will receive special prosecutorial attention and, if convicted to probation, will be put on strict-supervision probation regimes; groups and individuals with a history of violence will be screened for added attention by DEA and the U.S. Attorney. We will decide, over the next 2 weeks, where to direct those crackdowns. We will make our decisions based on whether, between now and then, there is any violence associated with your drug market.

Presumably at least one or two of these hypothetical markets are violent, and they receive crackdowns lasting 6 weeks. On July 15, new messages go out to the drug markets. The authorities say:

> We're gearing up again. We remind you that you've been warned before and that several markets broke the rules. Here's what happened to them. Once again, we warn you that any violence will bring serious consequences.

This cycle is repeated until drug market-related violence is controlled.

At this point, the authorities change their message to the following:

> The old rules still apply. Violence will bring consequences. But now that the violence is nearly gone, we're also going to insist on order. In 2 weeks, we're launching new crackdowns. We're going to assign them based on what is bothering the community the most: unruly buyers, late-night traffic, public drinking and urination, street-corner sales, and the like. (And, by the way, pick up your trash.)

Once again, the authorities repeat the cycle of communicating, responding, and communicating again until order is established.

The authorities then send a final message:

> The old rules still apply. Violence and disorder bring attention. (And, by the way, congratulations on behaving. We knew you were rational people.) We have one new rule. Don't use juveniles in your trade any more; the kids are off limits. And since those of you using juveniles are usually one or two steps removed from the streets, we're going to have to resort to serious investigations, in concert with DEA, to reach you. You don't want that. We don't want to have to do it. So pay attention.

It may not be unreasonable to think that such a strategy could address many of the worst problems associated with street drug markets. It would not address drug trafficking as such to any great extent; the market would no doubt reestablish itself in a safer, quieter, and more discreet fashion. But until we figure out how to stop the drug trade, this would be a considerable victory, and one many cities would be happy to win.

Conclusion

Community policing and problem-solving policing can be viewed as attempts to escape what have become the routine, and often extremely unsatisfactory, choices posed by traditional thinking about crime control. Deterrence, or, failing that, incapacitation, was the business of criminal justice, yet the ordinary case-processing business of criminal justice agencies often manifestly failed to deliver sufficient crime control. The other alternatives were root-cause strategies that prevent crime by making fundamental improvements in communities and the lives of the people and families that constitute them. Yet these too were uncertain, hard to carry out in the midst of high levels of local crime and fear, and offered little help to communities needing immediate help with serious public safety problems. Community policing and problem-solving policing have tried to escape that bind by borrowing from the repertoire of both enforcement and prevention, crafting strategic interventions for particular problems in concert with a wide variety of new partners. It may be that the "pulling levers" framework offers some useful guidance to shaping some of those interventions. Deterrence may not be so hard to come by after all. And, remarkably, it may be that a key aspect of getting the deterrence equation right is simply communicating directly with the last group that is usually considered for inclusion in crime control strategies: offenders themselves. It would be nice if this were so. Talk, after all, is cheap.

Notes

1. Berard, Darrin, "Turning Bad Apples Around," *Lowell Sun*, November 16, 1997.
2. Ibid.
3. Maguire, Kathleen, and Ann Pastore, eds., *Sourcebook of Criminal Justice Statistics 1995*, Washington, D.C.: U.S. Department of Justice, Bureau of Justice Statistics, 1996: 425, NCJ 158900 [hereinafter *1995 Sourcebook*].
4. Maguire, Kathleen, and Ann Pastore, eds., *1995 Sourcebook*: 509.
5. See Cuniff, Mark, *Sentencing Outcomes in 28 Felony Courts, 1985*, Washington, D.C.: U.S. Department of Justice, National Institute of Justice, 1987: 1, NCJ 107760.
6. Maguire, Kathleen, and Ann Pastore, eds., *1995 Sourcebook*: 540.

Operation Ceasefire was a 1997 Innovations in American Government program award winner. Every year, the Innovations in American Government program, administered by the John F. Kennedy School of Government at Harvard University, recognizes creative government initiatives. ✦

Chapter 27 Community Policing:

An Approach to Youth Gangs in a Medium-Sized City

Jim Weston

This brief article reports on an approach to gang policing that contrasts markedly with the strategies described in the two previous articles. While sharing the elements of selective targeting with the Westminster and Boston programs, the community policing strategy adopted in Reno focuses on engaging less-committed gang members in intervention programs, community awareness about gangs, and community collaboration in law enforcement operation and policy. Working with the media to report more accurately and better inform the public about gang matters is another distinctive feature of this approach. This is one variation of the community mobilization strategy described in the last Chapter of this volume.

Reno, Nevada, a tourist destination city of 135,000, serves a daily visitor population of 50,000 to 60,000. Its 315 sworn officers patrol 50 square miles, including several isolated geographical islands of the city. The 24-hour per day gaming and tourism industry draws a large number of transient, low-income service employees posing unique policing problems, such as a calls-for-service workload that frequently remains just as active on the late night shift as on the evening shift.

In 1986, after a series of violent crimes—including the gang rape of a 12-year-old girl—public outrage and demand for action prompted the Reno Police Department to form a gang unit, which was charged with developing a plan to gather gang intelligence information, adopt a zero-tolerance enforcement program targeted at gang members and educate the public concerning the dangers of youth gangs in the community.

Youths belonging to, or associated with, gangs were subject to constant scrutiny and arrest for a variety of violations. Drug sales activity being conducted by a black gang in a local park resulted in massive arrests and several violent confrontations between police and neighborhood youths. Although gang officers and detectives produced a high clearance rate for violent gang-motivated crime, gang membership continued to grow even as confrontations between police and neighborhood youths increased. Increased media attention to each gang incident fueled a public paranoia about the influence of gangs, although gang-motivated crime accounted for only a fraction of the violent crime in the city.

During this time, a survey revealed that 60 percent of Reno residents thought the police were not doing a good job and considered most officers to be "isolated and non-caring." The media portrayed the department as heavy-handed in its operations, and openly challenged the chief. The department had also suffered from 10 years of staff reductions coupled with increased workload, during which time two attempts to pass a ballot initiative to hire more officers were rejected by disgruntled voters.

Seeing a need for major change, then-Police Chief Robert Bradshaw embarked on a department-wide transformation to a community policing philosophy called "COP+." The "+" stood for a quality assurance bureau, which was charged with conducting contin-

Reprinted from: Jim Weston, "Community Policing: An Approach to Youth Gangs in a Medium-Sized City." In *The Police Chief,* 1993, 60(8):80–84.

uing public surveys to assess the department's performance and obtain public feedback concerning its operations. Captains formed neighborhood advisory groups (NAGs) to provide them with feedback about the department. The department's command structure was flattened out, and operations were decentralized to allow supervisors and commanders the ability to deal with neighborhood problems more effectively.

The department leadership instituted radical changes in the way officers went about their business in every section of the department, from traffic services to animal control to employee training. One change resulted in the abandonment of the enforcement-oriented war against gangs philosophy in favor of a new Community Action Team (CAT) designed to work with the community to address a wide range of youth gang issues.

Community Action Team (CAT)

Community policing normally means that the community is included as a partner with police in dealing with community issues, allocation of resources and problem solving. The Reno Police Department carried this philosophy a step further, designing the new CAT team with guidance from members of the local minority neighborhoods, community service agencies and political leaders. A general order defining what comprised a gang and the manner in which police would collect intelligence was developed with considerable public input.

The result was a decision not to wage a war against gangs, but to create a highly specialized team of officers to target the top 5 percent of violent gang members with a repeat offender program. At the same time, the team would assume responsibility for coordinating efforts to address the 80 percent of local gang members who were not involved in criminal activity and not considered to be "hard core." The minority community and police agreed that any effort to totally eliminate gangs would experience the same failure as the war against drugs. It was acknowledged that youth gangs fill a need in the lives of disadvantaged or neglected youth and that outlawing gang membership would simply worsen the problem.

Ten officers and two detectives were initially assigned to CAT; the team was subsequently expanded to include a drug dog handler and a Hispanic liaison officer. CAT team activities encompassed the following areas.

Intelligence Gathering

To lessen the tension between gang members and the police during field contacts, CAT team officers received cultural sensitivity training and were provided with "gang kits" consisting of cameras, field interview cards and tape recorders. A passive gang member identification technique was developed that encouraged local gang members to allow their photographs to be taken and to provide gang affiliation, addresses and other personal data.

Additionally, an officer regularly visits the regional jail to interview incarcerated gang members. The goal is not to obtain information about the specific case for which these gang members were arrested, but to obtain current gang intelligence information. Automated gang moniker files were developed that allow field officers with laptop computers to enter partial information about suspects involved in gang-motivated crime and have this information matched with specific gangs. This data base has resulted in the quick resolution of many violent crimes.

While many agencies have developed similar intelligence systems, Reno has taken the additional step of requiring names to be purged from the files for such reasons as a period of inactivity, no contact with police or—under certain circumstances—a personal request. The minority community in Reno felt that this purge system was very important, since it helps to prevent gang members from being labeled for life and provides a more realistic tally of current gang membership.

To minimize the negative perception of police held by many minorities during traffic stops or field contacts, a brochure titled, "What To Do When Stopped by Police," was prepared and distributed throughout the community. Developed with the assistance of the county Legal Aid Society, the brochure provides information as to what procedures police follow on traffic stops, as well as advice concerning rights of citizens who are contacted by police.

Since the program began, thousands of field contacts with gang members have been made without generating one formal complaint of harassment or heavyhandedness.

Repeat Offender Targeting

A core group of CAT officers was assigned to target the most violent gang members, as well as those involved in weapons violations. As with most crimes, officers found that the vast majority of gang-motivated crime in Reno was committed by 10 to 15 percent of the city's gang members.

In 1992, the FBI and five local law enforcement agencies created a Violent Crime Task Force to target the top 1 percent of gang members responsible for the most serious crimes. Again, the minority community was consulted during the formation process, and periodic meetings have continued with the group to discuss its progress. The Repeat Offender Program was designed specifically to avoid the perception that gang membership was a primary criterion for enforcement.

In conjunction with the targeting efforts, efforts by the state legislature to criminalize membership in youth gangs and outlaw youth gangs engaged in criminal activity were opposed by both the police department and the community, who agreed that these measures would have created an unenforceable and unwinnable situation for the police. Such legislation also would have done little to deal with the real issues underlying youth gang violence.

Community Awareness

The CAT team was designed to allow its officers to be free of the regular calls-for-service work load, which in turn allowed them time to deal directly with the families of many younger gang members or "wannabes." For example, officers encountering a gang member painting graffiti or participating in minor crimes were able to take the child home and speak directly to the parents concerning the offense. Literature and counseling referral services were provided for families who normally only heard the child's side of stories involving the police.

Officers developed relationships with many families, who in turn became invaluable sources of intelligence information concerning the worst offenders in neighborhood gangs. As a result, when major gang crimes occurred, neighborhood residents would usually support the department's efforts to deal with the problem. For example, one father of a Hispanic gang member wanted for a stabbing during a neighborhood gang incident provided the CAT officers with his son's whereabouts and then provided a news interview supporting the efforts of the police.

Intervention Programs

CAT officers became directly involved in efforts to deter gang membership. A jobs program with local trades was developed, allowing CAT officers to refer gang members into apprenticeship work programs at construction companies, auto body shops and other businesses that provide better opportunities than the typical low-paying service job.

In conjunction with a local, private gang counseling organization, CAT officers operated a bicycle shop that paid gang members to refurbish and rebuild bicycles to be donated to disadvantaged children. The building housing the bike shop, as well as ongoing expenses, was funded by local businesses and grants. At its peak, the program was providing a neutral territory for more than 50 individuals associated with 12 different gangs. Counseling, education and referral services were made available for gang members who brought friends or family members to the bike shop.

The department also conducts a variety of other outreach programs, including:

- An annual COPS + Kids picnic attracting over 2,500 underprivileged youth gives police officers an opportunity to educate kids and their parents about the department and its operations. Thousands of dollars of prizes, food and services are given away.

- PAL wrestling, backpacking, water skiing and boxing programs are targeted to underprivileged and gang youth.
- Police funds are provided to support a number of minority youth programs operated by local ministers.

Northern Nevada Youth Gang Task Force

In 1988, more than a dozen local agencies formed a Northern Nevada Youth Gang Task Force consisting of officers involved in gang intelligence operations. The group shared automated intelligence files, and most agencies began participating in the automated G.R.E.A.T. (Gang Resistance Education and Training) gang intelligence system operated by the Los Angeles County Sheriff's Department.

Most members of the group adopted the press policy established by the Reno Police Department to limit sensationalization of gang activities. The chiefs and sheriffs of the major agencies collaborated on media statements concerning gang-related issues in the county.

NAGs Provide Feedback

In conjunction with the police department's COP+ program, the chief of police and area captains developed Neighborhood Advisory Groups (NAGs) in geographical areas throughout the city to solicit feedback from the community. An advisory group of local minority leaders involved in youth gang issues was also organized, as was a NAG of gang members. In developing the gang NAG, the department did not recognize specific gangs as representatives, but did allow persons belonging to a variety of different gangs to join the group, where they were given access to the chief of police to air their concerns.

NAGs became very useful when new enforcement programs were adopted because the groups were able to participate in the programs' development and offer suggestions. As mentioned earlier, the FBI Violent Crime Task Force targeting gang crime utilized the groups during the formation process and for continuing feedback concerning operations.

The minority NAG initially voiced much fear of "secretive" FBI enforcement tactics that would exclude the media and public from any knowledge of the operations. Consequently, after several meetings with the FBI special agent in charge and heads of the participating law enforcement agencies, a number of safeguards were written into the task force agreement to address these concerns. The result was that the task force enjoyed the public support of the NAGs, the NAACP and a local Hispanic group.

Similarly, the input and blessing of the NAGs are typically sought prior to the implementation of major gang/drug enforcement projects in the neighborhoods to avoid controversy later when the media began reporting the arrests and neighborhood gang activity.

Media

A media policy, developed in conjunction with the NAGs and other local agencies that provide youth gang services, recommends that while law enforcement agencies should avoid identifying individual gangs or gang members by name or address, they should provide complete and accurate information when gang-motivated crime occurs.

A pool of statistical information was maintained to de-escalate periodic attempts by the media to overplay the gang crime issue. A semi-annual report, "Status of Gangs in the City of Reno," was prepared for the general public providing information on the total gang population, numbers and types of gang crimes committed and, most importantly, the results of gang intervention programs.

Gang-motivated crimes were repeatedly compared with total Part I felony crimes, showing that only a fraction of a percent of the total reported felony crime in Reno was attributable to gang members. The monthly gang crime and membership statistics made available to the media had a tendency to curtail journalistic efforts to overstate the gang problem.

The first question normally asked by reporters covering a violent crime was, "Is it gang related?" If an answer was not provided by the department, reporters typically approached neighbors, witnesses or anyone else who would comment and ask the same question. Unfortunately, residents would often label a crime as gang related whether it was or not. Consequently, the department made it a priority to determine as quickly as possible whether or not gang involvement was present and relay this information to the media. In the majority of cases, gang motivation was not present. Additionally, the department created a network of other agencies and sources that agreed to the same media policy to prevent the media from pitting the police against other groups when discussing the gang situation in Reno. One of these groups was the Gang Alternatives Partnership (GAP).

GAP

Formed in 1991 to coordinate the resources from public and private agencies involved in dealing with youth gangs, GAP included representatives from law enforcement, the district attorney's office, juvenile probation, the school district, several private agencies, businesses and private individuals. The group recognized early that any one group would have a limited impact on the youth gang issue. Thus, the partnership became invaluable in balancing the member agencies' enforcement, intervention and education efforts, as well as in providing a single source of information for the community on youth gang issues. Too often, the police had been targeted as the "experts" on youth gangs, resulting in a tendency for the media and community to focus on violence and enforcement programs.

Through community donations, a full-time executive director is being hired to administer grant programs, contribution drives and other resources. Public statements concerning the status of youth gangs, the effectiveness of intervention programs and the best approach to certain issues were jointly agreed upon and presented by the group.

Summary

In 1988, the citizens of Reno passed a ballot initiative that increased the number of police officers in Reno by 40 percent. Over the years since the first semi-annual community survey was conducted in 1987, the department's standing has improved to the point that nine out of every 10 residents report that they believe the police are doing a good job. A deputy chief responsible for the CAT team received the local NAACP chapter's Freedom Citation in recognition of the department's efforts, specifically with gang-related issues.

Youth gang violence in Reno has been minimal in comparison with total felony crime and, although gang membership continues to increase at a moderate rate, fear is no longer simply linked to an increase in gang membership. The minority community supports tough enforcement efforts against repeat violent offenders in gangs, and officers have been very effective in solving gang-related crime. Although it is difficult to prove definitively, it would appear that limited violence and limited growth in gang membership is related to the many success stories resulting from intervention efforts.

A lesson learned early in Reno was that there was no aspect of policing that could not benefit from a collaboration with the community. The traditional law enforcement mentality that the police are the expert "technicians" who know best how to deal with crime problems is simply a myth. There is no rule book that dictates how the police can best deal with crime or community issues, and there are certainly few proven methods for dealing with youth gang issues. One fact does remain, however. A community that participates in the process also willingly supports the efforts of the police. ✦

Chapter 28
Civil Gang Abatement:
A Community Based Policing Tool of the Office of the Los Angeles City Attorney

L.A. City Attorney
Gang Prosecution Section

The current thrust in gang policy is toward gang suppression and deterrence at the expense of prevention, rehabilitation, and efforts to change the social conditions that make gangs viable options for more and more youths today. Civil Gang Abatement provides an example of this approach, one which raises serious issues about the civil rights of gang members, as the use of civil abatement laws provides the police with the right to arrest individuals in gangs for acts that would otherwise be noncriminal. In addition to the fact that these measures are undertaken without also providing alternatives for gang youth, it is possible that these efforts will increase gang cohesiveness rather than diminish it. Without systematic evaluations of civil gang abatement strategies on gang processes and behavior, we cannot assess the impact of these increasingly popular approaches to gang intervention.

The L.A. City Attorney "Civil Gang Abatement" is a coordinated effort by police, prosecutors, and local residents to significantly reduce illegal gang, drug and other criminal activity while simultaneously identifying and providing resources to measurably improve the quality of life for residents of a targeted neighborhood. While the legal proceeding which is entitled "Civil Gang Abatement" is, by itself, a legal proceeding aimed at obtaining an injunction against a criminal element such as a street gang to prohibit them from engaging in conduct which facilitates criminal activity, the *ultimate* goal of the Civil Gang Abatement is to act as a *vehicle* for the coordination of various community-based policing efforts such as Neighborhood Watch, graffiti abatement, building abatements, at-risk youth identification, and employment recruitment as well as the more traditional law enforcement efforts to suppress narcotics trafficking and gang activity through undercover narcotics operations and the vertical (specialized) prosecution of hard-core gang members. When the Civil Gang Abatement is coordinated with other government and community-based efforts, as described in the "Broken Windows"[1] theory, crime is not only reduced but the neighborhood's *quality of life* is visibly improved and a mechanism remains to insure its continued improvement. Because the Civil Gang Abatement, by definition, begins through the mobilization of the community through meetings of local residents, police and prosecutors to identify problems which exist in the neighborhood in support of the prosecutor's request for an injunction, the Civil Gang Abatement also becomes a means to identify those resources which are necessary to improve the quality of life in a particular neighborhood. Such community meetings invariably identify needed community resources beyond law enforcement deployment, such as child care, parenting classes, street maintenance, graffiti removal, and increased employment opportunities. The Civil Gang Abatement is successful because it includes the coordination of resources to address these problems while simultaneously reducing criminal ac-

Prepared by the Gang Unit, Los Angeles City Attorney's Office, Los Angeles, CA. Martin Vranicar, Supervisor. Edited by Jule Bishop, Deputy City Attorney. Reprinted by permission.

tivity through the injunction and other law enforcement efforts. As such, the Civil Gang Abatement is a complete program which begins as a means to identify specific criminal elements and to provide an innovative legal solution to abate such criminal activity while simultaneously identifying other community needs and providing those resources which will bring about a measurable improvement in the quality of life for residents of the targeted area. The following is an illustration of how the Civil Gang Abatement can simultaneously mobilize a community through community based policing, identify and suppress drug dealing by a local street gang and also begin the revitalization of the community as a result of the community empowerment brought about by the Civil Gang Abatement process.

Gang-Related Drug Dealing Without a 'Civil Gang Abatement'

Without a "Civil Gang Abatement," *uniformed* police vainly attempt to enforce drug laws against street dealers. All day long, gang members stand at intersections known for drug sales, wear pagers, dress in gang attire, flash handsigns, and wave at and approach passing vehicles and pedestrians for what are certainly offers to buy drugs. Yet, because all of these activities (i.e. wearing pagers, flashing handsigns, waving at and approaching vehicles, etc.) are lawful conduct, the gang members are immune from arrest unless an actual exchange of money for drugs is observed. Since the uniformed officer typically observes only the lawful activity preceding the actual sale, he is forced to drive past in frustration while law abiding citizens look on in disgust.

Although it is true that an *undercover* officer may be able to successfully arrest and convict a limited number of gang members for drug sales and hopefully obtain lengthy prison terms (which is almost impossible in Los Angeles due to jail overcrowding), undercover enforcement fails to have any measurable impact on the *ability of the gang to profit*. This is because the "removal" of even a substantial number of drug dealing gang members by undercover officers, for no matter how long, merely creates a "vacancy" in the ranks of the gang's organization, with an endless supply of young recruits ready to assume that enviable position on the street corner dealing the gang's narcotics. Even under the best of circumstances, the gang will successfully consummate hundreds, if not thousands, of drug transactions while suffering only a handful of unsuccessful sales due to undercover enforcement. Add to this the fact that undercover narcotics officers are few in number and that all police departments rely, for the most part, upon uniformed personnel to achieve crime suppression and reduction, it is not surprising that while some gang members may serve long prison sentences, conspicuous drug dealing by the gang continues unabated.

Gang-Related Drug Dealing *With* a 'Civil Gang Abatement'

With a "Civil Gang Abatement," uniformed officers are given the tools to effectively impact a gang's ability to profit from drug dealing, while simultaneously providing the means for the community to improve the quality of life for all its residents. The legal procedure known as a "Civil Gang Abatement" is similar to a situs or building abatement.[2] However, unlike a building abatement which may result in a court ordered injunction against a *property owner*, the "Civil Gang Abatement" seeks a series of court orders against *members of a street gang*. For those unfamiliar with building abatements, the legal procedure known as a "Civil Gang Abatement" is easily understood when likened to an ordinary labor strike.

Consider, for a moment, an emotional labor strike wherein picketers grow in number and eventually become unruly, interfering with the ability of the employer and working employees to enter the work place. Once it becomes evident that routine police action will not be able to insure the protection of those choosing to cross the picket lines and violence appears certain, the employer and/or police provide evidence to a judge that the strikers are creating a dangerous nuisance. The court helps "abate" or reduce the nuisance by issuing orders which prohibit or "enjoin" the strikers from doing certain things, such as picketing too close to the entrance of the work place, limiting the number of picketers and other restrictions which will help to curb anticipated violence. These orders are in the form of an injunction which applies to every striker who chooses to picket and possibly interfere with the employer's ability to conduct business during the strike. If, after the strikers are formally notified of the injunction, they choose to ignore the orders of the court (e.g. picketing closer to the work entrance than the court injunction permits), the strikers are subject to arrest for Penal Code Section 166.4.[3]

Thus, aggressive enforcement of an injunction enables law enforcement to effectively *prevent* imminent criminal activity by arresting persons for *prohibited patterns of conduct which are known to precede and facilitate these crimes*. In the case of the strikers, this pattern of conduct includes strikers congregating in dangerously large groups, standing too close to a work place entrance and carrying signs which could be used as weapons. Since, in the case of gang activity, law enforcement can also identify many patterns of lawful activity by gang members which contribute to and normally precede the commission of certain crimes, such as drug dealing, the goal of the Civil Gang Abatement, as in the labor strike analogy, is to identify otherwise lawful conduct by gang members which precedes and furthers criminal activity and then seek to enjoin or prohibit it.[4]

Many gang members wear pagers, "dress down" in gang attire, flash "handsigns," approach and solicit business from pedestrians and passing vehicles, and congregate at known drug sales locations, all for the express purpose of selling illegal narcotics. If, however, this conduct is enjoined (prohibited) by a court, uniformed police are, for the first time, able to make arrests *before* drug deals are consummated, thus impairing the gang's ability to *profit* from drug dealing (which ultimately *prevents* gang-related drug dealing). Simply put, instead of consummating hundreds of illegal drug transactions and earning large profits before suffering an arrest for sale of narcotics, gang members are now subject to arrest for simply doing the things that are *necessary* for them to do *before* they can begin to sell the drugs and earn the profits. Since even standing on a particular corner or wearing a beeper can subject a gang member to arrest, the previously helpless *uniformed* officer is now able to *interfere* with and *reduce* the gang's ability to profit from drug sales by arresting the gang members *before* they are able to consummate a drug transaction. This effort, combined with undercover strategies, can effectively interfere with the gang's ability to profit while incarcerating an increasing number of drug dealing gang members.[5] Since the gang's potential for profits is diminished, the chronic and daily drug dealing on neighborhood street corners ceases and other forces are able to work together to significantly improve the overall quality of life for the residents of the community.

Civil Gang Abatement: How It Works

The L.A. City Attorney "Civil Gang Abatement" brings together specially assigned police, prosecutors and residents of the targeted neighborhood to gather the evidence which will prove to a judge that identified patterns of conduct such as the wearing of pagers, approaching pedestrians and passing vehicles and congregating at known drug locations furthers the illegal drug activity of the local gang and deserves to be enjoined by the court. Through the use of police, resident and community leader declarations, photographs and videos, crime and arrest statistics, and anything else that helps describe the gang's effect on the community, the Civil Gang Abatement persuades the judge to issue an injunction prohibiting the gang members, as a group, from engaging in the patterns of conduct identified by the community and police. Before the injunction is issued, a "Notice" by the City or District Attorney is distributed throughout the community warning the gang that if it does not stop (abate) its illegal criminal activities, the City or District Attorney's Office will seek an injunction against the gang.[6] If statistics and other evidence indicate that the gang is not complying with the Notice to Abate, then the prosecutor files a complaint requesting issuance of an injunction which includes court orders designed to help abate the criminal activity of the defendant street gang. Once the injunction is issued, the police can serve copies of the injunction on all gang members and immediately enforce the orders of the court through arrests for disobedience of a court order.[7] Ideally, those gang members arrested for violating the court injunction should be prosecuted by the City or District Attorney assigned to the Civil Gang Abatement. This special prosecutor not only will seek significant jail terms but more importantly, pursue probation conditions (such as "search and seizure" conditions, "do not associate with other gang members," and even "exclusion" from the neighborhood) which were not included in the terms of the civil injunction. Thus, even if a gang member violates the injunction and suffers only a small jail sentence with probation, a subsequent violation of probation can result in significant jail sentences and the virtual removal of that gang member from the neighborhood.[8]

Coordination of Other Efforts: 'The Community Impact Team'

While the effort to obtain an injunction against a drug dealing street gang can be, by itself, effective in interfering with a gang's ability to profit from drug dealing and thus reduce the gang's other criminal activities, the "Civil Gang Abatement" can and should be combined with other law enforcement strategies to address the many other problems that are certain to occur in the targeted neighborhood, as described in the "Broken Windows Theory." The creation of "Community Impact Teams" composed of specially assigned police and prosecutors facilitates the coordination of these efforts, as well as the gathering of the evidence necessary to obtain an injunction against the street gang.[9] For example, the Community Impact Team (or whatever name one assigns to such a group) schedules a number of community meetings attended by local residents, landlords, merchants, regular patrol and narcotics officers and probation officers. At these meetings, the "Community Impact Team" explains the concept of the "Civil Gang Abatement" and its reliance upon the participation of the community. Residents, merchants and property owners attending these meetings are asked to document how the local gang and its criminal activities have negatively impacted their quality of life. Citizens maintain diaries or "logs" of life in the area controlled or frequented by the gang. Not only is gang activity recorded but, importantly, the *consequences* of gang activity are also documented. As such, the logs not only include descriptions of gunshots going off each night and routine intimidation by gang members but also describe how municipal sanitation trucks avoid the neighborhood for fear of gang violence and streets remain in disrepair because maintenance workers are afraid to enter the area. These logs not only serve to mobilize the community against a local street gang but become the primary evidence in court to justify the issuance of an injunction.[10]

'Broken Windows Theory' and Community-Based Policing:[11] A Non-Traditional Approach to Law Enforcement

Because the consequences of gang activity include the deterioration of the normal municipal services such as street maintenance, garbage collection and other services critical to the quality of life of any community, the logs also become an important resource for use by the "Community Impact Team" in determining what other remedies are required to restore the quality of life in the neighborhood. For example, if residents describe trash and debris in alleys, the Team may discover that sanitation trucks do not regularly pick up trash in alleys for fear of violence or simply out of disgust because the gang quickly replaces the trash within hours of its pickup. The "Community Impact Team" thus, through its coordination with other governmental entities including the Department of Sanitation, takes necessary action to insure that future trash pickups include alleys in the targeted neighborhood. The "Civil Gang Abatement" is, accordingly, not only an effective and logical law enforcement tool for the permanent abatement of drug dealing street gangs, but a vehicle to assist a "Community Impact Team" in improving the *quality of life* in a neighborhood. Because the law enforcement activity is scheduled to occur *at the same time* that municipal services are restored by a "Community Impact Team," the lessons learned from the "Broken Window Theory" are realized and the community enjoys a renewed sense of calm as crime is reduced and the neighborhood actually begins to *look* and *feel* safer, all at the same time.

Some may question the wisdom of employing police and prosecutors, at significant taxpayer expense, to spearhead an effort to improve the quality of life for a neighborhood besieged by gangs and drugs. Why not use staff from offices of elected officials, especially since the "Broken Windows Theory" involves the coordination of municipal services normally not under the control or supervision of law enforcement? The reason, however, is simple. Since the coordination of all the efforts, both law enforcement strategies and municipal services, must be carefully timed in relation to when successes are achieved by police and prosecutors, only prosecutors and police are able to know *when* the restoration of municipal services is best implemented.

If, for instance, sanitation resumes trash collection in targeted areas before law enforcement has taken appropriate action to keep gang members from continually undermining sanitation efforts, trash collectors will quickly realize the futility in resuming trash collection and, once again, abandon the area. In addition, it is through the gathering of declarations from residents describing how the gang has negatively affected the community that one knows precisely what municipal services are required to improve the quality of life in the targeted neighborhood.

Moreover, it is the application of esoteric and little used laws (i.e. building abatement and nuisance laws, local codes and ordinances, special sentencing procedures) that require a special prosecutor who can use these laws to force compliance by landlords, residents and gang members. All too often, governmental entities responsible for insuring compliance with local laws (such as Building & Safety or Health & Safety Codes) are unsure of little used but effective legal strategies known to a prosecutor which can effectuate compliance and help contribute to the improved quality of life for the community. Thus, a building and safety inspector frustrated in his attempts to enforce Building and Safety Code violations against a property owner who allows gang and drug activity may be more successful if his efforts are linked with the strategies of the prosecutor and police of the Civil Gang Abatement.

In addition, the building inspector may not realize that in the course of inspecting a drug and gang infested building for code violations, the *timing* and *coordination* of his efforts with law enforcement could not only result in building code compliance but a marked reduction in gang activity. This, of course, is based on a fundamental concept that criminal activity can be dramatically reduced if the environment supporting the criminal activity is changed. Simply put, to the extent that the building inspector can use his legal weapons to force a property owner to improve a building's quality and appearance *at the same time* that other law enforcement efforts are in progress to abate gang and drug activity, he is able to create an environment in that building that will discourage criminal activity and likewise encourage occupancy by law abiding tenants. A building inspector who works closely with the Civil Gang Abatement prosecutor and local police can play a major role in bringing about a marked and permanent reduction in gang related crime in a neighborhood. On the other hand, a building inspector who fails to coordinate his efforts with an experienced prosecutor and local police will do little more than bring about temporary compliance with local codes and miss an opportunity to contribute to a community's enhanced quality of life.

Sadly, even when governmental agencies are knowledgeable about unusual or little used strategies, many prosecutors are not familiar with such strategies and thus fail to aggressively enforce such efforts in court. A specially assigned prosecutor, on the other hand, will not only aid in the discovery of effective albeit little used legal strategies, but insure their enforcement and support in court. Lastly, only a specially trained prosecutor working closely with police can insure that the Civil Gang Abatement is brought to a successful conclusion notwithstanding its uniqueness in our criminal justice system. Certainly, elected officials and other governmental representatives should be involved in the coordination effort. But, because this is clearly a law enforcement strategy in combination with other municipal efforts, law enforcement should and must take a leading role.

City of Los Angeles vs. the Playboy Gangster Crips

In the first application of the "Civil Gang Abatement" (against a West Los Angeles street gang, the Playboy Gangster Crips),[12] conspicuous street dealing was out of control while a number of apartment buildings were effectively controlled by the local street gang as a result of poor management by property owners. In coordination with the gathering of evidence for the civil injunction against the local street gang, the local prosecutor used California building abatement laws to force property owners to take corrective action to discourage gang and drug activity at their property locations. The prosecutor ordered the owners to remove graffiti daily, erect security gates, install lighting, remove abandoned vehicles, initiate evictions of known drug dealers and even trim shrubbery so as to effectively discourage gang and drug activity. Sample leases, property management advice, advice regarding enforcement of state trespass laws and other special police patrols were simultaneously offered to help the property owners effectively discourage and remove unwanted gang activity. In addition, the prosecutor applied pressure to other governmental entities to pave streets, restore street lighting, and improve garbage collection. Instead of merely seeking easily obtained court orders against the landlords, the prosecutor applied the concepts embodied in "community-based policing," and *proactively assisted* property owners in taking corrective steps *before* their property deteriorated to the point where prosecution was indicated.

Although prior efforts by police failed to reduce the gang's control over the neighborhood, the "Civil Gang Abatement" reduced criminal activity significantly and, in effect, forced the gang out of the community. More importantly, the "Civil Gang Abatement" not only *statistically* reduced crime but brought about a significant and visibly measurable improvement in the *quality of life* in the area. Residents, once again, were observed walking their dogs, watering their lawns and painting their homes. "For Sale" signs came down and property values went up. Potholes were repaired, street lights replaced and garbage was collected on a daily basis. The project was so effective that it provided the impetus for the Mayor to create a permanently established program to coordinate such community efforts, appropriately called the "Model Neighborhood Program." Lastly, because the "Civil Gang Abatement" not only reduces criminal activity but also mobilizes the community as an effective voice in government, a mechanism was in place to insure that long after the police and prosecutor have moved on to other neighborhoods, crime in the area would remain low while the quality of life would continue to improve.

In conclusion, while the "Civil Gang Abatement" can be effective as a single law enforcement tool, it is clearly most effective when used as a *vehicle* for the coordinated application of 1) aggressive law enforcement strategies (including traditional narcotics enforcement such as "buy-busts," specialized criminal prosecutions and building abatements); 2) efforts to mobilize the community; *and* 3) the restoration of critical municipal services which are essential for improving the quality of life for residents of the neighborhood. Moreover, while it is conceivable that police departments may be able to begin the abatement process on their own, the early formation of "Community Impact Teams" involving specially assigned police-prosecutor teams is critical to insure that the efforts of the police and other agencies are aggressively supported in court. Furthermore, this special police-prosecutor team is essential to *coordinate* the application of law enforcement strategies with the restoration of critical municipal services so as to bring about a noticeable improvement in quality of life. If police departments and prosecuting agencies are willing to assign the relatively few resources necessary to implement a Civil Gang Abatement, the rewards can be astonishing—a community that experiences significantly reduced gang activity, drug dealing and truancy while enjoying a noticeable and long lasting improvement in the quality of life for all its residents.

[Editors' note: We present below the original abatement notice used by the City Attorney's Office. Later notices have undergone some revisions.]

NOTICE TO ABATE PUBLIC NUISANCE AND OF INTENT TO SEEK A PRELIMINARY AND PERMANENT INJUNCTION IN LIEU OF VOLUNTARY ABATEMENT.

TO: *WATTS VARIO GRAPE STREET aka WVG, aka GRAPE STREET WATTS, aka GSW, aka GRAPE STREET, aka GS, aka WATTS BABY LOCO CRIPS, aka WBLC, aka BABY LOCO CRIPS, aka BLC, aka BABY LOCS, aka LOCO CRIPS, aka LOCS, aka TINY LOCO CRIPS, aka TLC, aka TINY LOCS, aka TL, aka EAST SIDE KIDS, aka ESK, aka PLAYBOY HOO RIDE CRIPS, aka PHRC, aka HOO RIDE CRIPS, aka HRC, aka SOUTH SIDE GRAPE STREET, aka SSG ST, aka YOUNG PANTHERS,* an UNINCORPORATED ASSOCIATION AND STREET GANG AS DEFINED IN CODE SECTION 186.22 OF THE CALIFORNIA PENAL CODE, AND ALL OF ITS MEMBERS, ASSOCIATES, AGENTS AND ALL OTHER PERSONS ACTING UNDER, IN CONCERN WITH, FOR THE BENEFIT OF, AT THE DIRECTION OF, OR IN ASSOCIATION WITH THEM:

THE PEOPLE OF THE STATE OF CALIFORNIA, BY AND THROUGH JAMES K. HAHN, CITY ATTORNEY FOR THE CITY OF LOS ANGELES, HEREBY PUT YOU ON NOTICE THAT:

You are creating, maintaining and encouraging, and permitting others to create and maintain, a public nuisance in that you are engaging in and encouraging, and permitting others to engage in, continuing, repeated and ongoing acts of:

a. murder;

b. open and conspicuous narcotics trafficking;

c. open and conspicuous narcotics possession and use;

d. assaults and other acts of violence;

e. use and possession of dangerous weapons and ammunition;

f. vandalism to public and private property including, but not limited to, graffiti;

g. congregating at locations including, but not limited to, the 2000 to 2100 blocks between 101st and 102nd Streets, the 2000 to 2200 blocks on the north side of 103rd Street, in the City of Los Angeles, so as to attract persons who seek to purchase narcotics and other contraband, and attract members of rival street gangs who intend to commit acts of violence and other violations of law;

h. congregating at or near Jordan Down Public Housing Project, in sufficiently large numbers and in such a rude and threatening manner, so as to interfere with lawful law enforcement investigations and activities and threaten the safety and well-being of law abiding citizens;

i. blocking the free flow of vehicular traffic and emergency vehicles by approaching passing vehicles and engaging passengers in conversation;

j. blocking and obstructing sidewalks and pedestrian thoroughfares so as to annoy, threaten and intimidate law abiding citizens;

k. wearing and possessing certain identifiable hats, shirts, belts, jackets, sweat shirts, shoe laces, handkerchiefs, and other articles of clothing which identify the wearer as a member or associate of the criminal street gang known as Watts Vario Grape Street, so as to intimidate law abiding citizens, facilitate recruitment of younger law abiding citizens to join said criminal street gang and commit illegal acts, and encourage and induce members of rival street gangs to acts of violence;

l. yelling of words and phrases and making certain identifiable hand and body movements in public which are intended to warn other gang members, narcotics traffickers, and potential customers of narcotics, that police officers and representatives of the Housing Authority of the City of Los Angeles are present;

m. soliciting, inducing and encouraging others, either verbally, in writing, or by hand and body movements, to commit acts of violence to law abiding citizens, police officers, and other gang members;

n. possessing paging devices (beepers) and portable and cellular telephones at or near narcotic locations described in paragraph g. (above) so as to facilitate the trafficking of narcotics by respondent street gang.

THE ABOVE DESCRIBED ACTIVITIES ARE A PUBLIC NUISANCE, ARE OFFENSIVE TO THE SENSES, ARE INJURIOUS TO HEALTH, AND ARE INDECENT, SO AS TO INTERFERE WITH THE COMFORTABLE ENJOYMENT OF LIFE AND PROPERTY BY AN ENTIRE NEIGHBORHOOD AND A CONSIDERABLE NUMBER OF PERSONS IN THE COMMUNITY.

THEREFORE, You are hereby commanded to halt, discontinue and abate the creation and maintenance of the public nuisance described above.

In the event that you should fail to abate said public nuisance, notice is hereby given that the People of the State of California, by and through James K. Hahn, City Attorney of the City of Los Angeles, will seek a preliminary and permanent injunction prohibiting the continuance of said nuisance.

THE VIOLATION OF AN INJUNCTION CAN BE PUNISHED BY CRIMINAL PROSECUTION AND CIVIL CONTEMPT RESULTING IN JAIL, FINES, OR BOTH!

JAMES K. HAHN

City Attorney

Notes

1. The "Broken Windows Theory" explains the deterioration of a community by comparing a building suffering a single broken window to the deterioration of a neighborhood riddled with crime. The theory states that when a single window is broken in an otherwise fit building but is not *immediately* repaired, soon afterwards many other windows will be vandalized in succession. It is a common phenomenon which many have observed in society. It follows that if a building *already* suffers from numerous broken windows, the only way to effectively restore the building to a fit condition is to repair *all* windows at the same time. Anything less than full *coordination* of the repairs will result in an endless attempt to keep fixing some windows while more are vandalized in the interim.

   By the same token, if government fails to *coordinate* its efforts to improve a neighborhood so that law enforcement strategies are timed with the restoration and improvement of municipal and social services, the entire effort will fail. If, for example, police make a major drive to reduce gang crime in winter, while municipal government doesn't take steps to repair streets, lighting and garbage collection until the summer, by the time government *begins* to restore municipal services, the successes achieved by the police during the winter months will have already been reversed and gone to nought. On the other hand, if municipal and social services are improved *at the same time* that police reduce gang crime, then the environment which supported the criminal activity will have been altered so as to sustain the successes achieved by the police.

2. Situs (building) abatement laws in California generally state that a property owner can suffer fines, jail and/or the loss of one's real property if he causes, maintains or permits a property to become a public nuisance. In real terms, this means that if a landlord fails to take reasonable steps to prevent illegal drug

or gang activity at a location, the landlord can face stiff penalties including the seizure of the property. In most cases, the property owner is held strictly liable and is *not* excused because the police were unable to control the problem. Not surprisingly, this is one of the most powerful and successful law enforcement tools in California.

3. California Penal Code §166.4 states, in pertinent part, that: "Every person guilty of any contempt of court . . . of the following kinds, is guilty of a misdemeanor: . . . Willful disobedience of any process or order lawfully issued by any court."
4. The "Civil Gang Abatement" can be based on any type of nuisance activity engaged in by a street gang. The most likely nuisance upon which to base a Civil Gang Abatement, however, is ongoing narcotic activity. This is simply because street sales of narcotics typically involve easily identifiable patterns of conduct (e.g. possession of pagers and approaching vehicles from known narcotics locations) which facilitate the gang's successful narcotics sales. Accordingly, an injunction prohibiting such conduct could be expected to be successful at abating such narcotic sales. However, this certainly does not preclude the use of a "Civil Gang Abatement" approach to other organized criminal activity where law enforcement can identify patterns of lawful conduct which, if enjoined by a court, would reduce or eliminate the illegal activity.
5. While undercover efforts, by themselves, are often ineffective in abating gang-motivated drug dealing, they should still be included as part of any drug abatement effort. To be sure, undercover officers are best able to identify and target gang *leaders* for felony arrests leading to significant jail and prison sentences, thus inhibiting continued recruitment and coordination of the gang's illegal activities.
6. The open distribution of the warning revitalizes community support and mobilizes the residents to further support the efforts of law enforcement, including their willingness to complete logs for the "Civil Gang Abatement." But even more striking, the distribution of this warning notice can be most effective in lawfully "intimidating" the targeted gang into abating its criminal activity. In Los Angeles, such a warning notice has been distributed three times in anticipation of a request for an injunction against three different local street gangs. In two instances (one against the notorious Grape Street Gang in Jordan Downs Housing Project, the other against the Harbor City Crips in the Harbor area of Los Angeles), the distribution of the warning notices themselves, without further court action, brought about a remarkable 50 percent reduction in gang related crime. Even more surprising, that reduction in crime was sustained for several months. This phenomenon has been observed with the distribution of other legal warnings to gangs (e.g. S.T.E.P. notices) with similar, although not quite as remarkable, reductions in crime. We leave it to sociologists and others to speculate on the reasons why the neighborhood distribution of such documents to gang members has such a dramatic and sometimes long lasting effect on their previously unabatable criminal activity.
7. A phenomenon was observed during the serving of the court orders on individual gang members that cannot go unnoticed. While it was *enforcement* of the terms of the injunction in combination with other efforts described in this paper that was largely responsible for the successes achieved during the first "Civil Gang Abatement," police noticed that gang members actually feared and went to great lengths to avoid being personally served with the court orders. Even though there was no attempt to intimidate gang members during service of the orders, something that was actually impossible due to wide scale media coverage of the event, gang members ran and hid when they observed a police officer holding the large manila envelope containing the court's injunction and proof of service. Gang members who once boldly sold drugs within a few steps of a uniformed officer now remained indoors to avoid receiving that most feared document, the civil injunction. Naturally, however, after most gang members had eventually been served, they resumed their open sales of narcotics. That is, of course, until the police and assigned prosecutors aggressively enforced the terms of the injunction.
8. Previous experience has shown, however, that abatement *deters* future violations of the injunction following the first few aggressive prosecutions for a violation of the injunction. In the first use of the Civil Gang Abatement in Los Angeles, several gang members "tested" the injunction by immediately violating the orders. One gang leader, for instance, threw the court order in the street minutes after being handed it by a police officer. He was immediately arrested for violating the injunc-

tion since one of the orders was not to litter. While clearly surprised to learn that he was going to eventually serve three days in jail for an apparently minor violation of law, he was even more shocked to learn that the prosecutor obtained (and his public defender recommended that he agree to) a condition of probation banishing him from the targeted neighborhood for two years! News of that sentence spread rapidly throughout the targeted gang and had the desired effect of virtually insuring future compliance of the injunction by all other members of the gang. Moreover, the littering gang leader obeyed his "banishment" condition and was never again seen in the targeted neighborhood, nor was he observed to participate in future gang activity.

9. While the creation of "Community Impact Teams" is not a necessary requirement for implementation of a Civil Gang Abatement, such teams can dramatically increase the effectiveness of the process by insuring coordination of the various efforts as called for in the "Broken Windows Theory" of community decline and restoration, as described herein.

10. Residents are, however, given assurances that their logs will only be included in the Civil Gang Abatement with their consent. Moreover, the prosecutor should request and will normally receive a court order "sealing" or "sanitizing" the logs to prevent gang members from obtaining sufficient information to retaliate against residents. If such an order is not obtained, then the logs can be removed from the court file and other evidence can be relied upon to justify the injunction, *including* the fact that residents were afraid to submit declarations for fear of retaliation.

11. A law enforcement philosophy which encourages police to work closely with residents, property owners and merchants to encourage compliance with the law. Instead of relying chiefly upon arrests and convictions, community-based policing is premised upon the fact that the quality of life of a neighborhood cannot improve unless citizens actively participate with police and elected officials in the restoration of the neighborhood. It also calls for police to attempt to secure compliance from cooperative citizens rather than relying exclusively upon confrontation and court proceedings.

12. The American Civil Liberties Union unsuccessfully challenged the L.A. City Attorney's request for an injunction against the local street gang, the Playboy Gangster Crips. Although the court did not enjoin all activity requested by the prosecutor, the court did find that the street gang was subject to a civil injunction and subsequently issued a number of useful injunctive orders. In the following year, twenty-six gang members were arrested for violation of the injunction. Twenty-two pled guilty while the remaining cases were dismissed for insufficient evidence. Many of the defendants who pled guilty complied with a probation order to stay out of the neighborhood for two years. ✦

Chapter 29
Public Policy Responses to Gangs:
Evaluating the Outcomes

Noelle E. Fearn, Scott H. Decker, and G. David Curry

Street gangs in the United States come in many forms. In this final chapter, the authors describe a plethora of federal and local governmental efforts initiated in the last decade to respond to gangs. These responses take the form of suppression, social intervention, organizational change, community mobilization, and the provision of social opportunities. How well does the response match the problem? Do the responses focus attention on the immediate or deep-rooted causes of gang activity? Do the responses take into account gang process and dynamics, the functions that gangs serve for disadvantaged youngsters? Sound policies rest on a thorough understanding of the phenomenon they attempt to address. Consider these initiatives in light of the depictions of gangs and gang activity provided in the prior sections of this volume. Is there a good fit between knowledge and response?

Introduction

Designing public policy to respond to gangs is difficult. Based on police respondents, the National Youth Gang Center estimated that in 1996, 51 percent of jurisdictions reported having a gang. These jurisdictions included 816,000 gang members in 30,500 youth gangs across the United States (National Youth Gang Center 1999). Moore and Cook (1999) summarized data from the 1998 National Youth Gang Survey and reported 28,700 gangs with 780,000 gang members nationwide. Others (Maxson and Klein 1994) document large movement of gang members across American cities. The current cycle of gang activity is different than in previous eras as it is spread across more cities, is more violent, and is more deeply entrenched than was the case earlier (Klein 1995). Contemporary gangs have greater access to automobiles and high-powered firearms than did their predecessors. The growth of the underclass has also contributed to the growth of gangs (Jackson 1991; Vigil 1988; Klein 1995). Gangs also appear to be spreading beyond the boundaries of cities and gaining a foothold in suburban and rural communities (Klein 1995). These circumstances make responding to gangs a difficult task.

It is a truism that we cannot respond effectively to gangs unless we understand them. Public perceptions of gangs are shaped more by media images, such as the evening news or movies, than by a solid understanding of what gangs are. Most understanding of gangs comes from the criminal justice system and is the by-product of reporting on only the most criminal or delinquent members of gangs. This is important given that our conceptions of gangs are critical to determining the way we respond to them. Decker and Leonard (1991) found that members of an anti-gang task force based their knowledge of gangs on the media, a source considered the least reliable. The popular perception sees gangs as well-organized groups of men committed to a profit-making enterprise and organized around a common set of goals. However, there is little or no evidence to support these views. These facts provide a backdrop for our attempts to compare the policy responses to gangs to the magnitude and nature of the gang problem.

Despite a veritable explosion of gang research in the past decade, there has been little effort to catalogue the responses to gang problems in a systematic fashion (but see Howell 1997 and 1998). These responses have been implemented by a variety of levels of government, and address the problem in different ways. While some interventions have been supported by the federal government, others have their locus in local governments. Some of these responses have emphasized prevention, while others have concentrated on intervention after the commission of an offense. We present this review by using the Spergel and Curry (1993) typology of responses to gang problems.

Responding to Gang-Related Crime and Delinquency

No response to gang-related crime and delinquency can hope to be effective unless it focuses attention on both the immediate causes of gangs, as well as background factors. Such efforts must be undertaken with the understanding that institutions in the community must be addressed at the same time that individual behavior is addressed by programs. The immediate causes of gangs include the threats that other gangs generate to personal safety, the values that reinforce violence, and the limited availability of legitimate activities where gang members live. Background factors that cause the growth of gangs include the concentration of poverty, unemployment, and the decline of the family in American cities. And no matter what level is chosen for intervention, solutions will not be easy.

Spergel and Curry (1993) surveyed law enforcement agencies in over 250 cities for the Office of Juvenile Justice and Delinquency Prevention (OJJDP) and identified five basic gang intervention strategies. The general categories of gang intervention include efforts oriented around suppression, social intervention, organizational change, community mobilization, and social opportunities provision. Interestingly, the survey reported that the response that was employed most often, suppression, was viewed as the least successful intervention strategy. Conversely, the social opportunities provision was viewed as the most successful strategy, though it was employed least often by the cities. The contrast between the perceptions of what was a successful strategy and what was used in these jurisdictions is quite notable.

Suppression strategies include law enforcement and criminal justice interventions such as arrest, imprisonment, and surveillance. Forty-four percent of the responding agencies reported that suppression was their primary strategy in responding to gangs. By itself, suppression will not affect the growth of gangs or the crimes committed by gang members. To be effective, suppression strategies need to be part of a larger group of responses to the crimes of gang members. Klein (1995) has argued that suppression efforts should not be implemented in ways that increase the status of gang members. Gang suppression may also exacerbate the racial disproportionality of arrest. It is likely that prison gangs will grow as a result of suppression efforts.

Social intervention approaches focus on short-term, more immediate interventions, particularly in response to acts of violence or personal crises. Thirty-two percent of the law enforcement agencies surveyed said that they used social intervention strategies such as crisis intervention, treatment for youths and their families, and social service referrals. Because gang members and their families often find themselves in personal crises, such as arrests, injuries, or threats to their personal well-being, the use of crisis intervention and the provision of social services to gang members and their families is an important response. Gang members frequently are victims of violence or witnesses to friends' victimization. The use of crisis intervention services in such instances is promising. Crisis responses should be available at emergency rooms and should be mobilized by law enforcement, health care, or community groups, and attempt to integrate families. Interventions targeted at families are important because of their focus on root causes and long-term change. In addition, most gang members have siblings or cousins whose well-being may be adversely affected by the gang member. This magnifies the potential impact of family interventions.

Organizational change requires the creation of a broad consensus about gang problems within cities. Forming a task force is typical of such a response. These task forces typically target the proximate causes of gangs and by themselves cannot solve gang problems. Organizational change was selected by 11 percent of the respondents. In general, organizational change and other efforts aimed at creating, modifying, and expanding policies, practices, and legislation regarding gangs can lead to an awareness of the gang problems in the community and mobilize efforts to address them, or produce a new set of relations among agencies and groups who respond to such problems. Putting together task forces and focus groups in order to address the needs of particular communities with local gang problems is an example of this type of response to gangs. Organizational change will only be successful if it has the support of the community and groups in those neighborhoods where gangs operate, optimally including local politicians and the private sector.

The fundamental causes of gangs are addressed by community mobilization strategies. This strategy coordinates and targets services so that the needs of gang members may be met more effectively. This strategy was selected by only nine percent of cities as their modal response to gangs. Community mobilization focuses on cooperation across agencies and is designed to produce better coordination of existing services and resident groups. City services are seldom offered or merged in ways that are effective in meeting the needs of gang members who often have little contact with social institutions. Effective community mobilization must include both immediate social institutions such as the family, but also schools, community agencies and groups, churches, public health agencies, and the criminal and juvenile justice systems.

Social opportunities attempt to expand job prospects and educational resources. Similar to community mobilization, this type of response confronts the fundamental causes of gang formation and gang membership. The smallest number of cities, five percent, reported that their primary response was to provide social opportunities to gang members. These gang intervention efforts incorporate job creation, training, and residential placements designed to reshape values, peer commitments, and institutional participation by gang members and those at risk for membership. The underlying value of such an approach is to expand social capital and create new values among gang members by integrating them into legitimate social institutions.

Contemporary Responses to Gangs

In the 1980s and 1990s, the United States came to depend increasingly on suppression as the major response to gang crime problems. Often the dependence on suppression leads to the exclusion of nonjustice agencies as well as other, more effective, responses to gang problems. As we noted above, the strategy of suppression was the most common response to gang problems reported by respondents to the 1988 OJJDP national survey. Despite this, most respondents regarded it as the least effective response and there is broad recognition that no single response can be effective in responding to gangs (Spergel and Curry 1993). Only a balanced approach that combines suppression and other interventions, especially social opportunities, can provide a successful intervention. Below, we review a number of major policy initiatives directed at gangs in the 1990s, frame these initiatives within the Spergel-Curry intervention typology, and assess their long-term prospects for success. Public policy responses to gang activity and gang membership can come from three government levels: federal, state, and local. The next section of this chapter presents the current response to gang problems by these distinct government levels. The responses may take on the identity of legislative and/or programmatic initiatives in order to provide prevention, intervention, and/or suppression of gang problems.

Gang Legislation

By 1993, 14 of the 50 states had enacted statutes specifically directed at criminal gang activity. A review conducted by the Institute for Law and Justice (1993) groups gang legislation into two major categories: (1) legislation that provides criminal sanctions for the justice system against offenders in gang-related crimes and (2) legislation that provides civil remedies for the victims of gang crime. Criminal sanction legislation most often enhances sentences for those found guilty of committing a gang-related crime or makes provisions for segregating incarcerated gang members. Civil remedy approaches have most often attempted to empower citizens to file civil suits against gang members collectively or individually. A major impediment to the effectiveness of gang legislation is court rulings that several specific legislative acts violate the First Amendment rights of gang members (e.g., United States Supreme Court ruling, June 10, 1999; *Chicago v. Moralez* No. 97–1121).

Gang legislation constitutes a unique kind of organizational development and change in response to gang-related crime. Many law enforcement agencies engage in efforts to initiate or modify legislation related to gangs or the gang problem or try to influence legislation pertaining to gangs. Perhaps the best known gang legislation and one that has served as a model for other jurisdictions is California's 1988 STEP (Street Terrorism Enforcement and Prevention) Act (California Penal Code Section 186). STEP provides a definition of a criminal street gang and enhanced penalties for individuals convicted under such statutes. In addition to the STEP Act, local ordinances in many California cities allow the police to obtain a civil injunction against named gang members that prohibit those gang members from congregating in public, carrying beepers, drinking in public, and other behaviors. In their review of gang legislation in California over a ten-year period, Jackson and Rudman (1993) argue that most gang legislation represented a form of moral panic that was overwhelmingly devoted to gang suppression and influenced by law enforcement. Thus, the legislation failed to include any of the provisions found in the more effective strategies aimed at the fundamental causes of gangs and gang membership.

Maxson and Allen (1997) provides the only evaluation of the impact of a civil injunction in California. Maxson reviews the process and outcome of the implementation of this civil process in Inglewood, CA. She notes that the gang members who were served with these injunctions (in the form of temporary restraining orders) seemed confused and unaware of what was happening when they were civilly served with the injunction on the street and during their court appearance. In addition, she noted that the grant funding was depleted before the injunction could be fully implemented and found no evidence that violent crime decreased in the target area following the issuance of the injunction.

Federal Policy and Gangs

DHHS's Youth Gang Drug Prevention Program

In 1988, the Youth Gang Drug Prevention Program was established in the Administration on Children, Youth, and Families (ACYF), part of the U.S. Department of Health and Human Services (DHHS). Applications for the first round of funding focused on single-purpose demonstration projects and innovative support programs for at-risk youths and their families. Sixteen consortium projects were funded for three years. In design, these programs constituted a federally initiated, coordinated, and monitored commitment to community organization strategic responses to gang crime problems. This commitment was on a scale that was historically without precedent. Nine more consortium projects were funded in 1992 with a total of $5.9 million, each for a period of five years for up to $750,000 per year. The consortium projects received the bulk of Youth Gang Drug Prevention Program funding. However, the ACYF program included a number of projects employing social intervention strategies. Over the five years of the program, projects provided peer counseling, family education, youth empowerment, mentoring, crisis intervention, community restitution, and recreation. Priority funding areas for the delivery of services also targeted intergenerational gang families, adolescent females, and new immigrant and refugee youth gangs.

The explicit goals of the Youth Gang Drug Prevention Program mandated by Congress in its creation included facilitating federal, state, and local cooperation and coordination of the agencies responding to gang and drug crime problems. Funding solicitations required applicant programs to incorporate a local evaluation plan, and an independent national level evaluation was funded for the 52 projects initially funded in 1989. The national evaluation (Cohen et al. 1995) concluded that while local programs were generally effective in reducing delinquency and drug use among youth participants, *the programs were not successful at preventing or reducing gang involvement*. In 1995, the gang component of the program came to an end.

OJJDP's Comprehensive Response to America's Gang Problem

The first national assessments of the U.S. gang problem and the establishment in 1988 of the National Youth Gang Suppression and Intervention Program by the Office of Juvenile Justice and Delinquency Prevention (OJJDP) were important parts of the federal response to gangs. The program set three goals: (1) identify and assess promising approaches and strategies for dealing with the youth gang problem, (2) develop prototypes or models from the information thereby gained, and (3) produce technical assistance manuals for those who would implement the models (Spergel and Curry 1993). The project included 12 prototypes or models for gang program development and 12 technical assistance manuals corresponding to each prototype. The major outcome of the project was OJJDP's resolution that community-wide responses were required for dealing with local level gang problems (Bryant 1989).

The Spergel Model. The Spergel model has become the driving force in the OJJDP response to gangs. It has a flexible format that is useful for responding to gang problems at the community level. It focuses on the formation of partnerships between local private and public agencies (including law enforcement) to provide educational, emotional, and treatment services for youth at risk of or already involved in gangs. Separate required components of the Spergel model focus on community mobilization and employment programs, with one agency acting as the lead or mobilizing agency. In addition, law enforcement plays a central role in this process. Key agencies that must be involved include the police, grassroots neighborhood organizations, and some form of employment or job training program. The guidelines for community mobilization are intended to facilitate interagency cooperation and minimize interagency conflict. Under funding from OJJDP, five demonstration sites received funding to implement and test the Spergel model in a variety of urban settings with coordinated technical assistance and a systematic evaluation led by Spergel. In addition, in the Chicago community of Little Village, Spergel (1994; Spergel and Grossman 1994) has been working with a network of police, outreach youth workers, probation officers, court service workers, and former gang members to reduce violence between two warring coalitions of Latino street gangs. Preliminary evaluation results of this project indicate a reduction in gang-related homicides, increased community organization and mobilization, and the channeling of gang-involved youths into educational programs and jobs (Spergel 1999).

Safe Futures. As the first few years of the 1990s brought record increases in levels of juvenile violence, OJJDP became convinced that the problems of serious, violent, and chronic offending and gang-related crime were related. The Comprehensive Strategy (another OJJDP program) focuses on strengthening the families, strengthening the juvenile justice system, providing opportunities for youth, mobilizing communities, and breaking the cycle of violence. This strategy is separated into two components: one for at-risk youth and one for delinquent youth. The difference between the Comprehensive Strategy and the Spergel model is the separate program objectives for at-risk versus delinquent youth. Social opportunities and prevention techniques are saved for at-risk youth while graduated sanctions, prosecution, and other suppression techniques are used on the delinquent youth. The Spergel model does not make the same separation. The Spergel model argues for a combination of all prevention and intervention strategies along with the formation of local partnerships. It was decided that a major effort needed to be undertaken to test the utility of both the Comprehensive Strategy and the Spergel model in specifically targeted geographic settings. The policy result was the Safe Futures Program. With funding from OJJDP, Safe Futures Programs have been established in four urban sites (Boston, Seattle, Contra Costa County, CA, and St. Louis), one rural site (Imperial Valley, CA), and one Indian Reservation (Fort Belknap, MT). Funding for Safe Futures projects is larger ($1.4 million per year) and extended over a longer period of time (a five-year commitment) than funding for previous comparable efforts. All sites were initially funded in the fall of 1996.

The Safe Futures programs incorporate specific suppression, opportunities provision, and neighborhood focused services. As such, they are consistent with the Spergel model, and likely to provide a full test of the effectiveness of this model, which integrates suppression with community mobilization. One key characteristic of Safe Futures is very close monitoring by OJJDP and a series of consultants hired through technical assistance contracts. Often it is difficult to determine the impact of a program. Programs look and operate substantially different from the initial plan. The technical assistance and close oversight is designed to overcome these difficulties. A local evaluation is mandated for each site, and all sites are participating in a national evaluation. It is too early in the funding cycle to know the effect of the interventions. However, one thing is clear: Mounting large-scale interventions designed to change the delivery of services to youths is very difficult. A few sites have struggled with local issues to implement the Spergel model. For example, in St. Louis, the Safe Futures site has had difficulty integrating law enforcement—a key component of the model—into service delivery and client identification.

Community-Oriented Policing Services

Anti-Gang Initiative. Community-oriented policing represents an even broader federal effort to respond to crime in a way that integrates law enforcement into a cooperative, community problem-solving framework. This strategy is aimed at establishing a partnership between law enforcement and people in the community. It focuses on getting officers more involved in their communities with the hopes that better and more familiar relationships between the police and the community will facilitate lower crime rates and strengthened community relationships. In 1996, the Community Oriented Policing Services (COPS) office in the Justice Department launched a 15 city Anti-Gang Initiative (AGI). Instead of being selected through a competitive application process, the 15 cities were selected for their consistency in providing gang-related crime statistics to the Justice Department surveys described above. Funding was mandated to be spent on community policing efforts, to improve data collection, to integrate law enforcement agencies into community-wide responses to gangs, and to provide a safer setting in which less suppressive response programs can be given a chance to develop. In total, $11 million was made available to the cities, in $1 million or $500,000 allocations depending on city size. The sites included Austin, Boston, Chicago, Dallas, Detroit, Indianapolis, Jersey City, Kansas City, Los Angeles, Miami, Oakland, Orange County, Phoenix, Salt Lake City, and St. Louis.

The Anti-Gang Initiative set three specific goals: (1) develop strategies to reduce gang-related problems, (2) develop strategies to reduce gang-related drug trafficking problems, and (3) reduce the fear instilled by gang-related activities. Each jurisdiction was required to develop a formal written characterization of their local gang problem to include the number of gangs, members, age ranges, reasons for joining a gang, source and location of recruitment, location of activities, reasons for migration, and incidents of gang-related crime. These characterizations called for considerable detail that in most cities was simply not available through traditional law enforcement data gathering. Local researchers were included in the process of developing the view of gangs in some cities.

Eight specific strategies were identified. Three of the departments (Detroit, Jersey City, and St. Louis) chose to use special curfew enforcement strategies to target juveniles out after curfew hours. Six jurisdictions (Boston, Indianapolis, Miami, Oakland, Phoenix, and St. Louis) emphasized the need to coordinate their funded activities with ongoing efforts to combat drugs and gangs that were already in place. In Boston, this meant that the AGI effort was specifically linked to the Safe Futures funding received from OJJDP, and in Phoenix a tie was developed between the G.R.E.A.T. program (Gang Resistance Education and Training, a school-based gang prevention program targeted at junior high students) and AGI efforts.

The most popular strategy was Organizational Development and Change. Spergel and Curry (1993) have identified this as a core response strategy of law enforcement to gang problems. Eleven of the 15 departments used some form of this strategy. Typically, this approach attempts to enhance existing interventions by changing an overall organization or strategic response by bringing new partners to the table. This often meant that police departments sought out the assistance of other law enforcement partners, but also turned to the schools or social service agencies for help. Six cities saw information sharing as a key strategy to be funded by AGI monies. Often this meant the use of enhanced technology to provide presentations, transfer data, or conduct analyses. For example, many cities took the opportunity to use Geographic Information System technology to map gang, drug, and youth crime activities.

Eight of the jurisdictions chose to track gang members through the use of an enhanced or expanded database. In this way, they sought to better understand the number and nature of membership, and use that information for developing additional strategies and tactics of suppression. Nine of the jurisdictions specifically included schools as a partner in their COPS funded Anti-Gang Initiative. Often this meant enhancing GREAT or PAL (Police Athletic League) activities, but in some cases new partnerships were developed. Finally, eight of the jurisdictions mounted a community organization strategy, seeking to engage citizens and neighborhoods in crime prevention and control. Typically this meant that presentations and meetings were held.

Each jurisdiction was required to set aside 5 percent of total funds for the purposes of conducting an evaluation. These evaluations were largely focused on process issues, given the small amount of money available and limited time frame. Unfortunately, to date there has been no effort to make those evaluations available in a form that could shed light on the feasibility, impact, or future of such interventions. What is clear from those sites with completed evaluations is that those areas of intervention that the police controlled themselves (i.e., suppression) generally worked according to plan. However, partnership ventures were considerably more difficult to accomplish. Given the Spergel model's insistence on linking suppression and opportunities provision, the likely impact of these efforts is temporary or quite small.

Youth Firearms Violence Initiative. Another COPS response to increased levels of firearm violence among youth was the Youth Firearms Violence Initiative (YFVI). This federal initiative targeted groups at high risk for the use of firearms in the commission of crimes, and youth gangs were one criterion for the design of interventions. Ten cities were selected to each receive $1 million for a one-year period to reduce violent firearms crime by youth. Departments were to develop innovative programs that enhanced proactive crime control efforts and prevention programs targeted at young persons. Specifically, the COPS office wanted evidence that the number of violent firearm crimes committed by youth declined. Additionally, the agency expected that the number of firearms-related gang offenses and the number of firearms-related drug offenses would decline. Each participating department was required to develop new initiatives in three areas: (1) innovative strategies or tactics, (2) community policing orientation, and (3) new information systems. The 10 cities included Birmingham, AL, Bridgeport, CT, Milwaukee, WI, Richmond, VA, Seattle, WA, Baltimore, MD, Cleveland, OH, Inglewood, CA, Salinas, CA, and San Antonio, TX. Local evaluations and a national evaluation were completed examining the efforts of each site.

There was considerable variation across the participating sites regarding the strategies and tactics employed to achieve these objectives. Not surprisingly, most strategies emphasized enforcement, although some combined enforcement with prevention. The tactics included such things as focusing on specific targets (gangs), neighborhoods, firearms crimes, and the use of dedicated units to address these issues specifically. Inglewood employed among the most innovative strategies. Inglewood is a medium-sized city in the Los Angeles area with predominantly African-American and Hispanic residents. Inglewood chose to target a single neighborhood of relatively small size. A full-time prosecutor and probation officer worked with the police department. The prosecutor worked to develop the civil injunction that was discussed above and is becoming a popular tactic in California. The probation officer was responsible for seizing hundreds of firearms from youth on probation, employing his powers to search the residences of his probationers. The officers' efforts serve as an example of the kind of innovative work that can be forged between different agencies of the criminal justice system. Unfortunately, these partnerships—seen as critical to the success of the prevention and suppression of crime—vanished when grant funding ended. This raises the important issue of sustainability, that is, the extent to which innovations and partnerships will continue once the federal money runs out.

The national evaluation demonstrated that these interventions, in most cities, were accompanied by reductions in gun offenses. A specific geographic area similar to the program area was chosen for comparison purposes and gun offenses were tracked by week. The tracking of gun offenses occurred during the two-year period prior to YFVI efforts and the one-year period after the program. In each of the five impact evaluation sites (Bridgeport, Seattle, Baltimore, Inglewood, Salinas), the decline in gun offenses per week was greater for the program area than for the comparison area. While this is not conclusive proof that YFVI was solely responsible for the observed declines, it is consistent with that hypothesis. In almost every case, YFVI was strictly a suppression program; only rarely did it effectively integrate the activities of social service or prevention activities. However, in those cities where such activities were integrated (especially Milwaukee and Seattle), those activities and relationships remained in place well after the conclusion of the program.

State and Local Policy Examples

The Illinois Gang Crime Prevention Center

In 1995, the governor of Illinois established the Governor's Commission on Gangs and appointed the Illinois attorney general to serve as the chairman. The Commission was to be responsible for generating practical solutions to the growing street gang problem in Illinois. Following nine months of research focused on examining the gang problem in Illinois as well as community mobilization, future legislation, public awareness and parental education, law enforcement, and safety in schools, the Commission recommended a comprehensive strategy to integrate suppression, prevention, and intervention strategies and the creation of an organization to focus on reducing gang activity statewide (Governor's Commission on Gangs 1996). The Gang Crime Prevention Center (GCPC) was designed and created to serve this function. The Center began operating on July 1, 1997. The GCPC was separated into four units: community mobilization, program development, research and information services, and operations. These units work together to develop, implement, and evaluate organization- and neighborhood-based programs.

The GCPC has utilized a seven-step program development process to create, fund, and implement five gang prevention pilot programs in Illinois: (1) collaboration and problem definition, (2) site assessment and target population, (3) approach and mission, (4) strategy and resource development, (5) implementation and operation, (6) monitoring and evaluation, and (7) modification and evolution. The five pilot programs, implemented in 1998, include two court-based (Early Intervention Probation and Evening Reporting Center) and three school-based (Student Covenant for the Future, Mentoring/Tutoring, and Right Track Truancy Reduction) programs. Each of these programs is concerned with preventing gang membership and intervention and suppression for active gang members (Leverentz 1999).

The Early Intervention Probation program focuses on youth already involved, to some extent, with gangs, delinquent activities, and the juvenile justice system. The Evening Reporting Center (ERC) also utilizes intervention and suppression techniques for youth previously exposed to the juvenile justice system. The ERC is modeled after the Eight Percent Solution in Orange County, California. This program, similar to the one in California, focuses on youth most likely to become the chronic, serious offenders of tomorrow. The programs identify and intervene with youth who are headed towards a criminal career. Objectives include both individual skill building and family-oriented services (Schumacher and Kurz 2000). As is the case with the two court-based programs, the three school-based programs are located in specific geographic locations throughout the state of Illinois. Lovejoy Elementary School is the home of the Mentoring/Tutoring program, Kelly High School houses the Student Covenant for the Future, and Springfield was chosen as the site of the Right Track Truancy Reduction program. These five sites were chosen by the Gang Crime Prevention Center because of the specific target population and objectives for each of the programs. The two court-based programs target youth already exposed to gangs and gang activities and utilize intervention and suppression strategies. The school-based programs, specifically the Mentoring/Tutoring Program, target younger recipients and opt for prevention as a goal. However, both the Student Covenant and Truancy programs include intervention and suppression strategies along with prevention measures. Without exception, all of these programs involve some kind of partnership between community agencies, schools, and/or law enforcement agencies. Some of the participants involved with the programs include the Attorney General's Office, the public school districts, the Illinois Retired Teachers' Association, probation and parole departments, the mental health department, the Department of Human Services, the Department of Children and Family Services, Social Service Programs, and law enforcement agencies.

The Gang Crime Prevention Center is currently being evaluated with regards to the implementation, process, and impact of its pilot programs and its role in developing, implementing, overseeing, evaluating, and replicating social programs. Preliminary implementation results indicate that with the exception of the Evening Reporting Center, the programs have broader foci than just gangs. Also, some of the programs (Mentoring/Tutoring, Student Covenant, and Right Track Truancy) do not emphasize gangs as a central program component. Participants in at least one of the programs, the Mentoring/Tutoring program, dissuade any discussion of gangs and gang membership. These participants focus on academic tutoring and emotional/social mentoring. This is so the youth will do better in school and thus stay there (in school) and (hopefully) away from gangs.

These programs provide social, emotional, behavioral, or academic benefits for the participants but do not seem to be targeting at-risk or gang-involved youth for the purposes expressed in the Governor's Commission on Gangs report (Governor's Commission on Gangs 1996). The direction of these programs has changed from the original plans (implementation changes) as well as during the life of the program (process changes). The sustainability and replicability of these pilot programs are problematic issues as the programs do not focus as much on gang prevention and intervention as originally intended. However, these programs represent an important state-level response in a state with serious gang problems.

The Boston Gun Suppression Project

Perhaps no single intervention in the 1990s has received as much public attention as the Boston Gun Suppression Project (Kennedy, Piehl, and Braga 1996; Boston Police Department and Partners 1997). Also known as Ceasefire, this project has been replicated in a number of cities across the country, including Minneapolis, where it has been carefully evaluated (Kennedy and Braga 1998). At its heart, Ceasefire employs the SARA (Scanning, Analysis, Response, and Assessment) problem-solving model to assess youth violence. The SARA model requires that local jurisdictions gather data to determine the nature of local problems, analyze those data, and, based on the results of those analyses, design a response to solve problems. The final step of the SARA model requires that the response be carefully assessed and recalibrated. The apparent success of this intervention largely rests on two features: (1) careful background work conducted to understand the nature of youth firearms markets and (2) partnerships among the participating groups. Kennedy and his colleagues determined that the youth firearm market was different from that of adults, was comprised of a relatively small group of serious offenders, was largely based on fear of attack by rival youth who often were gang members, and that the primary means of acquiring guns by young people was theft. These findings led Kennedy and his colleagues to conclude that traditional methods of intervention, such as intelligence gathering and arrest, by themselves may not be successful.

The Boston Gun Project involves a large interagency working group that consists of representatives from the local police department, the Bureau of Alcohol, Tobacco, and Firearms (ATF), the U.S. Attorney, the local prosecutor, the departments of probation and parole, city youth outreach workers, the school district, and Kennedy's research team. The working group met regularly to review research and operational findings, and it is from these meetings that a response plan was developed. Two complementary strategies were developed, one that attempted to disrupt the illegal firearms market on the supply side, and the other targeted at the demand side. On the supply side, ATF worked with local police, prosecutors, and the U.S. Attorney to step up gun tracing and prosecution efforts. It is the demand side where the most interesting interventions were developed, however. Probation and parole officers engaged in night visits to their clients to enforce routine conditions of sentence such as curfews and room searches that heretofore had not been regularly enforced. This was coupled with a series of dramatic meetings with local gang members attended by key law enforcement officials to announce and demonstrate the effects of a zero-tolerance policy for the use of guns by youth in a number of Boston neighborhoods.

The initial evaluations of the Boston Gun Project have demonstrated that the program was quite successful. Youth gun crime, particularly homicide, recorded dramatic declines in Boston, even greater declines than throughout the rest of the nation. Kennedy, Piehl, and Braga (1996) conducted both a process and outcome evaluation that demonstrated key components of the project. Kennedy and Braga (1998) replicated the Ceasefire project in Minneapolis with similar results. What are the key features of this effort to reduce gang firearm violence that appear to have made it successful? First, the intervention is based on data that come from local law enforcement and are presented in a way that leads naturally to policy interventions. Second, the use of data to guide the project did not end once the intervention began. Rather, the researchers continued to collect data and use it to refine the intervention on an on-going basis. Third, the intervention combined the efforts of a variety of committed groups and individuals. As Spergel and Curry remind us, no program based on a single form of intervention is likely to achieve success. By combining suppression at a number of levels (federal, state, and local) with social opportunities provision and broader based enforcement (probation and parole), Boston appears to have found ways to get a handle on its gang problem. These findings suggest that a mixture of Spergel-Curry strategies, especially combining suppression with social opportunities and perhaps crisis intervention, may be the most promising approach in responding to gangs.

A Different Public Policy Response for Female Gang Members?

Until the 1980s and 1990s, the majority of gang research focused on young men (Joe-Laidler and Hunt 1997; Curry 1998). Females were often overlooked, ignored, and/or marginalized in the literature regarding gang involvement and strategies for reducing gang activities and gang membership. Over the last 15 years, however, there has been an increase in research concerned with females and their roles within (and alongside) gangs (Curry 1998). While this "female-focused" body of gang research has continued to grow, there has been little change in the traditional response to gangs (i.e., suppression). This illuminates a critical gap since ideally policy responses should be theoretically grounded (Curry 1999). In other words, responses to gangs and gang membership should be implemented based on research that indicates its potential to affect decisions to join and maintain a relationship to a gang.

Most female gang research has been of a qualitative nature, utilizing in-depth interviews and ethnographic accounts (see for example, Fleisher 1998; Hunt, Mackenzie, and Joe-Laidler 2000; Joe-Laidler and Hunt 1997; Miller 2001). Much of the response to female gang involvement has come in the form of increased awareness and recognition of its existence. More and more research is being conducted on females and gangs and is seen by some as a response in itself. According to one gang researcher, "research on a subject increases in conjunction with increased public and policy concern and, perhaps just as important, funding resources" (Curry 1999:134). Thus, although research by itself might not be exactly what we think of as a response or a solution to the problem of female gang involvement, it is a beginning. While the female gang research continues to expand, public policy responses aimed at female gang involvement have been almost nonexistent.

Public policy responses to female gang members (aside from research) have taken on a social service and/or law enforcement focus. An NIJ law enforcement survey was conducted in 1992 and many of the law enforcement agencies provided either no information regarding female gang involvement or reported that they had no female gang members (Curry 1999). This contradicts the presence of females in gangs and female gangs described in other kinds of research (ethnographic and self-report studies; see Fleisher 1998; Hunt, Mackenzie, and Joe-Laidler 2000; Joe-Laidler and Hunt 1997; Miller 2001). The small number of reported female gang members (as compared to male members) and the lack of official statistics collected on female gang members and their activities has indeed contributed to the neglect of these individuals when policy decisions are being made. While the law enforcement response to females in gangs has been limited basically to increased reporting and suppression techniques, varied social services responses emerged (and have already begun to decline) in the early nineties (Curry 1999).

The majority of these social service programs were funded by Congress in 1989 under the administration of the Department of Health and Human Services Family Youth Services Bureau (FYSB). In 1990, the FYSB solicited programs for the prevention and intervention of female gang involvement. Overall 13 programs focused on preventing and intervening in female gang involvement were created and implemented in different sites by 1992. The services provided by these new programs varied and included: building self-esteem, providing social activities and recreation, individual and group counseling, education and employment support, mentoring, and conflict resolution skills. A couple of problems emerged with the focus and process of these programs. First, some of the programs received female participants from the juvenile court and many of these girls did not identify themselves as gang members. In addition, at least one of the programs would not allow current gang members and many of the participants in several of the programs were former gang members (Curry 1999). Thus, programs that were supposed to prevent female gang membership and activities were not actually recruiting, receiving, and accepting the proper target population. Out of all of these social service programs three were evaluated: Boston, Seattle and Pueblo, CO (Curry 1999). The evaluation results indicated that, "while the programs may have had some effect on reducing delinquency and drug-use, actual reductions in gang activity associated with program efforts could not be identified" (Curry 1999:149).

As a result of these evaluation findings, and a reemerging emphasis on law enforcement strategies, the FYSB programs gradually diminished. By 1995 all gang-focused program features had disappeared and by 1998 much of FYSB's program funding was withdrawn. As discussed in Curry (1999) this group of programs was the only federally funded attempt to prevent and intervene in female gang involvement. The disappearance of these programs is similar to (yet much more short-lived than) the continuous cycle of research, law enforcement, and social service responses to (male) gang involvement in which programs are initiated but fail to be accurately implemented, include the correct population, or provide viable services and opportunities for youth.

Conclusion

The last decade produced an unprecedented increase in gangs, gun assaults, and youth homicide. These increases have spurred federal and local governments to action. In the search for appropriate responses to these problems, suppression has been the strategy most often adopted. This makes sense for a variety of political and pragmatic reasons; after all, the police are a visible and generally popular resource in the effort to combat crime. However, such responses are not likely to be successful on their own. When suppression occurs in a vacuum, when it is not accompanied by other, more supportive, actions, the chances of making lasting changes in gang crime are diminished.

A number of federal initiatives that emphasize suppression or social opportunities provision have been undertaken in the last decade. The COPS Office's Anti-Gang Initiative is a good example of programs that were based almost exclusively on suppression. This is counterbalanced by the effort of DHHS in its Youth Gang Drug Prevention program. This heavily funded federal effort focused exclusively on opportunities provision. While the evaluation data do not enable a definitive conclusion about the effectiveness of these interventions, it is clear that they have not made substantial inroads into the gang problem in the communities where they were funded because of their failure to implement a balanced response. If there is a single message in this chapter, it is that law enforcement and social opportunities provision must work hand-in-hand if successful interventions are to be implemented.

The success of any initiative, as demonstrated by the Boston Gun Project, hinges largely on its ability to integrate a number of approaches. Gangs are not monolithic, as the recent work of Klein and Maxson (1995) has demonstrated. Klein and Maxson produced a typology of gang structures, based on the size of the gang, its age, involvement in crime, and other salient characteristics. Their typology reinforces the diversity of gangs, and consequently the need for a variety of responses. The key to a successful response to gangs is the recognition that gangs vary by type, within and between cities, and that successful responses must be built on a solid knowledge base. Klein is often critical of the police because they characterize gangs and gang members as overly organized, more seriously criminal, and more dedicated to the gang than is actually the case. He argues that this conception of gangs and gang members dominates the public and criminal justice understanding of this phenomenon, thereby distorting the fact that most gang members are loosely committed to their gang, that they are involved in a wide range of mostly minor criminal and delinquent acts, and that gangs are not effective vehicles for social organization. Without multiple sources of information and a coordinated response that involves suppression, community mobilization, and social opportunities provision, little progress will be made in responding to such gangs.

References

Allen-Hagen, B., and M. Sickmund. 1993. *Juveniles and Violence: Juvenile Offending and Victimization*. Office of Juvenile Justice and Delinquency Prevention. Washington, D.C.: U.S. Department of Justice.

American Psychological Association. 1993. "Violence and Youth: Psychology's Response." *Volume I: Summary Report of the American Psychological Association Commission on Violence and Youth*. Washington, D.C.: American Psychological Association.

Blumstein, A., and R. Rosenfeld. 1998. "Explaining Recent Trends in U.S. Homicide Rates." *Journal of Criminal Law and Criminology* 88:1–32.

Boston Police Department and Partners. 1997. *The Boston Strategy to Prevent Youth Violence*. Boston Police Department.

Bryant, D. 1989. *Community-Wide Responses Crucial for Dealing with Youth Gangs*. Washington, D.C.: Juvenile Justice Bulletin, Office of Juvenile Justice and Delinquency Prevention, U.S. Department of Justice.

Bureau of Justice Statistics. 1993. *Guns and Crime*. A BJS Crime Data Brief. Washington, D.C.: U.S. Department of Justice.

Cloward, R., and L. Ohlin. 1960. *Delinquency and Opportunity*. New York: Free Press.

Cohen, M., K. Williams, A. Beckman, and S. Crosse. 1995. "Evaluation of the National Youth Gang Drug Prevention Program," in M. Klein, C. Maxson, and J. Miller (Eds.) *The Modern Gang Reader*. Los Angeles: Roxbury, 266–275.

Curry, G. D. 1998. "Female Gang Involvement." *Journal of Research in Crime and Delinquency* 35:100–118.

Curry, G. D. 1999. "Responding to Female Gang Involvement," in M. Chesney-Lind and J. M. Hagedorn (Eds.) *Female Gangs in America: Essays on Girls, Gangs, and Gender*. Chicago: Lake View Press, 133–153.

Curry, G. D., R. Ball, and R. J. Fox. 1994. "Gang Crime and Law Enforcement Record-Keeping." *Research in Brief*. Washington, D.C.: National Institute of Justice.

Decker, S. H., and G. D. Curry. 1998. *Confronting Gangs: Crime and Community*. Los Angeles: Roxbury.

Decker, S. H., and K. L. Leonard. 1991. "Constructing Gangs: The Social Construction of Youth Activities." *Criminal Justice Policy Review* 4:271–291.

Fingerhut, L., J. Kleinman, E. Godfrey, and H. Rosenberg. 1991. *Firearm Mortality Among Children, Youth, and Young Adults 1–34 Years of Age, Trends and Current Status: United States, 1979–88*. Atlanta, GA: Public Health Service.

Fleisher, M. S. 1998. *Dead End Kids: Gang Girls and the Boys They Know*. Madison; London: University of Wisconsin Press.

Governor's Commission on Gangs. 1996. *Mobilizing Illinois: Report and Recommendations to the Governor*. Chicago: Office of the Attorney General of Illinois

Harries, K., and A. Powell. 1994. "Juvenile Gun Crime and Social Stress: Baltimore, 1980–1990." *Urban Geography* 15:45–63.

Howell, J. C. 1997. "Youth Gangs." Office of Juvenile Justice and Delinquency Prevention. Washington, D.C.: U.S. Department of Justice.

——. 1998. "Youth Gangs: An Overview." Office of Juvenile Justice and Delinquency Prevention. Washington,D.C.: U.S. Department of Justice.

Hunt, G., K. MacKenzie, and K. Joe-Laidler. 2000. "'I'm Calling My Mom': The Meaning of Family and Kinship Among Homegirls." *Justice Quarterly* 17:802–831.

Institute for Law and Justice. 1993. *Gang Prosecution Legislative Review*. Report prepared for the National Institute of Justice. Washington, D.C.: U.S. Department of Justice.

Jackson, P. I. 1991. "Crime, Youth Gangs, and Urban Transition: The Social Dislocations of Postindustrial Development." *Justice Quarterly* 8:379–398.

Jackson, P. J., with C. Rudman. 1993. "Moral Panic and the Response to Gangs in California," in S. Cummins and D. Monti (Eds.) *The Origins and Impact of Contemporary Youth Gangs in the United States*. Albany: SUNY Press, 257–275.

Joe-Laidler, K., and G. Hunt. 1997. "Violence and Social Organization in Female Gangs." *Social Justice* 24:148–169.

Kennedy, D., and A. Braga. 1998. "Homicide in Minneapolis." *Homicide Studies* 2:263–290.

Kennedy, D., A. Piehl, and A. Braga. 1996. "Youth Violence in Boston: Gun Markets, Serious Youth Offenders, and a Use-Reduction Strategy." *Law and Contemporary Problems* 59:147–196.

Klein, M. 1995. *The American Street Gang*. New York: Oxford.

Klein, M., and C. Maxson. 1994. "Gangs and Cocaine Trafficking," in D. MacKenzie and C. Uchida (Eds.) *Drugs and Crime: Evaluating Public Policy Initiatives*. Thousand Oaks, CA: Sage.

——. 1995. "Investigating Gang Structures." *Journal of Gang Research* 3:33–40.

Leverentz, Andrea. 1999. "Pilot Programs: An Interim Report." Research and Information Services Unit, Illinois Gang Crime Prevention Center.

Maxson, C. L. and T. Allen 1997. An Evaluation of the City of Inglewood's Youth Firearms Violence Initiative. University of Southern California, Los Angeles.

Maxson, C., and M. Klein. 1994. "The Scope of Street Gang Migration in the U.S." Presentation. Gangs Working Group. Washington, D.C.: National Institute of Justice.

Miller, J. 2001. *One of the Guys*. New York: Oxford University Press.

Miller, W. 1975. *Violence by Street Gangs and Youth Groups as a Crime Problem in Major American Cities*. National Institute for Juvenile Justice and Delinquency Prevention. Office of Justice Programs, U.S. Department of Justice. Washington, D.C.: U.S. Government Printing Office.

Moore, M. 1981. "Keeping Handguns from Criminal Offenders." *Annals of the American Academy of Political and Social Science* 455:92–109.

Moore, J. P., and I. L. Cook. 1999. "Highlights of the 1998 National Youth Gang Survey." *OJJDP Fact Sheet*. Washington, D.C.: Office of Juvenile Justice and Delinquency Prevention.

National Youth Gang Center. 1999. *1997 National Youth Gang Survey*. Washington, D.C.: U.S. Department of Justice, Office of Juvenile Justice and Delinquency Prevention.

Roberts, A. 1989. *Juvenile Justice: Policies, Programs, and Services*. Chicago: Dorsey.

Schumacher, M. A., and G. A. Kurz. 2000. *The 8% Solution: Preventing Serious, Repeat Juvenile Crime*. Thousand Oaks, CA: Sage Publications, Inc.

Shaw, C., and H. McKay. 1972. *Juvenile Delinquency and Urban Areas*. Chicago: University of Chicago Press.

Sheley, J., and J. Wright. 1993. *Drug Activity and Firearms Possession and Use by Juveniles*. A report to the National Institute of Justice and the Office of Juvenile Justice and Delinquency Prevention.

——. 1995. *In the Line of Fire*. New York: Aldine.

Sommerfeld, M. 1993. "About 10% of Youths Say They Have Fired a Gun or Been Shot at, New Survey Finds." *Education Week* (August): 11–23.

Spergel, I. 1994. *Gang Suppression and Intervention: Problem and Response*. Washington, D.C.: Office of Juvenile Justice and Delinquency Prevention.

——. 1999. *Evaluation of the Little Village Gang Violence Reduction Project*. Chicago: Illinois Criminal Justice Information Authority.

Spergel, I., and G. D. Curry. 1993. "The National Youth Gang Survey: A Research and Development Process," in A. P. Goldstein and C. R. Huff (Eds.) *Gang Intervention Handbook*. Champaign, IL: Research Press, pp. 359–400.

Spergel, I., and S. Grossman. 1994. *Gang Violence and Crime Theory: Gang Violence Reduction Project*. Presentation at the American Society of Criminology Annual Meetings. Miami, FL.

Vigil, J. D. 1988. *Barrio Gangs*. Austin: University of Texas Press. ✦

Recommended Readings

Battin, Sara R., Karl G. Hill, Robert D. Abbott, Richard F. Catalano, and J. David Hawkins. 1998. "The Contribution of Gang Membership to Delinquency Beyond Delinquent Friends." *Criminology* 36:93–115.

Chesney-Lind, Meda, and John M. Hagedorn. 1999. *Female Gangs in America: Essays on Girls, Gangs and Gender.* Chicago: Lakeview Press.

Chin, Ko-Lin. 1996. *Chinatown Gangs: Extortion, Enterprise, & Ethnicity.* New York: Oxford University Press.

Covey, Herbert C., Scott Menard, and Robert J. Franzere. 1997. *Juvenile Gangs*, 2nd Edition. Springfield, IL: Charles C. Thomas.

Curry, G. David, and Scott H. Decker. 1998. *Confronting Gangs: Crime and Community.* Los Angeles: Roxbury Publishing.

Decker, Scott H. 1996. "Collective and Normative Features of Gang Violence." *Justice Quarterly* 13(2):243–264.

Decker, Scott H., and Barrik Van Winkle. 1996. *Life in the Gang*. Cambridge: Cambridge University Press.

Esbensen, Finn-Aage, David Huizinga, and Anne W. Weiher. 1993. "Gang and Non-Gang Youth: Differences in Explanatory Factors." *Journal of Contemporary Criminal Justice* 9:94–116.

Fleisher, Mark S. 1998. *Dead End Kids: Gang Girls and the Boys They Know.* Madison: Wisconsin University Press.

Hagedorn, John M. 1998. *People and Folks: Gangs, Crime, and the Underclass in a Rustbelt City*, 2nd Edition. Chicago: Lakeview Press.

Hamm, Mark S. 1993. *American Skinheads: The Criminology and Control of Hate Crime*. Westport, CT: Praeger.

Horowitz, Ruth. 1983. *Honor and the American Dream*. New Brunswick, NJ: Rutgers University Press.

Huff, C. Ronald, ed. 1990. *Gangs in America*. Newbury Park, CA: Sage.

Huff, C. Ronald, ed. 1996. *Gangs in America*, 2nd Edition. Thousand Oaks, CA: Sage.

Klein, Malcolm W. 1995. *The American Street Gang: Its Nature, Prevalence and Control*. New York: Oxford University Press.

Klein, Malcolm W., Hans-Jurgen Kerner, Cheryl L. Maxson, and Elmar E. M. Weitekamp, eds. 2000. *The Eurogang Paradox: Youth Groups and Gangs in Europe and America*. The Hague: Kluwer.

Maxson, Cheryl L, Monica L. Whitlock, and Malcolm W. Klein. 1998. "Vulnerability to Street Gang Membership: Implications for Practice." *Social Service Review* (March):70–91.

Miller, Jody. 2001. *One of the Guys: Girls, Gangs and Gender.* New York: Oxford University Press.

Miller, Walter B. 1958. "Lower Class Culture as a Generating Milieu of Gang Delinquency." *Journal of Social Issues* 14:5–19.

Moore, Joan. 1991. *Going Down to the Barrio: Homeboys and Homegirls in Change*. Philadelphia: Temple University Press.

Rodriguez, Luis J. 1993. *Always Running: La Vida Loca*. Willimantic, CT: Curbstone Press.

Short, James F., and Fred L. Strodtbeck. 1965. *Group Process and Gang Delinquency.* Chicago: University of Chicago Press.

Spergel, Irving. 1995. *The Youth Gang Problem: A Community Approach*. New York: Oxford University Press.

Thornberry, Terence P., Marvin D. Krohn, Alan J. Lizotte and Deborah Chard-Wierschem. 1993. "The Role of Juvenile Gangs in Facilitating Delinquent Behavior." *Journal of Research in Crime and Delinquency* 30:75–85.

Thrasher, Frederic. 1927/1963. *The Gang: A Study of 1313 Gangs in Chicago*. Chicago: University of Chicago Press.

Vigil, James Diego. 1988. *Barrio Gangs: Street Life and Identity in Southern California*. Austin: University of Texas Press.

Zatz, Marjorie S. 1987. "Chicano Youth Gangs and Crime: The Creation of a Moral Panic." *Contemporary Crises* 11:129–158. ✦